The Complete
GILBERT & SULLIVAN
Opera Guide

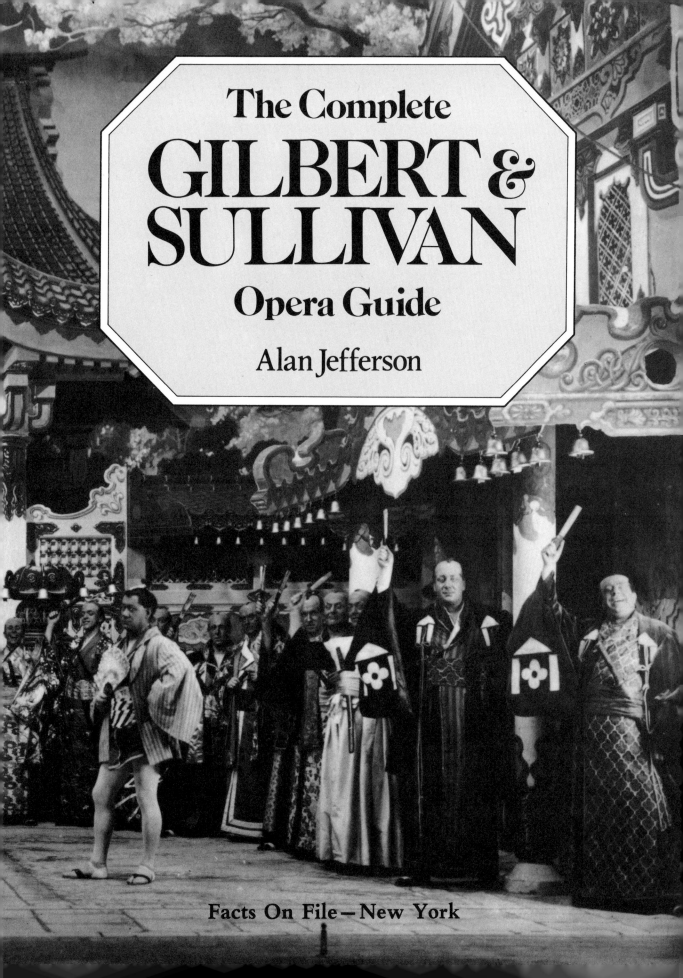

The Complete
GILBERT & SULLIVAN
Opera Guide

Alan Jefferson

Facts On File — New York

For Andreas

Previous pages: Mikado 1908, Savoy. Designer A. Terraine
(Theatre Museum)

Copyright © Alan Jefferson 1984

Picture research by Anne-Marie Ehrlich

Designed by Vic Giolitto

First published in Great Britain 1984 by Webb & Bower
(Publishers) Limited, 9 Colleton Crescent, Exeter, Devon EX2 4BY

First published in the United States by Facts On File, Inc.,
460 Park Avenue South, New York, N.Y. 10016

Library of Congress Cataloging in Publication Data

Jefferson, Alan.
  The complete Gilbert & Sullivan opera guide.

  Discography: p. 345
  Videography: p. 345
  Bibliography: p. 347
  Includes index.
  1. Sullivan, Arthur, Sir, 1842-1900. Operas.
  2. Operas—19th century—History and criticism.
  I. Title. II. Title: Complete Gilbert and Sullivan opera
  guide.
  ML410.S95J43 1984   782.81'092'4   83-20654
  ISBN 0-87196-857-6

Typeset in Great Britain by Busby's Typesetting and Design,
Exeter, Devon

Printed and bound in Hong Kong by Mandarin Offset International
Limited

10 9 8 7 6 5 4 3 2 1

CONTENTS

Preface

It has always been essential to know Gilbert's libretti in order to gain maximum enjoyment from his songs. In fact, when the operas were first produced, libretti were always available so that the audiences might follow the words during the performance. This book is intended as a listener's and viewer's guide to the Savoy Operas. Sullivan went out of his way to ensure that his music in no way obliterated Gilbert's words, but Gilbert's nonsensical rhymes and topsy-turvy ideas, following so closely in sequence, demand to be read and re-read.

Here the libretti are presented once more after about sixty years in the version checked and passed personally by Gilbert at the end of his life. Only *Thespis* was still to be approved: it lay on his desk at Grim's Dyke waiting for his attention on the day that he died.

The D'Oyly Carte 'tradition' was derived from Gilbert's prompt books, which are thoroughly explicit for succeeding producers. With the demise of the Company, this 'tradition' is already lost, for with the disbanding of the artists, there is no longer an ensemble brought up in it. Nevertheless, faded and stilted as it had become, this 'tradition' was based on Gilbert's own conception of his works. One of the most valuable legacies he has left is his collection of *Bab* drawings to illustrate his Savoyard Songs. These have been interpolated in the synopses to add some flavour of the real Gilbert and they will gradually gain in importance as time goes on.

The critical chapters take a retrospective look at the work of these two brilliant Victorian collaborators who, in the true spirit of their time, delved into tradition for their inspiration. They were both accused by their contemporaries of plagiarism, but rarely in any vein of denigration. Today there is a certain mystique surrounding Sullivan's music, partly due to an unreasonable witholding from publication of the orchestral scores.

The pattern that has emerged from these fourteen chapters, however, opens new fields for speculation. The study of Sullivan's sources today is fascinating and endless, and he has used his fund of inspiration with such subtlety that only with the aid of a tape cassette is one now able to decipher his ideas with greater ease.

In this new era of production, an understanding of these side-influences will enrich performances and carry the real tradition, not the 'tradition'—but the folk and operatic tradition on which these operas were first based—forward into the future.

I am very grateful to the individuals and organizations listed below for their invaluable help during research for, and writing of this book: Mrs Annette Bowen for access to the complete run of *Punch* in her library; Miyoko and Paul Freeman for Japanese translation; The Lord Greenway for advice on ceremony, and for photography; Basil Lam for receiving and generally answering random questions at all hours by telephone; Mrs Iona Molesworth-St Aubyn for permission to photograph her *Iolanthe* costumes at Pencarrow House; John Reed OBE and Nicholas Kerri for valued help; Peter Riley for general advice and encouragement, and for letting me quote his anecdote at the end of the introductory chapter; Roger Wild for information about early recordings; JHW and ADR for many things. Also to C. D. Paramor and Dr Terence Rees for being veritable mines of information and indicators of other likely sources; Phaidon Press for permission to quote from *Japanese Masters of the Colour Print* by J. Hillier; David Eden of The Sir Arthur Sullivan Society for useful information; Charles Haynes of Pavilion Records for kindly supplying transfers from 78; Janet Jessup of the D.P. Information Service; John Kehoe of Decca International; Peter Joslin for great help.

The Librarians of HM Tower of London, the Royal Society of Medicine, the Devon County Library, Torquay, and especially to the Librarian and indefatigable Staff of Devon County Library, Plymouth for their unstinting expertise, patience and help with my many awkward requests.

Alan Jefferson

DEVIOCK, CORNWALL

Introduction
The Operas and Gilbert and Sullivan

The operas of Gilbert and Sullivan are a British institution. From their inception, and through two world wars, professional companies played them in Britain and continued to do so until the closure of the D'Oyly Carte Opera Company in 1981 resulted in a new era. The American *Pirates of Penzance* was in production, soon to come to Drury Lane. With the introduction of special productions on film and video, this non-stop performance continues to be played to an ever-growing audience.

The operas are acceptable wherever the English language is spoken and, since the first 'pirated' production of *HMS Pinafore* in the USA, there have been countless performances—professional and amateur—throughout the old British Empire and, more recently, in garrison cities like Hong Kong and Singapore where the resident Service band accompanies local societies. As for amateur societies in Britain, they flourish as always.

The operas are inescapably Victorian in language and humour, but their deep-rooted foundation on folk tradition is responsible for their astonishing and enduring appeal. They can be compared with John Gay's *Beggar's Opera* of 1728 in their revival of past forms and styles, synchronized and updated.

Gilbert turns to the traditional folk theatre for his plots; for the most part his set of recurring characters are stereotyped pantomime ones: hero and heroine, clown and villain, old man and woman, pirate, policeman and Jack Tar. The situations are also based on timeless themes, thwarted love, highborn-lowborn transference, mistaken identity, curses. The libretti have none of the superficial sophistication of the French and Viennese operettas, but Gilbert's

alternatives in wit and topsy-turvydom make infinitely more absorbing entertainment.

Gilbert follows fashionable trends in the setting of his plots, and the undercurrents are always based on some aspect of the political or social status quo. His topsy-turvydom involves the class structure, both intellectual and social—including female emancipation, the services, the Law, and imperial rule.

Gilbert upsets all social *mores* to side with the reformers, but his *dénouements* invariably and rapidly resolve the intricately tangled situation by a reversion to the established pattern, Gilbert showing the rebels to be useless idealists.

As a result of the Industrial Revolution and the prosperity of Victorian England, the creative arts had reached a point of such high skill and ornamentation that the exponents turned to the simplicity of the past, or other cultures for new inspiration. The Aesthetic Movement embodied an almost limitless range of derivative styles and, in all the operas, Gilbert has drawn heavily on images created by the fashionable trend: the Classical, the Japanese, the Italian Renaissance, and Early English. In *Patience*,

his 'æsthetic opera', a suggested improvement of British military uniform embodies an interesting selection: ' ... there *is* a cobwebby grey velvet, with a tender bloom like cold gravy, which, made Florentine fourteenth-century, trimmed with Venetian leather and Spanish altar lace, and surmounted with something Japanese—it matters not what—would at least be Early English!' Kate Greenaway and Walter Crane were exponents of the folk revival in their idiosyncratic styles, and it is fairly obvious that Gilbert had keenly observed their work.

Above:
*c.*1870 card designed by Kate Greenaway for Messrs. Marcus Ward & Co. This picture was obviously copied by Gilbert for his *Bab* illustration 'Would you know?' Much of Gilbert's costume design was in Greenaway style. Constance's dress in *The Sorcerer* revival of 1884 was also based on this picture.
Above right:
'Would you know the kind of maid ...?' Gilbert's *Bab* illustration for Cyril's song in *Princess Ida*.

Another pervading trend, which Gilbert used as a basis for his plots (*The Sorcerer* and *Ruddigore*) was that of Spiritualism; in the last operas in the 1890s, he also played on the Cook's Tours and foreign travel aspect. There have been literary imitators of Gilbert. It is interesting that Benjamin Britten and his librettist, Eric Crozier, have used *mises-en-scène* for *Albert Herring* and *Billy Budd* identical with *The Sorcerer* and *HMS Pinafore*.

Gilbert was always insistent upon correct detail. In the course of preparing *HMS Pinafore*, *The Mikado* and *The Yeoman of the Guard* he visited HMS *Victory*, the Tower of London and the Japanese Exhibition in Knightsbridge, and personally supervised the costumes and properties. However, although his stage creations were correct in every detail, visually they were only accurate in Gilbert's context! The colourful and dramatic costumes for Orders of Knighthood in *Iolanthe* were made by Queen Victoria's Court robe-maker and in the Arcadian landscape of Act I (their 'bar of this House') the Peers sport these robes, completely spurious for their station. Sir Despard's roaring boys in *Ruddigore* have similarly accurate uniforms, contrived to turn them into officers and gentlemen, each of a different regiment: an amazing assortment to be found in a Cornish fishing village. Gilbert's knowledge of the Army was such as to make one believe he was poking fun at the Grenadier Guards when he called the sentry in *Iolanthe* 'Private'. Foibles like these have encouraged millions of people to take for granted Gilbert's topsy-turvy world.

Gilbert's peculiarly eccentric ideas are nearly all embodied in his *Bab Ballads*, written between 1861 and 1879. They are in the *Punch* tradition, both graphically (very similar to Richard Doyle), and in the ideals and characters they lampoon; though Mark Lemon, editor of *Punch* in the 1860s, rejected Gilbert's 'Yarn of the Nancy Bell' and in doing so yielded all the subsequent *Bab Ballads* to *Fun*. Gilbert's great originality lies in the ludicrous and ironic situations to which his characters are subjected. Unlike Edward Lear, Gilbert creates a serious credibility in his nonsense; Gilbert's language is just as sophisticated as Lear's but his words and lines are more calculated—full of puns and meaningful names, but less spontaneous. In this respect it is possible to discover mischievous *doubles ententes* among the lines of the libretti.

A Peer in Garter Robe and Marquis's coronet in the garden of Pencarrow House, Cornwall where, as a guest of Lady Molesworth in August 1892, Sullivan composed the March of the Peers.

In *The Mikado*, a transliterated Japanese warriors' song, 'Miya sama, miya sama ...' has no distinct, alternative erotic meaning. But that particular combination of words can have a suggestive meaning which depends solely on the mind of the interpreter. Gilbert enjoyed these little private jokes. If some of the phrases in *Patience*, for example, are examined it is possible to read more into them than the mere words say:

'Teasing Tom was a very bad boy,
A great big squirt was his favourite toy;...'

Apart from words, some of the situations Gilbert creates give cause for consideration. The relationships between the contralto and her protégé in *Pinafore*, *Pirates* and *The Mikado* are open to speculation as to whether there might not be blood-ties.

Gilbert's illustrations for the early *Bab Ballads* are

Bab drawing for 'The Yarn of the Nancy Bell', first published in *Fun* on 3 March 1866.

Bab illustration 'A Drop of Pantomime Water' in *The Graphic* on Christmas Day 1870.

grotesque but remarkably expressive. He later modified these and replaced them with others, far sweeter and more commonplace. Similarly, it is clear from Gilbert's libretti and stage directions that his original image of his characters and their surroundings was more striking than the one that finally emerged and became the prototype for every subsequent production.

Gilbert was known as a dramatic iconoclast but, in his time, lampoons on the parliamentary system,

class distinction, the clergy, and ageing females were legitimate in the pages of *Punch*, at least. The French thoroughly disliked his jingoistic attitude, particularly the ignominious 'defeat' of 'the Bold Mounseer' in *Ruddigore*. The allusion to Iolanthe's uncomfortable banishment 'among the frogs' was surely intended as another derogatory expression.

Gilbert is always, to all intents and purposes, 'proper', but as social values change, certain words and attitudes become unacceptable: Victorian references to ethnic races, and outmoded words. Gilbert's characterization of ageing women is constantly under attack, but it must be remembered

that his stock contralto character is a descendant of the ever-popular pantomime dame, and if one carefully examines Gilbert's feelings towards her in the operas, they are not without sympathy or pathos.

However, these are qualities which Gilbert seems almost afraid of expressing. They are always accompanied by a tongue-in-cheek self-consciousness which smacks of insincerity. Every time he launches into the truly poetical, there is irony. A Shakespearean chorus in the dramatic second act of *Yeoman* (a so-called serious work) contains ridiculous improbabilities, making a complete parody of the verse. In their search for the escaped Fairfax, the old soldiers have examined

> 'Every chink that holds a mouse,
> Every crevice in the keep,
> Where a beetle black could creep,
> Every outlet, every drain, ...'

The most poignant *coup* in this respect occurs in *The Mikado*, in Ko-Ko's wooing of Katisha. His song 'Tit Willow' ('The Suicide's Grave') is heart-rending, but its disappointing motive is cold, calculating self-interest.

Sullivan's music was entirely responsible for giving credibility to all Gilbert's heart-on-sleeve emotion. After *Princess Ida*, Sullivan was thoroughly disenchanted by Gilbert's irony: 'I should like to set a story of human interest and probability ... where if the situation were a tender or dramatic one, the words would be of a similar character. ...'. Although Sullivan must inevitably be ranked with the Victorian sentimentalists, his music, particularly the

love songs and ballads, transcend contemporary cliché and touch the deeper emotions. The inspiration of Gilbert's libretti has brought out an inventiveness in Sullivan which might otherwise have lain dormant.

Like all his British contemporaries, Sullivan draws on the past: folk songs, sea-shanties, the music of predecessors—Handel, Arne and others, as well as composers of grand opera, borrowed according to the mood and setting of the libretto. Musicologists dismiss Sullivan's operas for they cannot stand beside the giant creations of the nineteenth century, but Sullivan is a typically British miniaturist, a man of the people, writing for them with simple forms and harmonies.

So far as the operas were concerned, Sullivan was limited to as many players as would fit in a normal London orchestra pit—about thirty. This meant a small body of strings, only about sixteen; two flutes, one oboe, two clarinets and one bassoon—two bassoons from *The Yeomen* onwards; no trumpets, because cornets were customary and gave a gentler sound, and two, or occasionally three trombones. Of course there were two horns, but this instrument seems to have been the one deaf spot in all Sullivan's

11

wide and practical instrumental knowledge. In *The Mikado* there are two percussionists whose gong, cymbals and triangle, as well as the timpani, greatly assist in the oriental flavour.

The operas are not just pastiche. From his mixed gleanings, Sullivan has invented a quiet sort of entertainment which bears his indelible mark. Before the revival of British folk song and dance, Sullivan incorporated much traditional music into his work. The operas are musical stepping-stones between the popular music of the eighteenth and twentieth centuries.

It is interesting to know how Sullivan composed his operas, in Gilbert's own words: 'My usual practice is to furnish Sir Arthur Sullivan with the songs of the first act, and while he is setting them I proceed with the songs of act two. When these are practically finished I revert to the dialogue ... while he composes the music, and so it comes to pass that the pianoforte score and the libretto are usually completed at about the same date ...'

Gilbert's use of the word 'songs' does not mean the solo numbers, but all the set pieces, as Grossmith related: 'The music is always learned first. The choruses, finales etc., are composed first in order; then the quarters, the trios; the songs last. ... The greatest interest is evinced by all as the new vocal numbers arrive ... Sullivan will come suddenly, a batch of MS under his arm, and announce that there is something new. He plays over the new number— the vocal parts only are written. The conductor listens and watches and, after hearing them played over a few times, contrives to pick up all the harmonies, casual accompaniments etc. Sullivan is always strict in wishing that his music shall be sung exactly as he has written it.'

Sullivan was invariably short of time and often sought the help of Fred Clay (who died shortly before *Princess Ida* opened) and the Cellier brothers, Alfred and François, who were Sullivan's two conductors. When Alfred Cellier, musical director for *Iolanthe* in New York found himself without an Overture, Sullivan cabled him from London 'Write one yourself'.

Sullivan always composed the Overture last and there were apochryphal stories of pages of music manuscript being handed wet to the players during final rehearsal. On several occasions Sullivan had no time at all, through ill-health usually, to write the Overture himself, and it is not difficult to discern

where these instances occur. Overtures were always pot-pourris of tunes in the opera, with an eye to their becoming orchestral or military band pieces in their own right. Generally there was a repetition of an already familiar number for the finales, to send the audience out with a memorable tune.

This was an aspect of the partnership which always annoyed Gilbert. Apart from several catch-phrases (principally 'What, never?') the public tended to remember Sullivan's tunes and not Gilbert's words. Although the balance between dialogue and set numbers did not change uniformly, there is a considerable difference between the *durchkomponiert Trial by Jury* and the pages of speech in *The Grand Duke*. There was, on the other hand, an aspect of Gilbert's invention that cropped up several times in the partnership and which Sullivan refused to accept—the 'Lozenge Plot'. Whoever took the lozenge was able to change his personality according to his wish. Sullivan felt that this theme led too far in the direction of burlesque which allowed for no sincere human qualities. Despite this one constant rejection, on Sullivan's part, Gilbert was fortunate in having such a composer, who otherwise generally subjugated himself to his irascible librettist's demands.

William Schwenk Gilbert was born on 18 November 1836 in London. His father was a retired naval surgeon and his Scottish mother, Anne Morris, was a cold, hard woman. The parents frequently disagreed, and travelled abroad a good deal with their son and three older daughters, the changes in scene merely postponing the breakdown of their marriage. Gilbert's nickname was 'Bab', short for Baby, and this he retained, together with many foreign memories and experiences for later use. At the age of two he claims to have been snatched from his nursemaid by bandits in Naples and ransomed for £25. There is still speculation as to whether he

merely wandered off and got lost, but at any event the experience had a profound effect on him, and the event recurs in a number of his works.

Gilbert's drawing of Boulogne for the *Bab Ballad* in *Fun*, 12 September 1868.

He was educated in Boulogne, Ealing and at King's College, London and the abrupt end to the Crimean War prevented his applying for a regular commission in the Royal Artillery. Nevertheless he joined the Militia, rising to captain in twenty years, where he acquired a military insistence upon accuracy and obedience.

In 1856, Gilbert joined the Civil Service as a clerk in the Privy Council Office while reading for the Law, writing farces and extravaganzas, and visiting the theatre. Sharp differences with his mother forced him to live in lodgings instead of at home, but a small inheritance released him from the Civil Service and he was called to the Bar. Four years on the Northern Circuit ended in disaster, and since few briefs came to him he spent his spare time in writing and drawing.

In 1861, Gilbert sent an illustrated *Bab Ballad* to H. J. Byron, editor of a new paper, *Fun*, which was attempting to better *Punch*. Byron not only accepted it but engaged Gilbert on a permanent basis although he was only a tiro. So as to obtain a proper entrée into Fleet Street society, Gilbert founded (and fed every Saturday night) a society of promising journalistic and theatrical personalities called 'The Serious Family', including Tom Robertson.

Robertson—an important London dramatist of the 1860s and innovator in the art of production—encouraged Gilbert to attend his rehearsals and gave him a thorough, practical knowledge of stagecraft. Gilbert was recommended (by Robertson) to the St James's Theatre in December 1865, where his Christmas Extravaganza, based entirely on puns, ran for two weeks.

A year later, Gilbert's career as playwright was established at the same theatre with his burlesque *Dulcamara*, based on Donizetti's opera *L'Elisir d'Amore*. In producing it himself, Gilbert founded his personal reputation for autocracy in the theatre.

In his personal life Gilbert was equally autocratic. His rudeness and repartee were vicious in the case of anyone who annoyed him, whether a working partner, a neighbour, a cabby or a complete stranger; he was greedy for conquest and became involved in numerous law suits. A true *enfant terrible*, he risked his reputation by showing off and making outrageously provocative statements in public, and this tactlessness so offended the Establishment that his long awaited knighthood was never bestowed on him by Queen Victoria.

A self-confessing Gilbert emerges in the operas where leading male roles often embody his own worst traits. Bunthorne's insatiable desire for admiration, Gama's compulsive spite, the Mikado's sadistic love of punishment, Pooh-Bah's autocratic desires are all qualities for licensed mockery. Like his Sorcerer and Jack Point, Gilbert was highly conscious of being an entertainer at the mercy of the

Drawing by Gilbert of his wife 'Kitten' (Lucy Agnes *née* Turner).

Gilbert and his wife photographed shortly after their marriage in August 1867.

public. In Jack Point's case, creative output has become a neurosis and the enigmatic nature of this character may be better understood if one sees him as another reflection of his creator. Gilbert could not bear to be in the theatre during premières of his works, and spent the evening roaming about until it was time for him to take his call.

He was sensitive and keenly observant. His characters are often dismissed as stereotypes, but stilted lines badly spoken can conceal the flesh and blood Gilbert gave them. The women in the operas are particularly interesting. Gilbert's attitude to women in reality was eccentric. He understood women in that he was brought up in a predominantly female household—as 'Bab', the baby. Little is known about his long-suffering wife, 'Kitten', except that his letters to her when away from home were always charming and affectionate and she seems to have accepted the curious role of housekeeper and substitute mother-figure to which he subjected her. Gilbert was fascinated by young women, perhaps being so aware of and encumbered by the world of experience, he longed, like Lewis

Carroll, for the company of unspoiled innocence and was devoted to animals and children, although he was childless. But here the comparison ends for Lewis Carroll was puritanical and Gilbert, by all accounts, was distinctly bawdy behind the walls of his club.

His infatuation for girls was such that he would invite his protégées to spend holidays *à trois* with his wife and himself. At his own dinner parties the *men* were asked to retire at the end of the meal with their port, while Gilbert remained alone with the ladies, and he boasted of one room set aside in his house as a 'flirtorium'. At the Savoy Theatre, separate staircases led to male and female dressing-rooms, a theatrical innovation at Gilbert's insistence, and the sexes were only allowed to mix in the green room. He was a jealous guardian of his actresses, turning away all the stage-door Johnnies.

It is not surprising that living in such close proximity with women, Gilbert is so skilful a delineator of their emotions and way of thought. All Gilbert's heroines are different, according to their class: Rose Maybud, the village orphan, is the most

these has very individual characteristics. The worlds of Buttercup, Lady Blanche and the Duchess of Plaza Toro are widely separated.

This understanding of women could not have derived from observation alone. In many ways Gilbert was intuitive as his very topsy-turvydom—the ability to see all sides of a question—and his prolific output bear witness.

Perhaps the most curious manifestation of this trait was his obsession with water. In many of the *Bab Ballads* and in nine of the operas, water forms part of

simple and gullible; Patience, the milkmaid, more complex in her attempt to understand the foibles of the intellectual. Josephine and Mabel are somewhat hampered by being 'the sailor's bride' and the 'self-sacrificing heroine', but even they bear just as individual a mark as the self-centred teenagers, Phyllis, Tessa, Gianetta and Yum-Yum (whose spurious Japanese origin gives licence to her outrageous conceit). In *Yeomen of the Guard* the touchingly emotional Elsie and jealous Phoebe are well set in juxtaposition. At the other end of the scale Aline, Ida, Cassilda and Zara are intelligent women and to them must be added the warm and human Lady Psyche. Ida's 'The world is but a broken toy' (whether intended seriously or not) is a sad reflection on the fate of intelligent girls cast off socially as soon as they were beyond wearing white.

Ironically Gilbert's four most insinuating women have been given seraphic names: Angelina, Angela, Julia Jellicoe ('jellico' was a colloquial word for crystallized angelica) and Lady Blanche. Blanche belongs among the middle-aged contraltos who have been so criticized. On close examination each of

the scene, and in *Iolanthe, Princess Ida, The Mikado* and *The Yeomen* there are references to drowning or a similar situation.

Gilbert met his own real fate in the lake which had been made for him in the grounds of his house, Grim's Dyke, Harrow Weald in 1899. He had often spoken of dying in action, and in later years he had hopes of dying in his own garden on a summer's day. On 29 May 1911, two of his young visitors were swimming in the lake when one of the girls got into difficulties. Gilbert 'plunged himself into the billowy wave' and the effort was too much for him.

The shock of the cold water brought on a heart attack and his death was instantaneous. He died in action as he wished, a Don Quixote involving himself in unnecessary battles to the end. At times he imagined that Sullivan was his worst enemy, with an *idée fixe* that the composer was putting up barriers of music between his words and the audience. This was far from true.

Arthur Seymour Sullivan was born on 13 May 1842 in Lambeth, South London, the second son of a theatre clarinettist. From this humble start he was to become Sir Arthur Sullivan, intimate companion of princes and monarchs, familiar figure at the Monte Carlo Casino, England's leading composer-conductor and champion of British music and musicians.

Over a century later, Sullivan is not remembered for any of these achievements, but instead for his association with W. S. Gilbert and possibly as the composer of 'Onward, Christian Soldiers!', 'The Lost Chord' and a handful of other hymns and Victorian ballads.

Sullivan was born into a musical household. His father was an Irishman and his mother, though born with the Irish name of Coghlan, was of Italian descent and had a good voice. There was an elder brother, Frederic, who completed this happy and devoted family, living on the one guinea a week that clarinet-playing provided.

From an early age, Arthur spent many hours at the piano; and this, coupled with the domestic music-making, the attributes of a fine soprano voice, a wide musical knowledge for his age, remarkably good looks and an engaging personality earned him a place in the Chapel Royal Choir in 1852.

The Chapel Royal led naturally to a scholarship at the Royal Academy of Music (the first Mendelssohn Scholarship to be awarded) and thence to Leipzig, mecca of European musicians. Grieg was a fellow-student, but Sullivan also met Liszt, Spohr and Robert Schumann, and having learned to speak fluent German, he was able to converse with them naturally and with a flair that Liszt, for one, found attractive. Sullivan also acquired an easy and welcome place in German society which gave him the ambition to circulate among royalty.

Sullivan was given an extra year at Leipzig with the plea to accept it because: 'We do not want to see you go.' In this year, he composed his incidental music to *The Tempest* which he brought back with him to London and performed to great acclaim.

The culmination of his musical education came in 1866 with a festival of his own music, including a symphony, which clearly proved that he had 'arrived'. Academicians tipped him as the next Master of the Queen's Musick and everyone was convinced of the importance of this magnetic personality, so well endowed with social and musical gifts.

But drawing-rooms, songs and chamber music did not bring in enough to live on, and Sullivan became, over the next few years, organist-choirmaster at a fashionable Kensington church (where he reinforced a meagre group of voices by importing tenor and bass policemen from a local station); editor of Novello's operatic vocal scores; and resident organist at the Royal Opera House, Covent Garden (where on one occasion during a performance of *Faust* he daringly took the initiative and saved the finale when intercommunication between the conductor and himself had broken down).

An association with the remarkable George Grove (future editor of the music encyclopedia) led to a visit—with Grove and Charles Dickens—to Rossini in Paris. The cheerful old septagenarian played extempore variations on the piano with Sullivan who claimed that this meeting had imbued him with a desire to compose stage works. Sullivan accompanied Grove to Vienna where they unearthed Schubert's manuscript score of the 'lost' *Rosamunde* music, and also brought back to London a previously unknown overture and scores of two Schubert symphonies.

In 1866 a casual invitation from the witty and engaging F.C. Burnand (later editor of *Punch*) drew Sullivan into composing his libretto *Cox and Box*. It was given several times privately in London, with Sullivan 'pounding the piano in smoky atmosphere' and it was then performed with orchestra and three

Arthur Sullivan, *c.*1869.

professional singers in May 1867, with great success.

This, and *The Contrabandista* (a flop), Sullivan regarded as mere side-lines while composing the music, songs and chamber music generally expected from a musician of his calibre. It was with his oratorio 'The Prodigal Son' that Sullivan found himself at the cross-roads. The lure of the stage was strong and it paid well. Only a grand opera would enable him to combine true musical achievement with financial reward of the kind which would enable him to lead the life he so desired.

This was entirely based on his friendship with British and European royalty and high society. As time went on, Sullivan spent longer indulging his expensive hobby of entertaining, being entertained and giving lavish presents, and gambling at the fashionable casinos. This life was sometimes necessary as a palliative and recuperative process after bouts of his recurring kidney complaint, usually associated with hectic work during the last weeks of an opera production.

Because of his easy entrée to many grand houses and palaces, Sullivan was foremost among London's social lions. It was in this capacity that he met the beautiful American, Mrs Mary Ronalds, separated from her husband but not divorced. Their liaison was handled with the greatest tact, and was accepted everywhere as a purely platonic friendship, but it is fairly clear from Sullivan's earlier philanderings that he was hot-blooded and for twenty-four years—from *The Sorcerer* until the end of his life—Mrs Ronalds was Sullivan's mistress. They would probably have married, had she been free to do so, and the measure of his affection for her is shown by the letters he wrote to her every day, even when they were both in London.

Sullivan's male musical friends were Alfred, Duke of Edinburgh and Fred Clay, the composer and early partner with Sullivan in a passionate love-affair with two sisters. Sullivan could not help but charm people of both sexes. His talent for being a good listener and always seeming vitally interested in what other people were saying and doing, his gentleness and sympathy for the bereaved or the troubled, and his generosity and willingness to forgive all, marked him as a lovable man who was always entirely sincere.

It was through Fred Clay that Sullivan became associated with the German Reeds at the Royal Gallery of Illustration, where he first met Gilbert; and then later Clay acted as catalyst and mediator

Richard D'Oyly Carte, *c.*1885.

between the two of them until they were safely in the hands of their business manager, Richard D'Oyly Carte.

Carte's real name was Richard Doyle McCarthy, which seems to indicate Northern Irish origins. He was born on 3 May 1844 in Soho, son of the Carte family of instrument-makers and first importers to London of the saxophone. During a short spell in the family business, Richard studied composition and then founded a theatrical and lecture agency in the Charing Cross Road. His ambition to become a theatrical impresario began to be realized when he was appointed manager of the Royalty Theatre in Soho, which specialized in burlesques and operetta.

'Oily' Carte had managed the celebrated tenor Mario on his farewell tour of concerts in Britain, and he seems to have developed a nose for talent. It was he who suggested Sullivan as the composer of *Trial by Jury* and he who, after much opposition, welded Gilbert and Sullivan together under the auspices of the Comedy Opera Company which he founded by attracting backers, making them directors and then dispensing with their services when he refused to renew their working contract. By that time he had Gilbert and Sullivan safely in his pocket.

HMS Pinafore had been making £500 a week for the directors (the same sum as their initial investment) and so these rejected dissenters hired a gang of thugs to remove the scenery from the stage during a performance. They were seen off by members of the cast and stage staff, and a rival production, mounted simultaneously, but without the guidance of Gilbert, Sullivan or Carte, was a complete failure. Carte took them to court and subsequently won the case against them for the 'Pinafore Riot' of July 1879. Carte's mainly successful management of Gilbert-plus-Sullivan and their operas was based on five-year contracts. Carte firmly believed in contracts, and those he issued to artists virtually gave him licence to make them do anything, perform, sing or write anything that he wished.

In 1881, Carte built the Savoy Theatre on a vacant site off the Strand where John of Gaunt's old palace had once stood. It was a model of 'modern' theatrical architecture and management, was the first London theatre to be lit by electricity, to employ the queue system and to abolish cloakroom and programme charges. Once Carte had his own theatre and no longer had to rely upon renting the old Opéra Comique, the three-way partnership was reconstituted.

After a payment of £4000 a year rental of the Savoy and all running and production expenses, including salaries, Gilbert, Sullivan and Carte each received one third of the net proceeds. After *Patience* they were already rich men, but Carte was the richest of the three. He had the right touch in advertising, in public relations and a flair for continuing to pull in audiences. Gilbert and Sullivan could not have had a better business manager for he looked after his own side of the house and never interfered with theirs. Since the two creative artists frequently fell out, it was the diplomatic Carte, often aided by his highly capable secretary and *alter ago*, Helen Lenoir, who patched up the quarrels.

Carte became adept at subterfuge and trickery when it came to deceiving the American 'pirates' so as to prevent them from stealing a march on the London triumvirate. On a number of occasions he secretly sent companies to New York who arrived,

Programme covers representing simultaneous, rival productions of *HMS Pinafore* in 1881. The 'unofficial' version lasted for only 91 performances; D'Oyly Carte's ran for 571.

ready to open with the new opera and secure its American copyright, before the US 'pirates' were aware of their presence.

Between the unsuccessful *Ruddigore* and *The Yeomen*, things started to go wrong. Sullivan, not Gilbert, was Carte's best man at his wedding to Helen Lenoir at the Savoy Chapel in 1888; Sullivan was invited to become a director of Carte's new Savoy Hotel, not Gilbert; and when Queen Victoria suggested to Sullivan that he should compose a grand opera, it was interpreted as a Royal Command. Carte was prepared to build an opera house in Cambridge Circus which would enable him to extend his activities in a new direction with a flexible deployment of talent. Unfortunately it would naturally exclude Gilbert.

Apart from the fact that Sullivan was a more amenable partner, and more to Carte's taste as a companion—perhaps because they both had Irish blood—it was a great mistake to have emphasized a preference for Sullivan to the detriment of such a sensitive and touchy man as Gilbert.

Soon after the first performance of *The Gondoliers* in December 1889, Carte showed an item of £140, for new carpeting in the Savoy Theatre, on the joint account. Gilbert objected strongly but Sullivan did not demur and the 'Carpet Quarrel' divided the partners. Gilbert remained obdurate and unwisely took Carte to court, where he found Sullivan giving evidence for the other side. Gilbert lost, but in the course of his probings he is reported to have discovered several 'errors' in Carte's accounting elsewhere, one of as much as £1000.

At an auction of properties at the Savoy Theatre, from the original *Yeomen of the Guard* production, Gilbert bought the headsman's axe and block as a memento of his best work with Sullivan. He may have been sincere, for this was his favourite opera.

Carte's most disastrous error of judgement was in The 1891 *Ivanhoe*-Royal English Opera House affair. Sullivan did his best with a paltry libretto for his grand opera *Ivanhoe*, which ran for 155 performances non-stop. It created a record for grand opera which has never been beaten, but it was self-liquidating as a result. There was no back-up repertory, no far-seeing plans, only Messager's *French* opera, *La Basoche*, written specially for Carte's new house and succeeding well enough for a short run. Then the whole scheme folded. Carte had seriously misjudged his architect's capabilities, for the backstage facilities were cramped and impractical, and it was soon clear that the theatre was technically unsuitable for a repertory season of grand opera.

Ivanhoe has only since been given one professional production in London (of two performances). This was in Thomas Beecham's first 1910 opera season at Covent Garden. Carte lacked dynamic planning, all of a sudden, and his efforts to found English Opera were doomed. He lost a fortune and his ambitious dreams were shattered.

How large a part was played by Carte in the reconciliation between Gilbert and Sullivan before *Utopia Limited* is not clear, but it seems certain that he had lost his golden touch. Both Carte and Sullivan bent over backwards in allowing Gilbert's newest protégée (later his adopted daughter) the American amateur, Nancy McIntosh, to play the lead in this opera, although they afterwards insisted on her exclusion from *The Grand Duke*.

Gilbert and Sullivan appeared in public on the stage only once more, in September 1898 after a second revival of *The Sorcerer* and *Trial by Jury*. They took their call from opposite sides of the stage, with Carte between them, and walked off. There were no handshakes, and Gilbert ignored Sullivan. Attempts by Helen Carte to bring the three partners together again might have worked, at least temporarily, for Gilbert wrote a cordial note to Sullivan after the revival of *Patience* in early November 1900, regretting the composer's absence through illness, and hoping to find him recovered on his own return from Egypt. Gilbert was in Egypt when Sullivan died on 22 November, and read of his State Funeral and his burial in the crypt of St Paul's Cathedral.

Richard D'Oyly Carte, only fifty-seven, followed Sullivan on 2 April 1901, thus leaving the redoubtable Gilbert alive, cured of his tiresome gout, and enjoying his 'retirement' for another ten years. But the effects of Richard D'Oyly Carte's administration were to be felt up to 1981.

During the worst years of American 'piracy' in the late 1870s and the early 1880s, and until he learned how best to combat this canker, there was an urgent need for security of all music as well as strict secrecy concerning operas in production. This seems to have continued long after the need for it had

Sir Arthur Sullivan at the time of *Utopia, Limited*, 1893.

The mature Gilbert.

The D'Oyly Carte Company photographed on board HMS
Duchess of Atholl in September 1928 at the start of their
Canadian and American tour. Among them are Leslie Rands,
Darrell Fancourt, Henry Lytton, Bertha Lewis, Beatrice
Elburn, Pauline Wootten, Sydney Granville, Charles Goulding
and Martyn Green.

passed, for an atmosphere of suspicion and a fog of
uncertainty existed round the Company in later
years. From biographies and contemporary accounts
it seems likely that the early Savoyards (as they came
to be called) thoroughly enjoyed their peripatetic life
and had enormous fun together. Under later
administrations the approaching and fateful 'out of
copyright date' seemed to have a paralysing effect
upon the D'Oyly Carte Opera Company, whose
particular monopoly has never been matched. While
copyright still held, every amateur performance was
subject to scrutiny and could be stopped by the
visiting inspector from the D'Oyly Carte if it did not
conform to standards and traditions of presentation.

Today there is no D'Oyly Carte Opera Company
and perhaps their strict adherence to 'tradition' was
to blame for their demise, coupled with an
acknowledged bill for travelling which could no
longer be met out of box office receipts. But the
amateur societies continue as before, less restrained
and often with real guidance from a former Savoyard
whose ability to pass on his or her knowledge of the
Gilbert tradition must inevitably enrich any
performance.

Foremost among them today is John Reed,
D'Oyly Carte Company member from 1951, and
principal baritone between 1959 and 1977, an
inspiration to professionals and amateurs alike,
especially in the USA, where he also lectures at
universities. He enlivens performers and encourages
them to develop their own ideas, whether he is
producing or taking part in the production himself.

Gilbert's folk-tale traditions are everlasting and as
long as we can still enjoy pure melodic line in the
accepted European idiom, so is Sullivan's music. The
'big band sound' may take over temporarily, but it
cannot replace Sullivan's delicate, subtle and pure
instrumental line—the most significant aspect of this
British phenomenon.

At the end of a wearing tour of the USA, an
American impresario reassured the apologetic
D'Oyly Carte Manager: 'Don't worry how it looks,
son—they don't go out whistling the scenery!'

21

John Reed, OBE, Principal of the
D'Oyly Carte Opera Company 1959-79, in
'the twelve'. The last photograph represents
his unique concert performance as the
Grand Duke.

Thespis

or The Gods grown old

In November 1869 Sullivan first met Gilbert at the Gallery of Illustration, Lower Regent Street. They were already recognized as masters in their respective professions. Gilbert had been writing burlesques for London managements and their 'broad' entertainment since 1866; in 1869 he was writing and producing plays for Mr and Mrs German Reed who ran the Gallery as a family entertainment business providing clean fun, topical jokes and comic business.

Sullivan's one success in the operetta field had been *Cox and Box* in 1867 (to a libretto by Francis Burnand that might easily be mistaken for one by Gilbert); Sullivan's *Contrabandista* a few months later was a disastrous failure.

German Reed had attempted to bring Gilbert and Sullivan together in 1870 during a rehearsal of 'Ages Ago' but Sullivan had been put off by Gilbert's arrogant manner: he flippantly tricked Sullivan with a musical conundrum. But in the autumn of 1871, Sullivan changed his mind with regard to Gilbert and agreed to set *Thespis*, his 'Christmas operatic extravaganza'. This was the year of 'Onward, Christian Soldiers', some other short pieces and an oratorio, which did not produce anything like the financial return necessary to support Sullivan in his expensive life among titled and royal companions. Perhaps this was the reason for his decision to sign a contract with Gilbert and John Hollingshead, the enterprising manager of the (old) Gaiety Theatre in the Strand.

It was a coup for Hollingshead, who had already employed Gilbert as adaptor and producer of an operatic burlesque. Consequently Gilbert was familiar with the talents of the leading Gaiety artists for whom he wrote *Thespis*. This type of burlesque went back to Planché's 1832 'Olympic Revels' (at the Olympic Theatre, of course) where four Greek gods were discovered playing whist. Offenbach's *Orpheus in the Underworld*, given in two London productions in 1865 and 1869, had extended the popularity of Olympian farce; but while Offenbach's plot (by Crémieux and Halévy) is firmly based on the legend of Orpheus, Gilbert merely uses Greek trappings as a costume and scenic vehicle for a *Bab* burlesque, which he was to repeat almost exactly in *The Grand Duke*, twenty-five years later at the end of the partnership.

Green Room at the old Gaiety Theatre (demolished 1902). J. L. Toole (1830-1906), standing against the fireplace, played Thespis in the original production.

In later Savoy opera terms, *Thespis* was thrown upon the Gaiety stage with little more than a week's rehearsal. The leading players: J. L. Toole, Nellie Farren, Mlle Clary and Fred Sullivan (the composer's brother) were working at the Crystal Palace in the afternoons and unavailable to Gilbert. Carpenters were occupying the Gaiety stage when the players were there in the mornings, and consequently *Thespis* was presented to the Boxing Night audience in an under-rehearsed state. Together with its curtain-raiser, it over-ran for more than an hour and was booed. Hollingshead had faith in the burlesque, however, and after some tightening-up, *Thespis* ran comfortably for sixty-three performances—about the same duration as a normal London pantomime.

Contemporary press criticisms display an element of surprise at the quality of *Thespis*, which was above the heads of many in the audience, and all critics showed acute appreciation of the music.

There was a special benefit performance of *Thespis* after its run at the Gaiety, but thereafter it has never been revived professionally. Sullivan reclaimed his full score and band parts from Hollingshead some years afterwards, but then they disappeared and were not found among Sullivan's effects. A vocal score in the secret possession of a London firm of music publishers was destroyed by fire in the 1960s, and with it vanished all trace of the music, except for two numbers. While the libretto is printed here, in the uncorrected form as Gilbert left it, the opera can

Live performance of *Thespis*: (l to r) Fred Sullivan as Apollo, Frank Wood as Mars; John Maclean, Jupiter; J. L. Toole, Thespis; Fred Payne, Stupidas; Henry Payne, Preposteros; Nelly Farren, Mercury. *London Illustrated News*, 6 January 1872.

Thespis in rehearsal at the Gaiety. Gilbert second from right under the 'T-piece' gas-light. Pen and ink drawing by Alfred Bryan.

never be performed with Sullivan's music unless another score comes to light: not impossible, but unlikely.

SYNOPSIS

The scene is a ruined temple on Mount Olympus. An elderly Diana, clad in mackintosh and galoshes, argues with an Apollo in dressing-gown and smoking cap. This sets the level of the entertainment. An exceedingly decrepit Jupiter and frolicsome Mercury join them, only to hide from a group of mortals who, by climbing up Mount Olympus, are invading their time-honoured privacy. Two of the mortals appear. They are a boy (Sparkeion) and a girl (Nicemis) and it is their wedding day. They belong to a touring theatrical troupe and its manager, Thespis, has arranged for his company to have the day off so that they can all celebrate the wedding with a picnic on the mountain top. A quarrel ensues between the pair when Nicemis restrains Sparkeion's advances because they are 'not quite married'.

Nellie Farren (1848-1904), female star at the Gaiety and the original Mercury in *Thespis*. Gilbert was tied by the conventions of this theatre to condone the breeches role as well as a good deal of ad libbing.

The Thespians' arrival interrupts them, and as the actors appear, they sing the chorus 'Climbing over Rocky Mountain' which Sullivan was to use again in *The Pirates of Penzance*. It is a travelling song, ideally expressing their ascent and the pulling up of picnic baskets.

The Thespians settle down to their feast, and Thespis treats them all (for evidently the nth time) to his song about the director of a railway company at the North South East West Diddlesex Junction who was so benevolent that the company went into bankruptcy. According to contemporary press reports this was the most popular number in the opera. The orchestral accompaniment, with sand-blocks and whistles, and the actors chugging like pistons or whirring their arms round like wheels, combined to give an exciting and realistic impression of a railway train.

The gods appear and Thespis comes face to face with Jupiter. Recognizing each other as managers—though of different sorts—they agree that their respective companies shall change places for a year. Thespis maintains that it will be beneficial for the gods to test public reaction to themselves on earth, and thus repair their public image.

Act II opens on Olympus 'in a terrible muddle', for a year of rule by the deputy gods has wrought disaster. By delegating responsibility to his minions, the easy-going Thespis has failed as deputy Jupiter. Sparkeion is now deputy Apollo and he has forsaken Nicemis for Pretteia, now deputy Diana. He sings a song, 'Little Maid of Arcadee' which tells the story of the eternal triangle. (This song was published as a ballad and its music still exists.) Because deputy Apollo spends so much time with deputy Diana, the sun now shines by night as well as by day. Other seasonal upsets have resulted in a shoal of complaints from Greek mortals, and Mercury has collected them all.

The complaints are now to be heard, since it is the day of reckoning. Thespis presides over the court of enquiry at which the masked figures of three real gods are present as 'gentlemen of the Athenian press'. After four cases have been heard, the enraged gods reveal themselves and consign the actors to a fate of becoming 'eminent tragedians, whom no one ever goes to see!' As the Thespians return to earth, they and the gods all sing the refrain of the Diddlesex Junction song.

THESPIS;

OR

THE GODS GROWN OLD.

First produced at the Gaiety Theatre, 26 December 1871

DRAMATIS PERSONÆ

GODS.		THESPIANS.	
JUPITER		THESPIS	STUPIDAS
APOLLO	[Aged Deities]	SILLIMON	SPARKEION
MARS		TIMIDON	NICEMIS
DIANA		TIPSEION	PRETTEIA
VENUS		PREPOSTEROS	DAPHNE
MERCURY			CYMON

ACT I.

RUINED TEMPLE ON THE SUMMIT OF OLYMPUS.

ACT II.

THE SAME SCENE, WITH THE RUINS RESTORED, ONE YEAR LATER.

THESPIS;

OR,

THE GODS GROWN OLD.

ACT I

SCENE—*The ruins of The Temple of the Gods on summit of Mount Olympus. Picturesque shattered columns, overgrown with ivy, etc.,* R. *and* L., *with entrances to temple (ruined)* R. *Fallen columns on the stage. Three broken pillars* 2 R. E. *At the back of stage is the approach from the summit of the mountain. This should be "practicable" to enable large numbers of people to ascend and descend. In the distance are the summits of adjacent mountains. At first all this is concealed by a thick fog, which clears presently. Enter (through fog) Chorus of Stars coming off duty, as fatigued with their night's work*

CHORUS OF STARS

Throughout the night
  The constellations
Have given light
  From various stations.
When midnight gloom
  Falls on all nations,
We will resume
  Our occupations.

SOLO   Our light, it's true,
    Is not worth mention;
What can we do
    To gain attention,
When, night and noon,
    With vulgar glaring,
A great big Moon
    Is *always* flaring?

CHORUS   Throughout the night, etc.

During Chorus Enter DIANA, *an elderly Goddess. She is carefully wrapped up in Cloaks, Shawls, etc. A Hood is over her head, a Respirator in her mouth, and Goloshes on her feet. During the chorus she takes these things off, and discovers herself dressed in the usual costume of the Lunar Diana, the Goddess of the Moon*

DIA. *(shuddering)* Ugh! How cold the nights are! I don't know how it is, but I seem to feel the night air a great deal more than I used to. But it is time for the sun to be rising. *(Calls)* Apollo.

AP. *(within)* Hollo!

DIA. I've come off duty—it's time for you to be getting up.

Enter APOLLO. *(He is an elderly "buck" with an air of assumed juvenility, and is dressed in dressing gown and smoking cap*

AP. *(yawning)* I shan't go out to-day. I was out yesterday and the day before and I want a little rest. I don't know how it is, but I seem to feel my work a great deal more than I used to.

DIA. I'm sure these short days can't hurt you. Why, you don't rise till six and you're in bed again by five: you should have a turn at *my* work and see how you like that—out all night!

AP. My dear sister, I don't envy you—though I remember when I did—but that was when I was a younger sun. I don't think I'm quite well. Perhaps a little change of air will do me good. I've a great mind to show myself in London this winter, they'll be very glad to see me. No! I shan't go out to-day. I shall send them this fine, thick wholesome fog and they won't miss me. It's the best substitute for a blazing sun—and like most substitutes, nothing at all like the real thing. *(To fog)* Be off with you.

[*Fog clears away and discovers the scene described*

Hurried Music. MERCURY *shoots up from behind precipice at back of stage. He carries several parcels afterwards described. He sits down, very much fatigued*

MER. Home at last. A nice time I've had of it.

DIA. You young scamp you've been down all night again. This is the third time you've been out this week.

MER. Well *you're* a nice one to blow me up for that.

DIA. *I* can't help being out all night.

MER. And I can't help being down all night. The nature of Mercury requires that he should go down when the sun sets, and rise again, when the sun rises.

DIA. And what have you been doing?

MER. Stealing on commission. There's a set of false teeth and a box of Life Pills—that's for Jupiter—An invisible peruke and a bottle of hair dye—that's for Apollo—A respirator and a pair of goloshes—that's for Cupid—A full bottomed chignon, some auricomous fluid, a box of pearl-powder, a pot of rouge, and a hare's foot—that's for Venus.

DIA. Stealing! you ought to be ashamed of yourself!

MER. Oh, as the god of thieves I must do something to justify my position.

DIA. and AP. *(contemptuously).* Your position!

MER. Oh I know it's nothing to boast of, even on earth. Up here, it's simply contemptible. Now that you gods are to old for your work, you've made me the miserable drudge of Olympus—groom, valet, postman, butler, commissionaire, maid of all work, parish beadle, and original dustman.

AP. Your Christmas boxes ought to be something considerable.

MER. They ought to be but they're not. I'm treated abominably. I make everybody and I'm nobody—I go everywhere and I'm nowhere—I do everything and I'm nothing. I've made thunder for Jupiter, odes for Apollo, battles for Mars, and love for Venus. I've married couples for Hymen, and six weeks afterwards, I've divorced them for Cupid—and in return I get all the kicks while they pocket the halfpence. And in compensation for robbing me of the halfpence in question, what have they done for me?

AP. Why they've—ha! ha! they've made you the god of thieves!

MER. Very self-denying of them—there isn't one of them who hasn't a better claim to the distinction than I have.

SONG—MERCURY

Oh, I'm the celestial drudge,
　From morning to night I must stop at it,
On errands all day I must trudge,
　And I stick to my work till I drop at it!
In summer I get up to one
　(As a good-natured donkey I'm ranked for it),
Then I go and I light up the Sun,
　And Phœbus Apollo gets thanked for it!
　　Well, well, it's the way of the world,
　　　And will be through all its futurity;
　　Though noodles are baroned and earled,
　　　There's nothing for clever obscurity!

I'm the slave of the Gods, neck and heels,
　And I'm bound to obey, though I rate at 'em;
And I not only order their meals,
　But cook 'em, and serve 'em, and wait at 'em.
Then I make all their nectar—I do—
　(Which a terrible liquor to rack us is)
And whenever I mix them a brew,
　Why all the thanksgivings are Bacchus's!
　　Well, well, it's the way of the world, &c.

Then reading and writing I teach,
　And spelling-books many I've edited!
And for bringing those arts within reach,
　That donkey Minerva gets credited.
Then I scrape at the stars with a knife,
　And plate-powder the moon (on the days for it),
And I hear all the world and his wife
　Awarding Diana the praise for it!
　　Well, well, it's the way of the world, etc.

[*After song—very loud and majestic music is heard*

DIA. and MER. *(looking off)* Why, who's this? Jupiter, by Jove!

Enter JUPITER, *an extremely old man, very decrepit, with very thin straggling white beard, he wears a long braided dressing-gown, handsomely trimmed, and a silk night-cap on his head.* MERCURY *falls back respectfully as he enters*

JUP. Good day, Diana—ah Apollo—Well, well, well, what's the matter? what's the matter?

DIA. Why, that young scamp Mercury says that we do nothing, and leave all the duties of Olympus to him! Will you believe it, he actually says that our influence on earth is dropping down to *nil.*

JUP. Well, well—don't be hard on the lad—to tell you the truth, I'm not sure that he's very far wrong. Don't let it go any further, but, between ourselves, the sacrifices and votive offerings have fallen off terribly of late. Why, I can remember the time when people offered us human sacrifices—no mistake about it—human sacrifices! think of that!

DIA. Ah! those good old days!

JUP. Then it fell off to oxen, pigs, and sheep.

AP. Well, there are worse things than oxen, pigs, and sheep.

JUP. So I've found to my cost. My dear sir—between ourselves, it's dropped off from one thing to another until it has positively dwindled down to preserved Australian beef! What do you think of that?

AP. I don't like it at all.

JUP. You won't mention it—it might go further—

DIA. It couldn't fare worse.

JUP. In short, matters have come to such a crisis that there's no mistake about it—something must be done to restore our influence, the only question is, *What?*

QUARTETTE

MER. *(coming forward in great alarm)*

ENTER MARS

Oh incident unprecedented!
    I hardly can believe it's true!

MARS. Why, bless the boy, he's quite demented!
    Why, what's the matter, sir, with you?

AP. Speak quickly, or you'll get a warming!

MER. Why, mortals up the mount are swarming,
    Our temple on Olympus storming,
      In hundreds—aye in thousands, too!

ALL.   Goodness gracious,
      How audacious;
      Earth is spacious,
        Why come here?
      Our impeding
      Their proceeding
      Were good breeding,
        That is clear.

DIA. Jupiter, hear my plea;
    Upon the mount if *they* light,
    There'll be an end of me,
    I won't be seen by daylight!

AP. Tartarus is the place
    These scoundrels you should send to—
    Should they behold my face
    My influence there's an end to!

JUP. *(looking over precipice)* What fools to give
    themselves so much exertion!

DIA. *(looking over precipice)* A government survey
    I'll make assertion!

AP. *(looking over precipice)* Perhaps the Alpine club
    at their diversion!

MER. *(looking over precipice)* They seem to be more
    like a "Cook's Excursion."

ALL.   Goodness gracious, etc.

AP. If, Mighty Jove, you value your existence,
    Send them a thunderbolt with your regards!

JUP. My thunderbolts, though valid at a distance,

Are not effective at a hundred yards.

MER. Let the moon's rays, Diana, strike 'em flighty,
    Make 'em lunatics in various styles!

DIA. My Lunar rays unhappily are mighty
    Only at many hundred thousand miles.

ALL.   Goodness gracious, etc.

[*Exeunt* JUPITER, APOLLO, DIANA, *and* MERCURY *into ruined temple*

Enter SPARKEION *and* NICEMIS *climbing mountain at back*

SPAR. Here we are at last on the very summit, and we've left the others ever so far behind! Why, what's this?

NICE. A ruined palace! A palace on the top of a mountain. I wonder who lives here? Some mighty king, I dare say, with wealth beyond all counting, who came to live up here—

SPAR. To avoid his creditors! It's a lovely situation for a country house, though it's very much out of repair.

NICE. Very inconvenient situation.

SPAR. Inconvenient?

NICE. Yes—how are you to get butter, milk, and eggs up here? No pigs—no poultry—no postman. Why, I should go mad.

SPAR. What a dear little practical mind it is! What a wife you will make!

NICE. Don't be too sure—we are only partly married—the marriage ceremony lasts all day.

SPAR. I've no doubt at all about it. We shall be as happy as a king and queen, though we are only a strolling actor and actress.

NICE. It's very kind of Thespis to celebrate our marriage day by giving the company a pic-nic on this lovely mountain.

SPAR. And still more kind to allow us to get so much ahead of all the others. Discreet Thespis! [*Kissing her.*

NICE. There now, get away, do! Remember the marriage ceremony is not yet completed.

SPAR. But it would be ungrateful to Thespis's discretion not to take advantage of it by improving the opportunity.

NICE. Certainly not; get away.

SPAR. On second thoughts the opportunity's so good it don't admit of improvement. There! [*Kisses her.*

NICE. How dare you kiss me before we are quite married?

SPAR. Attribute it to the intoxicating influence of the mountain air.

NICE. Then we had better do down again. It is not right to expose ourselves to influences over which we have no control.

DUET—SPARKEION AND NICEMIS

SPAR.   Here far away from all the world,
      Dissension and derision,
    With Nature's wonders all unfurled
      To our delighted vision,
        With no one here
          (At least in sight)
        To interfere
          With our delight,
      And two fond lovers sever,
        Oh do not free,
          Thine hand from mine,
      I swear to thee
        My love is thine,
      For ever and for ever!

NICE.   On mountain top the air is keen,
And most exhilarating,
And we say things we do not mean
In moments less elating.
So please to wait,
For thoughts that crop,
En tête-á-tête,
On mountain top,
May not exactly tally
With those that you
May entertain,
Returning to
The sober plain
Of yon relaxing valley.

SPAR. Very well—if you won't have anything to say to me, I know who will.

NICE. Who will?

SPAR. Daphne will.

NICE. Daphne would flirt with anybody.

SPAR. Anybody would flirt with Daphne. She is quite as pretty as you and has twice as much back-hair.

NICE. She has twice as much money, which may account for it.

SPAR. At all events, *she* has appreciation. *She* likes good looks.

NICE. We all like what we haven't got.

SPAR. *She* keeps her eyes open.

NICE. Yes—one of them.

SPAR. Which one?

NICE. The one she doesn't wink with.

SPAR. Well, I was engaged to her for six months and if she still makes eyes at me, you must attribute it to force of habit. Besides —remember—we are only half-married at present.

NICE. I suppose you mean that you are going to treat me as shamefully as you treated her. Very well, break it off if you like. *I* shall not offer any objection. Thespis used to be very attentive to me, and I'd just as soon be a manager's wife as a fifth-rate actor's!

Chorus heard, at first below, then enter DAPHNE, PRETTEIA, PREPOSTEROS, STUPIDAS, TIPSEION, CYMON, *and other members of* THESPIS' *company climbing over rocks at back. All carry small baskets.*

Chorus—[with dance]

Climbing over rocky mountain,
Skipping rivulet and fountain,
Passing where the willows quiver,
By the ever rolling river,
Swollen with the summer rain.
Threading long and leafy mazes,
Dotted with unnumbered daisies,
Scaling rough and rugged passes,
Climb the hardy lads and lasses,
Till the mountain-top they gain.

FIRST VOICE   Fill the cup and tread the measure,
Make the most of fleeting leisure,
Hail it as a true ally,
Though it perish bye and bye!

SECOND VOICE   Every moment brings a treasure
Of its own especial pleasure,
Though the moments quickly die,
Greet them gaily as they fly!

THIRD VOICE   Far away from grief and care,
High up in the mountain air,
Let us live and reign alone,
In a world that's all our own.

FOURTH VOICE   Here enthroned in the sky,
Far away from mortal eye,
We'll be gods and make decrees,
Those may honour them who please.

CHORUS   Fill the cup and tread the measure,
etc.

After CHORUS *and* COUPLETS *enter* THESPIS *climbing over rocks*

THES. Bless you, my people, bless you. Let the revels commence. After all, for thorough, unconstrained unconventional enjoyment give me a pic-nic.

PREP. *(very gloomily)* Give him a pic-nic somebody!

THES. Be quiet, Preposteros—don't interrupt.

PREP. Ha! ha! shut up again! But no matter.

STUPIDAS *endeavours, in pantomime, to reconcile him. Throughout the scene* PREP. *shows symptoms of breaking out into a furious passion, and* STUPIDAS *does all he can to pacify and restrain him*

THES. The best of a pic-nic is that everybody contributes what he pleases, and nobody knows what anybody else has brought till the last moment. Now, unpack everybody, and let's see what there is for everybody.

NICE. I have brought you—a bottle of soda water—for the claret-cup.

DAPH. I have brought you—a lettuce for the lobster salad.

SPAR. A piece of ice—for the claret-cup.

PRETT. A bottle of vinegar—for the lobster-salad.

CYMON. A bunch of burrage for the claret-cup!

TIPS. A hard-boiled egg—for the lobster-salad!

STUP. One lump of sugar for the claret-cup!

PREP. He has brought one lump of sugar for the claret-cup? Ha! Ha! Ha!   *[Laughing melodramatically*

STUP. Well, Preposteros, and what have *you* brought?

PREP. *I* have brought *two* lumps of the very best salt for the lobster salad.

THES. Oh—is that all?

PREP. All! Ha! Ha! He asks if it is all!   *[STUPIDAS consoles him*

THES. But, I say—this is capital so far as it goes—nothing could be better, but it doesn't go far enough. The claret, for instance! I don't insist on claret—or a lobster—I don't insist on lobster, but a lobster salad without a lobster, why, it isn't lobster salad. Here, Tipseion!

TIPSEION *(a very drunken bloated fellow, dressed, however, with scrupulous accuracy and wearing a large medal round his neck).* My Master?   *[Falls on his knees to* THES. *and kisses his robe*

THES. Get up—don't be a fool. Where's the claret? We arranged last week that you were to see to that.

TIPS. True, dear master. But then I was a drunkard!

THES. You were.

TIPS. You engaged me to play convivial parts on the strength of my personal appearance.

THES. I did.

TIPS. You then found that my habits interfered with my duties as low comedian.

THES. True—

TIPS. You said yesterday that unless I took the pledge you would dismiss me from your company.

THES. Quite so.

TIPS. Good. I have taken it. It is all I have taken since yesterday. My preserver! [Embraces him

THES. Yes, but where's the wine?

TIPS. I left it behind, that I might not be tempted to violate my pledge.

PREP. Minion! [Attempts to get at him, is restrained by STUPIDAS

THES. Now, Preposteros, what is the matter with you?

PREP. It is enough that I am down-trodden in my profession. I will not submit to imposition out of it. It is enough that as your heavy villain I get the worst of it every night in a combat of six. I will not submit to insult in the day time. I have come out, ha! ha! to enjoy myself!

THES. But look here, you know—virtue only triumphs at night from seven to ten—vice gets the best of it during the other twenty-three hours. Won't that satisfy you?

[STUPIDAS endeavours to pacify him

PREP. (irritated to STUP.) Ye are odious to my sight! get out of it!

STUP. (in great terror) What have I done?

THES. Now what is it, Preposteros, what is it?

PREP. I a-hate him and would have his life!

THES. (to STUP.) That's it—he hates you and would have your life. Now go and be merry.

STUP. Yes, but why does he hate me?

THES. Oh—exactly. (To PREP.) Why do you hate him?

PREP. Because he is a minion!

THES. He hates you because you are a minion. It explains itself. Now go and enjoy yourselves. Ha! ha! It is well for those who can laugh—let them do so—there is no extra charge. The light-hearted cup and the convivial jest for them—but for me—what is there for me?

SILLIMON. There is some claret-cup and lobster salad.

[Handing some.

THES. (taking it) Thank you. (Resuming) What is there for me but anxiety—ceaseless gnawing anxiety that tears at my very vitals and rends my peace of mind asunder? There is nothing whatever for me but anxiety of the nature I have just described. The charge of these thoughtless revellers is my unhappy lot. It is not a small charge, and it is rightly termed a lot, because they are many. Oh why did the gods make me a manager?

SILL. (as guessing a riddle) Why did the gods make him a manager?

SPAR. Why did the gods make him a manager?

DAPH. Why did the gods make him a manager?

PRETT. Why did the gods make him a manager?

THES. No—no—what are you talking about? what do you mean?

DAPH. I've got it—don't tell us—

ALL. No—no—because—because—

THES. (annoyed) It isn't a conundrum—it's a misanthropical question. Why cannot I join you? [Retires up centre

DAPH. (who is sitting with SPARKEION to the annoyance of NICEMIS who is crying alone) I'm sure I don't know. We do not want you.

Don't distress yourself on our account—we are getting on very comfortably—aren't we, Sparkeion?

SPAR. We are so happy that we don't miss the lobster or the claret. What are lobster and claret compared with the society of those we love?

[Embracing DAPHNE

DAPH. Why, Nicemis, love, you are eating nothing. Aren't you happy, dear?

NICE. (spitefully). You are quite welcome to my share of everything. I intend to console myself with the society of my manager.

[Takes THESPIS' arm affectionately.

THES. Here I say—this won't do, you know—I can't allow it—at least before my company—besides, you are half-married to Sparkeion. Sparkeion, here's your half-wife impairing my influence before my company. Don't you know the story of the gentleman who undermined his influence by associating with his inferiors?

ALL. Yes, yes,—we know it.

PREP. (furiously) I do not know it! It's ever thus! Doomed to disappointment from my earliest years—

[STUPIDAS endeavours to console him

THES. There—that's enough. Preposteros—you shall hear it.

SONG—THESPIS

I once knew a chap who discharged a function
On the North South East West Diddlesex junction,
He was conspicuous exceeding,
For his affable ways and his easy breeding.
Although a Chairman of Directors,
He was hand in glove with the ticket inspectors,
He tipped the guards with brand-new fivers,
And sang little songs to the engine drivers
 T'was told to me with great compunction,
 By one who had discharged with unction,
 A Chairman of Director's Function,
 On the North South East West Diddlesex junction.
  Fol diddle, lol diddle, lol lol lay.

Each Christmas Day he gave each stoker
A silver shovel and a golden poker,
He'd button-hole flowers for the ticket sorters,
And rich Bath-buns for the outside porters.
He'd mount the clerks on his first-class hunters,
And he built little villas for the road-side shunters,
And if any were fond of pigeon shooting,
He'd ask them down to his place at Tooting.
 'Twas told to me, etc.

In course of time there spread a rumour
That he did all this from a sense of humour,
So instead of signalling and stoking,
They gave themselves up to a course of joking.
Whenever they knew that he was riding,
They shunted his train on lonely siding,
Or stopped all night in the middle of a tunnel,
On the plea that the boiler was a-coming through
  the funnel.
 'Twas told to me, etc.

If he wished to go to Perth or Stirling,
His train through several counties whirling,
Would set him down in a fit of larking,
At four a.m. in the wilds of Barking.
This pleased his whim and seemed to strike it,
But the general Public did not like it,
The receipts fell, after a few repeatings,
And he got it hot at the annual meetings,
    'Twas told to me, etc.

He followed out his whim with vigour,
The shares went down to a nominal figure,
These are the sad results proceeding
From his affable ways and his easy breeding!
The line, with its rails and guards and peelers,
Was sold for a song to marine store dealers,
The shareholders are all in the work'us,
And he sells pipe-lights in the Regent Circus.
    'Twas told to me with much compunction,
    By one who had discharged with unction
    A Chairman of Directors' function,
    On the North South East West Diddlesex junction,
      Fol diddle, lol diddle, lol lol lay!

                              [After song

THES. It's very hard. As a man I am naturally of an easy disposition. As a manager, I am compelled to hold myself aloof, that my influence may not be deteriorated. As a man, I am inclined to fraternize with the pauper—as a manager I am compelled to walk about like this: Don't know yah! Don't know yah! Don't know yah!

Strides haughtily about the stage, JUPITER, MARS, *and* APOLLO, *in full Olympian costume appear on the three broken columns. Thespians scream*

JUPITER, MARS AND APOLLO *(in recit.)* Presumptuous mortal!

THES. *(same business)* Don't know yah! don't know yah!

JUP. MARS and APOLLO *(seated on three broken pillars, still in recit.)* Presumptuous mortal!

THES. *(same business)* Don't know yah! Don't know yah!

JUP., MARS and APOLLO *(seated on three broken pillars, still in recit.)* Presumptuous mortal!

THES. *(recit.)* Remove this person.

                *[*STUP. *and* PREP. *seize* AP. *and* MARS.

JUP. *(speaking)* Stop, you evidently *don't* know me. Allow me to offer you my card.   *[Throws flash paper*

THES. Ah yes, it's very pretty, but we don't want any at present. When we do our Christmas piece I'll let you know. *(Changing his manner)* Look here, you know, this is a private party and we haven't the pleasure of your acquaintance. There are a good many other mountains about, if you must have a mountain all to yourself. Don't make me let myself down before my company. *(Resuming)* Don't know yah! Don't know yah!

JUP. I am Jupiter, the King of the Gods. This is Apollo. This is Mars.

                [All kneel to them except THESPIS

THES. Oh! then as I'm a respectable man, and rather particular about the company I keep, I think I'll go.

JUP. No—no—stop a bit. We want to consult you on a matter of great importance. There! Now we are alone. Who are you?

THES. I am Thespis of the Thessalian Theatres.

JUP. The very man we want. Now as a judge of what the public likes, are you impressed with my appearance as the father of the gods?

THES. Well to be candid with you, I am not. In fact I'm disappointed.

JUP. Disappointed?

THES. Yes, you see you're so much out of repair. No, you don't come up to my idea of the part. Bless you, I've played you often.

JUP. You have!

THES. To be sure I have.

JUP. And how have you dressed the part?

THES. Fine commanding party in the prime of life. Thunderbolt—full beard—dignified manner—A good deal of this sort of thing "Don't know yah! Don't know yah! Don't know yah!"   *[Imitating, crosses* L

JUP. *(much affected)* I—I'm very much obliged to you. It's very good of you. I—I—I used to be like that. I can't tell you how much I feel it. And do you find I'm an impressive character to play.

THES. Well no, I can't say you are. In fact we don't use you much out of burlesque.

JUP. Burlesque!   *[Offended, walks up*

THES. Yes, it's a painful subject, drop it, drop it. The fact is, you are not the gods you were—you're behind your age.

JUP. Well, but what are we to do? We feel that we ought to do something, but we don't know what.

THES. Why don't you all go down to Earth, incog., mingle with the world, hear and see what people think of you, and judge for yourselves as to the best means to take to restore your influence?

JUP. Ah, but what's to become of Olympus in the meantime?

THES. Lor bless you, don't distress yourself about that. I've a very good company, used to take long parts on the shortest notice. Invest us with your powers and we'll fill your places till you return.

JUP. *(aside)* The offer is tempting. But suppose you fail?

THES. Fail! Oh, we never fail in our profession. We've nothing but great successes!

JUP. Then it's a bargain?

THES. It's a bargain.   *[They shake hands on it*

JUP. And that you may not be entirely without assistance, we will leave you Mercury, and whenever you find yourself in a difficulty you can consult him.

ENTER MERCURY *[trap* C.]

QUARTETTE

JUP.   So that's arranged—you take my place, my boy,
      While we make trial of a new existence.
    At length I shall be able to enjoy
      The pleasures I have envied from a distance.

MER.   Compelled upon Olympus here to stop,
      While other gods go down to play the hero,
    Don't be surprised if on this mountain top
      You find your Mercury is down at zero!

AP.   To earth away to join in mortal acts,
      And gather fresh materials to write on,
    Investigate more closely several facts,
      That I for centuries have thrown some light on!

DIA.   I, as the modest moon with crescent bow,

Have always shown a light to nightly scandal,
I must say I should like to go below,
And find out if the game is worth the candle!

Enter all the Thespians, summoned by MERCURY

MER. Here come your people!
THES. People better now!

AIR—THESPIS

While mighty Jove goes down below
    With all the other deities,
I fill his place and wear his "clo",
    The very part for me it is.
To mother earth to make a track,
    They all are spurred and booted, too,
And you will fill, till they come back,
    The parts you best are suited to.

CHORUS   Here's a pretty tale for future Iliads and
                Odysseys,
            Mortals are about to personate the gods and
                goddesses.
            Now to set the world in order, we will work in
                unity.
            Jupiter's perplexity is Thespis's opportunity.

SOLO—SPARKEION

Phœbus am I, with golden ray,
The god of day, the god of day,
When shadowy night has held her sway,
    I make the goddess fly.
'Tis mine the task to wake the world,
In slumber curled, in slumber curled,
By me her charms are all unfurled,
    The god of day am I!

CHORUS   The god of day, the god of day,
                That part shall our Sparkeion play.
                    Ha! ha! etc.
                The rarest fun and rarest fare,
                That ever fell to mortal share!
                    Ha! ha! etc.

SOLO—NICEMIS

I am the moon, the lamp of night.
I show a light—I show a light.
With radiant sheen I put to flight
    The shadows of the sky.
By my fair rays, as you're aware,
Gay lovers swear—gay lovers swear,
While greybeards sleep away their care,
    The lamp of night am I!

CHORUS   The lamp of night—the lamp of night,
                Nicemis plays, to her delight.
                    Ha! ha! ha! ha!
                The rarest fun and rarest fare,
                That ever fell to mortal share.
                    Ha! ha! ha! ha!

SOLO—TIMIDON

Mighty old Mars, the God of War,
I'm destined for—I'm destined for—
A terribly famous conqueror,
    With sword upon his thigh.
When armies meet with eager shout,
And warlike rout, and warlike rout,
You'll find me there without a doubt.
    The God of War am I!

CHORUS   The God of War, the God of War.
                Great Timidon is destined for!
                    Ha! ha! ha! ha!
                The rarest fun and rarest fare,
                That ever fell to mortal share.
                    Ha! ha! ha! ha! etc.

SOLO—DAPHNE

When, as the fruit of warlike deeds,
The soldier bleeds, the soldier bleeds,
Calliope crowns heroic deeds,
    With immortality.
From mere oblivion I reclaim
The soldier's name, the soldier's name,
And write it on the roll of fame,
    The muse of fame am I!

CHORUS   The muse of fame, the muse of fame,
                Calliope is Daphne's name,
                    Ha! ha! ha! ha!
                The rarest fun and rarest fare,
                That ever fell to mortal share!
                    Ha! ha! ha! ha! &c.

TUTTI. Here's a pretty tale!

*Enter procession of old Gods, they come down very much
    astonished at all they see, then passing by, ascend the
    platform that leads to the descent at the back*
*Gods (*JUPITER, DIANA, *and* APOLLO) *in corner are together*

                We will go,
                Down below,
                Revels rare,
                We will share.
                    Ha! ha! ha!

                With a gay
                Holiday,
                All unknown,
                And alone.
                    Ha! ha! ha!

TUTTI.   Here's a pretty tale!

*The Gods, including those who have lately entered in procession
    group themselves on rising ground at back. The
    Thespians (kneeling) bid them farewell.*

ACT II

SCENE.—*The same scene as in Act I with the exception that in place of the ruins that filled the foreground of the stage, the interior of a magnificent temple is seen, showing the background of the scene of Act I, through the columns of the portico at the back. High throne L.U.E. Low seats below it*

All the substitute gods and goddesses (that is to say, Thespians) are discovered grouped in picturesque attitudes about the stage, eating, drinking, and smoking, and singing the following verses:—

CHORUS

Of all symposia,
    The best by half,
        Upon Olympus, here, await us,
We eat Ambrosia,
    And nectar quaff—
        It cheers but don't inebriate us.

We know the fallacies
    Of human food,
        So please to pass Olympian rosy,
We built up palaces,
    Where ruins stood,
        And find them much more snug and cosy.

SOLO—SILLIMON

To work and think, my dear,
    Up here, would be,
        The height of conscientious folly,
So eat and drink, my dear,
    I like to see,
        Young people gay—young people jolly.
Olympian food, my love,
    I'll lay long odds,
        Will please your lips—those rosy portals,
What is the good, my love
    Of being gods,
        If we must work like common mortals?

CHORUS Of all symposia, etc.

Exeunt all but NICEMIS, *who is dressed as* DIANA, *and* PRETTEIA, *who is dressed as* VENUS. *They take* SILLIMON'S *arm and bring him down*

SILLIMON. Bless their little hearts, I can refuse them nothing. As the Olympian stage-manager I ought to be strict with them and make them do their duty, but I can't. Bless their little hearts, when I see the pretty little craft come sailing up to me with a wheedling smile on their pretty little figure-heads, I can't turn my back on 'em. I'm all bow, though I'm sure I try to be stern!

PRETT. You certainly are a dear old thing.

SILL. She says I'm a dear old thing! Deputy Venus says I'm a dear old thing!

NICE. It's her affectionate habit to describe everybody in those terms. *I* am more particular, but still even *I* am bound to admit that you are certainly a very dear old thing.

SILL. Deputy Venus says I'm a dear old thing, and deputy Diana, who is much more particular, endorses it! Who could be severe with such deputy divinities?

PRETT. Do you know, I'm going to ask you a favour.

SILL. Venus is going to ask me a favour!

PRETT. You see, I am Venus.

SILL. No one who saw your face would doubt it.

NICE. *(aside)* No one who knew her *character* would.

PRETT. Well Venus, you know, is married to Mars.

SILL. To Vulcan, my dear, to Vulcan. The exact connubial relation of the different gods and goddesses is a point on which we must be extremely particular.

PRETT. I beg your pardon—Venus is married to Mars.

NICE. If she isn't married to Mars, she ought to be.

SILL. Then that decides it—call it married to Mars.

PRETT. Married to Vulcan or married to Mars, what does it signify?

SILL. My dear, it's a matter on which I have no personal feeling whatever.

PRETT. So that she is married to some one!

SILL. Exactly! so that she is married to some one. Call it married to Mars.

PRETT. Now here's my difficulty. Presumptios takes the place of Mars, and Presumptios is my father!

SILL. Then why object to Vulcan?

PRETT. Because Vulcan is my grandfather!

SILL. But, my dear, what an objection! you are playing a part till the real gods return. That's all! Whether you are supposed to be married to your father—or your grandfather, what does it matter? This passion for realism is the curse of the stage!

PRETT. That's all very well, but I can't throw myself into a part that has already lasted a twelvemonth, when I have to make love to my father. It interferes with my conception of the characters. It spoils the part.

SILL. Well, well, I'll see what can be done. *(Ext.* PRETTEIA *L.U.E.)* That's always the way with beginners, they've no imaginative power. A true artist ought to be superior to such considerations. *(Nicemis comes down* R.) Well, Nicemis—I should say Diana—what's wrong with you? Don't you like your part?

NICE. Oh, immensely! It's great fun.

SILL. Don't you find it lonely out by yourself all night?

NICE. Oh, but I'm *not* alone all night!

SILL. But—I don't want to ask any injudicious questions—but who accompanies you?

NICE. Who? why Sparkeion, of course.

SILL. Sparkeion? Well, but Sparkeion is Phœbus Apollo. *(Enter* SPARKEION) He's the Sun, you know.

NICE. Of course he is; I should catch my death of cold, in the night air, if he didn't accompany me.

SPAR. My dear Sillimon, it would never do for a young lady to be out alone all night. It wouldn't be respectable.

SILL. There's a good deal of truth in that. But still—the Sun—at night—I don't like the idea. The original Diana always went out alone.

NICE. I hope the original Diana is no rule for *me*. After all, what *does* it matter?

SILL. to be sure—what *does* it matter?

SPAR. The sun at night, or in the daytime!

SILL. So that he shines. That's all that's necessary. *(Exit* NICEMIS R.U.E.) But poor Daphne, what will she say to this?

SPAR. Oh, Daphne can console herself; young ladies soon get over this sort of thing. Did you never hear of the young lady who was engaged to Cousin Robin?

SILL. Never.

SPAR. Then I'll sing it to you.

SONG—SPARKEION

Little maid of Arcadee
Sat on Cousin Robin's knee,
Thought in form and face and limb,
Nobody could rival him.
He was brave and she was fair.
Truth, they made a pretty pair.
Happy little maiden, she—
Happy maid of Arcadee!

Moments fled as moments will
Happily enough, until,
After, say, a month or two,
Robin did as Robins do.
Weary of his lover's play,
Jilted her and went away.
Wretched little maiden, she—
Wretched maid of Arcadee!

To her little home she crept,
There she sat her down and wept,
Maiden wept as maidens will—
Grew so thin and pale—until
Cousin Richard came to woo!
Then again the roses grew!
Happy little maiden, she—
Happy maid of Arcadee!

[*Exit* SPARKEION

SILL. Well, Mercury, my boy, you've had a year's experience of us here. How do we do it? I think we're rather an improvement on the original gods—don't you?

MER. Well, you see, there's a good deal to be said on both sides of the question; you are certainly younger than the original gods, and, therefore, more active. On the other hand, they are certainly older than you, and have, therefore, more experience. On the whole I prefer *you,* because your mistakes amuse me.

SONG—MERCURY

Olympus is now in a terrible muddle,
    The deputy deities all are at fault;
They splutter and splash like a pig in a puddle,
    And dickens a one of 'em's earning his salt,
For Thespis as Jove is a terrible blunder,
    Too nervous and timid—too easy and weak—
Whenever he's called on to lighten or thunder,
    The thought of it keeps him awake for a week!

Then mighty Mars hasn't the pluck of a parrot,
    When left in the dark he will quiver and quail;
And Vulcan has arms that would snap like a carrot,
    Before he could drive in a tenpenny nail!
Then Venus's freckles are very repelling.
    And Venus should *not* have a squint in her eyes;
The learned Minerva is weak in her spelling,
    And scatters her h's all over the skies.

Then Pluto, in kindhearted tenderness erring,
    Can't make up his mind to let anyone die—
The *Times* has a paragraph ever recurring,
    "Remarkable instance of longevi*ty.*"
On some it has come as a serious onus,
    To others it's quite an advantage—in short,
While ev'ry Life Office declares a big bonus,
    The poor undertakers are all in the court!

Then Cupid, the rascal, forgetting his trade is
    To make men and women impartially smart,
Will only shoot at pretty young ladies,
    And never takes aim at a bachelor's heart.
The results of this freak—or whatever you term it—
    Should cover the wicked young scamp with disgrace,
While ev'ry young man is as shy as a hermit,
    Young ladies are popping all over the place!
This wouldn't much matter—for bashful and shy men,
    When skilfully handled, are certain to fall,
But, alas! that determined young bachelor Hymen
    Refuses to wed anybody at all!
He swears that Love's flame is the vilest of arsons,
    And looks upon marriage as quite a mistake;
Now, what in the world's to become of the parsons,
    And what of the artist who sugars the cake?

In short you will see from the facts that I'm showing,
    The start of the case is exceedingly sad;
If Thespis's people go on as they're going,
    Olympus will certainly go to the bad!
From Jupiter downwards there isn't a dab in it,
    All of 'em quibble and shuffle and shirk;
A premier in Downing Street, forming a Cabinet,
    Couldn't find people less fit for their work!

Enter THESPIS, L.U.E.

THES. Sillimon, you can retire.

SILL. Sir, I—

THES. Don't pretend you can't when I say you can. I've seen you do it—go! *(Exit* SILLIMON *bowing extravagantly,* THESPIS *imitates him)* Well, Mercury, I've been in power one year to-day.

MER. One year to-day. How do you like ruling the world?

THES. Like it! Why it's as straightforward as possible. Why there hasn't been a hitch of any kind since we came up here. Lor! The airs you gods and goddesses give yourselves are perfectly sickening. Why it's mere child's play!

MER. Very simple, isn't it?

THES. Simple? Why I could do it on my head.

MER. Ah—I daresay you will do it on your head very soon.

THES. What do you mean by *that,* Mercury?

MER. I mean that when you've turned the world *quite* topsy-turvy you won't know whether you're standing on your head or your heels.

THES. Well, but, Mercury, it's all right at present.

MER. Oh yes—as far as we know.

THES. Well, but, you know, we know as much as anybody knows; you know, I believe, that the world's still going on.

MER. Yes—as far as we can judge—much as usual.

THES. Well, then, give the Father of the Drama his due, Mercury. Don't be envious of the Father of the Drama.

MER. Well, but you see you leave so much to accident.

THES. Well, Mercury, if I do, it's my principle. I am an easy man, and I like to make things as pleasant as possible. What did I do the day we took office? Why I called the company together and I said to them: "Here we are, you know, gods and goddesses, no mistake about it, the real thing. Well, we have certain duties to discharge, let's discharge them intelligently. Don't let us be hampered by routine and red tape and precedent, let's set the original gods an example, and put a liberal interpretation on our duties. If it occurs to any one to try an experiment in his own department, let him try it, if he fails there's no harm done, if he succeeds it is a distinct gain to society. Take it easy," I said, "and at the same time, make experiments. Don't hurry your work, do it slowly, and do it well." And here we are after a twelvemonth, and not a single complaint or a single petition has reached me.

MER. No—not yet.

THES. What do you mean by "no, not yet"?

MER. Well, you see, you don't understand these things. All the petitions that are addressed by men to Jupiter pass through my hands, and it's my duty to collect them and present them once a year.

THES. Oh, only once a year?

MER. Only once a year.

THES. And the year is up—?

MER. To-day.

THES. Oh, then I suppose there are *some* complaints?

MER. Yes, there *are* some.

THES. *(disturbed)* Oh. Perhaps there are a good many?

MER. There are a good many.

THES. Oh. Perhaps there are a thundering lot?

MER. There are a thundering lot.

THES. *(very much disturbed)* Oh!

MER. You see you've been taking it so very easy—and so have most of your company.

THES. Oh, who has been taking it easy?

MER. Well, all except those who have been trying experiments.

THES. Well but I suppose the experiments are ingenious?

MER. Yes; they are ingenious, but on the whole ill-judged. But it's time to go and summon your court.

THES. What for?

MER. To hear the complaints. In five minutes they will be here.　　　　　　　　　　　　　　　　　　　　[*Exit.*

THES. *(very uneasy)* I don't know how it is, but there is something in that young man's manner that suggests that the Father of the Gods has been taking it *too* easy. Perhaps it would have been better if I hadn't given my company so much scope. I wonder what they've been doing. I think I will curtail their discretion, though none of them appear to have much of the article. It seems a pity to deprive 'em of what little they have.

Enter DAPHNE, *weeping.*

THES. Now then, Daphne, what's the matter with you?

DAPH. Well, you know how disgracefully Sparkeion—

THES. *(correcting her)* Apollo—

DAPH. Apollo, then—has treated me. He promised to marry me years ago, and now he's married to Nicemis.

THES. Now look here, I can't go into that. You're in Olympus now and must behave accordingly. Drop your Daphne—assume your Calliope.

DAPH. Quite so. That's it!　　　　　　　[*Mysteriously*

THES. Oh—that is it?　　　　　　　　　　　　　[*Puzzled*

DAPH. That is it, Thespis. I am Calliope, the Muse of Fame. Very good. This morning I was in the Olympian library, and I took down the only book there. Here it is.

THES. *(taking it)* Lemprière's Classical Dictionary. The Olympian Peerage.

DAPH. Open it at Apollo.

THES. *(opens it)* It is done.

DAPH. Read.

THES. "Apollo was several times married, among others to Issa, Bolina, Corinis, Chymene, Cyrene, Chione, Acacallis, and Calliope."

DAPH. *And* Calliope.

THES. *(musing)* Ha! I didn't know he was *married* to them.

DAPH. *(severely)* Sir! This is the Family Edition.

THES. Quite so.

DAPH. You couldn't expect a lady to read any other?

THES. On no consideration. But in the original version—

DAPH. I go by the Family Edition.

THES. Then by the Family Edition, Apollo is your husband.

Enter NICEMIS *and* SPARKEION

NICE. Apollo your husband? He is my husband.

DAPH. I beg your pardon. He is *my* husband.

NICE. Apollo is Sparkeion, and he's married to me.

DAPH. Sparkeion is Apollo, and he's married to me.

NICE. He's my husband.

DAPH. He's your brother.

THES. Look here, Apollo, whose husband are you? Don't let's have any row about it; whose husband are you?

SPAR. Upon my honour I don't know. I'm in a very delicate position, but I'll fall in with any arrangement Thespis may propose.

DAPH. I've just found out that he's my husband, and yet he goes out every evening with that "thing"!

THES. Perhaps he's trying an experiment.

DAPH. I don't like my husband to make such experiments. The question is, who are we all and what is our relation to each other.

QUARTETTE

SPAR.	You're Diana, I'm Apollo—
	And Calliope is she.
DAPH.	He's you're brother.
NICE.	You're another.
	He has fairly married me.
DAPH.	By the rules of this fair spot
	I'm his wife, and you are not—
SPAR. *and* DAPH.	By the rules of this fair spot,
	I'm ⎱ his wife, and you are not.
	She's ⎰
NICE.	By this golden wedding ring,
	I'm his wife, and you're a "thing."
DAPH., NICE *and* SPAR.	By this golden wedding ring,
	I'm ⎱ his wife, and you're a "thing".
	She's ⎰
ALL.	Please will some one kindly tell us,
	Who are our respective kin?
	All of ⎱ us ⎰ are very jealous,
	⎰ them ⎱

Neither of $\left\{\begin{array}{l}\text{us} \\ \text{them}\end{array}\right\}$ will give in.

NICE. He's my husband I declare,
I espoused him properlee.

SPAR. That is true, for I was there,
And I saw her marry me.

DAPH. He's your brother—I'm his wife,
If we go by Lemprière,

SPAR. So she is, upon my life,
Really that seems very fair.

NICE. You're my husband and no other

SPAR. That is true enough I swear,

DAPH. I'm his wife, and you're his brother.

SPAR. If we go by Lemprière.

NICE. It will surely be unfair.
To decide by Lemprière.
[Crying]

DAPH. It will surely be quite fair,
To decide by Lemprière,

SPAR. AND THES. How you settle I don't care,
Leave it all to Lemprière.
[Spoken] The Verdict.
As Sparkeion is Apollo
Up in this Olympian clime,
Why, Nicemis, it will follow,
He's her husband, for the time
—[indicating DAPHNE]
When Sparkeion turns to mortal,
Join once more the sons of men,
He may take you to his portal
[indicating NICEMIS]
He will be your husband then.
That oh that is my decision,
'Cording to my mental vision
Put an end to all collision,
That oh that is my decision.
My decision—my decision,

ALL. That oh that is his decision,
His decision—his decision! etc.

[Exeunt THES., NICE., SPAR., and DAPHNE, SPAR. with DAPHNE, NICEMIS weeping with THESPIS.

Mysterious Music. Enter JUPITER, APOLLO, and MARS, from below, at the back of stage. All wear cloaks as disguise and all are masked.

RECITATIVE

Oh rage and fury! Oh shame and sorrow!
We'll be resuming our ranks to-morrow,
Since from Olympus we have departed,
We've been distracted and brokenhearted,
Oh wicked Thespis! Oh villain scurvy;
Through him Olympus is topsy-turvy!
Compelled to silence to grin and bear it!
He's caused our sorrow, and he shall share it.
Where is the monster! Avenge his blunders,
He has awakened Olympian thunders.

Enter MERCURY

JUP.(recit.) Oh Monster!
AP. (recit.) Oh Monster!
MARS.(recit.) Oh Monster!

MER. (in great terror) Please sir, what have I done sir?
JUP. What did we leave you behind for?
MER. Please sir, that's the question I asked for when you went away.
JUP. Was it not that Thespis might consult you whenever he was in a difficulty?
MER. Well, here I've been, ready to be consulted, chockful of reliable information—running over with celestial maxims—advice gratis ten to four—after twelve ring the night bell in cases of emergency.
JUP. And hasn't he consulted you?
MER. Not he—he disagrees with me about everything.
JUP. He must have misunderstood me. I told him to consult you whenever he was in a fix.
MER. He must have thought you said insult. Why whenever I opened my mouth he jumps down my throat. It isn't pleasant to have a fellow constantly jumping down your throat—especially when he always disagrees with you. It's just the sort of thing I can't digest.
JUP. (in a rage) Send him here, I'll talk to him.

Enter THESPIS. He is much terrified.

JUP. (recit.) Oh Monster!
AP. (recit.) Oh Monster!
MARS.(recit.) Oh Monster!

THESPIS sings in great terror, which he endeavours to conceal.
JUP. Well Sir, the year is up to-day.
AP. And a nice mess you've made of it.
MARS. You've deranged the whole scheme of society.
THES. (aside) There's going to be a row! (Aloud and very familiarly) My dear boy—I do assure you—
JUP. (in recit.) Be respectful!
AP. (in recit.) Be respectful!
MARS.(in recit.) Be respectful!
THES. I don't know what you allude to. With the exception of getting our scene-painter to "run up" this temple, because we found the ruins draughty, we haven't touched a thing.
JUP. (in recit.) Oh story teller!
AP. (in recit.) Oh story teller!
MARS.(in recit.) Oh story teller!

Enter THESPIANS

THES. My dear fellows, you're distressing yourselves unnecessarily. The court of Olympus is about to assemble to listen to the complaints of the year, if any. But there are none, or next to none. Let the Olympians assemble!

Enter THESPIANS

THESPIS takes chair. JUP., AP. and MARS sit below him.

THES. Ladies and gentlemen. It seems that it is usual for the gods to assemble once a year to listen to mortal petitions. It doesn't seem to me to be a good plan, as work is liable to accumulate; but as I'm particularly anxious not to interfere with Olympian precedent, but to allow everything to go on as it has always been accustomed to go—why, we'll say no more about it. *(Aside)* But how shall I account for your presence?

JUP. Say we are gentlemen of the press.

THES. That all our proceedings may be perfectly open and above board I have communicated with the most influential members of the Athenian press, and I beg to introduce to your notice three of its most distinguished members. They bear marks emblematic of the anonymous character of modern journalism. *(Business of introduction.* THESPIS *very uneasy)* Now then, if you're all ready we will begin.

MER. *(brings tremendous bundles of petitions)* Here is the agenda.

THES. What's that? The petitions?

MER. Some of them. *(Opens one and reads)* Ah, I thought there'd be a row about it.

THES. Why, what's wrong now?

MER. Why, it's been a foggy Friday in November for the last six months and the Athenians are tired of it.

THES. There's no pleasing some people. This craving for perpetual change is the curse of the country. Friday's a very nice day.

MER. So it is, but a Friday six months long!—it gets monotonous.

JUP., AP. AND MARS. *(in recit. rising)* It's perfectly ridiculous.

THES. *(calling them)* It shall be arranged. Cymon!

CYM. *(as Time with the usual attributes)* Sir!

THES. *(introducing him to* THREE GODS) Allow me—Father Time—rather young at present but even Time must have a beginning. In course of Time, Time will grow older. Now then, Father Time, what's this about a wet Friday in November for the last six months?

CYM. Well, the fact is, I've been trying an experiment. Seven days in the week is an awkward number. It can't be halved. Two's into seven won't go.

THES. *(tries it on his fingers)* Quite so—quite so.

CYM. So I abolished Saturday.

JUP., AP. and MARS Oh but— [*Rising*

THES. Do be quiet. He's a very intelligent young man and knows what he is about. So you abolished Saturday. And how did you find it answer?

CYM. Admirably.

THES. You hear? He found it answer admirably.

CYM. Yes, only Sunday refused to take its place.

THES. Sunday refused to take its place?

CYM. Sunday comes after Saturday—Sunday won't go on duty after Friday, Sunday's principles are very strict. That's where my experiment sticks.

THES. Well, but why November? Come, why November?

CYM. December can't begin till November has finished. November can't finish because he's abolished Saturday. There again my experiment sticks.

THES. Well, but why wet? Come now, why wet?

CYM. Ah, that is your fault. You turned on the rain six months ago, and you forgot to turn it off again.

JUP., MARS and AP. *(rising—recitative)* Oh this is monstrous!

ALL. Order, order.

THES. Gentlemen, pray be seated. *(To the others)* The liberty of the press, one can't help it. *(To the three gods)* It is easily settled. Athens has had a wet Friday in November for the last six months. Let them have a blazing Tuesday in July for the next twelve.

JUP., MARS. and AP. But—

ALL. Order, order.

THES. Now then, the next article.

MER. Here's a petition from the Peace Society. They complain that there are no more battles.

MARS. *(springing up)* What!

THES. Quiet there! Good dog—soho; Timidon!

TIM. *(as* MARS) Here.

THES. What's this about there being no battles?

TIM. I've abolished battles; it's an experiment.

MARS. *(springing up)* Oh come, I say—

THES. Quiet then! *(To* TIM) Abolished battles?

TIM. Yes, you told us on taking office to remember two things, to try experiments and to take it easy. I found I couldn't take it easy while there are any battles to attend to, so I tried the experiment and abolished battles. And then I took it easy. The Peace Society ought to be very much obliged to me.

THES. Obliged to you! Why, confound it! since battles have been abolished war is universal.

TIM. War universal?

THES. To be sure it is! Now that nations can't fight, no two of 'em are on speaking terms. The dread of fighting was the only thing that kept them civil to each other. Let battles be restored and peace reign supreme.

MER. *(reads)* Here's a petition from the associated wine merchants of Mytilene.

THES. Well, what's wrong with the associated wine merchants of Mytilene? Are there no grapes this year?

MER. Plenty of grapes; more than usual.

THES. *(to the gods)* You observe, there is no deception; there are more than usual.

MER. There are plenty of grapes, only they are full of ginger beer.

THREE GODS Oh, come I say.

[*Rising, they are put down by* THESPIS.

THES. Eh? what. *(Much alarmed)* Bacchus?

TIPS. *(as* BACCHUS) Here!

THES. There seems to be something unusual with the grapes of Mytilene; they only grow ginger beer.

TIPS. And a very good thing too.

THES. It's very nice in its way, but it is not what one looks for from grapes.

TIPS. Beloved master, a week before we came up here, you insisted on my taking the pledge. By so doing you rescued me from my otherwise inevitable misery. I cannot express my thanks. Embrace me!

[*Attempts to embrace him*

THES. Get out, don't be a fool. Look here, you know you're the god of wine.

TIPS. I am.

THES. *(very angry)* Well, do you consider it consistent with your duty as the god of wine to make the grapes yield nothing but ginger beer?

TIPS. Do you consider it consistent with my duty as a total abstainer to grow anything stronger than ginger beer?

THES. But your duty as the god of wine—

TIPS. In every respect in which my duty as the god of wine can be discharged consistently with my duty as a total abstainer, I will discharge it. But when the functions clash, everything must give way to the pledge. My preserver! [*Attempts to embrace him.*

THES. Don't be a confounded fool! This can be arranged. We can't give over the wine this year, but at least we can improve the ginger beer. Let all the ginger beer be extracted from it immediately.

JUP., MARS, AP.
(aside)

We can't stand this,
We can't stand this,
It's much too strong,
We can't stand this.
    It would be wrong,
Extremely wrong,
If we stood this,
    If we stand this,
    If we stand this,
We can't stand this.

DAPH., SPAR., NICE.

Great Jove, this interference,
    Is more than we can stand;
Of them make a clearance,
    With your majestic hand.

JOVE

This cool audacity, it beats us hollow

(removing mask)

I'm Jupiter!

MARS.

I'm Mars!

AP.

I'm Apollo!

Enter DIANA and all the other gods and goddesses.

ALL [*kneeling with their foreheads on the ground*]

Jupiter, Mars and Apollo,
    Have quitted the dwellings of men;
The other gods quickly will follow,
    And what will become of us then.
Oh, pardon us, Jove and Apollo,
    Pardon us, Jupiter, Mars;
Oh, see us in misery wallow,
    Cursing our terrible stars.

CHORUS AND BALLET

ALL THE THESPIANS

Let us remain, we beg of you pleadingly!

THREE GODS

Let them remain, they beg of us pleadingly!

THES.

Life on Olympus suits us exceedingly.

GODS.

Life on Olympus suits them exceedingly

THES.

Let us remain, we pray in humility!

GODS

Let 'em remain, they pray in humility.

THES.

If we have shown some little ability.

GODS

If they have shown some little ability.
Let us remain, etc.

JUPITER

Enough, your reign is ended;
    Upon this sacred hill
Let him be apprehended,
    And learn our awful will,
Away to earth, contemptible comedians,
    And hear our curse, before we set you free;
You shall all be eminent tragedians,
    Whom no one ever goes to see!

ALL

We go to earth, contemptible comedians,
    We hear his curse before he sets us free,
We shall all be eminent tragedians,
    Whom no one ever, ever goes to see!

SILL.

Whom no one—

SPAR.

Whom no one—

THES.

Whom *no* one—

ALL

Ever, ever goes to see.

The Thespians are driven away by the gods, who group themselves in attitudes of triumph.

THES.

Now, here you see the arrant folly
Of doing your best to make things jolly.
I've ruled the world like a chap in his senses,
Observe the terrible consequences.
Great Jupiter, who nothing pleases,
Splutters and swears, and kicks up breezes,
And sends us home in a mood avengin',
In double quick time, like a railroad engine.
    And this he does without compunction,
    Because I have discharged with unction
    A highly complicated function,
    Complying with his own injunction.
        Fol, lol, lay.

CHORUS

All this he does, etc.

The gods drive the Thespians away. The Thespians prepare to descend the mountain as the curtain falls.

Trial by Jury

One of Gilbert's early contributions to *Fun* magazine was a skit on a breach-of-promise case, embellished with typical drawings. Five years later, in 1873, he filled out this scenario and offered it to Carl Rosa for his Drury Lane opera season. But Mme Rosa, for whom it was intended, died in early 1874 and Gilbert's libretto was returned to him.

Towards the end of that year Gilbert was talking to an acquaintance, Richard D'Oyly Carte, the ambitious and enterprising young manager of the Royalty Theatre, Soho. Carte was looking for a third item to form a triple bill that already had Offenbach's *La Périchole* as its centre-piece. Gilbert gave him *Trial by Jury* to read and Carte liked it so well that he immediately suggested Sullivan as the possible composer.

Gilbert called on Sullivan in early 1875 and read *Trial by Jury* to him. Gilbert was very self-conscious about it and gradually became more and more unsure of his piece as Sullivan's silent mirth increased. It went down so well with Sullivan that he agreed to set it at once, and within three weeks it was in rehearsal.

Fred Sullivan (from the Gaiety), the composer's brother, was cast as the Learned Judge. It was said that he conveyed—as no actor has done since—a unique mixture of condescension, dignity, sudden flashes of humour, perfect diction and a musical delivery. He helped considerably in the success of the piece. *Trial by Jury* ran for 300 performances over the next two years, often providing a ready-made production for charity and benefit matinées.

In many respects it is immature Sullivan, with its hotchpotch of styles, its reliance upon Offenbach for certain effects, and incomplete characterization of the roles. However, its through-composed style makes it go with such a swing that, as a light opera, it is first-class entertainment.

The entrance of the jilted bride, Angelina, with her Bridesmaids all in wedding garments, calls for comment.

In the stage directions to the first production, the Bridesmaids enter to a cheeky, bubbling introduction,

Gilbert's original *Trial by Jury* from *Fun.*

Fred Sullivan, the composer's brother, as the Learned Judge.

Trial by Jury at the Royalty Theatre. The Jury wear the Bridesmaids' rose garlands and the melodramatic farce is at its height. *Sporting and Dramatic News,* 1 May 1875.

'each bearing two palm branches, their arms crossed on their bosoms, and rose-wreaths on their arms'.

One does not find them obeying these instructions today, but if they did so, the effect would be similar to that of a Valentine in the Kate Greenaway style.

Looking at *Trial by Jury* in relation to a Valentine the whole work appears as a satire on love as well as on the High Court. At the first performance, and in the revival of 1898, the Bridesmaids gave their rose-wreaths to members of the Jury to wear. For the finale, these garlands were stretched out across the stage, radiating from the Judge's bench. It is unlikely that any implied Freudian motif was observed at the time, but in retrospect it is a provoking idea.

The whole work offers plenty of opportunities for improvisation. A descent of two plaster cupids—in early performances—and 'red, passionate fire' glowing from the wings, produced a burlesque effect which, when combined with a transformation scene by 'breaking' the Court set, removed the finale into the realms of pantomime. In a later production there was a Harlequinade, with Angelina as Columbine and all her Bridesmaids in wig and gown; and in the 1884 revival, which was given in a double bill after *The Sorcerer,* fire in the finale to both operas might have seemed repetitive.

None of these production tricks has been repeated in living memory, nor is there the necessity for so doing. *Trial by Jury* is strong enough and funny enough in text and in score to stand as an opera without the help of such subsidiary effects belonging to the Gaiety. Gilbert and Sullivan had, in the light of what followed, left all those behind them.

SYNOPSIS

After solemn drumbeats and a peremptory figure, repeated, the curtain rises to disclose a normal court scene. Jurymen, members of the public, Barristers, Counsel and Usher are all walking about and talking busily. The Jurymen and public hear ten o'clock striking, which is the signal for the beginning of the case. We hear, in choral *fugato*, that it concerns 'Edwin, sued by Angelina'. The Usher directs everyone to his proper place and advises the Jury that the trial must be without bias of any sort. He then goes on to express sympathy for the Plaintiff and total disregard for what the 'ruffianly Defendant' may have to say, interspersing his remarks with a reminder about bias. 'From bias free of every kind...' has a melody that may be found in the second movement of Mendelssohn's D major cello sonata.

The Defendant enters, with a guitar, and sensing the atmosphere of the Court, is half-prepared for the storm of abuse which he receives from the Jury. But he manages to hold their attention while he tells them his side of the story, although they make it clear that they are not in the mood to believe him. After tuning his instrument, the Defendant embarks upon a barcarolle, 'When first my old, old love I knew...' with its persuasive chorus, 'Tink-a-Tank' in which everyone joins. He explains that after adoring Angelina for some time, she became a bore to him until, one morning, he had fallen in love with another girl. The Jurymen have all experienced this condition, but ashamedly refuse to admit such vices, denying Edwin any sympathy in their growling chorus 'Now I was like that when a lad...' They end up with a jolly refrain, a pun which was much admired in early days: 'Trial-la-law!'

The Usher calls the Court to order as the Learned Judge appears to a mock-serious, mock-Arne refrain: 'All hail, great Judge!' He accepts their thanks, drily, and announces his intention of telling them how he came to be a judge, which they continue to delay with interruptions.

The Judge's Song is the first of a number of similar jolly and brazen autobiographies in the operas, related by a man who has achieved eminence and wealth by surprising methods. It is a light and easygoing song, not patter, often partly vocalized, with a firm spring in the light accompaniment. The Judge tells how he rose from being an impecunious young barrister to a highly successful one, thanks only to the munificence of an influential attorney in exchange for attention paid to his 'elderly ugly daughter'. As soon as he had reached the unassailable position of a judge, the attorney's daughter was thrown over and all disparagement went unheeded. This story is told with great satisfaction and received with much enjoyment.

The Usher swears in the Jury who disappear from view behind their box with groans and creaking joints. He then calls Angelina, the Plaintiff. Her Bridesmaids enter to a cheek, bubbling introduction, singing 'Comes the broken flower...' with great complacence. It is much in the style of the *Thespis* number 'Climbing over rocky mountain' though better, and the introduction is heard contrapuntally with the verse. The Judge eyes them all carefully and sends a note, via the Usher, to the first Bridesmaid, who kisses it and places it in her bosom. Angelina's entrance, with a verse to the same melody, makes it clear that she is more than ready to receive attention from another man. The Judge transfers his interest to her, calls back his note and has it rerouted to Angelina by the Usher. She goes through the same procedure with it.

The Judge confides to the Associate how taken he is with Angelina but the Jury overhear him; and although they shake their fingers reprovingly and call him 'Sly dog' their Foreman confirms his agreement with his Lordship. They all shout out at the Defendant, in best operatic angry style: 'Monster! Monster! Dread our fury!' The Usher calls again for silence, but nobody is speaking.

Counsel for the Plaintiff begins his prosecution. His attractive song 'With a sense of deep emotion...' increases in tempo and in excitement as he makes his points, emphasizing the Defendant's callous behaviour. All the time, the Plaintiff is cadging sympathy from the Jury, the Foreman, and then the Judge himself, actually sitting beside him on the Bench.

Edwin produces his own defence. Because 'Nature is constantly changing' he finds it utterly reasonable

to change his ways and his affections. In a light and airy 3/4 he obtains silence and consideration.

The Judge is taken with this 'reasonable proposition' and his wisdom is generally applauded, but the Plaintiff's Counsel confounds the proceedings by announcing that 'To marry two at once is Burglaree!' The Judge is flummoxed: 'A nice dilemma we have here!', he declares, and Counsel does not think that they can settle it. These sentiments as well as those of the Plaintiff and Defendant are brilliantly worked up, with the Foreman and Usher, in a sextet with chorus.

This is a double musical parody, of two Italian operatic ensembles familiar to audiences of the 1870s. It is set and laid out in the same key and style as the quartet 'D'un pensiero, e d'un accento' from Act I of Bellini's *La Sonnambula* (and Gilbert's libretto calls it 'quartette'); but by increasing the voices to six, it may also be seen as a parody of Donizetti's sextet 'Chi mi frena in tal momento?' from the second act of *Lucia di Lammermoor*.

The Plaintiff breaks the mood of doubt and uncertainty by declaring that she loves Edwin, in a passionate outburst which, by now, cannot be believed. Her ploy is to get substantial damages. Edwin retorts by drawing the worst possible picture of himself (to the same tune) — 'a ruffian — a bully — a sot', from which the Judge grasps a faint straw. He suggests that they make Edwin tipsy and find out whether he will truly behave as he claims.

There is a conflict of opinion now, at which the Judge expresses his impatience, since nothing he can suggest seems to please anybody. He suddenly announces grandly: 'Put your briefs upon the shelf, I will marry her myself!' He embraces Angelina, who is delighted, and there is general approbation expressing 'Joy unbounded' in a kind of restrained can-can — except from Edwin who wonders how long it will last. But there is universal consent that the Judge is a judge of beauty, and a good judge too, and to a general dance, the curtain falls.

Rutland Barrington, Learned Judge; Courtice Pounds, Defendant; Henry Lytton, Counsel; Walter Passmore, Usher; Ruth Vincent, Plaintiff; W. S. Gilbert, Associate, in the benefit matinée for Ellen Terry at Theatre Royal, Drury Lane, London, 5 June 1906.

TRIAL BY JURY.

SCENE.—*A Court of Justice.*

BARRISTERS, ATTORNEYS, *and* JURYMEN *discovered with* USHER.

CHORUS.

Hark, the hour of ten is sounding!
Hearts with anxious fears are bounding;
Hall of Justice crowds surrounding,
    Breathing hope and fear—
For to-day in this arena,
Summoned by a stern subpoena,
Edwin, sued by Angelina,
    Shortly will appear.

(*The* USHER *marshals the* JURY *into Jury-box.*)

SOLO. USHER.

Now, Jurymen, hear my advice—
All kinds of vulgar prejudice
    I pray you set aside:
With stern judicial frame of mind,
From bias free of every kind,
    This trial must be tried.

CHORUS.

From bias free of every kind
This trial must be tried.

(*During Choruses,* USHER *says, fortissimo, "Silence in Court!"*)

USHER.

Oh, listen to the plaintiff's case:
Observe the features of her face—
    The broken-hearted bride.
Condole with her distress of mind—
From bias free of every kind
    This trial must be tried!

CHORUS.

From bias free, etc.

USHER.

And when amid the plaintiff's shrieks,
The ruffianly defendant speaks—
    Upon the other side;
What *he* may say you needn't mind—
From bias free of every kind
    This trial must be tried.

CHORUS.

From bias free, etc.

Enter DEFENDANT.

DEFENDANT (*recit.*).

Is this the Court of the Exchequer?

ALL.

It is!

DEFENDANT *(aside).*

Be firm, my moral pecker,
Your evil star's in the ascendant!

ALL.

Who are you?

DEFENDANT.

I'm the Defendant!

Chorus of JURYMEN *(shaking their fists).*

Monster, dread our damages!
We're the jury,
Dread our fury!

DEFENDANT.

Hear me, hear me, if you please,
  These are very strange proceedings—
For, permit me to remark,
  On the merits of my pleadings,
You're at present in the dark.

(DEFENDANT *beckons to* JURYMEN—*they leave the box, and
gather round him as they sing the following):—*

Ha! ha! ha!
That's a very true remark—
On the merits of your pleadings,
We're entirely in the dark!
Ha! ha!—ha! ha!

SONG. DEFENDANT.

When first my old, old love I knew,
  My bosom swelled with joy;
My riches at her feet I threw—
  I was a love-sick boy!
No terms seemed extravagant
  Upon her to employ—
I used to mope, and sigh, and pant,
  Just like a love-sick boy!

But joy incessant palls the sense;
  And love, unchanged, will cloy,
And she became a bore intense
  Unto her love-sick boy!
With fitful glimmer burnt my flame
  And I grew cold and coy,
At last, one morning, I became
  Another's love-sick boy!

Chorus of JURYMEN *(advancing stealthily).*

Oh, I was like that when a lad;
A shocking young scamp of a rover!
I behaved like a regular cad;
But that sort of thing is all over.
I'm now a respectable chap
And shine with a virtue resplendent,
And therefore I haven't a scrap
Of sympathy with the defendant!
    He shall treat us with awe,
    If there isn't a flaw,
Singing so merrily—Trial-la-law!
Trial-la-law—Trial-la-law!
Singing so merrily—Trial-la-law!

RECIT. USHER.

Silence in Court, and all attention lend.
Behold your Judge! In due submission bend!

Enter JUDGE *on Bench.*

CHORUS.

All hail, great Judge!
  To your bright rays
We never grudge
  Ecstatic praise.
    All hail!
May each decree
  As statute rank,
And never be
  Reversed in banc.
    All hail!

RECIT. JUDGE.

For these kind words accept my thanks, I pray!
A Breach of Promise we've to try to-day:
But firstly, if the time you'll not begrudge,
I'll tell you how I came to be a judge.

ALL.

He'll tell us how he came to be a judge!

JUDGE.

Let me speak.

ALL.

Let him speak.

JUDGE.

Let me speak.

ALL.

Let him speak. Hush! hush!! hush!!!
(fortissimo) He'll tell us how he came to be a judge!

SONG. JUDGE.

When I, good friends, was called to the bar,
  I'd an appetite fresh and hearty,
But I was, as many young barristers are,
  An impecunious party:
I'd a swallow-tail coat of a beautiful blue—
  A brief which I bought of a booby—
A couple of shirts and a collar or two,
  And a ring that looked like a ruby!

CHORUS.

A couple of shirts, etc.

JUDGE.

In Westminster Hall I danced a dance,
  Like a semi-despondent fury;
For I thought I should never hit on a chance
  Of addressing a British jury—
But I soon got tired of third-class journeys,
  And dinners of bread and water;
So I fell in love with a rich attorney's
  Elderly, ugly daughter.

CHORUS.

So he fell in love, etc.

JUDGE.

The rich attorney he jumped with joy,
  And replied to my fond professions:
"You shall reap the reward of your pluck, my boy
  At the Bailey and Middlesex Sessions.
You'll soon get used to her looks," said he,
  "And a very nice girl you'll find her!
She may very well pass for forty-three
  In the dusk, with a light behind her!"

CHORUS.

"She may very well," etc.

JUDGE.

The rich attorney was good as his word:
  The briefs came trooping gaily,
And every day my voice was heard
  At the Sessions or Ancient Bailey.
All thieves who could my fees afford
  Relied on my orations,
And many a burglar I've restored
  To his friends and his relations.

CHORUS.

And many a burglar, etc.

JUDGE.

At length I became as rich as the Gurneys
  An incubus then I thought her,
So I threw over that rich attorney's
  Elderly, ugly daughter.
The rich attorney my character high
  Tried vainly to disparage—
And now, if you please, I'm ready to try
  This breach of promise of marriage!

CHORUS.

And now, if you please, etc.

JUDGE.

For now I am a Judge!

ALL.

And a good Judge too!

JUDGE.

Yes, now I am a Judge!

ALL.

And a good Judge too!

JUDGE.

Though all my law is fudge,
Yet I'll never, never budge,
But I'll live and die a Judge!

ALL.

And a good Judge too!

JUDGE (pianissimo).

It was managed by a job!

ALL.

And a good job too!

JUDGE.

It was managed by a job!

ALL.

And a good job too!

JUDGE.

It is patent to the mob,
That my being made a nob
Was effected by a job.

ALL.

And a good job too!

Enter COUNSEL *for* PLAINTIFF.

COUNSEL (recit.).

Swear thou the Jury!

USHER.

Kneel, Jurymen, oh! kneel!

(All the Jury kneel in the Jury-box, and so are hidden from audience).

USHER.

Oh, will you swear by yonder skies,
Whatever question may arise
'Twixt rich and poor—'twixt low and high,
That you will well and truly try?

JURY *(raising their hands, which alone are visible)*

To all of this we make reply,
By the dull slate of yonder sky:
That we will well and truly try.

(All rise with the last note, both hands in air.)

RECIT. USHER.

This blind devotion is indeed a crusher!
Pardon the tear-drop of the simple Usher!
(He weeps.)

RECIT. COUNSEL.

Call the plaintiff!

RECIT. USHER.

Oh, Angelina! Angelina!! Come thou into Court.

Enter the BRIDESMAIDS, *each bearing two palm branches, their arms crossed on their bosoms, and rose-wreaths on their arms.*

Chorus of BRIDESMAIDS.

Comes the broken flower—
    Comes the cheated maid—
Though the tempest lower,
    Rain and cloud will fade!
Take, O maid, these posies:
    Though thy beauty rare
Shame the blushing roses,
    They are passing fair!
        Wear the flowers till they fade:
        Happy by thy life, O maid!

(The JUDGE, *having taken a great fancy to* FIRST BRIDESMAID, *sends her a note by* USHER, *which she reads, kisses rapturously, and places in her bosom.)*

SOLO. ANGELINA.

O'er the season vernal
    Time may cast a shade;
Sunshine, if eternal,
    Makes the roses fade!
Time may do his duty;
    Let the thief alone—
Winter hath a beauty
    That is all his own.
        Fairest days are sun and shade:
        I am no unhappy maid!

(By this time the JUDGE *has transferred his admiration to* ANGELINA).

Chorus of BRIDESMAIDS.

Comes the broken flower, etc.

(During Chorus ANGELINA *collects wreaths of roses from* BRIDESMAIDS *and gives them to the* JURY, *who put them on, and wear them during the rest of the piece.)*

JUDGE *(to* ASSOCIATE).

Oh, never, never, never, since I joined the human race,
Saw I so exquisitely fair a face.

The JURY *(shaking their forefingers at* JUDGE).

Ah, sly dog! Ah, sly dog!

JUDGE *(to* JURY).

How say you, is she not designed for capture?

FOREMAN *(after consulting with the* JURY).

We've but one word, my lord, and that is—Rapture!

PLAINTIFF *(curtseying).*

Your kindness, gentlemen, quite overpowers!

The JURY.

We love you fondly, and would make you ours!

The BRIDESMAIDS *(shaking their forefingers at* JURY).

Ah, sly dogs! Ah, sly dogs!

COUNSEL *for* PLAINTIFF *(recit.).*

May it please you, my lud!
Gentlemen of the Jury!

ARIA.

With a sense of deep emotion,
    I approach this painful case;
For I never had a notion
    That a man could be so base,
Or deceive a girl confiding,
Vows, *etcætera*, deriding.

ALL.

He deceived a girl confiding,
Vows, *etcætera*, deriding.

(PLAINTIFF *falls sobbing on* COUNSEL'S *breast, and remains there.*)

COUNSEL.

See my interesting client,
    Victim of a heartless wile!
See the traitor all defiant
    Wears a supercilious smile!
Sweetly smiled my client on him,
Coyly woo'd and gently won him!

ALL.

Sweetly smiled, etc.

COUNSEL.

Swiftly fled each honeyed hour
    Spent with this unmanly male!
Camberwell became a bower,
    Peckham an Arcadian Vale,
Breathing concentrated otto!—
An existence *à la* Watteau.

ALL.

Bless us, concentrated otto! etc.

COUNSEL (*coming down with* PLAINTIFF, *who is still sobbing on his breast*).

Picture, then, my client naming
    And insisting on the day:
Picture him excuses framing—
    Going from her far away;
Doubly criminal to do so,
For the maid had brought her *trousseau!*

ALL.

Doubly criminal, etc.

COUNSEL (*to* PLANTIFF, *who weeps*).

Cheer up, my pretty—oh, cheer up!

JURY.

Cheer up, cheer up, we love you!

(COUNSEL *leads* PLAINTIFF *fondly into Witness-box; he takes a tender leave of her, and resumes his place in Court.*)

(PLAINTIFF *reels, as if about to faint.*)

JUDGE.

That she is reeling
    Is plain to me!

FOREMAN.

If faint you're feeling,
    Recline on me!

(*She falls sobbing on to the* FOREMAN'S *breast.*)

PLAINTIFF (*feebly*).

I shall recover
    If left alone.

ALL (*shaking their fists at* DEFENDANT).

Oh, perjured lover,
    Atone! atone!

FOREMAN.

Just like a father
    I wish to be. (*Kissing her.*)

JUDGE (*approaching her*).

Or, if you'd rather,
    Recline on me!

(*She staggers on to bench, sits down by the* JUDGE, *and falls sobbing on his breast.*)

COUNSEL.

Oh! fetch some water
    From far Cologne!

ALL.

For this sad slaughter
    Atone! atone!

JURY (*shaking fists at* DEFENDANT).

Monster, monster, dread our fury—
There's the Judge, and we're the Jury!

SONG. DEFENDANT.

Oh, gentlemen, listen, I pray,
  Though I own that my heart has been ranging,
Of nature the laws I obey,
  For nature is constantly changing.
The moon in her phases is found,
  The time and the wind and the weather,
The months in succession come round,
  And you don't find two Mondays together.
    Consider the moral, I pray,
      Nor bring a young fellow to sorrow,
    Who loves this young lady to-day,
      And loves that young lady to-morrow.

BRIDESMAIDS (*rushing forward, and kneeling to* JURY).

Consider the moral, etc.

You cannot eat breakfast all day,
  Nor is it the act of a sinner,
When breakfast is taken away,
  To turn your attention to dinner;
And it's not in the range of belief,
  That you could hold him as a glutton,
Who, when he is tired of beef,
  Determines to tackle the mutton.
    But this I am ready to say,
      If it will appease their sorrow,
    I'll marry one lady to-day,
      And I'll marry the other to-morrow.

BRIDESMAIDS (*rushing forward as before*).

But this he is ready to say, etc.

JUDGE (*recit.*).

That seems a reasonable proposition,
To which I think your client may agree.

ALL.

Oh, Judge discerning!

COUNSEL.

But, I submit, my lord, with all submission,
To marry two at once is Burglaree!

(*Referring to law book.*)

In the reign of James the Second,
It was generally reckoned
As a very serious crime
To marry two wives at one time.

(*Hands book up to* JUDGE, *who reads it.*)

ALL.

Oh, man of learning!

Quartette.

JUDGE.

A nice dilemma we have here,
  That calls for all our wit:

COUNSEL.

And at this stage it don't appear
  That we can settle it.

DEFENDANT.

If I to wed the girl am loth
  A breach 'twill surely be!

PLAINTIFF.

And if he goes and marries both
  It counts as Burglaree!

ALL.

A nice dilemma, etc.

DUET. PLAINTIFF *and* DEFENDANT.

PLANTIFF (*embracing* DEFENDANT *rapturously*).

I love him—I love him—with fervour unceasing,
  I worship and madly adore;
My blind adoration is always increasing,
  My loss I shall ever deplore.
Oh, see what a blessing—what love and caressing
  I've lost, and remember it, pray,
When you I'm addressing are busy assessing
  The damages Edwin must pay.

DEFENDANT (*repelling her furiously*).

I smoke like a furnace—I'm always in liquor,
  A ruffian—a bully—a sot.
I'm sure I should thrash her—perhaps I should kick her,
  I am such a very bad lot!
I'm not prepossessing, as you may be guessing,
  She couldn't endure me a day!
Recall my professing when you are assessing
  The damages Edwin must pay!

(*She clings to him passionately; he drags her round stage, and flings her to the ground.*)

JURY.

We would be fairly acting,
But this is most distracting!

JUDGE (*recit.*).

The question, gentlemen, is one of liquor,
  You ask for guidance—this is my reply:

This porcelain teapot, registered in 1882—the same year as *Patience*—by the Worcester Royal Porcelain Works, was a souvenir piece of the opera. The sunflower symbol ornaments Bunthorne while the lily is held by a maiden on the reverse side.

The influence of the graphic artist, Walter Crane, pervaded much of the art of his time and Gilbert obviously borrowed from him. His Patience is modelled on this milkmaid, and possibly the ogling gentleman added something to Bunthorne's character.

The traditional Pirate King was typified by H. Brock in this poster for the D'Oyly Carte Opera Company, current during the 1920s.

The British Tar, with cutlass and Union Flag was a standard Penny Plain-Twopence Coloured character on which Gilbert draw for his own stock characters in so many of the early operas.

If he, when tipsy, would assault and kick her,
Let's make him tipsy, gentlemen, and try!

COUNSEL.

With all respect
I do object!

ALL.

With all respect
We do object!

DEFENDANT.

I don't object!

ALL.

We do object!

JUDGE (tossing his books and papers about).

All the legal furies seize you!
No proposal seems to please you;
I can't stop up here all day,
I must shortly go away.
Barristers, and you, attorneys,
Set out on your homeward journeys;
Put your briefs upon the shelf,
I will marry her myself!

(He comes down from Bench to floor of Court.
He embraces Angelina.)

Finale.

PLAINTIFF.

Oh, joy unbounded!
With wealth surrounded,
The knell is sounded
    Of grief and woe

COUNSEL.

With love devoted
On you he's doated:
To castle moated
    Away they go!

DEFENDANT.

I wonder whether
They'll live together
In marriage tether
        In manner true?

USHER.

It seems to me, sir,
Of such as she, sir,
A judge is he, sir,
        A good judge too.

Chorus.

It seems to me, sir, etc.

JUDGE.

Oh yes, I am a Judge.

ALL.

And a good Judge too!

JUDGE.

Oh yes, I am a Judge.

ALL.

And a good Judge too!

JUDGE.

Though homeward as you trudge,
You declare my law is fudge,
Yet of beauty I'm a judge.

ALL.

And a good Judge too!

(JUDGE and PLAINTIFF dance back on to the Bench—the BRIDESMAIDS
    take the eight garlands of roses from behind the Judge's desk (where
    one end of them is fastened) and draw them across floor of Court,
    so that they radiate from the desk. Two plaster Cupids in bar wigs
    descend from flies. Red fire.)

The Sorcerer

The Sorcerer was the first collaboration commissioned by D'Oyly Carte for the Opéra Comique. It is based on the theme of a love potion, a subject which fascinated Gilbert. He had translated *L'Elisir d'Amore* for the English burlesque stage in 1866 and the idea re-emerged several times in his work. It is a variation of his 'Lozenge Plot' which he later offered to Sullivan over and over again, to the composer's unremitting dismay.

The Victorian village wedding and bun-fight which Gilbert has chosen as a setting for *The Sorcerer* gives him ample scope for the placing of his stock characters. The ageing aristocrats, the young social reformer, the vicar, the lowly pew-opener and her daughter, the local yokels are types who could have been found in the current pages of *Punch*. They are also characters who can legitimately be made figures of fun in the pantomime tradition.

The Sorcerer himself is a thinly disguised Demon King with all his fire and brimstone accoutrements, but there is an element of Harlequin in his role. Gilbert has portrayed him as an honest tradesman, a family sorcerer and purveyor of magic, with a lively, cheapjack manner which endears him to the audience despite his seedy appearance. One cannot but regret his going down in flames at the finale, donning white gloves and distributing trade cards as he disappears. In the 1870s, vendors of patent medicines were very much part of the country scene: the Beecham family in Lancashire had built up a highly successful business and their advertising was an inspiration.

The role of the Sorcerer in the opera was written with Fred Sullivan in mind as a result of his brilliant success in *Trial by Jury*, but his untimely death came several months before the libretto of *The Sorcerer* was finished. Eventually a replacement was found in George Grossmith Junior, a 'drawing-room entertainer'. Grossmith had not been trained as a professional actor but had made a great reputation for himself. He prized his frequent dates with the YMCA and religious bodies but professed serious qualms about the likelihood of their ever employing him again, were his début in comic opera to fail. Carte's directors were violently opposed to Grossmith's engagement but both Carte and Gilbert backed it strongly. Grossmith's musical audition with Sullivan consisted of singing a high D loudly, which Sullivan proclaimed to be 'Beautiful!', and then reciting 'My name is John Wellington Wells' to the composer's piano accompaniment, with which he was equally delighted. Grossmith was urged by a number of actor friends to accept the job, which he did, and remained with the company for the next eleven years, playing every new leading role.

Although Gilbert bullied Grossmith throughout rehearsals, he was able, as a natural comedian, to put much more into the character of Wells than Gilbert had, perhaps, first imagined. It is said that his 'squatter's run' backwards, holding the teapot and making noises like a railway engine, always brought the house down.

However, there are aspects of *The Sorcerer* which could have caused Grossmith grave embarrassment had he been forced to return at once to his former livelihood. Gilbert sails very close to the wind in religious matters. Although his vicar follows in the

George Grossmith as John Wellington Wells—his first G&S role.

Punch tradition (the Church was so much part of the Establishment as to be able to withstand the gentle satirist) Dr Daly prepares and administers — all unwittingly — the devilish love-potion. Gilbert's stage directions instruct the vicar to perform the ceremony 'scientifically' but, coupled with all the prescribed paraphernalia, 'ritualistically' might be a more suitable word.

Gilbert always had some cynical social comment in his libretti. His views on match-making and marriage are given full rein in *The Sorcerer*. He paints a sad picture of the ageing Sir Marmaduke and Lady Sangazure, lovers repressed by the conventions of their youth who never declared themselves. On the other hand he explodes the theory that mutual love is the ultimate perfection in marriage. Distinctions of age and class can make a relationship founded on love alone impossible. The great middle class was comparatively small in 1877 and the Labour movement was in its infancy.

Gilbert endows his 'hero' Alexis with the dogma of social reform, and it is Alexis who orders the love-potion to be administered in the interests of brotherly love. He is the typical youth with 'a mission', but Gilbert makes him drop his high ideals very hastily when he sees the old order vanishing.

Gilbert's heroes are more than bland juvenile leads, in fact they are rather bumptious and slightly unpleasant young men. Alexis is no exception. At the end of Gilbert's life he said that the tenor had been the curse of every piece he had written. Having endowed the young men with such unheroic characteristics, he may well have brought their antipathy upon himself.

Dr Daly, to whom Alexis refers as 'My dear old tutor and my valued pastor' is the most benevolent and lovable of all Gilbert's and Sullivan's operatic creations. For repertory purposes his part falls to the type of actor who plays the less pleasant 'Pooh-Bah roles'. Gilbert actually refers to Rutland Barrington, the first Dr Daly (foisted upon him *faute de mieux*) as 'a staid, solid swine' and in the future he wrote for him the kind of parts that would better fit this description. For the actors who were condemned to perform these supercilious roles in repertory, the few productions of *The Sorcerer* (it was not generally popular) could have been an uplifting experience.

The Bishop with his pastoral pipe (forerunner of Dr Daly) from Gilbert's story 'An Elixir of Love', from the Christmas *Graphic* 1876, on which *The Sorcerer* was based.

SYNOPSIS

The overture, with its suggestion of a village band and romantic atmosphere, sets the scene for the wedding celebration on which the curtain rises.

Sir Marmaduke Pointdextre, the squire, has laid on a village teaparty to celebrate the marriage of his Grenadier son, Alexis, to Aline, daughter of Lady Sangazure.

Before the happy pair arrives, Constance Partlet, the pew-opener's daughter, reveals to her mother her secret love for the gentle vicar, Dr Daly. Her touching song, 'When he is here...' is preceded by a recitative, in the grand operatic manner. The Vicar's subsequent entrance is accompanied by 'pastoral' bird-song and he comments on the all-pervading amorous atmosphere in his nostalgic ballad, with throbbing orchestration, 'Time was when Love and I were well acquainted...' He looks back on his curate days when he 'was loved beyond all other men'. Daly upsets Constance by innocently expressing hopes of marrying her to a suitable man one day. When he states his own resolve to die a bachelor, she leaves in tears. The Vicar muses wistfully over the 'comely little girl'.

Sir Marmaduke and Alexis arrive and, to the accompaniment of a Handelian-style minuet, Daly offers a flowery solecism to his beloved ex-pupil. When Alexis and his father are alone, Sir Marmaduke chides his son for his uninhibited display of affection towards Aline and divulges that when he and Lady Sangazure were in love, formality did not allow them ever to confess it.

The men retire as a Chorus of Country Wenches bring in Aline and her mother for the civil marriage. Aline sings a spirited waltz, 'Oh happy young heart...' in appreciation of her Grenadier husband. A Chorus number, 'With Heart and with Voice...' in

The exterior of Sir Marmaduke Pointdextre's Elizabethan mansion—the country setting for *The Sorcerer* from a quadrille music cover contemporary with the first production.

similar military tone (and very reminiscent of Dulcamara's entrance in Donizetti's *L'Elisir d'Amore*) heralds Alexis, and the ecstatic meeting of the young couple takes place. The relationship between Sir Marmaduke and Lady Sangazure still burns fiercely. To a staid gavotte, 'Welcome, joy adieu to sadness!...' they pay each other formal compliments while, to a counter melody, they declaim their love 'aside, with frantic vehemence' (as Gilbert directs).

An ancient Notary arrives and the wedding ceremony follows. 'All is prepared for sealing and for signing,' is in the form of a miniature Handelian cantata. The guests leave afterwards to a reprise of the military chorus, in canon, leaving Alexis and Aline alone. At once Alexis embarks on his pet hobby-horse: love, synonymous with marriage for all, regardless of rank, wealth or station. Aline has reservations but supports her husband's idealistic ballad, 'Love feeds on many kinds of food ...'. Alexis then breaks to Aline that he has engaged a family

'Demon souls, come here in shoals, this dreadful deed inspire!' John Wellington Wells brewing the philtre from the first production of *The Sorcerer. Illustrated London News*, 23 February 1878.

sorcerer, J.W. Wells, who by means of a magic philtre will bring love to the whole village. Despite Aline's disapproval and fear, Alexis sends his page, Hercules, to fetch Mr Wells from the marquee where he is 'refreshing'.

The little man introduces himself with a spoken

brochure of his firm's magic wares, followed by a jolly patter-song, 'Oh, my name is John Wellington Wells...' elaborating on their achievements with mention of 'the prophet who brings unbounded returns' and 'the resident djinn'. A sinister verse midway suggests genuine sorcery.

Alexis proceeds to do business with Wells and discovers that the philtre induces sleep and takes effect after twelve hours. On waking, a man will fall in love with the first unengaged woman he sees and their love will become mutual. Wells warns Alexis of the dangers, but the young man is determined to pursue his plan and forces unwilling Aline to fetch the all-important teapot.

Wells's Incantation, 'Sprites of earth and air...', proceeds on a darkened stage and, to the accompaniment of wind-machine and thunder effects, Wells invokes every conceivable demonaic spirit, with real horror music. Aline, terrified, pleads in a dramatic song 'Let us fly to a far-off land...' (her top B flat almost a scream) to be allowed to escape to a distant shore and live in eternal innocence. 'Too late!' the spirits intone. When the spell is completed, three phials are emptied into the teapot with flashes and impish *glissandi*. Here is an ironic parody of casting the magic bullets in Weber's *Der Freischütz*. Alexis and Aline plead once more for their isle of innocence while the demons take flight in a chorus of fiendish laughter.

Slowly light returns, and with it the village dance is heard, first in the minor, then modulating to the major key as daylight resumes. The wedding banquet has started, teacups are distributed by Mrs Partlet and Mr Wells, and in an unaccompanied Elizabethan catch, 'Now to the banquet we press...', the villagers eulogize the English tea complete with ham, jam and rollicking bun. While Sir Marmaduke welcomes his guests, and in a Teacup Brindisi recommends the tea 'brewed by the Vicar', the three conspirators comment in undertones. Daly, assisted by Constance, now performs his tea-making ritual for all to see. Then he takes up the Brindisi with benign voice, banishing all malignant elements.

In anticipation of the impending marriages, Alexis and Aline sing a Mendelssohnian anthem, 'Oh love, true love...'. The potion is beginning to work and the bemused villagers, singing 'Oh marvellous illusion! Oh terrible surprise!', struggle with drowsiness, reel and stagger, and finally fall to the ground as the act ends.

'Enough, Aline, I shall know how to interpret this refusal.'
Ruth Vincent, Aline and Robert Evett, Alexis in the 1898
Savoy revival of *The Sorcerer*.

Ominous wind chords, reminiscent of Verdi in his darkest *Macbeth* period, announce an all-pervading magic. The villagers are sprawled ('al-fresco-ly') over Sir Marmaduke's lawn in the moonlight, and the three conspirators come tiptoeing in to watch the great awakening. Alexis and Aline search for their parents and are relieved to hear that Wells tactfully had them removed, together with Dr Daly and the Notary, to their respective beds.

As the villagers begin to stir, the conspirators retire and, in Wells's words, 'Love, the housemaid, lights the kitchen fire'. Slowly the yokels come to their senses. 'Why, where be oi, and what be oi a doin'...?' begins the rustic scene of pairing. Snatches of folk song accompany the couples' vows to garden and cook for one another until, fully awake, the yokels embark on a rousing village hop.

However, all is not well: Constance, in tears, leads in the old Notary and beginning 'Dear friends, take pity on my lot,' she sings piteously of her long-standing love for the Vicar which her new and unwanted alliance with the lawyer has dissolved. Fortunately the 'very deaf old man', though struggling with his ear-trumpet, is unable to hear Constance's excited abuse.

Aline and Alexis survey the happy dancing villagers with approval. When they are alone, Aline comments on the ill-matched couples, but Alexis maintains that these unions are superior to conventional ones and that such conflicting personalities will reap untold benefits. Then Alexis insists that to seal their love, they must also drink the potion. Aline refuses and Alexis embarks on a jealous ballad, 'Thou hast the power thy vaunted love to sanctify', despising her vows of fidelity which he regards as temporal.

Dr Daly meets them and reflects on the number of forthcoming marriages, among them that of Sir Marmaduke. Alexis and Aline suppose that their parents are to marry each other but, to their horror, they see Sir Marmaduke approaching with Mrs Partlet. Alexis grudgingly congratulates, but plainly disapproves. Daly himself yearns for marriage, but sighs that 'all are engaged'.

Wells, regretting the dreadful havoc wrought by the potion, is pursued by a distraught Lady Sangazure. She swears to renounce her former life, to help Wells in his business, and to adopt all his working-class habits. He compassionately tries to ward her off, resorting at last to a guilty lie that he is engaged to a South Sea Island girl. Sangazure is mortified.

Aline finally takes the potion and is going to meet Alexis when she is intercepted by Dr Daly, playing his flageolet. 'Oh, my voice is sad and low ...' he sighs, relating how all his proposals to the village maidens have been turned down. When he sees Aline, they fall hopelessly in love.

Alexis arrives to find that Aline no longer loves him. He denounces her before the whole village, but Dr Daly defends her (shades of *La Traviata* Act III) reminding Alexis that he was responsible for the effects of the potion. Dr Daly proposes to leave the country rather than stand in Alexis' way.

Somewhat calmer, Alexis turns to Wells and learns the terrible truth that to undo the spell, one of them must die. Aline appeals for her future husband and eventually, by general consent, Wells is condemned. Bidding a happy future to all, he sinks sadly into the earth 'amid red fire'.

The spell is broken. All retrieve their former partners and Sir Marmaduke invites the villagers to another feast. The opera ends with a reprise of 'Now to the banquet we press' sung by the entire company.

THE SORCERER.

AN ENTIRELY ORIGINAL MODERN COMIC OPERA,

IN TWO ACTS.

First produced at the Opera Comique Theatre, 17 November, 1877.

DRAMATIS PERSONÆ

SIR MARMADUKE POINTDEXTRE [*an elderly Baronet*]	bass
ALEXIS [*of the Grenadier Guards—his Son*]	tenor
DR. DALY [*Vicar of Ploverleigh*]	baritone
JOHN WELLINGTON WELLS [*of J. W. Wells & Co., Family Sorcerers*]	baritone
NOTARY	bass
LADY SANGAZURE [*a Lady of ancient lineage*]	Contralto
ALINE [*her Daughter—betrothed to* ALEXIS]	Soprano
MRS. PARTLET [*a Pew-Opener*]	mezzo-soprano
CONSTANCE [*her Daughter*]	Soprano

CHORUS OF PEASANTRY.

ACT I.

GROUNDS OF SIR MARMADUKE'S MANSION

[*Half an hour is supposed to elapse between Acts I. and II.*]

ACT II.

MARKET-PLACE OF PLOVERLEIGH.

TIME—THE PRESENT DAY.

THE SORCERER.

ACT I.

SCENE.—*Garden of Sir Marmaduke's Elizabethan mansion. The end of a large marquee, open, and showing portion of table covered with white cloth, on which are joints of meat, teapots, cups, bread and butter, jam, etc. To the back a raised terrace with steps. A park in the background, with spire of church seen above the trees.*

CHORUS OF PEASANTRY.

Ring forth, ye bells,
  With clarion sound—
Forget your knells,
  For joys abound.

Forget your notes
  Of mournful lay,
And from your throats
  Pour joy to-day.

For to-day young Alexis—young Alexis Pointdextre
  Is betrothed to Aline—to Aline Sangazure,
And that pride of his sex is—of his sex is to be next her,
  At the feast on the green—on the green, oh, be sure!

    Ring forth, ye bells, etc.

[*At the end of chorus, exeunt the* MEN *into house.*

Enter MRS. PARTLET, *meeting* CONSTANCE, *her daughter.*

RECITATIVE.

MRS. P.   Constance, my daughter, why this strange
                depression?
          The village rings with seasonable joy,
          Because the young and amiable Alexis,
          Heir to the great Sir Marmaduke Pointdextre,
          Is plighted to Aline, the only daughter
          Of Annabella, Lady Sangazure.
          You, you alone are sad and out of spirits;
          What is the reason? Speak, my daughter, speak!
CON.   Oh, mother, do not ask! If my complexion
          From red to white should change in quick
                succession—
          And then from white to red, oh, take no notice!
          If my poor limbs shall tremble with emotion,
          Pay no attention, mother—it is nothing!
          If long and deep-drawn sighs I chance to utter,
          Oh, heed them not, their cause must ne'er be
                known!
MRS. P.   My child, be candid; think not to deceive
          The eagle-eyed pew-opener—you love!
CON. *(aside).* How guessed she that, my heart's most cherished
                secret?
(Aloud.)   I *do* love, fondly—madly—hopelessly!

ARIA.—CONSTANCE.

          When he is here,
             I sigh with pleasure;
          When he is gone,
             I sigh with grief.
          My hopeless fear
             No soul can measure;
          His love alone
             Can give my aching heart relief!
          When he is cold,
             I weep for sorrow;
          When he is kind,
             I weep for joy.
          My grief untold
             Knows no to-morrow.
          My woe can find
             No hope, no solace, no alloy!

[At the end of the song, MRS. PARTLET *silently motions to*
WOMEN *to leave them together. Exeunt* CHORUS.

MRS. P.   Come, tell me all about it! Do not fear—
          I, too, have loved; but that was long ago!
          Who is the object of your young affections?
CON.   Hush, mother! He is here!

Enter DR. DALY. *He is pensive, and does not see them. He sits on stool.*

MRS. P. *(amazed).*   **Our reverend vicar!**
CON.   Oh, pity me, my heart is almost broken!
MRS. P.   My child, be comforted. To such an union
          I shall not offer any opposition.

          Take him—he's yours! May you and he be
                happy!
CON.   But, mother dear, he is not yours to give!
MRS. P.   That's true, indeed!
CON.   He might object!
MRS. P.   He might.
          But come; take heart. I'll probe him on the
                subject.
          Be comforted; leave this affair to me.

RECITATIVE—DR. DALY.

The air is charged with amatory numbers—
   Soft madrigals, and dreamy lovers' lays.
Peace, peace, old heart! Why waken from its slumbers
   The aching memory of the old, old days?

BALLAD.

Time was when Love and I were well acquainted.
   Time was when we walked ever hand in hand,
A saintly youth, with worldly thought untainted—
   None better loved than I in all the land!
Time was when maidens of the noblest station,
   Forsaking even military men,
Would gaze upon me, rapt in adoration.
   Ah me! I was a fair young curate then!

Had I a headache? sighed the maids assembled;
   Had I a cold? welled forth the silent tear;
Did I look pale? then half a parish trembled;
   And when I coughed all thought the end was near.
I had no care—no jealous doubts hung o'er me;
   For I was loved beyond all other men.
Fled gilded dukes and belted earls before me.
   Ah me! I was a pale young curate then!

[At the conclusion of the ballad, MRS. PARTLET *comes forward with*
CONSTANCE.

MRS. P. Good day, reverend sir.

DR. D. Ah, good Mrs. Partlet, I am glad to see you. And your little daughter, Constance! Why, she is quite a little woman, I declare!

CON. *(aside).* Oh, mother, I cannot speak to him!

MRS. P. Yes, reverend sir, she is nearly eighteen, and as good a girl as ever stepped. *(Aside to* DR. D). Ah, sir, I'm afraid I shall soon lose her!

DR. D. *(aside to* MRS. P.). Dear me! you pain me very much. Is she delicate?

MRS. P. Oh no, sir; I don't mean that; but young girls look to get married.

DR. D. Oh, I take you. To be sure. But there's plenty of time for that. Four or five years hence, Mrs. Partlet, four or five years hence. But when the time *does* come, I shall have much pleasure in marrying her myself—

CON. *(aside).* Oh, mother!

DR. D. To some strapping young fellow in her own rank of life.

CON. (*in tears*). He does *not* love me!

MRS. P. I have often wondered, reverend sir (if you'll excuse the liberty) that *you* have never married.

DR. D. (*aside*). Be still, my fluttering heart!

MRS. P. A clergyman's wife does so much good in a village. Besides that, you are not so young as you were, and before very long you will want somebody to nurse you, and look after your little comforts.

DR. D. Mrs. Partlet, there is much truth in what you say. I am indeed getting on in years, and a helpmate would cheer my declining days. Time was when it might have been; but I have left it too long. I am an old fogey now, am I not, my dear? (*to Constance*)—a very old fogey indeed. Ha! ha! No, Mrs. Partlet, my mind is quite made up. I shall live and die a solitary old bachelor.

CON. Oh, mother, mother! (*Sobs on* MRS. PARTLET'S *bosom.*)

MRS. P. Come, come, dear one, don't fret. At a more fitting time we will try again—we will try again.

[*Exeunt* MRS. PARTLET *and* CONSTANCE.

DR. D. (*looking after them*). Poor little girl! I'm afraid she has something on her mind. She is rather comely. Time was when this old heart would have throbbed in double time at the sight of such a fairy form! But tush! I am puling! Here come the young Alexis, with his proud and happy father. Let me dry this tell-tale tear!

Enter SIR MARMADUKE *and* ALEXIS *from house.*

RECITATIVE.

DR. D. Sir Marmaduke—my dear young friend, Alexis—
On this most happy, most auspicious plighting,
Permit me, as a true old friend, to tender
My best, my very best congratulations!

SIR M. Sir, you are most obleeging!

ALEX.   Dr. Daly,
My dear old tutor and my valued pastor,
I thank you from the bottom of my heart!

(Spoken through music.)

DR. D. May fortune bless you! may the middle distance
Of your young life be pleasant as the foreground—
The joyous foreground! and, when you have reached
 it,
May that which now is the far-off horizon,
But which will then become the middle distance,
In fruitful promise be exceeded only
By that which will have opened, in the mean time,
Into a new and glorious horizon!

SIR M. Dear sir, that is an excellent example
Of an old school of stately compliment,
To which I have, through life, been much addicted.
Will you obleege me with a copy of it,
In clerkly manuscript, that I myself
May use it on appropriate occasions?

DR. D. Sir, you shall have a fairly written copy
Ere Sol has sunk into his western slumbers!

[*Exit* DR. DALY.

SIR M. (*to* ALEXIS, *who is in a reverie*). Come, come, my son—your *fiancée* will be here in five minutes. Rouse yourself to receive her.

ALEX. (*rising*). Oh, rapture!

SIR M. Yes, you are a fortunate young fellow, and I will not disguise from you that this union with the house of Sangazure realizes my fondest wishes. Aline is rich, and she comes of a sufficiently old family, for she is the seven thousand and thirty-seventh in direct descent from Helen of Troy. True, there was a blot on the escutcheon of that lady—that affair with Paris—but where is the family, other than my own, in which there is no flaw? You are a lucky fellow, sir—a very lucky fellow!

ALEX. Father, I am welling over with limpid joy! No sicklying taint of sorrow overlies the lucid lake of liquid love, upon which, hand in hand, Aline and I are to float into eternity!

SIR M. Alexis, I desire that of your love for this young lady you do not speak so openly. You are always singing ballads in praise of her beauty, and you expect the very menials who wait behind your chair to chorus your ecstasies. It is not delicate.

ALEX. Father, a man who loves as I love—

SIR M. Pooh, pooh, sir! fifty years ago I madly loved your future mother-in-law, the Lady Sangazure, and I have reason to believe that she returned my love. But were we guilty of the indelicacy of publicly rushing into each other's arms, exclaiming—

RECITATIVE.

"Oh, my adored one!"   "Beloved boy!"
"Ecstatic rapture!"   "Unmingled joy!"

which seems to be the modern fashion of love-making? No, it was, "Madam, I trust you are in the enjoyment of good health."—"Sir, you are vastly polite, I protest I am mighty well"—and so forth. Much more delicate—much more respectful. But see—Aline approaches; let us retire, that she may compose herself for the interesting ceremony in which she is to play so important a part.

[*Exeunt* SIR MARMADUKE *into house.*

Enter ALINE, *preceded by Chorus of* GIRLS.

CHORUS OF GIRLS.

With heart and with voice
 Let us welcome this mating:
To the youth of her choice,
 With a heart palpitating,
  Comes the lovely Aline!

May their love never cloy!
 May their bliss be unbounded!
With a halo of joy
 May their lives be surrounded!
  Heaven bless our Aline!

RECITATIVE.—ALINE.

My kindly friends, I thank you for this greeting,
And as you wish me every earthly joy,
I trust your wishes may have quick fulfilment!

ARIA.—ALINE.

Oh, happy young heart!
  Comes thy young lord a-wooing,
With joy in his eyes,
  And pride in his breast.
Make much of thy prize,
  For he is the best
That ever came a-suing.
    Yet—yet we must part,
        Young heart!
    Yet—yet we must part.

Oh, merry young heart,
  Bright are the days of thy wooing!
But happier far
  The days untried.
No sorrow can mar
  When Love has tied
The knot there's no undoing.
    Then, never to part,
        Young heart!
    Then, never to part!

Enter LADY SANGAZURE.

RECITATIVE.—LADY S.

My child, I join in these congratulations.
Heed not the tear that dims this aged eye!
Old memories crowd upon me. Though I sorrow,
'Tis for myself, Aline, and not for thee!

Enter ALEXIS *from house, preceded by Chorus of* MEN.

CHORUS OF MEN AND WOMEN.

With heart and with voice
  Let us welcome this mating:
To the maid of his choice,
  With a heart palpitating,
  Comes Alexis the brave!

SIR MARMADUKE *enters from house.* LADY SANGAZURE *and he exhibit signs of strong emotion at the sight of each other, which they endeavour to repress;* ALEXIS *and* ALINE *rush into each other's arms.*

RECITATIVE.

ALEX.   Oh, my adored one!
ALI.   Beloved boy!
ALEX.   Ecstatic rapture!
ALI.   Unmingled joy!

DUET.—SIR MARMADUKE *and* LADY SANGAZURE.

SIR M. *(with stately courtesy).*
  Welcome joy, adieu to sadness!

As Aurora gilds the day,
  So those eyes, twin orbs of gladness,
    Chase the clouds of care away.
Irresistible incentive,
  Bids me humbly kiss your hand;
I'm your servant most attentive,
  Most attentive to command.

(Aside, with frantic vehemence.)
  Wild with adoration!
  Mad with fascination!
  To indulge my lamentation
    No occasion do I miss!
  Goaded to distraction
  By maddening inaction,
  I find some satisfaction
    In apostrophe like this.
    "Sangazure immortal,
      Sangazure divine,
    Welcome to my portal,
      Angel, oh, be mine!"

(Aloud with much ceremony.)
  Irresistible incentive
    Bids me humbly kiss your hand,
  I'm your servant most attentive,
    Most attentive to command!

LADY S.   Sir, I thank you most politely
    For your graceful courtesee:
Compliment more true knightly
  Never yet was paid to me!
Chivalry is an ingredient
  Sadly lacking in our land.
Sir, I am your most obedient,
  Most obedient to command!

(Aside, with great vehemence.)
  Wild with adoration!
  Mad with fascination!
  To indulge my lamentation
    No occasion do I miss!
  Goaded to distraction
  By maddening inaction,
  I find some satisfaction
    In apostrophe like this:
    "Marmaduke immortal,
      Marmaduke divine,
    Take me to thy portal,
      Loved one, oh, be mine!"

(Aloud, with much ceremony.)
  Chivalry is an ingredient
    Sadly lacking in our land.
  Sir, I am your most obedient,
    Most obedient to command!

[*During this duet a small table has been placed upon stage, by* MRS. PARTLET. *The* COUNSEL *has entered, and prepares marriage contract behind table.*

RECITATIVE.—COUNSEL.

All is prepared for sealing and for signing,
The contract has been drafted as agreed;
Approach the table, oh ye lovers pining,
With hand and seal come execute the deed!

[ALEXIS *and* ALINE *advance and sign,* ALEXIS *supported by*
SIR MARMADUKE, ALINE *by her mother.*

CHORUS.

See they sign, without a quiver, it—
Then to seal proceed.
They deliver it—they deliver it
As their act and deed!
ALEX.   I deliver it—I deliver it
As my act and deed!
ALI.   I deliver it—I deliver it
As my act and deed!

CHORUS.

With heart and with voice
Let us welcome this mating:
Leave them here to rejoice,
With true love palpitating—
Alexis the brave,
And the lovely Aline!

[*Exeunt all but* ALEXIS *and* ALINE.

ALEX. At last we are alone! My darling, you are now irrevocably betrothed to me. Are you not very, very happy?

ALI. Oh, Alexis, can you doubt it? Do I not love you beyond all on earth, and am I not beloved in return? Is not true love, faithfully given and faithfully returned, the source of every earthly joy?

ALEX. Of that there can be no doubt. Oh that the world could be persuaded of the truth of that maxim! Oh that the world would break down the artificial barriers of rank, wealth, education, age, beauty, habits, taste, and temper, and recognize the glorious principle, that in marriage alone is to be found the panacea for every ill!

ALI. Continue to preach that sweet doctrine, and you will succeed, oh, evangel of true happiness!

ALEX. I hope so, but as yet the cause progresses but slowly. Still I have made some converts to the principle, that men and women should be coupled in matrimony without distinction of rank. I have lectured on the subject at Mechanics' Institutes, and the mechanics were unanimous in favour of my views. I have preached in workhouses, beershops, and lunatic asylums, and I have been received with enthusiasm. I have addressed navvies on the advantages that would accrue to them if they married wealthy ladies of rank, and not a navvy dissented.

ALI. Noble fellows! And yet there are those who hold that the uneducated classes are not open to argument! And what do the countesses say?

ALEX. Why, at present, it can't be denied, the aristocracy hold aloof.

ALI. The working man is the true Intelligence, after all!

ALEX. He is a noble creature when he is quite sober. Yes,

Aline, true happiness comes of true love, and true love should be independent of external influences. It should live upon itself and by itself—in itself love should live for love alone!

BALLAD.

ALEX. Love feeds on many kinds of food, I know.
Some love for rank, and some for duty;
Some give their hearts away for empty show,
And others love for youth and beauty.
To love for money all the world is prone;
Some love themselves, and live all lonely.
Give me the love that loves for love alone;
I love that love—I love it only!

What man for any other joy can thirst,
Whose loving wife adores him duly?
Want, misery, and care may do their worst,
If loving woman loves you truly.
A lover's thoughts are ever with his own;
None truly loved is ever lonely.
Give me the love that loves for love alone;
I love that love—I love it only!

ALI. Oh, Alexis, those are noble principles!

ALEX. Yes, Aline, and I am going to take a desperate step in support of them. Have you ever heard of the firm of J. W. Wells and Co., the old-established family sorcerers, in St. Mary Axe?

ALI. I have seen their advertisement.

ALEX. They have invented a philtre, which, if report may be believed, is simply infallible. I intend to distribute it through the village, and within half an hour of my doing so, there will not be an adult in the place who will not have learnt the secret of pure and lasting happiness. What do you say to that?

ALI. Well, dear, of course a filter is a very useful thing in a house; quite indispensable in the present state of Thames water; but still I don't quite see that it is the sort of thing that places its possessor on the very pinnacle of earthly joy.

ALEX. Aline, you misunderstand me. I didn't say a filter—I said philtre.

ALI. So did I, dear. *I* said a filter.

ALEX. No, dear, you said a filter. I don't mean a filter—I mean a philtre,—ph, you know.

ALI. *(alarmed).* You don't mean a love-potion?

ALEX. On the contrary—I *do* mean a love-potion.

ALI. Oh, Alexis, I don't think it would be right. I don't indeed. And then—a real magician! Oh, it would be downright wicked.

ALEX. Aline, is it, or is it not, a laudable object to steep the whole village up to its lips in love, and to couple them in matrimony, without distinction of age, rank, or fortune?

ALI. Unquestionably, but—

ALEX. Then, unpleasant as it must be to have recourse to supernatural aid, I must nevertheless pocket my aversion, in deference to the great and good end I have in view. *(Calling.)* Hercules!

Enter a PAGE *from tent.*

PAGE. Yes, sir.

ALEX. Is Mr. Wells there?

PAGE. He's in the tent, sir—refreshing.

ALEX. Ask him to be so good as to step this way.

PAGE. Yes, sir.   [*Exit* PAGE.

ALI. Oh, but, Alexis! A real sorcerer! Oh, I shall be frightened to death!

ALEX. I trust my Aline will not yield to fear while the strong right arm of her Alexis is here to protect her.

ALI. It's nonsense, dear, to talk of your protecting me with your strong right arm, in face of the fact that this Family Sorcerer could change me into a guinea-pig before you could turn round.

ALEX. He *could* change you into a guinea-pig, no doubt, but it is most unlikely that he would take such liberty. It's a most respectable firm, and I am sure he would never be guilty of so untradesmanlike an act.

Enter MR. WELLS *from tent.*

MR. W. Good day, sir.   [ALINE *much terrified.*

ALEX. Good day. I believe you are a sorcerer.

MR. W. Yes, sir, we practise necromancy in all its branches. We've a choice assortment of wishing-caps, divining-rods, amulets, charms, and counter-charms. We can cast you a nativity at a low figure, and we have a horoscope at three and six that we can guarantee. Our Abudah chests, each containing a patent hag who comes out and prophesies disasters, with spring complete, are strongly recommended. Our Aladdin lamps are very chaste, and our prophetic tablets, foretelling everything—from a change of ministry down to a rise in Turkish stock—are much inquired for. Our penny curse—one of the cheapest things in the trade—is considered infallible. We have some very superior blessings, too, but they're very little asked for. We've only sold one since Christmas—to a gentleman who bought it to send to his mother-in-law—but it turned out that he was afflicted in the head, and it's been returned on our hands. But our sale of penny curses, especially on Saturday nights, is tremendous. We can't turn 'em out fast enough.

SONG.—MR. WELLS.

Oh! my name is John Wellington Wells,
I'm a dealer in magic and spells,
    In blessings and curses,
    And ever-filled purses,
In prophecies, witches, and knells.

If you want a proud foe to "make tracks"—
If you'd melt a rich uncle in wax—
    You've but to look in
    On our resident Djinn,
Number seventy, Simmery Axe.

We've a first-class assortment of magic;
    And for raising a posthumous shade
With effects that are comic or tragic,
    There's no cheaper house in the trade.
Love-philtre—we've quantities of it!
    And for knowledge if any one burns,
We keep an extremely small prophet
    Who brings us unbounded returns:

Oh! he can prophesy
    With a wink *of* his eye,
Peep with security
    Into futurity,
Sum up your history,
    Clear up a mystery,
Humour proclivity
For a nativity—for a nativity;
    Mirrors so magical,
    Tetrapods tragical,
    Bogies spectacular,
    Answers oracular,
    Facts astronomical,
    Solemn or comical,
    And, if you want it, he
Makes a reduction on taking a quantity!

Oh!
If any one anything lacks,
He'll find it all ready in stacks,
    If he'll only look in
    On the resident Djinn,
Number seventy, Simmery Axe!

He can raise you hosts
    Of ghosts,
And that without reflectors;
    And creepy things
        With wings,
And gaunt and grisly spectres.
    He can fill you crowds
    Of shrouds,
And horrify you vastly;
    He can rack your brains
        With chains,
And gibberings grim and ghastly!

Then, if you plan it, he
Changes organity,
With an urbanity
Full of Satanity,
Vexes humanity
With an inanity
Fatal to vanity—
Driving your foes to the verge of insanity!
    Barring tautology,
    In demonology,
    'Lectro-biology,
    Mystic nosology,
    Spirit philology,
    High-class astrology,
    Such is his knowledge, he
Isn't the man to require an apology!

Oh!
My name is John Wellington Wells.
I'm a dealer in magic and spells,
    In blessings and curses,
    And ever-filled purses,
In prophecies, witches, and knells.

If any one anything lacks,
He'll find it all ready in stacks,
 If he'll only look in
 On the resident Djinn,
Number seventy, Simmery Axe!

ALEX. I have sent for you to consult you on a very important matter. I believe you advertise a Patent Oxy-Hydrogen Love-at-first-sight Philtre?

MR. W. Sir, it is our leading article. *(Producing a phial.)*

ALEX. Now, I want to know if you can confidently guarantee it as possessing all the qualities you claim for it in your advertisement?

MR. W. Sir, we are not in the habit of puffing our goods. Ours is an old-established house with a large family connection, and every assurance held out in the advertisement is fully realized. *(Hurt).*

ALI. *(aside).* Oh, Alexis, don't offend him! He'll change us into something dreadful—I know he will!

ALEX. I am anxious from purely philanthropical motives to distribute this philtre, secretly, among the inhabitants of this village. I shall of course require a quantity. How do you sell it?

MR. W. In buying a quantity, sir, we should strongly advise your taking it in the wood, and drawing it off as you happen to want it. We have it in four and a half and nine gallon casks—also in pipes and hogsheads for laying down, and we deduct 10 per cent. for prompt cash.

ALI. Oh, Alexis, surely you don't want to lay any down!

ALEX. Aline, the villagers will assemble to carouse in a few minutes. Go and fetch the teapot.

ALI. But, Alexis—

ALEX. My dear, you must obey me, if you please. Go and fetch the teapot.

ALI. *(going).* I'm sure Dr. Daly would disapprove it.

          [*Exit* ALINE *into tent.*

ALEX. And how soon does it take effect?

MR. W. In half an hour. Whoever drinks of it falls in love, as a matter of course, with the first lady he meets who has also tasted it, and his affection is at once returned. One trial will prove the fact.

Enter ALINE *from tent with large teapot.*

ALEX. Good: then, Mr. Wells, I shall feel obliged if you will at once pour as much philtre into this teapot as will suffice to affect the whole village.

ALI. But bless me, Alexis, many of the villagers are married people.

MR. W. Madam, this philtre is compounded on the strictest principles. On married people it has no effect whatever. But are you quite sure that you have nerve enough to carry you through the fearful ordeal?

ALEX. In the good cause I fear nothing.

MR. W. Very good; then we will proceed at once to the Incantation.

(The stage grows dark.)

INCANTATION.

MR. W. Sprites of earth and air—
     Fiends of flame and fire—

    Demon souls,
    Come here in shoals,
  This dreadful deed inspire!
   Appear, appear, appear!

MALE VOICES. Good master, we are here!

MR. W. Noisome hags of night—
    Imps of deadly shade—
     Pallid ghosts,
     Arise in hosts,
  And lend me all your aid!
   Appear, appear, appear!

FEMALE VOICES. Good master, we are here!

ALEX. *(aside).* Hark, they assemble,
      These fiends of the night!

ALI. *(aside).* Oh, Alexis, I tremble.
      Seek safety in flight!

ARIA.—ALINE.

Let us fly to a far-off land,
 Where peace and plenty dwell—
Where the sigh of the silver strand
 Is echoed in every shell.
To the joy that land will give,
 On the wings of Love we'll fly;
In innocence there to live—
 In innocence there to die!

CHORUS OF SPIRITS.

Too late—too late,
 It may not be!
That happy fate
 Is not for thee!

ALEXIS, ALINE, *and* MR. WELLS.

Too late—too late,
 That may not be!
That happy fate
 Is not for $\left\{ \begin{array}{l} \text{me!} \\ \text{thee!} \end{array} \right\}$

MR. W. Now, shrivelled hags, with poison bags,
    Discharge your loathsome loads!
  Spit flame and fire, unholy choir!
    Belch forth your venom, toads!
  Ye demons fell, with yelp and yell,
    Shed curses far afield—
  Ye fiends of night, your filthy blight
    In noisome plenty yield!

MR. W. *(pouring phial into teapot—flash).*
      Number One!

CHORUS.   It is done!

MR. W. *(pouring phial into teapot—flash).*
      Number Two!

CHORUS.   One too few!

MR. W. (*pouring phial into teapot—flash*).
            Number Three!
CHORUS.   Set us free!
            Set us free—our work is done.
            Ha! ha! ha!
            Set us free—our course is run!
            Ha! ha! ha!

ALINE and ALEXIS (*aside*).

Let us fly to a far-off land,
   Where peace and plenty dwell—
Where the sigh of the silver strand
   Is echoed in every shell.

CHORUS OF FIENDS.

Ha! ha! ha! ha! ha! ha! ha! ha! ha! ha!

[*Stage grows light. MR. WELLS beckons villagers.*

Enter villagers and all the dramatis personæ, dancing joyously. SIR MARMADUKE enters with LADY SANGAZURE from house. VICAR enters, absorbed in thought. He is followed by CONSTANCE. COUNSEL enters, followed by MRS. PARTLET. MRS. PARTLET and MR. WELLS distribute teacups.

CHORUS.

Now to the banquet we press;
   Now for the eggs, the ham,
Now for the mustard and cress,
   Now for the strawberry jam!
Now for the tea of our host,
   Now for the rollicking bun,
Now for the muffin and toast,
   Now for the gay Sally Lunn!
WOMEN. The eggs, and the ham, and the strawberry jam!
MEN.   The rollicking bun, and the gay Sally Lunn!
        The rollicking, rollicking bun!

RECITATIVE.—SIR MARMADUKE.

Be happy all—the feast is spread before ye,
   Fear nothing, but enjoy yourselves, I pray!
Eat, ay, and drink—be merry, I implore ye,
   For once let thoughtless Folly rule the day.

TEACUP BRINDISI.

Eat, drink, and be gay,
   Banish all worry and sorrow;
Laugh gaily to-day,
   Weep, if you're sorry, to-morrow!
Come, pass the cup round—
   I will go bail for the liquor;
It's strong, I'll be bound,
   For it was brewed by the vicar!

CHORUS.

None so knowing as he
At brewing a jorum of tea,
      Ha! ha!
A pretty stiff jorum of tea!

TRIO.—MR. WELLS, ALINE, and ALEXIS (*aside*).

See—see—they drink—
   All thought unheeding;
The teacups clink—
   They are exceeding!
Their hearts will melt
   In half an hour—
Then will be felt
   The potion's power!

[*During this verse CONSTANCE has brought a small teapot, kettle, caddy, and cosy to DR. DALY. He makes tea scientifically.*

BRINDISI, *2nd Verse.*—DR. DALY (*with the teapot*).

Pain, trouble, and care,
   Misery, heart-ache, and worry,
Quick, out of your lair!
   Get you all gone in a hurry!
Toil, sorrow, and plot,
   Fly away quicker and quicker—
Three spoons to the pot—
   That is the brew of your vicar!

CHORUS.

None so cunning as he
At brewing a jorum of tea,
      Ha! ha!
A pretty stiff jorum of tea!

[DR. DALY *places teapot on tray held by CONSTANCE. He covers it with the cosy. She takes tray into the house.*

ENSEMBLE.—ALEXIS and ALINE (*aside*).

Oh, love, true love—unworldly, abiding!
   Source of all pleasure—true fountain of joy—
Oh, love, true love—divinely confiding,
   Exquisite treasure that knows no alloy!
Oh, love, true love, rich harvest of gladness,
   Peace-bearing tillage—great garner of bliss—
Oh, love, true love, look down on our sadness—
   Dwell in this village—oh, hear us in this!

[*It becomes evident by the strange conduct of the characters that the charm is working. All rub their eyes.*

TUTTI (*aside*).   ALEXIS, MR. WELLS, and ALINE (*aside*).

Oh, marvellous illusion!   A marvellous illusion—
  Oh, terrible surprise!   A terrible surprise
What is this strange confusion Excites a strange confusion

That veils my aching eyes?   Within their aching eyes—
I must regain my senses,   They must regain their senses,
    Restoring Reason's law,   Restoring Reason's law,
Or fearful inferences   Or fearful inferences
    The company will draw!   The company will draw!

[*Those who have partaken of the philtre struggle against its effects, and
resume the Brindisi with a violent effort.*

TUTTI.

Eat, drink, and be gay,
    Banish all worry and sorrow,
Laugh gaily to-day,
    Weep, if you're sorry, to-morrow;
Come, pass the cup round—
    We will go bail for the liquor;
It's strong, I'll be bound,
    For it was brewed by the vicar!
None so cunning as he
At brewing a jorum of tea.
       Ha! ha!
At brewing a jorum of tea!

ACT II.

SCENE.—*Market-place in the Village. Rustic houses. In centre
a market cross.*

Enter PEASANTS *dancing, coupled two and two. An old* MAN *with a
young* GIRL. *Then an old* WOMAN *with a young* MAN. *Then
other ill-assorted couples.*

OPENING CHORUS.

Happy are we in our loving frivolity,
Happy and jolly as people of quality;
Love is the source of all joy to humanity,
Money, position, and rank are a vanity;
Year after year we've been waiting and tarrying,
Without ever dreaming of loving and marrying.
Though we've been hitherto deaf, dumb, and blind to it,
It's pleasant enough when you've made up your mind to it.

Enter CONSTANCE, *leading* NOTARY.

ARIA.—CONSTANCE.

Dear friends, take pity on my lot,
    My cup is not of nectar!
I long have loved—as who would not?—
    Our kind and reverend rector.
Long years ago my love began
    So sweetly—yet so sadly—
But when I saw this plain old man,
    Away my old affection ran—
    I found I loved him madly.
(*To*   Oh!
NOTARY.) You very, very plain old man,
    I love, I love you madly!

CHORUS. You very, very plain old man,
       She loves, she loves you madly!
NOTARY. I am a very deaf old man,
       And hear you very badly.

CON. I know not why I love him so;
       It is enchantment, surely!
He's dry and snuffy, deaf and slow.
       Ill-tempered, weak, and poorly!
He's ugly, and absurdly dressed,
       And sixty-seven nearly,
He's everything that I detest,
But if the truth must be confessed,
       I love him very dearly!
(*To*   Oh!
NOTARY.) You're everything that I detest,
       But still I love you dearly!
CHORUS. You're everything that girls detest,
       But still she loves you dearly!
NOTARY. I caught that line, but for the rest
       I did not hear it clearly!

[*During this verse* ALINE *and* ALEXIS *have entered at back, unobserved.*

ALINE *and* ALEXIS.

ALEX.   Oh, joy! oh, joy!
       The charm works well,
       And all are now united.
ALI.   The blind young boy
       Obeys the spell,
       Their troth they all have plighted!

ENSEMBLE.

ALINE *and* ALEXIS.	CONSTANCE.	NOTARY.
Oh, joy! oh, joy!	Oh, bitter joy!	Oh, joy! oh, joy!
The charm works well,	No words can tell	No words can tell
And all are now	How my poor	My state of mind
united.	heart is blighted!	delighted.
The blind young boy	They'll soon employ	They'll soon employ
Obeys the spell,	A marriage bell,	A marriage bell,
Their troth they all	To say that	To say that
have plighted.	we're united.	we're united.
True happiness	I do confess	True happiness
Reigns everywhere,	A sorrow rare	Reigns everywhere,
And dwells with	My humbled	And dwells with
both the sexes,	spirit vexes,	both the sexes,
And all will bless	And none will bless	And all will bless
The thoughtful care	Example rare	Example rare
Of their beloved	Of their beloved	Of their beloved
Alexis!	Alexis!	Alexis!

[*All, except* ALEXIS *and* ALINE, *dance off to symphony.*

ALI. How joyful they all seem in their new-found happiness!
The whole village has paired off in the happiest manner. And yet
not a match has been made that the hollow world would not
consider ill-advised!

ALEX. But we are wiser—far wiser—than the world. Observe

the good that will become of these ill-assorted unions. The miserly wife will check the reckless expenditure of her too frivolous consort, the wealthy husband will shower innumerable bonnets on his penniless bride, and the young and lively spouse will cheer the declining days of her aged partner with comic songs unceasing!

ALI. What a delightful prospect for him!

ALEX. But one thing remains to be done, that my happiness may be complete. We must drink the philtre ourselves, that I may be assured of your love for ever and ever.

ALI. Oh, Alexis, do you doubt me? Is it necessary that such love as ours should be secured by artificial means? Oh no, no, no!

ALEX. My dear Aline, time works terrible changes, and I want to place our love beyond the chance of change.

ALI. Alexis, it is already far beyond that chance. Have faith in me, for my love can never, never change!

ALEX. Then you absolutely refuse?

ALI. I do. If you cannot trust me, you have no right to love me—no right to be loved *by* me.

ALEX. Enough, Aline; I shall know how to interpret this refusal.

BALLAD.—ALEXIS.

Thou hast the power thy vaunted love
To sanctify, all doubt above,
    Despite the gathering shade:
To make that love of thine so sure
That, come what may, it must endure
    Till time itself shall fade.
        Thy love is but a flower
        That fades within the hour!
        If such thy love, oh, shame!
        Call it by other name—
            It is not love!

Thine is the power, and thine alone,
To place me on so proud a throne
    That kings might envy me!
A priceless throne of love untold,
More rare than orient pearl and gold.
    But no! Thou wouldst be free!
        Such love is like the ray
        That dies within the day!
        If such thy love, oh, shame!
        Call it by other name—
            It is not love!

Enter DR. DALY.

DR. D. *(musing)*. It is singular—it is very singular. It has overthrown all my calculations. It is distinctly opposed to the doctrine of averages. I cannot understand it.

ALI. Dear Dr. Daly, what has puzzled you?

DR. D. My dear, this village has not hitherto been addicted to marrying and giving in marriage. Hitherto the youths of this village have not been enterprising, and the maidens have been distinctly coy. Judge then of my surprise when I tell you that the whole village came to me in a body just now, and implored me to join them in matrimony with as little delay as possible. Even your excellent father has hinted to me that before very long it is not unlikely that he, also, may change his condition.

ALI. Oh, Alexis—do you hear that? Are you not delighted?

ALEX. Yes. I confess that a union between your mother and my father would be a happy circumstance indeed. *(Crossing to* DR. DALY.*)* My dear sir, the news that you bring us is very gratifying.

DR. D. Yes—still, in my eyes, it has its melancholy side. This universal marrying recalls the happy days—now, alas! gone for ever—when I myself might have—but tush! I am puling. I am too old to marry—and yet, within the last half-hour, I have greatly yearned for companionship. I never remarked it before, but the young maidens of this village are very comely. So likewise are the middle-aged. Also the elderly. All are comely—and *(with a deep sigh)* all are engaged!

ALI. Here comes your father.

Enter SIR MARMADUKE *with* MRS. PARTLET, *arm-in-arm.*

ALI. *and* ALEX. *(aside)*. Mrs. Partlet!

SIR M. Dr. Daly, give me joy. Alexis, my dear boy, you will, I am sure, be pleased to hear that my declining days are not unlikely to be solaced by the companionship of this good, virtuous, and amiable woman.

ALEX. *(rather taken aback)*. My dear father, this is not altogether what I expected. I am certainly taken somewhat by surprise. Still it can hardly be necessary to assure you that any wife of yours is a mother of mine. *(Aside to* ALINE.*)* It is not quite what I could have wished.

MRS. P. *(crossing to* ALEXIS*)*. Oh, sir, I entreat your forgiveness. I am aware that socially I am not everything that could be desired, nor am I blessed with an abundance of worldly goods, but I can at least confer on your estimable father the great and priceless dowry of a true, tender, and loving heart.

ALEX. *(coldly)*. I do not question it. After all, a faithful love is the true source of every earthly joy.

SIR M. I knew that my boy would not blame his poor father for acting on the impulse of a heart that has never yet misled him. Zorah is not, perhaps, what the world call beautiful—

DR. D. Still she is comely—distinctly comely! *(Sighs.)*

ALI. Zorah is very good, and very clean and honest, and quite sober in her habits; and that is worth far more than beauty, dear Sir Marmaduke.

DR. D. Yes; beauty will fade and perish, but personal cleanliness is practically undying, for it can be renewed whenever it discovers symptoms of decay. My dear Sir Marmaduke, I heartily congratulate you. *(Sighs.)*

QUINTETTE.

ALEXIS, ALINE, SIR MARMADUKE, ZORAH, *and* DR. DALY.

ALEX.   I rejoice that it's decided.
        Happy now will be his life,
     For my father is provided
        With a true and tender wife!

ENSEMBLE. She will tend him, nurse him, mend him,
        Air his linen, dry his tears.
     Bless the thoughtful fates that send him
        Such a wife to soothe his years!

ALI.   No young giddy thoughtless maiden,
        Full of graces, airs, and jeers—

Music cover for a ballad composed by Mrs Ronalds, published in London in c.1890.

Ages Ago was produced for the German Reeds in November 1869 with music by Fred Clay and words by Gilbert. Although it was farcical in nature, it shows how Gilbert re-used many early ideas when it came to *Ruddigore* and the identical theme of ancestors coming out of their frames in a picture gallery.

Mr & Mrs GERMAN REED'S ENTERTAINMENT
ROYAL GALLERY OF ILLUSTRATION, 14, REGENT STREET.

SCENE FROM

ADMISSION. 1/- 2/- STALLS, 3/- & 5/-

"Ages Ago"

ADMISSION. 1/- 2/- STALLS, 3/- & 5/-

EVERY EVENING (EXCEPT SATURDAY) AT 8, THURSDAY & SATURDAY AFTERNOON AT 3.

STANNARD & SON, 7, POLAND ST LONDON, W

Music cover for *The Pirates of Penzance*, published in London soon after the Opéra Comique première in April 1880.

HMS Pinafore, one of six posters commercially produced in the early 1920s for the use of amateur G&S societies. Space has been left for their promotional information.

But a sober widow, laden
  With the weight of fifty years!

SIR M. No high-born exacting beauty,
   Blazing like a jewelled sun—
  But a wife who'll do her duty,
   As that duty should be done!

MRS. P. I'm no saucy minx and giddy—
   Hussies such as they abound—
  But a clean and tidy widdy,
   Well be-known for miles around!

DR. D. All the village now have mated,
   All are happy as can be—
  I to live alone am fated:
   No one's left to marry me!

ENSEMBLE.   She will tend him, etc.

[*Exeunt* SIR MARMADUKE *and* MRS. PARTLET, ALINE *and* ALEXIS. DR. DALY *looks after them sentimentally, then exit with a sigh.* MR. WELLS, *who has overheard part of this Quintette, and who has remained concealed behind the market cross, comes down as they go off.*

RECITATIVE.—MR. WELLS.

Oh, I have wrought much evil with my spells!
 An ill I can't undo!
This is too bad of you, J. W. Wells—
 What wrong have they done you?
And see—another love-lorn lady comes—
 Alas, poor stricken dame!
A gentle pensiveness her life benumbs—
 And mine, alone, the blame!
       (*Sits at foot of market cross.*)

LADY SANGAZURE *enters. She is very melancholy.*

LADY S. Alas! ah me! and well-a-day!
   I sigh for love, and well I may,
   For I am very old and gray.
    But stay!
  (*Sees* MR. WELLS, *and becomes fascinated by him.*)

RECITATIVE.

LADY S. What is this fairy form I see before me?
MR. W. Oh, horrible!—she's going to adore me!
   This last catastrophe is overpowering!
LADY S. Why do you glare at me with visage lowering?
   For pity's sake, recoil not thus from me!
MR. W. My lady, leave me—this may never be!

DUET.—LADY SANGAZURE *and* MR. WELLS.

MR. W. Hate me! I drop my H's—have through life!
LADY S. Love me! I'll drop them too!
MR. W. Hate me! I always eat peas with a knife!
LADY S. Love me! I'll eat like you!
MR. W. Hate me! I spend the day at Rosherville!

LADY S. Love me! that joy I'll share!
MR. W. Hate me! I often roll down One Tree Hill!
LADY S. Love me! I'll join you there!

LADY S. Love me! my prejudices I will drop!
MR. W. Hate me! that's not enough!
LADY S. Love me! I'll come and help you in the shop!
MR. W. Hate me! the life is rough!
LADY S. Love me! my grammar I will all forswear!
MR. W. Hate me! abjure my lot!
LADY S. Love me! I'll stick sunflowers in my hair!
MR. W. Hate me! they'll suit you not!

RECITATIVE.—MR. WELLS.

  At what I am going to say be not enraged—
  I may not love you—for I am engaged!
LADY S. (*horrified*). Engaged!
MR. W.   Engaged!
  To a maiden fair,
  With bright brown hair,
   And a sweet and simple smile,
  Who waits for me
  By the sounding sea,
   On a South Pacific isle.

(*Aside.*)   A lie! No maiden waits me there!
 LADY S. (*mournfully*). She has bright brown hair!
 MR. W. (*aside*). A lie! No maiden smiles on me!
 LADY S. (*mournfully*). By the sounding sea!

ENSEMBLE.

LADY SANGAZURE.	MR. WELLS.
Oh, agony, rage, despair!	Oh, agony, rage, despair!
The maiden has bright brown hair!	Oh, where will this end— oh, where?
And mine is as white as snow!	I should like very much to know!
False man, it will be your fault	It will certainly be my fault
If I go to my family vault,	If she goes to her family vault,
And bury my life-long woe!	To bury her life-long woe!

BOTH. The family vault—the family vault.
  It will certainly be $\left\{ \begin{matrix} your \\ my \end{matrix} \right\}$ fault,

  If $\left\{ \begin{matrix} I\ go \\ she\ goes \end{matrix} \right\}$ to $\left\{ \begin{matrix} my \\ her \end{matrix} \right\}$ family vault,

   To bury $\left\{ \begin{matrix} my \\ her \end{matrix} \right\}$ life-long woe!

[*Exit* LADY SANGAZURE, *in great anguish*

RECITATIVE.—MR. WELLS.

On, hideous doom—to scatter desolation,
 And sow the seeds of sorrow far and wide!

To foster *mésalliances* through the nation,
   And drive high-born old dames to suicide!
Shall I subject myself to reprobation
   By leaving her in solitude to pine?
No! come what may, I'll make her reparation,
   So, aged lady, take me!—I am thine!

                  [*Exit* MR. WELLS.

Enter ALINE.

ALI. This was to have been the happiest day of my life—but I am very far from happy! Alexis insists that I shall taste the philtre—and when I try to persuade him that to do so would be an insult to my pure and lasting love, he tells me that I object because I do not desire that my love for him shall be eternal. Well *(sighing and producing a phial)*, I can at least prove to him that in that he is injust!

RECITATIVE.

Alexis! Doubt me not, my loved one! See,
Thine uttered will is sovereign law to me!
All fear—all thought of ill I cast away!
   It is my darling's will, and I obey!

               (She drinks the philtre.)

      The fearful deed is done,
        My love is near!
      I go to meet my own
        In trembling fear!
      If o'er us aught of ill
        Should cast a shade,
      It was my darling's will,
        And I obeyed!

[*As* ALINE *is going off, she meets* DR. DALY, *entering pensively. He is playing on a flageolet. Under the influence of the spell she at once becomes strangely fascinated by him, and exhibits every symptom of being hopelessly in love with him.*

SONG.—DR. DALY.

Oh, my voice is sad and low,
And with timid step I go—
For with load of love o'erladen
I enquire of every maiden,
"Will you wed me, little lady?
Will you share my cottage shady?"
   Little lady answers, "No!
   Thank you for your kindly proffer—
   Good your heart, and full your coffer;
   Yet I must decline your offer—
   I'm engaged to So-and-so!"
      So-and-so!
      So-and-so! *(flageolet).*
   She's engaged to So-and-so!
What a rogue young hearts to pillage!
What a worker on Love's tillage!
Every maiden in the village
   Is engaged to So-and-so!
      So-and-so!
      So-and-so! *(flageolet).*
   All engaged to So-and-so!

[*At the end of the song* DR. DALY *sees* ALINE, *and, under the influence of the potion, falls in love with her.*

ENSEMBLE.—ALINE *and* DR. DALY.

Oh, joyous boon! oh, mad delight!
Oh, sun and moon! oh, day and night!
   Rejoice, rejoice with me!
Proclaim our joy, ye birds above—
Ye brooklets, murmur forth our love,
   In choral ecstasy:

ALI.   Oh, joyous boon!
DR. D.   Oh mad delight!
ALI.   Oh, sun and moon!
DR. D.   Oh, day and night!
BOTH.   Ye birds and brooks and fruitful trees,
      With choral joy delight the breeze—
        Rejoice, rejoice with me!

Enter ALEXIS.

RECITATIVE.

ALEX. *(with rapture).* Aline, my only love, my happiness!
              The philtre—you have tasted it?
ALI. *(with confusion).*   Yes! Yes!
ALEX.   Oh, joy, mine, mine for ever and for aye.
                    [*Embraces her.*
ALI.   Alexis, don't do that—you must not!
            [DR. DALY *interposes between them.*
ALEX. *(amazed.)*   Why?

DUET.—ALINE *and* DR. DALY.

ALI.   Alas! that lovers thus should meet:
        Oh, pity, pity me!
      Oh, charge me not with cold deceit;
        Oh, pity, pity me!
      You bade me drink—with trembling awe
      I drank, and, by the potion's law,
      I loved the very first I saw!
        Oh, pity, pity me!

DR. D.   My dear young friend, consolèd be—
        We pity, pity you.
      In this I'm not an agent free—
        We pity, pity you.
      Some most extraordinary spell
      O'er us has cast its magic fell—
      The consequence I need not tell.
        We pity, pity you.

ENSEMBLE.

Some most extraordinary spell
O'er { us / them } has cast its magic fell—

The consequence { we / they } need not tell.

{ We / They } pity, pity { thee! / me! }

ALEX. *(furiously).* False one, begone—I spurn thee!
To thy new lover turn thee!
Thy perfidy all men shall know.

ALI. *(wildly).* I could not help it!

ALEX. *(calling off).* Come one, come all!

DR. D. We could not help it!

ALEX. *(calling off).* Obey my call!

ALI. *(wildly).* I could not help it!

ALEX. *(calling off).* Come, hither, run!

DR. D. We could not help it!

ALEX. *(calling off).* Come, every one!

Enter all the character except LADY SANGAZURE *and* MR. WELLS.

CHORUS.

Oh, what is the matter, and what is the clatter?
He's glowering at her, and threatens a blow!
Oh, why does he batter the girl he did flatter?
And why does the latter recoil from him so?

RECITATIVE.—ALEXIS.

Prepare for sad surprises—
My love Aline despises!
No thought of sorrow shames her—
Another lover claims her!
Be his, false girl, for better or for worse—
But, ere you leave me, may a lover's curse—

DR. D. *(coming forward).* Hold! Be just. This poor child drank the philtre at your instance. She hurried off to meet you —but, most unhappily, she met me instead. As you had administered the potion to both of us, the result was inevitable. But fear nothing from me—I will be no man's rival. I shall quit the country at once—and bury my sorrow in the congenial gloom of a colonial bishopric.

ALEX. My excellent old friend! *(Taking his hand—then turning to* MR. WELLS, *who has entered with* LADY SANGAZURE.*)* Oh, Mr. Wells, what, what is to be done?

MR. W. I do not know—and yet—there is one means by which this spell may be removed.

ALEX. Name it—oh, name it!

MR. W. Or you or I must yield up his life to Ahrimanes. I would rather it were you. I should have no hesitation in sacrificing my own life to spare yours, but we take stock next week, and it would not be fair on the Co.

ALEX. True. Well, I am ready!

ALI. No, no—Alexis—it must not be! Mr. Wells, if he must die that all may be restored to their old loves, what is to become of me? I should be left out in the cold, with no love to be restored to!

MR. W. True—I did not think of that. *(To the others.)* My friends, I appeal to you, and I will leave the decision in your hands.

FINALE.

MR. W. Or I or he
Must die!
Which shall it be?
Reply!

SIR M. Die thou!
Thou art the cause of all offending!

LADY S. Die thou!
Yield thou to this decree unbending!

ALL. Die thou!

MR. W. So be it! I submit! My fate is sealed.
To popular opinion thus I yield! *(Falls.)*
Be happy all—leave me to my despair—
I go—it matters not with whom—or where! *(Gong.)*

[*All quit their present partners, and rejoin their old lovers.* SIR MARMADUKE *leaves* MRS. PARTLET, *and goes to* LADY SANGAZURE. ALINE *leaves* DR. DALY, *and goes to* ALEXIS. DR. DALY *leaves* ALINE, *and goes to* CONSTANCE. NOTARY *leaves* CONSTANCE, *and goes to* MRS. PARTLET. *All the* CHORUS *make a corresponding change.*

ALL.

GENTLEMEN. Oh, my adored one!

LADIES. Unmingled joy!

GENTLEMEN. Ecstatic rapture!

LADIES. Beloved boy! *(They embrace.)*

SIR M. Come to my mansion, all of you! At least
We'll crown our rapture with another feast.

ENSEMBLE.

SIR MARMADUKE, LADY SANGAZURE, ALEXIS, *and* ALINE.

Now to the banquet we press;
Now for the eggs and the ham,
Now for the mustard and cress,
Now for the strawberry jam!

CHORUS. Now to the banquet, etc.

DR. DALY, CONSTANCE, NOTARY, *and* MRS. PARTLET.

Now for the tea of our host,
Now for the rollicking bun,
Now for the muffin and toast,
Now for the gay Sally Lunn!

CHORUS. Now for the tea, etc.

(General Dance.)

HMS Pinafore

or The Lass that loved a Sailor

HMS Pinafore was the first Gilbert and Sullivan 'smash hit', not only in London but in pirated productions all over the USA and in several European countries — though not France. The French took umbrage at the thoroughly British sentiments that Gilbert open-handedly presents. *Pinafore* also saw the end of the Opéra Comique Company with its board of grabbing directors, and the establishment of Carte's own English Opera Company.

Pinafore has all the ingredients and all the characters of the next seven operas, set in a neat topsy-turvy plot of mistaken identity at birth (to be repeated with variations in *The Pirates of Penzance* and *The Gondoliers*). It is set upon the water, and it has roots in about a dozen *Bab Ballads*, of which these offer the main ideas: 'Captain Reece', 'Joe Golightly', 'General John' and 'The Baby's Vengeance', 'The Martinet' and 'The Bumboat Woman's Story'.

The casting involved an important acquisition to the company — Jessie Bond. As a singer she declined to tackle the largish part of Cousin Hebe as it stood, so Gilbert cut the dialogue and Jessie Bond afterwards played his leading roles up to *The Gondoliers*.

George Grossmith's assumption of Sir Joseph Porter was a triumph, and the resemblance to Lord Nelson in his make-up was in order to direct criticism away from Disraeli's First Lord, Mr W.H. Smith. Smith, a self-made man, was the celebrated newsagent, and Gilbert's savage attack on his origins and puritanism — which were all part of Sir Joseph Porter — was explained away as being an attack on the *system* instead. But even Disraeli, who disliked *Pinafore*, always referred to his First Lord as 'Pinafore Smith'. Gilbert was sailing close to the wind by offending the Queen and the Establishment, a policy which delayed his knighthood for over twenty years.

On the other hand, the public adored it all. The phrases 'What, never?...' became current jargon at home and abroad. They were passwords between early theatregoers to the Opéra Comique, they eventually became clichés in the press and in conversation. But the music did a very great deal to ensure the run of 571 performances in the first production, during which George Grossmith never missed a single one.

Sullivan's score is as breezy as the scene, as British as the Royal Navy and as unashamedly jingoistic as Queen Victoria's England. 'For he is an Englishman' could well be the national anthem, and 'A British tar

is a soaring soul' is full of national pride — and a touch of 'Tom Bowling'. There is far more music than speech in *HMS Pinafore*, which is a true *opéra-comique* (like *Fidelio* or *Carmen*) where the stretches of dialogue are short and it is the music which matters.

The set, a facsimile of *HMS Victory's* quarter-deck, was the background for Gilbert's production in which officers, sailors and marines all behaved as though they were in the service. The tremendous fire and energy in the playing of the piece caught the public fancy in a manner beyond the experience of every theatregoer.

Another of Gilbert's daring strokes was the use of the word 'Damn!', first hinted at in '...never use a big, big D—!' and then spoken outright by Captain Corcoran as 'Damme!' Uttered before women on the stage (in the opera) and before ladies in the audience, it was regarded by many people as offensive. A susequent production of the opera at Savoy Theatre matinées by children in 1879-80, when the boy who played Captain Corcoran said 'Damme!', occasioned a sharp and pained reproof by the Rev. Dodgson (Lewis Carroll). It is the only occasion in all the libretti when a swear-word is printed, and it seems that Gilbert had gone too far for the manners of the time.

George Grossmith and Jessie Bond as Sir Joseph and Cousin Hebe in the first production of *HMS Pinafore*. Observe Grossmith's expressive legs.

The full Chorus of *HMS Pinafore* in the 1908 revival at the Savoy.

Rosina Brandram, an early Little Buttercup, at the Opéra Comique.

Pinafore was the first opera to excite American 'pirates' and to cause many thousands of dollars' loss of royalties to its creators, because the USA did not subscribe to international copyright laws. It was necessary for a 'copyright performance' on American soil to substantiate ownership, but even that did not stop the many low-grade and unauthorized productions there, stuffed with topical allusions, popular tunes and — in one instance — a *male* Little Buttercup, seven feet tall. But in a backhanded way, even this was a compliment to Gilbert and Sullivan from a nation of theatregoers greedy for something entirely new. The copyright production on Broadway in 1879 was a modified success because all the tunes were familiar and the shine of novelty was off *HMS Pinafore* soon after it had reached New York, in spite of Gilbert's fine production and the elegant playing of the orchestra.

Pinafore contains a theme expressed already in *the Sorcerer:* the mixture of social classes and the failure of idealistic socialism when put into practice. The very idea of a Naval Captain's daughter marrying a simple tar is anathema to the Captain and occasions the utterance of 'Damme!'. But when the secret of infant transference is revealed by Mrs Cripps (a jolly, lovely character, quite the most endearing of all the contraltos) the social levels click into place, and she is at liberty to pair off with the former captain, now a tar, whom she has always loved.

SYNOPSIS

Theatrical drum-rolls give way to the jolly and boisterous opening of the Overture, a tune resembling 'A Hundred Pipers'. A short 'love' interlude follows and then another rousing tune later to be heard in the opera as 'Never mind the why and wherefore...', not unlike an Offenbach can-can. A fanfare and more drum-rolls begin what amounts to a prelude as the curtain goes up to reveal the quarter-deck of *HMS Pinafore*. The ship is at anchor off Portsmouth and sailors are performing their off-shore duties with 'Ahoys' like the sailors in Wagner's *Flying Dutchman*. Mrs Cripps, the bumboat woman, known as Little Buttercup, comes aboard with her wares. Her song, 'For I'm called Little Buttercup...' is almost like a street cry in its hurdy-gurdy simplicity. During her conversation with the genial Boatswain it transpires that, despite her happy exterior, Buttercup has a guilty secret. The disparaging remarks of the hunchbacked AB, Dick Deadeye, bring this villain of the piece to the fore, and Buttercup's interest in the youthful sailor, Ralph Rackstraw, introduces the hero. From Buttercup's cry of 'Remorse! Remorse!' it is obvious that he is part of her murky past.

Ralph's Madrigal, a kind of Ode to a Nightingale, is Mendelsshonian with earlier additions. He is in love 'above his station' with the Captain's daughter, Josephine. His ballad, 'A Maiden fair to see' is similar in character to Alexis' two love songs in *The Sorcerer,* but Ralph's verses are interspersed with a muted chorus.

Captain Corcoran's entrance is attended by warm solicitations from his crew, and his catalogue of self-approbation ends with the boast 'I never use a big, big D—' 'What, *never?*' sing the incredulous Crew; 'Hardly ever!' he admits.

Alone with Buttercup, the Captain sadly tells her

that his daughter Josephine rejects the idea of her eligible suitor, Sir Joseph Porter, First Lord of the Admiralty.

Josephine's subsequent ballad, 'Sorry her lot who loves too well' is unique in Sullivan's work in its portrayal of a grief-stricken maiden. The song is Schubertian in inspiration, though there is more than a hint of Irish folk song there, too. Josephine confesses to her father that she is in love with a humble sailor, but the Captain, despite his professed liberalism, cannot condone the match socially. As Sir Joseph's barge is seen approaching, Josephine is sent to her cabin (with Sir Joseph's photograph as an inducement to bring her 'to a more reasonable frame of mind').

A gently rocking barcarolle, distantly sung by Sir Joseph's entourage of Sisters, Cousins and Aunts, brings the Crew of *Pinafore* on deck. They take up the welcoming chorus whose change of rhythm suggests choppy water, as the barge comes alongside. The Ladies archly step on board as the two choruses continue in counterpoint.

The Captain calls from the poop for three cheers, and to a side-drum roll Sir Joseph enters, accompanied by Cousin Hebe. His introductory song, 'I am the monarch of the sea,...' has lines that are echoed by Hebe and taken up by the other relatives. Sir Joseph follows it with an autobiographical account of his rise to position: 'When I was a lad I served a term ...'. He then conducts a patronizing cross-questioning of the Captain and Crew, and sermonizes on manners and equality. He singles out Ralph and presents him with a song he has composed for the encouragement of the 'lower branches of the service'.

Following his departure to discuss 'a tender and sentimental subject' with the Captain, the Crew discuss Sir Joseph's lecture. Dick Deadeye blandly points out the social flaws, whereas Ralph resolves to take advantage of the First Lord's broadminded views on social equality by proposing to Josephine. The Crew show their approval with a rendering of Sir Joseph's *a cappella* glee, reminiscent of the old public school songs: 'A British tar is a soaring soul, ...'. This is followed by a hornpipe in which all the Sailor Chorus joins.

Ralph is left musing alone as Josephine emerges from her cabin, expressing disenchantment with Sir Joseph. Ralph confesses his love in ornate and convoluted sentences while Josephine (with loving

'A British tar is a soaring soul'—Henry Lytton, Walter Passmore and Robert Evett in the 1899 revival at the Savoy.

asides) haughtily rejects him. 'Refrain, audacious tar, ...' is a melodramatic outburst, conjuring up a typical penny-plain situation. Ralph, incensed by Josephine's attitude, takes up in hot-tempered reply. But each gives way to love in an amorous verse to follow their declamation, and they part after a tender duet.

But Ralph is hurt. At his summons 'Messmates, ahoy! Come here! Come here!' (momentarily reminiscent of Wagner's *Dutchman* motif) the Sailors and Female Relatives come flocking on deck; all are sympathetic except Dick Deadeye, with his 'I told you so!' Ralph embarks on a sentimental Victorian suicide piece, reducing all to tears (Verdi's *Don Carlo*, end of Act I, Fontainebleau). As Ralph puts a pistol to his head and the Sailors stop their ears, the music mounts to a crescendo and Josephine rushes on to the deck. 'Ah! Stay your hand! I love you!' she cries. The ensemble of happy reunion is undermined by Deadeye who adopts the vocal role of an Osmin (guardian of the harem in Mozart's *Il Seraglio*). In breathless, clipped phrases, Josephine, Hebe, Ralph and the Boatswain make plans for a secret marriage that night. Excitement mounts as the Female Relatives repeat the plans and Deadeye utters dire warnings from the hatchway. The merry company dismiss him with 'Back, vermin, back, you shock us!' and then, to a reprise of the melody first heard in the Overture, they sing 'Let's give three cheers for the sailor's bride!' followed by a variation of Sir Joseph's glee.

The short interlude to Act II comprises mandolin and foghorn effects (*Flying Dutchman* again) and a full orchestral reprise of Buttercup's song. The Captain is discovered on the poop-deck in moonlight, accompanying his song 'Fair moon, to thee I sing' on a mandolin, while Buttercup fondly gazes up at him from below, lamenting her secret love for him and hinting that he also has a part in her mysterious secret. They then confess mutual affection but the Captain explains that his rank forbids anything more than friendship. However, Buttercup predicts change, and with a list of appropriate proverbs beginning 'Things are seldom what they seem', she puzzles the Captain. Not to be outdone, he replies with a somewhat disconnected list of his own. In keeping with this parody of grand-opera-fatal-gypsy, Buttercup makes a melodramatic exit.

Sir Joseph enters and tells Captain Corcoran that his overtures to Josephine have failed, but the Captain persuades him that modesty alone is responsible for her reticence. Meanwhile Josephine wonders whether she has not made a rash decision. In a passionate recitative she weighs her own 'luxurious' home full of antiques 'and everything that isn't old, from Gillow's...' against the sordid slum she expects to find herself in — a marvellous Dickensian description here. The aria which follows, 'A simple sailor, lowly born,...' is in the truly classical Schubert/Mendelssohn tradition and the most difficult soprano aria in all the operas.

Sir Joseph now proposes once more to Josephine and drawing from him the statement that 'love is a platform upon which all ranks meet', she announces that she has made her decision, and rejoices with her father and Sir Joseph. 'Never mind the why and wherefore,...' (first of the 'encore' trios) repeats the carefree tune first heard in the Overture to Act I, and has innuendos for each member of the trio.

The Captain's elation is marred by Dick Deadeye who tells him in a roundabout manner of the planned elopement of Ralph and Josephine. Their duet, 'Sing hey, the merry maiden and the tar' derives from

Pinafore on video. Peter Marshall, Captain Corcoran and Frankie Howerd, Sir Joseph. Brent-Walker 1981.

English folk song and has similarities with 'There were three crows...'

Quickly donning 'a mysterious cloak', the Captain is just in time to see the Crew arriving on tiptoe to meet Josephine. Accompanied by Buttercup, she emerges from her cabin equipped for flight, and with more cautious tiptoeing, all prepare to leave. The enraged Captain stamps, provoking a moment's general alarm. Dick Deadeye's 'It was the cat' reassures the elopers and they miss the Captain's confirmation as he brandishes his cat-o'-nine-tails.

At last the Captain unmasks, and to a turbulent tune he enquires where his daughter is going 'with these sons of the brine'. Ralph's defiance and his agitated rejoinder are taken up by Josephine and the Crew, gradually rising to a crescendo with the all-excusing words: 'For he is an Englishman'. The Captain, biting his lip, reprimands Ralph with typical English self-control, until he finally lapses into the frustrated 'Why, damme, it's too bad!' The Female Relatives witness the outburst and Sir Joseph arrives to hear a repeat performance. Horror ensues and, despite the Captain's excuses, he is sent to his cabin, disgraced. Josephine follows him. Sir Joseph's anger is equally repressed:

> 'My pain and my distress,
> I find it is not easy to express;
> My amazement — my surprise —
> You may learn from the expression of my
> eyes!'

His subsequent moral treatise on swearing is sung to 'I am the monarch of the sea...' and then supported by the Company with 'For he is an Englishman!' once more.

Sir Joseph questions Ralph on the reason for the Captain's outburst, and grandly dismisses the sailor's self-confessed lowliness. He only understands when Josephine comes rushing into Ralph's arms. Ralph is forthwith handcuffed and condemned to the ship's dungeon. 'Farewell, my own,...' beginning in the Irish folk-song tradition, has verses of parting for Ralph and Josephine. Variations follow for Hebe, Buttercup, Sir Joseph and the three principal members of the Crew, with full chorus, to make the only octet in all the operas. Once more Sir Joseph expresses 'My pain and my distress,...' and it seems as though an impasse has been reached.

Buttercup now reveals her secret. A short introduction, imitative of Schubert's baby-snatching

'They're right, it was the cat!' Henry Lytton as Captain Corcoran in the 1899 revival.

'Erlkönig', leads into 'A many years ago...' a fatal chant of confession. Buttercup was a baby farmer and fostered two children: one lowly born, the other 'upper crust'. But she mixed them up and they were not reared as befitted their true station. These babies were the Captain and Ralph.

Sir Joseph orders them to be fetched, and to prove their identity, Ralph is now dressed as the captain, and Corcoran as a common sailor. Josephine flies to her father's arms and at once identifies with him. Sir Joseph now singles out Corcoran, just as he did Ralph, earlier. He informs him that marriage with Josephine is out of the question, and to Corcoran's protest that love levels all ranks, Sir Joseph replies 'not as much as that', and hands Josephine to Ralph.

Corcoran and Buttercup are united, but now Sir Joseph is without a partner. Reluctantly he gives his hand to Cousin Hebe. The finale is a reprise of 'Oh joy, oh rapture unforeseen...; What, never?...; I'm called Little Buttercup...; I am the monarch of the sea...' and ends patriotically with 'For he is an Englishman!'

H.M.S. PINAFORE;

OR,

THE LASS THAT LOVED A SAILOR.

ACT I.

SCENE—*Quarter-deck of H.M.S. Pinafore. View of Portsmouth in distance.* SAILORS, *led by* BOATSWAIN, *discovered cleaning brasswork, splicing rope, etc.*

CHORUS.

We sail the ocean blue,
　And our saucy ship's a beauty;
We're sober men, and true,
　And attentive to our duty.
When the balls whistle free o'er the bright blue sea,

We stand to our guns all day;
When at anchor we ride on the Portsmouth tide,
We have plenty of time to play.

Enter LITTLE BUTTERCUP, *with large basket on her arm.*

RECITATIVE.

Hail, men-o'-war's men—safeguards of your nation,
Here is an end, at last, of all privation;
You've got your pay—spare all you can afford
To welcome Little Buttercup on board.

ARIA.

For I'm called Little Buttercup, dear Little Buttercup,
    Though I could never tell why,
But still I'm called Buttercup, poor Little Buttercup,
    Sweet Little Buttercup, I.
I've snuff, and tobaccy, and excellent jacky;
    I've scissors, and watches, and knives;
I've ribbons and laces to set off the faces
    Of pretty young sweethearts and wives.
I've treacle and toffee and excellent coffee,
    Soft tommy and succulent chops;
I've chickens and conies and pretty polonies,
    And excellent peppermint drops.
Then buy of your Buttercup—dear Little Buttercup,
    Sailors should never be shy;
So buy of your Buttercup—poor Little Buttercup,
    Come, of your Buttercup buy!

BOAT. Ay, Little Buttercup—and well called—for you're the rosiest, the roundest, and the reddest beauty in all Spithead.

BUT. Red, am I? and round—and rosy! Maybe, for I have dissembled well! But hark ye, my merry friend—hast ever thought that beneath a gay and frivolous exterior there may lurk a cankerworm which is slowly but surely eating its way into one's very heart?

BOAT. No, my lass, I can't say I've ever thought that.

Enter DICK DEADEYE. *He pushes through* SAILORS.

DICK. *I have thought it often. (All recoil from him.)*

BUT. Yes, you look like it! What's the matter with the man? Isn't he well?

BOAT. Don't take no heed of *him;* that's only poor Dick Deadeye.

DICK. I say—it's a beast of a name, ain't it—Dick Deadeye?

BUT. It's not a nice name.

DICK. I'm ugly too, ain't I?

BUT. You are certainly plain.

DICK. And I'm three-cornered too, ain't I?

BUT. You are rather triangular.

DICK. Ha! ha! That's it. I'm ugly, and they hate me for it; for you all hate me don't you?

BOAT. *(crossing).* Well, Dick, we wouldn't go for to hurt any fellow-creature's feelings, but you can't expect a chap with such a name as Dick Deadeye to be a popular character—now, can you?

DICK. No.

BOAT. It's asking too much, ain't it?

DICK. It is. From such a face and form as mine the noblest sentiments sound like the black utterances of a depraved imagination. It is human nature—I am resigned.

RECITATIVE.

BUT. *(looking down hatchway).*
    But, tell me—who's the youth whose faltering feet
    With difficulty bear him on his course?
BOAT. *(crossing).*
    That is the smartest lad in all the fleet—
    Ralph Rackstraw!
BUT.   Ha! that name! Remorse! remorse!

Enter RALPH *from hatchway.*

MADRIGAL.—RALPH.

        The nightingale.
    Loved the pale moon's bright ray,
        And told his tale
    In his own melodious way!
    He sang "Ah, well-a-day!"

ALL.   He sang "Ah, well-a-day!"

        The lowly vale
    For the mountain vainly sighed;
        To his humble wail
    The echoing hills replied.
        They sang "Ah, well-a-day!"

ALL.   They sang "Ah, well-a-day!"

RECITATIVE.

    I know the value of a kindly chorus,
        But choruses yield little consolation,
    When we have pain and trouble too before us!
        I love—and love, alas, above my station!

BUT. *(aside).* He loves—and loves a lass above his station!
ALL. *(aside).* Yes, yes, the lass is much above his station!

BALLAD.—RALPH.

        A maiden fair to see,
        The pearl of minstrelsy,
            A bud of blushing beauty,
        For whom proud nobles sigh,
        And with each other vie,
            To do her menial's duty.

ALL.   To do her menial's duty.

        A suitor, lowly born,
        With hopeless passion torn,
            And poor beyond concealing,
        Has dared for her to pine

At whose exalted shrine
  A world of wealth is kneeling.

ALL.   A world of wealth is kneeling!

Unlearnèd he in aught
Save that which love has taught.
  (For love had been his tutor)
Oh, pity, pity me—
Our captain's daughter she,
  And I that lowly suitor!

ALL.   And he that lowly suitor!

[*Exit* LITTLE BUTTERCUP.

BOAT. Ah, my poor lad, you've climbed too high: our worthy captain's child won't have nothin' to say to a poor chap like you. Will she, lads?

DICK. No, no captains' daughters don't marry foremast hands.

ALL (*recoiling from him*). Shame! shame!

BOAT. (*crossing*). Dick Deadeye, them sentiments o' yourn are a disgrace to our common natur'.

RALPH. But it's a strange anomaly, that the daughter of a man who hails from the quarter-deck may not love another who lays out on the fore-yard arm. For a man is but a man, whether he hoists his flag at the maintruck or his slacks on the maindeck.

DICK. Ah, it's a queer world!

RALPH. Dick Deadeye, I have no desire to press hardly on you, but such a revolutionary sentiment is enough to make an honest sailor shudder.

BOAT. (*who has gone on poop-deck, returns*). My lads, our gallant captain has come on deck; let us greet him as so brave an officer and so gallant a seaman deserves.

RECITATIVE.

CAPT. My gallant crew, good morning.

ALL (*saluting*).   Sir, good morning!

CAPT. I hope you're all well.

ALL (*as before*).   Quite well; and you, sir?

CAPT. I am reasonable in health, and happy
    To meet you all once more.

ALL (*as before*).   You do us proud, sir!

SONG.—CAPTAIN.

CAPT.   I am the Captain of the Pinafore!
ALL.   And a right good captain, too!
CAPT.   You're very, very good,
      And be it understood
    I command a right good crew.
ALL.   We're very, very good,
      And be it understood
    He commands a right good crew.
CAPT.   Though related to a peer,
    I can hand, reef, and steer,
      And ship a selvagee;
    I am never known to quail
    At the fury of a gale,
      And I'm never, never sick at sea!

ALL.   What, never?
CAPT.   No, never!
ALL.   What, *never?*
CAPT.   Hardly ever!
ALL.   He's hardly ever sick at sea!
    Then give three cheers, and one cheer more,
    For the hardy Captain of the Pinafore!
CAPT.   I do my best to satisfy you all—
ALL.   And with you we're quite content.
CAPT.   You're exceedingly polite,
    And I think it only right
    To return the compliment.
ALL.   We're exceedingly polite,
    And he thinks it's only right
    To return the compliment.
CAPT.   Bad language or abuse,
    I never, never use,
    Whatever the emergency;
      Though, "bother it," I may
      Occasionally say,
    I never use a big, big D——
ALL.   What, never?
CAPT.   No, never!
ALL.   What, *never?*
CAPT.   Hardly ever!
ALL.   Hardly ever swears a big, big D——
    Then give three cheers, and one cheer more,
    For the well-bred Captain of the Pinafore!

[*After song exeunt all but* CAPTAIN.

Enter LITTLE BUTTERCUP.

RECITATIVE.

BUT.   Sir, you are sad. The silent eloquence
    Of yonder tear that trembles on your eyelash
    Proclaims a sorrow far more deep than common;
    Confide in me—fear not—I am a mother!
CAPT.   Yes, Little Buttercup, I'm sad and sorry—
    My daughter, Josephine, the fairest flower
    That ever blossomed on ancestral timber,
    Is sought in marriage by Sir Joseph Porter,
    Our Admiralty's First Lord, but for some reason,
    She does not seem to tackle kindly to it.
BUT.   (*with emotion*).
    Ah, poor Sir Joseph! Ah, I know too well
    The anguish of a heart that loves but vainly!
    But see, here comes your most attractive daughter.
    I go—Farewell!   [*Exit.*
CAPT.   (*looking after her*). A plump and pleasing person!

Enter JOSEPHINE *on poop. She comes down, twining some flowers which she carries in a small basket.*

BALLAD.—JOSEPHINE.

Sorry her lot who loves too well,
  Heavy the heart that hopes but vainly,
Sad are the sighs that own the spell
  Uttered by eyes that speak too plainly;
    Heavy the sorrow that bows the head

When love is alive and hope is dead!
Sad is the hour when sets the sun—
    Dark is the night to earth's poor daughters,
When to the ark the wearied one
Flies from the empty waste of waters!
    Heavy the sorrow that bows the head
    When love is alive and hope is dead!

CAPT. My child, I grieve to see that you are a prey to melancholy. You should look your best to-day, for Sir Joseph Porter, K.C.B., will be here this afternoon to claim your promised hand.

Jos. Ah, father, your words cut me to the quick. I can esteem—reverence—venerate Sir Joseph, for he is a great and good man; but oh, I cannot love him! My heart is already given.

CAPT. (aside). It is, then, as I feared. (Aloud.) Given? And to whom? Not to some gilded lordling?

Jos. No, father—the object of my love is no lordling. Oh, pity me, for he is but a humble sailor on board your own ship!

CAPT. Impossible!

Jos. Yes, it is true—too true.

CAPT. A common sailor? Oh, fie!

Jos. I blush for the weakness that allows me to cherish such a passion. I hate myself when I think of the depth to which I have stooped in permitting myself to think tenderly of one so ignobly born, but I love him! I love him! I love him! (Weeps.)

CAPT. Come, my child, let us talk this over. In a matter of the heart I would not coerce my daughter—I attach but little value to rank or wealth, but the line must be drawn somewhere. A man in that station may be brave and worthy, but at every step he would commit solecisms that society would never pardon.

Jos. Oh, I have thought of this night and day. But fear not, father. I have a heart, and therefore I love; but I am your daughter, and therefore I am proud. Though I carry my love with me to the tomb, he shall never, never know it.

CAPT. You *are* my daughter, after all. But see, Sir Joseph's barge approaches, manned by twelve trusty oarsmen and accompanied by the admiring crowd of female relatives that attend him wherever he goes. Retire, my daughter, to your cabin—take this, his photograph, with you—it may help to bring you to a more reasonable frame of mind.

Jos. My own thoughtful father.   [*Exit* JOSEPHINE.

BARCAROLLE (without.)

Over the bright blue sea
Comes Sir Joseph Porter, K.C.B.,
Wherever he may go
Bang-bang the loud nine-pounders go!
Shout o'er the bright blue sea
For Sir Joseph Porter, K.C.B.

[*During this the* CREW *have entered on tiptoe, listening attentively to the song.*

CHORUS OF SAILORS.

We sail the ocean blue,
    And our saucy ship's a beauty;
We're sober men, and true,
    And attentive to our duty.
We're smart and sober men,

And quite devoid of fe-ar,
In all the Royal N.
    None are so smart as we are.

Enter SIR JOSEPH'S FEMALE RELATIVES. They dance round stage.

REL.   Gaily tripping,
                Lightly skipping,
        Flock the maidens to the shipping.
SAIL.   Flags and guns and pennants dipping
        All the ladies love the shipping.

REL.   Sailors sprightly
                Always rightly
        Welcome ladies so politely.
SAIL.   Ladies who can smile so brightly,
        Sailors welcome most politely.

Enter SIR JOSEPH *with* COUSIN HEBE.

CAPT. (from poop). Now give three cheers, I'll lead the way.
ALL.   Hurrah! hurrah! hurrah! hurray!   (Repeat.)

SONG.—SIR JOSEPH.

        I am the monarch of the sea,
            The Ruler of the Queen's Navee,
        Whose praise Great Britain loudly chants.
COUSIN H. And we are his sisters, and his cousins, and his
            aunts!
REL.   And we are his sisters, and his cousins, and his
            aunts!
SIR J.   When at anchor here I ride,
                My bosom swells with pride,
        And I snap my fingers at a foeman's taunts.
COUSIN H. And so do his sisters, and his cousins, and his aunts!
ALL.   And so do his sisters, and his cousins, and his aunts!
SIR J.   But when the breezes blow,
                I generally go below,
        And seek the seclusion that a cabin grants!
COUSIN H. And so do his sisters, and his cousins, and his aunts!
ALL.   And so do his sisters, and his cousins, and his aunts!
                His sisters and his cousins,
                Whom he reckons up by dozens,
                    And his aunts!

SONG.—SIR JOSEPH.

When I was a lad I served a term
As office boy to an attorney's firm.
I cleaned the windows and I swept the floor,
And I polished up the handle of the big front door.
    I polished up that handle so carefullee
    That now I am the Ruler of the Queen's Navee!
        CHORUS.—He polished, etc.

As office boy I made such a mark
That they gave me the post of a junior clerk.
I served the writs with a smile so bland,
And I copied all the letters in a big round hand—
    I copied all the letters in a hand so free,

That now I am the Ruler of the Queen's Navee!
   Chorus.—He copied, etc.

In serving writs I made such a name
That an articled clerk I soon became;
I wore clean collars and a brand-new suit
For the pass examination at the Institute.
   And that pass examination did so well for me,
   That now I am the Ruler of the Queen's Navee!
      Chorus.—And that pass examination, etc.

Of legal knowledge I acquired such a grip
That they took me into the partnership,
And that junior partnership, I ween,
Was the only ship that I ever had seen.
   But that kind of ship so suited me,
   That now I am the Ruler of the Queen's Navee!
      Chorus.—But that kind, etc.

I grew so rich that I was sent
By a pocket borough into Parliament.
I always voted at my party's call,
And I never thought of thinking for myself at all.
   I thought so little, they rewarded me
   By making me the Ruler of the Queen's Navee!
      Chorus.—He thought so little, etc.

Now, landsmen all, whoever you may be,
If you want to rise to the top of the tree,
If your soul isn't fettered to an office stool,
Be careful to be guided by this golden rule—
   Stick close to your deck and never go to sea,
   And you all may be Rulers of the Queen's Navee!
      Chorus.—Stick close, etc.

Sir J. You've a remarkably fine crew, Captain Corcoran.

Capt. It *is* a fine crew, Sir Joseph.

Sir J. *(examining a very small midshipman).* A British sailor is a splendid fellow, Captain Corcoran.

Capt. A splendid fellow indeed, Sir Joseph.

Sir J. I hope you treat your crew kindly, Captain Corcoran.

Capt. Indeed, I hope so, Sir Joseph.

Sir J. Never forget that they are the bulwarks of England's greatness, Captain Corcoran.

Capt. So I have always considered them, Sir Joseph.

Sir J. No bullying, I trust—no strong language of any kind, eh?

Capt. Oh, never, Sir Joseph.

Sir J. What, *never?*

Capt. Hardly ever, Sir Joseph. They are an excellent crew, and do their work thoroughly without it.

Sir J. *(reproving).* Don't patronize them, sir—pray, don't patronize them.

Capt. Certainly not, Sir Joseph.

Sir J. That you are their captain is an accident of birth. I cannot permit these noble fellows to be patronized because an accident of birth has placed you above them and them below you.

Capt. I am the last person to insult a British sailor, Sir Joseph.

Sir J. You are the last person who did, Captain Corcoran. Desire that splendid seaman to step forward.

Capt. Ralph Rackstraw, come here.

Sir J. *(sternly).* If what?

Capt. I beg your pardon—

Sir J. If you *please.*

Capt. Oh yes, of course. If you *please.* [Ralph *steps forward.*

Sir J. You're a remarkably fine fellow.

Ralph. Yes, your honour.

Sir J. And a first-rate seaman, I'll be bound.

Ralph. There's not a smarter topman in the navy, your honour, though I say it who shouldn't.

Sir J. Not at all. Proper self-respect, nothing more. Can you dance a hornpipe?

Ralph. No, your honour.

Sir J. That's a pity: all sailors should dance hornpipes. I will teach you one this evening, after dinner. Now, tell me—don't be afraid—how does your captain treat you, eh?

Ralph. A better captain don't walk the deck, your honour.

All. Hear!

Sir J. Good. I like to hear you speak well of your commanding officer; I dare say he don't deserve it, but still it does you credit. Can you sing?

Ralph. I can hum a little, your honour.

Sir J. Then hum this at your leisure. *(Giving him MS. music.)* It is a song that I have composed for the use of the Royal Navy. It is designed to encourage independence of thought and action in the lower branches of the service, and to teach the principle that a British sailor is any man's equal, excepting mine. Now, Captain Corcoran, a word with you in your cabin, on a tender and sentimental subject.

Capt. Ay, ay, Sir Joseph. Boatswain, in commemoration of this joyous occasion, see that extra grog is served out to the ship's company at one bell.

Boat. Beg pardon. If what, your honour?

Capt. If what? I don't think I understand you.

Boat. If you *please,* your honour.

Capt. What!

Sir J. The gentleman is quite right. If you *please.*

Capt. *(stamping his foot impatiently).* If you please!

Sir J.   For I hold that on the seas
           The expression, "If you please,"
   A particularly gentlemanly tone implants.

Cousin H. And so do his sisters, and his cousins, and his aunts!

All.   And so do his sisters, and his cousins, and his aunts!

        [*Exeunt* Captain *and* Sir Joseph *into cabin.*

Boat. Ah! Sir Joseph's a true gentleman: courteous and considerate to the very humblest.

Ralph. True, Boatswain; but we are not the very humblest. Sir Joseph has explained our true position to us. As he says, a British seaman is any man's equal excepting his; and if Sir Joseph says that, is it not our duty to believe him?

All. Well spoke! well spoke!

Dick. You're on a wrong tack, and so is he. He means well, but he don't know. When people have to obey other people's orders, equality's out of the question.

All *(recoiling).* Horrible! horrible!

Boat. Dick Deadeye, if you go for to infuriate this here ship's company too far, I won't answer for being able to hold 'em in. I'm shocked! that's what I am—shocked!

Ralph *(coming forward).* Messmates, my mind's made up. I'll speak to the captain's daughter, and tell her, like an honest man, of the honest love I have for her.

All. Hurrah!

RALPH. Is not my love as good as another's? Is not my heart as true as another's? Have I not hands and eyes and ears and limbs like another?

ALL. Ay, ay.

RALPH. True, I lack birth—

BOAT. You've a berth on board this very ship.

RALPH. Well said—I had forgotten that. Messmates, what do you say? do you approve my determination?

ALL. We do.

DICK. I don't.

BOAT. What is to be done with this here hopeless chap? Let us sing him the song that Sir Joseph has kindly composed for us. Perhaps it will bring this here miserable creetur to a proper state of mind.

GLEE.—RALPH, BOATSWAIN, BOATSWAIN'S MATE, *and* CHORUS.

A British tar is a soaring soul,
  As free as a mountain bird!
His energetic fist should be ready to resist
  A dictatorial word.
His nose should pant and his lip should curl,
His cheeks should flame and his brow should furl,
His bosom should heave and his heart should glow,
And his fist be ever ready for a knock-down blow.
    CHORUS.—His nose should pant, etc.

His eyes should flash with an inborn fire,
  His brow with scorn be wrung;
He never should bow down to a domineering frown,
  Or the tang of a tyrant tongue.
His foot should stamp and his throat should growl,
His hair should twirl and his face should scowl,
His eyes should flash and his breast protrude,
And this should be his customary attitude! *(Pose.)*
    CHORUS.—His foot should stamp, etc.

[*All strike attitude and then dance off to hornpipe down hatchway, excepting* RALPH, *who remains, leaning pensively against bulwark.*

Enter JOSEPHINE *from cabin.*

Jos. It is useless—Sir Joseph's attentions nauseate me. I know that he is a truly great and good man, but to me he seems tedious, fretful, and dictatorial. Yet his must be a mind of no common order, or he would not dare to teach my dear father to dance a hornpipe on the cabin table. *(Sees* RALPH.) Ralph Rackstraw! *(Overcome by emotion.)*

RALPH. Ay, lady—no other than poor Ralph Rackstraw!

Jos. *(aside).* How my head beats! *(Aloud.)* And why poor, Ralph?

RALPH. I am poor in the essence of happiness, lady—rich only in never-ending unrest. In me there meet a combination of antithetical elements which are at eternal war with one another. Driven hither by objective influences—thither by subjective emotions—wafted one moment into blazing day by mocking hope—plunged the next into the Cimmerian darkness of tangible despair, I am but a living ganglion of irreconcilable antagonisms. I hope I make myself clear, lady?

Jos. Perfectly. *(Aside.)* His simple eloquence goes to my heart. Oh, if I dared—but no, the thought is madness. *(Aloud.)* Dismiss these foolish fancies, they torture you but needlessly. Come, make one effort.

RALPH *(aside).* I will—one. *(Aloud.)* Josephine!

Jos. *(indignantly).* Sir!

RALPH. Ay, even though Jove's armoury were launched at the head of. the audacious mortal whose lips, unhallowed by relationship, dared to breathe that precious word, yet would I breathe it once, and then perchance be silent evermore. Josephine, in one brief breath I will concentrate the hopes, the doubts, the anxious fears of six weary months. Josephine, I am a British sailor, and I love you!

Jos. Sir, this audacity! *(Aside.)* Oh, my heart, my heart! *(Aloud.)* This unwarrantable presumption on the part of a common sailor! *(Aside.)* Common! oh, the irony of the word! *(Aloud.)* Oh, sir, you forget the disparity in our ranks.

RALPH. I forget nothing, haughty lady. I love you desperately, my life is in thy hand—I lay it at your feet! Give me hope, and what I lack in education and polite accomplishments, that I will endeavour to acquire. Drive me to despair, and in death alone I shall look for consolation. I am proud, and cannot stoop to implore. I have spoken, and I wait your word!

Jos. You shall not wait long. Your proffered love I haughtily reject. Go, sir, and learn to cast your eyes on some village maiden in your own poor rank—they should be lowered before your captain's daughter!

DUET.—JOSEPHINE *and* RALPH.

Jos.	Refrain, audacious tar,
	Your suit from pressing,
	Remember what you are,
	And whom addressing!
	Proud lords to seek my hand
	In throngs assemble,
	The loftiest in the land
	Bow down and tremble!
Aside.)	I'd laugh my rank to scorn
	In union holy,
	Were he more highly born
	Or I more lowly!
RALPH.	Proud lady, have your way
	Unfeeling beauty!
	You speak and I obey,
	It is my duty!
	I am the lowliest tar
	That sails the water.
	And you, proud maiden, are
	My captain's daughter!
(Aside.)	My heart with anguish torn
	Bows down before her,
	She laughs my love to scorn,
	Yet I adore her.

[*Repeat refrain ensemble, then exit* JOSEPHINE *into cabin.*

RECITATIVE.—RALPH.

Can I survive this overbearing
Or live a life of mad despairing,
My proffered love despised, rejected!

No, no, it's not to be expected!
(Calling off.) Messmates, ahoy!
Come here! Come here!

Enter SAILORS, HEBE *and* RELATIVES.

ALL. Ay, ay, my boy,
    What cheer, what cheer?
     Now tell us, pray,
     Without delay,
    What does she say—
    What cheer, what cheer?

RALPH *(to* COUSIN HEBE*)*.
  The maiden treats my suit with scorn,
   Rejects my humble love, my lady;
  She says I am ignobly born,
   And cuts my hopes adrift, my lady.

ALL.   Oh, cruel one!
DICK. She spurns your suit? Oho! Oho!
   I told you so, I told you so.

SAIL. *and* REL. Shall { we / they } submit? Are { we / they } but slaves?
   Love comes alike to high and low—
  Britannia's sailors rule the waves,
   And shall they stoop to insult? No!

DICK. You must submit, you are but slaves;
   A lady she! Oho! Oho!
  You lowly toilers of the waves,
   She spurns you all—I told you so! *(Goes off.)*

RALPH *(drawing a pistol)*.
  My friends, my leave of life I'm taking,
  For oh, for oh, my heart is breaking.
  When I am gone, oh, prithee tell
  The maid that, as I died, I loved her well!
         (Loading it.)

ALL *(turning away, weeping)*.
  Of life, alas! his leave he's taking,
  For, ah! his faithful heart is breaking.
  When he is gone we'll surely tell
  The maid that, as he died, he loved her well.
    (During chorus he has loaded pistol.)
RALPH. Be warned, my messmates all
   Who love in rank above you—
   For Josephine I fall!

(Puts pistol to his head. All the sailors stop their ears.)

Enter JOSEPHINE.

JOS. Ah! stay your hand! I love you!
ALL. Ah! stay your hand—she loves you!
RALPH *(incredulously)*. Loves me?
JOS.   Loves you!
ALL. Yes, yes—ah, yes—she loves you!

ENSEMBLE.

SAILORS *and* RELATIVES, *and* JOSEPHINE.

Oh, joy! oh, rapture unforeseen!
For now the sky is all serene;
The god of day—the orb of love,
Has hung his ensign high above,
 The sky is all a-blaze.
With wooing words and loving song,
We'll chase the lagging hours along.
And if { I find / we find } the maiden coy,
I'll / We'll } murmur forth decorous joy
  In dreamy roundelays!

DICK DEADEYE.

He thinks he's won his Josephine,
But though the sky is now serene,
A frowning thunderbolt above
May end their ill-assorted love
 Which now is all a-blaze.
Our captain, ere the day is gone,
Will be extremely down upon
The wicked men who art employ
To make his Josephine his coy
 In many various ways.

JOS.   This very night,
HEBE.   With bated breath
RALPH. And muffled oar—
JOS.   Without a light,
HEBE.   As still as death,
RALPH. We'll steal ashore.
JOS.   A clergyman
RALPH. Shall make us one
BOAT.   At half-past ten,
JOS.   And then we can
RALPH. Return, for none
BOAT.   Can part us then!
ALL.   This very night, etc.

(DICK appears at hatchway.)

DICK. Forbear, nor carry out the scheme you've planned,
  She is a lady—you a foremast hand!
  Remember, she's your gallant captain's daughter,
  And you the meanest slave that crawls the water.
ALL.   Back, vermin, back,
    Nor mock us!
   Back, vermin, back,
    You shock us!
Let's give three cheers for the sailor's bride
Who casts all thought of rank aside—
Who gives up house and fortune too
For the honest love of a sailor true!
For a British tar is a soaring soul
 As free as a mountain bird!
His energetic fist should be ready to resist
 A dictatorial word!

His foot should stamp and his throat should growl,
His hair should twirl and his face should scowl,
His eyes should flash and his breast protrude,
And this should be his customary attitude. (*Pose.*)

(*General Dance.*)

ACT II.

Same Scene. Night. Moonlight.

CAPTAIN *discovered singing on poop-deck, and accompanying himself on a mandolin.* LITTLE BUTTERCUP *seated on quarter-deck, near gun, gazing sentimentally at him.*

SONG.—CAPTAIN.

Fair moon, to thee I sing,
　　Bright regent of the heavens;
Say, why is everything
　　Either at sixes or at sevens?
I have lived hitherto
　　Free from breath of slander,
Beloved by all my crew—
　　A really popular commander.
But now my kindly crew rebel;
　　My daughter to a tar is partial;
Sir Joseph storms, and, sad to tell,
　　He threatens a court martial!
Fair moon, to thee I sing,
　　Bright regent of the heavens;
Say, why is everything
　　Either at sixes or at sevens?

BUT. How sweetly he carols forth his melody to the unconscious moon! Of whom is he thinking? Of some high-born beauty? It may be! (*Sighing.*) Who is poor Little Buttercup that she should expect his glance to fall on one so lowly! And yet if he knew—
　　　　　　　　　　[CAPTAIN *has come down from poop-deck.*

CAPT. Ah! Little Buttercup, still on board? That is not quite right, little one. It would have been more respectable to have gone on shore at dusk.

BUT. True, dear Captain—but the recollection of your sad pale face seemed to chain me to the ship. I would fain see you smile before I go.

CAPT. Ah! Little Buttercup, I fear it will be long before I recover my accustomed cheerfulness, for misfortunes crowd upon me, and all my old friends seem to have turned against me!

BUT. Oh no—do not say "all," dear Captain. That were unjust to one, at least.

CAPT. True, for you are staunch to me. (*Aside.*) If ever I gave my heart again, methinks it would be to such a one as this! (*Aloud.*) I am deeply touched by your innocent regard for me, and were we differently situated, I think I could have returned it. But as it is, I fear I can never be more to you than a friend.

BUT. (*change of manner*). I understand! You hold aloof from me because you are rich and lofty—and I, poor and lowly. But take care! The poor bumboat woman has gipsy blood in her veins, and she can read destinies. There is a change in store for you!

CAPT. A change!

BUT. Ay—be prepared!

DUET.—LITTLE BUTTERCUP *and* CAPTAIN.

BUT.　　Things are seldom what they seem;
　　　　Skim milk masquerades as cream;
　　　　Highlows pass as patent leathers;
　　　　Jackdaws strut in peacocks' feathers.

CAPT. (*puzzled*).　Very true,
　　　　　　　　So they do.

BUT.　　Black sheep dwell in every fold
　　　　All that glitters is not gold;
　　　　Storks turn out to be but logs;
　　　　Bulls are but inflated frogs.

CAPT. (*puzzled*).　So they be,
　　　　　　　　Frequentlee.

BUT.　　Drops the wind and stops the mill;
　　　　Turbot is ambitious brill;
　　　　Gild the farthing if you will,
　　　　But it is a farthing still.

CAPT. (*puzzled*).　Yes, I know
　　　　　　　　That is so.
　　　　Though to catch your drift I'm striving,
　　　　　　It is shady—it is shady;
　　　　I don't see at what you're driving,
　　　　　　Mystic lady—mystic lady,

(*Aside.*)　Stern conviction's o'er me stealing,
　　　　That the mystic lady's dealing
　　　　In oracular revealing.

BUT. (*aside*). Stern conviction's o'er him stealing,
　　　　That the mystic lady's dealing
　　　　In oracular revealing.

BOTH.　　　Yes, I know
　　　　　　That is so!

CAPT.　　Though I'm anything but clever,
　　　　I could talk like that for ever:
　　　　Once a cat was killed by care;
　　　　Only brave deserve the fair.

BUT.　　　Very true,
　　　　　So they do.

CAPT.　　Wink is often good as nod;
　　　　Spoils the child who spares the rod;
　　　　Thirsty lambs run foxy dangers;
　　　　Dogs are found in many mangers.

BUT.　　　Frequentlee,
　　　　　I agree.

CAPT.　　Paw of cat the chestnut snatches;
　　　　Worn-out garments show new patches;
　　　　Only count the chick that hatches;
　　　　Men are grown up catchy-catchies.

BUT.　　　Yes, I know
　　　　　That is so.

(*Aside.*)　Though to catch my drift he's striving,
　　　　　I'll dissemble—I'll dissemble;
　　　　When he sees at what I'm driving,
　　　　　Let him tremble—let him tremble!

ENSEMBLE.

Though a mystic tone $\left\{ {I \atop you} \right\}$ borrow,

$\left\{ {\text{I shall} \atop \text{You will}} \right\}$ learn the truth with sorrow,

Here to-day and gone to-morrow;
    Yes, I know
    That is so!

[At the end exit LITTLE BUTTERCUP, *melo-dramatically.*

CAPT. Incomprehensible as her utterances are, I nevertheless feel that they are dictated by a sincere regard for me. But to what new misery is she referring? Time alone can tell!

Enter SIR JOSEPH.

SIR J. Captain Corcoran, I am much disappointed with your daughter. In fact, I don't think she will do.

CAPT. She won't do, Sir Joseph!

SIR J. I'm afraid not. The fact is, that although I have urged my suit with as much eloquence as is consistent with an official utterance, I have done so hitherto without success. How do you account for this?

CAPT. Really, Sir Joseph, I hardly know. Josephine is, of course, sensible of your condescension.

SIR J. She naturally would be.

CAPT. But perhaps your exalted rank dazzles her.

SIR J. You think it does?

CAPT. I can hardly say; but she is a modest girl, and her social position is far below your own. It may be that she feels she is not worthy of you.

SIR J. That is really a very sensible suggestion, and displays more knowledge of human nature than I had given you credit for.

CAPT. See, she comes. If your lordship would kindly reason with her, and assure her, officially, that it is a standing rule at the Admiralty that love levels all ranks, her respect for an official utterance might induce her to look upon your offer in its proper light.

SIR J. It is not unlikely. I will adopt your suggestion. But soft, she is here. Let us withdraw, and watch our opportunity.

Enter JOSEPHINE *from cabin.* SIR JOSEPH *retires up and watches her.*

SCENA.—JOSEPHINE.

The hours creep on apace,
    My guilty heart is quaking!
Oh that I might retract
    The step that I am taking.
Its folly it were easy to be showing,
What I am giving up and whither going.

On the one hand, papa's luxurious home,
    Hung with ancestral armour and old brasses,
Carved oak and tapestry from distant Rome,
    Rare "blue and white" Venetian finger-glasses,
Rich Oriental rugs, luxurious sofa pillows,
And everything that isn't old, from Gillow's.
And on the other, a dark dingy room
    In some back street, with stuffy children crying,
Where organs yell, and clacking housewives fume,
    And clothes are hanging out all day a-drying;
With one cracked looking-glass to see your face in,
And dinner served up in a pudding basin!

A simple sailor, lowly born,
    Unlettered and unknown,
Who toils for bread from early morn
    Till half the night has flown!
No golden rank can he impart—
    No wealth of house or land—
No fortune save his trusty heart
    And honest brown right hand!
And yet he is so wondrous fair
That love for one so passing rare,
So peerless in his manly beauty,
Were little else than solemn duty!
Oh, god of love, and god of reason, say,
Which of you twain shall my poor heart obey!

SIR J. *(coming forward).* Madam, it has been represented to me that you are appalled by my exalted rank; I desire to convey to you, officially, my assurance that if your hesitation is attributable to that circumstance, it is uncalled for.

JOS. Oh! then your lordship is of opinion that married happiness is *not* inconsistent with discrepancy in rank?

SIR J. I am officially of that opinion.

JOS. That the high and the lowly may be truly happy together, provided that they truly love one another?

SIR J. Madam, I desire to convey to you, officially, my opinion that love is a platform upon which all ranks meet.

JOS. I thank you, Sir Joseph. I *did* hesitate, but I will hesitate no longer. *(Aside.)* He little thinks how eloquently he has pleaded his rival's cause!

CAPTAIN *has entered; during this speech he comes forward.*

TRIO.—SIR JOSEPH, CAPTAIN, *and* JOSEPHINE.

CAPT.	Never mind the why and wherefore,
	Love can level ranks, and therefore,
	Though his lordship's station's mighty,
	Though stupendous be his brain,
	Though your tastes are mean and flighty
	And your fortune poor and plain—
CAPT. *and*	Ring the merry bells on board ship,
SIR J.	Rend the air with warbling wild,
	For the union of $\left\{ \begin{matrix} his \\ my \end{matrix} \right\}$ lordship
	With a humble captain's child!
CAPT.	For a humble captain's daughter—
JOS. *(aside).*	For a gallant captain's daughter—
SIR J.	And a lord who rules the water—
JOS. *(aside).*	And a *tar* who ploughs the water!
ALL.	Let the air with joy be laden,
	Rend with songs the air above,
	For the union of a maiden
	With the man who owns her love!
SIR J.	Never mind the why and wherefore,
	Love can level ranks, and therefore,
	Though your nautical relation *(alluding to*
	CAPTAIN*)*
	In my set could scarcely pass—
	Though you occupy a station
	In the lower middle class—

Capt. *and*   Ring the merry bells on board ship,
Sir J.   Rend the air with warbling wild,

For the union of $\begin{Bmatrix} his \\ my \end{Bmatrix}$ lordship

With a humble captain's child?
Sir J.   For a humble captain's daughter—
Jos. *(aside).* For a gallant captain's daughter—
Capt.   And a lord who rules the water—
Jos. *(aside).* And a *tar* who ploughs the water!
All.   Let the air with joy be laden,
       Fill with songs the air above,
       For the union of a maiden
       With the man who owns her love!

Jos.   Never mind the why and wherefore,
       Love can level ranks, and therefore
       I admit its jurisdiction;
         Ably have you played your part;
       You have carried firm conviction
       To my hesitating heart.
Capt. *and* Sir J. Ring the merry bells on board ship,
       Rend the air with warbling wild,

For the union of $\begin{Bmatrix} his \\ my \end{Bmatrix}$ lordship

With a humble captain's child!
Capt. *and* Sir J. For a humble captain's daughter—
Jos. *(aside).* For a gallant captain's daughter—
Capt. *and* Sir J. And a lord who rules the water—
Jos. *(aside).* And a *tar* who ploughs the water!
(Aloud.) Let the air with joy be laden,
Capt. *and* Sir J. Ring the merry bells on board ship—
Jos.   For the union of a maiden—
Capt. *and* Sir J. For the union with his lordship.
All.   Rend with songs the air above
       For the man who owns her love!

                    [*Exit* JOSEPHINE.

Capt. Sir Joseph, I cannot express to you my delight at the happy result of your eloquence. Your argument was unanswerable.

Sir J. Captain Corcoran, it is one of the happiest characteristics of this glorious country that official utterances are invariably regarded as unanswerable. [*Exit* SIR JOSEPH *into cabin.*

Capt. At last my fond hopes are to be crowned. My only daughter is to be the bride of a Cabinet Minister. The prospect is Elysian.

During this speech DICK DEADEYE *has entered.*

Dick. Captain!

Capt. Deadeye! You here? Don't! *(Recoiling from him.)*

Dick. Ah, don't shrink from me, Captain. I'm unpleasant to look at, and my name's agin me, but I ain't as bad as I seem.

Capt. What would you with me?

Dick *(mysteriously).* I'm come to give you warning.

Capt. Indeed! Do you propose to leave the Navy, then?

Dick. No, no, you misunderstand me; listen.

DUET.—CAPTAIN *and* DICK DEADEYE.

Dick. Kind Captain, I've important information,
      Sing hey, the kind commander that you are!

About a certain intimate relation;
      Sing hey, the merry maiden and the tar!
Both.   The merry maiden and the tar!

Capt. Good fellow, in conundrums you are speaking,
      Sing hey, the mystic sailor that you are!
The answer to them vainly I am seeking;
      Sing hey, the merry maiden and the tar!
Both.   The merry maiden and the tar!

Dick. Kind Captain, your young lady is a-sighing,
      Sing hey, the simple captain that you are!
This very night with Rackstraw to be flying;
      Sing hey, the merry maiden and the tar!
Both.   The merry maiden and the tar!

Capt. Good fellow, you have given timely warning,
      Sing hey, the thoughtful sailor that you are!
I'll talk to Master Rackstraw in the morning;
      Sing hey, the cat-o'-nine-tails and the tar!
                 (Producing a "cat.")
Both.   The merry cat-o'-nine-tails and the tar!

Capt. Dick Deadeye, I thank you for your warning; I will at once take means to arrest their flight. This boat-cloak will afford me ample disguise. So! *(Envelopes himself in a mysterious cloak, holding it before his face.)*

Dick. Ha! ha! They are foiled—foiled—foiled!

Enter CREW *on tiptoe, with* RALPH *and* BOATSWAIN, *meeting* JOSEPHINE, *who enters from cabin on tiptoe, with bundle of necessaries, and accompanied by* LITTLE BUTTERCUP. *The* CAPTAIN, *shrouded in his boat-cloak, watches them unnoticed.*

ENSEMBLE.

Carefully on tiptoe stealing,
    Breathing gently as we may,
Every step with caution feeling,
    We will softly steal away.

*(*CAPTAIN *stamps—chord.)*

All *(much alarmed).* Goodness me!
             Why, what was that?
Dick.   Silent be,
            It was the cat!
All *(reassured).* It was—it was the cat!
Capt. *(producing cat-o'-nine-tails).*
             They're right, it was the cat!

Pull ashore, in fashion steady,
    Hymen will defray the fare,
For a clergyman is ready
    To unite the happy pair!

(Stamp as before, and chord.)

All.   Goodness me!
          Why, what was that?
Dick.   Silent be,
         Again the cat!

ALL.   It was again that cat!

CAPT. *(aside).*   They're right, it was the cat!

(Throwing off cloak.)   Hold! *(All start.)*

> Pretty daughter of mine,
> I insist upon knowing
> Where you may be going
> With these sons of the brine;
> For my excellent crew,
> Though foes they could thump any,
> Are scarcely fit company,
> My daughter, for you.

CREW.   Now, hark at that, do!
> Though foes we could thump any,
> We are scarcely fit company
> For a lady like you!

RALPH. Proud officer, that haughty lip uncurl!
> Vain man, suppress that supercilious sneer,
> For I have dared to love your matchless girl,
> A fact well known to all my messmates here!

CAPT.   Oh, horror!

RALPH *and* JOS. $\left\{\begin{array}{l} \text{I,} \\ \text{He,} \end{array}\right\}$ humble, poor, and lowly born,
> The meanest in the port division—
> The butt of epauletted scorn—
> The mark of quarter-deck derision—
> $\left\{\begin{array}{l} \text{Have} \\ \text{Has} \end{array}\right\}$ dared to raise $\left\{\begin{array}{l} \text{my} \\ \text{his} \end{array}\right\}$ wormy eyes
> Above the dust to which you'd mould $\left\{\begin{array}{l} \text{me,} \\ \text{him,} \end{array}\right\}$
> In manhood's glorious pride to rise.
> $\left\{\begin{array}{l} \text{I am} \\ \text{He is} \end{array}\right\}$ an Englishman—behold $\left\{\begin{array}{l} \text{me!} \\ \text{him!} \end{array}\right\}$

ALL.   He is an Englishman!

BOAT.   He is an Englishman!
> For he himself has said it,
> And it's greatly to his credit,
> That he is an Englishman!

ALL.   That he is an Englishman!

BOAT.   For he might have been a Roosian,
> A French, or Turk, or Proosian,
> Or perhaps Itali-an!

ALL.   Or perhaps Itali-an!

BOAT.   But in spite of all temptations
> To belong to other nations,
> He remains an Englishman!

ALL.   Hurrah!
> For the true-born Englishman!

CAPT. *(trying to repress his anger).*
> In uttering a reprobation
> To any British tar,
> I try to speak with moderation,
> But you have gone too far.
> I'm very sorry to disparage
> A humble foremast lad,
> But to seek your captain's child in marriage,
> Why, damme, it's too bad!

During this COUSIN HEBE *and* FEMALE RELATIVES *have entered.*

ALL *(shocked).*   Oh!

CAPT.   Yes, damme, it's too bad!

CAPT. *and* DICK DEADEYE. Yes, damme, it's too bad.

During this SIR JOSEPH *has appeared on poop-deck.*
He is horrified at the bad language.

HEBE.   Did you hear him—did you hear him?
> Oh, the monster overbearing!
> Don't go near him—don't go near him—
> He is swearing—he is swearing.

SIR J. *(with impressive dignity).*
> My pain and my distress
> I find it is not easy to express;
> My amazement—my surprise—
> You may learn from the expression of my eyes!

CAPT. My lord, one word—the facts are known before you;
> The word was injudicious, I allow—
> But hear my explanation, I implore you,
> And you will be indignant, too, I vow!

SIR J.   I will hear of no defence,
> Attempt none if you're sensible.
> That word of evil sense
> Is wholly indefensible.
> Go, ribald, get you hence
> To your cabin with celerity.
> This is the consequence
> Of ill-advised asperity!

[*Exit* CAPTAIN, *disgraced, followed by* JOSEPHINE.]

ALL.   Behold the consequence
> Of ill-advised asperity!

SIR J   For I'll teach you all, ere long,
> To refrain from language strong.
> For I haven't any sympathy for ill-bred taunts!

HEBE. No more have his sisters, nor his cousins, nor his aunts.

ALL.   For he is an Englishman, etc.

SIR J. Now, tell me, my fine fellow—for you *are* a fine fellow—

RALPH. Yes, your honour.

SIR J. How came your captain so far to forget himself? I am quite sure you had given him no cause for annoyance.

RALPH. Please your honour, it was thus wise. You see, I'm only a topman—a mere foremast hand—

SIR J. Don't be ashamed of that. Your position as a topman is a very exalted one.

RALPH. Well, your honour, love burns as brightly in the foksle as it does on the quarter-deck, and Josephine is the fairest bud that ever blossomed upon the tree of a poor fellow's wildest hopes.

Enter JOSEPHINE; *she rushes to* RALPH's *arms.* SIR JOSEPH *horrified.*

She's the figurehead of my ship of life—the bright beacon that guides me into my port of happiness—the rarest, the purest gem that ever sparkled on a poor but worthy fellow's trusting brow.

ALL. Very pretty.

Sir J. Insolent sailor, you shall repent this outrage. Seize him!

[*Two* Marines *seize him and handcuff him.*

Jos. Oh, Sir Joseph, spare him, for I love him tenderly.

Sir J. Away with him. I will teach this presumptuous mariner to discipline his affections. Have you such a thing as a dungeon on board?

All. We have!

Sir J. Then load him with chains and take him there at once!

OCTETTE.

RALPH.	Farewell, my own!
	Light of my life, farewell!
	For crime unknown
	I go to a dungeon cell.
All.	For crime, etc.
Jos.	In the mean time, farewell!
	And all alone
	Rejoice in your dungeon cell!
All.	And all, etc.
Sir J.	A bone, a bone
	I'll pick with this sailor fell;
	Let him be shown
	At once to his dungeon cell.
All.	Let him, etc.
Boat. }	He'll hear no tone
Dick. }	Of the maiden he loves so well!
Hebe. }	No telephone
	Communicates with his cell!
All.	No telephone, etc.
But.	But when is known
(*mysteriously*).	The secret I have to tell,
	Wide will be thrown
	The door of his dungeon cell.
All.	Wide will be thrown
	The door of his dungeon cell!

[*All repeat respective verses, ensemble. At the end* RALPH *is led off in custody.*

Sir J. Josephine, I cannot tell you the distress I feel at this most painful revelation. I desire to express to you, officially, that I am hurt. You, whom I honoured by seeking in marriage—you, the daughter of a captain in the Royal Navy!

But. Hold! *I* have something to say to that?

Sir J. You?

But. Yes, I!

SONG.—BUTTERCUP.

A many years ago,
When I was young and charming,
As some of you may know
I practised baby-farming.

All. Now this is most alarming!
When she was young and charming,
She practised baby-farming,
A many years ago.

But. Two tender babes I nussed:
One was of low condition,
The other, upper crust,
A regular patrician.

All. (*explaining to each other*).
Now, this is the position:
One was of low condition,
The other a patrician,
A many years ago.

But. Oh, bitter is my cup!
However could I do it?
I mixed those children up,
And not a creature knew it!

All. However could you do it?
Some day, no doubt, you'll rue it,
Although no creature knew it,
So many years ago.

But. In time each little waif
Forsook his foster-mother.
The well-born babe was Ralph—
Your captain was the other!

All. They left their foster-mother.
The one was Ralph, our brother—
Our captain was the other,
A many years ago.

Sir J. Then I am to understand that Captain Corcoran and Ralph were exchanged in childhood's happy hour—that Ralph is really the Captain and the Captain is Ralph?

But. That is the idea I intended to convey?

Sir J. You have done it very well. Let them appear before me, at once!

RALPH *enters as Captain;* CAPTAIN *as a common sailor.* JOSEPHINE *rushes to his arms.*

Jos. My father—a common sailor!

Capt. It is hard, is it not, my dear?

Sir J. This is a very singular occurrence; I congratulate you both. (*To* RALPH.) Desire that remarkably fine seaman to step forward.

Ralph. Cocoran, come here.

Capt. If what? If you *please.*

Sir J. Perfectly right. If you *please.*

Ralph. Oh. If you *please.*   [CAPTAIN *steps forward.*

Sir J. (*to* CAPTAIN). You are an extremely fine fellow.

Capt. Yes, your honour.

Sir J. So it seems that you were Ralph, and Ralph was you.

Capt. So it seems, your honour.

Sir J. Well, I need not tell you that after this change in your condition, a marriage with your daughter will be out of the question.

Capt. Don't say that, your honour—love levels all ranks.

Sir J. It does to a considerable extent. But it does not level them as much as that. (*Handing* JOSEPHINE *to* RALPH.) Here—take her, sir, and mind you treat her kindly.

RALPH *and* Jos.	Oh, bliss! oh, rapture!
Sir J.	Sad my lot, and sorry,
	What shall I do? I cannot live alone!

All.	What will he do? he cannot live alone!
Hebe.	Fear nothing—while I live I'll not desert you.
	I'll soothe and comfort your declining days.
Sir J.	No, don't do that.
Hebe.	Yes, but indeed I'd rather.
Sir J. *(resigned).*	
	To-morrow morn our vows shall all be plighted,
	Three loving pairs on the same day united!

DUET.—RALPH *and* JOSEPHINE.

Oh, joy! oh, rapture unforeseen!
The clouded sky is now serene;
The god of day—the orb of love,
Has hung his ensign high above,
   The sky is all ablaze.

With wooing words and loving song,
We'll chase the lagging hours along;
And if $\begin{Bmatrix} \text{he finds} \\ \text{I find} \end{Bmatrix}$ the maiden coy,
We'll murmur forth decorous joy,
   In dreamy roundelays.

Capt.	For he is the Captain of the Pinafore.
All.	And a right good captain too!
Capt.	And though before my fall
	I was Captain of you all,
	I'm a member of the crew.
All.	Although before his fall, etc.

Capt.	I shall marry with a wife
	In my own rank of life! *(Turning to* BUTTERCUP.*)*
	And you, my love, are she.
	I must wander to and fro,
	But wherever I may go,
	I shall never be untrue to thee!
All.	What, never?
Capt.	No, never!
All.	What, *never?*
Capt.	Hardly ever!
All.	Hardly ever be untrue to thee.
	Then give three cheers, and one cheer more,
	For the faithful seamen of the Pinafore.
But.	For he loves Little Buttercup, dear Little Buttercup,
	I'm sure I shall never know why;
	But still he loves Buttercup, poor Little Buttercup,
	Sweet Little Buttercup, ay!
All.	For he loves, etc.
Sir J.	I'm the monarch of the sea,
	And when I've married thee *(to* HEBE*)*
	I'll be true to the devotion that my love implants.
Hebe.	Then good-bye to his sisters, and his cousins, and his aunts,
	Especially his cousins,
	Whom he reckons up by dozens,
	His sisters, and his cousins, and his aunts!
All.	For he is an Englishman,
	And he himself hath said it,
	And it's greatly to his credit
	That he is an Englishman!

The Pirates of Penzance

or The Slave of Duty

The Pirates, as an export commodity, is in the tradition of the British Penny Plain-Twopence Coloured Toy Theatre. The setting is the romantic, rugged Cornish coastline, happy hunting ground for smugglers, and offering provoking opportunities for paddling damsels. The moonlit Gothic mausoleum of the second act gives further melodramatic possibilities. Although the construction of the plot allows for the recently established stock characters of *Pinafore*, the boisterous Pirates, the bumpkin Policemen, the Pantaloonish Major-General — even the caravanserai of eligible Daughters — come straight from pantomime. In fact, Gilbert's burlesque 'Our Island Home' for the Gallery of Illustration in 1870, had a similar plot with a Pirate king whose obligation to murder terminated on his twenty-first birthday.

The characters in *The Pirates* have none of the flesh and blood of R.L.Stevenson's *Treasure Island* of 1883, but because of this they have the advantage that they can be converted into alternative stereotyped characters to suit the fashion of the day. The Pirate King of the 1980s new romantic era is a kind of Rock hero. Frederic, the pawn of good and bad, is a pop star, while the Stanley Sisters, instead of being a group of unmarried daughters, are individualized (possibly as Gilbert first conceived them). The changing of Sullivan's orchestration (much brass and no strings) works with this opera.

Ruth and Mabel are equally Victorian scrapbook characters but Sullivan's music for Mabel transcends that of melodrama and endows her with a sympathy that makes her ridiculous plight and heroic vows almost credible. On the other hand, Ruth is a blatant parody of the glamorous and fatal Bohemian girl. She emulates the current mezzo-soprano operatic Spanish gypsy (Bizet's *Carmen* was first heard in London in 1878, and Verdi's *La Forza del Destino* was first heard there eleven years earlier). But Ruth is a figure of fun, middle-aged and lumpish, her black leather belt stuffed with pistols.

The one really human character in the plot is the Major-General, a typically *Bab* creation with his

Richard Temple as the first Pirate King, Opéra Comique London, 4 April 1880. *Illustrated Sporting & Dramatic News.*

initial one-upmanship and his subsequent gnawing remorse.

Sullivan has obviously been inspired by the seaside setting: there is a definite affinity with Neapolitan folk song in the waltz rhythms of the first act, while the Pirates have many affinities, both in text and score, with Purcell's *Dido and Aeneas,* set on the Carthaginian shore. Purcell's sailors are synonymous with the Pirates, the witches with the united Pirate King and Ruth, the parting scenes and choruses of female agitation similar: Elizabethan song and snatches of Verdi creep in. Nevertheless, the overall spontaneity of Sullivan's work makes for irresistible enjoyment which the more sophisticated, later operas seldom match.

'Free "Shakespeare" in the Park'. *The Pirates of Penzance* in Central Park, New York 1980.

Alice Barnett, the first Ruth in the New York *Pirates of Penzance*, 31 December 1879.

SYNOPSIS

Act I opens at 11.30 on the morning of 1 March 1873. On a Cornish beach the Pirate band is regaling Frederic with sherry on his coming of age. He has achieved pirate status but he now causes astonishment by announcing his intention of leaving the Band to which he was only apprenticed in error. His Nursemaid Ruth, now a Pirate Maid-of-all-Work, confirms in her one solo 'When Frederic was a little lad' that her orders had been to apprentice him to a *pilot*, but she misheard. Her solo, in the minor key, a club-footed Habañera, suggests a musical joke. (Sullivan later used much the same idea — major mode this time — for the Duke of Plaza Toro.)

Frederic, now 'out of his indentures', expresses his

disgust with the Pirates' methods. They are orphans, and as such they release any captive who claims the same predicament. Frederic talks of his duty to avenge their cowardice by extermination and tries unsuccessfully to persuade the Pirates to give up their calling. The Pirate King defends their profession in 'Oh, better far to live and die under the brave black flag I fly...' This echoes Verdi in his *Don Carlo* period, and the importance of the number lies in its choral catch-phrase 'For I am a Pirate King' later developed as '...Major-General', '...Orphan Boy'. (The melody of the first four bars of this declaration theme was later adopted by the cartoon character, Popeye, as his signature tune.)

Frederic is left, rather unwillingly, with Ruth to accompany him on his mission. She is the only woman he has seen during the last thirteen years, and while she recommends herself to him as a fine example of womanhood (though forty-seven years old), he has doubts.

'A bevy of beautiful maidens' approaches the beach to paddle and Frederic sees that Ruth has indeed deceived him; despite her entreaties, he denounces her. The Girls' opening chorus 'Climbing over rocky mountain' is introduced by an idyllic conceit. (This is the number said to have been lifted from *Thespis*.) Frederic hides from the girls because of his uncouth costume, but as soon as each takes off a shoe, he cannot resist making himself known. His lyrical, though short, aria 'Oh, is there not one maiden breast...?' is his proposal to any one of them who will have him and its second stanza takes up the Victorian joke:

'Oh, is there not one maiden here
Whose homely face and bad complexion..?'

The assembled Sisters reject him and as Frederic begins to lose hope of acquiring even the plainest of them, Mabel — the youngest and not at all plain — appears. Her instant love for Frederic is inspired by her sense of duty which she expresses in her coloratura aria 'Poor wandering one!' — a show-stopper. Its similarities with the Neapolitan idiom evoke the sunny seashore, while its waltz tempo gives it a buoyancy as well as a touching quality so apt to form part of the Act II finale. Their *rapprochement* is observed with a hint of scepticism by the Sisters who discreetly (and contrapuntally) sing about the weather.

Martyn Green as Major-General Stanley.

Frederic suddenly remembers the Pirates, but he is too late, for they have crept up unseen. The Sisters are surrounded and each Pirate seizes a Girl, demanding instant *marriage*. Only Mabel stands up to them, announcing that they are Wards in Chancery and that their father is a Major-General.

His title echoes and re-echoes as Major-General Stanley makes an imposing entrance. He opens 'cold' with the patter-song 'I am the very model of a modern Major-General' which is a catalogue of self-approbation. Not until he has effected a polite introduction to the Pirate King does he realize the gravity of the situation: that the Pirates of Penzance are menacing his family. He instantly recalls the formula for reprieve and pleads that he is an orphan.

The Pirates' brash intentions change to sympathy and the Pirate King introduces one of the most memorable musical moments in the whole opera, 'Hail, Poetry, thou heaven-born maid!' It is set to an almost hymn-tune for four-part unaccompanied mixed chorus, and it puts the Pirate King definitely on the side of the angels, in keeping with the general

93

The magnificent tableau of fraternity at the end of Act I—Opéra Comique, London. *Illustrated Sporting & Dramatic News*, 12 April 1880.

'Know ye not, oh rash ones, that I have doomed you to extermination?' *Illustrated Sporting & Dramatic News*, 12 April 1880.

topsy-turvydom. The Act ends in a magnificent tableau of fraternity. Stanley, now an honorary Pirate, waves the Union Flag while the Pirate King brandishes the Skull and Crossbones above the gleeful Pirates. At the height of the celebration Ruth breaks in to seek the Pirates' affection once more but they pour scorn on her. Rejected by all, she collapses in their midst.

At the beginning of Act II Stanley is discovered surrounded by his Daughters in a moonlit, Gothic ruin. 'The chilly night air is damp, and the dews are falling fast!' sets the musical scene with cool woodwind chords. Stanley's remorse over the lie he has told leads him to hold a nightly vigil in the mausoleum of the now dishonoured ancestors he inherited when he bought the estate. His conscience remains unassuaged and he fears the Pirates' vengeance. Frederic awaits the local Police to lead them in a sortie against the Pirates. They march in, interpolating nervous sentiment with their war-cry 'Tarantara!' The Sisters' exhortations to battle and glorious death are met by a definite cooling of enthusiasm on the part of the Police, who persist in delaying their fateful departure. They march out, the Stanleys take leave of Frederic, and he is about to prepare himself for the assault when he is prevented.

The Pirate King and Ruth appear and hold him at pistol-point, appealing to him to postpone his revenge until he has been told of the 'startling paradox' they have discovered. They explain that because he was born on 29 February, he has not had twenty-one birthdays after all, and is 'still a little boy of five'. Frederic enjoys the joke with them until the Pirate King produces a document showing the termination of his apprenticeship to be on his *twenty-first birthday*. Frederic's sense of duty aligns him once more with the Pirates and he is obliged to betray General Stanley. In a vengeance trio, 'Away, away! my heart's on fire...' the Pirate King and Ruth vow to kill Stanley and his Daughters that night.

Frederic tearfully tells all to Mabel. She rejoices in his courageous call to duty, and their duet 'Ah, leave me not to pine alone and desolate...' is a Victorian version of the Elizabethan love-song, winsome and very English. Hints of the rescue-opera idea in *Pirates* are reinforced in the following ensemble when Mabel and Frederic exchange vows and she promises to wait for him until 1940. 'Oh, here is love, and here is truth...' is in the manner of Leonore and Florestan in 'O namenlose Freude' from Beethoven's *Fidelio*. Even in this romantic and apparently sincere moment, Gilbert finds irony irresistible as he makes the lovers sing:

> 'He
> She will be faithful to his
> her sooth
> Till we are wed, and even after.'

Mabel is left to explain Frederic's absence to the Police. They fail to comprehend his motives, but *duty*

they *do* understand and the Sergeant embarks on a homily about constabulary duty and the irksome lot of curbing the pleasures of fellow-creatures. 'When a felon's not engaged in his employment...' is a

working-class moan which strikes a balance between simple enjoyment and the wretchedness of duty. The musical accompaniment offers a chirpy melody over a tramping bass.

The 'burglar-Pirates' are heard noisily approaching 'with cat-like tread'. Their lusty chorus 'Come, friends, who plough the sea,...' has become a popular American camp-fire song. The Police hide and watch a distribution of burglary implements until Stanley, in night attire, appears with a light, searches, and finds no one. Action is temporarily suspended while the old man sings his delicate ballad, 'Sighing softly to the river comes the loving breeze...' The delicate setting makes this an unexpectedly emotional moment.

The Daughters arrive on the scene, *en peignoir*, anxious for their father. 'Oh, what is this, and what is that...?' is immediately followed by the Pirates' assault. Stanley is to die despite his Daughters' pleadings. At this critical moment, the Police spring out and in the ensuing struggle the Pirates are victorious. 'We triumph now!' is ironically similar to the 'Friendship Duet' from Verdi's *Don Carlo*. From his prostrate position the Sergeant of Police calls: 'We charge you yield, in Queen Victoria's name!'

Magically, the Pirates surrender, their sense of duty to the real Monarch prevailing. The Police are about to lead them away when Ruth halts the proceedings and proclaims that the Pirates are 'all noblemen who have gone wrong'. Stanley offers instant forgiveness and hands his Daughters to them 'because, with all our faults, we love our House of Peers!'

THE PIRATES OF PENZANCE;

OR

THE SLAVE OF DUTY*

AN ENTIRELY ORIGINAL COMIC OPERA,

IN TWO ACTS.

First produced at the Royal Bijou Theatre, Paignton, on 30 December 1879
Then at Fifth Avenue Theater, New York, on 31 December 1879
First London production at the Opéra Comique, on 3 April 1880

* A Sense of Duty (*Gilbert's Original*)
Love and Duty (Paignton)

DRAMATIS PERSONÆ

MAJOR-GENERAL STANLEY		baritone
THE PIRATE KING[1]		bass-baritone
SAMUEL [*his Lieutenant*]		baritone
FREDERIC [*the Pirate Apprentice*]		tenor
SERGEANT OF POLICE[2]		bass
GENERAL STANLEY'S DAUGHTERS:	MABEL	soprano
	EDITH	soprano
	KATE	mezzo
	ISABEL	mezzo
RUTH [*a Pirate Maid-of-all-Work*][3]		contralto

Chorus of Pirates, Police and General Stanley's Daughters.

[1] Richard, a Pirate Chief) New York 1879
[2] Edward, a Sergeant of Police) New York 1879
[3] Ruth, Frederic's Nurse   Paignton 1879

ACT I.

A ROCKY SEA-SHORE ON THE COAST OF CORNWALL.

ACT II.

A RUINED CHAPEL BY MOONLIGHT.

THE PIRATES OF PENZANCE

OR,

THE SLAVE OF DUTY.

ACT I.

SCENE—*A rocky sea-shore on the coast of Cornwall. Under the rock is a cavern. In the distance is a calm sea, on which a schooner is lying at anchor. As the curtain rises groups of* PIRATES *are discovered— some drinking, some playing cards.* SAMUEL, *the pirate lieutenant, is going from one group to the other, filling the cups from a flask.* FREDERIC *is seated in a despondent attitude at the back of the scene.* RUTH *kneels at his feet.*

OPENING CHORUS.

SAM.   Pour, oh, pour the pirate sherry;
        Fill, oh, fill the pirate glass;
        And, to make us more than merry,
        Let the pirate bumper pass.

Solo. }
SAM. }   For to-day our pirate 'prentice
        Rises from indenture freed;
        Strong his arm and keen his scent is,
        He's a pirate now indeed!

ALL.   Here's good luck to Frederic's ventures!
        Frederic's out of his indentures.

Solo. }
SAM. }   Two and twenty now he's rising,
        And alone he's fit to fly,
        Which we're bent on signalizing
        With unusual revelry.

ALL.   Here's good luck to Frederic's ventures!
        Frederic's out of his indentures,
        So pour, oh, pour the pirate sherry, etc.

[FREDERIC *rises and comes forward with* PIRATE KING.

KING. Yes, Frederic, from to-day you rank as a full-blown member of our band.

ALL. Hurrah!

FRED. My friends, I thank you all, from my heart, for your kindly wishes. Would that I could repay them as they deserve!

KING. What do you mean?

FRED. To-day I am out of my indentures, and to-day I leave you for ever.

KING. But this is quite unaccountable; a keener hand at scuttling a Cunarder or cutting out a White Star never shipped a handspike.

FRED. Yes, I have done my best for you. And why? It was my duty under my indentures, and I am the slave of duty. As a child I was regularly apprenticed to your band. It was through an error—no matter, the mistake was ours, not yours, and I was in honour bound by it.

SAM. An error? What error?

FRED. I may not tell you; it would reflect upon my well-loved Ruth.   [RUTH *comes down to* FREDERIC.

RUTH. Nay, dear master, my mind has long been gnawed by the cankering tooth of mystery. Better have it out at once.

SONG.—RUTH.

When Frederic was a little lad he proved so brave and daring,
His father thought he'd 'prentice him to some career
    seafaring.
I was, alas, his nursery-maid, and so it fell to *my* lot
To take and bind the promising boy apprentice to a *pilot*—
A life not bad for a hardy lad, though certainly not a high lot.
Though I'm a nurse, you might do worse than make your
    boy a pilot.

I was a stupid nursery-maid, on breakers always steering,
And I did not catch the word aright, through being hard of
    hearing;
Mistaking my instructions, which within my brain did gyrate,
I took and bound this promising boy apprentice to a *pirate*.
A sad mistake it was to make and doom him to a vile lot.
I bound him to a pirate—you—instead of to a pilot.

I soon found out, beyond all doubt, the scope of this disaster,
But I hadn't the face to return to my place, and break it to
    my master.
A nursery-maid is never afraid of what you people *call* work,
So I made up my mind to go as a kind of piratical maid of all
    work;
And that is how you find me now a member of your shy lot,
Which you wouldn't have found, had he been bound
    apprentice to a pilot.

(Kneeling at his feet.) Oh, pardon! Frederic, pardon!

FRED. Rise, sweet one; I have long pardoned you.

RUTH *(rises).* The two words were so much alike.

FRED. They were. They still are, though years have rolled over their heads. (RUTH *goes up with* SAMUEL.) But this afternoon my obligation ceases. Individually I love you all with affection unspeakable, but collectively, I look upon you with a disgust that amounts to absolute detestation. Oh! pity me, my beloved friend, for such is my sense of duty, that once out of my indentures I shall feel myself bound to devote myself heart and soul to your extermination!

ALL. Poor lad! poor lad! *(All weep.)*

KING. Well, Frederic, if you conscientiously feel that it is your duty to destroy us, we cannot blame you for acting on that conviction. Always act in accordance with the dictates of your conscience, my boy, and chance the consequences.

SAM. Besides, we can offer you but little temptation to remain with us. We don't seem to make piracy pay. I'm sure I don't know why, but we don't.

FRED. *I* know why, but, alas! I mustn't tell you; it wouldn't be right.

KING. Why not, my boy? It's only half-past eleven, and you are one of us until the clock strikes twelve.

SAM. True, and until then you are bound to protect our interests.

ALL. Hear, hear!

FRED. Well, then, it is my duty, as a pirate, to tell you that you are too tender-hearted. For instance, you make a point of never attacking a weaker party than yourselves, and when you attack a stronger party, you invariably get thrashed.

KING. There is some truth in that.

FRED. Then, again, you make a point of never molesting an orphan!

SAM. Of course; we are orphans ourselves, and know what it is.

FRED. Yes, but it has got about, and what is the consequence? Every one we capture says he's an orphan. The last three ships we took proved to be manned entirely by orphans, and so we had to let them go. One would think that Great Britain's mercantile navy was recruited solely from her orphan asylums—which we know is not the case.

SAM. But, hang it all, you wouldn't have us absolutely merciless?

FRED. There's my difficulty; until twelve o'clock I would, after twelve I wouldn't. Was ever a man placed in so delicate a situation!

RUTH. And Ruth, your own Ruth, whom you love so well, and who has won her middle-aged way into your boyish heart, what is to become of *her?*

KING. Oh, he will take you with him.

FRED. Well, Ruth, I feel some little difficulty about you. It is true that I admire you very much, but I have been constantly at sea since I was eight years old, and yours is the only woman's face I have seen during that time. I think it is a sweet face!

RUTH. It is, oh, it is!

FRED. I say I *think* it is; that is my impression. But as I have never had an opportunity of comparing you with other women, it is just possible I may be mistaken.

KING. True.

FRED. What a terrible thing it would be if I were to marry this innocent person, and then find out that she is, on the whole, plain!

KING. Oh, Ruth is very well, very well indeed.

SAM. Yes, there are the remains of a fine woman about Ruth.

FRED. Do you really think so? Then I will not be so selfish as to take her from you. In justice to her, and in consideration for you, I will leave her behind. *(Hands* RUTH *to* KING.)

KING. No, Frederic, this must not be. We are rough men, who lead a rough life, but we are not so utterly heartless as to deprive thee of thy love. I think I am right in saying that there is not one here who would rob thee of this inestimable treasure for all the world holds dear.

ALL *(loudly)*. Not one!

KING. No, I thought there wasn't. Keep thy love, Frederic, keep thy love. *(Hands her back to* FREDERIC.)

FRED. You're very good, I'm sure.

KING. Well, it's the top of the tide, and we must be off. Farewell, Frederic. When your process of extermination begins,

let our deaths be as swift and painless as you can conveniently make them.

FRED. I will! By the love I have for you, I swear it! Would that you could render this extermination unnecessary by accompanying me back to civilization!

KING. No, Frederic, it cannot be. I don't think much of our profession, but, contrasted with respectability, it is comparatively honest. No, Frederic, I shall live and die a pirate king.

SONG.—PIRATE KING.

Oh, better far to live and die
Under the brave black flag I fly,
Than play a sanctimonious part,
With a pirate head and a pirate heart.
Away to the cheating world go you,
Where pirates all are well to do;
But I'll be true to the song I sing,
And live and die a pirate king.
        For I am a pirate king.

ALL.   You are!
        Hurrah for our pirate king!
KING.   And it is, it is a glorious thing
        To be a pirate king.
ALL.   Hurrah! *(Cheering action by* PIRATES.)
        Hurrah for our pirate king!
KING.   When I sally forth to seek my prey
        I help myself in a royal way:
        I sink a few more ships, it's true,
        Than a well-bred monarch ought to do;
        But many a king on a first-class throne,
        If he wants to call his crown his own,
        Must manage somehow to get through
        More dirty work than ever *I* do,
            Though I am a pirate king.
ALL.   You are!
        Hurrah for our pirate king!
KING.   And it is, it is a glorious thing
        To be a pirate king!
ALL.   It is!
        Hurrah for our pirate king!

[*After song, the* KING, SAMUEL, *and all the Pirates, excepting* FREDERIC *and* RUTH, *go off;* FREDERIC *comes, followed by* RUTH.)

RUTH. Oh, take me with you! I cannot live if I am left behind.

FRED. Ruth, I will be quite candid with you: you are very dear to me, as you know, but I must be circumspect. You see, you are considerably older than I. A lad of twenty-one usually looks for a wife of seventeen.

RUTH. A wife of seventeen! You will find me a wife of a thousand!

FRED. No, but I shall find you a wife of forty-seven, and that is quite enough. Ruth, tell me candidly, and without reserve—compared with other women, how are *you?*

RUTH. I will answer you truthfully, master; I have a slight cold, but otherwise I am quite well.

FRED. I am sorry for your cold, but I was referring rather to your personal appearance. Compared with other women—are you beautiful?

RUTH (*bashfully*). I have been told so, dear master.

FRED. Ah, but lately?

RUTH. Oh no, years and years ago.

FRED. What do you think of yourself?

RUTH. It is a delicate question to answer, but I think I am a fine woman.

FRED. That is your candid opinion?

RUTH. Yes, I should be deceiving you if I told you otherwise.

FRED. Thank you, Ruth; I believe you, for I am sure you would not practise on my inexperience. I wish to do the right thing, and if—I say if—you are really a fine woman, your age shall be no obstacle to our union. (*Shakes hands with her. Chorus of* GIRLS *heard in the distance, "Climbing over rocky mountain," etc. See entrance of* GIRLS.) Hark! Surely I hear voices! Who has ventured to approach our all but inaccessible lair? Can it be Custom House? No, it does not sound like Custom House.

RUTH (*aside*). Confusion! it is the voices of young girls! If he should see them I am lost.

FRED. (*climbing rocky arch and looking off*). By all that's marvellous, a bevy of beautiful maidens!

RUTH (*aside*). Lost! lost! lost!

FRED. How lovely! how surpassingly lovely is the plainest of them! What grace! what delicacy! what refinement! And Ruth—Ruth told me she was beautiful!

RECITATIVE.

FRED. Oh, false one, you have deceived me.

RUTH. I have deceived you?

FRED. Yes, deceived me. (*Denouncing her.*)

DUET.—FREDERIC *and* RUTH.

FRED. You told me you were fair as gold!

RUTH (*wildly*). And, master, am I not so?

FRED. And now I see you're plain and old.

RUTH. I am sure I am not a jot so.

FRED. Upon my ignorance you play.

RUTH. I'm not the one to plot so.

FRED. Your face is lined, your hair is grey.

RUTH. It's gradually got so.

FRED. Faithless woman to deceive me,
  I who trusted so!

RUTH Master, master, do not leave me.
  Hear me, ere you go.
  My love, without reflecting,
  Oh, do not be rejecting.
Take a maiden tender—her affection, raw and green,
  At very highest rating,
  Has been accumulating
Summers seventeen—summers seventeen.
  Don't, belovèd master,
  Crush me with disaster.
What is such a dower to the dower I have here?
  My love, unabating,
  Has been accumulating
Forty-seven year—forty-seven year!

ENSEMBLE.

RUTH.	FREDERIC.
Don't, beloved master,	Yes, your former master
Crush me with disaster.	Saves you from disaster.
What is such a dower	Your love would be
to the dower	uncomfortably fervid,
I have here, etc.	it is clear,
	If, as you are stating,
	It's been accumulating
	Forty-seven year—forty-seven
	year.

[*At the end he renounces her, and she goes off in despair.*

RECITATIVE.—FREDERIC.

What shall I do? Before these gentle maidens,
I dare not show in this detested costume.
No, better far remain in close concealment
Until I can appear in decent clothing.

[*Hides in cave as they enter, climbing over the rocks and through arched rock.*

GIRLS. Climbing over rocky mountain,
  Skipping rivulet and fountain;
  Passing where the willows quiver
  By the ever-rolling river,
    Swollen with the summer rain;
  Threading long and leafy mazes
  Dotted with unnumbered daisies;
  Scaling rough and rugged passes,
  Climb the hardy little lasses,
    Till the bright sea-shore they gain.

EDITH. Let us gaily tread the measure,
  Make the most of fleeting leisure;
    Hail it as a true ally
    Though it perish by-and-by.

ALL.   Hail it as a true ally
    Though it perish by-and-by.

EDITH. Every moment brings a treasure
  Of its own especial pleasure.
  Though the moments quickly die,
  Greet them gaily as they fly.

KATE.   Far away from toil and care,
  Revelling in fresh sea air,
  Here we live and reign alone
  In a world that's all our own,
  Here in this our rocky den,
  Far away from mortal men,
  We'll be queens, and make decrees;
  They may honour them who please.

ALL.   Let us gaily tread the measure, etc.

KATE. What a picturesque spot! I wonder where we are!

EDITH. And I wonder where papa is. We have left him ever so far behind.

ISA. Oh, he will be here presently! Remember, poor papa is not as young as we are, and we have come over a rather difficult country.

KATE. But how thoroughly delightful it is to be so entirely alone! Why, in all probability we are the first human beings who ever set foot on this enchanting spot.

ISA. Except the mermaids—it's the very place for mermaids.

KATE. Who are only human beings down to the waist!

EDITH. And who can't be said strictly to set *foot* anywhere. Tails they may, but feet they *cannot*.

KATE. But what shall we do until papa and the servants arrive with the luncheon? [*All rise and come down.*

EDITH. We are quite alone, and the sea is as smooth as glass. Suppose we take off our shoes and stockings and paddle.

ALL. Yes, yes. The very thing!

[*They prepare to carry out the suggestion. They have all taken off one shoe, when* FREDERIC *comes forward from cave.*

RECITATIVE.

FRED.   Stop, ladies, pray!
ALL (*hopping on one foot*).   A man!
FRED.   I had intended
Not to intrude myself upon your notice
In this effective but alarming costume,
But under these peculiar circumstances
It is my bounden duty to inform you
That your proceedings will not be unwitnessed.
EDITH.   But who are you, sir? Speak! (*All hopping.*)
FRED.   I am a pirate.
ALL (*recoiling hopping*).
          A pirate! Horror!
FRED.   Ladies, do not shudder!
This evening I renounce my vile profession;
And to that end, oh, pure and peerless maidens!
Oh, blushing buds of ever-blooming beauty!
I, sore of heart, implore your kind assistance.
EDITH.   How pitiful his tale!
KATE.   How rare his beauty!
ALL.   How pitiful his tale! How rare his beauty!

[*Put on their shoes, and group in semicircle.*

SONG.—FREDERIC.

Oh! is there not one maiden breast
   Which does not feel the moral beauty
Of making worldly interest
   Subordinate to sense of duty?
Who would not give up willingly
   All matrimonial ambition,
To rescue such a one as I
   From his unfortunate position?

ALL.   Alas! there's not one maiden breast
      Which seems to feel the moral beauty
   Of making worldly interest
      Subordinate to sense of duty.

FRED.   Oh, is there not one maiden here,
      Whose homely face and bad complexion
   Have caused all hopes to disappear

Of ever winning man's affection?
To such a one, if such there be,
   I swear by heaven's arch above you,
If you will cast your eyes on me—
   However plain you be—I'll love you!

ALL.   Alas! there's not one maiden here,
      Whose homely face and bad complexion
   Have caused all hope to disappear
      Of ever winning man's affection.

FRED. (*in despair*). Not one!
ALL.   No, no—not one!
FRED.   Not one?
                No, no!

MABEL *enters through arch.*

MAB.   Yes, one!
ALL.   'Tis Mabel!
MAB.   Yes, 'tis Mabel!

RECITATIVE.—MABEL.

Oh, sisters, deaf to pity's name,
                For shame!
It's true that he has gone astray,
                But pray,
Is that a reason good and true
                Why you
Should all be deaf to pity's name?
                For shame!

ALL   The question is, had he not been a thing of beauty,
(*aside*).   Would she be swayed by quite as keen a sense of duty?

SONG.—MABEL.

Poor wandering one,
Though thou hast surely strayed,
Take heart of grace,
Thy steps retrace,
Be not afraid.
Poor wandering one,
If such poor love as mine
Can help thee find
True peace of mind—
Why, take it, it is thine!
Take heart, fair days will shine.
Take any heart—take mine.
ALL.   Take heart; no danger lowers.
      Take any heart—but ours.

[MABEL *and* FREDERIC *exit into cave and converse.* KATE *beckons her sisters, who form in a semicircle around her.*

EDITH.

What ought we to do,
   Gentle sisters, pray?
Propriety, we know,
   Says we ought to stay;

While sympathy exlaims,
"Free them from your tether—
Play at other games—
Leave them here together."

KATE.

Her case may, any day,
Be yours, my dear, or mine.
Let her make her hay
While the sun doth shine.
Let us compromise
(Our hearts are not of leather);
Let us shut our eyes,
And talk about the weather.

LADIES. Yes, yes; let's talk about the weather.
[EDITH, KATE, and GIRLS *retire and sit two and two, facing each other, in a line across.*

MABEL *and* FREDERIC *enter from cave.*

CHATTERING CHORUS.

How beautifully blue the sky,
The glass is rising very high,
Continue fine I hope it may,
And yet it rained but yesterday;
To-morrow it may pour again
(I hear the country wants some
    rain);
Yet people say, I know not why,
That we shall have a warm July.

(*During* MABEL'S *solo the* GIRLS *continue chatter pianissimo, but listening eagerly all the time.*

SOLO.—MABEL.

Did ever maiden wake
    From dream of homely duty,
To find her daylight break
    With such exceeding beauty?
Did ever maiden close
    Her eyes on waking sadness,
To dream of goodness knows
    How much exceeding gladness?

FRED. Oh yes—ah, yes; this is exceeding gladness.
[FREDERIC *and* MABEL *turn and see that the* GIRLS *are listening; detected, they continue their chatter forte.*

GIRLS.   How beautifully blue the sky, etc.

SOLO.—FREDERIC.

[*During this,* GIRLS *continue their chatter pianissimo as before, but listening intently all the time.*

Did ever pirate roll
    His soul in guilty dreaming,
And wake to find that soul

With peace and virtue beaming?
Did ever pirate loathed
    Forsake his hideous mission,
To find himself betrothed
    To lady of position?

MAB. Ah, yes—ah, yes; I am a lady of position.
[MABEL *and* FREDERIC *turn as before;* GIRLS *resume their chatter forte.*

ENSEMBLE.

MABEL.	FRED.	GIRLS.
Did ever maiden wake, etc.	Did ever pirate loathed, etc.	How beautifully blue the sky, etc.

RECITATIVE.—FRED.

Stay, we must not lose our senses;
Men who stick at no offences
    Will anon be here.
Piracy their dreadful trade is;
Pray you, get you hence, young ladies,
    While the coast is clear.

GIRLS.   No, we must not lose our senses
If they stick at no offences.
Piracy their dreadful trade is—
Nice associates for young ladies!
    Let us disappear.

[*During this chorus the* PIRATES *have entered stealthily, and formed in a semicircle behind the* GIRLS. *As the* GIRLS *move to go off, each* PIRATE *seizes a girl.* [KING *seizes* EDITH, SAMUEL *seizes* KATE.

ALL.   Too late!
PIRATES.   Ha! Ha!
ALL.   Too late!
PIR.   Ha! Ha!
    Ha! ha! ha! ha! Ha! ha! ha! ha!

ENSEMBLE.

(PIRATES *pass in front of* LADIES.)   (LADIES *pass in front of* PIRATES.)

PIRATES.	LADIES.
Here's a first-rate opportunity	We have missed our
To get married with	opportunity
impunity,	Of escaping with impunity;
And indulge in the felicity	So farewell to the felicity
Of unbounded domesticity	Of our maiden domesticity.
You shall quickly be	We shall quickly be
parsonified,	parsonified,
Conjugally matrimonified	Conjugally matrimonified
By a doctor of divinity,	By a doctor of divinity,
Who is located in this vicinity.	Who is located in this vicinity.

RECITATIVE.—MABEL (*coming forward*).

How, monsters! Ere your pirate caravanserai

Proceed, against our will, to wed us all,
Just bear in mind that we are wards in Chancery,
And father is a major-general!

SAM. *(cowed).*   We'd better pause, or danger may befall;
Their father is a major-general.

LADIES. Yes, yes; he is a major-general.

The MAJOR-GENERAL *has entered unnoticed on rock.*

GEN.   Yes, I am a major-general.
ALL.   You are!
         Hurrah for the Major-General!
GEN.   And it is a glorious thing
    To be a major-general.
ALL.   It is!
         Hurrah for the Major-General!

SONG.—MAJOR-GENERAL.

I am the very pattern of a modern major-gineral,
I've information vegetable, animal, and mineral;
I know the kings of England, and I quote the fights
    historical
From Marathon to Waterloo, in order categorical;
I'm very well acquainted too with matters mathematical;
I understand equations, both the simple and quadratical;
About binomial theorem I'm teeming with a lot o'
    news—
(Bothered for next rhyme.)—Lot o' news—lot o'
    news—*(struck with an idea)*
With many cheerful facts about the square of the
    hypotenuse.
(Joyously.) With many cheerful facts about the square of
    the hypotenuse.
ALL. With many cheerful facts, etc.
GEN. I'm very good at integral and differential calculus;
I know the scientific names of beings animalculous.
In short, in matters vegetable, animal, and mineral,
I am the very model of a modern major-gineral.
ALL. In short, in matters vegetable, animal, and mineral,
He is the very model of a modern major-gineral.

GEN. I know our mythic history, King Arthur's and Sir
    Caradoc's,
I answer hard acrostics, I've a pretty taste for paradox,
I quote in elegiacs all the crimes of Heliogabalus,
In conics I can floor peculiarities parabolous.
I can tell undoubted Raphaels from Gerard Dows and
    Zoffanies;
I know the croaking chorus from the ''Frogs'' of
    Aristophanes.
Then I can hum a fugue, of which I've heard the music's
    din afore,
(Bothered for next rhyme.)—Din afore, din afore, din
    afore—*(struck with an idea)*
And whistle all the airs from that infernal nonsense
    ''Pinafore.''
(Joyously.) And whistle all the airs, etc.
ALL. And whistle all the airs, etc.
GEN. Then I can write a washing bill in Babylonic cuneiform,
And tell you every detail of Caractacus's uniform.

In short, in matters vegetable, animal, and mineral,
I am the very pattern of a modern major-gineral.
ALL. In short, in matters vegetable, animal, and mineral,
He is the very pattern of a modern major-gineral.

GEN. In fact, when I know what is meant by mamelon and
    ravelin,
When I can tell at sight a chassepôt rifle from a javelin,
When such affairs as sorties and surprises I'm more wary
    at,
And when I know precisely what is meant by
    commissariat,
When I have learnt what progress has been made in
    modern gunnery,
When I know more of tactics than a novice in a
    nunnery;
In short, when I've a smattering of elemental strategy,
(Bothered for next rhyme.)—Strategy, strategy—*(struck with
    an idea)*
You'll say a better major-gener*al* has never *sat* a gee—
(Joyously.) You'll say a better major-gener*al* has never *sat* a
    gee!
ALL. You'll say a better, etc.
GEN. For my military knowledge, though I'm plucky and
    adventury,
Has only been brought down to the beginning of the
    century,
But still in learning vegetable, animal, and mineral, etc.
ALL. But still in learning vegetable, animal, and mineral,
He is the very model of a modern major-gineral.

GEN. And now that I've introduced myself I should like to
have some idea of what's going on.

KATE. Oh, papa—we—

SAM. Permit me, I'll explain in two words: we propose to
marry your daughters.

GEN. Dear me!

GIRLS. Against our wills, papa—against our wills!

GEN. Oh, but you mustn't do that. May I ask—this is a
picturesque costume, but I'm not familiar with it—what are
you?

KING. We are all single gentlemen.

GEN. Yes, I gathered that—anything else?

KING. No, nothing else.

EDITH. Papa, don't believe them, they are pirates—the famous
Pirates of Penzance!

GEN. The Pirates of Penzance? I have often heard of them.

MAB. All except this gentleman—*(indicating* FREDERIC*)*—who
was a pirate once, but who is out of his indentures to-day, and
who means to lead a blameless life evermore.

GEN. But wait a bit. I object to pirates as sons-in-law.

KING. We object to major-generals as fathers-in-law. But we
waive that point. We do not press it. We look over it.

GEN. *(aside).* Hah! an idea! *(Aloud.)* And do you mean to say
that you would deliberately rob me of these the sole remaining
props of my old age, and leave me to go through the remainder of
life unfriended, unprotected, and alone?

KING. Well, yes, that's the idea.

GEN. Tell me, have you ever known what it is to be an
orphan?

PIRATES *(disgusted).* Oh, dash it all!

KING. Here we are again!

GEN. I ask you, have you ever known what it is to be an orphan?

KING. Often!

GEN. Yes, orphan. Have you ever known what it is to be one?

KING. I say, often.

ALL (disgusted). Often, often, often. (Turning away.)

GEN. I don't think we quite understand one another. I ask you, have you ever known what it is to be an orphan, and you say "orphan". As I understand you, you are merely repeating the word "orphan" to show that you understand me.

KING. I didn't repeat the word often.

GEN. Pardon me, you did indeed.

KING. I only repeated it once.

GEN. True, but you repeated it.

KING. But not often.

GEN. Stop, I think I see where we are getting confused. When you said "orphan," did you mean "orphan"—a person who has lost his parents; or often—frequently?

KING. Ah, I beg pardon, I see what you mean—frequently.

GEN. Ah, you said often—frequently.

KING. No, only once.

GEN. (irritated). Exactly, you said often, frequently, only once.

FINALE.

RECITATIVE.—GENERAL.

Oh, men of dark and dismal fate,
    Forego your cruel employ;
Have pity on my lonely state,
    I am an orphan boy.

KING.   An orphan boy?
GEN.   An orphan boy!
PIRATES.   How sad—an orphan boy!

SOLO.—GENERAL.

These children whom you see
    Are all that I can call my own!
PIR.   Poor fellow!
GEN. Take them away from me
    And I shall be indeed alone.
PIR.   Poor fellow!
GEN. If pity you can feel,
    Leave me my sole remaining joy.
See, at your feet they kneel;
    Your hearts you cannot steel
Against the sad, sad tale of the lonely orphan boy!
PIR. (sobbing).   Poor fellow!
See, at our feet they kneel;
    Our hearts we cannot steel
Against the sad, sad tale of the lonely orphan boy.
KING.   The orphan boy!
SAM.   The orphan boy!
ALL.   The lonely orphan boy! Poor fellow!

[GENERAL comes down. PRINCIPALS come down.
LADIES rise.

ENSEMBLE.

GENERAL.	GIRLS (aside).	PIRATES (aside).
I'm telling a terrible story,	He's telling a terrible story,	If he's telling a terrible story
But it doesn't diminish my glory;	Which will tend to diminish his glory.	He shall die by a death that is gory,
For they would have taken my daughters	Though they would have taken his daughters	One of the cruellest slaughters
Over the billowy waters,	Over the billowy waters,	That ever were known in these waters;
If I hadn't, in elegant diction,	It's easy, in elegant diction,	And we'll finish his moral affliction
Indulged in an innocent fiction;	To call it an innocent fiction;	By a very complete malediction,
Which is not in the same category	But it comes in the same category	As a compliment valedictory,
As a regular terrible story.	As a regular terrible story.	If he's telling a terrible story.

KING.

Although our dark career
    Sometimes involves the crime of stealing,
We rather think that we're
    Not altogether void of feeling.
Although we live by strife,
    We're always sorry to begin it,
And what, we ask, is life
    Without a touch of Poetry in it?

ALL (kneeling).

Hail, Poetry, thou heaven-born maid,
Thou gildest e'en the pirate's trade!
Hail, flowing fount of sentiment!
All hail, Divine Emollient! (All rise.)

KING.

You may go, for you're at liberty, our pirate rules protect you,
And honorary members of our band we do elect you.
SAM.   For he is an orphan boy.
CHORUS.   He is an orphan boy.
GEN.   And it sometimes is a useful thing
            To be an orphan boy.
CHORUS.   It is! Hurrah for the orphan boy!
QUARTETTE. Oh, happy day, with joyous glee
            We will away and merry be!
            Should it befall auspiciouslee,
            My sisters all will bridesmaids be.
CHORUS.   Oh, happy day, with joyous glee
            They will away, and merry be;
            Should it befall auspiciouslee,
            Our sisters all will bridesmaids be!

RUTH enters, and comes down to FREDERIC, and kneels.

RUTH. Oh, master, hear one word, I do implore you!
    Remember Ruth, your Ruth, who kneels before you!

[PIRATES *come in front of* LADIES.

CHORUS. Yes, yes, remember Ruth who kneels before you.
FRED. (PIRATES *threaten* RUTH).
        Away, you did deceive me!
CHORUS.   Away, you did deceive him!
RUTH.   Oh, do not leave me!
CHORUS.   Oh, do not leave her!
FRED.   Away, you grieve me!
CHORUS.   Away, you grieve her!
FRED.   I wish you'd leave me.

[FREDERIC *casts* RUTH *from him. Exit* RUTH.

ENSEMBLE.

Pray observe the magnanimity
  We }
  They } display to lace and dimity;
Never was such opportunity
To get married with impunity,
But { we }
    { they } give up the felicity
Of unbounded domesticity,
Though a doctor of divinity
Is located in this vicinity.

KING.   For we are all orphan boys,
ALL.   We are,
      Hurrah for the orphan boys!
GEN.   And it sometimes is a useful thing
      To be an orphan boy.
ALL.   It is.
      Hurrah for the orphan boy!

[GIRLS *and* GENERAL *go up rocks, while* PIRATES *indulge in a wild dance of delight. The* GENERAL *produces a British flag, and the* PIRATE KING, *on arched rock, produces a black flag with skull and cross-bones. Picture.*

ACT II.

SCENE.—*A ruined chapel by moonlight. Aisles divided by pillars and arches; ruined Gothic windows at back.* GENERAL STANLEY *discovered seated pensively, surrounded by his daughters.*

CHORUS.

Oh, dry the glistening tear
  That dews that martial cheek;
Thy loving children hear,
  In them thy comfort seek.
With sympathetic care
  Their arms around thee creep,
For oh, they cannot bear
  To see their father weep.

Enter MABEL.

SOLO.—MABEL.

Dear father, why leave your bed
  At this untimely hour,
When happy daylight is dead,
  And darksome dangers lower?
See, heaven has lit her lamp,
  The midnight hour is past,
The chilly night air is damp,
  And the dews are falling fast!
Dear father, why leave your bed
  When happy daylight is dead?

FREDERIC *enters down aisle.*

MAB. Oh, Frederic, cannot you reconcile it with your conscience to say something that will relieve my father's sorrow?
FRED. I will try, dear Mabel. But why does he sit, night after night, in this draughty old ruin?
GEN. Why do I sit here? To escape from the pirates' clutches, I described myself as an orphan, and I am no orphan! I come here to humble myself before the tombs of my ancestors, and to implore their pardon for having brought dishonour on the family escutcheon.
FRED. But you forget sir, you only bought the property a year ago, and the stucco in your baronial hall is scarcely dry.
GEN. Frederic, in this chapel are ancestors; you cannot deny that. With the estate, I bought the chapel and its contents. I don't know whose ancestors they *were*, but I know whose ancestors they *are*, and I shudder to think that their descendant by purchase (if I may so describe myself) should have brought disgrace upon what, I have no doubt, was an unstained escutcheon.
FRED. Be comforted. Had you not acted as you did, these reckless men would assuredly have called in the nearest clergyman, and have married your large family on the spot.
GEN. I thank you for your proffered solace, but it is unavailing. At what time does your expedition march against these scoundrels?
FRED. At eleven; and before midnight I hope to have atoned for my involuntary association with the pestilent scourges by sweeping them from the face of the earth. And then, my Mabel, you will be mine!
GEN. Are your devoted followers at hand?
FRED. They are; they only wait my orders.

RECITATIVE.—GENERAL.

Then, Frederic, let your escort lion-hearted
Be summoned to receive a general's blessing,
Ere they depart upon their dread adventure.

FRED. Dear sir, they come.

Enter POLICE, *marching in double file. Form in line facing audience.*

SONG—SERGEANT.

When the foeman bares his steel,
        Tarantara! tarantara!
We uncomfortable feel,
        Tarantara!

And we find the wisest thing,
      Tarantara! tarantara!
Is to slap our chests and sing.
      Tarantara!
For when threatened with emeutes,
      Tarantara! tarantara!
And your heart is in your boots,
      Tarantara!
There is nothing brings it round,
      Tarantara! tarantara!
Like the trumpet's martial sound.
      Tarantara!
Tarantara, ra-ra-ra-ra!

ALL.   Tarantara, ra-ra-ra-ra!

MAB.   Go, ye heroes, go to glory;
Though you die in combat gory
Ye shall live in song and story.
    Go to immortality.
Go to death, and go to slaughter;
Die, and every Cornish daughter
With her tears your grave shall water.
    Go, ye heroes; go and die.

ALL.   Go, ye heroes; go and die.

POL.   Though to us it's evident,
      Tarantara! tarantara!
These attentions are well meant,
      Tarantara!
Such expressions don't appear,
      Tarantara! tarantara!
Calculated men to cheer,
      Tarantara!
Who are going to meet their fate
In a highly nervous state,
      Tarantara!
Still to us it's evident
These attentions are well meant.
      Tarantara!

EDITH.   Go and do your best endeavour,
And before all links we sever
We will say farewell for ever;
    Go to glory and the grave.
For your foes are fierce and ruthless,
False, unmerciful, and truthless.
Young and tender, old and toothless,
    All in vain their mercy crave.

ALL.   Yes, your foes are fierce and ruthless, etc.

SERG.   We observe too great a stress
On the risks that on us press,
And of reference a lack
To our chance of coming back.
Still perhaps it would be wise
Not to carp or criticise,
For it's very evident
These attentions are well meant.

ALL.   Yes, to them it's evident
Our attentions are well meant.
      Tarantara, ra-ra-ra-ra!
Go, ye heroes, go to glory, etc.

GEN.   Away, away.
POL. (without moving). Yes, yes, we go.
GEN.   These pirates slay.
POL.   Yes, yes, we go.
GEN.   Then do not stay.
POL.   We go, we go.
GEN.   Then why all this delay?
POL.   All right—we go, we go,
Yes, forward on the foe,
    Ho, ho! Ho, ho!
We go, we go, we go!
    Tarantara-ra-ra!
Then forward on the foe!
ALL.   Yes, forward!
POL.   Yes, forward!
GEN.   Yes, but you don't go!
POL.   We go, we go, we go!
ALL.   At last they really go—Tarantara-ra-ra!

ENSEMBLE.

CHORUS OF ALL BUT POLICE.	CHORUS OF POLICE.
Go and do your best endeavour,	Such expressions don't appear,
	Tarantara! tarantara!
And before all links we sever	Calculated men to cheer,
We will say farewell for ever;	Tarantara!
Go to glory and the grave.	Who are going to their fate,
For your foes are fierce and	Tarantara! tarantara!
ruthless,	In a highly nervous state.
False, unmerciful and	Tarantara!
truthless,	We observe too great a stress,
Young and tender, old and	Tarantara! tarantara!
toothless,	On the risks that on us press,
All in vain their mercy crave.	Tarantara!
	And of reference a lack,
	Tarantara! tarantara!
	To our chance of coming back.
	Tarantara!

[MABEL *tears herself from* FREDERIC *and exit, followed by her sisters, consoling her. The* GENERAL *and others follow the* POLICE *off.* FREDERIC *remains.*

RECITATIVE.—FREDERIC.

Now for the pirate's lair! Oh, joy unbounded!
Oh, sweet relief! Oh, rapture unexampled!
At last I may atone, in some slight measure,
For the repeated acts of theft and pillage
Which, at a sense of duty's stern dictation,
I, circumstance's victim, have been guilty.

[*The* PIRATE KING *and* RUTH *appear at the window armed.*

KING.   Young Frederic! (*Covering him with pistol.*)
FRED.   Who calls?
KING.   Your late commander! (*Coming down.*)
RUTH.   And I, your little Ruth! (*Covering him with pistol.*)
FRED.   Oh, mad intruders,
How dare ye face me? Know ye not, oh rash ones,
That I have doomed you to extermination?

[KING *and* RUTH *hold a pistol to each ear.*

KING. Have mercy on us, hear us, ere you slaughter.
FRED. I do not think I ought to listen to you.
  Yet, mercy should alloy our stern resentment,
  And so I will be merciful—say on.

TRIO.—RUTH, KING, *and* FRED.

When first you left our pirate fold
  We tried to cheer our spirits faint,
According to our customs old,
  With quips and quibbles quaint.
But all in vain the quips we heard,
  We lay and sobbed upon the rocks,
Until to somebody occurred
  A curious paradox.

FRED.   A paradox!
KING *(laughing).*   A paradox.
RUTH.   A most ingenious paradox.
  We've quips and quibbles heard in flocks,
  But none to beat this paradox!
  Ha! ha! ha! ha! ho! ho! ho! ho!

KING.   We knew your taste for curious quips,
  For cranks and contradictions queer,
  And with the laughter on our lips,
  We wished you had been there to hear.
  We said, "If we could tell it him,
    How Frederic would the joke enjoy,"
  And so we've risked both life and limb
    To tell it to our boy.
FRED. *(interested).*
    That paradox? That paradox!
KING *and* RUTH *(laughing).*
    That most ingenious paradox!
  We've quips and quibbles heard in flocks,
  But none to beat that paradox!
  Ha, ha, ha, ha! ho, ho, ho, ho!

CHANT.—KING.

For some ridiculous reason, to which, however, I've no desire to
  be disloyal,
Some person in authority, I don't know who—very likely the
  Astronomer Royal—
Has decided that, although for such a beastly month as February
  twenty-eight days as a general rule are plenty,
One year in every four his days shall be reckoned as nine and
  twenty.
Through some singular coincidence—I shouldn't be surprised if it
  were owing to the agency of an ill-natured fairy—
You are the victim of this clumsy arrangement, having been born
  in leap year, on the twenty-ninth of February,
And so, by a simple arithmetical process, you'll easily discover,
That though you've lived twenty-one years, yet, if we go by
  birthdays, you're only five and a little bit over!
RUTH.   Ha! ha! ha! ha!
KING.   Ho! ho! ho! ho!
FRED.   Dear me!

Let's see! *(Counting on fingers.)*
Yes, yes; with yours my figures do agree!

ALL. Ha, ha, ha, ha! Ho, ho, ho, ho! *(FREDERIC more amused
than any.)*

FRED.   How quaint the ways of paradox!
  At common sense she gaily mocks!
  Though counting in the usual way,
    Years twenty-one I've been alive,
  Yet, reckoning by my natal day,
    I am a little boy of five!
ALL.   He is a little boy of five. Ha, ha!
  At common sense she gaily mocks;
  So quaint a way is paradox.
ALL.   Ha, ha, ha, ha!
KING.   Ho, ho, ho, ho!
RUTH.   Ha, ha, ha, ha!
FRED.   Ha, ha, ha, ha!
ALL. Ho, ho, ho, ho!
    [RUTH *and* KING *throw themselves back on seats,*
        exhausted with laughter.]
FRED. Upon my word, this is most curious—most absurdly
whimsical. Five and a quarter! No one would think it to look at
me.
RUTH. You are glad now, I'll be bound, that you spared us.
You would never have forgiven yourself when you discovered
that you had killed *two of your comrades.*
FRED. My comrades?
KING. I'm afraid you don't appreciate the delicacy of your
position. You were apprenticed to us—
FRED. Until I reached my twenty-first year.
KING. No, until you reached your twenty-first *birthday*
(producing document), and, going by birthdays, you are as yet only
five and a quarter.
FRED. You don't mean to say you are going to hold me to
that?
KING. No, we merely remind you of the fact, and leave the rest
to your sense of duty.
FRED. *(wildly).* Don't put it on that footing! As I was merciful
to you just now, be merciful to me! I implore you not to insist on
the letter of your bond just as the cup of happiness is at my lips!
RUTH. We insist on nothing; we content ourselves with
pointing out to you *your duty.*
FRED. *(after a pause).* Well, you have appealed to my sense of
duty, and my duty is only too clear. I abhor your infamous
calling; I shudder at the thought that I have ever been mixed up
with it; but duty is before all—at any price I will do my duty!
KING. Bravely spoken. Come, you are one of us once more.
FRED. Lead on; I follow. *(Suddenly.)* Oh, horror!
KING *and* RUTH. What is the matter?
FRED. Ought I to tell you? No, no, I cannot do it; and yet, as
one of your band—
KING. Speak out, I charge you, by that sense of conscien-
tiousness to which we have never yet appealed in vain.
FRED. General Stanley, the father of my Mabel—
KING *and* RUTH. Yes, yes!
FRED. He escaped from you on the plea that he was an orphan?
KING. He did.
FRED. It breaks my heart to betray the honoured father of the
girl I adore, but, as your apprentice, I have no alternative. It is
my duty to tell you that General Stanley is no orphan.

KING and RUTH. What!

FRED. More than that, he never was one!

KING. And I to understand that, to save his contemptible life, he dared to practise on our credulous simplicity? (FREDERIC *nods as he weeps*.) Our revenge shall be swift and terrible. We will go and collect our band and attack Tremorden Castle this very night.

FRED. But—

KING. Not a word. He is doomed. *(Goes up and down stage.)*

TRIO.

KING *and* RUTH.	FREDERIC.
Away, away, my heart's on fire,	Away, away, ere I expire—
I burn this base deception to repay,	I find my duty hard to do to-day!
This very day my vengeance dire	My heart is filled with anguish dire,
Shall glut itself in gore.	It strikes me to the core.
Away, away!	Away, away!

KING.   With falsehood foul
        He tricked us of our brides.
        Let vengeance howl;
        The pirate so decides.
        Our nature stern
        He softened with his lies,
        And in return,
        To-night the traitor dies.

ALL.   Yes, yes; to-night the traitor dies.

RUTH *(crosses to* FREDERIC*)*.
        To-night he dies.

KING.   Yes, or early to-morrow.

FRED.   His girls likewise?

RUTH.   They will welter in sorrow.

KING.   The one soft spot—

FRED.   In their natures they cherish,
        And all who plot—

RUTH.   To abuse it shall perish!

ALL.   Yes, all who plot—

KING.   To abuse it shall perish!
        Away, away, etc.

[*Exeunt* KING *and* RUTH. FREDERIC *throws himself on a stone in blank despair.*

Enter MABEL.

RECITATIVE.—MABEL.

All is prepared, your gallant crew await you.
My Frederic in tears? It cannot be
That lion-heart quails at the coming conflict?

FRED. No, Mabel, no. A terrible disclosure
Has just been made! Mabel, my dearly loved one,
I bound myself to serve the pirate captain
until I reached my one and twentieth birthday—

MAB. But you are twenty-one?

FRED.   I've just discovered
That I was born in leap year, and that birthday
Will not be reached by me till 1940.

MAB. Oh, horrible! catastrophe appalling!

FRED. And so, farewell!

MAB.   No, no! Oh, Frederic, hear me.

DUET.—MABEL *and* FREDERIC.

MAB.   Stay, Frederic, stay!
        They have no legal claim;
        No shadow of a shame
        Will fall upon thy name.
        Stay, Frederic, stay!

FRED.   Nay, Mabel, nay,
        To-night I quit these walls.
        The thought my soul appals,
        But when stern duty calls,
        I must obey.

MAB.   Stay, Frederic, stay—

FRED.   Nay, Mabel, nay—

MAB.   They have no claim—

FRED.   But duty's name!
        The thought my soul appals,
        But when stern duty calls,
        I must obey.

BALLAD.—MABEL *(kneels)*.

Oh, leave me not to pine
   Alone and desolate;
No fate seemed fair as mine,
   No happiness so great.
And nature, day by day,
   Has sung, in accents clear,
This joyous roundelay,
   ''He loves thee—he is here.
        Fal-la, fa-la, fa-la.''

FRED.   Ah, must I leave thee here
        In endless night to dream,
        Where joy is dark and drear,
        And sorrow all supreme!
        Where nature, day by day,
        Will sing, in altered tone,
        This weary roundelay,
        ''He loves thee—he is gone.
           Fa-la, fa-la, fa-la.''
        He loves thee, he is gone. *(Rises.)*

FRED.   In 1940 I of age shall be.
        I'll then return, and claim you—I declare it.

MAB.   It seems so long!

FRED.   Swear that, till then, you will be true to me.

MAB.   Yes, I'll be strong!
        By all the Stanleys dead and gone,
        I swear it!

ENSEMBLE.

Oh, here is love, and here is truth,
   And here is food for joyous laughter.
He }
She } will be faithful to { his } { her } sooth
   Till we are wed, and even after.

What joy to know that though $\left\{ \begin{array}{c} He \\ I \end{array} \right\}$ must

Embrace piratical adventures,

$\left. \begin{array}{c} He \\ She \end{array} \right\}$ will be faithful to $\left\{ \begin{array}{c} his \\ her \end{array} \right\}$ trust

Till $\left\{ \begin{array}{c} he\ is \\ I\ am \end{array} \right\}$ out of $\left\{ \begin{array}{c} his \\ my \end{array} \right\}$ indentures.

FRED. Farewell! Adieu!

BOTH. Farewell! Adieu!

[FREDERIC *rushes to window and leaps out.*]

MAB. *(feeling pulse).*

Yes, I am brave! Oh, family descent,
How great thy charm, thy sway how excellent!
Come, one and all, undaunted men in blue;
A crisis, now, affairs are coming to.

Enter POLICE, marching in single file.

SERG.　　Though in body and in mind,
　　　　　　　　Tarantara! tarantara!
　　　We are timidly inclined,
　　　　　　　　Tarantara!
　　　And anything but blind,
　　　　　　　　Tarantara! tarantara!
　　　To the danger that's behind,
　　　　　　　　Tarantara!
　　　Yet, when the danger's near,
　　　　　　　　Tarantara! tarantara!
　　　We manage to appear
　　　　　　　　Tarantara!
　　　As insensible to fear
　　　As anybody here.
　　　　　　　　Tarantara!
　　　Tarantara! tarantara, ra—ra—ra—ra!

MAB. Sergeant, approach. Young Frederic was to have led you to death and glory.

ALL. That is not a pleasant way of putting it.

MAB. No matter; he will not so lead you, for he has allied himself once more with his old associates.

ALL. He has acted shamefully.

MAB. You speak falsely. You know nothing about it. He has acted nobly.

ALL. He has acted nobly.

MAB. Dearly as I loved him before, his heroic sacrifice to his sense of duty has endeared him to me tenfold. He has done his duty. I will do mine. Go ye, and do yours.　　　[*Exit* MABEL.

ALL. Very well.

SERG. This is perplexing.

ALL. We cannot understand it at all.

SERG. Still he is actuated by a sense of duty—

ALL. That makes a difference, of course. At the same time we repeat, we cannot understand it at all.

SERG. No matter; our course is clear. We must do our best to capture these pirates alone. It is most distressing to us to be the agents whereby our erring fellow-creatures are deprived of that liberty which is so dear to all—but we should have thought of that before we joined the force.

ALL. We should.

SERG. It is too late now!

ALL. It is.

SONG.—SERGEANT.

　　　　When a felon's not engaged in his employment—
ALL.　　　　　　　　His employment,
　　　　Or maturing his felonious little plans—
ALL.　　　　　　　　Little plans,
SERG.　His capacity for innocent enjoyment—
ALL.　　　　　　　　'Cent enjoyment,
SERG.　Is just as great as any honest man's—
ALL.　　　　　　　　Honest man's.
SERG.　Our feelings we with difficulty smother—
ALL.　　　　　　　　'Culty smother,
SERG.　When constabulary duty's to be done—
ALL.　　　　　　　　To be done,
SERG.　Ah, take one consideration with another—
ALL.　　　　　　　　With another,
SERG.　A policeman's lot is not a happy one.
ALL.　When constabulary duty's to be done,
　　　　The policeman's lot is not a happy one.

SERG.　When the enterprising burglar's not a-burgling—
ALL.　　　　　　　　Not a-burgling,
SERG.　When the cut-throat isn't occupied in crime—
ALL.　　　　　　　　'Pied in crime,
SERG.　He loves to hear the little brook a-gurgling—
ALL.　　　　　　　　Brook a-gurgling,
SERG.　And listen to the merry village chime—
ALL.　　　　　　　　Village chime.
SERG.　When the coster's finished jumping on his mother—
ALL.　　　　　　　　On his mother,
SERG.　He loves to lie a-basking in the sun—
ALL.　　　　　　　　In the sun.
SERG.　Ah, take one consideration with another—
ALL.　　　　　　　　With another,
SERG.　The policeman's lot is not a happy one.
　　　　When constabulary duty's to be done—
　　　　　　　　To be done,
　　　　The policeman's lot is not a happy one—
　　　　　　　　Happy one.

CHORUS OF PIRATES *(without, in the distance).*

A rollicking band of pirates we,
Who, tired of tossing on the sea,
Are trying their hands in a burglaree,
　　　With weapons grim and gory.

SERG. Hush, hush! I hear them on the manor poaching;
With stealthy step the pirates are approaching.

CHORUS OF PIRATES *(resumed nearer).*

We are not coming for plate of gold—
A story General Stanley's told—
We seek a penalty fifty-fold
　　　For General Stanley's story.

POL.　　They seek a penalty—
PIR. *(without).*　　　　　Fifty-fold;
　　　We seek a penalty—
POL.　　　　　　　　Fifty-fold;
ALL.　$\left\{ \begin{array}{c} We \\ They \end{array} \right\}$ seek a penalty fifty-fold

POL.   For General Stanley's story.
           They come in force, with stealthy stride,
           Our obvious course is now—to hide.

[POLICE conceal themselves in aisle. As they do so, the PIRATES, with
RUTH and FREDERIC, are seen appearing at ruined window. They
enter cautiously. SAMUEL is laden with burglarious tools and pistols,
etc.

CHORUS.—PIRATES *(very loud).*

           With cat-like tread,
               Upon our prey we steal;
           In silence dread
               Our cautious way we feel.
POL. *(pianissimo).*   Tarantara! tarantara!
PIR.   No sound at all,
               We never speak a word,
           A fly's foot-fall
               Could be distinctly heard—
POL.   Tarantara! tarantara!
PIR.   Ha! ha!
               Ho! ho!
           So stealthily the pirate creeps
           While all the household soundly sleeps.
               Ha! ha! ho! ho!
POL. *(pianissimo).*   Tarantara! tarantara!
(Forte.)   Tarantara!
SAM. *(distributing implements to various members of the gang).*
           Here's your crowbar and your centrebit,
           Your life preserver—you may want to hit;
           Your silent matches, your dark lantern seize,
           Take your file and your skeletonic keys.
ALL *(fortissimo).*   With cat-like tread, etc.

RECITATIVE.

FRED.   Hush, not a word. I see a light inside.
           The Major-General comes, so quickly hide.
GEN. *(without).*
               Yes, yes, the Major-General comes.
PIR.   He comes.
GEN. *(entering in dressing-gown, carrying a light).*
               Yes, yes, I come.
POL.   He comes.
GEN.   Yes, yes, I come.
ALL.   The Major-General comes.   [*Exit* FREDERIC.

SOLO.—GENERAL.

           Tormented with the anguish dread
               Of falsehood unatoned,
           I lay upon my sleepless bed,
               And tossed and turned and groaned.
           The man who finds his conscience ache
               No peace at all enjoys,
           And as I lay in bed awake
               I thought I heard a noise.
PIR.   He thought he heard a noice—ha! ha!
POL.   He thought he heard a noise—ha! ha!   *(Very loud.)*
GEN.   No, all is still
               In dale, on hill;

           My mind is set at ease.
               So still the scene—
               It must have been
           The sighing of the breeze.

BALLAD.—GENERAL.

           Sighing softly to the river
               Comes the loving breeze,
           Setting nature all a-quiver,
               Rustling through the trees—
ALL.   Through the trees.
GEN.   And the brook in rippling measure
               Laughs for very love,
           While the poplars, in their pleasure,
               Wave their arms above.
                                   (Goes up stage and returns.)
POL. *and* PIR. Yes, the trees, for very love,
           Wave their leafy arms above,
               River, river, little river,
               May thy loving prosper ever.
           Heaven speed thee, poplar tree;
           May thy wooing happy be.

GEN.   Yet, the breeze is but a rover;
               When he wings away,
           Brook and poplar mourn a lover!
               Sighing well-a-day!
ALL.   Well-a-day!
GEN.   Ah, the doing and undoing
               That the rogue could tell!
           When the breeze is out a-wooing,
               Who can woo so well?
POL. *and* PIR. Shocking tales the rogue could tell,
           Nobody can woo so well.
               Pretty brook, thy dream is over,
               For thy love is but a rover
           Sad the lot of poplar trees
           Courted by the fickle breeze.

Enter the GENERAL'S *daughters, all in white peignoirs and*
nightcaps, and carrying lighted candles.

GIRLS. Now, what is this, and what is that, and why does father
           leave his rest
       At such a time as this, so very incompletely dressed?
       Dear father is, and always was, the most methodical of
           men;
       It's his invariable rule to go to bed at half-past ten.
       What strange occurrence can it be that calls dear father
           from his rest
       At such a time of night as this, so very incompletely
           dressed?
KING *(springing up).*
           Forward, my men, and seize that General there!
                       [*They seize the* GENERAL.
PIR.   Ha! ha! we are the pirates, so despair—
KING.   With base deceit
               You worked upon our feelings
           Revenge is sweet,
               And flavours all our dealings.
           With courage rare

And resolution manly,
For death prepare,
Unhappy General Stanley!

FRED. *(coming forward).*
Alas, alas, unhappy General Stanley!

GEN.   Frederic here! Oh, joy! Oh, rapture!
Summon your men and effect their capture.

MAB.   Frederic, save us!

FRED.   Beautiful Mabel,
I would if I could, but I am not able.

PIR.   He's telling the truth, he is not able.

POL. *(pianissimo).*   Tarantara! tarantara.

MAB. *(wildly).* Is he to die, unshriven—unannealed?

GIRLS.   Oh, spare him!

MAB.   Will no one in his cause a weapon wield?

GIRLS.   Oh, spare him!

POL. *(springing up).*
Yes, we are here, though hitherto concealed!

GIRLS.   Oh, rapture!

POL.   So to our prowess, pirates, quickly yield!

GIRLS.   Oh, rapture!

[*A struggle ensues between* PIRATES *and* POLICE. *Eventually the* POLICE *are overcome, and fall prostrate, the* PIRATES *standing over them with drawn swords.* LADIES *run down.*

CHORUS *of* POLICE *and* PIRATES.

You }
We } triumph now, for well we trow
Our mortal career's cut short,
No pirate band will take its stand
At the Central Criminal Court.

SERG.   To gain a brief advantage you've contrived,
But your proud triumph will not be long-lived.

KING.   Don't say you are orphans, for we know that game.

SERG.   On your allegiance we've a nobler claim.
We charge you yield, in Queen Victoria's name!

KING. *(baffled).*   You do!

POL.   We do;
We charge you yield, in Queen Victoria's name!
[PIRATES *kneel,* POLICE *stand over them triumphantly.*

KING.   We yield at once, with humbled mien,
Because, with all our faults, we love our Queen,

POL.   Yes, yes; with all their faults, they love their Queen.

LADIES. Yes, yes; with all, *etc.*
[POLICE, *holding* PIRATES *by the collar, take out handkerchiefs and weep.*

RUTH *enters.*

GEN.   Away with them, and place them at the bar.

RUTH.   One moment; let me tell you who they are.
They are no members of the common throng;
They are all noblemen, who have gone wrong!

GEN., POL., *and* GIRLS. What, *all* noblemen?

KING *and* PIR.   Yes, all noblemen!

GEN., POL., *and* GIRLS. What, *all*?

KING.   Well, nearly all!

GEN.   No Englishmen unmoved that statement hears,
Because, with all our faults, we love our House of
      Peers.
[*All kneel to* PIRATES.

RECITATIVE.—GENERAL.

I pray you, pardon me, ex-Pirate King,
Peers will be peers, and youth will have its fling.
Resume your ranks and legislative duties,
And take my daughters, all of whom are beauties.

FINALE.

MAB.   Poor wandering ones,
Though ye have surely strayed,
Take heart of grace,
Your steps retrace,
   Poor wandering ones!
Poor wandering ones,
If such poor love as ours
   Can help you find
   True peace of mind,
Why, take it, it is yours!

ALL.   Poor wandering ones, *etc.*

THE END.

Patience

or Bunthorne's Bride

Patience is known as the Aesthetic Opera. It is indeed a lampoon on the æsthetic movement which was in full bloom in the 1880s, and there have been numerous speculations on the personalities said to be represented by Bunthorne and Grosvenor (Morris, Rosetti, Swinburne, Whistler and Wilde). Gilbert had been intending to make an opera out of his *Bab Ballad* of 1867, 'The Rival Curates', but realizing how tasteless a mockery of the clergy would be, his curates became rival æsthetes. This unique, contemporary artistic-social movement offered a far

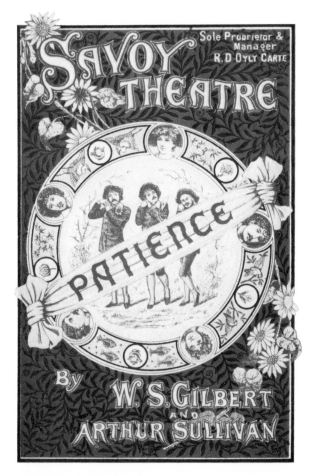

Block-printed æsthetic programme cover, with portraits of characters and relevant motifs, for the transfer of *Patience* to the new Savoy Theatre on 10 October 1881.

greater range of dramatic possibilities than the Church.

Gilbert portrays a complete social stratum of idle rich, ultimately searching for true simplicity but getting ensnared by false idols on the way. The pre-Raphaelite concept of mediaeval courtly love — love including eroticism and all that goes with it except for physical sex — is epitomized by the twenty rapturous Lovesick Maidens (county Ladies) in unanimous pursuit of the æsthetic poet Bunthorne. They are obviously jealous of the simple milkmaid Patience, the one woman in whom their poet shows an interest, and they temporarily manage, by æsthetic indoctrination, to destroy her simplicity.

On the male side, the straightforward and patriotic Colonel Calverley, who stands for the Dragoons, is forced to ape the æsthetes in order to regain the women's lost attentions.

Whereas Archibald Grosvenor is only too glad of the excuse to become an everyday young man after languishing in poetic intensity, Bunthorne, the older and more self-indulgent of the two, is unable to drop the pose. There is more than a hint of homosexuality in Bunthorne.

The Baby's Opera of 1877 by Walter Crane, traditional nursery rhymes illustrated with his highly sophisticated æsthetic drawings, may well have been another inspiration for *Patience*, and in any case this curious mixture of traditional simplicity and affectation pervades the opera, being totally realistic in its artificiality.

The ordinary is always too ordinary, and it is this everlasting reality which has made *Patience* one of the most popular and often-performed of all Gilbert and Sullivan operas.

SYNOPSIS

A languorous, hymn-like beginning to the Overture suggests the all-pervading pre-Raphaelite atmosphere of *Patience*, and after lapsing into a bright polka, the music returns to preciousness, making a rather static, stained-glass effect for the twenty rapturous Lovesick Maidens who are waiting outside the pseudo-mediaeval Castle Bunthorne.

The Ladies Angela, Ella and Saphir eulogize the hopelessness of their love but are brought to earth by the mature Lady Jane who informs them that their beloved æsthetic poet, Reginald Bunthorne, is in love with Patience the milkmaid. Their disapproving remarks are cut short by Patience herself, a breath of fresh air in the cloying atmosphere. She pities the Maidens, and her song 'I cannot tell what this love may be' is in skipping, nursery-rhyme style with a 'My Pretty Maid' melody. The Maidens disparage Patience for never having loved and she, in turn, gives them news that their fiancés of the previous year — the Heavy Dragoons — have arrived in the village. Angela disdainfully informs Patience that now, 'etherealized', the Maidens despise their former lovers, and they forthwith file off to greet Bunthorne with a morning carol.

A quick march heralds the Officers of the Dragoons led by their Major, and the rhythm changes to a slow trot for the entrance of the Colonel. His patter song, 'If you want a receipt for that popular mystery...' is a ridiculous list of remarkable personalities, past and contemporary who, when all melted down in a crucible, will produce the Heavy Dragoon.

Lieutenant the Duke of Dunstable, who has joined the Dragoons in order to become ordinary, bemoans the fate that wealth and rank have bestowed upon him. However, his introvert musings are interrupted by the arrival of Bunthorne in the throes of composition and pursued by the Ladies. They ignore the Dragoons and continue their adulation of Bunthorne, while the affronted soldiers chorus their amazement. Bunthorne, revelling in these attentions, slyly peers round his book to see the Ladies kneeling in supplication. The Colonel, the Major and Duke question their respective fiancées Angela, Saphir and Jane on the meaning of their change of heart. 'Bunthorne — he has idealized us!' replies Jane.

With a tremendous show of giving birth to his composition, Bunthorne completes it, and the Dragoons are obliged to witness a rendering of it

The twenty love-sick maidens idolizing Bunthorne (C. H. Workman) while their former loves, the Dragoon Guards, survey them angrily.

addressed to Patience who has just arrived. It is a mock heroic verse, 'Oh, Hollow! Hollow! Hollow!', cynically deploring the poet's inability to portray the agonies of a suffering maiden because he is aware that a chemist's prescription will provide instant cure. Patience, although frightened by Bunthorne's attentions, unashamedly pronounces the verse to be nonsense.

Now, having witnessed the cause of the Ladies' infatuation, the Dragoons object. But they are quashed by an attack on their nonentity: 'Oh, be Early English ere it is too late!' cries Saphir. Lady Jane deplores the primary colours of their uniforms and makes suggested improvements, derived from all ages, to which the Colonel objects with his rousing 'When I first put this uniform on...'. Although in quick march time, with an underlying rat-at-tat, Sullivan endows it with a smack of inimitable patriotism.

Alone at last, Bunthorne makes a melodramatic confesssion. He is a sham, and detests the poses he adopts. 'If you're anxious for to shine in the high æsthetic line as a man of culture rare,...' is a recipe offering qualifications for joining the Aesthetic Movement and echoes the Colonel's song 'If you want a receipt ...'.

Bunthorne welcomes Patience's arrival and attempts to make suggestive overtures to her. She misunderstands him, is frightened of him, says she could not possibly love him and expresses a dislike of his poetry. He goes so far as to agree with her but begs her to keep the secret from his admirers. Rejected, Bunthorne exits on his poem, 'Heart Foam' — 'the dust of an earthy today is the earth of a dusty tomorrow'.

Patience, in tears, is confronted by Angela and she demands to know the meaning of this upsetting love. 'It is the one unselfish emotion in this whirlpool of grasping greed...' Angela explains, somewhat disdainfully. She then quizzes Patience about her never having loved and coaxingly suggests that there must have been someone. Angela disqualifies Patience's great-aunt, but readily urges Patience on in the baby-tripping duet, 'Long years ago — fourteen, maybe...' where Patience describes her childhood playfellow — a little boy!

Patience, now smarting with shame and guilt at loving no one, determines to find a lover. At once, a handsome young stranger — Archibald Grosvenor the idyllic poet — appears and launches into his charming and simple love song, 'Willow Waly', the melody a variant on 'My Pretty Maid'.

Grosvenor is Patience's childhood love, grown out of recognition. In a happy reunion he explains that his good looks make him beloved by any woman who sets eyes on him. Patience suggests he should moderate his picturesque style, but he believes that his mission is to display his beauty for the delectation of others. However, he declares his fifteen-year-old love for Patience and she momentarily vows everlasting love for him. Suddenly smitten by conscience, she declares that to monopolize Archibald would be selfish. Nothing should prevent him from loving her but she may not love him. She bids farewell in a reprise of 'Willow Waly'.

Bunthorne is about to choose a bride. He is led in by the Maidens 'classically dancing and playing their archaic instruments in Grecian mode'. Bunthorne is decked in rose garlands and led on strings of roses like a prize bull, by Angela and Saphir. By contrast, the Dragoons enter to a businesslike march and question the proceedings. Bunthorne explains that on his Solicitor's advice he has decided to put himself up 'to be raffled for'. The Dragoons are as apprehensive as the Maidens are excited, and appeal to their fiancés not to take part. The Duke makes a mock-heroic appeal in Irish tenor style, forcing the Dragoons to sigh, kneel and weep with him at the appropriate moments.

Bunthorne impatiently starts up an auctioneering patter, exalting himself as a 'judge of blue and white', to get the ticket-selling started. All the Ladies crowd round him while the Dragoons affect indifference. Bunthorne is horrified to find Jane last in the queue for a ticket. Nevertheless she joins the Maidens in their half-peeping blindfold waltz, a kind of pass-the-parcel number, when one is aware that a coup will take place at any moment. Almost *parlando* in the background, Bunthorne asks Jane to draw. 'He loves me best!' she cries. 'I want to know the worst!' he asides. As Jane is about to draw, Patience dashes in, stops the proceedings and offers herself to Bunthorne. To the disgust of the Ladies Bunthorne accepts the Milkmaid's overtures, smugly suggesting that she has secretly been in love with him for weeks. 'No, Mr Bunthorne, no — you're wrong again;...' and Patience goes on to explain that the dutiful mission of loving Bunthorne would be love indeed. 'Exactly so!' echo the Dragoons, to the tune of 'You're wrong again' after each of Patience's remarks. The raffle is abandoned, there is no chance for anyone but Patience, so the Ladies return happily to their former lovers. The sextet of reconciliation is a kind of Old Lang Syne, with words by Gilbert in 'The Lost Chord' vein — almost challenging Sullivan to produce a parody on his own work. (It is said to be in imitation of Smart.)

A Bizet-like melody heralds the approach of Archibald Grosvenor, reading and ignoring everybody. The Ladies, embracing their lovers, are 'strangely fascinated' by him and, withdrawing from the Dragoons, they fall in love with Archibald. The Dragoons are disgusted, Bunthorne is jealous and Patience despairing over her fickle fiancé.

Jane is discovered alone in a sylvan glade leaning on her cello. The chorus of Maidens is heard in the distance. They have deserted Bunthorne and only Jane remains faithful to him. Still hoping to 'catch' Bunthorne, she bemoans her encroaching middle age in a melodramatic, grand operatic recitative. Gilbert's words are so graphic that the sentiment is

Alice Barnett as the first Lady Jane, wearing the costume designed for her by Gilbert and embodying a variety of Japanese and classical styles.

too unvarnished to be funny: 'Silvered is the raven hair,...' is a toddling, nostalgic song enumerating the traits of middle age against those of youth.

Grosvenor appears, pursued by Maidens just as Bunthorne was. His thoughts are of Patience, but he cannot resist the admiration of the Ladies and is persuaded by them to read some of his own poems — banal if not suggestive. The entranced Maidens beg for more, and before taking a half day, after a week of being followed, Grosvenor sings them the fable of 'The Magnet and the Churn', a tale in Edward Lear vein, embroidered with Gilbertian puns — a nursery-rhyme tune with an accompaniment suggestive of hardware.

When the Maidens have departed, Patience appears and a ridiculous love scene ensues. She vows she only loves Bunthorne out of duty, making fond approaches to Grosvenor but refusing to let him near her. They bid a fond adieu and Patience is left crying as Bunthorne approaches, trying to shake off Lady Jane. He is obviously jealous of Grosvenor, tired of Patience and accuses her of not knowing what love is. Her charming ballad, 'Love is a plaintive song', is a waltz in the line of 'Poor Wandering One' from *The Pirates of Penzance*. Patience goes away weeping, but Bunthorne is too preoccupied with trying to outdo Grosvenor to notice. Lady Jane finally manages to ingratiate herself by offering to assist him and 'Sing "Booh to you — Pooh, pooh to you" ' (the spirited number that forms part of the Overture), is a discussion between Jane and Bunthorne of the means they will use to tackle Grosvenor.

Now the Colonel, the Major and the Duke enter, transformed into æsthetes, contorting themselves to emulate the correct poses. In the trio, 'You hold yourself like this...' (reminiscent of a halting 'Looby Loo') they practise their attitudes. Angela and Saphir discover them and are touched and delighted. The Colonel makes a quick military reckoning on how the two girls shall be apportioned, and it is finally decided by the Duke, in an abandoned dancing quintet, that the Colonel shall have Angela, and the Major Saphir.

In the confrontation between Grosvenor and Bunthorne, Archibald is persuaded, after ugly threats from Bunthorne, to give up his æstheticism and become absolutely 'commonplace'. Both æsthetes are immensely relieved, their jolly duet 'When I go out of door,' contrasts the 'Out of the way young man' with the 'Every day young man', and is a witty

'Suppose for one moment I were to curse you?' George
Grossmith as Bunthorne threatening Grosvenor (Rutland
Barrington). First production of *Patience*, 23 April 1881.

and much-quoted social document. Bunthorne is still
dancing with delight when Patience finds him. She is
amazed at the change and doubts that he will keep
his resolution to model himself on Grosvenor and be
'mildly cheerful'. When he insists that he really is
reformed, Patience is delighted, but a second later
she is smitten with the realization that it would be
wrong to love such a perfect being.

Bunthorne is about to retract when Grosvenor
appears, followed by the Maidens who have paired
off with the Dragoons and now dance cheerfully—
their languishing attitudes discarded. Patience is
horrified to find her Archibald with hair cut, and
commonplace, but suddenly she realizes that he is no
longer perfect and that she is free to love him. They
fall into each other's arms. 'Crushed again!' moans
Bunthorne. Jane, still æsthetic, sees her moment has
come and rushes to his side. This time he welcomes
her advances. But now a fanfare announces the
Colonel, the Major and the Duke, and the Colonel
proclaims that the Duke will select a bride. In
response to the Duke's call for the truly lovely to
step forward, all comply except Jane and Patience.
The Duke then unexpectedly selects plain Jane, who
leaves Bunthorne and flies to him. 'Crushed again!'
Bunthorne reiterates.

There is a reprise of the dancing quintet as the
happy couples rejoice, their song ending:
  'Each of us will wed the other,
  Nobody be Bunthorne's Bride!'

PATIENCE;

OR

BUNTHORNE'S BRIDE.

AN ENTIRELY NEW AND ORIGINAL ÆSTHETIC OPERA,

IN TWO ACTS.

First produced at the Opéra Comique Theatre, 23 April 1881

DRAMATIS PERSONÆ

COLONEL CALVERLEY		bass
MAJOR MURGATROYD	[*Officers of Dragoon Guards*]	baritone
LIEUT. THE DUKE OF DUNSTABLE		tenor
REGINALD BUNTHORNE [*a Fleshly Poet*]		baritone
ARCHIBALD GROSVENOR [*an Idyllic Poet*]		baritone
MR. BUNTHORNE'S SOLICITOR		

Chorus of Officers of Dragoon Guards.

THE LADY ANGELA		mezzo-soprano
THE LADY SAPHIR	[*Rapturous Maidens*]	soprano
THE LADY ELLA		soprano
THE LADY JANE		contralto
PATIENCE [*a Dairy Maid*]		soprano

Chorus of Rapturous Maidens.

ACT I.

EXTERIOR OF CASTLE BUNTHORNE.

ACT II.

A GLADE.

PATIENCE;

OR,

BUNTHORNE'S BRIDE.

ACT I.

SCENE—*Exterior of Castle Bunthorne. Entrance to castle by draw-bridge over moat. Young* LADIES *dressed in æsthetic draperies are grouped about the stage. They play on lutes, mandolines, etc., as they sing, and all are in the last stage of despair.* ANGELA, ELLA, *and* SAPHIR *lead them.*

CHORUS.

Twenty love-sick maidens we,
Love-sick all against our will.
Twenty years hence we shall be
Twenty love-sick maidens still!

SOLO.—ANGELA.

Love feeds on hope, they say, or love will die—
ALL.   Ah, miserie!
Yet my love lives, although no hope have I!
ALL.   Ah, miserie!
Alas, poor heart, go hide thyself away—
ALL.   Ah, miserie!
To weeping concords tune thy roundelay!
ALL.   Ah, miserie!

CHORUS.

All our love is all for one,
Yet that love he heedeth not,
He is coy and cares for none,
Sad and sorry is our lot!
Ah, miserie!

SOLO.—ELLA.

Go, breaking heart,
Go, dream of love requited!
Go, foolish heart,
Go, dream of lovers plighted;
Go, madcap heart,
Go, dream of never waking;
And in thy dream
Forget that thou art breaking!

ALL.   Ah, miserie!

ANG. There is a strange magic in this love of ours! Rivals as we all are in the affections of our Reginald, the very hopelessness of our love is a bond that binds us to one another!

SAPH. Jealousy is merged in misery. While he, the very cynosure of our eyes and hearts remains icy insensible—what have we to strive for?

ELLA. The love of maidens is, to him, as interesting as the taxes!

SAPH. Would that it were! He pays his taxes.

ANG. And cherishes the receipts!

Enter LADY JANE.

JANE *(suddenly)*. Fools!

ANG. I beg your pardon?

JANE. Fools and blind! The man loves—wildly loves!

ANG. But whom? None of us!

JANE. No, none of us. His weird fancy has lighted, for the nonce, on Patience—the village milkmaid!

SAPH. On, Patience? Oh, it cannot be!

JANE. Bah! But yesterday I caught him in her dairy, eating fresh butter with a table-spoon. To-day he is not well!

SAPH. But Patience boasts that she has never loved—that love is, to her, a sealed book! Oh, he cannot be serious.

JANE. 'Tis but a fleeting fancy—'twill quickly pass away. *(Aside.)* Oh, Reginald, if you but knew what a wealth of golden love is waiting for you, stored up in this rugged old bosom of mine, the milkmaid's triumph would be short indeed!

[*All sigh wearily.*

[PATIENCE *appears on an eminence. She looks down with pity on the despondent* LADIES.

RECITATIVE.

PA.   Still brooding on their mad infatuation!
        I thank thee, Love, thou comest not to me;
    Far happier I, free from thy ministration,
        Than dukes or duchesses who love, can be!

SAPH. *(looking up)*. 'Tis Patience—happy girl! Loved by a Poet!

PA.   Your pardon, ladies. I intrude upon you! *(Going.)*

ANG.   Nay, pretty child, come hither. Is it true
        That you have never loved?

PA.   Most true indeed.

SOPRANOS. Most marvellous!

CONTRALTOS.   And most deplorable!

SONG.—PATIENCE.

I cannot tell what this love may be
That cometh to all but not to me.
It cannot be kind as they'd imply,
Or why do these gentle ladies sigh?
It cannot be joy and rapture deep,
Or why do these gentle ladies weep?
It cannot be blissful, as 'tis said,
Or why are their eyes so wondrous red?

Though everywhere true love I see
A-coming to all, but not to me,
I cannot tell what this love may be!
    For I am blithe and I am gay,
    While they sit sighing all night, all day.
    Think of the gulf 'twixt them and me,
    "Fal la la la!"—and "Miserie!"

CHORUS.   Yes, she is blithe, etc.

PA.   If love is a thorn, they show no wit

Who foolishly hug and foster it.
If love is a weed, how simple they
Who gather and gather it, day by day!
If love is a nettle that makes you smart,
Why do you wear it next your heart?
And if it be none of these, say I,
Why do you sit and sob and sigh?
        Though everywhere, etc.

CHORUS.   For she is blithe, etc.

ANG. Ah, Patience, if you have never loved, you have never known true happiness! *(All sigh.)*

PA. But the truly happy always seem to have so much on their minds. The truly happy never seem quite well.

JANE. There is a transcendentality of delirium—an acute accentuation of supremest ecstacy—which the earthy might easily mistake for indigestion. But it is *not* indigestion—it is æsthetic transfiguration! *(To the others.)* Enough of babble. Come!

PA. But I have some news for you. The 35th Dragoon Guards have halted in the village, and are even now on their way to this very spot.

ANG. The 35th Dragoon Guards!

SAPH. They are fleshly men, of full habit!

ELLA. We care nothing for Dragoon Guards!

PA. But, bless me, you were all in love with them a year ago!

SAPH. A year ago!

ANG. My poor child, you don't understand these things. A year ago they were very well in our eyes, but since then our tastes have been etherealized, our perceptions exalted. *(To the others.)* Come! it is time to lift up our voices in morning carol to our Reginald. Let us to his door.

[*The* LADIES *go off two and two into the Castle, singing refrain of "Twenty love-sick maidens we," and accompanying themselves on harps and mandolins.* PATIENCE *watches them in surprise, as she climbs the rock by which she entered.*

March. Enter OFFICERS OF DRAGOON GUARDS, *led by* MAJOR.

CHORUS OF DRAGOONS.

The soldiers of our Queen
    Are linked in friendly tether;
Upon the battle scene
    They fight the foe together.
There every mother's son
    Prepared to fight and fall is;
The enemy of one
    The enemy of all is!

Enter COLONEL.

SONG.—COLONEL.

If you want a receipt for that popular mystery,
    Known to the world as a Heavy Dragoon,
Take all the remarkable people in history,
    Rattle them off to a popular tune.
The pluck of Lord Nelson on board of the Victory—
    Genius of Bismarck devising a plan;
The humour of Fielding (which sounds contradictory)—
    Coolness of Paget about to trepan—

The science of Jullien, the eminent musico—
    Wit of Macaulay, who wrote of Queen Anne—
The pathos of Paddy, as rendered by Boucicault—
    Style of the Bishop of Sodor and Man—
The dash of a D'Orsay, divested of quackery—
Narrative powers of Dickens and Thackeray—
Victor Emmanuel—peak-haunting Peveril—
Thomas Aquinas, and Doctor Sacheverell—
Tupper and Tennyson—Daniel Defoe—
Anthony Trollope and Mr. Guizot!
    Take of these elements all that is fusible,
    Melt them all down in a pipkin or crucible,
    Set them to simmer and take off the scum,
    And a Heavy Dragoon is the residuum!

CHORUS.   Yes! yes! yes! yes!
        A Heavy Dragoon is the residuum!

COL. If you want a receipt for this soldierlike paragon,
    Get at the wealth of the Czar (if you can)—
The family pride of a Spaniard from Arragon—
    Force of Mephisto pronouncing a ban—
A smack of Lord Waterford, reckless and rollicky—
    Swagger of Roderick, heading his clan—
The keen penetration of Paddington Pollaky—
    Grace of an Odalisque on a divan,
The genius strategic of Cæsar or Hannibal—
Skill of Sir Garnet in thrashing a cannibal—
Flavour of Hamlet—the Stranger, a touch of him—
Little of Manfred (but not very much of him)—
Beadle of Burlington—Richardson's show—
Mr. Micawber and Madame Tussaud!
    Take of these elements all that is fusible—
    Melt 'em all down in a pipkin or crucible—
    Set 'em to simmer and take off the scum,
    And a Heavy Dragoon is the residuum!

ALL.   Yes! yes! yes! yes!
        A Heavy Dragoon is the residuum!

COL. Well, here we are again on the scene of our former triumphs. But where's the Duke?

Enter DUKE, *listlessly, and in low spirits.*

DUKE. Here I am! *(Sighs.)*
COL. Come, cheer up, don't give way!
DUKE. Oh, for that, I'm as cheerful as a poor devil can be expected to be, who has the misfortune to be a duke, with a thousand a day!
MAJ. Humph! Most men would envy you!
DUKE. Envy *me*? Tell me, Major, are you fond of toffee?
MAJ. Very!
COL. We are all fond of toffee.
ALL. We are!
DUKE. Yes, and toffee in moderation is a capital thing. But to *live* on toffee—toffee for breakfast, toffee for dinner, toffee for tea—to have it supposed that you care for nothing *but* toffee, and that you would consider yourself insulted if anything but toffee were offered to you—how would you like *that*?
COL. I can believe that, under those circumstances, even toffee would become monotonous.

DUKE. For "toffee" read flattery, adulation, and abject deference, carried to such a pitch that I began, at last, to think that man was born bent at an angle of forty-five degrees! Great heavens, what is there to adulate in me! Am I particularly intelligent, or remarkably studious, or excruciatingly witty, or unusually accomplished, or exceptionally virtuous?
COL. You're about as commonplace a young man as ever I saw.
ALL. You are!
DUKE. Exactly! That's it exactly! That describes me to a T! Thank you all very much! Well, I couldn't stand it any longer so I joined this regiment. In the army, thought I, I shall be occasionally snubbed, perhaps even bullied, who knows? The thought was rapture, and here I am.
COL. *(looking off).* Yes, and here are the ladies!
DUKE. But who is the gentleman with the long hair?
COL. I don't know.
DUKE. He seems popular!
COL. He *does* seem popular!

BUNTHORNE *enters followed by* LADIES, *two and two, singing and playing on harps as before. He is composing a poem and quite absorbed. He sees no one, but walks across stage, followed by* LADIES. *They take no notice of* DRAGOONS—*to the surprise and indignation of those* OFFICERS.

CHORUS OF LADIES.

In a melancholy train
    Two and two we walk all day—
Pity those who love in vain
    None so sorrowful as they
        Who can only sigh and say,
        Woe is me, alackaday!

CHORUS OF DRAGOONS.

Now is not this ridiculous—and is not this preposterous?
    A thorough-paced absurdity—explain it if you can.
Instead of rushing eagerly to cherish us and foster us,
    They all prefer this melancholy literary man.
        Instead of slyly peering at us,
        Casting looks endearing at us,
    Blushing at us, flushing at us—flirting with a fan;
They're actually sneering at us, fleering at us, jeering at us!
        Pretty sort of treatment for a military man!
        Pretty sort of treatment for a military man!

ANG.   Mystic poet, hear our prayer,
            Twenty love-sick maidens we—
        Young and wealthy, dark and fair—
            And we die for love of thee!
        Yes, we die for love of thee—
        Twenty love-sick maidens we!

BUN. *(aside—slyly).*   Though my book I seem to scan,
            In a rapt ecstatic way,
        Like a literary man
            Who despises female clay;
        I hear plainly all they say,
        Twenty love-sick maidens they!

OFFICERS (to each other).   He hears plainly, etc.

ELLA.   Though so excellently wise,
       For a moment mortal be,
      Deign to raise thy purple eyes
      From thy heart-drawn poesy.
      Twenty love-sick maidens see—
      Each is kneeling on her knee! (All kneel.)

CHO. of LADIES.   Twenty love-sick, etc.

BUN. (aside).   Though as I remarked before,
       Any one convinced would be
      That some transcendental lore
       Is monopolizing me,
      Round the corner I can see
      Each is kneeling on her knee!

OFFICERS (to each other). Round the corner, etc.

ENSEMBLE.

OFFICERS.	LADIES.	BUNTHORNE (aside).
Now is not this ridiculous, etc.	Mystic poet, hear our prayers, etc.	Though my book I seem to scan, etc.

COL. Angela! what is the meaning of this?

ANG. Oh, sir, leave us; our minds are but ill-attuned to light love-talk.

MAJ. But what in the world has come over you all?

JANE. Bunthorne! *He* has come over us. He has come among us, and he has idealized us.

DUKE. Has he succeeded in idealizing *you?*

JANE. He has!

DUKE. Bravo, Bunthorne!

JANE. My eyes are open; I droop despairingly; I am soulfully intense; I am limp, and I cling!

[*During this* BUNTHORNE *is seen in all the agonies of composition. The* LADIES *are watching him intently as he writhes. At last, he hits on the word he wants and writes it down. A general sense of relief.*

BUN. Finished! At last! Finished!

[*He staggers, overcome with the mental strain, into arms of* COLONEL.

COL. Are you better now?

BUN. Yes—oh, it's you—I am better now. The poem is finished, and my soul had gone out into it. That was all. It was nothing worth mentioning, it occurs three times a day. (*Sees* PATIENCE, *who has entered during this scene.*) Ah, Patience! Dear Patience! (*Holds her hand; she seems frightened.*)

ANG. Will it please you read it to us, sir?

SAPH. This we supplicate. (*All kneel.*)

BUN. Shall I?

All the DRAGOONS. No!

BUN. (annoyed—to PATIENCE). I will read it if *you* bid me!

PA. (much frightened). You can if you like!

BUN. It is a wild, weird, fleshly thing; yet very tender, very yearning, very precious. It is called, "Oh, Hollow! Hollow! Hollow!"

PA. Is it a hunting song?

BUN. A hunting song? No, it is *not* a hunting song. It is the wail of the poet's heart on discovering that everything is commonplace. To understand it, cling passionately to one another and think of faint lilies. (*They do so, as he recites.*)

"OH, HOLLOW! HOLLOW! HOLLOW!"

What time the poet hath hymned
The writhing maid, lithe-limbed,
  Quivering on amaranthine asphodel,
How can he paint her woes,
Knowing, as well he knows,
  That all can be set right with calomel?

When from the poet's plinth
The amorous colocynth
  Yearns for the aloe, faint with rapturous thrills,
How can he hymn their throes
Knowing, as well he knows,
  That they are only uncompounded pills?

Is it, and can it be,
Nature hath this decree,
  Nothing poetic in the world shall dwell?
Or that in all her works
Something poetic lurks,
  Even in colocynth and calomel?
      I cannot tell.

ANG. How purely fragrant!

SAPH. How earnestly precious!

DUKE. Well, it seems to me to be nonsense.

SAPH. Nonsense; yes, perhaps—but, oh, what precious nonsense!

ALL. Ah!

COL. This is all very well; but you seem to forget that you are engaged to us!

SAPH. It can never be. You are not Empyrean. You are not Della Cruscan. You are not even Early English. Oh, be Early English ere it is too late! (OFFICERS *look at each other in astonishment.*)

JANE (looking at uniform). Red and yellow! Primary colours! Oh, South Kensington!

DUKE. We didn't design our uniforms, but we don't see how they could be improved.

JANE. No, you wouldn't. Still there *is* a cobwebby grey velvet, with a tender bloom like cold gravy, which, made Florentine fourteenth century, trimmed with Venetian leather and Spanish altar lace, and surmounted with something Japanese—it matters not what—would at least be Early English! Come maidens.

[*Exeunt* MAIDENS, *two and two, singing, refrain of "Twenty love-sick maidens we." The* OFFICERS *watch them off in astonishment.*

DUKE. Gentlemen, this is an insult to the British uniform.

COL. A uniform that has been as successful in the courts of Venus as in the field of Mars!

SONG.—COLONEL.

When I first put this uniform on,
  I said, as I looked in the glass,
    "It's one to a million
    That any civilian,

My figure and form will surpass.
  Gold lace has a charm for the fair,
  And I've plenty of that, and to spare,
    While a lover's professions,
    When uttered in Hessians,
  Are eloquent everywhere!''
    A fact that I counted upon,
    When I first put this uniform on!

CHORUS OF DRAGOONS.

By a simple coincidence, few
  Could ever have reckoned upon,
The same thing occurred to me, too,
  When I first put this uniform on!

COL.   I said, when I first put it on,
  "It is plain to the veriest dunce
    That ever beauty
    Will feel it her duty
  To yield to its glamour at once.
  They will see that I'm freely gold-laced
  In a uniform handsome and chaste''—
    But the peripatetics
    Of long-haired æsthetics,
  Are very much more to their taste—
    Which I never counted upon
    When I first put this uniform on!

COL.   By a simple coincidence, few
  Could ever have counted upon,
I didn't anticipate that,
  When I first put this uniform on!

[*The* DRAGOONS *go off angrily.*
[*As soon as he is alone,* BUNTHORNE *changes his manner and becomes intensely melodramatic.*

RECITATIVE AND SONG.—BUNTHORNE.

Am I alone,
    And unobserved? I am!
Then let me own
    I'm an æsthetic sham!
This air severe
    Is but a mere
      Veneer
This cynic smile
    Is but a wile
      Of guile!
This costume chaste
    Is but good taste
      Misplaced!

Let me confess!
A languid love for lilies does *not* blight me!
Lank limbs and haggard cheeks do *not* delight me!
I do *not* care for dirty greens
    By any means.
I do *not* long for all one sees
    That's Japanese.
I am *not* fond of uttering platitudes

In stained-glass attitudes.
In short, my mediævalism's affectation,
Born of a morbid love of admiration!

SONG.

If you're anxious for to shine in the high æsthetic line as a man of culture rare,
You must get up all the germs of the transcendental terms, and plant them everywhere.
You must lie upon the daisies, and discourse in novel phrases of your complicated state of mind,
The meaning doesn't matter if it's only idle chatter of a transcendental kind.
    And every one will say,
    As you walk your mystic way,
"If this young man expresses himself in terms too deep for *me*,
Why what a very singularly deep young man this deep young man must be!''

Be eloquent in praise of the very dull old days which have long since passed away,
And convince 'em, if you can, that the reign of good Queen Anne was Culture's palmiest day.
Of course you will pooh-pooh whatever's fresh and new, and declare it's crude and mean,
For Art stopped short in the cultivated court of the Empress Josephine.
    And every one will say,
    As you walk your mystic way,
"If that's not good enough for him which is good enough for *me*,
Why what a very cultivated kind of youth this kind of youth must be!''

Then a sentimental passion of a vegetable fashion must excite your languid spleen,
An attachment *à la* Plato for a bashful young potato, or a not-too-French French bean!
Though the Philistines may jostle, you will rank as an apostle in the high æsthetic band,
If you walk down Piccadilly with a poppy or a lily in your mediæval hand.
    And every one will say,
    As you walk your flowery way,
"If he's content with a vegetable love, which would certainly not suit *me*,
Why what a most particularly pure young man this pure young man must be!''

At the end of his song PATIENCE *enters. He sees her.*

BUN. Ah! Patience, come hither. I am pleased with thee. The bitter-hearted one, who finds all else hollow, is pleased with thee. For you are not hollow. *Are* you?

PA. I beg your pardon—I interrupt you.

BUN. Life is made up of interruptions. The tortured soul, yearning for solitude, writhes under them. Oh, but my heart is a-weary! Oh, I am a cursed thing! Don't go.

PA. Really, I'm very sorry—

BUN. Tell me, girl, do you ever yearn?

PA. *(misunderstanding him).* I earn my living.

BUN. *(impatiently)*. No, no! Do you know what it is to be heart-hungry? Do you know what it is to yearn for the Indefinable, and yet to be brought face to face, daily, with the Multiplication Table? Do you know what it is to seek oceans and to find puddles?—to long for whirlwinds and to have to do the best you can with the bellows? That's my case. Oh, I am a cursed thing!

PA. If you please, I don't understand you—you frighten me!

BUN. Don't be frightened—it's only poetry.

PA. If that's poetry, I don't like poetry.

BUN. *(eagerly)*. Don't you? *(Aside.)* Can I trust her? *(Aloud.)* Patience, you don't like poetry—well, between you and me, *I* don't like poetry. It's hollow, unsubstantial—unsatisfactory. What's the use of yearning for Elysian Fields when you know you can't get 'em, and would only let 'em out on building leases if you had 'em?

PA. Sir, I—

BUN. Don't go. Patience, I have long loved you—let me tell you a secret. I am not as bilious as I look. If you like I will cut my hair. There is more innocent fun within me than a casual spectator would imagine. You have never seen me frolicsome. Be a good girl—a very good girl—and you shall.

PA. Sir, I will speak plainly. In the matter of love I am untaught, I have never loved but my great-aunt. But I am quite certain that, under any circumstances, I couldn't possibly love *you*.

BUN. Oh, you think not?

PA. I'm quite sure of it. Quite sure. Quite.

BUN. *(releasing her)*. Very good. Life is henceforth a blank. I don't care what becomes of me. I have only to ask that you will not abuse my confidence; though *you* despise me, I am extremely popular with the other young ladies.

PA. I only ask that you will leave me and never renew the subject.

BUN. Certainly. Broken-hearted and desolate I go. *(Recites.)*

> "Oh, to be wafted away
>   From this black Aceldama of sorrow,
> Where the dust of an earthy to-day
>   Is the earth of a dusty to-morrow!"

It is a little thing of my own. I call it "Heart Foam." I shall not publish it. Farewell!   [*Exit* BUNTHORNE.

PA. What on earth does it all mean? Why does he love me? Why does he expect me to love him? He's not a relation! It frightens me!

Enter ANGELA.

ANG. Why, Patience, what is the matter?

PA. Lady Angela, tell me two things. Firstly, what on earth is this love that upsets everybody; and secondly, how is it to be distinguished from insanity?

ANG. Poor blind girl! Oh, forgive her, Eros! Why, love is of all passions the most essential! It is the embodiment of purity, the abstraction of refinement; it is the one unselfish emotion in this whirlpool of grasping greed!

PA. Oh dear, oh! *(Beginning to cry.)*

ANG. Why are you crying?

PA. To think that I have lived all these years without having experienced this ennobling and unselfish passion! Why, what a wicked girl I must be! For it *is* unselfish, isn't it?

ANG. Absolutely. Love that is tainted with selfishness is no love. Oh, try, try, try to love! It really isn't difficult if you give your whole mind to it.

PA. I'll set about it at once. I won't go to bed until I'm head over ears in love with somebody.

ANG. Noble girl. But is it possible that you have never loved anybody?

PA. Yes, one.

ANG. Ah, whom?

PA. My great-aunt.

ANG. Your great-aunt doesn't count.

PA. Then there's nobody. At least—no, nobody. Not since I was a baby. But *that* don't count, I suppose.

ANG. I don't know—tell me all about it.

DUET.—PATIENCE *and* ANGELA.

PA.
> Long years ago, fourteen, maybe,
>   When but a tiny babe of four,
> Another baby played with me,
>   My elder by a year or more.
> A little child of beauty rare,
> With marvellous eyes and wondrous hair,
> Who, in my child-eyes, seemed to me
> All that a little child should be!
>   Ah, how we loved, that child and I,
>   How pure our baby joy!
>   How true our love—and, by-the-by,
>   *He* was a little boy!

ANG.
> Ah, old, old tale of Cupid's touch!
> I thought as much—I thought as much!
>   He *was* a little boy!

PA. *(shocked)*.
> Pray don't misconstrue what I say—
> Remember, pray—remember, pray,
>   He was a *little* boy!

ANG.
> No doubt, yet spite of all your pains,
> The interesting fact remains—
>   He was a little *boy!*

ENSEMBLE.

> Ah, yes } in spite of all { my } pains, etc.
> No doubt }   { her }

[*Exit* ANGELA.

PA. It's perfectly appalling to think of the dreadful state I must be in! I had no idea that love was a duty. No wonder they all look so unhappy. Upon my word, I hardly like to associate with myself. I don't think I'm respectable. I'll go at once and fall in love with—

Enter GROSVENOR.

PA. A stranger!

DUET.—PATIENCE *and* GROSVENOR.

GROS.
> Prithee, pretty maiden—prithee tell me true,
>   (Hey, but I'm doleful, willow willow waly!)
> Have you e'er a lover a dangling after you?

> Hey willow waly O!
>   I would fain discover
>   If you have a lover?
> Hey willow waly O!

PA.   Gentle sir, my heart is frolicsome and free—
>   (Hey, but he's doleful, willow willow waly!)
>   Nobody I care for comes a courting me—
>   Hey willow waly O!
>   Nobody I care for
>   Comes a courting—therefore,
>   Hey willow waly O!

GROS.   Prithee, pretty maiden, will you marry me?
>   (Hey, but I'm hopeful, willow willow waly!)
>   I may say, at once, I'm a man of propertee—
>   Hey willow waly O!
>   Money, I despise it,
>   But many people prize it,
>   Hey willow waly O!

PA.   Gentle sir, although to marry I design—
>   (Hey, but he's hopeful—willow willow waly!)
>   As yet I do not know you, and so I must decline.
>   Hey willow waly O!
>   To other maidens go you—
>   As yet I do not know you,
>   Hey willow waly O!

GROS. Patience! Can it be that you don't recognize me?

PA. Recognize you? No, indeed I don't!

GROS. Have fifteen years so greatly changed me?

PA. Fifteen years. What do you mean?

GROS. Have you forgotten the friend of your youth, your Archibald?—your little playfellow? Oh, Chronos, Chronos, this is too bad of you!

PA. Archibald! Is it possible? Why, let me look! It is! It is! It must be! Oh, how happy I am! I thought we should never meet again! And how you've grown!

GROS. Yes, Patience, I am much taller and much stouter than I was.

PA. And how you're improved!

GROS. Yes, Patience, I am very beautiful! *(Sighs.)*

PA. But surely *that* doesn't make you unhappy?

GROS. Yes, Patience. Gifted as I am with a beauty which probably has not its rival on earth—I am, nevertheless, utterly and completely miserable.

PA. Oh, but why?

GROS. My child-love for you has never faded. Conceive, then, the horror of my situation when I tell you that it is my hideous destiny to be madly loved by every woman I come across!

PA. But why do you make yourself so picturesque? Why not disguise yourself, disfigure yourself, anything to escape this persecution?

GROS. No, Patience, that may not be. These gifts—irksome as they are—have been confided to me for the enjoyment and delectation of my fellow-creatures. I am a trustee for Beauty, and it is my duty to see that the conditions of my trust are faithfully discharged.

PA. And you, too, are a Poet?

GROS. Yes, I am the Apostle of Simplicity. I am called "Archibald the All-right"—for I am infallible!

PA. And is it possible that you condescend to love such a girl as I?

GROS. Yes, Patience, is it not strange? I have loved you with a Florentine fourteenth-century frenzy for full fifteen years!

PA. Oh, marvellous! I have hitherto been deaf to the voice of love—I seem now to know what love is! It has been revealed to me—it is Archibald Grosvenor!

GROS. Yes, Patience, it is! *(Embrace.)*

PA. *(as in a trance).* We will never, never part!

GROS. We will live and die together!

PA. I swear it!

GROS. We both swear it! *(Embrace.)*

PA. *(recoiling from him).* But—oh, horror!

GROS. What's the matter?

PA. Why, you are perfection! A source of endless ecstasy to all who know you!

GROS. I know I am—well?

PA. Then, bless my heart, there can be nothing unselfish in loving *you!*

GROS. Merciful powers, I never thought of that!

PA. To monopolize those features on which all women love to linger! It would be unpardonable!

GROS. Why, so it would! Oh, fatal perfection, again you interpose between me and my happiness!

PA. Oh, if you were but a thought less beautiful than you are!

GROS. Would that I were; but candour compels me to admit that I'm not!

PA. Our duty is clear; we must part, and for ever!

GROS. Oh, misery! And yet I cannot question the propriety of your decision. Farewell, Patience!

PA. Farewell, Archibald! But stay!

GROS. Yes, Patience?

PA. Although I may not love *you*—for you are perfect—there is nothing to prevent your loving *me.* I am plain, homely, unattractive!

GROS. Why, that's true!

PA. The love of such a man as you for such a girl as I must be unselfish!

GROS. Unselfishness itself!

DUET.—PATIENCE *and* GROSVENOR.

PA.   Though to marry you would very selfish be—
GROS.   Hey, but I'm doleful—willow willow waly!
PA.   You may all the same continue loving me—
GROS.   Hey, but I'm doleful—willow willow waly!
BOTH.   All the world ignoring,
>   You ⎫
>   I'll ⎬ go on adoring—
>   Hey willow waly O!

[At the end, exeunt despairingly, in opposite directions

Enter BUNTHORNE, *crowned with roses and hung about with garlands, and looking very miserable. He is led by* ANGELA *and* SAPHIR *(each of whom holds an end of the rose-garland by which he is bound), and accompanied by procession of* MAIDENS. *They are dancing classically, and playing on cymbals, double pipes, and other archaic instruments.*

CHORUS.

Let the merry cymbals sound,
  Gaily pipe Pandæan pleasure,
With a Daphnephoric bound
  Tread a gay but classic measure.
Every heart with hope is beating,
For at this exciting meeting
  Fickle Fortune will decide
  Who shall be our Bunthorne's bride!

Enter DRAGOONS, *led by* COLONEL, MAJOR, *and* DUKE.
They are surprised at proceedings.

CHORUS OF DRAGOONS.

Now tell us, we pray you,
Why thus you array you—
Oh, poet, how say you—
    What is it you've done?

DUKE. Of rite sacrificial,
       By sentence judicial,
       This seems the initial,
           Then why don't you run?

COL.   They cannot have led you,
       To hang or behead you,
       Nor may they *all* wed you,
           Unfortunate one!

CHORUS OF DRAGOONS.

Then tell us, we pray you,
Why thus they array you—
Oh, poet, how say you—
    What is it you've done?

RECITATIVE.—BUNTHORNE.

Heart-broken at my Patience's barbarity,
  By the advice of my solicitor *(introducing his*
                                     solicitor),
In aid—in aid of a deserving charity,
  I've put myself up to be raffled for!

MAIDENS. By the advice of his solicitor
          He's put himself up to be raffled for!

DRAGOONS. Oh, horror! urged by his solicitor,
          He's put himself up to be raffled for!

MAIDENS. Oh, Heaven's blessing on his solicitor!

DRAGOONS. A hideous curse on his solicitor!

[*The* SOLICITOR, *horrified at the* DRAGOONS' *curse, rushes off.*

COL.   Stay, we implore you,
       Before our hopes are blighted!
       You see before you
       The men to whom you're plighted!

CHORUS OF DRAGOONS.

Stay we implore you,
For we adore you;
To us you're plighted
To be united—
    Stay we implore you!

SOLO.—DUKE.

Your maiden hearts, ah, do not steel
  To pity's eloquent appeal,
  Such conduct British soldiers feel.
(*Aside to* DRAGOONS.)   Sigh, sigh, all sigh!   [*They all sigh.*

To foeman's steel we rarely see
A British soldier bend the knee,
Yet, one and all, they kneel to ye—
(*Aside to* DRAGOONS.)   Kneel, kneel, all kneel!   [*They all kneel.*

Our soldiers very seldom cry,
  And yet—I need not tell you why—
  A tear-drop dews each martial eye!
(*Aside to* DRAGOONS.)   Weep, weep, all weep!   [*They all weep.*

ENSEMBLE.

Our soldiers very seldom cry
And yet—I need not tell you why—
A tear-drop dews each manly eye!
    Weep, weep, all weep!

BUNTHORNE (*who has been impatient during the appeal*).
Come, walk up, and purchase with avidity,
Overcome your diffidence and natural timidity,
Tickets for the raffle should be purchased with avidity,
  Put in half a guinea and a husband you may gain—
Such a judge of blue-and-white, and other kinds of pottery—
From early Oriental, down to modern terra-cotta-ry—
Put in half a guinea—you may draw him in a lottery—
  Such an opportunity may not occur again.

CHORUS. Such a judge of blue-and-white, etc.

[MAIDENS *crowd up to purchase tickets—during this* DRAGOONS
  dance in single file round stage—to express their indifference.

DRAGOONS. We've been thrown over, we're aware,
          But we don't care—but we don't care!
          There's fish in the sea, no doubt of it,
          As good as ever came of it,
          And some day we shall get our share,
          So we don't care—so we don't care!
[*During this the* GIRLS *have been buying tickets. At last,* JANE
  presents herself. BUNTHORNE *looks at her with aversion.*

RECITATIVE.

BUN.   And are *you* going, a ticket for to buy?
JANE (*surprised*). Most certainly I am; why should not I?
BUN. (*aside*).   Oh, Fortune this is hard! (*Aloud.*) Blindfold
                  your eyes;

Two minutes will decide who wins the prize!
[GIRLS *blindfold themselves.*

CHORUS OF MAIDENS.

Oh, Fortune, to my aching heart be kind;
Like us, thou are blindfolded, but not blind!
(Each uncovers one eye.)
Just raise your bandage, thus, that you may see,
And give the prize, and give the prize to me!
(They cover their eyes again.)
BUN. Come, Lady Jane, I pray you draw the first!
JANE *(joyfully)*. He loves me best!
BUN. *(aside)*. I want to know the worst!
[JANE *draws a paper, and is about to open it, when* PATIENCE
enters. PATIENCE *snatches paper from* JANE *and tears it up.*

PA. Hold! Stay your hand!
ALL *(uncovering their eyes)*. What means this interference?
Of this bold girl I pray you make a clearance!
JANE. Away with you, and to your milk-pails go?
BUN. *(suddenly)*. She wants a ticket! Take a dozen!!
PA. No!

SOLO.—PATIENCE, *kneeling to* BUNTHORNE.

If there be pardon in your breast
    For a poor penitent,
Who with remorseful thought opprest,
    Sincerely doth repent.
If you, with one so lowly, still
    Desire to be allied,
Then you may take me, if you will,
    For I will be your bride!

ALL.   Oh, shameless one!
                    Oh, boldfaced thing!
                Away you run—
                    Go, take you wing,
                You shameless one!
                    You boldfaced thing!

BUN. How strong is love! For many and many a week,
She's loved me fondly and has feared to speak
But Nature, for restraint too mighty far,
Has burst the bonds of Art—and here we are!

PA. No, Mr. Bunthorne, no—you're wrong again,
Permit me—I'll endeavour to explain!

SONG.—PATIENCE.

True love must single-hearted be—
BUN.   Exactly so!
PA. From every selfish fancy free—
BUN.   Exactly so!
PA. No idle thought of gain or joy,
    A maiden's fancy should employ—
    True love must be without alloy.
ALL.   Exactly so!

PA. Imposture to contempt must lead—

COL.   Exactly so!
PA. Blind vanity's dissension's seed—
MAJ.   Exactly so!
PA. It follows then, a maiden who
    Devotes herself to loving *you (indicating* BUNTHORNE),
    Is prompted by no selfish view!
ALL.   Exactly so!

SAPH. *(taking* BUNTHORNE *aside).* Are you resolved to wed this
shameless one?
ANG. Is there no chance for any other?
BUN. *(decisively)*.   None!
[*Embraces* PATIENCE.
[ANGELA, SAPHIR *and* ELLA *take* COLONEL, DUKE, *and* MAJOR
down, while GIRLS *gaze fondly at other* OFFICERS.

SESTETTE.

I hear the soft note of the echoing voice
    Of an old old love, long dead—
It whispers my sorrowing heart ''rejoice''—
    For the last sad tear is shed—
The pain that is all but a pleasure we'll change
    For the pleasure that's all but pain,
And never, oh, never, this heart will range
    From that old old love again!
[GIRLS *embrace* OFFICERS.

CHORUS.   Yes, the pain that is all, etc.   [*Embrace.*

[*As the* DRAGOONS *and* GIRLS *are embracing, enter* GROSVENOR
    *reading. He takes no notice of them, but comes slowly down,
    still reading. The* GIRLS *are all strangely fascinated by him
    and gradually withdrawn from* DRAGOONS.

ANG.   But who is this, whose god-like grace
             Proclaims he comes of noble race?
             And who is this, whose manly face
             Bears sorrow's interesting trace?

ENSEMBLE.—TUTTI.

Yes, who is this? etc.

GROS.   I am a broken-hearted troubadour,
         Whose mind's æsthetic, and whose tastes are pure!
ANG.   Æsthetic! He is æsthetic!
GROS.   Yes, yes—I am æsthetic
             And poetic!
All the LADIES. Then, we love you!

[*The* GIRLS *leave* DRAGOONS *and group, kneeling, around*
    GROSVENOR. *Fury of* BUNTHORNE, *who recognizes a rival.*

DRAGOONS.   They love him! Horror!
BUN. *and* PA. They love him! Horror!
GROS.   They love me! Horror! Horror! Horror!

ENSEMBLE.—TUTTI.

GIRLS.   GROSVENOR.
Oh, list while we a love confess   Again my cursed comeliness

That words imperfectly express,
Those shell-like ears, ah, do not close
To blighted love's distracting woes!
Nor be distressed, nor scandalized
If what we do is ill-advised,
Or we shall seek within the tomb
Relief from our appalling doom!

Spreads hopeless anguish and distress,
Thine ears, O Fortune, did not close
To my intolerable woes.
Let me be hideous, undersized,
Contemned, degraded, loathed, despised.
Or bid me seek within the tomb
Relief from my detested doom!

Spectacled the limped eye,
　Little will be left of me,
　　In the coming by-and-by!

Fading is the taper waist—
　Shapeless grows the shapely limb,
And although securely laced,
　Spreading is the figure trim!
Stouter than I used to be,
　Still more corpulent grow I—
There will be too much of me
　In the coming by-and-by!　　　　[*Exit* JANE.

PATIENCE.

List, Reginald, while I confess
A love that's all unselfishness,
That it's unselfish, goodness knows,
You won't dispute it, I suppose.
For you are hideous— undersized,
And everything that I've despised,
And I shall love you, I presume,
Until I sink into the tomb!

BUN.

My jealousy I can't express,
Their love they openly confess,
His shell-like ear he does not close
To their recital of their woes—
I'm more than angry and surprised,
I'm pained, and shocked, and scandalized,
But he shall meet a hideous doom
Prepared for him by—I know whom!

Enter GROSVENOR, *followed by* MAIDENS, *two and two, each playing on an archaic instrument, as in Act I. He is reading abstractedly, as* BUNTHORNE *did in Act I., and pays no attention to them.*

CHORUS OF MAIDENS.

Turn, oh, turn, in this direction,
　Shed, oh, shed a gentle smile,
With a glance of sad perfection
　Our poor fainting hearts beguile!
On such eyes as maidens cherish
　Let thy fond adorers gaze,
Or incontinently perish,
　In their all consuming rays;

[*He sits—they group around him.*

GROS. (*aside*). The old old tale. How rapturously these maidens love me, and how hopelessly! Oh, Patience, Patience, with the love of thee in my heart, what have I for these poor mad maidens but an unvalued pity? Alas, they will die of hopeless love for me, as I shall die of hopeless love for thee!

ANG. Sir, will it please you read to us? (*Kneels.*)

GROS. (*sighing*). Yes, child, if you will. What shall I read?

ANG. One of your own poems.

GROS. One of my own poems? Better not, my child. *They* will not cure thee of thy love.

ELLA. Mr. Bunthorne used to read us a poem of his own every day.

SAPH. And, to do him justice, he read them extremely well.

GROS. Oh, did he so? Well, who am I that I should take upon myself to withhold my gifts from you? What am I but a trustee? Here is a decalet—a pure and simple thing, a very daisy—a babe might understand it. To appreciate it it is not necessary to think of anything at all.

ANG. Let us think of nothing at all!

GROSVENOR *recites.*

Gentle Jane was as good as gold,
She always did as she was told.
She never spoke when her mouth was full,
Or caught blue-bottles their legs to pull;
Or spilt plum jam on her nice new frock,
Or put white mice in the eight-day clock,
Or vivisected her last new doll,
Or fostered a passion for alcohol.
And when she grew up she was given in marriage
To a first-class earl who keeps his carriage!

ACT II.

SCENE.—*A glade. In the centre a small sheet of water.* JANE *is discovered leaning on a violoncello, upon which she presently accompanies herself.*

JANE. The fickle crew have deserted Reginald and sworn allegiance to his rival, and all, forsooth, because he has glanced with passing favour on a puling milkmaid! Fools! Of that fancy he will soon weary—and then I, who alone am faithful to him, shall reap my reward. But do not dally too long, Reginald, for my charms are ripe, Reginald, and already they are decaying. Better secure me ere I have gone too far?

RECITATIVE.—JANE.

Sad is that woman's lot who, year by year,
Sees, one by one, her beauties disappear,
When Time, grown weary of her heart-drawn sighs,
Impatiently begins to "dim her eyes!"
Compelled, at last, in life's uncertain gloamings,
To wreathe her wrinkled brow with well-saved "combings,"
Reduced, with rouge, lipsalve and pearly grey,
To "make up" for lost time, as best she may!

SONG.—JANE.

Silvered is the raven hair—
　Spreading is the parting straight,
Mottled the complexion fair,
　Halting is the youthful gait.
Hollow is the laughter free,

GROS. I believe I am right in saying that there is not one word in that decalet which is calculated to bring the blush of shame to the cheek of modesty.

ANG. Not one; it is purity itself.

GROS. Here's another.

> Teasing Tom was a very bad boy;
> A great big squirt was his favourite toy;
> He put live shrimps in his father's boots,
> And sewed up the sleeves of his Sunday suits;
> He punched his poor little sisters' heads,
> And cayenne-peppered their four-post beds;
> He plastered their hair with cobbler's wax,
> And dropped hot halfpennies down their backs.
>> The consequence was he was lost totally,
>> And married a girl in the *corps de bally!*

ANG. Marked you how grandly—how relentlessly—the damning catalogue of crime strode on, till Retribution, like a poisëd hawk, came swooping down upon the Wrong-Doer. Oh, it was terrible!

ELLA. Oh, sir, you are indeed a true poet, for you touch our hearts, and they go out to you!

GROS. *(aside).* This is simply cloying. *(Aloud.)* Ladies, I am sorry to distress you, but you have been following me about ever since Monday, and this is Saturday. I should like the usual half-holiday, and if you will kindly allow me to close early to-day, I shall take it as a personal favour.

SAPH. Oh, sir, do not send us from you!

GROS. Poor, poor girls! It is best to speak plainly. I know that I am loved by you, but I never can love you in return, for my heart is fixed elsewhere! Remember the fable of the Magnet and the Churn!

ANG. *(wildly).* But we don't know the fable of the Magnet and the Churn!

GROS. Don't you? Then I will sing it to you.

SONG.—GROSVENOR.

> A magnet hung in a hardware shop,
> And all around was a loving crop
> Of scissors and needles, nails and knives,
> Offering love for all their lives;
> But for iron the magnet felt no whim,
> Though he charmed iron, it charmed not him,
> From needles and nails and knives he'd turn,
> For he'd set his love on a Silver Churn!

ALL. A Silver Churn!

GROS. A Silver Churn!
>> His most æsthetic,
>> Very magnetic
>> Fancy took this turn—
>> "If I can wheedle
>> A knife or needle,
>> Why not a Silver Churn?"

CHOR. His most æsthetic, etc.

GROS. And Iron and Steel expressed surprise,
> The needles opened their well-drilled eyes,
> The pen-knives felt "shut up," no doubt,
> The scissors declared themselves "cut out,"

> The kettles they boiled with rage, 'tis said,
> While every nail went off its head,
> And hither and thither began to roam,
> Till a hammer came up—and drove them home.

ALL. It drove them home?

GROS. It drove them home;
>> While this magnetic
>> Peripatetic
>> Lover he lived to learn,
>> By no endeavour,
>> Can magnet ever
>> Attract a Silver Churn!

ALL. While this magnetic, etc.

[They go off in low spirits, gazing back at him from time to time.

GROS. At last they are gone! What *is* this mysterious fascination that I seem to exercise over all I come across. A curse on my fatal beauty, for I am sick of conquests!

PATIENCE *appears.*

PA. Archibald!

GROS. *(turns and sees her).* Patience!

PA. I have escaped with difficulty from my Reginald. I wanted to see you so much that I might ask you if you still love me as fondly as ever?

GROS. Love you? If the devotion of a lifetime— *(Seizes her hand.)*

PA. *(indignantly).* Hold! Unhand me, or I scream. *(He releases her.)* If you are a gentleman, pray remember that I am another's! *(Very tenderly.)* But you *do* love me, don't you?

GROS. Madly, hopelessly, despairingly!

PA. That's right! I can never be yours; but that's right!

GROS. And you love this Bunthorne?

PA. With a heart-whole ecstasy that withers, and scorches, and burns, and stings! *(Sadly.)* It is my duty.

GROS. Admirable girl! But you are not happy with him?

PA. Happy? I am miserable beyond description!

GROS. That's right! I never can be yours; but that's right!

PA. But go now—I see dear Reginald approaching. Farewell, dear Archibald, I cannot tell you how happy it has made me to know that you still love me.

GROS. Ah, if I only dared— *(Advances towards her.)*

PA. Sir! This language to one who is promised to another! *(Tenderly.)* Oh, Archibald, think of me sometimes, for my heart is breaking! He is so unkind to me, and you would be so loving!

GROS. Loving! *(Advances towards her.)*

PA. Advance one step, and as I am a good and pure woman, I scream! *(Tenderly.)* Farewell, Archibald! *(Sternly.)* Stop there! *(Tenderly.)* Think of me sometimes! *(Angrily.)* Advance at your peril! Once more, adieu!

[GROSVENOR sighs, gazes sorrowfully at her, sighs deeply, and exit. She bursts into tears.

Enter BUNTHORNE, followed by JANE. He is moody and preoccupied.

JANE *sings.*

In a melancholy train,
　One and one I walk all day;
Pity those who love in vain—
　None so sorrowful as they,
　　Who can only sigh and say,
　　Woe is me, alack a-day!

BUN. *(seeing* PATIENCE*)*. Crying eh? What are you crying about?

PA. I've only been thinking how dearly I love you!

BUN. Love me! Bah!

JANE. Love him! Bah!

BUN. *(to* JANE*).* Don't you interfere.

JANE. He always crushes me!

PA. *(going to him).* What is the matter, dear Reginald? If you have any sorrow, tell it to me, that I may share it with you. *(Sighing.)* It is my duty!

BUN. *(snappishly).* Whom were you talking with, just now?

PA. With dear Archibald.

BUN. *(furiously).* With dear Archibald! Upon my honour, this is too much!

JANE. A great deal too much!

BUN. *(angrily to* JANE*).* Do be quiet!

JANE. Crushed again!

PA. I think he is the noblest, purest, and most perfect being I have ever met. But I don't love him. It is true that he is devotedly attached to me, but indeed I don't love *him.* Whenever he grows affectionate, I scream. It is my duty! *(Sighing).*

BUN. I dare say!

JANE. So do I. *I* dare say!

PA. Why, how could I love him and love you too? You can't love two people at once!

BUN. I don't believe you know what love is!

PA. *(sighing).* Yes, I do! There was a happy time when I didn't, but a bitter experience has taught me!

BALLAD.—PATIENCE.

Love is a plaintive song,
　Sung by a suffering maid,
Telling a tale of wrong,
　Telling of hope betrayed.
Tuned to each changing note,
　Sorry when *he* is sad.
Blind to his every mote,
　Merry when he is glad!
　　Love that no wrong can cure,
　　Love that is always new,
　　That is the love that's pure,
　　That is the love that's true!

Rendering good for ill,
　Smiling at every frown,
Yielding your own self-will,
　Laughing your tear-drops down,
Never a selfish whim,
　Trouble, or pain to stir;
Everything for him,
　Nothing at all for her!
　　Love that will aye endure,

Though the rewards be few,
　That is the love that's pure,
　That is the love that's true!

[*At the end of ballad, exit* PATIENCE, *weeping.*

BUN. Everything has gone wrong with me since that smug-faced idiot came here. Before that I was admired; I may say, loved.

JANE. Too mild. Adored!

BUN. Do let a poet soliloquize! The damozels used to follow me wherever I went; now they all follow him!

JANE. Not all! *I* am still faithful to you.

BUN. Yes, and a pretty damozel *you* are!

JANE. No, not pretty. Massive. Cheer up! I will never leave you, I swear it!

BUN. Oh, thank you! I know what it is; it's his confounded mildness. They find me too highly spiced, if you please! And no doubt I *am* highly spiced.

JANE. Not for my taste!

BUN. *(savagely).* No; but I am for theirs. But I can be as mild as he. If they want insipidity, they shall have it. I'll meet this fellow on his own ground and beat him on it.

JANE. You shall. And I will help you.

BUN. You will? Jane, there's a good deal of good in you, after all!

DUET.—BUNTHORNE *and* JANE.

JANE. So go to him and say to him, with compliment
　　　　ironical—
BUN. 　　　Sing "Hey to you—
　　　　　　Good day to you"—
　　　　And that's what I shall say!
JANE. "Your style is much too sanctified—your cut is too
　　　　canonical—"
BUN. 　　　Sing "Bah to you—
　　　　　　Ha! ha! to you"—
　　　　And that's what I shall say!
JANE. "I was the beau ideal of the morbid young æsthetical—
　　　　To doubt my inspiration was regarded as heretical—
　　　　Until you cut me out with your placidity emetical."
BUN. 　　　Sing "Booh to you—
　　　　　　Pooh, pooh, to you"—
　　　　And that's what I shall say!
BOTH. 　Sing "Hey to you, good day to you"—
　　　　Sing "Bah to you, ha! ha! to you"
　　　　Sing "Booh to you, pooh, pooh"—
　　　　And that's what $\left\{ \begin{matrix} you \\ I \end{matrix} \right\}$ shall say!
BUN. I'll tell him that unless he will consent to be more
　　　　jocular—
JANE. 　　　Say "Booh to you—
　　　　　　Pooh, pooh, to you"
　　　　And that's what you should say!
BUN. To cut his curly hair, and stick an eye-glass in his
　　　　ocular—
JANE. 　　　Sing "Bah to you—
　　　　　　Ha! ha! to you"—
　　　　And that's what you should say!
BUN. To stuff his conversation full of quibble and of quiddity,
　　　　To dine on chops and roly-poly pudding with avidity—
　　　　He'd better clear away with all convenient rapidity.

JANE. Sing "Hey to you—
　　　　Good day to you"—
　　　And that's what you should say!
BOTH. Sing "Booh to you—pooh, pooh, to you,"
　　　Sing "Bah to you—ha! ha! to you,"
　　　Sing "Hey to you—good day to you—"
　　　And that's what $\left\{ \begin{matrix} I \\ you \end{matrix} \right\}$ shall say!

[*Exeunt* JANE *and* BUNTHORNE *together.*

[*Enter* DUKE, COLONEL *and* MAJOR. *They have abandoned their uniforms, and are dressed and made up in imitation of Æsthetics. They have long hair, and other outward signs of attachment to the brotherhood. As they sing they walk in stiff, constrained, and angular attitudes—a grotesque exaggeration of the attitudes adopted by Bunthorne and the young* LADIES *in Act I.*

TRIO.

DUKE, COLONEL, *and* MAJOR.

It's clear that mediæval art alone retains its zest,
To charm and please its devotees we've done our little best.
We're not quite sure if all we do has the Early English ring;
But, as far as we can judge, it's something like this sort of thing;
　　　You hold yourself like this *(attitude),*
　　　You hold yourself like that *(attitude),*
By hook and crook you try to look both angular and flat *(attitude).*
　　　We venture to expect
　　　That what we recollect,
Though but a part of true High Art, will have its due effect.

If this is not exactly right, we hope you won't upbraid,
You can't get high Æsthetic tastes like trousers, ready made.
True views on Mediævalism, Time alone will bring,
But, as far as we can judge, it's something like this sort of thing:
　　　You hold yourself like this *(attitude),*
　　　You hold yourself like that *(attitude),*
By hook and crook you try to look both angular and flat *(attitude).*
　　　To cultivate the trim
　　　Rigidity of limb,
You ought to get a Marionette, and form your style on him
　(attitude).

COL. *(attitude).* Yes, it's quite clear that our only chance of making a lasting impression on these young ladies is to become as æsthetic as they are.

MAJ. *(attitude).* No doubt. The only question is how far we've succeeded in doing so. I don't know why, but I've an idea that this is not quite right.

DUKE *(attitude).* I don't like it. I never did. I don't see what it means. I do it, but I don't like it.

COL. My good friend, the question is not whether we like it, but whether they do. They understand these things—we don't. Now, I shouldn't be surprised if this is effective enough—at a distance.

MAJ. I can't help thinking we're a little stiff at it. It would be extremely awkward if we were to be "struck" so!

COL. I don't think we shall be struck so. Perhaps we're a little awkward at first—but everything must have a beginning. Oh, here they come! 'Tention!

They strike fresh attitudes, as ANG. *and* SAPHIR *enter.*

ANG. *(seeing them).* Oh, Saphir—see—see! The immortal fire has descended on them, and they are of the Inner Brotherhood—perceptively intense and consummately utter! *(The* OFFICERS *have some difficulty in maintaining their constrained attitudes.)*

SAPH. *(in admiration).* How Botticellian! How Fra Angelican! Oh, Art! I thank thee for this boon!

COL. *(apologetically).* I'm afraid we're not quite right.

ANG. Not supremely, perhaps, but, oh, so all-but! *(To* SAPHIR.) Oh, Saphir, are they not quite too all-but?

SAPH. They are indeed jolly utter.

MAJ. *(in agony).* What do the Inner Brotherhood usually recommend for cramp?

COL. Ladies, we will not deceive you. We are doing this at some personal inconvenience with a view of expressing the extremity of our devotion to you. We trust that it is not without its effect.

ANG. We will not deny that we are much moved by this proof of your attachment.

SAPH. Yes, your conversion to the principles of Æsthetic Art in its highest development has touched us deeply.

ANG. And if Mr. Grosvenor should remain obdurate—

SAPH. Which we have every reason to believe he will—

MAJ. *(aside, in agony).* I wish they'd make haste.

ANG. We are not prepared to say that our yearning hearts will not go out to you.

COL. *(as giving a word of command).* By sections of threes—Rapture! *(All strike a fresh attitude, expressive of æsthetic rapture.)*

SAPH. Oh, it's extremely good—for beginners it's admirable.

MAJ. The only question is, who will take who?

SAPH. Oh, the Duke choose first, as a matter of course.

DUKE. Oh, I couldn't think of it—you are really too good!

COL. Nothing of the kind. You are a great matrimonial fish, and it's only fair that each of these ladies should have a chance of hooking you.

DUKE. It's perfectly simple. Observe, suppose you choose Angela, I take Saphir, Major takes nobody. Suppose you choose Saphir, Major takes Angela, I take nobody. Suppose you choose neither, I take Angela, Major takes Saphir. Clear as day!

QUINTETTE.

DUKE, COLONEL, MAJOR, ANGELA, *and* SAPHIR.

DUKE *(taking* SAPHIR*).*
If Saphir I choose to marry,
　I shall be fixed up for life;
Then the Colonel need not tarry,
　Angela can be his wife.
　　　[*Handing* ANGELA *to* COLONEL.
[DUKE *dances with* SAPHIR, COLONEL *with* ANGELA, MAJOR *dances alone.*

MAJOR *(dancing alone).*
In that case unprecedented,
　Single I shall live and die—
I shall have to be contented
　With their heartfelt sympathy!

ALL (*dancing as before*).
He will have to be contented
With our heartfelt sympathy!

DUKE (*taking* ANGELA).
If on Angy I determine,
At my wedding she'll appear,
Decked in diamond and ermine,
Major then can take Saphir!
[*Handing* SAPHIR *to* MAJOR.
[DUKE *dances with* ANGELA, MAJOR *with* SAPHIR, COLONEL
dances alone.

COLONEL (*dancing*).
In that case unprecedented,
Single I shall live and die,
I shall have to be contented
With their heartfelt sympathy!

ALL (*dancing as before*).
He will have to be contented
With our heartfelt sympathy!

DUKE (*taking both* ANGELA *and* SAPHIR).
After some debate internal,
If on neither I decide,
Saphir then can take the Colonel,
[*Handing* SAPHIR *to* COLONEL.
Angy be the Major's bride!
[*Handing* ANGELA *to* MAJOR.
[COLONEL *dances with* SAPHIR, MAJOR *with* ANGELA, DUKE
dances alone.

DUKE (*dancing*).
In that case unprecedented,
Single I must live and die,
I shall have to be contented
With their heartfelt sympathy!

ALL (*dancing as before*).
He will have to live contented
With our heartfelt sympathy!

[*At the end,* DUKE, COLONEL, *and* MAJOR, *and two* GIRLS
dance off arm in arm.

Enter GROSVENOR.

GROS. It is very pleasant to be alone. It is pleasant to be able to
gaze at leisure upon those features which all others may gaze
upon at their good will! (*Looking at his reflection in hand-mirror.*)
Ah! I am a very Narcissus!

Enter BUNTHORNE, *moodily.*

BUN. It's no use, I can't live without admiration! Since
Grosvenor came here, insipidity has been at a premium. Ah, he is
there!

GROS. Ah, Bunthorne, come here—look! Very graceful, isn't
it?

BUN. (*taking hand-mirror*). Yes, it is graceful.

GROS. (*re-taking hand-mirror*). Oh! good gracious not that—
this—

BUN. You don't mean that. Bah! I am in no mood for trifling.

GROS. And what is amiss?

BUN. Ever since you came here, you have entirely monopolized
the attentions of the young ladies. I don't like it, sir!

GROS. My dear sir, how can I help it? They are the plague of
my life. My dear Mr. Bunthorne with your personal
disadvantages, you can have no idea of the inconvenience of being
madly loved, at first sight, by every woman you meet.

BUN. Sir, until you came here I was adored!

GROS. Exactly—until I came here. That's my grievance. I cut
everybody out! I assure you, if you could only suggest some
means whereby, consistently with my duty to society, I could
escape these inconvenient attentions, you would earn my
everlasting gratitude.

BUN. I will do so at once. However popular it may be with the
world at large, your personal appearance is highly objectionable
to *me*.

GROS. It is? (*Shaking his hand.*) Oh, thank you, thank you!
How can I express my gratitude?

BUN. By making a complete change at once. Your conversation must henceforth be perfectly matter-of-fact. You must cut
your hair, and have a back parting. In appearance and costume
you must be absolutely commonplace.

GROS. (*decidedly*). No. Pardon me, that's impossible.

BUN. Take care. When I am thwarted I am very terrible.

GROS. I can't help that. I am a man with a mission. And that
mission must be fulfilled.

BUN. I don't think you quite appreciate the consequences of
thwarting me.

GROS. I don't care what they are.

BUN. Suppose—I won't go so far as to say that I will do
it—but suppose for one moment, I were to curse you?
(GROSVENOR *quails.*) Ah! Very well. Take care.

GROS. But surely you would never do that? (*In great alarm.*)

BUN. I don't know. It would be an extreme measure, no
doubt. Still—

GROS. (*wildly*). But you would not do it—I am sure you would
not. (*Throwing himself at* BUNTHORNE'S *knees, and clinging to him.*)
Oh, reflect! reflect! You had a mother once.

BUN. Never!

GROS. Then you had an aunt! (BUNTHORNE *affected.*) Ah! I see
you had! By the memory of that aunt, I implore you to pause ere
you resort to this last fearful expedient. Oh, Mr. Bunthorne,
reflect, reflect! (*Weeping.*)

BUN. (*aside, after a struggle with himself*). I must not allow myself
to be unmanned! (*Aloud.*) It is useless. Consent at once, or may a
nephew's curse—

GROS. Hold. Are you absolutely resolved?

BUN. Absolutely.

GROS. Will nothing shake you?

BUN. Nothing. I am adamant.

GROS. Very good. (*Rising.*) Then I yield.

BUN. Ha! You swear it?

GROS. I do. Cheerfully. I have long wished for a reasonable
pretext for such a change as you suggest. It has come at last. I do
it on compulsion!

BUN. Victory! I triumph!

DUET.—BUNTHORNE *and* GROSVENOR.

BUN.
When I go out of door,
Of damozels a score
    (All sighing and burning,
    And clinging and yearning)
Will follow me as before.
I shall, with cultured taste,
Distinguish gems from paste,
    And "High diddle diddle"
    Will rank as an idyll,
If I pronounce it chaste!

A most intense young man,
A soulful-eyed young man,
An ultra poetical, super-æsthetical,
Out-of-the-way young man.

BOTH.   A most intense young man, etc.

GROS.
Conceive me, if you can,
An everyday young man;
    A commonplace type,
    With a stick and a pipe,
And a half-bred black-and-tan.
    Who thinks suburban "hops,"
    More fun than "Monday pops."
Who's fond of his dinner,
    And doesn't get thinner
    On bottled beer and chops.

A commonplace young man—
A matter-of-fact young man—
A steady and stolid-y, jolly Bank-holiday
Everyday young man!

BUN.
A Japanese young man—
A blue-and-white young man—
Francesca di Rimini, miminy, piminy,
Je-ne-sais-quoi young man.

GROS.
A Chancery Lane young man—
A Somerset House young man—
A very delectable, highly respectable,
Threepenny-bus young man!

BUN.
A pallid and thin young man—
A haggard and lank young man—
A greenery-yallery, Grosvenor Gallery,
Foot-in-the-grave young man!

GROS.
A Sewell and Cross young man—
A Howell and James young man—
A pushing young particle—
    "What's the next article"—
Waterloo House young man!

ENSEMBLE.

BUN.	GROS.
Conceive me, if you can,	Conceive me, if you can,

A crotchety, cracked young
    man,
An ultra-poetical, super-
    æsthetical,
Out-of-the-way young man!

A matter-of-fact young
    man,
An alphabetical, arithmetical,
Everyday young man!

[*At the end,* GROSVENOR *dances off.* BUNTHORNE *remains.*

BUN. It is all right! I have committed my last act of ill-nature, and henceforth I'm a reformed character.

[*Dances about stage, humming refrain of last air.*

PA. Reginald! Dancing! And—what in the world is the matter with you?

BUN. Patience. I'm a changed man. Hitherto, I've been gloomy, moody, fitful—uncertain in temper, and selfish in disposition—

PA. You have indeed! *(Sighing.)*

BUN. All that is changed. I have reformed. I have modelled myself upon Mr. Grosvenor. Henceforth I am mildly cheerful. My conversation will blend amusement with instruction. I shall still be æsthetic; but my æstheticism will be of the most pastoral kind.

PA. Oh, Reginald! Is all this true?

BUN. Quite true. Observe how amiable I am. *(Assuming a fixed smile.)*

PA. But, Reginald, how long will this last?

BUN. With occasional intervals for rest and refreshment, as long as I do.

PA. Oh, Reginald, I'm so happy! *(In his arms.)* Oh, dear, dear Reginald, I cannot express the joy I feel at this change. It will no longer be a duty to love you, but a pleasure—a rapture, an ecstasy!

BUN. My darling!

PA. But—oh, horror! *(Recoiling from him.)*

BUN. What's the matter?

PA. Is it quite certain that you have absolutely reformed—that you are henceforth a perfect being—utterly free from defect of any kind?

BUN. It is quite certain. I have sworn it!

PA. Then I never can be yours!

BUN. Why not?

PA. Love, to be pure, must be absolutely unselfish, and there can be nothing unselfish in loving so perfect a being as you have now become!

BUN. But, stop a bit, I don't want to reform—I'll relapse—I'll be as I was—

PA. No; love should purify—it should never debase.

BUN. But, I assure you, I—interrupted!

Enter GROSVENOR, *followed by all the young* LADIES, *who are followed by chorus of* DRAGOONS. *He has had his hair cut, and is dressed in an ordinary suit of dittos and a pot hat. They all dance cheerfully round the stage in marked contrast to their former languor.*

CHORUS.—GROSVENOR *and* LADIES.

GROS.	LADIES.
I'm a Waterloo House young man,	We're Swears and Wells young girls,

A Sewell and Cross young man,
A steady and stolid-y, jolly Bank-holiday,
    Everyday young man.

We're Madame Louise young girls,
We're prettily pattering, cheerily chattering,
    Everyday young girls.

GROS.   I'm a Waterloo House young man!
GIRLS.   We're Swears and Wells young girls!
GROS.   I'm a Sewell and Cross young man!
GIRLS.   We're Madam Louise young girls!
GROS.   ⎱ I'm a steady and stolid-y, jolly Bank-holiday,
                 Everyday young man!
LADIES.   ⎰ We're prettily pattering, cheerily chattering,
                 Everyday young girls!

BUN. Angela—Ella—Saphir—what—what does this mean?

ANG. It means that Archibald the All-right cannot be wrong; and if the All-right chooses to discard æstheticism, it proves that æstheticism ought to be discarded.

PA. Oh, Archibald! Archibald! I'm shocked—surprised—horrified!

GROS. I can't help it. I'm not a free agent. I do it on compulsion.

PA. This is terrible. Go! I shall never set eyes on you again. But—oh, joy!

GROS. What is the matter?

PA. Is it quite, quite certain that you will always be a commonplace young man?

GROS. Always—I've sworn it.

PA. Why then, there's nothing to prevent my loving you with all the fervour at my command!

GROS. Why, that's true.

PA. My Archibald!

GROS. My Patience! *(They embrace.)*

BUN. Crushed again!

Enter JANE.

JANE *(who is still æsthetic).* Cheer up! I am still here. I have never left you, and I never will!

BUN. Thank you, Jane. After all, there is no denying it, you're a fine figure of a woman!

JANE. My Reginald!

BUN. My Jane!

Flourish. Enter COLONEL, DUKE, and MAJOR.

COL. Ladies, the Duke, has at length determined to select a bride! *(General excitement.)*

DUKE. I have a great gift to bestow. Approach, such of you as are truly lovely. *(All come forward, bashfully, except JANE and PATIENCE.)* In personal beauty you have all that is necessary to make a woman happy. In common fairness, I think I ought to choose the only one among you who has the misfortune to be distinctly plain. (GIRLS *retire disappointed.)* Jane!

JANE *(leaving BUNTHORNE's arms).* Duke! *(JANE and DUKE embrace. BUNTHORNE is utterly disgusted.)*

BUN. Crushed again!

FINALE.

DUKE.   After much debate internal
              I on Lady Jane decide,
              Saphir now may take the Colonel,
              Angy be the Major's bride!

[SAPHIR *pairs off with* COLONEL, ANGELA *with the* MAJOR, ELLA *with* SOLICITOR.

BUN.   In that case unprecedented,
              Single I must live and die,
            I shall have to be contented
              With a tulip or li*ly!*

[*Takes a lily from button-hole, and gazes affectionately at it.*

ALL.   He will have to be contented
              With a tulip or li*ly!*

ALL.   Greatly pleased with one another,
              To get married we decide,
            Each of us will wed the other,
              Nobody be Bunthorne's Bride!

DANCE.

CURTAIN.

Iolanthe

or The Peer and The Peri

A conflict between politicians and fairies seems an extraordinary plot to have maintained popularity for over a hundred years. It was considered strange at the time, even allowing for the Victorian leaning towards satire and weekly graphic representations of Parliamentary figures in *Punch*, with fairies in fairly close proximity. Gilbert shared the contemporary fascination for fairies which Hans Andersen and the folk-tale revival had started. But Gilbert's fairies were of the pantomime genre, synonymous with ballet dancers and pretty girls. He had already set fairies among the clergy in his provocative *Bab Ballad*, 'The Fairy Curate', of which *Iolanthe* is a development.

It is Gilbert's most directly satirical opera, an attack on the British legal and Parliamentary systems and on female participation in politics but an attack so embroidered with charm, colour and pathos that, as it stands now, it never sinks below the level of fun. Two particularly aggressive numbers were, in fact, withdrawn and have never been reinstated.

Parliamentary reform was in the wind in the 1880s. The growth of social reform threatened the ancient foundations of the British Parliamentary system for which Gilbert's peers, led by Mountararat (dating from the flood) and Tolloller (a *pretty* good fellow) stand. They are severely threatened by the Radical Arcadian Strephon — half a fairy — who is also an obstruction in the competition for Phyllis. It seems that their professed love for Phyllis is only in the interest of male conquest (Tolloller's masculinity is in question as he was traditionally played falsetto). The situation parallels that of the *Bab* 'Periwinkle Girl' where the rival dukes in pursuit of her are condemned for their vice.

Mr Kenneth Baker (a Conservative MP) once proposed that Strephon was based on Lord Randolph Churchill, and also suggested that the Fairy Queen represents Queen Victoria, and the Lord Chancellor, Gladstone. The off-hand manner in which Queen Victoria's Prime Minister is known to have treated her is echoed in the Lord Chancellor's dismissive attitude towards the Fairy Queen. Private Willis, the guardsman who so attracts the Fairy Queen, is said to represent John Brown, Queen Victoria's ghillie and confidant.

This is speculation, but the role of the Fairy Queen has been written with a subtlety that has created more than a mere puppet. Gilbert has given her the authority and loneliness of a leader, with added

The Fairies, led by their Queen, complete with the novelty of electric light halos, in Palace Yard Westminster. Detail from music cover contemporary with first production.

compassion and feminine frailty. These aspects were particularly noticeable in a production of *Iolanthe* when she was characterized as Mrs Thatcher.

In this opera, male superiority, social snobbery and the law of the land hold no weight against fairy law. Women, in the guise of fairies, put men to shame

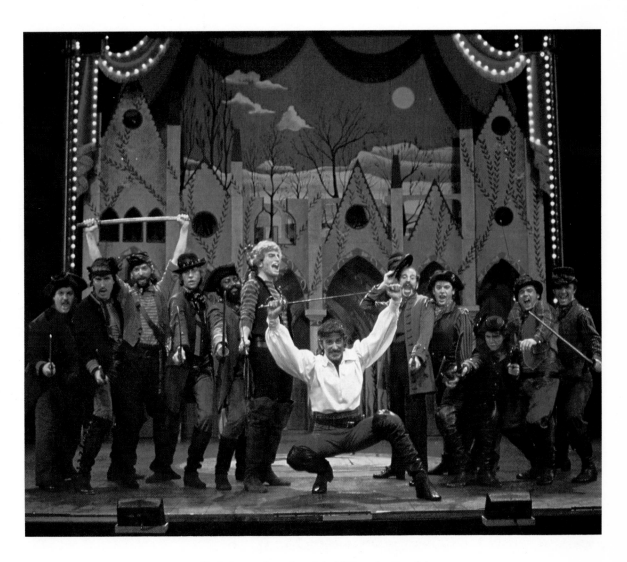

Typical scene from the original US production of the
'new' Pirates which transferred from Central Park
(see picture on page 92) to Broadway in
1980. Kevin Kline is the Pirate King here.

Derek Hammond-Stroud as Bunthorne and Emil
Belcourt as Algernon in the English National Opera's
production of *Patience* at the London Coliseum in
November 1972. The set with gazebo and lily pond
was by John Stoddart.

but finally, as in every Gilbert libretto, all revert to the *status quo*.

Early audiences enjoyed *Iolanthe* enormously, and individual performances were especially remarkable. It ran for almost four hundred performances at the Savoy, from November 1882 until New Year's Day 1884, but it was not heard again in London until the end of 1901, when Sullivan was dead. Among the unexpected criticisms of *Iolanthe* was one in *The Stage* which stated: 'It will not last ... the music is not tuneful enough even to become popular'.

Iolanthe is the most ambitious and inventive of Sullivan's scores. When all the unusual aspects are examined, it seems clear that he may have had several scores of Wagner's operas beside him during composition. Sullivan saw the plot in a Wagnerian idiom. Because of this his score is invested with unexpected, quasi-Wagnerian themes, modulations, harmonies and instrumental effects. These are accompanied by more chromaticism and greater use of the minor mode than usual, which is especially noticeable at the beginning of the Overture. The fairy music is Mendelssohnian in its gentler moments, but Sullivan's writing for this particular female chorus excels when he becomes more ambitious. Their 'Aiaiah! Willaloo!' cries of foreboding recall the plaints of the Rhinemaidens at the end of *Das Rheingold*; and Iolanthe's 'Now let me die!' has triplet semi-quaver and quaver groups reminiscent of the Rhine motif at the beginning of the *Ring* cycle.

It is also interesting to consider the confrontation between the Fairy Queen and the Lord Chancellor in the finale of Act I as a parallel to the Brünnhilde-Wotan scene in Act III of *Die Walküre* ('Wo ist Brünnhild' ...?') with its chorus of chanting Walküren. Alice Barnett, the first, towering Fairy Queen, was dressed like Brünnhilde, and Wotan's 'Wrath' motif may be the source for the Lord Chancellor's (much lightened) little descending theme which always comes with him.

Although Wagner's *Tristan und Isolde* had been heard in Munich as early as 1865, it was not given in London until June 1882, at about the time when Sullivan began composition of *Iolanthe*. Sullivan was undoubtedly familiar with Wagner's revolutionary masterpiece and there is a remarkable similarity in the oboe solo for Iolanthe's rising from the stream in Act I, and the shepherd's cor anglais solo at the start to Act III of *Tristan*. The mood of Iolanthe's opening

words on her 'awakening' has some resemblance to Tristan's as he awakes at Kareol: 'Die alte Weise'. ...'.

Sullivan's own feelings at the time were deeply affected by bereavement. His mother had died in May 1882 and when he started composing *Iolanthe* shortly afterwards, he was thoroughly dissatisfied with his efforts. He finally began working in earnest while staying at Pencarrow in Cornwall, as the guest of Lady Molesworth. The woodlands and the terraced lawns were an inspiration for the fairy setting, and the reality derived from them has transformed this incongruous story into one of the most human and fluent of all the Gilbert and Sullivan operas.

SYNOPSIS

Notes of foreboding begin the Overture in which Fairies, Arcadian Shepherds and the Peerage are all introduced. It has some resemblance to Mendelssohn's *Midsummer Night's Dream*, both in the music and in the dramatic differentiation of characters. A cool, magic woodwind sound pervades and, unlike most of the other Sullivan Overtures, none of the rousing star numbers, to be heard later, destroy the effect.

The scene opens on an Arcadian landscape — Watteau in style — with Fairies flitting aimlessly; their sole purpose is to hover round lovers, but they are bored. They fondly reminisce about Iolanthe, their favourite sister, who transgressed twenty-five years ago and married a mortal. Her punishment of death was commuted by the Fairy Queen to penal servitude on condition that she never saw her husband again. She is now serving her sentence on her head at the bottom of the adjoining stream and the Fairies beg their Queen to forgive her and restore her to them. Rhinemaiden ripples accompany the Fairy Queen's invocation, and she is backed by the Wagnerian call of the Fairies: 'Iolanthe! Iolanthe!' — the haunting four notes which punctuate the Overture.

Iolanthe rises from the stream and explains that she took up her abode 'among the frogs' in order to be near her son Strephon, an Arcadian Shepherd. He is now twenty-four and engaged to Phyllis, a Ward in Chancery. When the Fairies disapprove of the liaison, Iolanthe explains that he is a fairy to the waist, with mortal legs.

A classical, pastoral piping brings on Strephon. The Fairies retire as he joyfully greets his mother with the news, 'I'm to be married today!' He tells her that although the Lord Chancellor has refused permission, he intends to defy him. He then sees the other Fairies — his aunts. Strephon divulges that Phyllis knows nothing of his fairyhood, and to him it is nothing but a curse because his mortal half is always preventing his fairy half from accomplishing its purpose. The Fairy Queen recommends that, with a fairy brain, Strephon should go into Parliament, and she offers to help him to a seat. The Fairies' farewell to Strephon has similarities with Sangazure's 'Sir, I am your most obedient...' from *The Sorcerer*. They promise help if he should be in need, and trip away.

Now Phyllis greets Strephon, 'Good morrow, good lover!' to the same Arcadian tune as that which Strephon has addressed his mother ('For we're to be married today...'). Phyllis has reservations about the forbidden marriage and dwells on the penalties, but

Strephon is unwilling to wait, knowing that numerous Peers are ready to woo Phyllis.

'None shall part us from each other...' is a love duet in Mendelssohnian style. The complementary phrases, splitting the melody, are unique to this opera, but they are harmonized in the typical, Victorian choral tradition.

A side-drum roll brings in — ideally — a section of the Grenadier Guards Band, heralding the Peers with a series of fanfares. A magnificent display of pageantry follows — a proud parade of robed and coroneted nobility, all metaphorically blowing their own trumpets with 'Tantantara! Tzing! Boom!'. Then 'Bow, bow, ye lower middle classes!' they proclaim in unison. At this climax, the Lord Chancellor appears with his train-bearer.

His foreboding signature tune suggests that he is a villain with a dark secret, but his song 'The Law is the true embodiment Of everything that's excellent.' belies, at least, this dark tone. He revels in his guardianship of 'pretty young Wards in Chancery,' but admits the temptations, being 'such a susceptible Chancellor'. The assembled Peers are

Richard Temple and Leonora Braham, the original Strephon and Phyllis, Savoy Theatre 25 November 1882.

vying for Phyllis's hand and the Lord Chancellor has come to bestow her on the Peer of her choice. He confesses that he is in love with Phyllis himself, and considers the problems of coming under his own jurisdiction.

The Lords Tolloller and Mountararat are first in the line of competitors for Phyllis. She arrives in answer to the Lord Chancellor's summons and immediately the two Lords make overtures in an Arcadian vein, deigning patronizingly — and somewhat tentatively — to come down to a rustic level. Phyllis is insulted and the fatal tones of the Lord Chancellor creep into her recitative: 'Nay, tempt me not ... In lowly cot is virtue found...'. The

Clara Dow as Phyllis in the 1907 revival at the Savoy.

Peers refute her allegations and Tolloller's ballad, 'Spurn not the nobly born With love affected,..' is a pompous and heartfelt plea to Phyllis, full of nostalgic patriotism:

> 'Hearts just as pure and fair
> May beat in Belgrave Square
> As in the lowly air
> Of Seven Dials!'

is the prize sentiment in inverted snobbery.

Phyllis then confesses her love for Strephon, who forthwith appears. He introduces himself in a variation of 'Over the hills and far away'. The Morris Dance rhythm soon changes into a quick march as the Peers break into seething disquiet, desperately attempting to retain composure. Minor modulations and an unrepressed glissando build up to the fanfares and a reprise of 'Tantantara!' on which they make their 'dignified and stately' exit.

Phyllis is sent away and Strephon, confronted by the Lord Chancellor, becomes the rebellious hero, proclaiming that Nature, in all her manifestations, has given him authority to love Phyllis. The Lord Chancellor is patiently sceptical, deploring the lack of real evidence such as 'an affidavit from a thunderstorm' and so on. When Strephon begs him to be less prosaic, the Lord Chancellor launches into his autobiographical rise to position, 'Said I to myself, said I', listing all the legal wiles which his conscience does *not* allow him to employ.

Iolanthe discovers Strephon weeping over the Lord Chancellor's cruelty. 'Oh, if he did but know!' she hints, enigmatically, and she promises to plead Strephon's cause with the Fairy Queen.

The Peers have returned unnoticed, led by Mountararat and Tolloller on either side of Phyllis. They tiptoe up to enquire into Strephon's new attachment. An almost sleazy, swaggering man-about-town tune opens the quartet, 'When darkly looms the day,'. Strephon declares his faith in Iolanthe, and she in turn promises him an ark of refuge. Their words are misheard, however, and the delighted Peers report to Phyllis plans for a lurid assignation in St James's Park.

In a dramatic musical climax, Phyllis declares that all is over between herself and Strephon. His statement, 'This lady's my mother!' is greeted with universal laughter. The same Wagnerian undertones herald the Lord Chancellor's arrival to assess the situation. Iolanthe hastily veils herself while the Peers give their side of the story in a song of guffawing mockery into which the Lord Chancellor is drawn. Strephon then explains, by way of proving Iolanthe's identity, that she nurtured him in babyhood and saved him from dying. It is in the line of Sullivan's 'baby-tripping' music but its tone is stronger than usual. It has been suggested that it derives from the Tsar's aria 'Sonst spielt ich mit Zepter und Kron!' from Lortzing's *Zar und Zimmermann*.

Strephon attracts the Lord Chancellor's exaggerated sympathy but the Peers are jealous, '...let's pipe our eye! Because our Strephon did not die!'

Meanwhile Iolanthe has escaped, and Strephon is left to take the brunt of Phyllis's rage. Her ballad, 'For riches and rank I do not long...' is a variation on the Arcadian 'Goodmorrows' of earlier. She then gives way to despair in a quasi-Verdian passage, also reminiscent of that between Wells and Lady Sangazure in *The Sorcerer*, and throws herself recklessly at the 'richest and rankiest' of the Peers, Mountararat and Tolloller, disregarding preference.

'Mighty Protectress, hasten to my aid!' calls Strephon, and at once the Fairies appear. An agitated explanation from Strephon is interspersed with taradiddles and disbelieving statements from the Peers.

The mood changes to one of rebuff as the Lord Chancellor tries to dismiss the Fairy Queen:

> 'Go away, madam;
> I should say, madam,
> You display, madam,
> Shocking taste.'

but the Fairies stand their ground, taking up his refrain in defiance. This repeated, upward thrust in the melody is strangely reminiscent of the 'Fate' theme in Verdi's *Forza del Destino*. The Queen furiously threatens vengeance and she reprimands the Lord Chancellor for his lack of respect in the face of 'an influential Fairy!'; he realizes that he has acted injudiciously in taking her for 'the proprietor of a Ladies' Seminary!'

A Mendelssohnian fanfare opens the Fairy Queen's pronouncement. Strephon is to be the instrument of punishment. He is to go into Parliament and his departure from Arcadia is announced by the Fairy Queen in a nursery rhyme, horse-and-driver trot.

She then delivers her decree *parlando* over rising *vibrato* accompaniment, with interjections of horror from the Peers. All bills that Strephon proposes shall automatically be passed and special privileges enjoyed by the Lords shall be abolished. Finally, she commands that:

> '...a Duke's exalted station
> Be attainable by Com-
> Petitive Examination!'

A rumbustious 'taking-off' song follows, reminiscent of the Act I final chorus from Verdi's *Un Ballo in Maschera*, and the Peers threaten vengeance should the base 'canaille', the 'plebs', or the οἱ πολλοί! interfere with their 'prestige'. The Fairies mock their attempt at intellectual superiority: 'One Latin word, one Greek remark, and one that's French!' They force the Peers, with their wands, to plead for mercy. Phyllis begs Strephon to relent but he is adamant, and she falls fainting into the arms of Lords Mountararat and Tolloller.

Private Willis, a sentry, stands on guard outside Westminster Hall. His song, in the eighteenth-century English patriotic style is a reflection on the Parliamentary system: 'I am an intellectual chap, And think of things that would astonish you.' The cynical surprises are, however, shrouded in ridiculous banalities.

The Fairies, with their three leaders Celia, Leila and Fleta, skip round the Yard. Their triumphant chorus, 'Strephon's a Member of Parliament!' is in the nature of a children's singing game. The Peers enter and take up the song, telling of Strephon's all-powerful Parliamentary sway. They chide the Fairies for their interference which threatens to ruin the balance of British politics. Mountararat upholds the efficiency of that ancient institution, the House of Peers, in his patriotic, eighteenth-century style song, enumerating great British victories when the House of Peers 'did nothing in particular and did it very well'. Leila and Ceila are charmed. They still express hate in a tantalizing duet against the light violin

Captain (later Sir) Eyre Massey Shaw (1830-1908), one of the most popular men in London and Chief of the Metropolitan Fire Brigade. His name, invoked by the Fairy Queen, created a sensation.

pizzicato accompaniment, but intersperse each phrase with a breathless 'Don't go!' Seeing how the Fairies weaken, the Lords now play 'hard-to-get' and take their leave.

The Fairy Queen is shocked to find her troupe in the throes of transgressing by falling in love with mortals. She gives the Fairies a practical lecture on restraint taking, as the object of her admiration, Private Willis. In a passionate, lilting song (previously heard in the Overture) she invokes the 'hose of common sense' to quell her ardour. The second stanza is addressed to Captain Shaw, Chief of the London Fire Brigade (a popular man-about-town later cited in a divorce case but cleared of impropriety).

Still believing Strephon to be unfaithful, Phyllis halfheartedly courts the attentions of Mountararat and Tolloller. They vie for her affections in the true 'old boy' spirit and finally reach no conclusion as to which shall take her. The quartet for the two Lords, Phyllis and Willis, 'In Friendship's name...' begins with a Haydnesque melody, reverting to a pure Sullivan *tutti* with a one-line *estravaganza* for Willis.

The Lord Chancellor's love for Phyllis has become an obsession. His Nightmare Song is surrealistic — Gilbert at his most witty and evocative:

'You get a good spadesman to plant a small tradesman
    (first take off his boots with a boot-tree),
And his legs will take root, and his fingers will
    shoot ...'

The song opens with the Lord Chancellor's motif and has appropriate nightmarish accompaniment, complete with ship's siren. After his rendering of this longest and fastest patter-song in all the operas, the Lord Chancellor falls exhausted on a seat.

He is discovered by Tolloller and Mountararat, who are distressed by his condition and his quandary of dual capacity in Phyllis's case. Mountararat sympathetically urges the Lord Chancellor to apply to himself once more with deference and live up to the maxim 'Faint heart never won Fair Lady'. Their dancing trio of wise sayings, 'If you go in You're sure to win —' is another 'taking-off' piece.

Strephon is tired of his political advantages and in a confrontation with Phyllis he confesses his fairy origins. Their duet of reconciliation is sung to the Arcadian theme first heard in the Overture.

Now Iolanthe appears and joyfully accepts Phyllis

as her daughter-in-law. Strephon begs his mother to plead his cause with the Lord Chancellor. 'Impossible!' she replies, and at last divulges that the Lord Chancellor is her husband. However, he believes that his wife is dead and she may not disillusion him.

As she speaks, the Lord Chancellor appears and she hastily veils herself. Phyllis and Strephon go off and she is left alone with her husband.

He is in high spirits having, with much heartrending, reconciled his two capacities. 'I may now consider myself engaged to Phyllis!' His self-interested hypocrisy, with all its wit, becomes excruciatingly out of place at this tense moment. Solemnly Iolanthe kneels before him and pleads for Strephon in a Tristanesque recitative. Her ballad, 'He loves! If in the bygone years...' is touchingly sentimental in the Victorian tradition. Iolanthe evokes memory of herself. 'If, in the eventide of life, sad thoughts of her arise,' she then reminds him of the treasured wedding relics. He is moved, but

Durward Lely, Lord Tolloller; George Grossmith, Lord Chancellor; Rutland Barrington, Mountararat in the first production of *Iolanthe*. 'If you go in, you're sure to win!'

doggedly determined to marry Phyllis. Iolanthe realizes that she is doomed to confess her identity. An unseen Chorus of wailing Fairies try to prevent her, but she is beyond restraint. She declares herself and the Lord Chancellor recognizes her. The wailing mounts as the Queen appears with the Fairies and proclaims Iolanthe's fate. At this point of desperation, the Peers and Private Willis enter and the two Fairies Leila and Celia step forward, declaring that if Iolanthe must die, so must they all, for they have all committed themselves to the Peers.

The Fairy Queen examines her regal scroll, declaring that 'every fairy must die who marries a mortal', but now the Lord Chancellor steps in and,

Bertha Lewis, Fairy Queen; Henry Lytton, Lord Chancellor; Marjorie Eyre, Iolanthe at the climax of the opera.

as 'an old equity draughtsman', he inserts the word 'doesn't' before 'marry'.

Only the Fairy Queen and Willis are without partners. The Queen summons Willis to her and invites him to become a fairy guardsman. As he accepts, wings sprout from his shoulders; the Fairies likewise implore the Peers to become fairies. In a reprise of the 'taking-off' song, 'If you go in...' they all fly to Fairyland, exchanging House of Peers for House of Peris.

IOLANTHE;

OR

THE PEER AND THE PERI

First produced at the Savoy Theatre, 25 November 1882

DRAMATIS PERSONÆ

THE LORD CHANCELLOR	baritone
EARL OF MOUNTARARAT	bass
EARL TOLLOLLER	tenor
PRIVATE WILLIS [*of the Grenadier Guards*].	baritone
STREPHON [*an Arcadian Shepherd*].	baritone
QUEEN OF THE FAIRIES	contralto
IOLANTHE [*a Fairy, Strephon's Mother*].	soprano
CELIA ⎫	
LEILA ⎬ *Fairies*	soprano
FLETA ⎭	
PHYLLIS [*an Arcadian Shepherdess and Ward in Chancery*].	
	soprano

Chorus of DUKES, MARQUISES, EARLS, VISCOUNTS, BARONS AND FAIRIES.

ACT I.

AN ARCADIAN LANDSCAPE.

ACT II.

PALACE YARD, WESTMINSTER.

IOLANTHE;

OR,

THE PEER AND THE PERI

ACT I.

SCENE—*An Arcadian Landscape. A river runs around the back of the Stage.*

A rustic bridge crosses the river.

Enter Fairies, led by LEILA, CELIA, *and* FLETA. *They trip around the stage singing as they dance.*

CHORUS.

Tripping hither, tripping thither,
Nobody knows why or whither;
We must dance and we must sing,
Round about our fairy ring!

SOLO.—CELIA.

We are dainty little fairies,
  Ever singing, ever dancing;
We indulge in our vagaries
  In a fashion most entrancing.
If you ask the special function
  Of our never-ceasing motion,
We reply, without compunction,
  That we haven't any notion!

CHORUS.

No, we haven't any notion!
Tripping hither, etc.

SOLO.—LEILA.

If you ask us how we live,
Lovers all essentials give—
We can ride on lovers' sighs,
Warm ourselves in lovers' eyes,
Bathe ourselves in lovers' tears,
Clothe ourselves in lovers' fears,
Arm ourselves with lovers' darts,
Hide ourselves in lovers' hearts.
When you know us, you'll discover
That we almost live on lover!

CHORUS.

Tripping hither, etc.

(At the end of chorus, all sigh wearily.)

CELIA. Ah, it's all very well, but since our Queen banished Iolanthe, fairy revels have not been what they were!

LEILA. Iolanthe was the life and soul of fairy land. Why, she wrote all our songs and arranged all our dances! We sing her songs and we trip her measures, but we don't enjoy ourselves!

FLETA. To think that five and twenty years have elapsed since she was banished! What could she have done to have deserved so terrible a punishment?

LEILA. Something awful! She married a mortal!

FLETA. Oh! Is it injudicious to marry a mortal?

LEILA. Injudicious? It strikes at the root of the whole fairy system. By our laws, the fairy who marries a mortal, dies!

CELIA. But Iolanthe didn't die!

Enter FAIRY QUEEN.

QUEEN. No, because your Queen, who loved her with a surpassing love, commuted her sentence to penal servitude for life, on condition that she left her husband and never communicated with him again!

LEILA *(aside to CELIA).* That sentence of penal servitude she is now working out, on her head, at the bottom of that stream!

QUEEN. Yes, but when I banished her, I gave her all the pleasant places of the earth to dwell in. I'm sure I never intended that she should go and live at the bottom of a stream! It makes me perfectly wretched to think of the discomfort she must have undergone!

LEILA. Think of the damp! And her chest was always delicate.

QUEEN. And the frogs! Ugh! I never shall enjoy any peace of mind until I know why Iolanthe went to live among the frogs!

FLETA. Then why not summon her and ask her?

QUEEN. Why? Because if I set eyes on her I should forgive her at once!

CELIA. Then why not forgive her? Twenty-five years—it's a long time!

LEILA. Think how we loved her!

QUEEN. Loved her? What was your love to mine? Why, she was invaluable to me! Who taught me to curl myself inside a buttercup? Iolanthe! Who taught me to swing upon a cobweb? Iolanthe! Who taught me to dive into a dewdrop—to nestle in a nutshell—to gambol upon gossamer? Iolanthe!

LEILA. She certainly did surprising things!

FLETA. Oh, give her back to us, great Queen, for your sake if not for ours! *(All kneel in supplication.)*

QUEEN *(irresolute).* Oh, I should be strong, but I am weak! I should be marble, but I am clay! Her punishment has been heavier than I intended. I did not mean that she should live among the frogs—and—well, well, it shall be as you wish—it shall be as you wish!

INVOCATION.—QUEEN.

Iolanthe!
From thy dark exile thou art summoned!
Come to our call—
Come, Iolanthe!

CELIA.   Iolanthe!
LEILA.   Iolanthe!
ALL.   Come to our call,
Come, Iolanthe!

[IOLANTHE *rises from the water. She is clad in water-weeds. She approaches the* QUEEN *with head bent and arms crossed.*

IOL.   With humbled breast
And every hope laid low,
To thy behest,
Offended Queen, I bow!

QUEEN. For a dark sin against our fairy laws,
We sent thee into lifelong banishment;
But Mercy holds her sway within our hearts—
Rise—thou art pardoned!

IOL.   Pardoned!
ALL.   Pardoned!
IOL. Ah!

[*Her weeds fall from her, and she appears clothed as a fairy. The* QUEEN *places a diamond coronet on her head, and embraces her. The others also embrace her*

CHORUS.

Welcome to our hearts again,
Iolanthe! Iolanthe!
We have shared thy bitter pain,
Iolanthe! Iolanthe!
Every heart and every hand
In our loving little band
Welcome thee to fairy land,
Iolanthe!

QUEEN. And now, tell me, with all the world to choose from, why on earth did you decide to live at the bottom of that stream?

IOL. To be near my son, Strephon.

QUEEN. Bless my heart, I didn't know you had a son!

IOL. He was born soon after I left my husband by your royal command—but he does not even know of his father's existence!

FLETA. How old is he?

IOL. Twenty-four.

LEILA. Twenty-four! No one, to look at you, would think you had a son of twenty-four! But that's one of the advantages of being immortal. We never grow old! Is he pretty?

IOL. He's extremely pretty, but he's inclined to be stout.

ALL (disappointed). Oh!

QUEEN. I see no objection to stoutness, in moderation.

CEL. And what is he?

IOL. He's an Arcadian shepherd—and he loves Phyllis, a ward in Chancery.

CEL. A mere shepherd! and he half a fairy!

IOL. He's a fairy down to the waist—but his legs are mortal.

ALL. Dear me!

QUEEN. I have no reason to suppose that I am more curious than other people, but I confess I should like to see a person who is a fairy down to the waist, but whose legs are mortal.

IOL. Nothing easier, for here he comes!

Enter STREPHON, *singing and dancing and playing on a flageolet. He does not see the fairies, who retire up stage as he enters.*

SONG.—STREPHON.

Good morrow, good mother!
  Good mother, good morrow!
By some means or other,
  Pray banish your sorrow!
    With joy beyond telling
    My bosom is swelling,
    So join in a measure
    Expressive of pleasure.
For I'm to be married to-day—to-day—
Yes, I'm to be married to-day!

CHORUS. (aside) Yes, he's to be married to-day—to-day—
Yes, he's to be married to-day!

IOL. Then the Lord Chancellor has at last given his consent to your marriage with his beautiful ward, Phyllis?

STREPH. Not he, indeed. To all my tearful prayers he answers me, "A shepherd lad is no fit helpmate for a ward of Chancery." I stood in court, and there I sang him songs of Arcadee, with flageolet accompaniment—in vain. At first he seemed amused, so did the Bar; but quickly wearying of my song and pipe, bade me get out. A servile usher, then, in crumpled bands and rusty bombazine, led me, still singing, into Chancery Lane! I'll go no more! I'll marry her to-day, and brave the upshot, be it what it may! (sees Fairies). But who are these?

IOL. Oh, Strephon! rejoice with me, my Queen has pardoned me!

STREPH. Pardoned you, mother? This is good news indeed!

IOL. And these ladies are my beloved sisters.

STREPH. Your sisters! Then they are—my aunts! (Kneels.)

QUEEN. A pleasant piece of news for your bride on her wedding day.

STREPH. Hush! My bride knows nothing of my fairyhood. I dare not tell her, lest it frighten her. She thinks me mortal, and prefers me so.

LEILA. Your fairyhood doesn't seem to have done you much good.

STREPH. Much good! It's the curse of my existence! What's the use of being half a fairy? My body can creep through a keyhole, but what's the good of that, when my legs are left kicking behind? I can make myself invisible down to the waist, but that's of no use, when my legs remain exposed to view? My brain is a fairy brain, but from the waist downwards I'm a gibbering idiot. My upper half is immortal, but my lower half grows older every day, and some day or other must die of old age. What's to become of my upper half when I've buried my lower half I really don't know!

QUEEN. I see your difficulty, but with a fairy brain you should seek an intellectual sphere of action. Let me see. I've a borough or two at my disposal. Would you like to go into Parliament?

IOL. A fairy Member! That would be delightful!

STREPH. I'm afraid I should do no good there—you see, down to the waist, I'm a Tory of the most determined description, but my legs are a couple of confounded Radicals, and, on a division, they'd be sure to take me into the wrong lobby. You see they're two to one, which is a strong working majority.

QUEEN. Don't let that distress you; you shall be returned as a Liberal-Conservative, and your legs shall be our peculiar care.

STREPH. (bowing). I see your Majesty does not do things by halves.

QUEEN. No, we are fairies down to the feet.

ENSEMBLE.

QUEEN.	Fare thee well, attractive stranger.
FAIRIES.	Fare thee well, attractive stranger.
QUEEN.	Shouldst thou be in doubt or danger,
	Peril or perplexitee,
	Call us, and we'll come to thee!
FAIRIES.	Call us, and we'll come to thee!
	Tripping hither, tripping thither.
	Nobody knows why or whither.
	We must now be taking wing
	To another fairy ring!

[*Fairies and* QUEEN *trip off.* IOLANTHE, *who takes an affectionate farewell of her son, going off last.*

Enter PHYLLIS, *singing and dancing, and accompanying herself on a flageolet.*

SONG.—PHYLLIS.

Good morrow, good lover!
  Good lover, good morrow!
I prithee discover,
  Steal, purchase, or borrow,
    Some means of concealing
    The care you are feeling,
    And join in a measure
    Expressive of pleasure.
For we're to be married to-day—to-day!
For we're to be married to-day!

BOTH. Yes, we're to be married, etc.

STREPH. (embracing her). My Phyllis! And to-day we are to be made happy for ever!

PHYL. Well, we're to be married.

STREPH. It's the same thing.

PHYL. I suppose it is. But, oh, Strephon, I tremble at the step I'm taking! I believe it's penal servitude for life to marry a ward of Court without the Lord Chancellor's consent! I shall be of age in two years. Don't you think you could wait two years?

STREPH. Two years! Why, you can't have seen yourself? Here, look at that *(showing her a pocket mirror)*, and tell me if you think it rational to expect me to wait two years?

PHYL. *(looking at herself)*. No. You're quite right—it's asking too much. One must be reasonable.

STREPH. Besides, who knows what will happen in two years? Why, you might fall in love with the Lord Chancellor himself by that time!

PHYL. Yes. He's a clean old gentleman.

STREPH. As it is, half the House of Lords are sighing at your feet.

PHYL. The House of Lords are certainly extremely attentive.

STREPH. Attentive? I should think they were! Why did five-and-twenty Liberal Peers come down to shoot over your grass-plot last autumn? It couldn't have been the sparrows. Why did five-and-twenty Conservative Peers come down to fish your pond? Don't tell me it was the gold-fish! No, no; delays are dangerous, and if we are to marry, the sooner the better.

DUET.—STREPHON *and* PHYLLIS.

None shall part us from each other.
    One in life and death are we:
All in all to one another—
    I to thee and thou to me!
Thou the tree and I the flower—
    Thou the idol; I the throng—
Thou the day and I the hour—
    Thou the singer; I the song!

All in all since that fond meeting
    When, in joy, I woke to find
Mine the heart within thee beating,
    Mine the love that heart enshrined!
Thou the stream and I the willow—
    Thou the sculptor; I the clay—
Thou the ocean; I the billow—
    Thou the sunrise; I the day!

[*Exeunt* STREPHON *and* PHYLLIS *together.*

March. Enter Procession of Peers.

CHORUS.

Loudly let the trumpet bray!
        Tantantara!
Gaily bang the sounding brasses!
        Tzing!
As upon its lordly way
    This unique procession passes,
        Tantantara! Tzing! Boom!
Bow, bow, ye lower middle classes!
Bow, ye tradesmen! bow, ye masses!
Blow the trumpets, bang the brasses!
        Tantantara! Tzing! Boom!
We are peers of highest station,
Paragons of legislation,
Pillars of the British nation!
        Tantantara! Tzing! Boom!

Enter the LORD CHANCELLOR, *followed by his trainbearer.*

SONG.—LORD CHANCELLOR.

The Law is the true embodiment
Of everything that's excellent.
It has no kind of fault or flaw,
And I, my Lords, embody the Law.

The constitutional guardian I
Of pretty young wards in Chancery,
All very agreeable girls—and none
Are over the age of twenty-one.
    A pleasant occupation for
    A rather susceptible Chancellor!
ALL.   A pleasant, etc.

But though the compliment implied
Inflates me with legitimate pride,
It nevertheless can't be denied
That it has its inconvenient side.
For I'm not so old, and not so plain,
And I'm quite prepared to marry again,
But there'd be the deuce to pay in the Lords
If I fell in love with one of my wards!
    Which rather tries my temper, for
    I'm *such* a susceptible Chancellor!
ALL.   Which rather, etc.

And every one who'd marry a ward
Must come to me for my accord,
And in my court I sit all day,
Giving agreeable girls away,
With one for him—and one for he—
And one for you—and one for ye—
And one for thou—and one for thee—
But never, oh never a one for me!
    Which is exasperating, for
    A highly susceptible Chancellor!
ALL.   Which is, etc.

Enter Lord TOLLOLLER.

LD. TOLL. And now, my Lords, to the business of the day.

LD. CH. By all means. Phyllis, who is a ward of Court, has so powerfully affected your Lordships, that you have appealed to me in a body to give her to whichever one of you she may think proper to select, and a noble lord has just gone to her cottage to request her immediate attendance. It would be idle to deny that I, myself, have the misfortune to be singularly attracted by this young person. My regard for her is rapidly undermining my constitution. Three months ago I was a stout man. I need say no more. If I could reconcile it with my duty, I should unhesitatingly award her to myself, for I can conscientiously say that I know no man who is so well fitted to render her exceptionally happy. But such an award would be open to misconstruction, and therefore, at whatever personal inconvenience, I waive my claim.

LD. TOLL. My Lord, I desire, on the part of this House, to express its sincere sympathy with your Lordship's most painful position.

LD. CH. I thank your Lordships. The feelings of a Lord Chancellor who is in love with a ward of Court are not to be envied. What is his position? Can he give his own consent to his own marriage with his own ward? Can he marry his own ward without his own consent? And if he marries his own ward without his own consent, can he commit himself for contempt of his own Court? And if he commit himself for contempt of his own Court, can he appear by counsel before himself, to move for arrest of his own judgment? Ah, my Lords, it is indeed painful to have to sit upon a woolsack which is stuffed with such thorns as these!

Enter LORD MOUNTARARAT.

LD. MOUNT. My Lords, I have much pleasure in announcing that I have succeeded in inducing the young person to present herself at the Bar of this House.

Enter PHYLLIS.

Recit.—PHYLLIS.   My well-beloved Lord and Guardian dear,
                  You summoned me, and I am here!

Chorus of PEERS.   Oh, rapture, how beautiful!
                How gentle! how dutiful!

SOLO.—LORD TOLLOLLER.

Of all the young ladies I know,
   This pretty young lady's the fairest,
Her lips have the rosiest show,
   Her eyes are the richest and rarest.
Her origin's lowly, it's true,
   But of birth and position we've plenty;
We've grammar and spelling for two,
   And blood and behaviour for twenty!

CHORUS.   Her origin's lowly, it's true,
         But we've grammar and spelling for two;
        Of birth and position we've plenty,
        With blood and behaviour for twenty!

SOLO.—EARL OF MOUNTARARAT.

Though the views of the House have diverged
   On every conceivable motion,
All questions of Party are merged
   In a frenzy of love and devotion;
If you ask us distinctly to say
   What Party we claim to belong to,
We reply, without doubt or delay,
   The Party I'm singing this song to!

CHORUS.   If you ask us distinctly to say,
        We reply, without doubt or delay,
        That the Party we claim to belong to
        Is the Party we're singing this song to!

SOLO.—PHYLLIS.

I'm very much pained to refuse,
   But I'll stick to my pipes and my tabors;
I can spell all the words that I use,
   And my grammar's as good as my neighbours'.
As for birth—I was born like the rest,
   My behaviour is rustic but hearty,
And I know where to turn for the best,
   When I want a particular Party!

CHORUS.   Though her station is none of the best,
        I suppose she was born like the rest;
        And she knows where to look for her hearty,
        When she wants a particular Party!

RECIT.—PHYLLIS.

Nay, tempt me not.
   To rank I'll not be bound;
In lowly cot
   Alone is virtue found!

CHORUS. Nay, do not shrink from us—we will not hurt you—
        The Peerage is not destitute of virtue.

BALLAD.—LORD TOLLOLLER.

Spurn not the nobly born
   With love affected,
Nor treat with virtuous scorn
   The well connected.

High rank involves no shame—
   We boast an equal claim
With him of humble name
   To be respected!
Blue blood! Blue blood!
     When virtuous love is sought,
     Thy power is nought,
Though dating from the Flood,
     Blue blood!
CHORUS.   Blue blood! Blue blood! etc.

Spare us the bitter pain
   Of stern denials,
Nor with lowborn disdain
   Augment our trials.
Hearts just as pure and fair
May beat in Belgrave Square
As in the lowly air
   Of Seven Dials!
Blue blood! Blue blood!
     Of what avail art thou
     To serve us now?
Though dating from the Flood,
     Blue blood!
CHORUS.   Blue blood! Blue blood! etc.

RECIT.—PHYLLIS.

My Lord, it may not be.
   With grief my heart is riven!
You waste your words on me,
   For ah! my heart is given!

ALL.   Given!
PHYLL.   Given!
ALL.   Oh, horror!!!

RECIT.—LORD CHANCELLOR.

And who has dared to brave our high displeasure,
And thus defy our definite command?

Enter STREPHON—PHYLLIS *rushes to his arms.*

STREPH. 'Tis I—young Strephon! mine this priceless treasure.
         Against the world I claim my darling's hand!
         A shepherd I—

ALL.   A shepherd he!
STREPH.   Of Arcady—
ALL.   Of Arcadee!
STREPH.   Betrothed are we!
ALL.   Betrothed are they—
STREPH.   And mean to be—
ALL.   Espoused to-day!

ENSEMBLE.

STREPH. A shepherd I   THE OTHERS. A shepherd he
         Of Arcady,   Of Arcadee,
         Betrothed are we,   Betrothed is he,
         And mean to be   And means to be
         Espoused to-day!   Espoused to-day!

DUET.—LORD MOUNT, *and* LORD TOLL. *(aside to each other).*

         'Neath this blow,
             Worse than stab of dagger—
         Though we mo-
             Mentarily stagger,
         In each heart
             Proud are we innately—
         Let's depart,
             Dignified and stately!

ALL.   Let's depart,
             Dignified and stately!

Chorus of Peers.

Though our hearts she's badly bruising,
In another suitor choosing,
Let's pretend it's most amusing.
         Ha! ha! ha! ha! Tzing! Boom!

[*Exeunt all the Peers marching round stage with much dignity.* LORD
CHANCELLOR *separates* PHYLLIS *from* STREPHON, *and orders her
off. She follows Peers. Manent* LORD CHANCELLOR *and*
STREPHON.

LORD CH. Now, sir, what excuse have you to offer for having
disobeyed an order of the Court of Chancery?

STREPH. My Lord, I know no Courts of Chancery; I go by
Nature's Acts of Parliament. The bees—the breeze—the seas—
the rocks—the brooks—the gales—the vales—the fountains and
the mountains, cry, "You love this maiden—take her we
command you!" 'Tis writ in heaven by the bright barbèd dart
that leaps forth into lurid light from each grim thundercloud.
The very rain pours forth her sad and sodden sympathy! When
chorussed Nature bids me take my love, shall I reply, "Nay, but
a certain Chancellor forbids it"? Sir, you are England's Lord
High Chancellor, but are you Chancellor of birds and trees, King
of the winds, and Prince of thunderclouds?

LORD CH. No. It's a nice point. I don't know that I ever met it
before. But my difficulty is that at present there's no evidence
before the Court that chorussed Nature has interested herself in
the matter.

STREPH. No evidence! You have my word for it. I tell you that
she bade me take my love.

LORD CH. Ah! but, my good sir, you mustn't tell us what she
told you—it's not evidence. Now an affidavit from a
thunderstorm, or a few words on oath from a heavy shower,
would meet with all the attention they deserve.

STREPH. And have you the heart to apply the prosaic rules of
evidence to a case which bubbles over with poetical emotion?

LORD CH. Distinctly. I have always kept my duty strictly
before my eyes, and it is to that fact that I owe my advancement
to my present distinguished position.

SONG.—LORD CHANCELLOR.

When I went to the Bar as a very young man,
      (Said I to myself—said I,)
I'll work on a new and original plan,
      (Said I to myself—said I,)
I'll never assume that a rogue or a thief
Is a gentleman worthy implicit belief,
Because his attorney has sent me a brief,
      (Said I to myself—said I!)

I'll never throw dust in a juryman's eyes,
      (Said I to myself—said I,)
Or hoodwink a judge who is not over-wise,
      (Said I to myself—said I,)
Or assume that the witnesses summoned in force
In Exchequer, Queen's Bench, Common Pleas, or
      Divorce,
Have perjured themselves as a matter of course,
      (Said I to myself—said I!)

Ere I go into court I will read my brief through,
      (Said I to myself—said I,)
And I'll never take work I'm unable to do,
      (Said I to myself—said I.)
My learned profession I'll never disgrace
By taking a fee with a grin on my face,
When I haven't been there to attend to the case,
      (Said I to myself—said I!)

In other professions in which men engage,
      (Said I to myself—said I,)
The Army, the Navy, the Church, and the Stage,
      (Said I to myself—said I,)
Professional licence, if carried too far,

Your chance of promotion will certainly mar—
And I fancy the rule might apply to the Bar,
(Said I to myself—said I!).

[*Exit* LORD CHANCELLOR.

To STREPHON, *who is in tears, enter* IOLANTHE.

STREPH. Oh, Phyllis, Phyllis! To be taken from you just as I was on the point of making you my own! Oh, it's too much—it is too much!

IOL. My son in tears—and on his wedding day!

STREPH. My wedding day! Oh, mother, weep with me, for the Law has interposed between us, and the Lord Chancellor has separated us for ever!

IOL. The Lord Chancellor! (*aside*). Oh, if he did but know!

STREPH. (*overhearing her*). If he did but know what?

IOL. No matter! The Lord Chancellor has no power over you. Remember you are half a fairy. You can defy him—down to the waist.

STREPH. Yes, but from the waist downwards he can commit me to prison for years! Of what avail is it that my body is free, if my legs are working out seven years' penal servitude?

IOL. True. But take heart—our Queen has promised you her special protection. I'll go to her and lay your peculiar case before her.

STREPH. My beloved mother! How can I repay the debt I owe you?

FINALE.

QUARTET.

[*As it commences, the Peers appear at the back, advancing unseen and on tiptoe.* MOUNTARARAT *and* TOLLOLLER *lead* PHYLLIS *between them, who listens in horror to what she hears.*)

STREPH. (*to* IOLANTHE). When darkly looms the day,
　　　　And all is dull and grey,
　　　　To chase the gloom away
　　　　　　On thee I'll call!

PHYL. (*speaking aside to* MOUNT.). What was that?

MOUNT. (*aside to* PHYLLIS). I think I heard him say,
　　　　That on a rainy day,
　　　　To while the time away,
　　　　　　On her he'd call!

CHORUS. We think we heard him say, etc.

(PHYLLIS *much agitated at her lover's supposed faithlessness.*)

IOL. (*to* STREPHON). When tempests wreck thy bark,
　　　　And all is drear and dark,
　　　　If thou shouldst need an Ark,
　　　　　　I'll give thee one!

PHYL. (*speaking aside to* TOLLOLLER). What was that?

TOL. (*aside to* PHYLLIS). I heard the minx remark,
　　　　She'd meet him after dark,
　　　　Inside St. James's Park,
　　　　　　And give him one!

ALL. The prospect's not so bad,
　{ My }
　{ Thy } heart so sore and sad
　　May very soon be glad
　　　　As summer sun;
　　But while the sky is dark,
　　And tempests wreck { my } { thy } bark,
　　If { I should } { thou shouldst } need an Ark,
　　{ Thou'lt } { I'll } give { me } { thee } one!

PHYL. (*revealing herself*). Ah!

(IOLANTHE *and* STREPHON *much confused.*)

PHYL. Oh, shameless one, tremble!
　　　　Nay, do not endeavour
　　　　Thy fault to dissemble,
　　　　　　We part—and for ever!
　　　　I worshipped him blindly,
　　　　He worships another—

STREPH. Attend to me kindly,
　　　　This lady's my mother!

PHYL. This lady's his *what*?

STREPH. This lady's my mother!

TENORS. This lady's his *what*?

BASSES. He says she's his mother!

(*They point derisively to* IOLANTHE, *laughing heartily at her. She for protection to* STREPHON.)

Enter LORD CHANCELLOR. IOLANTHE *veils herself.*

LORD CH. What means this mirth unseemly,
　　　　That shakes the listening earth?

LORD TOL. The joke is good extremely,
　　　　And justifies our mirth.

LORD MOUNT. This gentleman is seen,
　　　　With a maid of seventeen,
　　　　A taking of his *dolce far niente;*
　　　　And wonders he'd achieve,
　　　　For he asks us to believe
　　She's his mother—and he's nearly five-and-twenty!

LORD CH.
(*sternly*). Recollect yourself, I pray,
　　　　And be careful what you say—
　　As the ancient Romans said, *festina lente.*
　　　　For I really do not see
　　　　How so young a girl could be
　　The mother of a man of five-and-twenty.

ALL. Ha! ha! ha! ha! ha!

STREPH.   My Lord, of evidence I have no dearth—
           She is—has been—my mother, from my birth!

BALLAD.

In babyhood
Upon her lap I lay,
With infant food
She moistened my clay:
Had she withheld
The succour she supplied,
By hunger quelled,
Your Strephon might have died!

LORD CH. *(much moved).* Had that refreshment been denied,
        Indeed our Strephon might have died!

ALL *(much affected).* Had that refreshment been denied,
        Indeed our Strephon might have died!

LD. MOUNT. But as she's not
       His mother, it appears,
     Why weep these hot
       Unnecessary tears?
     And by what laws
       Should we, so joyously,
     Rejoice, because
       Our Strephon didn't die?
     Oh, rather let us pipe our eye,
     Because our Strephon didn't die!

ALL.   That's very true—let's pipe our eye
     Because our Strephon didn't die!

(All weep. IOLANTHE, *who has succeeded in hiding her face from the* LORD CHANCELLOR, *escapes unnoticed.)*

PHYL.   Go, traitorous one—for ever we must part:
     To one of you, my Lords, I give my heart!
ALL.   Oh, rapture!
STREPH.   Hear me, Phyllis, ere you leave me!
PHYL.   Not a word—you did deceive me!
ALL.   Not a word—you did deceive her!

BALLAD.—PHYLLIS.

For riches and rank I do not long—
   Their pleasures are false and vain:
I gave up the love of a lordly throng
   For the love of a simple swain.

But now that that simple swain's untrue,
With sorrowful heart I turn to you—
   A heart that's aching,
   Quaking, breaking,
As sorrowful hearts are wont to do!

The riches and rank that you befall
   Are the only baits you use,
So the richest and rankiest of you all
   My sorrowful heart shall choose.
As none are so noble—none so rich

As this couple of lords, I'll find a niche,
   In my heart that's aching,
   Quaking, breaking,
For one of you two—and I don't care which!

ENSEMBLE.

PHYL. *(to* LD. MOUNT. *and* LD. TOLL.). To you I give my heart so
   rich!
ALL. *(puzzled).* To which?
PHYL.   I do not care!
       To you I yield—it is my doom;
ALL.   To whom?
PHYL.   I'm not aware!
       I'm yours for life if you but choose.
ALL.   She's whose?
PHYL.   That's your affair.
       I'll be a countess, shall I not?
ALL.   Of what?
PHYL.   I do not care!

ALL.   Lucky little lady!
     Strephon's lot is shady;
     Rank, it seems, is vital,
     "Countess" is the title,
      But of what I'm not aware!

STREPH.   Can I inactive see my fortune fade?
        No, no!
     Mighty protectress, hasten to my aid!

Enter Fairies, tripping, headed by CELIA, LEILA, *and* FLETA,
and followed by QUEEN.

Chorus of FAIRIES.

Tripping hither, tripping thither,
Nobody knows why or whither;
   Why you want us we don't know,
   But you've summoned us, and so
   Enter all the little fairies
     To their usual tripping measure!
   To oblige you all our care is—
     Tell us, pray, what is your pleasure!

STREPH. The lady of my love has caught me talking to another—
ALL.   Oh, fie! Strephon is a rogue!
STREPH. I tell her very plainly that the lady is my mother—
ALL.   Taradiddle, taradiddle, tol lol lay!
STREPH. She won't believe my statement, and declares we must
      be parted,
    Because on a career of double dealing I have started,
    Then gives her hand to one of these, and leaves me
      broken-hearted—
ALL.   Taradiddle, taradiddle, tol lol lay!
QUEEN. Ah, cruel ones, to part two faithful lovers from each
    other!

ALL. Oh, fie! Strephon is a rogue!

QUEEN. You've done him an injustice, for the lady *is* his mother!

ALL. Taradiddle, taradiddle, tol lol lay!

LORD CH. (*aside*). That fable perhaps may serve his turn as well as
any other.
I didn't see her face, but if they fondled one another,
And she's but seventeen—I don't believe it was his
mother!

ALL. Taradiddle, taradiddle, tol lol lay!

LORD TOLL. I've often had a use
For a thorough-bred excuse
Of a sudden (which is English for *"repentè"*)
But of all I ever heard
This is much the most absurd,
For she's seventeen and he is five-and-twenty!

ALL. He says she is his mother, and he's four or five-and-twenty!
Oh, fie! Strephon is a rogue!

LORD MOUNT. Now listen, pray, to me,
For this paradox will be
Carried nobody at all *contradicente*.
Her age, upon the date
of his birth was *minus* eight,
If she's seventeen, and he is five-and-twenty!

ALL. To say she is his mother is an utter bit of folly!
Oh, fie! Strephon is a rogue!
Perhaps his brain is addled, and it's very melancholy!
Taradiddle, taradiddle, tol lol lay!
I wouldn't say a word that could be construed as injurious,
But to find a mother younger than her son is very curious,
And that's a kind of mother that is usually spurious.
Taradiddle, taradiddle, tol lol lay!

LD. CH. Go away, madam;
I should say, madam,
You display, madam,
Shocking taste.

It is rude, madam,
To intrude, madam,
With your brood, madam,
Brazen-faced!

You come here, madam,
Interfere, madam,
With a peer, madam.
(I am one.)

You're aware, madam,
What you dare, madam,
So take care, madam,
And begone!

ENSEMBLE.

FAIRIES (*to* QUEEN).	PEERS.
Let us stay, madam,	Go away, madam;
I should say, madam,	I should say, madam,
They display, madam,	You display, madam,
Shocking taste.	Shocking taste.
It is rude, madam,	It is rude, madam,
To allude, madam,	To intrude, madam,
To your brood, madam,	With your brood, madam,
Brazen-faced!	Brazen-faced!
We don't fear, madam,	You come here, madam,
Any peer, madam,	Interfere, madam,
Though, my dear madam,	With a peer, madam.
This is one.	(I am one.)
They will stare, madam,	You're aware, madam,
When aware, madam,	What you dare, madam,
What they dare, madam—	To take care, madam,
What they've done!	And begone!

QUEEN (*furious*). Bearded by these puny mortals!
I will launch from fairy portals
All the most terrific thunders
In my armoury of wonders!

PHYL. (*aside*). Should they launch terrific wonders,
All would then repent their blunders.

QUEEN. Oh! Chancellor unwary,
It's highly necessary
Your tongue to teach
Respectful speech—
Your attitude to vary!

Your badinage so airy,
Your manner arbitrary,
Are out of place
When face to face
With an influential Fairy!

All the PEERS (*aside*). I never knew
We were speaking to
An influential Fairy!

LORD CH. A plague on this vagary!
I'm in a nice quandary!
Of hasty tone
With dames unknown;
I ought to be more chary!
It seems that she's a fairy
From Andersen's library,
And I took her for
The proprietor
Of a Ladies' Seminary!

ALL. { He }
{ We } took her for
The proprietor
Of a Ladies' Seminary!

QUEEN. When next your Houses do assemble,
   You may tremble!

CELIA. Our wrath, when gentlemen offend us,
   Is tremendous!

LEILA. They meet, who underrate our calling,
   Doom appalling!

QUEEN. Take down our sentence as we speak it,
   And *he* shall wreak it!
       (Indicating STREPHON.)

QUEEN. Henceforth, Strephon, cast away
   Crooks and pipes and ribbons so gay—
   Flocks and herds that bleat and low;
   Into Parliament you shall go!

FAIRIES. Into Parliament he shall go!
   Backed by our supreme authority,
   He'll command a large majority!
   Into Parliament he shall go!

QUEEN. In the Parliamentary hive,
   Liberal or Conservative—
   Whig or Tory—I don't know—
   But into Parliament you shall go!

FAIRIES. Into Parliament, etc.

PEERS. Ah, spare us!

   QUEEN *(speaking through music).*

Every Bill and every measure
That may gratify his pleasure,
Though your fury it arouses,
Shall be passed by both your Houses!
You shall sit, if he sees reason,
Through the grouse and salmon season!
He shall end the cherished rights
You enjoy on Wednesday nights:
He shall prick that annual blister,
Marriage with deceased wife's sister!
Titles shall ennoble, then,
All the Common Councilmen:
 Peers shall teem in Christendom,
 And a Duke's exalted station
Be attainable by Com-
Petitive Examination!

PEERS.	FAIRIES *and* PHYLLIS.
Oh, horror!	Their horror! They can't dissemble Nor hide the fear that makes them tremble!

      ENSEMBLE.

PEERS.	FAIRIES *and* PHYLLIS.

Young Strephon is the kind
 of lout
We do not care a fig about!
  We cannot say
  What evils may,
 Result in consequence.
	With Strephon for your foe,
	 no doubt,
	A fearful prospect opens out,
	  And who shall say
	  What evils may
	 Result in consequence?

But lordly vengeance will
 pursue
All kinds of common people
 who
  Oppose our views,
  Or boldly choose
 To offer us offence.
	A hideous vengeance will
	 pursue
	All noblemen who venture
	 to
	  Oppose his views
	  Or boldly choose
	 To offer him offence.

He'd better fly at humbler
 game,
Or our forbearance he must
 claim
  If he'd escape
  In any shape
 A very painful wrench!
	'Twill plunge them into grief
	 and shame;
	His kind forbearance they
	 must claim
	  If they'd escape
	  In any shape
	 A very painful wrench.

Your powers we dauntlessly
 pooh-pooh:
A dire revenge will fall on
 you,
  If you besiege
  Our high *prestige*—
(The word *"prestige"* is
French).
	Although our threats you
	 now pooh-pooh,
	A dire revenge will fall on
	 you,
	  Should he besiege
	  Your high *prestige*—
	(The word *"prestige"* is
	French).

PEERS.   Our lordly style
     You shall not quench
    With base *canaille!*
FAIRIES.   (That word is French.)
PEERS.   Distinction ebbs
     Before a herd
    Of vulgar *plebs!*
FAIRIES.   (A Latin word.)
PEERS.   'Twould fill with joy,
     And madness stark
    The οἱ πολλοί!
FAIRIES.   (A Greek remark.)

PEERS.	FAIRIES.
You needn't wait: Away you fly! Your threatened hate We thus defy!	We will not wait: We go sky-high! Our threatened hate You won't defy!

FAIRIES.   Your lordly style
     We'll quickly quench
    With base *canaille!*
PEERS.   (That word is French!)

Patricia Leonard as the Fairy Queen and Kenneth
Sandford as Private Willis in the D'Oyly Carte's 1977
production of *Iolanthe*.

D'Oyly Carte Company poster for the première of
Princess Ida at the Savoy Theatre, January 1884.

FAIRIES.   Distinction ebbs
                 Before a herd
                 Of vulgar *plebs!*
PEERS.   (A Latin word.)
FAIRIES.   'Twill fill with joy
                 And madness stark
                 The οἱ πολλοί!
PEERS.   (A Greek remark.)

PEERS.   FAIRIES.

You needn't wait: We will not wait:
  Away you fly!   We go sky-high!
Your threatened hate Our threatened hate
We won't defy!   You won't defy!

[*Fairies threaten Peers with their wands. Peers kneel as begging for mercy.* PHYLLIS *implores* STREPHON *to relent. He casts her from him, and she falls fainting into the arms of* LORD MOUNTARARAT *and* LORD TOLLOLLER.

END OF ACT I.

ACT II.

SCENE.—*Palace Yard, Westminster. Westminster Hall,* L. *Clock tower up* R.C.

PRIVATE WILLIS *discovered on sentry,* R. *Moonlight.*

SONG.—WILLIS.

When all night long a chap remains
  On sentry-go, to chase monotony
He exercises of his brains,
  That is, assuming that he's got any.
Though never nurtured in the lap
  Of luxury, yet I admonish you,
I am an intellectual chap,
  And think of things that would astonish you.
    I often think it's comical—Fal, lal, la!
    How Nature always does contrive—Fal, lal, la!
      That every boy and every gal,
        That's born into the world alive,
      Is either a little Liberal,
        Or else a little Conservative!
      Fal, lal, la!

When in that House M.P.'s divide,
  If they've a brain and cerebellum, too,
They've got to leave that brain outside,
  And vote just as their leaders tell 'em to.
But then the prospect of a lot
  Of dull M.P.'s in close proximity,
All thinking for themselves, is what
  No man can face with equanimity.
    Then let's rejoice with loud Fal lal—Fal, lal, la!
    That Nature wisely does contrive—Fal, lal, la!
      That every boy and every gal,
        That's born into the world alive,
      Is either a little Liberal,

        Or else a little Conservative!
      Fal, lal, la!

Enter Fairies, with CELIA, LEILA, *and* FLETA. *They trip round stage.*

Chorus of FAIRIES.

Strephon's a Member of Parliament!
  And carries every Bill he chooses.
To his measures all assent;—
    Showing that fairies have their uses.
      Whigs and Tories
      Dim their glories,
Giving an ear to all his stories—
Lords and Commons are both in the blues:
Strephon makes them shake in their shoes!
      Shake in their shoes!
      Shake in their shoes!
Strephon makes them shake in their shoes!

Enter Peers from Westminster Hall.

Chorus of PEERS.

Strephon's a Member of Parliament!
  Running a-muck at all abuses.
His unqualified assent
    Somehow nobody now refuses.
      Whigs and Tories
      Dim their glories,
Giving an ear to all his stories—
Carrying every Bill he may wish:
Here's a pretty kettle of fish!
      Kettle of fish!
      Kettle of fish!
Here's a pretty kettle of fish!

Enter LORD MOUNTARARAT *and* LORD TOLLOLLER *from Westminster Hall.*

CELIA. You seem annoyed.

LD. MOUNT. Annoyed? I should think so! Why, this ridiculous *protégé* of yours is playing the deuce with everything! To-night is the second reading of his Bill to throw the Peerage open to Competitive Examination!

LD. TOLL. And he'll carry it, too!

LD. MOUNT. Carry it? Of course he will! He's a Parliamentary Pickford—he carries everything!

LEILA. Yes. If you please, that's our fault!

LD. MOUNT. The deuce it is!

CELIA. Yes; we influence the members, and compel them to vote just as he wishes them to.

LEILA. It's our system. It shortens the debates.

LD. TOLL. Well, but think what it all means. I don't so much mind for myself, but with a House of Peers with no grandfathers worth mentioning, the country must go to the dogs!

LEILA. I suppose it must!

LD. MOUNT. I don't want to say a word against brains—I've a great respect for brains—I often wish I had some myself—but with a House of Peers composed exclusively of people of intellect, what's to become of the House of Commons?

LEILA. I never thought of that!

LD. MOUNT. This comes of women interfering in politics. It so happens that if there is an institution in Great Britain which is not susceptible of any improvement at all, it is the House of Peers!

SONG.—LD. MOUNT.

When Britain really ruled the waves—
(In good Queen Bess's time)
The House of Peers made no pretence
To intellectual eminence,
    Or scholarship sublime;
Yet Britain won her proudest bays
In good Queen Bess's glorious days!

CHORUS. Yes, Britain won, etc.

When Wellington thrashed Bonaparte,
    As every child can tell,
The House of Peers, throughout the war,
Did nothing in particular,
    And did it very well:
Yet Britain set the world a-blaze
In good King George's glorious days!

CHORUS. Yes, Britain set, etc.

And while the House of Peers withholds
    Its legislative hand,
And noble statesmen do not itch
To interfere with matters which
    They do not understand,
As bright will shine Great Britain's rays,
As in King George's glorious days!

CHORUS. As bright will shine, etc.

LEILA (who has been much attracted by the Peers during this song). Charming persons, are they not?

CELIA. Distinctly. For self-contained dignity, combined with airy condescension, give me a British Representative Peer!

LD. TOLL. Then pray stop this protégé of yours before it's too late. Think of the mischief you're doing!

LEILA (crying). But we can't stop him now. (Aside to CELIA) Aren't they lovely! (Aloud.) Oh, why did you go and defy us, you great geese!

DUET.—LEILA and CELIA.

LEILA. In vain to us you plead—
    Don't go!
   Your prayers we do not heed—
    Don't go!
    It's true we sigh,
     But don't suppose
    A tearful eye
     Forgiveness shows.
    Oh, no!
   We're very cross indeed—
    Don't go!
   It's true we sigh, etc.

CELIA. Your disrespectful sneers—
    Don't go!
   Call forth indignant tears!

Don't go!
You break our laws—
You are our foe!
We cry because
We hate you so!
You know!
You very wicked Peers!
Don't go!

FAIRIES.	LORDS MOUNT. and TOLL.
You break our laws—	We break their laws—
You are our foe!	They are our foe!
We cry because	They cry because
We hate you so!	They hate us so!
You know!	Oh, ho!
You very wicked Peers!	If that's the case, my dears,
Don't go!	We'll go!

Exeunt MOUNTARARAT, TOLLOLLER, *and Peers. Fairies gaze wistfully after them. Enter* FAIRY QUEEN.

QUEEN. Oh, shame—shame upon you! Is this your fidelity to the laws you are bound to obey? Know ye not that it is death to marry a mortal?

LEILA. Yes, but it's not death to *wish* to marry a mortal!

FLETA. If it were, you'd have to execute us all!

QUEEN. Oh, this is weakness! Subdue it!

CELIA. We know it's weakness, but the weakness is so strong!

LEILA. We are not all as tough as you are!

QUEEN. Tough! Do you suppose that I am insensible to the effect of manly beauty? Look at that man (referring to sentry). A perfect picture! (To sentry) Who are you, sir?

WILLIS (coming to "attention"). Private Willis, B Company 1st Grenadier Guards.

QUEEN. You're a very fine fellow, sir.

WILLIS. I am generally admired.

QUEEN. I can quite understand it. (To Fairies.) Now here is a man whose physical attributes are simply god-like. That man has a most extraordinary effect upon me. If I yielded to a natural impulse, I should fall down and worship that man. But I mortify this inclination: I wrestle with it, and it lies beneath my feet! That is how I treat my regard for that man!

SONG.—FAIRY QUEEN.

Oh, foolish fay,
    Think you, because
His brave array
    My bosom thaws,
I'd disobey
    Our fairy laws?
Because I fly
    In realms above.
In tendency
    To fall in love
Resemble I
    The amorous dove?
(aside) Oh, amorous dove!
        Type of Ovidius Naso!
        This heart of mine

Is soft as thine,
Although I dare not say so!

CHORUS.   Oh, amorous dove, etc.

On fire that glows
    With heat intense
I turn the hose
    Of common sense,
And out it goes
    At small expense!
We must maintain
    Our fairy law;
That is the main
    On which to draw—
In that we gain
    A Captain Shaw!
(aside) Oh, Captain Shaw!
        Type of true love kept under!
            Could thy Brigade
            With cold cascade
        Quench my great love, I wonder!

CHORUS.   Oh, Captain Shaw! etc.

[*Exeunt Fairies and* FAIRY QUEEN, *sorrowfully*

Enter PHYLLIS.

PHYL. *(half crying)*. I can't think why I'm not in better spirits! I'm engaged to two noblemen at once. That ought to be enough to make any girl happy. But I'm miserable! Don't suppose it's because I care for Strephon, for I hate him! No girl *could* care for a man who goes about with a mother considerably younger than himself!

Enter LORD MOUNTARARAT *and* LORD TOLLOLLER.

LD. MOUNT. Phyllis! My darling!

LD. TOLL. Phyllis! My own!

PHYL. Don't! How dare you? Oh, but perhaps you're the two noblemen I'm engaged to?

LD. MOUNT. I am one of them.

LD. TOLL. I am the other.

PHYL. Oh, then, my darling! *(to* MOUNTARARAT). My own! *(to* TOLLOLLER). Well, have you settled which it's to be?

LD. TOLL. Not altogether. It's a difficult position. It would be hardly delicate to toss up. On the whole we would rather leave it to you.

PHYL. How can it possibly concern me? You are both Earls, and you are both rich, and you are both plain.

LD. MOUNT. So we are. At least I am.

LD. TOLL. So am I.

LD. MOUNT. No, no!

LD. TOLL. I am indeed. Very plain.

LD. MOUNT. Well, well—perhaps you are.

PHYL. There's really nothing to choose between you. If one of you would forego his title, and distribute his estates among his Irish tenantry, why, then I should then see a reason for accepting the other.

LD. MOUNT. Tolloller, are you prepared to make this sacrifice?

LD. TOLL. No!

LD. MOUNT. Not even to oblige a lady?

LD. TOLL. No!

LD. MOUNT. Then the only question is, which of us shall give way to the other? Perhaps, on the whole, she would be happier with me. I don't know. I may be wrong.

LD. TOLL. No. I don't know that you are. I really believe she would. But the awkward part of the thing is that if you rob me of the girl of my heart, one of us must die. It's a family tradition that I have sworn to respect. It's a painful position, for I have a very strong regard for you, George.

LD. MOUNT. *(much affected)*. My dear Thomas!

LD. TOLL. You are very dear to me, George. We were boys together—at least *I* was. If I were to survive you, my existence would be hopelessly embittered.

LD. MOUNT. Then, my dear Thomas, you must not do it. I say it again and again—if it will have this effect upon you, you must not do it. No, no. If one of us is to destroy the other, let it be me!

LD. TOLL. No, no.

LD. MOUNT. Ah, yes!—by our boyish friendship I implore you!

LD. TOLL. *(much moved)*. Well, well, be it so. But, no, no; I cannot consent to an act which would crush you with unavailing remorse.

LD. MOUNT. But it would not do so. I should be very sad at first—oh, who would not be?—but it would wear off. I like you *very much*—but not, perhaps, as much as you like me.

LD. TOLL. George, you're a noble fellow, but that tell-tale tear betrays you. No, George; you are very fond of me, and I cannot consent to give you a week's uneasiness on my account.

LD. MOUNT. But, dear Thomas, it would not last a week! Remember, you lead the House of Lords! on your demise I shall take your place! Oh, Thomas, it would not last a day!

PHYL. *(coming down)*. Now I do hope you're not going to fight about me, because it's really not worth while.

LD. TOLL. *(looking at her)*. Well, I don't believe it is!

LD. MOUNT. Nor I. The sacred ties of Friendship are paramount.

QUARTETTE.—MOUNTARARAT, TOLLOLLER, PHYLLIS, *and* WILLIS.

LD. TOLL.   Though p'raps I may incur your blame,
                The things are few
                I would not do
            In Friendship's name!

LD. MOUNT.   And I may say I think the same;
                Not even love
                Should rank above
            True Friendship's name!

PHYL.   Then free me, pray; be mine the blame;
                Forget your craze
                And go your way
            In Friendship's name!

WILLIS.   Accept, O Friendship, all the same,
                This sacrifice to thy dear name!

ALL.   Oh, many a man, in Friendship's name,
                Has yielded fortune, rank, and fame!

But no one yet, in the world so wide,
Has yielded up a promised bride!

[*Exeunt* MOUNTARARAT *and* TOLLOLLER, *lovingly, in one direction,
and* PHYLLIS *in another.*

Enter LORD CHANCELLOR, *very miserable.*

RECIT.—LORD CHANCELLOR.

Love, unrequited, robs me of my rest:
  Love, hopeless love, my ardent soul encumbers:
Love, nightmare like, lies heavy on my chest,
  And weaves itself into my midnight slumbers!

SONG.—LORD CHANCELLOR.

When you're lying awake with a dismal headache, and repose is
  taboo'd by anxiety,
I conceive you may use any language you choose to indulge in,
  without impropriety;
For your brain is on fire—the bedclothes conspire of usual
  slumber to plunder you:
First your counterpane goes, and uncovers your toes, and your
  sheet slips demurely from under you;
Then the blanketing tickles—you feel like mixed pickles—so
  terribly sharp is the pricking,
And you're hot, and you're cross, and you tumble and toss till
  there's nothing 'twixt you and the ticking.
Then the bedclothes all creep to the ground in a heap, and you
  pick 'em all up in a tangle;
Next your pillow resigns and politely declines to remain at its
  usual angle!
Well, you get some repose in the form of a doze, with hot
  eyeballs and head ever aching,
But your slumbering teems with such horrible dreams that you'd
  very much better be waking;
For you dream you are crossing the Channel, and tossing about
  in a steamer from Harwich—
Which is something between a large bathing-machine and a very
  small second-class carriage—
And you're giving a treat (penny ice and cold meat) to a party of
  friends and relations—
They're a ravenous horde—and they all came on board at Sloane
  Square and South Kensington Stations.
And bound on that journey you find your attorney (who started
  that morning from Devon);
He's a bit undersized, and you don't feel surprised when he tells
  you he's only eleven.
Well, you're driving like mad with this singular lad (by-the-bye
  the ship's now a four-wheeler),
And you're playing round games, and he calls you bad names
  when you tell him that "ties pay the dealer;"
But this you can't stand, so you throw up your hand, and you
  find you're as cold as an icicle,
In your shirt and your socks (the black silk with gold clocks),
  crossing Salisbury Plain in a bicycle:
And he and the crew are on bicycles too—which they've
  somehow or other invested in—
And he's telling the tars, all the particulars of a company he's
  interested in—

It's a scheme of devices, to get at low prices, all goods from
  cough mixtures to cables
(Which tickled the sailors) by treating retailers, as though they
  were all vegetables—
You get a good spadesman to plant a small tradesman, (first take
  off his boots with a boot-tree),
And his legs will take root, and his fingers will shoot, and they'll
  blossom and bud like a fruit-tree—
From the greengrocer tree you get grapes and green pea,
  cauliflower, pineapple and cranberries,
While the pastry-cook plant, cherry brandy will grant, apple
  puffs, and three-corners, and Banburys—
The shares are a penny, and ever so many are taken by Rothschild
  and Baring,
And just as a few are allotted to you, you awake with a shudder
  despairing—
You're a regular wreck, with a crick in your neck, and no
  wonder you snore, for your head's on the floor, and you've
  needles and pins from your soles to your shins, and your
  flesh is a-creep, for your left leg's asleep, and you've cramp
  in your toes, and a fly on your nose, and some fluff in your
  lung, and a feverish tongue, and a thirst that's intense, and a
  general sense that you haven't been sleeping in clover;
But the darkness has passed, and it's daylight at last, and the
  night has been long—ditto ditto my song—and thank goodness they're both of them over!

(LORD CHANCELLOR *falls exhausted on a seat.*)

LORDS MOUNTARARAT *and* TOLLOLLER *come forward.*

LD. MOUNT. I am much distressed to see your Lordship in this
condition.

LD. CH. Ah, my Lords, it is seldom that a Lord Chancellor has
reason to envy the position of another, but I am free to confess
that I would rather be two Earls engaged to Phyllis than any
other half-dozen noblemen upon the face of the globe!

LD. TOLL. (*without enthusiasm*). Yes. It's an enviable position
when you're the only one.

LD. MOUNT. Oh yes, no doubt—most enviable. At the same
time, seeing you thus, we naturally say to ourselves, "This is
very sad. His Lordship is constitutionally as blithe as a bird—he
trills upon the bench like a thing of song and gladness. His series
of judgments in F sharp, given *andante* in six-eight time, are
among the most remarkable effects ever produced in a Court of
Chancery. He is, perhaps, the only living instance of a judge
whose decrees have received the honour of a double *encore*. How
can we bring ourselves to do that which will deprive the Court of
Chancery of one of its most attractive features?"

LD. CH. I feel the force of your remarks, but I am here in two
capacities, and they clash, my Lord, they clash! I deeply grieve to
say that in declining to entertain my last application, I presumed
to address myself in terms which render it impossible for me ever
to apply to myself again. It was a most painful scene, my
Lord—most painful!

LD. TOLL. This is what it is to have two capacities! Let us be
thankful that we are persons of no capacity whatever.

LD. MOUNT. Come, come. Remember you are a very just and
kindly old gentleman, and you need have no hesitation in
approaching yourself, so that you do so respectfully and with a
proper show of deference.

Ld. Ch. Do you really think so? Well, I will nerve myself to another effort, and, if that fails, I resign myself to my fate!

TRIO.—LORD CHANCELLOR, LORDS MOUNTARARAT *and* TOLLOLLER.

Ld. MOUNT.
    If you go in
    You're sure to win—
Yours will be the charming maidie:
    Be your law
    The ancient saw,
"Faint heart never won fair lady!"

ALL.
Faint heart never won fair lady!
    Every journey has an end—
    When at the worst affairs will mend—
    Dark the dawn when day is nigh—
    Hustle your horse and don't say die!

Ld. TOLL.
    He who shies
    At such a prize
Is not worth a maravedi,
    Be so kind
    To bear in mind—
"Faint heart never won fair lady!"

ALL.
Faint heart never won fair lady!
    While the sun shines make your hay—
    Where a will is, there's a way—
    Beard the lion in his lair—
    None but the brave deserve the fair!

Ld. CH.
    I'll take heart
    And make a start—
Though I fear the prospect's shady—
    Much I'd spend
    To gain my end—
Faint heart never won fair lady!

ALL.
Faint heart never won fair lady!
    Nothing venture, nothing win—
    Blood is thick, but water's thin—
    In for a penny, in for a pound—
    It's Love that makes the world go round!

[*Dance, and exeunt arm-in-arm together.*

Enter STREPHON, *in very low spirits.*

STREPH. I suppose one ought to enjoy one's self in Parliament when one leads both parties, as I do! But I'm miserable, poor, broken-hearted, fool that I am! Oh Phyllis, Phyllis!—

Enter PHYLLIS.

PHYL. Yes?
STREPH. (*surprised*). Phyllis! But I suppose, I should say "My Lady". I have not yet been informed which title your Ladyship has pleased to select?
PHYL. I—I haven't quite decided. You see I have no *mother* to advise *me!*
STREPH. No. I have.
PHYL. Yes; a *young* mother.

STREPH. Not very—a couple of centuries or so.
PHYL. Oh! She wears well.
STREPH. She does. She's a fairy.
PHYL. I beg your pardon—a what?
STREPH. Oh, I've no longer any reason to conceal the fact—she's a fairy.
PHYL. A fairy! Well, but—that would account for a good many things! Then—I suppose *you're* a fairy?
STREPH. I'm half a fairy.
PHYL. Which half?
STREPH. The upper half—down to the waistcoat.
PHYL. Dear me! (*prodding him with her fingers*). There is nothing to show it! But why didn't you tell me this before?
STREPH. I thought you would take a dislike to me. But as it's all off, you may as well know the truth—I'm only half a mortal!
PHYL. (*crying*). But I'd rather have half a mortal I do love, than half a dozen I don't!
STREPH. Oh, I think not—go to your half-dozen.
PHYL. (*crying*). It's only two! and I hate 'em! Please forgive me!
STREPH. I don't think I ought to. Besides, all sorts of difficulties will arise. You know, my grandmother looks quite as young as my mother. So do all my aunts.
PHYL. I quite understand. Whenever I see you kissing a very young lady, I shall know it's an elderly relative.
STREPH. You will? Then, Phyllis, I think we shall be very happy! (*embracing her*).
PHYL. We won't wait long.
STREPH. No; we might change our minds. We'll get married first.
PHYL. And change our minds afterwards?
STREPH. That's the usual course.

DUET.—STREPHON *and* PHYLLIS.

STREPH.
If we're weak enough to tarry
    Ere we marry,
        You and I,
Of the feeling I inspire
    You may tire
        By-and-bye.
For Peers with flowing coffers
    Press their offers—
        That is why
I think we will not tarry
    Ere we marry
        You and I!

PHYL.
If we're weak enough to tarry
    Ere we marry,
        You and I,
With some more attractive maiden,
    Jewel-laden,
        You may fly.
If by chance we should be parted,
    Broken-hearted
        I should die—
So I think we will not tarry
    Ere we marry,
        You and I!

PHYL. But does your mother know you're— I mean, is she aware of an engagement?

Enter IOLANTHE.

IOL. She is—and thus she welcomes her daughter-in-law! *(kisses her).*

PHYL. She kisses just like other people! But the Lord Chancellor!

STREPH. I forgot him! Mother, none can resist your fairy eloquence: you will go to him, and plead for us?

IOL. *(much agitated).* No, no; impossible!

STREPH. But our happiness—our very lives, depend on our obtaining his consent!

PHYL. Oh, madam, you cannot refuse to do this!

IOL. You know not what you ask! The Lord Chancellor is—my husband!

STREPH. *and* PHYL. Your husband!

IOL. My husband and your father! *(addressing* STREPHON, *who is much moved).*

PHYL. Then our course is plain: on his learning that Strephon is his son, all objection to our marriage will be at once removed!

IOL. No, he must never know! He believes me to have died childless, and dearly as I love him, I am bound, under penalty of death, not to undeceive him. But see—he comes! Quick—my veil! *(They retire up as* IOLANTHE *veils herself.)*

Enter LORD CHANCELLOR.

LD. CH. Victory! Victory! Success has crowned my efforts, and I may consider myself engaged to Phyllis! At first I wouldn't hear of it—it was out of the question. But I took heart. I pointed out to myself that I was no stranger to myself—that, in point of fact, I had been personally acquainted with myself for some years. This had its effect. I admitted that I had watched my professional advancement with considerable interest, and I handsomely added that I yielded to no one in admiration for my private and professional virtues. This was a great point gained. I then endeavoured to work upon my feelings. Conceive my joy when I distinctly perceived a tear glistening in my own eye! Eventually, after a severe struggle with myself, I reluctantly—most reluctantly—consented!

IOLANTHE *comes down veiled*—STREPHON *and* PHYLLIS *go off on tip-toe.*

RECIT.—IOLANTHE.

My Lord, a suppliant at your feet I kneel,
Oh, listen to a mother's fond appeal!
Hear me to-night! I come in urgent need—
'Tis for my son, young Strephon, that I plead!

BALLAD.—IOLANTHE.

He loves! If the bygone years
Thine eyes have ever shed
Tears—bitter, unavailing tears,
For one untimely dead—
If in the eventide of life
Sad thoughts of her arise,
Then let the memory of thy wife
Plead for my boy—he dies!

He dies! If fondly laid aside
In some old cabinet,
Memorials of thy long-dead bride
Lie, dearly treasured yet,
Then let her hallowed bridal dress—
Her little dainty gloves—
Her withered flowers—her faded tress—
Plead for my boy—he loves!

The LORD CHANCELLOR *is moved by this appeal. After a pause*—

LD. CH. It may not be—for so the Fates decide:
Learn thou that Phyllis is my promised bride!

IOL. *(in horror).* Thy bride! No! no!

LD. CH. It shall be so!
Those who would separate us woe betide!

IOL. My doom thy lips have spoken—
I plead in vain!

Chorus of Fairies (without). Forbear! forbear!

IOL. A vow already broken
I break again!

Chorus of Fairies (without). Forbear! forbear!

IOL. For him—for her—for thee
I yield my life.
Behold—it may not be!
I am thy wife!

Chorus of Fairies (without). Aiaiah! Aiaiah! Willaloo!

LD. CH. *(recognizing her).* Iolanthe! thou livest?

IOL. Aye!
I live! Now let me die!

Enter FAIRY QUEEN *and Fairies.* IOLANTHE *kneels to her.*

QUEEN. Once again thy vows are broken:
Thou thyself thy doom hath spoken!

Chorus of Fairies. Aiaiah! Aiaiah!
Willahalah! Willaloo!
Laloiah! Laloiah!
Willahalah! Willaloo!

QUEEN. Bow thy head to Destiny:
Death thy doom, and thou shalt die!

Chorus of Fairies. Aiaiah! Aiaiah! etc.

The Peers and STREPHON *enter. The* QUEEN *raises her spear.*

LEILA. Hold! If Iolanthe must die, so must we all; for, as she has sinned, so have we!

QUEEN. What! *(Peers and Fairies kneel to her—*LORD MOUNTARARAT *with* CELIA; LORD TOLLOLLER *with* LEILA).

CELIA. We are all fairy duchesses, marchionesses, countesses, viscountesses, and baronesses.

LD. MOUNT. It's our fault. They couldn't help themselves.

QUEEN. It seems they *have* helped themselves, and pretty freely, too! *(After a pause.)* You have all incurred death; but I can't slaughter the whole company! And yet *(unfolding a scroll)* the law is clear—every fairy must die who marries a mortal!

LD. CH. Allow me, as an old Equity draughtsman, to make a suggestion. The subtleties of the legal mind are equal to the emergency. The thing is really quite simple—the insertion of a single word will do it. Let it stand that every fairy shall die who *don't* marry a mortal, and there you are, out of your difficulty at once!

QUEEN. We like your humour. Very well! (*Altering the MS. in pencil.*) Private Willis!

SENTRY (*coming forward*). Ma'am!

QUEEN. To save my life, it is necessary that I marry at once. How should you like to be a fairy guardsman?

SENTRY. Well, ma'am, I don't think much of the British soldier who wouldn't ill-convenience himself to save a female in distress.

QUEEN. You are a brave fellow. You're a fairy from this moment (*wings spring from Sentry's shoulders*). And you, my Lords, how say you? Will you join our ranks?

(*Fairies kneel to Peers and implore them to do so.*)

LD. MOUNT. (*to* LD. TOLLOLLER). Well, now that the Peers are to be recruited entirely from persons of intelligence, I really don't see what use *we* are, down here.

LD. TOL. None whatever.

QUEEN. Good! (*Wings spring from shoulders of Peers.*) Then away we go to Fairyland.

FINALE.

PHYL.
Soon as we may,
Off and away!
We'll commence our journey airy—
Happy are we—
As you can see,
Every one is now a fairy!

Every one is now a fairy!

IOL., QUEEN, *and* PHYL. Though as a general rule we know
Two strings go to every bow,
Make up your minds that grief 'twill bring
If you've two beaux to every string.

ALL.
Though as a general rule, etc.

LD. CH.
Up in the sky,
Ever so high,
Pleasures come in endless series;
We will arrange
Happy exchange—
House of Peers for House of Peris!

ALL.
House of Peers for House of Peris!

LD. CH., MOUNT., *and* TOLL. Up in the air, sky-high, sky-high,
Free from wards in Chancery,
$\left\{ \begin{matrix} \text{I} \\ \text{He} \end{matrix} \right\}$ will be surely happier, for
$\left\{ \begin{matrix} \text{I'm} \\ \text{He's} \end{matrix} \right\}$ such a susceptible Chancellor!

Up in the air, etc.

CURTAIN.

THE END.

Princess Ida

or Castle Adamant

The inspiration for this opera originated in Tennyson's poem 'The Princess — A Medley', published in 1847 as a comment on the prevailing trend towards women's higher education. Gilbert unashamedly made use of Tennyson's text in his own play of 1870, 'The Princess — A Whimsical Allegory', which lampooned the real establishment of university colleges for women. This burlesque, in Tennysonian heroic metre, was successfully played at the Olympic Theatre with lyrics (not carried forward to *Princess Ida*) set to popular operatic melodies by Offenbach and Hervé. The curious casting of this play was all female, except for the roles of the opposing Kings Gama and Hildebrand.

Scene from Gilbert's play *The Princess* (Olympic Theatre, 1870). *Illustrated Sporting & Dramatic News*. The three 'men' are women *en travesti* redisguised as women.

In early 1883, Gilbert resurrected 'The Princess', restructured it, and rewrote the songs. He retains the Tennysonian inspiration which transcends his usual work, and also uses Tennyson's choice of names with great relish: Gama (the crooked-legged); Hildebrand (the battle sword); and Ida (the Greek summit of scenes of love and war).

Gilbert's 'Per-version' of Tennyson's poem obviously appealed to Sullivan, for his music bubbles with merriment, witty allusions and ingenious descriptions of mood. Sullivan was temporarily at peace with Gilbert and seems to have been enjoying life, especially since his knighthood in May 1883.

Princess Ida has several similarities with Thackeray's 'Rose and the Ring' of 1855: the infant marriage, the Crusades, the pseudo-Italian mixed with the Victorian, and the accent upon learning. Gilbert has given *Ida* a quasi-Florentine setting, but

from existing illustrations it is clear that lush Victorianism prevailed. There are also topical jokes on the latest nineteenth-century scientific discoveries.

Sullivan's music follows his own interpretation based on the familiar operatic repertoire. Rossini's comic opera, *Le Comte Ory*, with a similar plot to *Princess Ida*, is said to have originated in an old Picard legend from Crusader times. Taking this theme as a lead, Sullivan has turned to Handel — his *Rinaldo* is a Crusader opera; and then with Turks in mind, Sullivan looks at Beethoven's *Ruins of Athens* (incidental music to Kotzebue's play dealing with the Turkish ravages of Athens and the awakening of Minerva after 2000 years). This Beethoven work not only influences the battle scenes in *Princess Ida* but permeates some of the other episodes.

Gilbert's biting satire is softened, though not lessened in any way, by Sullivan. Although at first sight *Ida* is an attack on women, Gilbert and Sullivan do not take sides. Their men are as boorish as their women are fanciful or bossy. The lyrical Prince Hilarion (though a tenor) is virtually excused from entering into the category of male chauvinism to

Gilbertian self-confession which pervades all the operas from *Patience*, and which Gilbert's drawing on page 13 bears out.

Ida, by contrast, is one of Gilbert's most human and admirable characters, in spite of her implicit belief in a lost cause. She has that dignity which ridicule cannot penetrate. One is led to believe in her superiority and to feel compassion for her when, abandoned, she admits her folly. Lady Psyche too, Professor of Humanities, lives up to her name, and her real warmth contrasts with the prosaic coldness of the calculating Lady Blanche. The interweaving of gentle feminine versus hard masculine makes for a new departure in Sullivan's music.

Although the score of *Princess Ida* is undoubtedly one of Sullivan's best, the opera did not achieve the usual success: possibly the musical allusion was too intellectual, and the subject-matter, though acceptable in a *Punch* cartoon, was not so palatable in a three-act opera before a mixed audience. This sort of sex-war did not provide thoroughly comfortable family entertainment in the 1880s, nor even later, for the opera was banished from the London stage until the end of 1919.

Punch cartoon 26 January 1884.

SYNOPSIS

The Overture opens with battle music, a Turkish theme derived from Beethoven's *Ruins of Athens*. A short progression leads into the sonorous, Mendelssohnian music of Ida.

The scene opens on a royal pavilion overlooking a mountainous panorama. King Hildebrand's courtiers

which the other men belong. They are depicted as unimaginative and synonymous with Darwinian man — a monkey. But both Hildebrand and the belligerent little King Gama are not without more than a touch of humour. Gama has been compared with Gilbert. He is just another fragment of and soldiers anxiously await the arrival of Princess Ida, daughter of King Gama. They speculate as to whether she will come and as they scan the horizon with optical instruments, their pacing is sentry-like and ungracious.

Ida has been wedded in infancy to Hildebrand's son, Hilarion, and now that she is twenty-one, the marriage contract must be fulfilled. In a warlike gallop with chorus, Hildebrand threatens dire vengeance on Gama if he fails to bring his daughter.

Following this bombastic opening the music becomes lyrical for Hilarion's speculation on his childhood bride. In his ballad, 'Ida was a twelvemonth old...', tripping baby steps evoke the sentimentalized Victorian infant.

News is brought that King Gama has been sighted without Ida, and has only brought his three sons, Arac, Guron and Scynthius. A fanfare heralds the arrival of these three moronic individuals. To a clanking of chain mail and armour, Arac boorishly introduces them in his monosyllabic 'We are warriors three...'. Battle cries and war clangour

Peter Pratt as King Gama. His fantastic costume is typical of the surrealistic designs by James Wade for the 1954 Savoy Theatre revival. *Princess Ida* had been out of the repertory since 1939.

increase as the song progresses — this is the first subject of the overture.

Then the crabbed, ill-tempered Gama displays his contrary whims in an apoplectic, wheezing song, 'If you give me your attention, I will tell you what I am...'. He continues by courting abuse from Hilarion's companions, Cyril and Florian, and trying to excuse Ida's absence by implying that she is too good for such low people.

Hildebrand furiously threatens Gama until the old man divulges that his daughter is running a women's university in one of his many properties, Castle Adamant, and that she has abjured everything male. Gama suggests that Hilarion might have some success by going to Ida in person. 'P'raps if you address the lady most politely, most politely...' is charming, tight-lipped and threatening. The second verse of the duet is taken up by Hildebrand, expressing his intention of hanging Gama ('most politely') should Hilarion be harmed.

Gama and his sons are led away while Hilarion and his friends, left to themselves, look forward to the exciting prospect of wooing. Hilarion starts tentatively: 'Expressive glances shall be our lances...', and following the chorus 'Oh dainty Triolet! Oh fragrant violet!...', Cyril and Florian each sing a verse in different keys, becoming progressively more daring, musically and verbally. Gama and his sons are led in 'heavily ironed'. The rousing rataplan-like trio for the Brothers 'For a month to dwell in a dungeon cell...' is full of battle sounds, and the *tutti*, 'For the rum-tum-tum of the military drum...', makes an exciting finale.

Act II opens on a garden with a rustic bridge leading over a river to the distant Castle Adamant. A group of girl graduates sit at the feet of Lady Psyche, Professor of Humanities. In a chorus influenced by the *Ruins of Athens* music they express their mutual intention to soar to the Empyrean heights of learning, but the descending bass figure in the orchestra suggests that their 'easy flights' are somewhat short-lived. Lady Psyche is acting as the all-knowing aunt in a kind of Enquire Within on the classics. Her answers are accompanied throughout by chattering strings. The subject inevitably turns to Man: 'Nature's sole mistake'.

An emotional chorus of adulation welcomes Ida. Her first aria, an invocation to Minerva, might be part of a Victorian oratorio. In a denouncement of men, Ida resolves to conquer by demonstrating female superiority. Should this fail, the next step will be to neglect all feminine duties conceived to please man.

The university is ruled by a triumvirate: Ida, Lady Psyche and Lady Blanche, but already jealousy is creeping in. Lady Blanche, Professor of Abstract Science, gives an exposé, veiled in philosophical terms, of her ambition to become Number One instead of Number Two. Her song, 'Come, mighty Must! Inevitable Shall!' is a complaint with a Gilbertian play on words. The cold and calculating theme did not inspire Sullivan to his usual sympathetic writing for the ageing mezzo, which is possibly why this number is generally cut nowadays.

Hilarion, Cyril and Florian are seen scaling a wall. Like sniggering boys, the Prince and his companions enter the precinct. Hilarion and Cyril, with mock seriousness, deliver a list of ludicrous feminine ideals. 'They intend to send a wire to the moon...' has a repeated phrase in every second line which is evocative of laughter after each comment. The men then dress in academic gowns which they discover on the ground and, to a slow jig with a barrel-organ-like accompaniment, Hilarion roguishly begins 'I am a maiden, cold and stately'.

They collect themselves as Ida enters, and do their best to emulate three prospective female under-graduates (Cyril failing hopelessly). The ingenuous Ida, having satisfied herself that they will love their schoolfellows, welcomes her new disciples without reserve. The quartet, 'The world is but a broken toy...' despite the gentle mocking tone taken up by the men, remains a serious and compassionate love-song amid all the frivolity.

The men's ribald rejoicing on Ida's exit is observed by Lady Psyche. To make matters worse, Florian recognizes her as his sister and they have to divulge their plot. Psyche tries to justify Ida's renunciation of man with the Darwinian theory of descent from the ape. Her song about the Darwinian man — the well-behaved ape who did all he could, without success, to rise in the social scale for the love of a lady — evokes a barrel-organ complete with monkey. This idea has been extended and the ape characterized in Hans Werner Henze's opera of 1965, *Der Junge Lord,* said to have been based on *Der Affe als Mensch* (Ape as Man) by the early nineteenth-century German writer, Wilhelm Hauff.

During Lady Psyche's story Melissa, daughter of Lady Blanche, has been watching the men unobserved. She has been brought up in total seclusion and now, amazed and delighted by this new experience, she swears to keep the intruders' secret. They all rejoice that 'the truth is found'. 'The woman of the wisest wit...' is a take-leave-of-convention quintet (similar to the flight of the peers and fairies in *Iolanthe*). Lady Blanche has seen this latest frolic and quizzes Melissa with ever-growing sarcasm. Melissa insists that the new students are girls until her mother triumphantly discovers cigars inside a supposed needlework *étui* that has been dropped. Lady Blanche is persuaded to back Hilarion's mission. The eighteenth-century nursery-rhyme style duet is a pot-pourri of old English clichés. 'Now wouldn't you like to rule the roast...?' is charming but, at the same time, leaves one in no doubt that Blanche is the hardest of Gilbert's middle-aged women.

Florian has already fallen in love with Melissa and she is ready to elope with him, but he decides to lunch first. In a miniature form of Handelian cantata, the next scene, beginning 'Merrily ring the luncheon bell...' in canon, has the community settling down to an alfresco meal (of cold roast lamb).

Ida, sitting beside Hilarion, questions her new student about the court of King Hildebrand and enquires about the Prince. Cyril, getting tipsy, interrupts with indiscretions for which Hilarion tries to excuse him. Unrelenting, Cyril breaks into a risqué song, 'Would you know the kind of maid sets my heart aflame-a...?', the music following on from the luncheon cantata, yet with apishness creeping into the compulsive refrain, 'Oh, kiss me, kiss me, kiss me, kiss me...'

Ida is horrified. Hilarion strikes Cyril furiously, Cyril in turn protests, addressing the prince as Hilarion, and they are found out. Ida runs to the bridge and, with a supreme effort to take control, falls into the stream. Hilarion dives in to save her and, amid pessimistic speculation from Blanche and optimism from Psyche, he rescues Ida. A busy and frightened Chorus of Ladies implores Ida to spare the brave Hilarion. Relentlessly she speaks out: 'Stand forth, ye three, whoe'er ye be,...' the music parodying 'Here comes the Bride' from *Lohengrin*. The men beg for mercy but Ida, angry, dripping and breathless, firmly orders them to be arrested.

Hilarion's love song 'Whom thou has chained must wear his chain...' is in a mollifying 6/8, and as the three intruders are led away bound by the

Daughters of the Plough, warlike clangour is heard and Hildebrand's army storms the castle. With *Iolanthe*-like wailing the women protest against the soldiers' martial orders to them. Ida dramatically defies Hildebrand and he, with a definite twinkle of dismissal, embarks on a pedestrian but threatening solo, 'Some years ago, no doubt you know...' reminding her of her marriage vow to Hilarion.

Ida's brothers, still chained, have accompanied the army and they now persuade Ida in another 'plain' trio to yield, on pain of their death.

Ida's delightfully feminine and tripping (Elgarian) recitative of disbelief is smartly countermanded by Hildebrand's assurance that her brothers will be hanged unless Hilarion is released (a minute section of Mozartian ensemble occurs here).

To a cavalry march rhythm, Ida refuses to submit. Furthermore she orders Hilarion's imprisonment despite her apparent admiration for him. A high solo

'Audacious tyrant, do you dare to beard a maiden in her lair?' Ida upbraids King Hildebrand. First production of *Princess Ida*, Savoy Theatre 5 January 1884. *Illustrated Sporting & Dramatic News*

line for her above the chorus sopranos helps to give her a Joan of Arc image as she stands, surrounded by kneeling maidens and encircled by soldiers.

In the courtyard of Castle Adamant the undergraduates, armed with battleaxes, sing their war cry 'Death to the Invader!' It shortly gives way to Melissa's timid little 'Please you, do not hurt us. ...' until, anticipating Ida's imminent arrival, the women resume their battle cry.

The Princess enters, armed and attended by Blanche and Psyche. She rallies her troops but finds them all reluctant and full of excuses. Contemptuously she dismisses them and vows to face the men alone. Her Mendelssohnian song, 'I built upon a rock ...' has a funereal fanfare motif throughout, and movingly expresses the fall of all her idealistic hopes. Deserted, Ida lifts her ban on men and allows her father to visit her. Gama proposes that as Hildebrand will not fight women, Ida's brothers should be matched against Hilarion and his two friends. When Ida deplores Gama's lack of faith in her, he tells her tearfully of the tortures he has suffered. Hildebrand has ordered that all his

164

unreasonable whims be satisfied, nobody is allowed to contradict him, and he complains, in a hurdy-gurdy song, '...And isn't your life extremely flat with nothing whatever to grumble at!' Ida gives way when he falls sobbing on a seat.

Hildebrand's soldiers now gather in the courtyard and sing a military patter-song, a variation of 'The Grand Old Duke of York' in which the girls, now on the battlements, join them. Gama gives his stifled wit full rein when the Daughters of the Plough bring in Hilarion, Cyril and Florian still bound and in women's clothes. The old king challenges them to fight his sons.

Ida's Brothers then perform a feat of disarming. Arac leads the ridiculous Handelian song, reminiscent of 'Let the Bright Seraphim' from *Samson*, as they throw off all their uncomfortable and cumbersome accoutrements. In the desperate fight which ensues, Ida's brothers are cheered on by her dutiful supporters, but as they fall wounded, the cry goes up: 'Hilarion! Hilarion! Hilarion!'

Ida surveys her brothers on the ground, their victors standing over them, and reluctantly surrenders. She unwillingly consigns the university to Blanche and admits that she erred in her simple belief that her scheme would benefit Posterity. Psyche and Melissa have already accepted Cyril and Florian, so Ida turns happily to Hilarion, full of love and new aspirations; and to a reprise of 'O dainty Triolet!' they sing:

> 'It were profanity for poor humanity
> To treat as vanity the sway of love ...'

Below left:

Arac, Guron and Scinthius, Princess Ida's brothers, from music cover of 'The Princess Ida Lancers'.

Below:

'My Lady Blanche, how do you solve this riddle?' 'Don't ask me—Abstract Philosophy won't answer it.' Muriel Dickson and Dorothy Gill as Ida and Blanche in the D'Oyly Carte American Tour, September 1934.

PRINCESS IDA;

OR

CASTLE ADAMANT.

*A RESPECTFUL OPERATIC PER-VERSION OF
TENNYSON'S "PRINCESS,"*

IN THREE ACTS.

First produced at the Savoy Theatre, 5 January 1884

DRAMATIS PERSONÆ

KING HILDEBRAND	baritone
HILARION [his Son]	tenor
CYRIL	tenor
FLORIAN } [Hilarion's Friends]	baritone
KING GAMA	baritone
ARAC	bass
GURON } [his Sons]	bass
SCYNTHIUS	bass
PRINCESS IDA [Gama's Daughter]	soprano
LADY BLANCHE [Professor of Abstract Science]	contralto
LADY PSYCHE [Professor of Humanities]	soprano
MELISSA [Lady Blanche's Daughter]	soprano
SACHARISSA	soprano
CHLOE } [Girl Graduates]	soprano
ADA	mezzo-soprano

Soldiers, Courtiers, Girl Graduates, Daughters of the Plough, etc.

ACT I.

PAVILION IN KING HILDEBRAND'S PALACE.

ACT II.

GARDENS OF CASTLE ADAMANT.

ACT III.

COURTYARD OF CASTLE ADAMANT.

PRINCESS IDA;

OR,

CASTLE ADAMANT.

ACT I.

SCENE—*Pavilion attached to* KING HILDEBRAND'S *Palace.* SOLDIERS *and* COURTIERS *discovered looking out through opera-glasses, telescopes, etc.* FLORIAN *leading.*

CHORUS.

Search throughout the panorama
For a sign of royal Gama,
   Who to-day should cross the water
   With his fascinating daughter—
   Ida is her name.

Some misfortune evidently
Has detained them—consequently
   Search throughout the panorama
   For the daughter of King Gama,
   Prince Hilarion's flame!

SOLO.

FLOR. Will Prince Hilarion's hopes be sadly blighted?
ALL.   Who can tell?
FLOR. Will Ida break the vows that she has plighted?
ALL.   Who can tell?
FLOR. Will she back out, and say she did not mean them?
ALL.   Who can tell?
FLOR. If so, there'll be the deuce to pay between them!
ALL.   No, no—we'll not despair,
           For Gama would not dare
           To make a deadly foe
           Of Hildebrand, and so,
               Search throughout etc.

Enter KING HILDEBRAND, *with* CYRIL.

HILD. See you no sign of Gama?
FLOR.   None, my liege!
HILD. It's very odd indeed. If Gama fail
To put in an appearance at our Court
Before the sun has set in yonder west,
And fail to bring the Princess Ida here,
To whom our son Hilarion was betrothed
At the extremely early age of one,
There's war between King Gama and ourselves!
(*Aside to* CYRIL.) Oh, Cyril, how I dread this interview,
It's twenty years since he and I have met.
He was a twisted monster—all awry—
As though dame Nature, angry with her work,
Had crumpled it in fitful petulance!
  CYR. But, sir, a twisted and ungainly trunk
Often bears goodly fruit. Perhaps he was
A kind, well-spoken gentlemen?

HILD.   Oh, no!
For, adder-like his sting lay in his tongue.
(His "sting" is present, though his "stung" is past.)
 FLOR. *(looking through glass).* But stay, my liege; o'er yonder
     mountain's brow
Comes a small boy, bearing Gama's arms;
And now, I look more closely at it, sir,
I see attached to it King Gama's legs;
From which I gather this corollary
That that small body must be Gama's own!
 HILD. Ha! Is the Princess with him?
 FLOR.   Well, my liege,
Unless her highness is full six feet high,
And wears moustachios too—and smokes cigars—
And rides *en cavalier* in coat of steel—
I do not think she is.
 HILD.   One never knows.
She's a strange girl, I've heard, and does odd things!
Come, bustle there!
For Gama place the richest robes we own—
For Gama place the coarsest prison dress—
For Gama let our best spare bed be aired—
For Gama let our deepest dungeon yawn—
For Gama lay the costliest banquet out—
For Gama place cold water and dry bread!
For as King Gama brings the Princess here,
Or brings her not, so shall King Gama have
Much more than everything—much less than nothing!

SONG AND CHORUS.

HILD.   Now hearken to my strict command
         On every hand, on every hand—

CHORUS.

         To your command,
         On every hand,
         We dutifully bow!

HILD.   If Gama bring the Princess here
         Give him good cheer, give him good cheer.

CHORUS.

         If she come here
         We'll give him a cheer,
         And we will show you how.
     Hip, hip, hurrah! hip, hip, hurrah!
     Hip, hip, hurrah! hip, hip, hurrah!
         We'll shout and sing
         Long live the king,
         And his daughter, too, I trow!
     Then shout ha! ha! hip, hip, hurrah!
     For the fair Princess and her good papa,
         Hip, hip, hurrah!
         Hip, hip, hurrah!
         Hip, hip, hurrah! hurrah!

HILD.   But if he fail to keep his troth,
         Upon our oath, we'll trounce them both!

CHORUS.

         He'll trounce them both,
         Upon his oath.
         As sure as quarter day!

HILD.   We'll shut him up in a dungeon cell,
         And toll his knell on a funeral bell.

CHORUS.

         From dungeon cell,
         His funeral knell,
         Shall strike him with dismay!
     And we'll shout ha! ha! hip, hip, hurrah!
     Hip, hip, hurrah! hip, hip, hurrah!
         As up we string,
         The faithless King,
         In the old familiar way!
     We'll shout ha! ha! hip, hip, hurrah!
     As we make an end of her false papa.
         Hip, hip, hurrah!
         Hip, hip, hurrah!
     Hip, hip, hurrah! hurrah!   [*Exeunt all.*

Enter HILARION.

RECITATIVE.—HILARION.

To-day we meet—my baby bride and I—
   But, ah, my hopes are balanced by my fears!
What transmutations have been conjured by
   The silent alchemy of twenty years!

BALLAD.—HILARION.

         Ida was a twelvemonth old,
             Twenty years ago!
         I was twice her age, I'm told,
             Twenty years ago!
         Husband twice as old as wife
         Argues ill for married life
         Baleful prophecies were rife
             Twenty years ago!

         Still, I was a tiny prince
             Twenty years ago.
         She has gained upon me, since
             Twenty years ago.
         Though she twenty-one, it's true,
         I am barely twenty-two—
         False and foolish prophets you,
             Twenty years ago!

Enter HILDEBRAND.

 HIL. Well, father, is there news for me at last?
 HILD. King Gama is in sight, but much I fear
With no Princess!
 HIL.   Alas, my liege, I've heard
That Princess Ida has forsworn the world,
And, with a band of women, shut herself

Within a lonely country house, and there
Devotes herself to stern philosophies!
   HILD. Then I should say the loss of such a wife
Is one to which a reasonable man
Would easily be reconciled.
   HIL.   Oh no!
Or I am not a reasonable man.
She *is* my wife—has been for twenty years!
(Looking through glass.) I think I see her now.
   HILD.   Ha! let me look!
   HIL. In my mind's eye, I mean—a blushing bride,
All bib and tucker, frill and furbelow!
How exquisite she looked, as she was borne,
Recumbent, in her foster-mother's arms;
How the bride wept—nor would be comforted
Until the hireling mother-for-the-nonce,
Administered refreshment in the vestry.
And I remember feeling much annoyed
That she should weep at marrying with me.
But then I thought, "These brides are all alike.
You cry at marrying me? How much more cause
You'd have to cry if it were broken off!"
These were my thoughts; I kept them to myself,
For at that age I had not learnt to speak.

Enter COURTIERS, *with* CYRIL *and* FLORIAN.

CHORUS. From the distant panorama
          Come the sons of royal Gama.
             Who, to-day, should cross the water
             With his fascinating daughter—
               Ida is her name!

Enter ARAC, GURON, *and* SCYNTHIUS.

SONG.—ARAC.

    We are warriors three,
      Sons of Gama, Rex,
    Like most sons are we,
      Masculine in sex.

ALL THREE.   Yes, yes,
          Masculine in sex.

ARAC.   Politics we bar,
       They are not our bent;
    On the whole we are
       Not intelligent.

ALL THREE.   No, no,
         Not intelligent.

ARAC.   But with doughty heart,
       And with trusty blade
    We can play our part—
       Fighting is our trade.

ALL THREE.   Yes, yes,
         Fighting is our trade.

ALL THREE. Bold, and fierce, and strong, ha! ha!
         For a war we burn,
    With its right or wrong, ha! ha!
         We have no concern.
    Order comes to fight, ha! ha!
         Order is obeyed,

    We are men of might, ha! ha!
         Fighting is our trade.
         Yes, yes,
    Fighting is our trade, ha! ha!
         Fighting is our trade.

CHORUS.   They are men of might, ha! ha!
    Order comes to fight, ha! ha!
    Order is obeyed, ha! ha!
         Fighting is their trade!

Enter KING GAMA.

SONG.—GAMA.

If you give me your attention, I will tell you what I am!
I'm a genuine philanthropist—all other kinds are sham.
Each little fault of temper and each social defect
In my erring fellow-creatures, I endeavour to correct.
To all their little weaknesses I open people's eyes
And little plans to snub the self-sufficient I devise;
I love my fellow-creatures—I do all the good I can—
Yet everybody says I'm such a disagreeable man!
        And I can't think why!

To compliments inflated I've a withering reply,
And vanity I always do my best to mortify;
A charitable action I can skilfully dissect;
And interested motives I'm delighted to detect;
I know everybody's income and what everybody earns;
And I carefully compare it with the income-tax returns;
But to benefit humanity however much I plan,
Yet everybody says I'm such a disagreeable man!
        And I can't think why!

I'm sure I'm no ascetic; I'm as pleasant as can be;
You'll always find me ready with a crushing repartee,
I've an irritating chuckle, I've a celebrated sneer,
I've an entertaining snigger, I've a fascinating leer.
To everybody's prejudice I know a thing or two;
I can tell a woman's age in half a minute—and I do.
But although I try to make myself as pleasant as I can,
Yet everybody says I'm such a disagreeable man!
        And I can't think why!

   GAMA. So this is Castle Hildebrand? Well, well!
Dame Rumour whispered that the place was grand;
She told me that your taste was exquisite,
Superb, unparalleled!

HILD. (*gratified*).   Oh, really, king!

GAMA. But she's a liar! Why, how old you've grown!
Is this Hilarion! Why, you've changed too—
You were a singularly handsome child!
(*To* FLORIAN.) Are you a courtier? Come, then, ply your
        trade,
Tell me some lies. How do you like your king?
Vile rumour says he's all but imbecile.
Now, that's not true?

FLO.   My lord, we love our king
His wise remarks are valued by his court
As precious stones.

GAMA.   And for the selfsame cause,
Like precious stones, his sensible remarks
Derive their value from their scarcity!
Come now, be honest, tell the truth for once!
Tell it of me. Come, come, I'll harm you not.
This leg is crooked—this foot is ill-designed—
This shoulder wears a hump! Come, out with it!
Look, here's my face! Now, am I not the worst
of Nature's blunders?

CYRIL.   Nature never errs.
To those who know the workings of your mind,
Your face and figure, sir, suggest a book
Appropriately bound.

GAMA (*enraged*).   Why, hark ye, sir,
How dare you bandy words with me?

CYRIL.   No need,
To bandy aught that appertains to you.

GAMA (*furiously*). Do you permit this, king?

HILD.   We are in doubt
Whether to treat you as an honoured guest,
Or as a traitor knave who plights his word,
And breaks it.

GAMA (*quickly*). If the casting vote's with me,
I give it for the former!

HILD.   We shall see.
By the terms of our contract, signed and sealed,
You're bound to bring the Princess here to-day;
Why is she not with you?

GAMA.   Answer me this;
What think you of a wealthy purse-proud man,
Who, when he calls upon a starving friend,
Pulls out his gold and flourishes his notes,
And flashes diamonds in the pauper's eyes?
What name have you for such an one?

HILD.   A snob.

GAMA. Just so. The girl has beauty, virtue, wit,
Grace, humour, wisdom, charity, and pluck.
Would it be kindly, think you, to parade,
These brilliant qualities before *your* eyes?
Oh no, King Hildebrand, I am no snob!

HILD. (*furiously*). Stop that tongue,
Or you shall lose the monkey head that holds it!

GAMA. Bravo! your king deprives me of my head,
That he and I may meet on equal terms!

HILD. Where is she now?

GAMA.   In Castle Adamant,
One of my many country houses.
She rules a woman's University,
With full a hundred girls, who learn of her.

CYRIL. A hundred girls! A hundred ecstasies!

GAMA. But no mere girls, my good young gentleman;
With all the college learning that you boast,
The youngest there will prove a match for *you*.

CYRIL. With all my heart, if she's the prettiest!
(*To* FLO.) Fancy a hundred matches—all alight!—
That's if I strike them as I hope to do!

GAMA. Despair your hope; their hearts are dead to men.
He who desires to gain their favour must
Be qualified to strike their teeming brains,
And not their hearts. They're safety matches, sir,
And they light only on the knowledge box—
So *you've* no chance!

FLO. Are there no males whatever in those walls?

GAMA. None, gentlemen, excepting letter mails—
And they are driven (as males often are
In other large communities) by women.
Why, bless my heart, she's so particular
She'll scarcely suffer Dr. Watt's hymns—
And all the animals she owns are "hers"!
The ladies rise at cockcrow every morn—

CYRIL. Ah, then they have male poultry?

GAMA.   Not at all,
(*Confidentially.*) The crowing's done by an accomplished hen!

DUET.—GAMA *and* HILDEBRAND.

GAMA.   Perhaps if you address the lady
              Most politely, most politely—
          Flatter and impress the lady,
              Most politely, most politely—
          Humbly beg and humbly sue—
          She may deign to look on you,
          But your doing you must do
              Most politely, most politely!

ALL.   Humbly beg and humbly sue, etc.

HILD.   Go you, and inform the lady,
              Most politely, most politely,
          If she don't, we'll storm the lady,
              Most politely, most politely!
(*To* GAMA). You'll remain as hostage here;
          Should Hilarion disappear,
          We will hang you, never fear,
              Most politely, most politely!

ALL.   ⎰ He'll ⎱
       ⎱ I'll ⎰ remain as hostage here, etc.
         You'll

[GAMA, ARAC, GURON, *and* SCYNTHIUS *are marched off in
custody,* HILDEBRAND *following.*

RECITATIVE.—HILARION.

Come, Cyril, Florian, our course is plain,
    To-morrow morn fair Ida we'll engage;
But we will use no force her love to gain,
    Nature has armed us for the war we wage!

HIL.
Expressive glances
Shall be our lances,
 And pops of Sillery
 Our light artillery.
We'll storm their bowers
With scented showers
Of fairest flowers
 That we can buy!

CHOR.
 Oh, dainty triolet!
 Oh, fragrant violet!
 Oh, gentle heigho-let
  (Or little sigh)
On sweet urbanity,
Though mere inanity,
To touch their vanity
 We will rely!

CYR.
When day is fading,
With serenading
 And such frivolity
 We'll prove our quality.
A sweet profusion
Of soft allusion
This bold intrusion
 Shall justify.

CHOR.
 Oh, dainty triolet, etc.

FLO.
We'll charm their senses
With verbal fences,
 With ballads amatory
 And declamatory.
And little heeding
Their pretty pleading
Our love exceeding
 We'll justify!

CHOR.
 Oh, dainty triolet, etc.

Re-enter GAMA, ARAC, GURON, *and* SCYNTHIUS *heavily ironed.*

RECITATIVE.

GAMA. Must we, till then, in prison cell be thrust?
HILD.   You must!
GAMA. This seems unnecessarily severe!
ARAC, GURON, *and* SCYNTHIUS.   Hear, hear!

TRIO.—ARAC, GURON *and* SCYNTHIUS.

For a month to dwell
In a dungeon cell;
 Growing thin and wizen
 In a solitary prison,
Is a poor look out
For a soldier stout,
 Who is longing for the rattle
 Of a complicated battle—
For the rum-tum-tum
Of the military drum,
 And the guns that go boom! boom!

ALL.
Boom! boom! boom! boom!
Rum-tummy-tummy-tum!
Boom! boom!

HILD.
When Hilarion's bride
Has at length compiled
 With the just conditions
 Of our requisitions,
You may go in haste
And indulge your taste
 For the fascinating rattle
 Of a complicated battle.

For the rum-tum-tum,
Of the military drum,
 And the guns that go boom! boom!

ALL.
 Boom! boom! etc.

ALL.
But till that time $\left\{ \begin{matrix} \text{we'll} \\ \text{you'll} \end{matrix} \right\}$ here remain,

And bail $\left\{ \begin{matrix} \text{they} \\ \text{we} \end{matrix} \right\}$ will not entertain,

Should she $\left\{ \begin{matrix} \text{his} \\ \text{our} \end{matrix} \right\}$ mandate disobey,

$\left. \begin{matrix} \text{Our} \\ \text{Your} \end{matrix} \right\}$ lives the penalty will pay!

[GAMA, ARAC, GURON, *and* SCYNTHIUS *are marched off.*

ACT II.

Gardens in Castle Adamant. A river runs across the back of the stage, crossed by a rustic bridge. Castle Adamant in the distance. GIRL *graduates discovered seated at the feet of* LADY PSYCHE.

CHORUS.

Towards the empyrean heights
 Of every kind of lore,
We've taken several easy flights,
 And mean to take some more.
In trying to achieve success
 No envy racks our heart,
And all the knowledge we possess
 We mutually impart.

SOLO.—MELISSA.

Pray what authors should she read
Who in Classics would succeed?

PSYCHE.

If you'd cross the Helicon,
You should read Anacreon,
Ovid's Metamorphoses,
Likewise Aristophanes,
And the works of Juvenal:
These are worth attention, all;

But, if you will be advised.
You will get them Bowdlerized!

CHORUS.

Yes, we'll do as we're advised,
We will get them Bowdlerized!

SOLO.—SACHARISSA.

Pray you, tell us, if you can,
What's the thing that's known as Man?

PSYCHE.

Man will swear, and Man will storm—
Man is not at all good form—
Man is of no kind of use—
Man's a donkey—Man's a goose—
Man is coarse and Man is plain—
Man is more or less insane—
Man's a ribald—Man's a rake,
Man is Nature's sole mistake!

CHORUS.

We'll a memorandum make—
Man is Nature's sole mistake!

And thus to empyrean height
Of every kind of lore,
In search of wisdom's pure delight,
Ambitiously we soar.
In trying to achieve success
No envy racks our heart,
For all we know and all we guess,
We mutually impart!

Enter LADY BLANCHE. *All stand up demurely.*

BLA. Attention, ladies, while I read to you
The Princess Ida's list of punishments.
The first is Sacharissa. She's expelled!
ALL. Expelled!
BLA.   Expelled, because although she knew
No man of any kind may pass our walls,
She dared to bring a set of chessmen here!
SACH. *(crying)*. I meant no harm; they're only men of wood!
BLA. They're men with whom you give each other mate,
And that's enough! The next is Chloe.
CHLOE.   Ah!
BLA. Chloe will lose three terms, for yesterday,
When looking through her drawing-book, I found
A sketch of a perambulator!
ALL *(horrified)*.   Oh!
BLA. *Double* perambulator, shameless girl!
That's all at present. Now, attention, pray!
Your Principal the Princess comes to give
Her usual inaugural address
To those young ladies who joined yesterday.

Enter the PRINCESS.

CHORUS.

Mighty maiden with a mission,
    Paragon of common sense,
Running fount of erudition,
    Miracle of eloquence,
    We are blind, and we would see;
    We are bound, and would be free;
    We are dumb, and we would talk;
    We are lame, and we would walk.
Mighty maiden with a mission—
    Paragon of common sense;
Running fount of erudition—
    Miracle of eloquence!

PRIN. *(Recit.)* Minerva! hear me:

ARIA.

At this my call
    A fervent few
    Have come to woo
The rays that from thee fall.

Oh, goddess wise
    That lovest light,
    Endow with sight,
    Their unillumined eyes.
Let fervent words and fervent thoughts be mine,
That I may lead them to thy sacred shrine!

Women of Adamant, fair Neophytes—
Who thirst for such instruction as we give,
Attend, while I unfold a parable.
The elephant is mightier than Man,
Yet Man subdues him. Why? The elephant
Is elaphantine everywhere but here *(tapping her forehead)*.
And Man, whose brain is to the elephant's,
As Woman's brain to Man's—(that's rule of three)—
Conquers the foolish giant of the woods,
As Woman, in her turn, shall conquer Man.
In Mathematics, Woman leads the way—
The narrow-minded pedant still believes
That two and two make four! Why we can prove,
We women—household drudges as we are—
That two and two make five—or three—or seven;
Or five and twenty, if the case demands!
Diplomacy? The wiliest diplomate
Is absolutely helpless in our hands,
He wheedles monarchs—woman wheedles him!
Logic? Why, tyrant Man himself admits
It's waste of time to argue with a woman!
Then we excel in social qualities:
Though Man professes that he holds our sex
In utter scorn, I venture to believe
He'd rather spend the day with one of you,
Than with five hundred of his fellow-men!
In all things we excel. Believing this,
A hundred maidens here have sworn to place
Their feet upon his neck. If we succeed,

We'll treat him better than he treated us:
But if we fail, why then let hope fail too!
Let no one care a penny how she looks—
Let red be worn with yellow—blue with green—
Crimson with scarlet—violet with blue!
Let all your things misfit, and you yourselves,
At inconvenient moments come undone!
Let hair-pins lose their virtue: let the hook
Disdain the fascination of the eye—
The bashful button modestly evade
The soft embraces of the button-hole!
Let old associations all dissolve,
Let Swan secede from Edgar—Gask from Gask,
Sewell from Cross—Lewis from Allenby!
In other words—let Chaos come again!
(Coming down) Who lectures in the Hall of Arts to-day?

BLA. I, madam, on Abstract Philosophy.
There I propose considering, at length,
Three points—The Is, the Might Be, and the Must:
Whether the Is, from being actual fact,
Is more important than the vague Might Be,
Or the Might Be, from taking wider scope,
Is for that reason greater than the Is:
And lastly, how the Is and Might Be stand
Compared with the inevitable Must!
    PRIN. The subject's deep—how do you treat it, pray?
    BLA. Madam, I take three possibilities,
And strike a balance, then, between the three!
As thus: The Princess Ida Is our head,
The Lady Psyche Might Be—Lady Blanche,
Neglected Blanche, inevitably Must.
Given these three hypotheses—to find
The actual betting against each of them!
    PRIN. Your theme's ambitious: pray you bear in mind
Who highest soar fall farthest. Fare you well,
You and your pupils! Maidens, follow me.
        [Exeunt PRINCESS and MAIDENS, singing refrain of chorus,
        "And thus to empyrean heights," etc. Manet LADY
        BLANCHE.
    BLA. I should command here—I was born to rule.
But do I rule? I don't. Why? I don't know.
I shall some day. Not yet. I bide my time.
I once was Some One—and the Was Will Be.
The Present as we speak becomes the Past,
The Past repeats itself, and so is Future!
This sounds involved. It's not. It's right enough.

SONG.—LADY BLANCHE.

Come mighty Must!
   Inevitable Shall!
In thee I trust.
   Time weaves my coronal!
Go, mocking Is!
   Go, disappointing Was!
That I am this
   Ye are the cursed cause!
Yet humble second shall be first,
   I ween;
And dead and buried be the curst
   Has Been!

Oh, weak Might Be!
   Oh, May, Might, Could, Would, Should!
How powerless ye
   For evil or for good!
In every sense
   Your moods I cheerless call,
Whate'er your tense
   Ye are Imperfect, all!
Ye have deceived the trust that I've shown
   In ye!
Away! The Mighty Must alone
   Shall be!

                [Exit LADY BLANCHE.

Enter HILARION, CYRIL, and FLORIAN, climbing over wall, and
creeping cautiously among the trees and rocks at the back of the
stage.

TRIO.—HILARION, CYRIL, FLORIAN.

Gently, gently,
Evidently,
   We are safe so far,
After scaling
Fence and paling,
   Here, at last, we are!
In this college
Useful knowledge
   Everywhere one finds,
And already,
Growing steady,
   We've enlarged our minds.

CYR.   We've learnt that prickly cactus
        Has the power to attract us
             When we fall.

ALL.   When we fall!

HIL.   That nothing man unsettles
        Like a bed of stinging nettles,
             Short or tall.

ALL.   Short or tall!

FLOR.   That bull-dogs feed on throttles—
        That we don't like broken bottles
             On a wall.

ALL.   On a wall!

HIL.   That spring-guns breathe defiance!
        And that burglary's a science
             After all.

ALL.   After all!

RECITATIVE.—FLORIAN.

A Woman's college! maddest folly going!
What can girls learn within its walls worth knowing?

I'll lay a crown (the Princess shall decide it)
I'll teach them twice as much in half an hour outside it.

HILARION.

Hush, scoffer; ere you sound your puny thunder,
List to their aims, and bow your head in wonder!

They intend to send a wire
    To the moon—to the moon;
And they'll set the Thames on fire
    Very soon—very soon;
Then they learn to make silk purses
    With their rigs—with their rigs
From the ears of Lady Circe's
    Piggy-wigs—piggy-wigs.
And weazels at their slumbers
    They trepan—they trepan;
To get sunbeams from cucumbers
    They've a plan—they've a plan.
They've a firmly rooted notion
They can cross the Polar Ocean,
And they'll find Perpetual Motion,
    If they can—if they can.

    These are the phenomena
    That every pretty domina
      Hopes that we shall see
      At this Universitee.

ALL.
    These are the phenomena
    That every pretty domina
      Hopes that we shall see
      At this Universitee!

CYR.   As for fashion, they forswear it,
    So they say—so they say—
And the circle—they will square it
    Some fine day—some fine day—
Then the little pigs they're teaching
    For to fly—for to fly;
And the niggers they'll be bleaching,
    By-and-by—by-and-by!
Each newly joined aspirant
    To the clan—to the clan—
Must repudiate the tyrant
    Known as Man—known as Man—
They mock at him and flout at him,
For they do not care about him,
And they're "going to do without him"
    If they can—if they can!

    These are the phenomena
    That every pretty domina
      Hopes that we shall see
      At this Universitee.

ALL.   These are the phenomena, etc.

HIL. So that's the Princess Ida's castle! Well,
They must be lovely girls, indeed, if it requires
Such walls as those to keep intruders off!

CYR. To keep men off is only half their charge,
And that the easier half. I much suspect
The object of these walls is not so much
To keep men off as keep the maidens in!
    FLO. But what are these?
                  [Examining some collegiate robes.
    HIL. *(looking at them).* Why, Academic robes,
Worn by the lady undergraduates,
When they matriculate. Let's try them on.   *[They do so.*
Why, see—we're covered to the very toes.
Three lovely lady undergraduates
Who, weary of the world and all its wooing—
    FLO. And penitent for deeds there's no undoing—
    CYR. Looked at askance by well-conducted maids—
    ALL. Seek sanctuary in these classic shades!

TRIO.—HILARION, CYRIL, FLORIAN.

HIL.   I am a maiden, cold and stately,
      Heartless I, with a face divine.
    What do I want with a heart innately?
      Every heart I meet is mine!

ALL.   Haughty, humble, coy, or free,
        Little care I what maid may be.
      So that a maid is fair to see,
        Every maid is the maid for me!   *[Dance.*

CYR.   I am a maiden frank and simple,
      Brimming with joyous roguery;
    Merriment lurks in every dimple,
      Nobody breaks more hearts than I!

ALL.   Haughty, humble, coy, or free,
        Little care I what maid may be.
      So that a maid is fair to see,
        Every maid is the maid for me!   *[Dance.*

FLO.   I am a maiden coyly blushing,
      Timid I as a startled hind;
    Every suitor sets me flushing:
      I am the maid that wins mankind!

ALL.   Haughty, humble, coy, or free,
        Little care I what maid may be.
      So that a maid is fair to see,
        Every maid is the maid for me!

Enter the PRINCESS, *reading. She does not see them.*

FLO. But who comes here? The Princess, as I live!
What shall we do?
    HIL. *(aside).*   Why, we must brave it out!
(Aloud). Madam, accept our humblest reverence.
        [They bow, then suddenly recollecting themselves, curtsy.
    PRIN. *(surprised).* We greet you, ladies. What would you with
us?
    HIL. *(aside).* What shall I say? *(Aloud.)* We are three students,
ma'am,
Three well-born maids of liberal estate,
Who wish to join this University.

[HILARION *and* FLORIAN *curtsy again.* CYRIL *bows
extravagantly, then, being recalled to himself by*
FLORIAN, *curtsys.*

PRIN. If, as you say, you wish to join our ranks,
And will subscribe to all our rules, 'tis well.

FLO. To all your rules we cheerfully subscribe.

PRIN. You say you're noblewomen. Well, you'll find
No sham degrees for noblewomen here.
You'll find no sizars here, or servitors,
Or other cruel distinctions, meant to draw
A line 'twixt rich and poor: you'll find no tufts
To mark nobility, except such tufts
As indicate nobility of brain.
As for your fellow-students, mark me well:
There are a hundred maids within these walls,
All good, all learned, and all beautiful:
They are prepared to love you: will you swear
To give the fulness of your love to them?

HIL. Upon our words and honours, ma'am, we will!

PRIN. But we go further: will you undertake
That you will never marry any man?

FLO. Indeed we never will!

PRIN.   Consider well,
You must prefer our maids to all mankind!

HIL. To all mankind we much prefer your maids!

CYR. We should be dolts indeed, if we did not,
Seeing how fair—

HIL. *(aside to* CYRIL). Take care—that's rather strong!

PRIN. But have you left no lovers at your home
Who may pursue you here?

HIL.   No, madam, none.
We're homely ladies, as no doubt you see,
And we have never fished for lover's love.
We smile at girls who deck themselves with gems,
False hair, and meretricious ornament,
To chain the fleeting fancy of a man,
But do not imitate them. What we have
Of hair, is all our own. Our colour, too,
Unladylike, but not unwomanly,
Is Nature's handiwork, and man has learnt
To reckon Nature an impertinence.

PRIN. Well, beauty counts for naught within these walls;
If all you say is true, you'll spend with us
A happy, happy time!

CYR.   If, as you say,
A hundred lovely maidens wait within,
To welcome us with smiles and open arms,
I think there's very little doubt we shall!

QUARTETTE.—PRINCESS, HILARION, CYRIL, FLORIAN.

PRIN.   The world is but a broken toy,
            Its pleasure hollow—false its joy,
              Unreal its loveliest hue.
                              Alas!
              Its pains alone are true,
                              Alas!
              Its pains alone are true.

HIL.   The world is everything you say
            The world we think has had its day,

Its merriment is slow,
                Alas!
We've tried it, and we know,
                Alas!
We've tried it, and we know.

TUTTI.

PRINCESS.	HILARION, CYRIL, FLORIAN.
The world is but a broken toy,	The world is but a broken toy,
Its pleasures hollow—	We freely give it up
false its joy,	with joy,
Unreal its loveliest hue.	Unreal its loveliest hue.
Alas!	Alas!
Its pains alone are true,	We quite agree with you,
Alas!	Alas!
Its pains alone are true!	We quite agree with you!

[*Exit* PRINCESS. *The three* GENTLEMEN *watch her off.*

LADY PSYCHE *enters, and regards them with amazement.*

HIL. I'faith, the plunge is taken, gentlemen!
For, willy-nilly, we are maidens now,
And maids against our will we must remain!

[*All laugh heartily.*

PSY. *(aside).* These ladies are unseemly in their mirth.

[*The* GENTLEMEN *see her, and, in confusion, resume their
modest demeanour.*

FLO. *(aside.)* Here's a catastrophe, Hilarion!
This is my sister! She'll remember me,
Though years have passed since she and I have met!

HIL. *(aside to* FLORIAN). Then make a virtue of necessity
And trust our secret to her gentle care.

FLOR. *(to* PSYCHE, *who has watched* CYRIL *in amazement)*
    Psyche.
Why, don't you know me? Florian!

PSY. *(amazed).* Why! Florian!

FLOR.   My sister! *(Embraces her.)*

PSY.   Oh, my dear!
What are you doing here—and who are these?

HIL. I am that Prince Hilarion to whom
Your Princess is betrothed. I come to claim
Her plighted love. Your brother Florian
And Cyril, come to see me safely through.

PSY. The Prince Hilarion? Cyril too? How strange!
My earliest playfellows!

HIL.   Why, let me look!
Are you that learned little Psyche who
At school alarmed her mates because she called
A buttercup "rananculus bulbosus?"

CYR. Are you that indeed that Lady Psyche who
At children's parties drove the conjuror wild,
Explaining all his tricks before he did them?

HIL. Are you that learned little Psyche, who
At dinner parties, brought into dessert,
Would tackle visitors with "You don't know
Who first determined longitude—I do—
Hipparchus 'twas—B.C. one sixty-three!"
Are you indeed that small phenomenon?

PSY. That small phenomenon indeed am I!
But, gentlemen, 'tis death to enter here:
We have all promised to renounce mankind!

FLO. Renounce mankind? On what ground do you base
This senseless resolution?
PSY.   Senseless? No.
We are all taught, and, being taught, believe
That Man, sprung from an Ape, is Ape at heart.
CYR. That's rather strong.
PSY.   The truth is always strong.

SONG.—LADY PSYCHE.

The Ape and the Lady.

A Lady fair, of lineage high,
Was loved by an Ape, in the days gone by—
The Maid was radiant as the sun,
The Ape was a most unsightly one—
    So it would not do—
    His scheme fell through,
For the Maid, when his love took formal shape,
    Expressed such terror
    At his monstrous error,
That he stammered an apology and made his 'scape,
The picture of a disconcerted Ape.

With a view to rise in the social scale,
He shaved his bristles, and he docked his tail,
He grew moustachios, and he took his tub,
And he paid a guinea to a toilet club—
    But it would not do,
    The scheme fell through—
For the Maid was Beauty's fairest Queen,
    With golden tresses,
    Like a real princess's,
While the Ape, despite his razor keen,
Was the apiest Ape that ever was seen!

He bought white ties, and he bought dress suits,
He crammed his feet into bright tight boots—
And to start in life on a bran new plan,
He christened himself Darwinian Man!
    But it would not do,
    The scheme fell through—
For the Maiden fair, whom the monkey craved,
    Was a radiant Being,
    With a brain far-seeing—
While a Man, however well-behaved,
At best is only a monkey shaved!

During this MELISSA *has entered unobserved: she looks on in
amazement.*

MEL. *(coming down).* Oh, Lady Psyche!
PSY. *(terrified).*   What! you heard us then?
Oh, all is lost!
MEL.   Not so! I'll breathe no word!
                    [*Advancing in astonishment to* FLORIAN.
How marvellously strange! and are you then
Indeed young men?
FLO.   Well, yes, just now we are—
But hope by dint of study to become,
In course of time, young women.

MEL. *(eagerly).*   No, no, no—
Oh, don't do that! Is this indeed a man?
I've often heard of them, but, till to-day,
Never set eyes on one. They told me men
Were hideous, idiotic, and deformed!
They're quite as beautiful as women are!
As beautiful, they're infinitely more so!
Their cheeks have not that pulpy softness which
One gets so weary of in womankind:
Their features are more marked—and—oh, their chins!
How curious!   [*Feeling his chin.*
FLO.   I fear it's rather rough.
MEL. *(eagerly).* Oh, don't apologize—I like it so!

QUINTETTE.—PSYCHE, MELISSA, HILARION, CYRIL, FLORIAN.

PSY.   The woman of the wisest wit
            May sometimes be mistaken, O!
        In Ida's views, I must admit,
            My faith is somewhat shaken, O!

CYR.   On every other point than this,
            Her learning is unshaken, O!
        But Man's a theme with which she is
            Entirely unacquainted, O!
                —acquainted, O!
                —acquainted, O!
            Entirely unacquainted, O!

ALL.   Then jump for joy and gaily bound,
        The truth is found—the truth is found!
        Set bells a-ringing through the air—
        Ring here and there and everywhere—
        And echo forth the joyous sound,
        The truth is found—the truth is found!   [*Dance.*

MEL.   My natural instinct teaches me
            (And instinct is important, O!)
        You're everything you ought to be,
            And nothing that you oughtn't, O!

HIL.   That fact was seen at once by you
            In casual conversation, O!
        Which is most creditable to
            Your powers of observation, O!
                —servation, O!
                —servation, O!
            Your powers of observation, O!

ALL.   Then jump for joy, etc.

[*Exeunt* PSYCHE, HILARION, CYRIL, *and* FLORIAN. MELISSA
going.

Enter LADY BLANCHE.

BLA. Melissa!
MEL. *(returning).* Mother!
BLA.   Here—a word with you.
Those are the three new students?
MEL. *(confused).*   Yes, they are.
They're charming girls.

BLA.   Particularly so.
So graceful, and so very womanly!
So skilled in all a girl's accomplishments!
   MEL. *(confused).* Yes—very skilled.
   BLA.   They sing so nicely too!
   MEL. They *do* sing nicely!
   BLA.   Humph! It's very odd.
One is a tenor, two are baritones!
   MEL. *(much agitated).* They've all got colds!
   BLA.   Colds! Bah! D'ye think I'm blind?
These "girls" are men disguised!
   MEL.   Oh no—indeed!
You wrong these gentlemen—I mean—why see,
Here is an *étui* dropped by one of them *(picking up an étui),*
Containing scissors, needles, and—
   BLA. *(opening it.)*   Cigars!
Why these *are* men! And you knew this, you minx.
   MEL. Oh, spare them—they are gentlemen indeed.
The Prince Hilarion (married years ago
To Princess Ida) with two trusted friends!
Consider, mother, he's her husband now,
And has been, twenty years! Consider too,
You're only second here—you should be first.
Assist the Prince's plan, and when he gains
The Princess Ida, why, you *will* be first.
You will design the fashions—think of that—
And always serve out all the punishments!
The scheme is harmless, mother—wink at it!
   BLA. *(aside).* The prospect's tempting! Well, well, well,
                       I'll try—
Though I've not winked at anything for years!
'Tis but one step towards my destiny—
The mighty Must! the inevitable Shall!

DUET.—MELISSA *and* LADY BLANCHE.

MEL.   Now wouldn't you like to rule the roast,
        And guide this University?
BLA.   I must agree
          'Twould pleasant be.
          (Sing hey a Proper Pride!)

MEL.   And wouldn't you like to clear the coast
        Of malice and perversity?
BLA.   Without a doubt
         I'll bundle 'em out,
         Sing hey, when I preside!

BOTH.   Sing, hoity, toity! Sorry for some!
     Marry come up, and { my / her } day will come!
        Sing Proper Pride
        Is the horse to ride,
        And Happy-go-lucky, my Lady, O!

BLA.   For years I've writhed beneath her sneers,
        Although a born Plantagenet!
MEL.   You're much too meek,
        Or you would speak.
        (Sing hey, I'll say no more!)

BLA.   Her elder I, by several years,
        Although you'd never imagine it.
MEL.   Sing, so I've heard
        But never a word
        Have I ever believed before!

BOTH.   Sing, hoity, toity! Sorry for some!
     Marry come up, { my / her } day will come!
        Sing, she shall learn
        That a worm will turn.
        Sing, Happy-go-lucky, my Lady, O!
               [*Exit* LADY BLANCHE.

   MEL. Saved for a time, at least!

Enter FLORIAN, *on tiptoe.*

   FLO. *(whispering).*   Melissa—come!
   MEL. Oh, sir! you must away from this at once—
My mother guessed your sex! It was my fault—
I blushed and stammered so that she exclaimed,
"Can these be men?" Then, seeing this, "Why these—"
"*Are men,*" she would have added, but "*are men*"
Stuck in her throat! She keeps your secret, sir,
For reasons of her own—but, fly from this
And take me with you—that is—no—not that!
   FLO. I'll go, but not without you! *(Bell.)* Why, what's
     that?
   MEL. The luncheon bell.
   FLO.   I'll wait for luncheon then!

Enter HILARION *with* PRINCESS, CYRIL *with* PSYCHE, LADY
   BLANCHE *and* LADIES. *Also* "DAUGHTERS OF THE PLOUGH"
   bearing luncheon, which they spread on the rocks.

CHORUS.

   Merrily ring the luncheon bell!
   Here in meadow of asphodel,
   Feast we body and mind as well,
   So merrily ring the luncheon bell!

SOLO.—BLANCHE.

   Hunger, I beg to state,
   Is highly indelicate,
   This is a fact profoundly true
   So learn your appetites to subdue.
ALL.   Yes, yes,
      We'll learn our appetites to subdue!

SOLO.—CYRIL *(eating).*

   Madam, your words so wise,
   Nobody should despise,
   Cursed with an appetite keen I am
      And I'll subdue it—
      And I'll subdue it—
   And I'll subdue it with cold roast lamb!

ALL.   Yes, yes,
      We'll subdue it with cold roast lamb!

CHORUS. Merrily ring, etc.

PRIN. You say you know the court of Hildebrand?
There is a Prince there—I forget his name—
HIL. Hilarion?
PRIN.   Exactly—is he well?
HIL. If it be well to droop and pine and mope,
To sigh "Oh, Ida! Ida!" all day long,
"Ida! my love! my life! Oh come to me!"
If it be well, I say, to do all this,
Then Prince Hilarion is very well.
    PRIN. He breathes *our* name? Well, it's a common one!
And is the booby comely?
HIL.   Pretty well.
I've heard it said that if I dressed myself
In Prince Hilarion's clothes (supposing this
Consisted with my maiden modesty),
I might be taken for Hilarion's self.
But what is this to you or me, who think
Of all mankind with undisguised contempt?
    PRIN. Contempt? Why, damsel, when I think of man,
Contempt is not the word.
    CYR. (getting tipsy).   I'm sure of that,
Or if it is, it surely should not be!
    HIL. (aside to CYRIL). Be quiet, idiot, or they'll find us out.
    CYR. The Prince Hilarion's a goodly lad!
    PRIN. You know him then?
    CYR. (tipsily).   I rather think I do!
We are inseparables!
    PRIN.   Why, what's this?
You love him then?
    CYR.   We do indeed—all three!
    HIL. Madam, she jests! (Aside to CYRIL.) Remember where
      you are!
    CYR. Jests? Not at all! Why, bless my heart alive,
You and Hilarion, when at the Court,
Rode the same horse!
    PRIN. (horrified).   Astride?
    CYR.   Of course! Why not?
Wore the same clothes—and once or twice, I think,
Got tipsy in the same good company!
    PRIN. Well, these are nice young ladies, on my word!
    CYR. (tipsy). Don't you remember that old kissing-song
He'd sing to blushing Mistress Lalage,
The hostess of the Pigeons? Thus it ran:

SONG.—CYRIL.

[During symphony HILARION and FLORIAN try to stop CYRIL.
    He shakes them off angrily.

    Would you know the kind of maid
      Sets my heart a flame-a?
    Eyes must be downcast and staid,
      Cheeks must flush for shame-a!
        She may neither dance nor sing,
        But, demure in everything,
        Hang her head in modest way,
        With pouting lips that seem to say
      "Kiss me, kiss me, kiss me, kiss me,
        Though I die of shame-a,"
      Please you, that's the kind of maid
        Sets my heart a flame-a!

    When a maid is bold and gay
      With a tongue goes clang-a,
    Flaunting it in brave array,
      Maiden may go hang-a!
        Sunflower gay and hollyhock
        Never shall my garden stock;
        Mine the blushing rose of May,
        With pouting lips that seem to say,
      "Oh, kiss me, kiss me, kiss me, kiss me,
        Though I die for shame-a!"
    Please you that's the kind of maid
      Sets my heart a flame-a!

    PRIN. Infamous creature, get you hence away!
    [HILARION, *who has been with difficulty restrained by* FLORIAN
      during this song, breaks from him and strikes CYRIL *furiously*
      on the breast.
    HIL. Dog! there is something more to sing about!
    CYR. (sobered). Hilarion, are you mad?
    PRIN. (horrified).   Hilarion? Help!
Why these are men! Lost! lost! betrayed! undone!
              [Running on to bridge.
Girls, get you hence! Man-monsters, if you dare
Approach one step, I— Ah!
        [Loses her balance, and falls into the stream.
PSY.   Oh! save her, sir!
BLA. It's useless, sir—you'll only catch your death!
              [HILARION springs in.
SACH. He catches her!
MEL.   And now he lets her go!
Again she's in his grasp—
PSY.   And now she's not.
He seizes her back hair!
BLA. (not looking).   And it comes off!
PSY. No, no! She's saved!—she's saved!—she's
    saved!
    [HILARION *is seen swimming with* PRINCESS *in one arm.*
    The PRINCESS *and he are brought to land.*

FINALE.

CHORUS OF LADIES.

    Oh! joy, our chief is saved,
      And by Hilarion's hand;
    The torrent fierce he braved,
      And brought her safe to land!
        For his intrusion we must own
        This doughty deed may well atone;

PRIN.   Stand forth ye three,
          Whoe'er ye be,
    And hearken to our stern decree;

HIL., CYR., *and* FLO. Have mercy, lady—disregard your oaths!

PRIN. I know not mercy, men in women's clothes.
      The man whose sacrilegious eyes
      Invade our strict seclusion, dies.
      Arrest these coarse intruding spies!
    [They are arrested by the "DAUGHTERS OF THE PLOUGH."

177

FLO., CYR., and LADIES. Have mercy lady—disregard your oaths!

PRIN. I know not mercy, men in women's clothes.

[CYRIL and FLORIAN are bound.

SONG.—HILARION.

Whom thou hast chained must wear his chain,
   Thou canst not set him free,
He wrestles with his bonds in vain
   Who lives by loving thee!
If heart of stone for heart of fire,
   Be all thou hast to give,
If dead to me my heart's desire,
   Why should I wish to live?

No word of thine—no stern command
   Can teach my heart to rove,
Then rather perish by thy hand,
   Than live without thy love!
A loveless life apart from thee
   Were hopeless slavery,
If kindly death will set me free,
   Why should I fear to die?

[He is bound by two of the attendants, and the three GENTLEMEN
are marched off.

Enter MELISSA.

MEL.   Madam, without the castle walls
        An armed band
     Demand admittance to our halls
        For Hildebrand!

ALL.   Oh, horror!

PRIN.   Deny them;
     We will defy them!

ALL.   Too late—too late!
     The castle gate
     Is battered by them!

[The gate yields. HILDEBRAND and SOLDIERS rush in. ARAC.
GURON, and SCYNTHIUS are with them, but with their hands
handcuffed.

ALL (SOLDIERS and LADIES).   Too late—too late,
     The castle gate
     Is battered by them!

ENSEMBLE.

GIRLS.	MEN.
Rend the air with wailing,	Walls and fences scaling,
Shed the shameful tear!	Promptly we appear;
Walls are unavailing,	Walls are unavailing,
Man has entered here!	We have entered here.
Shame and desecration	Female execration
Are his staunch allies,	Stifle if you're wise,

Let your lamentation	Stop your lamentation,
Echo to the skies!	Dry your pretty eyes!

RECITATIVE.

PRIN.   Audacious tyrant, do you dare
     To beard a maiden in her lair?

KING.   Since you inquire,
       We've no desire
     To beard a maiden here, or anywhere!

SOL.   No, no—we've no desire
     To beard a maiden here, or anywhere!

SOLO.—HILDEBRAND.

   Some years ago,
   No doubt you know
(And if you don't I'll tell you so),
   You gave your troth
   Upon your oath
To Hilarion my son.
   A vow you make
   You must not break
(If you think you may, it's a great mistake,)
   For a bride's a bride
   Though the knot were tied
     At the early age of one!
      And I'm a peppery kind of King,
      Who's indisposed for parleying
      To fit the wit of a bit of a chit,
      And that's the long and the short of it!

ALL.   For he's a peppery kind of King, etc.

   If you decide
   To pocket your pride,
And let Hilarion claim his bride,
   Why, well and good,
   It's understood
We'll let bygones go by—
   But if you choose
   To sulk in the blues,
I'll make the whole of you shake in your shoes.
   I'll storm your walls,
   And level your halls,
     In the twinkling of an eye!
      For I'm a peppery Potentate,
      Who's little inclined his claim to bate,
      To fit the wit of a bit of a chit,
      And that's the long and the short of it.

TRIO.—ARAC, GURON, and SCYNTHIUS.

We may remark, though nothing can
       Dismay us,
That, if you thwart this gentleman,
       He'll slay us,
We don't fear death, of course—we're taught
       To shame it;

But still upon the whole we thought
    We'd name it,
(To each other). Yes, yes, better perhaps to name it.

Our interests we would not press
    With chatter,
Three hulking brothers more or less
    Don't matter;
If you'd pooh-pooh this monarch's plan,
    Pooh-pooh it,
But when he says he'll hang a man,
    He'll do it.
(To each other). Yes, yes, devil doubt he'll do it.

PRIN. *(Recit.).* Be reassured, nor fear his anger blind,
  His menaces are idle as the wind.
  He dares not kill you—vengeance lurks behind!

AR., GUR., SCYN. *We* rather think he dares, but never mind;
     No, no,—never, never mind

KING. Enough of parley—as a special boon—
  We give you till to-morrow afternoon!
  Release Hilarion, then, and be his bride,
  Or you'll incur the guilt of fratricide!

ENSEMBLE.

PRINCESS.	THE OTHERS.
To yield at once to such a foe	Oh! yield at once, 'twere better
With shame were rife;	so
So quick; away with him,	Than risk a strife!
although	And let the Prince Hilarion go—
He saved my life!	He saved thy life!
That he is fair, and strong,	Hilarion's fair, and strong,
and tall,	and tall—
Is very evident to all,	A worse misfortune might
Yet I will die before I call	befal—
Myself his wife!	It's not so dreadful, after all,
	To be his wife!

SOLO.—PRINCESS.

Though I am but a girl,
Defiance thus I hurl,
 Our banners all
 On outer wall
We fearlessly unfurl.

ALL. Though she is but a girl, etc.

PRINCESS.	THE OTHERS.
That he is fair, etc.	Hilarion's fair, etc.

[The PRINCESS *stands, surrounded by the* GIRLS *kneeling. The* KING *and* SOLDIERS *stand on built rocks at back and sides of stage. Picture.*

CURTAIN.

ACT III

SCENE.— *Outer walls and courtyard of Castle Adamant.* MELISSA, SACHARISSA, *and* LADIES *discovered, armed with battle-axes.*

CHORUS.

Death to the invader!
 Strike a deadly blow,
As an old Crusader
 Struck his Paynim foe!
  Let our martial thunder
  Fill his soul with wonder,
  Tear his ranks asunder,
   Lay the tyrant low!

SOLO.—MELISSA.

Thus our courage, all untarnished
 We're instructed to display;
But, to tell the truth unvarnished,
 We are more inclined to say,
"Please you, do not hurt us."

ALL.	"Do not hurt us, if it please you!"
MEL.	"Please you let us be."
ALL.	"Let us be—let us be!"
MEL.	"Soldiers disconcert us."
ALL.	"Disconcert us, if it please you!"
MEL.	"Frightened maids are we."
ALL.	"Maids are we—maids are we!"

MELISSA.

But 'twould be an error
To confess our terror,
So, in Ida's name,
Boldly we exclaim:

CHORUS.

Death to the invader
 Strike a deadly blow,
As an old Crusader
 Struck his Paynim foe
  Let our martial thunder
  Fill his soul with wonder,
  Tear his ranks asunder,
   Lay the tyrant low!

Flourish. Enter PRINCESS, *armed, attended by* BLANCHE *and* PSYCHE.

PRIN. I like your spirit, girls! We have to meet
Stern bearded warriors in fight to-day:
Wear naught but what is necessary to
Preserve your dignity before their eyes,
And give your limbs full play.
 BLA.   One moment, ma'am,
Here is a paradox we should not pass
Without inquiry. We are prone to say

"This thing is Needful—that, Superfluous"—
Yet they invariably co-exist!
We find the Needful comprehended in
The circle of the grand Superfluous,
Yet the Superfluous cannot be bought
Unless you're amply furnished with the Needful.
These singular considerations are—
PRIN. Superfluous, yet not Needful—so you see
The terms may independently exist.
(To LADIES.) Women of Adamant, we have to show
That Woman, educated to the task,
Can meet Man, face to face, on his own ground,
And beat him there. Now let us set to work;
Where is our lady surgeon?
SAC.   Madam, here!
PRIN. We shall require your skill to heal the wounds
Of those that fall.
SAC. *(alarmed).* What, heal the wounded?
PRIN.   Yes!
SAC. And cut off real live legs and arms?
PRIN.   Of course!
SAC. I wouldn't do it for a thousand pounds!
PRIN. Why, how is this? Are you faint-hearted, girl?
You've often cut them off in theory!
SAC. In theory I'll cut them off again,
With pleasure, and as often as you like,
But not in practice.
PRIN.   Coward! get you hence,
I've craft enough for that, and courage too;
I'll do your work. My fusiliers, advance!
Why, you are armed with axes! Gilded toys!
Where are your rifles, pray?
CHLOE.   Why, please you, ma'am,
We left them in the armoury, for fear
That in the heat and turmoil of the fight
They might go off!
PRIN.   "They might!" Oh, craven souls!
Go off yourselves! Thank Heaven, I have a heart
That quails not at the thought of meeting men;
I will discharge your rifles! Off with you!
Where's my bandmistress?
ADA.   Please you, ma'am, the band
Do not feel well, and can't come out to-day!
PRIN. Why, this is flat rebellion! I've no time
To talk to them just now. But, happily,
I can play several instruments at once,
And I will drown the shrieks of those that fall
With trumpet music, such as soldiers love!
How stand we with respect to gunpowder?
My Lady Psyche—you who superintend
Our lab'ratory—are you well prepared
To blow these bearded rascals into shreds?
PSY. Why, madam—
PRIN.   Well?
PSY.   Let us try gentler means.
We can dispense with fulminating grains
While we have eyes with which to flash our rage!
We can dispense with villainous saltpetre
While we have tongues with which to blow them up!
We can dispense, in short, with all the arts
That brutalize the practical polemist!

PRIN. *(contemptuously).* I never knew a more dispensing
chemist!
Away, away—I'll meet these men alone,
Since all my women have deserted me!
    [*Exeunt all but* PRINCESS, *singing refrain of "Death to the
    Invader," pianissimo.*
PRIN. So fail my cherished plans—so fails my faith—
And with it hope, and all that comes of hope!

SOLO.—PRINCESS.

I built upon a rock;
    But ere Destruction's hand
        Dealt equal lot
        To Court and cot,
    My rock had turned to sand!
        Ah, faithless rock,
        My simple faith to mock!

I leant upon an oak;
    But in the hour of need,
        Alack-a-day,
        My trusted stay
    Was but a bruised reed!
        Ah, trait'rous oak,
        Thy worthlessness to cloak!

I drew a sword of steel;
    But when to home and hearth
        The battle's breath
        Bore fire and death,
    My sword was but a lath!
        Ah, coward steel,
            That fear can unanneal!
                [*She sinks on a bank*

Enter CHLOE *and all the* LADIES.

CHLOE. Madam, your father and your brothers claim
An audience!
PRIN.   What do they do here?
CHLOE.   They come
To fight for you!
PRIN.   Admit them!
BLA.   Infamous!
One's brothers, ma'am, are men!
PRIN.   So I have heard;
But all my women seem to fail me when
I need them most. In this emergency,
Even one's brothers may be turned to use.

Enter GAMA, *quite pale and unnerved.*

GAMA. My daughter!
PRIN.   Father! thou art free!
GAMA.   Ay, free!
Free as a tethered ass! I come to thee
With words from Hildebrand. Those duly given,
I must return to black captivity.
I'm free so far.
PRIN.   Your message.
GAMA.   Hildebrand

Is loth to war with women. Pit my sons,
My three brave sons, against these popinjays,
These tufted jack-a-dandy featherheads,
And on the issue let thy hand depend!
   PRIN. Insult on insult's head! Are we a stake
For fighting men? What fiend possesses thee,
That thou hast come with offers such as these
From such as he to such an one as I?
   GAMA. I am possessed
By the pale devil of a shaking heart!
My stubborn will is bent. I dare not face
That devilish monarch's black malignity!
He tortures me with torments worse than death,
I haven't anything to grumble at!
He finds out what particular meats I love,
And gives me them. The very choicest wines,
The costliest robes—the richest rooms are mine:
He suffers none to thwart my simplest plan,
And gives strict orders none should contradict me!
He's made my life a curse!   [*Weeps.*
   PRIN.   My tortured father!

SONG.—GAMA.

    Whene'er I spoke
    Sarcastic joke
Replete with malice spiteful,
    This people mild
    Politely smiled,
And voted me delightful!
    Now when a wight
    Sits up all night
Ill-natured jokes devising,
    And all his wiles
    Are met with smiles,
It's hard, there's no disguising!
Oh, don't the days seem lank and long
When all goes right and nothing goes wrong,
And isn't your life extremely flat
With nothing whatever to grumble at!

    When German bands
    From music stands
Played Wagner imper*fectly*—
    I bade them go—
    They didn't say no,
But off they went directly!
    The organ boys
    They stopped their noise
With readiness surprising,
    And grinning herds
    Of hurdy-gurds
Retired apologizing!
Oh, don't the days seem lank and long, etc.

    I offered gold
    In sums untold
To all who'd contradict me—
    I said I'd pay
    A pound a day
To any one who kicked me—

    I bribed with toys
    Great vulgar boys
To utter something spiteful,
    But, bless you, no!
    They *would* be so
Confoundedly politeful!

In short, these aggravating lads
They tickle my tastes, they feed my fads,
They give me this and they give me that,
And I've nothing whatever to grumble at!
      [*He bursts into tears, and falls sobbing on a bank.*
   PRIN. My poor old father! How he must have suffered!
Well, well, I yield!
   GAMA. (*hysterically*). She yields! I'm saved, I'm saved!
   PRIN. Open the gates—admit these warriors,
Then get you all within the castle walls.
    [*The gates are opened, and the* GIRLS *mount the battlements as*
    HILDEBRAND *enters with* SOLDIERS. *Also* ARAC,
    GURON, *and* SCYNTHIUS.

CHORUS OF SOLDIERS.

When anger spreads his wing,
   And all seems dark as night for it,
   There's nothing but to fight for it,
But ere you pitch your ring,
   Select a pretty site for it,
   (This spot is suited quite for it),
And then you gaily sing,

"Oh, I love the jolly rattle
Of an ordeal by battle,
There's an end of tittle-tattle,
    When your enemy is dead.
It's an arrant molley coddle,
Fears a crack upon the noddle,
And he's only fit to swaddle,
    In a downy feather-bed!—

  ALL.   For a fight's a kind of thing
    That I love to look upon,
      So let us sing,
      Long live the King,
    And his son Hilarion!

    [*During this,* HILARION, FLORIAN, *and* CYRIL *are brought out
    by the* "DAUGHTERS OF THE PLOUGH." *They are still
    bound and wear the robes.*

   GAMA. Hilarion! Cyril! Florian! dressed as women!
Is this indeed Hilarion?
   HIL.   Yes, it is!
   GAMA. Why, you look handsome in your women's clothes!
Stick to 'em! men's attire becomes you not!
(*To* CYRIL *and* FLORIAN.) And you, young ladies, will you
      please to pray
King Hildebrand to set me free again?
Hang on his neck and gaze into his eyes,
He never could resist a pretty face!
   HIL. You dog, you'll find though I wear woman's garb,
My sword is long and sharp!

GAMA.   Hush, pretty one!
Here's a virago! Here's a termagant!
If length and sharpness go for anything,
You'll want no sword while you can wag your tongue!
    CYRIL. What need to waste your words on such as he?
He's old and crippled.
    GAMA.   Ay, but I've three sons,
Fine fellows, young, and muscular, and brave,
They're well worth talking to! Come, what d'ye say?
    ARAC. Ay, pretty ones, engage yourselves with us,
If three rude warriors affright you not!
    HIL. Old as you are I'd wring your shrivelled neck
If you were not the Princess Ida's father.
    GAMA. If I were not the Princess Ida's father,
And so had not her brothers for my sons,
No doubt you'd wring my neck—in safety too!
Come, come, Hilarion, begin, begin!
Give them no quarter—they will give you none.
You've this advantage over warriors
Who kill their country's enemies for pay—
You know what you are fighting for—look there!
                    [*Pointing to* LADIES *on the battlements.*

SONG.—ARAC.

This helmet, I suppose,
Was meant to ward off blows,
    It's very hot,
    And weighs a lot,
As many a guardsman knows,
So off that helmet goes.

THE THREE KNIGHTS. Yes, yes,
    So off that helmet goes!
                [*Giving their helmets to attendants.*

ARAC.   This tight-fitting cuirass
    Is but a useless mass,
        It's made of steel,
        And weighs a deal,
    A man is but an ass
    Who fights in a cuirass,
    So off goes that cuirass.

ALL THREE.   Yes, yes,
    So off goes that cuirass!   [*Removing cuirasses.*

ARAC.   These brassets, truth to tell,
    May look uncommon well,
        But in a fight
    They're much too tight,
    They're like a lobster shell!

ALL THREE.   Yes, yes,
    They're like a lobster shell.
                [*Removing their brassets.*

ARAC.   These things I treat the same,   [*Indicating leg pieces.*
    (I quite forget their name)
        They turn one's legs
        To cribbage pegs
    Their aid I thus disclaim,
    Though I forget their name.

ALL THREE.   Yes, yes,
    Though we forget their name,
    Their aid we thus disclaim!

[*They remove their leg pieces and wear close fitting shape suits.*
[*Desperate fight between the three* PRINCES *and the three* KNIGHTS *during which the* LADIES *on the battlements and the* SOLDIERS *on the stage sing the following chorus*—

This is our duty plain towards
    Our Princess all immaculate
We ought to bless her brothers' swords
    And piously ejaculate:
        Oh, Hungary!
        Oh, Hungary!
    Oh, doughty sons of Hungary!
        May all success
        Attend and bless
    Your warlike ironmongery!

[*By this time,* ARAC, GURON, *and* SCYNTHIUS *are on the ground, wounded*—HILARION, CYRIL *and* FLORIAN *stand over them.*
    PRIN. (*entering through gate and followed by* LADIES.)
        Hold! stay your hands!—we yield ourselves to you!
Ladies, my brothers all lie bleeding there!
Bind up their wounds—but look the other way.
(*Coming down.*) Is this the end? (*Bitterly to* LADY BLANCHE.)
        How say you, Lady Blanche—
Can I with dignity my post resign?
And if I do, will you then take my place?
    BLA. To answer this, it's meet that we consult
The great Potential Mysteries; I mean
The five Subjunctive Possibilities—
The May, the Might, the Would, the Could, the Should.
Can you resign? The prince May claim you; if
He Might, you Could—and if you Should, I Would!
    PRIN. I thought as much! Then, to my Fate I yield—
So ends my cherished scheme! Oh, I had hoped
To band all women with my maiden throng,
And make them all abjure tyrannic Man!
    HILD. A noble aim!
    PRIN.   You ridicule it now;
But if I carried out this glorious scheme,
At my exalted name Posterity
Would bow in gratitude!
    HILD.   But pray reflect—
If you enlist all women in your cause,
And make them all abjure tyrannic Man,
The obvious question then arises, "How
Is this Posterity to be provided?"
    PRIN. I never thought of that! My Lady Blanche,
How do you solve the riddle?
    BLA.   Don't ask me—
Abstract Philosophy won't answer it.
Take him—he is your Shall. Give in to Fate!
    PRIN. And you desert me. I alone am staunch!
    HILD. Madam, you placed your trust in Woman—well,
Woman has failed you utterly—try Man,
Give him one chance, it's only fair—besides,
Women are far too precious, too divine

To try unproven theories upon.
Experiments, the proverb says, are made
On humble subjects—try our grosser clay,
And mould it as you will!
    CYR.   Remember, too,
Dear Madam, if at any time you feel,
A-weary of the Prince, you can return
To Castle Adamant, and rule your girls
As heretofore, you know.
    PRIN.   And shall I find
The Lady Psyche here?
    PSY.   If Cyril, ma'am,
Does not behave himself, I think you will.
    PRIN. And you, Melissa, shall I find *you* here?
    MEL. Madam, however Florian turns out,
Unhesitatingly I answer, No!
    GAMA. Consider this, my love, if your mamma
Had looked on matters from your point of view
(I wish she had), why where would you have been?
    BLA. There's an unbounded field of speculation,
On which I could discourse for hours!
    PRIN.   No doubt!
We will not trouble you. Hilarion,
I have been wrong—I see my error now.
Take me, Hilarion—"We will walk the world
Yoked in all exercise of noble end!
And so through those dark gates across the wild
That no man knows! Indeed, I love thee—Come!"

FINALE.

PRINCESS.

With joy abiding,
Together gliding
    Through life's variety
    In sweet society,
And thus enthroning
The love I'm owning,
On this atoning
    I will rely!

CHORUS.

It were profanity
For poor humanity
To treat as vanity
    The sway of Love.
In no locality
Or principality
Is our mortality
    Its sway above!

HILARION.

When day is fading,
With serenading
    And such frivolity
    Of tender quality—
With scented showers
Of fairest flowers,
The happy hours
    Will gaily fly!

CHORUS.

It were profanity, etc.

CURTAIN.

The Mikado

or The Town of Titipu

It is said that an ornamental Japanese sword, dropping from the wall in Gilbert's library, was the inspiration for *The Mikado*. This may well be, but his choice of a Japanese setting was a falling-in with the most popular artistic influence of the second half of the nineteenth century. From the fifties onwards there had been Japanese exhibitions, an enormous import of Japanese goods, and the leading artists and craftsmen all drew on the Japanese style.

The adoption of a 'barbarian' setting gave Gilbert licence to play with ideas and names which were absolutely *Bab* in conception, though in fact only a few actually derive from the Ballads. In a vein of the lightest humour Gilbert describes tortures, executions, outrageous little girls, corrupt officials.

Advertisement for the Japanese Village in Knightsbridge which was well established before *The Mikado* was written.

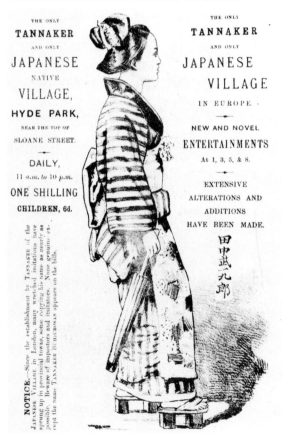

He interweaves cliché: bowing and scraping, the sun and moon, suicide, volcanoes (the willow and the cheap tailor border on the Chinese) among his lines; and though the sentiment is still totally British, he creates an evocative atmosphere which has inspired some of Sullivan's most original music.

The 'flirting' aspect on which the whole plot hangs is more complex. This was one of Gilbert's pet themes recurring in the earlier plays but certainly he had no reason to suggest that the Japanese girls infringed their strict etiquette any more than Victorian English girls. But Japanese erotica from prints readily available may have encouraged Gilbert to introduce this sort of *frisson* into *The Mikado*.

James Hillier, writing on Japanese art after the revolution of 1868, says: 'There is something febrile and unbalanced. It is a world of rigid etiquette and extreme fastidiousness in dress where, quite apart from the drama, men are often posed in feminine attire, and yet a world of the utmost grossness and brutality where self-immolation is decreed for a pecadillo and any crime sanctioned in the cause of revenge. ...'

The brazen Katisha is the villain, the most grotesque of Gilbert's contraltos with her self-confessed bloodthirsty tastes. Were it not for the other side of Katisha, so movingly portrayed by Gilbert, this raging bully might have been conceived by him as a transvestite role. (The suggested pantomime tone of *The Mikado* has resulted in several female renderings of Nanki-Poo.) The liaison between Katisha and Ko-Ko (he abhors marriage) can be interpreted in several ways. But when Katisha breaks down in the face of general opposition, she is definitely the pathetic and unloved middle-aged feminine figure.

After *Princess Ida* there was a bitter disagreement between author and composer, when all Gilbert could offer in the way of a new libretto was a revised version of the 'Lozenge Plot'. After declaring that he was not going to compose any more operas for Carte, Sullivan relented when Gilbert gave him *The Mikado*. Sullivan had given in to Gilbert's insistence on the importance of his words and allowed for long stretches of spoken dialogue, making his contribution in set pieces with little recitative. As always, Sullivan's music rises to the scene. The Japanese theme aroused new and witty musical ideas, but towards the end of the opera he reverted to an English folk-song style. Although the plot is involved, there is less action entailed than in most of the other operas and the story is relatively simple. This factor, coupled with the innocuous buffoonery, must be responsible for its enormous popularity.

SYNOPSIS

The Overture to *The Mikado* was constructed by Hamilton Clarke with Sullivan's prompting as to the sequence of numbers, and Sullivan's promised alternative has never materialized. The initial Japanese atmosphere created by the opening chords is lost in the pot-pourri of best numbers.

The scene opens on the courtyard of the Lord High Executioner's palace in the Japanese provincial town of Titipu. A chattering chorus of Nobles in Japanese-print attitudes are taking their ease. They are diverted by the arrival of a Wandering Minstrel in a state of great excitement. He asks the whereabouts of Ko-Ko's ward, Yum-Yum and they,

in turn, ask who he is. In reply he strikes up his 'native guitar' and from his sheaf of ballads begins 'A wandering minstrel I — '. The wide musical intervals give this song a definitely 'foreign' — if not Eastern — tone, and yet it is one of Sullivan's best tenor ballads in his own idiom. It is followed with a verse in spanking military style, then a sea-shanty, before a return to the ballad.

Nanki-Poo (the Mikado's son in disguise) has returned to Titipu to claim the girl he fell in love with a year ago when he was a member of the town band. Yum-Yum was then betrothed to her guardian Ko-Ko, a cheap tailor, but Ko-Ko has since been condemned to death for flirting. However, Nanki-Poo finds his hopes thwarted. Pish-Tush, an officious nobleman, informs him in a bowing-and-scraping song, with a definite hint of sniggering among the Chorus, that although the Mikado made flirting a capital offence (in order to steady young men) the wily citizens of Titipu have managed to get round the distasteful edict by releasing Ko-Ko — next in line for the axe — and promoting him to Lord High

'And you are right, and we are right, and all is right as right can be!': Leicester Tunks, Pish-Tush and Strafford Moss, Nanki-Poo. The lavish revival at the Savoy in 1908 with set by A. Terraine.

Executioner. Thus, until Ko-Ko executes himself, no further decapitations can take place.

This is confirmed by the haughty Pooh-Bah, who claims an extraordinary ancestral line dating back to a protoplasmal, primordial, atomic globule. Ko-Ko's appointment as the highest ranking official in the Titipu hierarchy has caused upheaval, all other officers refusing to serve under an ex-tailor. All vacant posts have been commandeered by Pooh-Bah, who uses his multiple capacities solely for his own gain, and thrives on bribery. Pish-Tush is his sounding-board and dogsbody.

In a dismissive, throat-clearing trio, the two 'noblemen' inform Nanki-Poo that Yum-Yum is about to return from school for her wedding to Ko-Ko. Words and accompaniment suggest petty pomp as they give details of the arrangement in 'Young man, despair,...'.

Hectic fanfares announce the arrival of Ko-Ko, and a martial chorus (to the tune of 'A Fine old English Gentleman') complete with ceremonial bowing leads into Ko-Ko's giddy song 'Taken from a county jail ...'. Ko-Ko has no illusions about his position: 'As some day it may happen that a victim must be found, I've got a little list...'. This song, in the same clownish vein as his first, enumerates 'society offenders who might well be underground'.

Ko-Ko holds a conference with the omnipotent Pooh-Bah who gives him conflicting advice from each of his official standpoints. The distinguished advisers can only be squared with a very considerable bribe. At this point they are interrupted by the arrival of Yum-Yum and her two sisters, Peep-Bo and Pitti-Sing. Their chattering chorus 'Comes a train of little ladies ...' (reminiscent of the Bridesmaids in *Trial by Jury*) has a graceful, airy line, and speculation on life not unlike Princess Ida's

> 'Are its palaces and pleasures
> Fantasies that fade?
> And the glory of its treasures
> Shadows of a shade?'

The following trio for the Sisters, 'Three little maids from school are we ...' is bubbling with life and schoolgirl mirth, emphasized by Sullivan's rare, and mocking use of solo bassoon.

Ko-Ko approaches Yum-Yum and after consultation with Pooh-Bah embraces her, but quite obviously she has no feelings for him, and as soon as she sets eyes on Nanki-Poo, Ko-Ko is forgotten. The three girls rush to Nanki-Poo, overwhelming him with babbling chatter, while Ko-Ko and Pooh-Bah — in the most polite manner — have Nanki-Poo removed. Pooh-Bah has no time for Ko-Ko's three wards, who proceed to make fun of him. Ko-Ko chides Pooh-Bah for his dismissive attitude to the girls and he is forced, at great expense to his pride, to acknowledge them. Their apology, 'So please you, Sir, we must regret ...' is the most Offenbach-like of their three consecutive choral pieces. The second verse, for Pooh-Bah, is adapted to his own stilted vein, but inevitably breaks into a dance.

Nanki-Poo returns to find Yum-Yum alone, and because she has doubts about marrying an itinerant musician, he reveals his true identity. He explains that he fled his father's court on pain of death because the elderly Lady Katisha claimed him in marriage (misrepresenting his 'customary affability' for affection).

The following love scene is a ridiculous parody on the Japanese art of love-making, Yum-Yum responding in a roundabout way to all Nanki-Poo's roundabout advances. Their kissing duet, 'Were you not to Ko-Ko plighted' begins with a love-song for

'Three Little Maids from school are we': Sybil Grey, Leonore Braham and Jessie Bond in the first production, Savoy Theatre, 14 March 1885.

Nanki-Poo parodying 'Mag der Himmel Euch vergeben' from Flotow's *Martha*. Yum-Yum responds to his final kiss with an excited change of rhythm, reminding Nanki-Poo of Ko-Ko. Once more Nanki-Poo steadies his passion, then it breaks loose in an abandoned flight of kisses:

> 'This, oh, this, oh, this, oh, this,
> This is what I'll never do...'

Gilbert's alliteration allows for the kisses not permitted on stage in early productions. Finally, Nanki-Poo reverts to heavy mock-seriousness.

As they go their separate ways, Ko-Ko observes Yum-Yum and he reflects 'It hardly seems worth while! Oh, matrimony! ...' His thoughts are interrupted by Pish-Tush with a decree from the Mikado that an execution must take place within a month. Otherwise the post of Lord High Executioner will be abolished and Titipu will lose its status and become a village. Pish-Tush and Pooh-Bah feel that Ko-Ko, the condemned, should sacrifice himself, but Ko-Ko is all for appointing Pooh-Bah a Lord High Substitute. An ingenious trio of speculation follows, reminiscent of that between Osmin, Pedrillo and Belmonte in Mozart's *Il Seraglio*. Pooh-Bah begins 'I am so proud'; Ko-Ko follows with a quicker, playing-for-time song; and Pish-Tush gives a hard and sadistic exposé on execution. The three are then sung together and this trio ends with the celebrated chorus in dread of

> '... the short sharp shock
> From a cheap and chippy chopper
> on a big black block.'

Pooh-Bah and Pish-Tush leave Ko-Ko bemoaning his fate. He is interrupted by the entrance of Nanki-Poo with a rope, threatening suicide. Here is Ko-Ko's substitute! He persuades Nanki-Poo to accept execution after a month's marriage to Yum-Yum.

The finale to this act is in cantata form. The Nobles enter on a note of foreboding to enquire how Ko-Ko intends to act on the Mikado's decree. They hail Nanki-Poo, the volunteer, in patriotic unison, and then with a snatch of sentimental regret, Ko-Ko hands Yum-Yum to Nanki-Poo. General rejoicing is expressed in a hectic, Offenbach-like can-can. Pooh-Bah's interlude to propose the toast, 'Long life to

Nanki-Poo!' is in public school song style with the message repeated in a sonorous cadenza. The Chorus take up his words in a repetition of the can-can.

Sudden, melodramatic chords herald the entrance of Katisha: 'I claim my perjured lover, Nanki-Poo!' she cries. The Chorus take on the role of furies (as in Gluck's *Orfeo*) as they try to turn her away and then, hearing her story, they take sides with her against Nanki-Poo. He tries to escape with Yum-Yum but Katisha holds him. In typically Verdian style she reprimands him and curses Yum-Yum in multiple operatic climaxes:

> 'Thy doom is nigh,
> Pink cheek, bright eye!'

At the darkest moment and in true Gilbertian manner, Pitti-Sing unravels the tangle. To a pert, *pizzicato* accompaniment in the minor she says simply that Katisha's claims are of no concern, and then breaking into the major key she states: 'For he's going to marry Yum-Yum!' All join in the gleeful, skipping chorus: Katisha is snubbed and breaks down. Relenting, the Chorus becomes subdued for her pathetic aria, 'The hour of gladness...' There are

Rutland Barrington, the original Pooh-Bah and creator of the line of somewhat unpleasant characters known as the 'Pooh-Bah roles'.

marked similarities between some of her phrases and those of Florestan bemoaning his lost Leonore in Act II of Beethoven's *Fidelio*. No sooner has Katisha won sympathy than she rallies and ruthlessly attempts to expose Nanki-Poo's identity. This time Yum-Yum takes the initiative, and leading the Chorus in a string of Japanese words that mean something in the nature of 'She devil! Surprise! — hiccup!' she contrives, with the aid of the Chorus, to blot out Katisha's dramatic attempts to unmask Nanki-Poo. In a grandiose, patriotic and Verdian ensemble, Katisha rages, and makes a melodramatic exit, sweeping the Crowd aside as she goes.

In Ko-Ko's garden, Yum-Yum is being dressed for her wedding. A cool, gentle melody reflecting 'Rose lip, bright eye' precedes the lilting and graceful chorus 'Braid the raven hair' with its verse for the arch Pitti-Sing. Yum-Yum, left alone, extols her own beauty quite shamelessly which, as a child of Nature in a country where Nature is worshipped, Gilbert feels she should. Her song 'The sun whose rays...' is one of Sullivan's masterpieces, peaceful and contemplative, beautiful in its apparent simplicity of line. And yet its originality lies in the modulations and hesitant rhythm, evocative of a wondering bride-to-be, followed by a change to utter confidence with 'I mean to rule the earth...'.

Yum-Yum's euphoria is dispelled when her sister, Peep-Bo, reminds her that her happiness is soon to be curtailed. Yum-Yum is in tears when Nanki-Poo and Pish-Tush arrive and the mood of depression prevails despite forced attempts at jollity. 'Brightly dawns our wedding day' is, on the face of it, a straight four-part English madrigal, but in keeping with Gilbert's mournful words the preliminary rejoicing wanes as each verse progresses and wilts at the end into lump-in-throat tearfulness.

Ko-Ko spreads an even deeper gloom when he informs the lovers of his discovery that the wife of a beheaded man must be buried alive. 'Here's a how-de-do!' is a comic trio of agitation, almost in music-hall style. Yum-Yum, with second thoughts about marriage, leaves Nanki-Poo and Ko-Ko. Nanki-Poo now reverts to his suicide plan and Ko-Ko desperately tries to dissuade him.

At this point, Pooh-Bah brings news that the arrival of the Mikado is imminent. Ko-Ko still tries to make Nanki-Poo act as Executioner's victim, so Nanki-Poo challenges him to chop off his head immediately, and Pooh-Bah presses Ko-Ko to do so.

After multiple excuses, Ko-Ko breaks down, weeping: 'I can't kill anything!' Then he has an idea. He connives with Pooh-Bah (for a large sum) to fake Nanki-Poo's death certificate. He then orders Pooh-Bah as Archbishop of Titipu, to marry Nanki-Poo and Yum-Yum, who must escape and never come back.

No sooner has he given his orders than drums herald the Mikado's procession. His troops chant 'Miya sama...' the Japanese war song of the 1870s — the 'Tokotonyare' — as the Mikado and Katisha make their entrance. Sullivan develops the real Japanese music with gong effects for the Mikado's stiff introductory self-appraisal. At every stage, the Emperor is outdone by the egotistical comments of the irrepressible and overruling Katisha. 'Bow, bow, to his daughter-in-law elect!' demands the obeisance which Sullivan's music dictates.

The Mikado becomes more confidential in his solo 'A more humane Mikado ...' in which he outlines his pet antipathies and the dire punishments he accords to them. The song, as it stands, is a perfect piece of sadistic wit in no need of the raucous laughs, said to have been introduced by Darrell Fancourt in about 1924.

Pooh-Bah, Ko-Ko and Pitti-Sing now kneel before the Mikado and Ko-Ko presents the death certificate. At the Mikado's request, they describe the execution, building up a gruesome fiction in the line of such narrative ballads as 'Widdecombe Fair'. Pitti-Sing's account of the prisoner's kissing his hand to her is enhanced by a piccolo *obbligato* of 'The Girl I left behind me'.

The Mikado now explains that the purpose of his visit is to discover the whereabouts of Nanki-Poo and while the conspirators try to find a way out of their dilemma, Katisha discovers Nanki-Poo's name on the death certificate. Smiling and suave, the Mikado condemns the conspirators, protesting ignorance and innocence, to death in boiling oil. He sympathizes with them, 'but it's an unjust world and virtue is triumphant only in theatrical performance'. The glee for five voices in eighteenth-century style, 'See how the fates their gifts allot', bears out this homily in scholastic vein, taking A and B to represent the unworthy and the worthy.

Nanki-Poo and Yum-Yum, married and preparing to depart, are approached by Ko-Ko who begs Nanki-Poo to reveal himself to his father, but Nanki-Poo will only comply if Ko-Ko marries the vengeful

Katisha — 'When Katisha is married, existence will be as welcome as the flowers in spring.'

'The flowers that bloom in the Spring' is a country dance (more sophisticated than that in *The Sorcerer*) with a verse of rejoicing for Nanki-Poo and one of resignation for Ko-Ko.

Dramatic minor chords accompany Katisha's despairing entrance. her recitative, 'Alone and yet alive,...' has nostalgic harmonies reminiscent of Beethoven, and the pulsating accompaniment to her aria, 'Hearts do not break' has a definite affinity with a moment in the dungeon scene in *Fidelio*. Ko-Ko approaches Katisha timidly and pleads for mercy. But she meets his overtures with recrimination and abuse: Ko-Ko has deprived her of her only love—'Oh, where shall I find another?' 'Here! Here!' cries Ko-Ko and proceeds to make an exaggerated and convincing confession of his secret passion for Katisha, swearing that he will perish of a broken heart if she fails him. To counter her scepticism he sings her the touching story of the little tom-tit who died of blighted affection. The words almost certainly derive from Desdemona's Willow Song—the song of suicide—in Shakespeare's *Othello*:

'The poor soul sat sighing by a sycamore tree Sing all a green willow ...'

Sullivan's tune is similar to that of an eighteenth-century setting by Arne.

The end of Ko-Ko's song leaves Katisha almost in tears; she melts and gives herself to Ko-Ko. The match is made in a duet where she divulges her somewhat brazen tastes. 'There is beauty in the bellow of the blast' conjures up the warlike images of Japanese figurative art—'the tiger a-lashing of his tail and the flight of thunderbolts ...'. Ko-Ko's rejoinder expresses the clownish tone of the duet:

'Won't you wait until you're eighty in the shade...
There's a fascination frantic
In a ruin that's romantic ...'

and the verses end with a happy dancing 'Sing derry down derry'.

A flourish of 'trumpets' heralds the Mikado who, having lunched, has come to watch the executions. He is amazed when Katisha asks for a reprieve and explains that she has married Ko-Ko. As the Mikado states that he cannot absolve Ko-Ko from the execution of his son, Nanki-Poo and Yum-Yum appear. Katisha is furious with Ko-Ko, but the Mikado is sympathetic and allows Ko-Ko to give his explanation—a piece of convincing talk which satisfies the Emperor. To a reprise of 'For he's going to marry Yum-Yum ...' all celebrate with the happy couple.

THE MIKADO;

OR

THE TOWN OF TITIPU.

AN ENTIRELY NEW AND ORIGINAL JAPANESE OPERA,

IN TWO ACTS.

Produced at the Savoy Theatre, 14 March 1885

DRAMATIS PERSONÆ

THE MIKADO OF JAPAN	bass
NANKI-POO [*his Son, disguised as a wandering minstrel, and in love with* YUM-YUM]	tenor
KO-KO [*Lord High Executioner of Titipu*]	baritone
POOH-BAH [*Lord High Everything Else*]	baritone
PISH-TUSH [*a Noble Lord*]	baritone
YUM-YUM	soprano
PITTI-SING [*Three Sisters—Wards of* KO-KO]	soprano
PEEP-BO	soprano
KATISHA [*an elderly Lady, in love with* NANKI-POO]	contralto

Chorus of School Girls, Nobles, Guards, and Coolies.

ACT I.

COURTYARD OF KO-KO'S OFFICIAL RESIDENCE.

ACT II.

KO-KO'S GARDEN.

THE MIKADO;

OR,

THE TOWN OF TITIPU.

ACT I.

SCENE—*Courtyard of* KO-KO's *Palace in Titipu. Japanese* NOBLES *discovered standing and sitting in attitudes suggested by native drawings.*

CHORUS.

If you want to know who we are,
  We are gentlemen of Japan:
On many a vase and jar—
  On many a screen and fan,
    We figure in lively paint:
    Our attitudes queer and quaint—
    You're wrong if you think it ain't.

If you think we are worked by strings,
    Like a Japanese marionette,
You don't understand these things:
    It is simply Court etiquette.
        Perhaps you suppose this throng
        Can't keep it up all day long?
        If that's your idea, you're wrong.

Enter NANKI-POO *in great excitement. He carries a native guitar on his
back, and a bundle of ballads in his hand.*

RECITATIVE.—NANKI-POO.

Gentlemen, I pray you tell me,
Where a lovely maiden dwelleth,
Named Yum-Yum, the ward of Ko-Ko,
In pity speak—oh, speak, I pray you!

A NOBLE. Why, who are you who ask this question?
NANK.   Come, gather round me, and I'll tell you.

SONG.—NANKI-POO.

A wandering minstrel I—
    A thing of shreds and patches,
    Of ballads, songs, and snatches,
A dreamy lullaby!

My catalogue is long,
    Through every passion ranging,
    And to your humours changing
I tune my supple song!

        Are you in sentimental mood?
        I'll sigh with you,
            Oh, willow, willow!
        On maiden's coldness do you brood?
        I'll do so too—
            Oh, willow, willow!
        I'll charm your willing ears
        With songs of lover's fears,
        While sympathetic tears
            My cheeks bedew—
            Oh, willow, willow!

But if patriotic sentiment is wanted,
    I've patriotic ballads cut and dried;
For where'er our country's banner may be planted
    All other local banners are defied!
Our warriors, in serried ranks assembled,
    Never quail—or they conceal it if they do—
And I shouldn't be surprised if nations trembled
    Before the mighty troops of Titipu!

And if you call for a song of the sea,
    We'll heave the capstan round,
With a yeo heave ho, for the wind is free,
    Her anchor's a-trip and her helm's a-lee,
    Hurrah for the homeward bound!
        Yeo-ho—heave ho—
    Hurrah for the homeward bound!

To lay aloft in a howling breeze
    May tickle a landsman's taste,
But the happiest hours a sailor sees
    Is when he's down
    At an inland town,
With his Nancy on his knees, yeo ho!
    And his arm around her waist!

        Then man the capstan—off we go,
        As the fiddler swings us round,
        With a yeo heave ho,
        And a rumbelow.
            Hurrah for the homeward bound!

A wandering minstrel I, etc.

Enter PISH-TUSH.

PISH. And what may be your business with Yum-Yum?
NANK. I'll tell you. A year ago I was a member of the Titipu
town band. It was my duty to take the cap round for
contributions. While discharging this delicate office, I saw Yum-
Yum. We loved each other at once, but she was betrothed to her
guardian, Ko-Ko, a cheap tailor, and I saw that my suit was
hopeless. Overwhelmed with despair, I quitted the town. Judge
of my delight when I heard, a month ago, that Ko-Ko had been
condemned to death for flirting! I hurried back at once, in the
hope of finding Yum-Yum at liberty to listen to my
protestations.
PISH. It is true that Ko-Ko was condemned to death for
flirting; but he was reprieved at the last moment, and raised to
the exalted rank of Lord High Executioner under the following
remarkable circumstances:—

SONG.—PISH-TUSH.

Our great Mikado, virtuous man,
When he to rule our land began,
    Resolved to try
    A plan whereby
    Young men might best be steadied.
So he decreed, in words succinct,
That all who flirted, leered, or winked
(Unless connubially linked),
    Should forthwith be beheaded.
        And I expect you'll all agree
        That he was right to so decree.
        And I am right,
        And you are right,
        And all is right as right can be!

CHORUS.   And I expect, etc.

This stern decree, you'll understand,
Caused great dismay throughout the land;
    For young and old
    And shy and bold
    Were equally affected.
The youth who winked a roving eye,
Or breathed a non-connubial sigh,
Was thereupon condemned to die—
    He usually objected.

And you'll allow, as I expect,
That he was right to so object.
And I am right,
And you are right,
And everything is quite correct!

CHORUS.　　　And you'll allow, as I expect, etc.

And so we straight let out on bail
A convict from the county jail,
Whose head was next,
On some pretext,
Condemnëd to be mown off,
And made *him* Headsman, for we said,
"Who's next to be decapited
Cannot cut off another's head
Until he's cut his own off."

And we are right, I think you'll say,
To argue in this kind of way,
And I am right,
And you are right,
And all is right—too-looral-lay!

CHORUS.　　　And they were right, etc.

[*Exeunt* CHORUS.

Enter POOH-BAH.

NANK. Ko-Ko, the cheap tailor, Lord High Executioner of Titipu! Why, that's the highest rank a citizen can attain!

POOH. It is. Our logical Mikado, seeing no moral difference between the dignified judge, who condemns a criminal to die, and the industrious mechanic who carries out the sentence, has rolled the two offices into one, and every judge is now his own executioner.

NANK. But how good of you (for I see that you are a nobleman of the highest rank) to condescend to tell all this to me, a mere strolling minstrel!

POOH. Don't mention it. I am, in point of fact, a particularly haughty and exclusive person, of pre-Adamite ancestral descent. You will understand this when I tell you that I can trace my ancestry back to a protoplasmal primordial atomic globule. Consequently, my family pride is something inconceivable. I can't help it. I was born sneering. But I struggle hard to overcome this defect. I mortify my pride continually. When all the great officers of State resigned in a body, because they were too proud to serve under an ex-tailor, did I not unhesitatingly accept all their posts at once?

PISH. And the salaries attached to them? You did.

POOH. It is consequently my degrading duty to serve this upstart as First Lord of the Treasury, Lord Chief Justice, Commander-in-Chief, Lord High Admiral, Master of the Buckhounds, Groom of the Back Stairs, Archbishop of Titipu, and Lord Mayor, both acting and elect, all rolled into one. And at a salary! A Pooh-Bah paid for his services! I a salaried minion! But I do it! It revolts me, but I do it.

NANK. And it does you credit.

POOH. But I don't stop at that. I go and dine with middle-class people on reasonable terms. I dance at cheap suburban parties for a moderate fee. I accept refreshment at any hands, however lowly. I also retail State secrets at a very low figure. For instance,

any further information about Yum-Yum would come under the head of a State secret. (NANKI-POO *takes the hint, and gives him money.*) *(Aside.)* Another insult, and, I think, a light one!

SONG.—POOH-BAH.

Young man, despair,
Likewise go to,
Yum-Yum the fair
You must not woo.
It will not do:
I'm sorry for you,
You very imperfect ablutioner!
This very day
From school Yum-Yum
Will wend her way,
And homeward come
With beat of drum,
And a rum-tum-tum,
To wed the Lord High Executioner!
And the brass will clash,
And the trumpets bray,
And they'll cut a dash
On their wedding-day.
From what I say, you may infer
It's as good as a play for him and her
She'll toddle away, as all aver,
With the Lord High Executioner!

It's a hopeless case
As you may see,
And in your place
Away I'd flee;
But don't blame me—
I'm sorry to be
Of your pleasure a diminutioner.
They'll vow their pact
Extremely soon,
In point of fact
This afternoon
Her honeymoon,
With that buffoon,
At seven, commences, so *you* shun her!
ALL.　　　The brass will crash, etc.

RECITATIVE.

NANK. And have I journeyed for a month, or nearly,
To learn that Yum-Yum, whom I love so dearly,
This day to Ko-Ko is to be united!

POOH. The fact appears to be as you've recited;
But here he comes, equipped as suits his station;
He'll give you any further information.

Enter KO-KO, *attended.*

CHORUS.

Behold the Lord High Executioner!
A personage of noble rank and title—
A dignified and potent officer,

Whose functions are particularly vital.
Defer, defer,
To the noble Lord High Executioner!

SOLO.—KO-KO.

Taken from the county jail
By a set of curious chances;
Liberated then on bail,
On my own recognizances;
Wafted by a favouring gale
As one sometimes is in trances
To a height that few can scale,
Save by long and weary dances;
Surely, never had a male
Under such like circumstances
So adventurous a tale,
Which may rank with most romances.

CHORUS.

Behold the Lord High Executioner, etc.

KO. Gentlemen, I'm much touched by this reception. I can only trust that by strict attention to duty I shall ensure a continuance of those favours which it will ever be my study to deserve. Gentlemen, I expect my three beautiful wards, Yum-Yum, Peep-Bo, and Pitti-Sing, in a few minutes. If you will kindly receive them with a show of abject deference, I shall feel obliged to you. I know how painful it must be to noblemen of your rank to have to humiliate yourselves before a person of my antecedents, but discipline must be observed. (Chorus *bow and exeunt.*) Pooh-Bah, it seems that the festivities in connection with my approaching marriage must last a week. I should like to do it handsomely, and I want to consult you as to the amount I ought to spend upon them.

POOH. Certainly. In which of my capacities? As First Lord of the Treasury, Lord Chamberlain, Attorney-General, Chancellor of the Exchequer, Privy Purse, or Private Secretary?

KO. Suppose we say as Private Secretary.

POOH. Speaking as your Private Secretary, I should say that, as the city will have to pay for it, don't stint yourself, do it well.

KO. Exactly—as the city will have to pay for it. That is your advice.

POOH. As Private Secretary. Of course you will understand that, as Chancellor of the Exchequer, I am bound to see that due economy is observed.

KO. Oh. But you said just now "Don't stint yourself, do it well."

POOH. As Private Secretary.

KO. And now you say that due economy must be observed.

POOH. As Chancellor of the Exchequer.

KO. I see. Come over here, where the Chancellor can't hear us. *(They cross stage.)* Now, as my Solicitor, how do you advise me to deal with this difficulty?

POOH. Oh, as your Solicitor, I should have no hesitation in saying, "Chance it—"

KO. Thank you. *(Shaking his hand.)* I will.

POOH. If it were not, that, as Lord Chief Justice, I am bound to see that the law isn't violated.

KO. I see. Come over here where the Chief Justice can't hear us. *(They cross the stage.)* Now, then, as First Lord of the Treasury?

POOH. Of course, as First Lord of the Treasury, I could propose a special vote that would cover all expenses, if it were not that, as leader of the Opposition, it would be my duty to resist it, tooth and nail. Or, as Paymaster-General, I could so cook the accounts, that as Lord High Auditor I should never discover the fraud. But then, as Archbishop of Titipu, it would be my duty to denounce my dishonesty and give myself into my own custody as First Commissioner of Police.

KO. That's extremely awkward.

POOH. I don't say that all these people couldn't be squared; but it is right to tell you that I shouldn't be sufficiently degraded in my own estimation unless I was insulted with a very considerable bribe.

KO. The matter shall have my careful consideration. But my bride and her sisters approach, and any little compliment on your part, such as an abject grovel in a characteristic Japanese attitude, would be esteemed a favour.

Enter procession of YUM-YUM's *schoolfellows, heralding* YUM-YUM, PEEP-BO, *and* PITTI-SING.

CHORUS.

Comes a train of little ladies
From scholastic trammels free,
Each a little bit afraid is,
Wondering what the world can be!

Is it but a world of trouble—
Sadness set to song?
Is its beauty but a bubble
Bound to break ere long?

Are its palaces and pleasures
Fantasies that fade?
And the glory of its treasures
Shadow of a shade?

Schoolgirls we, eighteen and under,
From scholastic trammels free,
And we wonder—how we wonder!—
What on earth the world can be!

TRIO.—YUM-YUM, PEEP-BO, *and* PITTI-SING.

THE THREE.   Three little maids from school are we,
              Pert as a schoolgirl well can be,
              Filled to the brim with girlish glee,
                  Three little maids from school

YUM-YUM.   Everything is a source of fun. *(Chuckle).*
PEEP-BO.   Nobody's safe, for we care for none! *(Chuckle).*
PITTI-SING.   Life is a joke that's just begun! *(Chuckle).*
THE THREE.   Three little maids from school!

All (dancing).   Three little maids who, all unwary,
                   Come from a ladies' seminary,
                   Freed from its genius tutelary—
THE THREE *(suddenly demure).* Three little maids from school!

YUM-YUM.   One little maid is a bride, Yum-Yum—
PEEP-BO.   Two little maids in attendance come—
PITTI-SING.   Three little maids is the total sum.

THE THREE.   Three little maids from school!

YUM-YUM.   From three little maids take one away—
PEEP-BO.   Two little maids remain, and they—
PITTI-SING.   Won't have to wait very long, they say—
THE THREE.   Three little maids from school!

ALL *(dancing).*   Three little maids who, all unwary,
                   Come from a ladies' seminary.
                   Freed from its genius tutelary
THE THREE *(suddenly demure).* Three little maids from school!

Ko. At last, my bride that is to be! *(About to embrace her.)*
YUM. You're not going to kiss me before all these people?
Ko. Well, that was the idea.
YUM. *(aside to PEEP-BO).* It seems odd, don't it?
PEEP. It's rather peculiar.
PITTI. Oh, I expect it's all right. Must have a beginning, you know.
YUM. Well, of course, I know nothing about these things; but I've no objection if it's usual.
Ko. Oh, it's quite usual, I think. Eh, Lord Chamberlain? *(Appealing to POOH-BAH.)*
POOH. I have known it done. (KO-KO *embraces her.*)
YUM. That's over! *(Sees NANKI-POO, and rushes to him).* Why, that's never you? *The Three GIRLS rush to him and shake his hands, all speaking at once.)*

> YUM. Oh, I'm so glad! I haven't seen you for ever so long, and I'm right at the top of the school, and I've got three prizes, and I've come home for good, and I'm not going back any more!
>
> PEEP. And have you got an engagement?—Yum-Yum's got one, but she don't like it, and she'd ever so much rather it was you. I've come home for good, and I'm not going back any more!
>
> PITTI. Now tell us all the news, because you go about everywhere, and we've been at school; but, thank goodness, that's all over now, and we've come home for good, and we're not going back any more!

        [These three speeches are spoken together in one breath.
Ko. I beg your pardon. Will you present me?
YUM. ⌈ Oh, this is the musician who used—
PEEP. ⟨ Oh, this is the gentleman who used—
PITTI. ⌊ Oh, it is only Nanki-Poo who used—
Ko. One at a time, if you please.
YUM. He's the gentleman who used to play so beautifully on the—on the—
PITTI. On the Marine Parade.
YUM. Yes, I think that was the name of the instrument.
NANK. Sir, I have the misfortune to love your ward, Yum-Yum—oh, I know I deserve your anger!
Ko. Anger! Not a bit, my boy. Why, I love her myself. Charming little girl, isn't she? Pretty eyes, nice hair. Taking little thing, altogether. Very glad to hear my opinion backed by a competent authority. Thank you very much. Good-bye, *(To* PISH-TUSH.) Take him away. (PISH-TUSH *removes him.)*
PITTI. *(who has been examining* POOH-BAH). I beg your pardon, but what is this? Customer come to try on?
Ko. That is a Tremendous Swell. *(She starts back in alarm.)*
POOH. Go away, little girls. Can't talk to little girls like you. Go away, there's dears.
Ko. Allow me to present you, Pooh-Bah. These are my three

wards. The one in the middle is my bride elect.
POOH. What do you want me to do to them? Mind, I *will not* kiss them.
Ko. No, no, you shan't kiss them: a little bow—a mere nothing—you needn't mean it, you know.
POOH. It goes against the grain. They are not young ladies, they are young persons.
Ko. Come, come, make an effort, there's a good nobleman.
POOH *(aside to KO-KO).* Well, I shan't mean it. *(With a great effort.)* How de do, How de do, little girls! *(Aside.)* Oh, my protoplasmal ancestor!
Ko. That's very good. (GIRLS *indulge in suppressed laughter.)*
POOH. I see nothing to laugh at. It is very painful to me to have to say "How de do, How de do, little girls," to young persons. I'm not in the habit of saying "How de do, How de do, little girls" to anybody under the rank of a Stockbroker.
Ko. *(aside to* GIRLS). Don't laugh at him—he's under treatment for it. *(Aside to* POOH-BAH.) Never mind them, they don't understand the delicacy of your position.
POOH. We know how delicate it is, don't we?
Ko. I should think we did! How a nobleman of your importance can do it at all is a thing I never can, never shall understand.   [KO-KO *retires up and goes off.*

QUARTETTE *and* CHORUS.

YUM-YUM, PEEP-BO, *and* PITTI-SING.

So please you, sir, we much regret
If we have failed in etiquette
Towards a man of rank so high—
We shall know better by-and-by.
But youth, of course, must have its fling,
        So pardon us,
        So pardon us,
And don't in girlhood's happy spring,
        Be hard on us,
        Be hard on us,
If we're disposed to dance and sing,
        Tra la la, etc. *(Dancing.)*

CHORUS OF GIRLS. But youth of course, etc.

POOH.   I think you ought to recollect
             You cannot show too much respect
             Towards the highly-titled few;
             But nobody does, and why should you?
That youth at us should have its fling,
             Is hard on us,
             Is hard on us;
To our prerogative we cling—
             So pardon us,
             So pardon us,
If we decline to dance and sing—
             Tra la la, etc. *(Dancing.)*

CHORUS OF GIRLS. But youth, of course, must have its fling, etc.

        [Exeunt all but YUM-YUM.
YUM. How pitiable is the condition of a young and innocent child brought from the gloom of a ladies' academy into the full blown blaze of her own marriage ceremony; and with a man for

whom I care nothing! True, he loves me; but everybody does that.

Enter NANKI-POO.

NANK. Yum-Yum, at last we are alone! I have sought you night and day for three weeks, in the belief that your guardian was beheaded, and I find that you are about to be married to him this afternoon!

YUM. Alas, yes!

NANK. But you do not love him?

YUM. Alas, no!

NANK. Modified rapture! But why do you not refuse him?

YUM. What good would that do? He's my guardian, and he wouldn't let me marry you!

NANK. But I would wait until you were of age!

YUM. You forget that in Japan girls do not arrive at years of discretion until they are fifty.

NANK. True; from seventeen to fifty-nine are considered years of indiscretion.

YUM. Besides, a wandering minstrel, who plays a wind instrument outside tea-houses, is hardly a fitting husband for the ward of a Lord High Executioner.

NANK. But— *(Aside.)* Shall I tell her? Yes! She will not betray me! *(Aloud.)* What if it should prove that, after all, I am no musician!

YUM. There! I was certain of it, directly I heard you play!

NANK. What if it should prove that I am no other than the son of his Majesty the Mikado?

YUM. The son of the Mikado! But why is your Highness disguised? And what has your Highness done? And will your Highness promise never to do it again?

NANK. Some years ago I had the misfortune to captivate Katisha, an elderly lady of my father's court. She misconstrued my customary affability into expressions of affection, and claimed me in marriage, under my father's law. My father, the Lucius Junius Brutus of his race, ordered me to marry her within a week, or perish ignominiously on the scaffold. That night I fled his court and, assuming the disguise of a Second Trombone, I joined the band in which you found me when I had the happiness of seeing you! *(Approaching her.)*

YUM. *(retreating)*. If you please, I think your Highness had better not come too near. The laws against flirting are excessively severe.

NANK. But we are quite alone, and nobody can see us.

YUM. Still that don't make it right. To flirt is illegal, and we must obey the law.

NANK. Deuce take the law!

YUM. I wish it would, but it won't!

NANK. If it were not for that, how happy we might be!

YUM. Happy indeed!

NANK. If it were not for the law, we should now be sitting side by side, like that. *(Sits by her.)*

YUM. Instead of being obliged to sit half a mile off, like that. *(Crosses and sits at other side of stage.)*

NANK. We should be gazing in each other's eyes, like that. *(Approaching and gazing at her sentimentally.)*

YUM. Breathing vows of unutterable love—like that. *(Sighing and gazing lovingly at him.)*

NANK. With our arms round each other's waists like that. *(Embracing her.)*

YUM. Yes, if it wasn't for the law.

NANK. If it wasn't for the law.

YUM. As it is, of course, we couldn't do anything of the kind.

NANK. Not for worlds!

YUM. Being engaged to Ko-ko, you know!

NANK. Being engaged to Ko-ko!

NANK.   So, in spite of all temptation,
               Such a theme I'll not discuss,
          And on no consideration
               Will I kiss you fondly thus—*(kissing her)*
          Let me make it clear to you,
               This, oh, this, oh, this, oh, this—*(kissing her)*
          This is what I'll never do!

[*Exeunt in opposite directions*

Enter KO-KO.

KO. *(looking after* YUM-YUM). There she goes! To think how entirely my future happiness is wrapped up in that little parcel! Really, it hardly seems worth while! Oh, matrimony!

Enter POOH-BAH *and* PISH-TUSH.

Now then, what is it? Can't you see I'm soliloquizing? You have interrupted an apostrophe, sir!

PISH. I am the bearer of a letter from His Majesty the Mikado.

KO. *(taking it from him reverentially)*. A letter from the Mikado! What in the world can he have to say to me? *(Reads letter.)* Ah, here it is at last! I thought it would come! The Mikado is struck by the fact that no executions have taken place in Titipu for a year, and decrees that, unless somebody is beheaded within one month, the post of Lord High Executioner shall be abolished, and the city reduced to the rank of a village!

PISH. But that will involve us all in irretrievable ruin!

KO. Yes. There's no help for it, I shall have to execute somebody. The only question is, who shall it be?

POOH. Well, it seems unkind to say so, but as you're already under sentence of death for flirting, everything seems to point to *you*.

KO. To me? What are you talking about? I can't execute myself, Recorder!

POOH. Why not?

KO. Why not? Because, in the first place, self-decapitation is an extremely difficult, not to say dangerous, thing to attempt; and, in the second, it's suicide, and suicide is a capital offence.

POOH. That is so, no doubt.

PISH. We might reserve that point.

POOH. True, it could be argued six months hence, before the full Court.

KO. Besides, I don't see how a man *can* cut off his own head.

POOH. A man might try.

PISH. Even if you only succeed in cutting it half off, that would be something.

POOH. It would be taken as an earnest of your desire to comply with the Imperial will.

KO. No. Pardon me, but there I am adamant. As official Headsman, my reputation is at stake, and I can't consent to embark on a professional operation unless I see my way to a successful result.

POOH. This professional conscientiousness is highly creditable to *you*, but it places us in a very awkward position.

Ko. My good sir, the awkwardness of your position is grace itself compared with that of a man engaged in the act of cutting off his own head.

Pish. I am afraid that, unless you can obtain a substitute—

Ko. A substitute? Oh, certainly—nothing easier. *(To* Pooh-Bah.) Pooh-Bah, I appoint you my substitute.

Pooh. I should like it above all things. Such an appointment would realize my fondest dreams. But no, at any sacrifice, I must set bounds to my insatiable ambition!

TRIO.

Ko-Ko.	Pooh-Bah.	Pish-Tush.
My brain it teems	I am so proud,	I heard one day,
With endless schemes,	If I allowed	A gentleman say
Both good and new	My family pride	That criminals who
For Titipu;	To be my guide,	Are cut in two
But if I flit,	I'd volunteer	Can hardly feel
The benefit	To quit this sphere	The fatal steel,
That I'd diffuse	Instead of you,	And so are slain
The town would lose!	In a minute or two,	Without much pain.
Now every man	But family pride	If this is true
To aid his clan	Must be denied,	It's jolly for you;
Should plot and plan	And set aside,	Your courage screw
As well as he can,	And mortified,	To bid us adieu,
And so,	And so,	And go
Although	Although	And show
I'm ready to go,	I wish to go,	Both friend and foe
Yet recollect	And greatly pine	How much you dare,
'Twere disrespect	To brightly shine,	I'm quite aware
Did I neglect	And take the line	It's your affair,
To thus effect	Of a hero fine,	Yet I declare
This aim direct,	With grief condign	I'd take your share,
So I object—	I must decline—	But I don't much care—
So I object—	I must decline—	I don't much care—
So I object—	I must decline—	I don't much care—

All. To sit in solemn silence in a dull, dark dock,
In a pestilential prison, with a life-long lock,
Awaiting the sensation of a short, sharp shock,
From a cheap and chippy chopper on a big black block!

[*Exeunt all but* Ko-Ko.

Ko. This is simply appalling! I, who allowed myself to be respited at the last moment, simply in order to benefit my native town, am now required to die within a month, and that by a man whom I have loaded with honours! Is this public gratitude? Is this—

Enter Nanki-Poo, *with a rope in his hands.*

Go away, sir? How dare you? Am I never to be permitted to soliloquize?

Nank. Oh, go on—don't mind me.

Ko. What are you going to do with that rope?

Nank. I am about to terminate an unendurable existence.

Ko. Terminate your existence? Oh, nonsense! What for!

Nank. Because you are going to marry the girl I adore.

Ko. Nonsense, sir. I won't permit it. I am a humane man, and if you attempt anything of the kind I shall order your instant arrest. Come, sir, desist at once, or I summon my guard.

Nank. That's absurd. If you attempt to raise an alarm, I instantly perform the Happy Despatch with this dagger.

Ko. No, no, don't do that. This is horrible! *(Suddenly.)* Why, you cold-blooded scoundrel, are you aware that, in taking your life, you are committing a crime which—which—which is—Oh! *(Struck by an idea.)*

Nank. What's the matter?

Ko. Is it *absolutely certain* that you are resolved to die?

Nank. Absolutely!

Ko. Will *nothing* shake your resolution?

Nank. Nothing.

Ko. Threats, entreaties, prayers—all useless?

Nank. All! My mind is made up.

Ko. Then, if you really mean what you say, and if you are absolutely resolved to die, and if nothing whatever will shake your determination—don't spoil yourself by committing suicide, but be beheaded handsomely at the hands of the Public Executioner!

Nank. I don't see how that would benefit me.

Ko. You don't? Observe: you'll have a month to live, and you'll live like a fighting-cock at my expense. When the day comes, there'll be a grand public ceremonial—you'll be the central figure—no one will attempt to deprive you of that distinction. There'll be a procession—bands—dead march—bells tolling—all the girls in tears—Yum-Yum distracted—then, when it's all over, general rejoicings, and a display of fireworks in the evening. *You* won't see them, but they'll be there all the same.

Nank. Do you think Yum-Yum would really be distracted at my death?

Ko. I am convinced of it. Bless you, she's the most tender-hearted little creature alive.

Nank. I should be sorry to cause her pain. Perhaps, after all, if I were to withdraw from Japan, and travel in Europe for a couple of years, I might contrive to forget her.

Ko. Oh, I don't think you could forget Yum-Yum so easily and, after all, what is more miserable than a love-blighted life?

Nank. True.

Ko. Life without Yum-Yum—why, it seems absurd!

Nank. And yet there are a good many people in the world who have to endure it.

Ko. Poor devils, yes! You are quite right not to be of their number.

Nank. *(suddenly).* I *won't* be of their number!

Ko. Noble fellow!

Nank. I'll tell you how we'll manage it. Let me marry Yum-Yum to-morrow, and in a month you may behead me.

Ko. No, no. I draw the line at Yum-Yum.

Nank. Very good. If you can draw the line, so can I. *(Preparing rope.)*

Ko. Stop, stop—listen one moment—be reasonable. How can I consent to your marrying Yum-Yum, if I'm going to marry her myself?

Nank. My good friend, she'll be a widow in a month, and you can marry her then.

Ko. That's true, of course. I quite see that, but, dear me, my position during the next month will be most unpleasant—most unpleasant!

Nank. Not half as unpleasant as my position at the end of it.

Ko. But—dear me—well—I agree. After all, it's only putting off my wedding for a month. But you won't prejudice her against me, will you? You see, I've educated her to be my wife; she's been taught to regard me as a wise and good man. Now, I shouldn't like her views on that point disturbed.

NANK. Trust me, she shall never learn the truth from me.

FINALE.

Enter CHORUS, POOH-BAH, *and* PISH-TUSH.

CHORUS.

With aspect stern
   And gloomy stride,
We come to learn
   How you decide.

Don't hesitate
   Your choice to name,
A dreadful fate
   You'll suffer all the same.

POOH. To ask you what you mean to do we punctually
     appear.
KO.   Congratulate me, gentlemen, I've found a Volunteer!
ALL.   The Japanese equivalent for Hear, Hear, Hear!
KO. *(presenting him).*   'Tis Nanki-Pooh!
ALL.   Hail, Nanki-Pooh!
KO.   I think he'll do?
ALL.   Yes, yes, he'll do!
KO.   He yields his life if I'll Yum-Yum surrender;
    Now, I adore that girl with passion tender,
    And could not yield her with a ready will,
       Or her allot,
       If I did not
    Adore myself with passion tenderer still!
ALL.   Ah, yes!
    He loves himself with passion tenderer still!
KO. *(to* NANKI-POO.) Take her—she's yours!

Enter YUM-YUM, PEEP-BO, *and* PITTI-SING.

NANK. *and* YUM-YUM.   Oh, rapture!

ENSEMBLE.

YUM-YUM *and*
NANKI-POO. The threatened cloud has passed away,
    And brightly shines the dawning day;
    What though the night may come too soon,
    There's yet a month of afternoon!
       Then let the throng
         Our joy advance,
       With laughing song,
         And merry dance,
    With joyous shout and ringing cheer,
    Inaugurate our brief career!

CHORUS.   Then let the throng, etc.

PITTI-SING.   A day, a week, a month, a year—
    Or be it far, or be it near,
    Life's eventime comes much too soon,
    You'll live at least a honeymoon!

ALL.   Then let the throng, etc.

SOLO.—POOH-BAH.

As in three weeks you've got to die,
   If Ko-Ko tells us true,
'Twere empty compliment to cry
   Long life to Nanki-Poo!
But as you've got three weeks to live
   As fellow citizen,
This toast with three times three we'll give—
   "Long life to you—till then!"

CHORUS.   May all good fortune prosper you,
    May you have health and riches too,
    May you succeed in all you do.
      Long life to you—till then!

DANCE.

Enter KATISHA, *melodramatically.*

KAT.   Your revels cease—assist me all of you!
CHORUS.   Why, who is this whose evil eyes
      Rain blight on our festivities?
KAT.   I claim my perjured lover, Nanki-Poo!
    Oh, fool! to shun delights that never cloy!
    Come back, oh, shallow fool! come back to joy!
CHORUS.   Go, leave thy deadly work undone;
      Away, away! ill-favoured one!
NANK. *(aside to* YUM-YUM).   Ah!
      'Tis Katisha!
      The maid of whom I told you.
      (About to go.)
KAT. *(detaining him).*   No!
      You shall not go,
      These arms shall thus enfold you!

SONG.—KATISHA.

(Addressing NANKI-POO.) Oh fool, that fleest
        My hallowed joys!
      Oh blind, that seest
        No equipoise!
      Oh rash, that judgest
        From half, the whole!
      Oh base, that grudgest
        Love's lightest dole!
         Thy heart unbind,
         Oh fool, oh blind!
         Give me my place,
         Oh rash, oh base!

CHORUS.   If she's thy bride, restore her place
    Oh fool, oh blind, oh rash, oh base!

KAT. *(addressing* YUM-YUM).   Pink cheek, that rulest
                Where wisdom serves!
         Bright eye, that foolest
                Steel-tempered nerves;
         Rose-lip, that scornest
                Lore-laden years—
         Sweet tongue, that warnest
                Who rightly hears—
                  Thy doom is nigh,
                  Pink cheek, bright eye!
                  Thy knell is rung,
                  Rose-lip, sweet tongue.

CHORUS.   If true her tale, thy knell is rung,
        Pink cheek, bright eye, rose-lip, sweet tongue!

PITTI-SING.   Away, nor prosecute your quest—
        From our intention well expressed,
           You cannot turn us!
        The state of your connubial views
        Towards the person you accuse
           Does not concern us!
        For he's going to marry Yum-Yum—

ALL.   Yum-Yum!

PITTI.   Your anger pray bury,
          For all will be merry,
        I think you had better succumb—

ALL.   Cumb—cumb!

PITTI.   And join our expressions of glee,
        On this subject I pray you be dumb—

ALL.   Dumb—dumb!

PITTI.   You'll find there are many
         Who'll wed for a penny—
        The word for your guidance is, "Mum"—

ALL.   Mum—mum!

PITTI.   There's lots of good fish in the sea!

ALL.   There's lots of good fish in the sea!
        And you'll find there are many, etc.

SOLO.—KATISHA.

The hour of gladness
    Is dead and gone;
In silent sadness
    I live alone!
The hope I cherished
    All lifeless lies,
And all has perished
    Save love, which never dies!
Oh, faithless one, this insult you shall rue!
In vain for mercy on your knees you'll sue.
    I'll tear the mask from you disguising!

NANK. *(aside).*   Now comes the blow!

KAT.   Prepare yourself for news surprising!

NANK. *(aside).*   How foil my foe?

KAT.   No minstrel he, despite bravado!

YUM. *(aside, struck by an idea).* Ha! ha! I know!

KAT.   He is the son of your—

[NANKI-POO *and* YUM-YUM, *interrupting, sing Japanese
    words to drown her voice.*
      O ni! bikkuri shakkuri to!
      O sa! bikkuri shakkuri to!

KAT.   In vain you interrupt with this tornado:
    He is the only son of your—

ALL.   O ni! bikkuri shakkuri to!

KAT.   I'll spoil—

ALL.   O ni! bikkuri shakkuri to!

KAT.   Your gay gambado!
    He is the son—

ALL.   O ni! bikkuri shakkuri to!

KAT.   Of your—

ALL.   O ni! bikkuri shakkuri to!

ENSEMBLE.

KATISHA.	THE OTHERS.
Ye torrents roar!	We'll hear no more
Ye tempests howl!	Ill-omened owl,
Your wrath outpour	To joy we soar,
With angry growl!	Despite your scowl
Do ye your worst, my	The echoes of our festival
vengeance call	Shall rise triumphant over all!
Shall rise triumphant over all!	Away you go,
Prepare for woe,	Collect your hordes;
Ye haughty lords,	Proclaim your woe
At once I go	In dismal chords;
Mikado-wards.	We do not heed their dismal
And when he learns his son is	sound,
found,	For joy reigns everywhere
My wrongs with vengeance	around!
will be crowned!	

[KATISHA *rushes furiously up stage, clearing the crowd away
    right and left, finishing on steps at the back of stage.*

ACT II.

SCENE.—KO-KO's *Garden.* YUM-YUM *discovered seated at her bridal
    toilet, surrounded by* MAIDENS, *who are dressing her hair and
    painting her face and lips, as she judges of the effect in a mirror.*

CHORUS.

Braid the raven hair—
    Weave the supple tress—
Deck the maiden fair
    In her loveliness—
Paint the pretty face—
    Dye the coral lip—
Emphasize the grace
    Of her ladyship!
Art and nature, thus allied,
Go to make a pretty bride!

SOLO.—PITTI-SING.

Sit with downcast eye—
    Let it brim with dew—
Try if you can cry—
    We will do so, too.
When you're summoned, start,
    Like a frightened roe—
Flutter, little heart,

Colour, come and go!
Modesty at marriage-tide
Well becomes a pretty bride!

CHORUS.

Braid the raven hair, etc.   [*Exeunt* CHORUS.

YUM. (*looking at herself in glass*). Yes, I am indeed beautiful! Sometimes I sit and wonder, in my artless Japanese way, why it is that I am so much more attractive than anybody else in the whole world? Can this be vanity? No! Nature is lovely and rejoices in her loveliness. I am a child of Nature, and take after my mother.

SONG.—YUM-YUM.

The sun, whose rays
Are all ablaze
    With ever living glory,
Does not deny
His majesty—
    He scorns to tell a story!
He don't exclaim,
"I blush for shame,
    So kindly be indulgent."
But, fierce and bold,
In fiery gold,
    He glories all effulgent!

    I mean to rule the earth,
        As he the sky—
    We really know our worth,
        The sun and I!

Observe his flame,
That placid dame,
    The moon's Celestial Highness;
There's not a trace
Upon her face
    Of diffidence or shyness:
She borrows light
That, through the night,
    Mankind may all acclaim her!
And, truth to tell,
She lights up well,
    So I, for one, don't blame her!

    Ah, pray make no mistake,
        We are not shy;
    We're very wide awake,
        The moon and I!

YUM. Yes, everything seems to smile upon me. I am to be married to-day to the man I love best, and I believe I am the very happiest girl in Japan!

PEEP. The happiest girl indeed, for she is indeed to be envied who has attained happiness in all but perfection.

YUM. In "all but" perfection?

PEEP. Well, dear, it can't be denied that the fact that your husband is to be beheaded in a month is, in its way, a drawback.

PITTI. I don't know about that. It all depends!

PEEP. At all events, *he* will find it a drawback.

PITTI. Not necessarily. Bless you, it all depends!

YUM. (*in tears*). I think it very indelicate of you to refer to such a subject on such a day. If my married happiness *is* to be—to be—

PEEP. Cut short.

YUM. Well, cut short—in a month, can't you let me forget it? (*Weeping.*)

Enter NANKI-POO *followed by* PISH-TUSH.

NANK. Yum-Yum in tears—and on her wedding morn!

YUM. (*sobbing*). They've been reminding me that in a month you're to be beheaded! (*Bursts into tears.*)

PITTI. Yes, we've been reminding her that you're to be beheaded. (*Bursts into tears.*)

PEEP. It's quite true, you know, you *are* to be beheaded! (*Bursts into tears.*)

NANK. (*aside*). Humph! How some bridegrooms would be depressed by this sort of thing! (*Aloud.*) A month? Well, what's a month? Bah! These divisions of time are purely arbitrary. Who says twenty-four hours make a day?

PITTI. There's a popular impression to that effect.

NANK. Then we'll efface it. We'll call each second a minute—each minute an hour—each hour a day—and each day a year. At that rate we've about thirty years of married happiness before us!

PEEP. And at that rate, this interview has already lasted four hours and three-quarters!   [*Exit* PEEP-BO.

YUM. (*still sobbing*). Yes. How time flies when one is thoroughly enjoying one's self!

NANK. That's the way to look at it! Don't let's be downhearted! There's a silver lining to every cloud.

YUM. Certainly. Let's—let's be perfectly happy! (*Almost in tears.*)

PISH. By all means. Let's—let's thoroughly enjoy ourselves.

PITTI. It's—it's absurd to cry! (*Trying to force a laugh.*)

YUM. Quite ridiculous! (*Trying to laugh.*)

[*All break into a forced and melancholy laugh.*

QUARTETTE.

YUM-YUM, PITTI-SING, NANKI-POO, *and* PISH-TUSH.

Brightly dawns our wedding-day;
    Joyous hour, we give thee greeting!
    Whither, whither art thou fleeting?
Fickle moment, prithee stay!
    What though mortal joys be hollow?
    Pleasures come, if sorrows follow:
Though the tocsin sound, ere long,
    Ding dong! Ding dong!
Yet until the shadows fall
Over one and over all,
Sing a merry madrigal—
        A madrigal!

    Fal-la—fal-la! etc. (*Ending in tears.*)

Let us dry the ready tear,
    Though the hours are surely creeping,
    Little need for woeful weeping,
Till the sad sundown is near.
    All must sip the cup of sorrow—
    I to-day and thou to-morrow:

This the close of every song—
　　Ding dong! Ding dong!
What, though solemn shadows fall,
Sooner, later, over all?
Sing a merry madrigal—
　　A madrigal!

Fal-la—fal-la! etc. *(Ending in tears.)*

　　　　　　　[*Exeunt* PITTI-SING *and* PISH-TUSH.

NANKI-POO *embraces* YUM-YUM. *Enter* KO-KO.
NANKI-POO *releases* YUM-YUM.

KO. Go on—don't mind me.

NANK. I'm afraid we're distressing you.

KO. Never mind, I must get used to it. Only please do it by degrees. Begin by putting your arm round her waist. (NANKI-POO *does so.*) There; let me get used to that first.

YUM. Oh, wouldn't you like to retire? It must pain you to see us so affectionate together!

KO. No, I must learn to bear it! Now oblige me by allowing her head to rest on your shoulder. *(He does so—*KO-KO *much affected.)* I am much obliged to you. Now—kiss her! *(He does so—*KO-KO *writhes with anguish.)* Thank you—it's simple torture!

YUM. Come, come, bear up. After all, it's only for a month.

KO. No. It's no use deluding one's self with false hopes.

NANK. *and* YUM. *(together).* What do you mean?

KO. *(to* YUM-YUM*).* My child—my poor child. *(Aside.)* How shall I break it to her? *(Aloud.)* My little bride that was to have been.

YUM. *(delighted). Was* to have been!

KO. Yes; you never can be mine!

YUM. *(in ecstasy).* What!!!

KO. I've just ascertained that, by the Mikado's law, when a married man is beheaded his wife is buried alive.

NANK. *and* YUM. *(together).* Buried alive!

KO. Buried alive. It's a most unpleasant death.

NANK. But whom did you get that from?

KO. Oh, from Pooh-Bah. He's my solicitor.

YUM. But he may be mistaken!

KO. So I thought, so I consulted the Attorney-General, the Lord Chief Justice, the Master of the Rolls, the Judge Ordinary, and the Lord Chancellor. They're all of the same opinion. Never knew such unanimity on a point of law in my life!

NANK. But, stop a bit! This law has never been put in force?

KO. Not yet. You see, flirting is the only crime punishable with decapitation, and married men never flirt.

NANK. Of course they don't. I quite forgot that! Well, I suppose I may take it that my dream of happiness is at an end!

YUM. Darling, I don't want to appear selfish, and I love you with all my heart—I don't suppose I shall ever love anybody else half as much—but when I agreed to marry you, my own, I had no idea, pet, that I should have to be buried alive in a month!

NANK. Nor I! It's the very first I've heard of it!

YUM. It—it makes a difference, doesn't it?

NANK. It *does* make a difference, of course!

YUM. You see—burial alive—it's such a stuffy death! You see my difficulty, don't you?

NANK. Yes; and I see my own. If I insist on your carrying out your promise, I doom you to a hideous death; if I release you, you marry Ko-Ko at once!

TRIO.—YUM-YUM, NANKI-POO *and* KO-KO.

YUM.　　Here's a how-de-do!
　　　　If I marry you,
　　When your time has come to perish,
　　Then the maiden whom you cherish
　　　　Must be slaughtered too!
　　　　Here's a how-de-do!

NANK.　　Here's a pretty mess!
　　　　In a month, or less,
　　I must die, without a wedding!
　　Let the bitter tears I'm shedding
　　　　Witness my distress,
　　　　Here's a pretty mess!

KO.　　Here's a state of things!
　　　　To her life she clings!
　　Matrimonial devotion
　　Doesn't seem to suit her notion—
　　　　Burial it brings!
　　　　Here's a state of things!

ENSEMBLE.

YUM-YUM *and* NANKI-POO.	KO-KO.
With a passion that's intense	With a passion that's intense
I worship and adore,	You worship and adore,
But the laws of common sense	But the laws of common sense
We oughtn't to ignore.	You oughtn't to ignore.
If what he says is true,	If what I say is true,
It is death to marry you!	It is death to marry you!
Here's a pretty state of things!	Here's a pretty state of things!
Here's a pretty how-de-do!	Here's a pretty how-de-do!

　　　　　　　[*Exit* YUM-YUM.

KO. *(going up to* NANKI-POO*).* My poor boy, I'm really very sorry for you.

NANK. Thanks, old fellow. I'm sure you are.

KO. You see I'm quite helpless.

NANK. I quite see that.

KO. I can't conceive anything more distressing than to have one's marriage broken off at the last moment. But you shan't be disappointed of a wedding—you shall come to mine.

NANK. It's awfully kind of you, but that's impossible.

KO. Why so?

NANK. To-day I die.

KO. What do you mean?

NANK. I can't live without Yum-Yum. This afternoon I perform the Happy Despatch.

KO. No, no—pardon me—I can't allow that.

NANK. Why not?

KO. Why, hang it all, you're under contract to die by the hand of the Public Executioner in a month's time! If you kill yourself, what's to become of me? Why, I shall have to be executed in your place!

NANK. It would certainly seem so!

Enter POOH-BAH.

KO. Now then, Lord Mayor, what is it?

POOH. The Mikado and his suite are approaching the city, and will be here in ten minutes.

KO. The Mikado! He's coming to see whether his orders have been carried out! (To NANKI-POO.) Now, look here, you know—this is getting serious—a bargain's a bargain, and you really mustn't frustrate the ends of justice by committing suicide. As a man of honour and a gentleman, you are bound to die ignominiously by the hands of the Public Executioner.

NANK. Very well, then—behead me.

KO. What, now?

NANK. Certainly; at once.

KO. My good sir, I don't go about prepared to execute gentlemen at a moment's notice. Why, I never even killed a blue-bottle!

POOH. Still, as Lord High Executioner—

KO. My good sir, as Lord High Executioner I've got to behead him in a month. I'm not ready yet. I don't know how it's done. I'm going to take lessons. I mean to begin with a guinea-pig, and work my way through the animal kingdom till I come to a second trombone. Why, you don't suppose that, as a humane man, I'd have accepted the post of Lord High Executioner if I hadn't thought the duties were purely nominal? I *can't* kill you—I can't kill anything! (Weeps.)

NANK. Come, my poor fellow, your feelings do you credit; but you must nerve yourself to this—you must, indeed. We all have unpleasant duties to discharge at times; and when these duties present themselves we must nerve ourselves to an effort. Come, now—after all, what is it? If I don't mind, why should you? Remember, sooner or later it must be done.

KO. (springing up suddenly). Must it? I'm not so sure about that!

NANK. What do you mean?

KO. Why should I kill you when making an affidavit that you've been executed will do just as well? Here are plenty of witnesses—the Lord Chief Justice, and Lord High Admiral, Commander-in-Chief, Secretary of State for the Home Department, First Lord of the Treasury, and Chief Commissioner of Police. They'll all swear to it—won't you? (To POOH-BAH.)

POOH. Am I to understand that all of us high Officers of State are required to perjure ourselves to ensure your safety?

KO. Why not? You'll be grossly insulted as usual.

POOH. Will the insult be cash down, or at a date?

KO. It will be a ready-money transaction.

POOH. (aside). Well, it will be a useful discipline. (Aloud.) Very good. Choose your fiction, and I'll endorse it! (Aside.) Ha! ha! Family Pride, how do you like *that*, my buck?

NANK. But I tell you that life without Yum-Yum—

KO. Oh, Yum-Yum, Yum-Yum! Bother Yum-Yum! Here, Commissionaire (to POOH-BAH), go and fetch Yum-Yum. (Exit POOH-BAH.) Take Yum-Yum and marry Yum-Yum, only go away and never come back again.

Enter POOH-BAH *with* YUM-YUM *and* PITTI-SING.

Here she is. Yum-Yum, are you particularly busy?

YUM. Not particularly.

KO. You've five minutes to spare?

YUM. Yes.

KO. Then go along with his Grace the Archbishop of Titipu; he'll marry you at once.

YUM. But if I'm to be buried alive?

KO. Now don't ask any questions, but do as I tell you, and Nanki-Poo will explain all.

NANK. But one moment—

KO. Not for worlds. Here comes the Mikado, no doubt to ascertain whether I've obeyed his decree, and if he finds you alive, I shall have the greatest difficulty in persuading him that I've beheaded you. (Exeunt NANKI-POO and YUM-YUM, followed by POOH-BAH.) Close thing that, for here he comes!

March. Enter procession, heralding MIKADO, *with* KATISHA.

CHORUS.

"March of the Mikado's troops."

> Miya sama, miya sama,
> On ma no mayé ni
> Pira-Pira suru no wa
> Nan gia na
> Toko tonyaré tonyaré na!

DUET.—MIKADO *and* KATISHA.

MIKADO.	From every kind of man
	Obedience I expect;
	I'm the Emperor of Japan.
KAT.	And I'm his daughter-in-law elect!
	He'll marry his son
	(He has only got one)
	To his daughter-in-law elect.
MIK.	My morals have been declared
	Particularly correct;
KAT.	But they're nothing at all, compared
	With those of his daughter-in-law elect!
	Bow! Bow!
	To his daughter-in-law elect!
ALL.	Bow! Bow!
	To his daughter-in-law elect.
MIK.	In a fatherly kind of way
	I govern each tribe and sect,
	All cheerfully own my sway—
KAT.	Except his daughter-in-law elect!
	As tough as a bone,
	With a will of her own,
	Is his daughter-in-law elect!
MIK.	My nature is love and light—
	My freedom from all defect—
KAT.	Is insignificant quite,
	Compared with his daughter-in-law elect!
	Bow! Bow!
	To his daughter-in-law elect!
ALL.	Bow! Bow!
	To his daughter-in-law elect.

SONG.—MIKADO.

> A more humane Mikado never
> Did in Japan exist,
> To nobody second,
> I'm certainly reckoned
> A true philanthropist.

It is my very humane endeavour
To make, to some extent,
Each evil liver
A running river
Of harmless merriment.
My object all sublime
I shall achieve in time—
To let the punishment fit the crime—
The punishment fit the crime;
And make each prisoner pent
Unwillingly represent
A source of innocent merriment,
Of innocent merriment!

All prosy dull society sinners,
Who chatter and bleat and bore,
Are sent to hear sermons
From mystical Germans
Who preach from ten to four.
The amateur tenor, whose vocal villainies
All desire to shirk,
Shall, during off-hours,
Exhibit his powers
To Madame Tussaud's waxwork.

My object all sublime, etc.

The lady who dies a chemical yellow,
Or stains her grey hair puce,
Or pinches her figger,
Is blacked like a nigger
With permanent walnut juice.
The idiot who, in railway carriages,
Scribbles on window panes,
We only suffer
To ride on a buffer
In parliamentary trains.

My object all sublime, etc.

The advertising quack who wearies
With tales of countless cures,
His teeth, I've enacted,
Shall all be extracted
By terrified amateurs.
The music-hall singer attends a series
Of masses and fugues and "ops"
By Bach, interwoven
With Spohr and Beethoven,
At classical Monday Pops.

My object all sublime, etc.

The billiard sharp whom any one catches,
His doom's extremely hard—
He's made to dwell—
In a dungeon cell
On a spot that's always barred.
And there he plays extravagant matches
In fitless finger-stalls
On a cloth untrue
With a twisted cue,
And elliptical billiard balls!

My object all sublime, etc.

Enter POOH-BAH, *who hands a paper to* KO-KO.

KO. I am honoured in being permitted to welcome your Majesty. I guess the object of your Majesty's visit—your wishes have been attended to. The execution has taken place.

MIK. Oh, you've had an execution, have you?

KO. Yes. The Coroner has just handed me his certificate.

POOH. I am the Coroner. (KO-KO *hands certificate to* MIKADO.)

MIK. (*reads*). "At Titipu, in the presence of the Lord Chancellor, Lord Chief Justice, Attorney-General, Secretary of State for the Home Department, Lord Mayor, and Groom of the Second Floor Front."

POOH. They were all present, your Majesty. I counted them myself.

MIK. Very good house. I wish I'd been in time for the performance.

KO. A tough fellow he was, too—a man of gigantic strength. His struggles were terrific. It was really a remarkable scene.

TRIO.—KO-KO, PITTI-SING, *and* POOH-BAH.

KO.   The criminal cried, as he dropped him down,
                In a state of wild alarm—
        With a frightful frantic, fearful frown
                I bared my big right arm.
        I seized him by his little pig-tail,
                And on his knees fell he,
                        As he squirmed and struggled
                        And gurgled and guggled,
                I drew my snickersnee!
                        Oh, never shall I
                        Forget the cry,
        Or the shriek that shriekèd he,
                        As I gnashed my teeth,
                        When from its sheath
                I drew my snickersnee!

CHORUS.

                We know him well,
                He cannot tell
        Untrue or groundless tales—
                He always tries
                To utter lies,
        And every time he fails.

PITTI-SING.   He shivered and shook as he gave the sign
                For the stroke he didn't deserve;
        When all of a sudden his eye met mine,
                And it seemed to brace his nerve,
        For he nodded his head and kissed his hand,
                And he whistled an air, did he,
                        As the sabre true
                        Cut cleanly through
                His cervical vertebræ!
                        When a man's afraid,
                        A beautiful maid
                Is a cheering sight to see,
                        And it's oh, I'm glad
                        That moment sad
                Was soothed by sight of me!

CHORUS.

Her terrible tale
You can't assail,
With truth it quite agrees;
Her taste exact
For faultless fact
Amounts to a disease.

POOH.   Now though you'd have said that head was dead
(For its owner dead was he),
It stood on its neck with a smile well bred,
And bowed three times to me!

It was none of your impudent off-hand nods,
But as humble as could be;
For it clearly knew
The deference due
To a man of pedigree!
And it's oh, I vow,
This deathly bow
Was a touching sight to see;
Though trunkless, yet
It couldn't forget
The deference due to me!

CHORUS.

This haughty youth
He speaks the truth
Whenever he finds it pays,
And in this case
It all took place
Exactly as he says!   [*Exeunt* CHORUS.

MIK. All this is very interesting, and I should like to have seen it. But we came about a totally different matter. A year ago my son, the heir to the throne of Japan, bolted from our imperial court.

Ko. Indeed? Had he any reason to be dissatisfied with his position?

KAT. None whatever. On the contrary, I was going to marry him—yet he fled!

POOH. I am surprised that he should have fled from one so lovely!

KAT. That's not true. You hold that I am not beautiful because my face is plain. But you know nothing; you are still unenlightened. Learn, then, that it is not in the face alone that beauty is to be sought. But I have a left shoulder-blade that is a miracle of loveliness. People come miles to see it. My right elbow has a fascination that few can resist. It is on view Tuesdays and Fridays, on presentation of visiting-card. As for my circulation, it is the largest in the world. Observe this ear.

Ko. Large.

KAT. Large? Enormous! But think of its delicate internal mechanism. It is fraught with beauty! As for this tooth, it almost stands alone. Many have tried to draw it, but in vain.

Ko. And yet he fled!

MIK. And is now masquerading in this town, disguised as a second trombone.

Ko., POOH., *and* PITTI. *(together)*. A second trombone!

MIK. Yes; would it be troubling you too much if I asked you to produce him? He goes by the name of Nanki-Poo.

Ko. Oh no; not at all—only—

MIK. Yes?

Ko. 'It's rather awkward; but, in point of fact, he's gone abroad!

MIK. Gone abroad? His address!

Ko. Knightsbridge.

KAT. *(who is reading certificate of death)*. Ha!

MIK. What's the matter?

KAT. See here—his name—Nanki-Poo—beheaded this morning! Oh, where shall I find another! Where shall I find another! [KO-KO, POOH-BAH, *and* PITTI-SING *fall on their knees.*

MIK. *(looking at paper)*. Dear, dear, dear; this is very tiresome. *(To* KO-KO.*)* My poor fellow, in your anxiety to carry out my wishes, you have beheaded the heir to the throne of Japan!

Together. { Ko. But I assure you we had no idea—
POOH. But, indeed, we didn't know—
PITTI. We really hadn't the least notion—

MIK. Of course you hadn't. How could you? Come, come my good fellow, don't distress yourself—it was no fault of yours. If a man of exalted rank chooses to disguise himself as a second trombone, he must take the consequences. It really distresses me to see you take on so. I've no doubt he thoroughly deserved all he got. *(They rise.)*

Ko. We are infinitely obliged to your Majesty.

MIK. Obliged? Not a bit. Don't mention it. How *could* you tell?

POOH. No, of course we couldn't know that he was the Heir Apparent.

PITTI. It wasn't written on his forehead, you know.

Ko. It might have been on his pocket-handkerchief, but Japanese don't use pocket-handkerchiefs! Ha! ha! ha!

MIK. Ha! ha! ha! *(To* KAT.*)* I forget the punishment for compassing the death of the Heir Apparent.

Ko., POOH., *and* PITTI. *(together)*. Punishment! *(They drop down on their knees again.)*

MIK. Yes. Something lingering, with boiling oil in it, I fancy. Something of that sort. I think boiling oil occurs in it, but I'm not sure. I know it's something humorous, but lingering, with either boiling oil or melted lead. Come, come, don't fret—I'm not a bit angry.

Ko. *(in abject terror)*. If your Majesty will accept our assurance, we had no idea—

MIK. Of course you hadn't. That's the pathetic part of it. Unfortunately the fool of an Act says "compassing the death of the Heir Apparent." There's not a word about a mistake, or not knowing, or having no notion. There should be, of course, but there isn't. That's the slovenly way in which these Acts are drawn. However, cheer up, it'll be all right. I'll have it altered next session.

Ko. What's the good of that?

MIK. Now, let's see—will after luncheon suit you? Can you wait till then?

Ko., PITTI. *and* POOH. Oh yes—we can wait till then!

MIK. Then we'll make it after luncheon. I'm really very sorry for you all, but it's an unjust world, and virtue is triumphant only in theatrical performances.

GLEE.

MIKADO, KATISHA, KO-KO, POOH-BAH, *and* PITTI-SING.

MIK. *and* KAT.	See how the Fates their gifts allot,
	For A is happy—B is not.
	Yet B is worthy, I dare say,
	Of more prosperity than A!
KO., POOH., *and* PITTI.	*Is* B more worthy?
MIK. *and* KAT.	I should say
	He's worth a great deal more than A.

ENSEMBLE.

> Yet A is happy!
> Oh, so happy!
> Laughing, Ha! ha!
> Chaffing, Ha! ha!
> Nectar quaffing, Ha! ha! ha! ha!
> Ever joyous ever gay,
> Happy, undeserving A!

KO., POOH., *and* PITTI.	If I were fortune—which I'm not—
	B should enjoy A's happy lot,
	And A should die in miserie,
	That is, assuming I am B.
MIK. *and* KAT.	But *should* A perish?
KO., POOH., *and* PITTI.	That should he,
	(Of course assuming I am B).

> B should be happy!
> Oh, so happy!
> Laughing, Ha! ha!
> Chaffing, Ha! ha!
> Nectar quaffing, Ha! ha! ha! ha!
> But condemned to die is he,
> Wretched, meritorious B!

[*Exeunt* MIKADO *and* KATISHA.

KO. Well! a nice mess you've got us into, with your nodding head and the deference due to a man of pedigree!

POOH. Merely corroborative detail, intended to give artistic verisimilitude to a bald and unconvincing narrative.

PITTI. Corroborative detail indeed! Corroborative fiddlestick!

KO. And you're just as bad as he is, with your cock-and-a-bull stories about catching his eye, and his whistling an air. But that's so like you! You must put in your oar!

POOH. But how about your big right arm?

PITTI. Yes, and your snickersnee!

KO. Well, well, never mind that now. There's only one thing to be done. Nanki-Poo hasn't started yet—he must come to life again at once.

Enter NANKI-POO, *and* YUM-YUM *prepared for journey.*

Here he comes. Here, Nanki-Poo, I've good news for you—you're reprieved.

NANK. Oh, but it's too late. I'm a dead man, and I'm off for my honeymoon.

KO. Nonsense. A terrible thing has just happened. It seems you're the son of the Mikado.

NANK. Yes; but that happened some time ago.

KO. Is this a time for airy persiflage? Your father is here, and with Katisha.

NANK. My father! And with Katisha!

KO. Yes; he wants you particularly.

POOH. So does she.

YUM. Oh, but he's married now.

KO. But, bless my heart, what has that to do with it?

NANK. Katisha claims me in marriage, but I can't marry her because I'm married already—consequently she will insist on my execution, and if I'm executed, my wife will have to be buried alive.

YUM. You see our difficulty.

KO. Yes. I don't know what's to be done.

NANK. There's one chance for you. If you could persuade Katisha to marry you, she would have no further claim on me, and in that case I could come to life without any fear of being put to death.

KO. I marry Katisha!

YUM. I really think it's the only course.

KO. But, my good girl, have you seen her? She's something appalling!

PITTI. Ah, that's only her face. She has a left elbow which people come miles to see!

POOH. I am told that her right heel is much admired by connoisseurs.

KO. My good sir, I decline to pin my heart upon any lady's right heel.

NANK. It comes to this: while Katisha is single, I prefer to be a disembodied spirit. When Katisha is married, existence will be as welcome as the flowers in spring.

DUET.—NANKI-POO *and* KO-KO.

NANK.	The flowers that bloom in the spring,
	Tra la,
	Breathe promise of merry sunshine—
	As we merrily dance and we sing,
	Tra la,
	We welcome the hope that they bring,
	Tra la,
	Of a summer of roses and wine;
	And that's what we mean when we say that a thing
	Is welcome as flowers that bloom in the spring.
	Tra la la la la la, etc.
ALL.	And that's what we mean, etc.
KO.	The flowers that bloom in the spring,
	Tra la,
	Have nothing to do with the case.
	I've got to take under my wing,
	Tra la,
	A most unattractive old thing,
	Tra la,
	With a caricature of a face;
	And that's what I mean when I say, or I sing,
	"Oh bother the flowers that bloom in the spring!"
	Tra la la la la la, etc.

ALL. And that's what he means when he ventures to sing, etc.

[*Dance and exeunt* NANKI-POO, YUM-YUM, POOH-BAH, *and* PITTI-SING.

Enter KATISHA.

RECITATIVE.

Alone, and yet alive! Oh sepulchre!
My soul is still my body's prisoner!
Remote the peace that Death alone can give—
My doom to wait! My punishment to live!

SONG.

Hearts do not break!
They sting and ache
For old sake's sake,
    But do not die!
Though with each breath
They long for death,
As witnesseth
    The living I!
      Oh living I!
      Come, tell me why,
      When hope is gone
      Dost thou stay on?
      Why linger here,
      Where all is drear?
    May not a cheated maiden die?

KO. *(approaching her timidly).* Katisha!

KAT. The miscreant who robbed me of my love! But vengeance pursues—they are heating the cauldron!

KO. Katisha—behold a suppliant at your feet! Katisha—mercy!

KAT. Mercy? Had you mercy on him? See here, you! You have slain my love. He did not love *me*, but he would have loved me in time. I am an acquired taste—only the educated palate can appreciate *me*. I was educating *his* palate when he left me. Well, he is dead, and where shall I find another? It takes years to train a man to love me—am I to go through the weary round again, and, at the same time, implore mercy for you who robbed me of my prey—I mean my pupil—just as his education was on the point of completion? Oh, where shall I find another!

KO. *(suddenly, and with great vehemence).* Here!—Here!

KAT. What!!!

KO. *(with intense passion).* Katisha, for years I have loved you with a white-hot passion that is slowly but surely consuming my very vitals! Ah, shrink not from me! If there is aught of woman's mercy in your heart, turn not away from a love-sick suppliant whose every fibre thrills at your tiniest touch! True it is that, under a poor mask of disgust, I have endeavoured to conceal a passion whose inner fires are broiling the soul within me. But the fire will not be smothered—it defies all attempts at extinction, and, breaking forth, all the more eagerly for its long restraint, it declares itself in words that will not be weighed—that cannot be schooled—that should not be too severely criticized! Katisha, I dare not hope for your love—but I will not live without it!

KAT. You, whose hands still reek with the blood of my betrothed, dare to address words of passion to the woman you have so foully wronged!

KO. I do—accept my love, or I perish on the spot!

KAT. Go to! Who knows so well as I that no one ever yet died of a broken heart!

KO. You know not what you say. Listen!

SONG.—KO-KO.

On a tree by a river a little tom-tit
    Sang, "Willow, titwillow, titwillow!"
And I said to him, "Dicky-bird, why do you sit
    Singing 'Willow, titwillow, titwillow'?"
"Is it weakness of intellect, birdie?" I cried,
"Or a rather tough worm in your little inside?"
With a shake of his poor little head he replied,
    "Oh, willow, titwillow, titwillow!"

He slapped at his chest, as he sat on that bough,
    Singing, "Willow, titwillow, titwillow!"
And a cold perspiration bespangled his brow,
    Oh, willow, titwillow, titwillow!
He sobbed and he sighed, and a gurgle he gave,
Then he threw himself into the billowy wave,
And an echo arose from the suicide's grave—
    "Oh, willow, titwillow, titwillow!"

Now, I feel just as sure as I'm sure that my name
    Isn't willow, titwillow, titwillow.
That 'twas blighted affection that made him exclaim,
    "Oh, willow, titwillow, titwillow!"
And if you remain callous and obdurate, I
Shall perish as he did, and you will know why,
Though I probably shall not exclaim as I die,
    "Oh, willow, titwillow, titwillow!"

[*During this song* KATISHA *has been greatly affected, and at the end is almost in tears.*

KAT. *(whimpering).* Did he really die of love?

KO. He really did.

KAT. All on account of a cruel little hen?

KO. Yes.

KAT. Poor little chap!

KO. It's an affecting tale, and quite true. I knew the bird intimately.

KAT. Did you? He must have been very fond of her!

KO. His devotion was something extraordinary.

KAT. *(still whimpering).* Poor little chap! And—and if I refuse you, will you go and do the same?

KO. At once.

KAT. No, no—you mustn't! Anything but that! *(Falls on his breast.)* Oh, I'm a silly little goose!

KO. *(making a wry face).* You are!

KAT. And you won't hate me because I'm just a little teeny weeny wee bit blood-thirsty, will you?

KO. Hate you? Oh, Katisha! is there not beauty even in blood-thirstiness?

KAT. My idea exactly!

DUET.—KO-KO *and* KATISHA.

KAT. There is beauty in the bellow of the blast,
    There is grandeur in the growing of the gale,
      There is eloquent out-pouring
      When the lion is a-roaring,
    And the tiger is a-lashing of his tale!

Ko.   Yes, I like to see a tiger
From the Congo or the Niger,
And especially when lashing of his tail!

Kat.   Volcanoes have a splendour that is grim,
And earthquakes only terrify the dolts,
But to him who's scientific
There's nothing that's terrific
In the falling of a flight of thunderbolts!

Ko.   Yes, in spite of all my meekness,
If I have a little weakness,
It's a passion for a flight of thunderbolts.

Both.   If that is so,
Sing derry down derry!
It's evident, very,
Our tastes are one.
Away we'll go,
And merrily marry,
Nor tardily tarry
'Till day is done!

Ko.   There is beauty in extreme old age—
Do you fancy you are elderly enough?
Information I'm requesting
On a subject interesting:
Is a maiden all the better when she's tough?

Kat.   Throughout this wide dominion
It's the general opinion
That she'll last a good deal longer when she's tough.

Ko.   Are you old enough to marry do you think?
Won't you wait 'till you are "eighty in the shade"?
There's a fascination frantic
In a ruin that's romantic;
Do you think you are sufficiently decayed?

Kat.   To the matter that you mention
I have given some attention,
And I think I am sufficiently decayed.

Both.   If that is so,
Sing derry down derry!
It's evident, very,
Our tastes are one!
Away we'll go,
And merrily marry,
Not tardily tarry
Till day is done!   [*Exeunt together.*

Flourish. Enter the Mikado, *attended by* Pish-Tush, *and Court.*

Mik. Now then, we've had a capital lunch, and we're quite ready. Have all the painful preparations been made?

Pish. Your Majesty, all is prepared.

Mik. Then produce the unfortunate gentleman and his two well-meaning but misguided accomplices.

Enter Ko-Ko, Katisha, Pooh-Bah, *and* Pitti-Sing.
They throw themselves at the Mikado's *feet.*

Kat. Mercy! Mercy for Ko-Ko! Mercy for Pitti-Sing! Mercy even for Pooh-Bah!

Mik. I beg your pardon, I don't think I quite caught that remark.

Kat. Mercy! My husband that was to have been is dead, and I have just married this miserable object.

Mik. Oh! You've not been long about it!

Ko. We were married before the Registrar.

Pooh. *I* am the Registrar.

Mik. I see. But my difficulty is that, as you have slain the Heir-Apparent—

Enter Nanki-Poo *and* Yum-Yum. *They kneel.*

Nank. The Heir-Apparent is *not* slain.

Mik. Bless my heart, my son!

Yum. And your daughter-in-law elected!

Kat. *(seizing* Ko-Ko). Traitor, you have deceived me!

Mik. Yes, you are entitled to a little explanation, but I think he will give it better whole than in pieces.

Ko. Your Majesty, it's like this. It is true that I stated that I had killed Nanki-Poo—

Mik. Yes, with most affecting particulars.

Pooh. Merely corroborative detail intended to give verisimilitude to a bald and—

Ko. *Will* you refrain from putting in your oar? *(To* Mik.) It's like this: when your Majesty says, "Let a thing be done," it's as good as done—practically, it *is* done—because your Majesty's will is law. Your Majesty says, "Kill a gentleman," and a gentleman is told off to be killed. Consequently that gentleman is as good as dead—practically he *is* dead—and if he is dead, why not say so?

Mik. I see. Nothing could possibly be more satisfactory.

FINALE.

Yum. *and* Nank.   The threatened cloud has passed away,
And brightly shines the dawning day;
What though the night may come too soon,
We've years and years of afternoon!

Pli.   Then let the throng
Our joy advance,
With laughing song
And merry dance,
With joyous shout and ringing cheer,
Inaugurate our new career!

           Then let the throng, etc.

Ruddigore

or The Witch's Curse

Ruddigore was a disappointment. *The Mikado* was still running to full houses at the Savoy Theatre when it was taken off to make way for the new opera, and the new opera in no way matched it.

In 1869 Gilbert produced his burlesque 'Ages Ago', from which the second act of *Ruddigore* was derived. The scene was set in a baronial hall.

In *Ruddigore* Gilbert leaves the fantastic world of *Iolanthe*, *Princess Ida* and *The Mikado*, and returns to semi-reality. The setting and characters might have come from a Victorian photograph album: the Cornish fishing village, the pious, buttoned-up heroine, the wedding couples, the army officers and the ancestors are very much part of country life.

There is always an element in Gilbert's work which jars with conventional morality, but even the original title of *Ruddygore* shocked the puritanical section of society.

It has been called a parody of the traditional, popular melodrama with its truly villainous villains and gallant heroes. In *Ruddigore* the wicked are reformed and the pious are forced to be party to corruption. Rose Maybud, reared strictly on her book of etiquette and—by her speech—the Bible, becomes unwittingly betrothed to Richard Dauntless, a reckless bounder; while Mad Margaret and Sir Despard, the relentless wrongdoers, turn to religious reform.

Mad Margaret is one of Gilbert's most interesting characters and her part is enhanced by Sullivan's music. It was written for the remarkable singing-actress, Jessie Bond, who played Margaret as a half-naked gypsy. Margaret's ironic conversion to a Sunday School teacher (in Salvation Army garb) was considered offensive and the religious connotation had to be removed. Gilbert describes her as a 'typical character of theatrical madness' and it is possible that his inspiration derived from the findings of Jacques Charcot whose researches into female hysteria and hypnotism were taking place in Paris in the 1880s. Gilbert enjoyed investigating the macabre and, in spite of the fact that *Ruddigore* did not receive universal acclaim, Gilbert regarded it as one of his favourite operas.

Elsie Griffin, Rose Maybud in the 1920 revival of *Ruddigore*. 'Where can it be? Now let me see—Yes, yes! It's contrary to etiquette!'

Sir Roderic, the spokesman of the accursed ancestors, sadistically tortures his innocent—yet guilty—nephew. His villainous image is completed with vampire outfit and gloating description of the ghosts' midnight socials.

On the other hand, the would-be Lotharios, the Bucks and Blades of the evil Sir Despard's company, surprisingly appear in the smart guise of army officers, and as such they are above reproach. In similar vein the power of the Union Jack is invoked to ward off evil; but this joke was not appreciated.

There is a distinctly Elizabethan flavour to *Ruddigore*. Gilbert borrows from Shakespeare's *Hamlet* and *As You Like It*, and Sullivan's music is, for the most part, descended from English folk tune.

Act I met with the usual first-night enthusiasm

Jessie Bond as Mad Margaret in the original production, Savoy Theatre, 22 January 1887.

but Sullivan's inventive ghost music weighed heavily on Act II, and it was booed, an unprecedented event at the Savoy. Gilbert complained that the music was too operatic and not suitably humorous, whereas Sullivan was anxious to escape from being a mere song-writer for Gilbert's plays.

Act II was radically altered and abridged within the first month of the run, and although it has never been satisfactory, it would have worked perfectly well in its original state with the right emphasis upon melodrama.

SYNOPSIS

The story of the curse on the Murgatroyds, Baronets of Ruddigore, is related by the elderly Dame Hannah who was betrothed to the late Sir Roderic until she discovered his identity. The first baronet burned a witch, and in revenge she declared each succeeding baronet must commit one crime a day or die.

The opera centres round Rose Maybud, an orphan, found with her book of etiquette in a plated dish-cover hung on the knocker of the workhouse door. A Chorus of Professional Bridesmaids awaits her wedding day; but although she is the prettiest girl in the village, Rose's inhibitions, created by the book—her mentor—forbid any male overtures. She will not confess her love for Robin Oakapple. In her waltz, 'If somebody there chance to be', her proposed advances are always halted by the 'don'ts' of her book. Robin, shy and retiring, is afraid to woo Rose, but eventually in 'I know a youth who loves a little maid' there is an exchange of words when each lover, in nursery-rhyme style, pretends to seek advice from the other on behalf of a third party.

Disguised as a farmer, Robin is in fact Sir Ruthven Murgatroyd, the present Baronet of Ruddigore who fled from home twenty years previously to escape the curse that must fall on him at his uncle's—Sir Roderic's—death. Ten years ago, Robin's brother Despard inherited the title, believing Robin dead.

Now general rejoicing heralds the arrival of Richard Dauntless, Robin's sailor step-brother. Richard introduces a collection of sea-songs that matches Sir Henry Wood's. 'The Bold Mounseer', a riproaring shanty, leads into a light 'Jack's the Lad' hornpipe which almost surpasses the real thing. An interlude for Robin 'My boy you may take it from me' follows in the same nautical vein although Robin is airing his intellectual talents. This song is reintroduced in variation by Richard in Act II.

Robin tells Richard of his hopeless love for Rose, and Richard offers to woo her, on Robin's behalf. But on seeing Rose, Richard decides to take her himself, and a sailor's love song 'The Battle's roar is over, oh my love' unites them. Robin, seeing them together, thinks that Rose has been won for him and unhesitatingly embraces her. At every anticipated match, the Professional Bridesmaids appear to give chirpy greeting to the happy pair, transferring allegiance as required and exasperating Robin. Finding that he must now compete for Rose, Robin's inhibitions all vanish as he pursues a subtle campaign against Richard. In an Offenbach-like trio with Richard and Rose 'My heart says ...', Robin convinces Rose of his superior assets and wins her back.

The arrival of Sir Despard with his 'huntin'' Bucks and Blades is heralded by Mad Margaret. Her prelude, 'Merrily carols the lark' is a miniature

The Bucks and Blades, officers from a wide variety of regiments in the correct dress uniforms of 1815. *Illustrated Sporting & Dramatic News*, 26 February 1887.

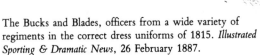

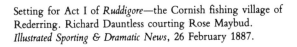

Setting for Act I of *Ruddigore*—the Cornish fishing village of Rederring. Richard Dauntless courting Rose Maybud. *Illustrated Sporting & Dramatic News*, 26 February 1887.

English masterpiece of a mad scene, parody or no. Her subsequent Mendelssohnian 'To a garden full of posies' takes the favourite downtrodden violet symbol originated by Goethe, and compares it with the preferable Rose.

Threatening to kill Rose for stealing her lover, Margaret warns her that Sir Despard has intentions on her. In fact Sir Despard's intended crime for the day is to abduct Rose (for which he means to atone by erecting a cathedral). But Richard waylays him and betrays Robin as Ruthven, Despard's elder brother. The following duet, 'You understand? - I think I do', is in the nature of a children's singing game.

Robin and Rose are about to be married. The assembled company rejoice in a madrigal with a distinctly Elizabethan flavour, 'When the buds are blossoming', and dance to a gavotte in the style of Purcell. Suddenly Sir Despard storms in and declares Robin to be the rightful heir to Ruddigore. Rose flies to Sir Despard, but his affections are with Margaret, so Richard reclaims Rose. The Bridesmaids chorus relentlessly as Robin bemoans his cursed fate, and amid general rejoicing to an Irish jig, he falls senseless as the act ends.

In the portrait gallery at Ruddigore Castle, Robin and his faithful old retainer, Adam, regret the dreadful change that has come over them. They adopt the guise of pantomime demons and hatch evil plots which they do not, however, wish to put into practice.

Rose and Richard arrive with the inevitable Bridesmaids to ask permission to marry. Rose is saved from Robin's abduction plan by Richard's waving a protective Union Jack. Rose's nostalgic and hymnlike farewell plea to Robin, 'In bygone days', harks back melodically to 'I know a youth...' Robin yields and consents to Rose's marriage with Richard.

Robin prays to the portraits of his ancestors for mercy, but they descend from their frames, rebuking him. Their dirge, 'Painted emblems ...' starts with the first two bars of 'Onward, Christian Soldiers' in the minor mode, making it also sound like the start to the middle section of Schubert's song, 'Der Wanderer'.

Last of all, the late Sir Roderic descends and, refusing to accept Robin's compassion, declares that—contrary to belief—the ghosts lead an enjoyable social life. In vampire costume Sir Roderic delivers the gruesome 'When the night wind howls'. The macabre words are accompanied by

George Grossmith, Robin Oakapple tortured by his ancestors.

'We only cut respectable capers.' Fred Billington, Sir Despard and Kate Forster, Mad Margaret in the production which left for New York in 1887. The semi-reformed Mad Margaret still holds up her farmyard pattens.

ingenious instrumental effects for wind and percussion. Robin has to submit to an inquisition on his week's crime, which amounts to very little. Fortunately, the ghosts, being 'foggy', accept—if somewhat grudgingly—Robin's slender defence of his misdeeds. Sir Roderic is not at all satisfied and now commands Robin, on pain of death, to abduct a maiden—immediately. When Robin hesitates, he is invisibly tortured. At last he gives in and Adam is sent to carry out the abduction.

Meanwhile Sir Despard and Margaret, now dressed as religious reformers, arrive to convert Robin. They are finding life somewhat dull and their 'fantastic' dance, 'I once was a very abandoned person', recalls former days when the scandals surrounding them 'got into all the papers'. They are trying a method of controlling Margaret's mad flights: the word 'Basingstoke' seems to have a sedative effect.

Despard reminds Robin that he must take responsibility for the wicked deeds of the past ten years. At this, Robin decides to defy his ancestors

and die if necessary. The patter-trio, 'It really doesn't matter', is enhanced by the crazy verse for Mad Margaret and the demolishing rejoinder, 'her opinion doesn't matter'.

Adam returns with a maiden—the furious Dame Hannah. She hands Robin a dagger and challenges him to a fight. Terrified, he calls on Sir Roderic who emerges from his frame and discovers his 'little Nannikin', his youthful love. Hannah tearfully confesses her undying love for him in her song, 'The Great Oak Tree'—a variation on Margaret's violet theme. In the reunion of the old couple, Robin's predicament is forgotten.

But Robin finds a solution to the curse. To disobey the ancestors amounts to suicide: suicide is illegal, so all the deaths for disobedience were invalid. Robin, no longer a bad baronet, once more takes Rose from Richard—he is content with another girl. Roderic and Hannah are united, and before the repeat of the little jig which formed the first finale, Despard and Margaret decide to move to the calmer air of Basingstoke.

RUDDIGORE;

OR

THE WITCH'S CURSE.

AN ENTIRELY ORIGINAL SUPERNATURAL OPERA,

IN TWO ACTS.

First produced at the Savoy Theatre, 22 January 1887

DRAMATIS PERSONÆ

MORTALS.

ROBIN OAKAPPLE [*a Young Farmer*]	baritone
RICHARD DAUNTLESS [*his Foster-brother—a Man-o'-war's-man*]	tenor
SIR DESPARD MURGATROYD [*of Ruddigore—a Wicked Baronet*]	baritone
OLD ADAM GOODHEART [*Robin's Faithful Servant*]	bass
ROSE MAYBUD [*a Village Maiden*]	soprano
MAD MARGARET	soprano
DAME HANNAH [*Rose's Aunt*]	contralto
ZORAH } RUTH } [*Professional Bridesmaids*]	sopranos

GHOSTS.

SIR RUPERT MURGATROYD [*the First Baronet*]

SIR JASPER MURGATROYD [*the Third Baronet*]

SIR LIONEL MURGATROYD [*the Sixth Baronet*]

SIR CONRAD MURGATROYD [*the Twelfth Baronet*]

SIR DESMOND MURGATROYD [*the Sixteenth Baronet*]

SIR GILBERT MURGATROYD [*the Eighteenth Baronet*]

SIR MERVYN MURGATROYD [*the Twentieth Baronet*]

SIR RODERIC MURGATROYD [*the Twenty-first Baronet*]

Chorus of Officers, Ancestors, and Professional Bridesmaids.

ACT I.

THE FISHING VILLAGE OF REDERRING, IN CORNWALL.

ACT II.

PICTURE GALLERY IN RUDDIGORE CASTLE.

TIME—EARLY IN THE PRESENT CENTURY.

RUDDIGORE;

OR,

THE WITCH'S CURSE.

ACT I.

SCENE.—*The fishing village of Rederring (in Cornwall).*
ROSE MAYBUD'S *cottage is seen.*

Enter CHORUS OF BRIDESMAIDS. *They range themselves in front of*
ROSE'S *cottage.*

CHORUS OF BRIDESMAIDS.

Fair is Rose as the bright May-day;
  Soft is Rose as the warm west-wind;
Sweet is Rose as the new-mown hay—
  Rose is the queen of maiden-kind!
    Rose, all glowing
      With virgin blushes, say—
    Is anybody going
      To marry you to-day?

SOLO.—ZORAH.

Every day, as the days roll on,
Bridesmaids' garb we gaily don,
Sure that a maid so fairly famed
Won't very long remain unclaimed.
Hour by hour, and day by day,
Several months have passed away.
And though she's the fairest flower that blows,
Nobody, yet has married Rose!

CHORUS.

Rose, all glowing
  With virgin blushes, say—
Is anybody going
  To marry you to-day?

Enter OLD HANNAH, *from cottage.*

HAN. Nay, gentle maidens, you sing well but vainly, for Rose is still heart-free, and looks but coldly upon her many suitors.

ZOR. It's very disappointing. Every young man in the village is in love with her, but they are appalled by her beauty and modesty, and won't declare themselves; so, until she makes her own choice, there's no chance for anybody else.

RUTH. This is, perhaps, the only village in the world that possesses an endowed corps of professional bridesmaids who are bound to be on duty every day from ten to four—and it is at least six months since our services were required. The pious charity by which we exist is practically wasted!

ZOR. We shall be disendowed—that will be the end of it! Dame Hannah—you're a nice old person—*you* could marry if you liked. There's old Adam—Robin's faithful servant—he loves you with all the frenzy of a boy of fourteen.

HAN. Nay—that may never be, for I am pledged!

ALL. To whom?

HAN. To an eternal maidenhood! Many years ago I was betrothed to a god-like youth who woo'd me under an assumed name. But on the very day upon which our wedding was to have been celebrated, I discovered that he was no other than Sir Roderic Murgatroyd, one of the bad Baronets of Ruddigore, and the uncle of the man who now bears that title. As a son of that accursed race he was no husband for an honest girl, so, madly as I loved him, I left him then and there. He died but ten years since, but I never saw him again.

ZOR. But why should you not marry a bad Baronet of Ruddigore?

RUTH. All baronets are bad; but was he worse than other baronets?

HAN. My child, he was accursed.

ZOR. But who cursed him? Not you, I trust!

HAN. The curse is on all his line, and has been ever since the time of Sir Rupert, the first Baronet. Listen, and you shall hear the legend.

LEGEND.—HANNAH.

Sir Rupert Murgatroyd
   His leisure and his riches
He ruthlessly employed
   In persecuting witches.
With fear he'd make them quake—
He'd duck them in his lake—
   He'd break their bones
   With sticks and stones,
And burn them at the stake!

CHORUS.   This sport he much enjoyed,
   Did Rupert Murgatroyd—
     No sense of shame
     Or pity came
   To Rupert Murgatroyd!

Once, on the village green,
   A palsied hag he roasted,
And what took place, I ween,
   Shook his composure boasted;
For, as the torture grim
Seized on each withered limb,
   The writhing dame,
   'Mid fire and flame,
Yelled forth this curse on him:—

"Each lord of Ruddigore,
   Despite his best endeavour,
Shall do one crime, or more,
   Once, every day, for ever!
This doom he can't defy
However he may try,
   For should he stay
   His hand, that day
In torture he shall die!"

The prophecy came true:
   Each heir who held the title
Had, every day, to do
   Some crime of import vital;
Until, with guilt o'erplied,
"I'll sin no more!" he cried,
   And on the day
   He said that say,
In agony he died!

CHORUS.   And thus, with sinning cloyed,
   Has died each Murgatroyd,
     And so shall fall,
     Both one and all,
   Each coming Murgatroyd!

[*Exeunt* CHORUS OF BRIDESMAIDS.

Enter ROSE MAYBUD *from cottage, with small basket on her arm.*

HAN. Whither away, dear Rose? On some errand of charity, as is thy wont?

ROSE. A few gifts, dear aunt, for deserving villagers. Lo, here is some peppermint rock for old gaffer Gadderby, a set of false teeth for pretty little Ruth Rowbottom, and a pound of snuff for the poor ophan girl on the hill.

HAN. Ah, Rose, pity that so much goodness should not help to make some gallant youth happy for life! Rose, why dost thou harden that little heart of thine? Is there none hereaway whom thou couldst love?

ROSE. And if there were such an one, verily it would ill become me to tell him so.

HAN. Nay, dear one, where true love is, there is little need of prim formality.

ROSE. Hush, dear aunt, for thy words pain me sorely. Hung in a plated dish-cover to the knocker of the workhouse door, with nought that I could call mine own, save a change of baby-linen and a book of etiquette, little wonder if I have always regarded that work as a voice from a parent's tomb. This hallowed volume (*producing a book of etiquette*), composed, if I may believe the title-page, by no less an authority than the wife of a Lord Mayor, has been, through life, my guide and monitor. By its solemn precepts I have learnt to test the moral worth of all who approach me. The man who bites his bread, or eats peas with a knife, I look upon as a lost creature, and he who has not acquired the proper way of entering and leaving a room is the object of my pitying horror. There are those in this village who bite their nails, dear aunt, and nearly all are wont to use their pocket-combs in public places. In truth I could pursue this painful theme much further, but behold, I have said enough.

HAN. But is there not one among them who is faultless, in thine eyes? For example—young Robin. He combines the manners of a Marquis with the morals of a Methodist. Couldst thou not love *him*?

ROSE. And even if I could, how should I confess it unto him? For lo, he is shy, and sayeth nought!

BALLAD.—ROSE.

If somebody there chanced to be
   Who loved me in a manner true,
My heart would point him out to me,
   And I would point him out to you.

(Referring to book.) But here it says of those who point,
>> Their manners must be out of joint—
>> You *may* not point—
>> You *must* not point—
>> It's manners out of joint, to point!

>> Had I the love of such as he,
>> Some quiet spot he'd take me to,
>> Then he could whisper it to me,
>> And I could whisper it to you;
(Referring to book.) But whispering, I've somewhere met,
>> Is contrary to etiquette:
>> Where can it be? *(Searching book.)*
>> Now let me see— *(Finding reference.)*
>> Yes, Yes!
>> It's contrary to etiquette!
>>>> [*Showing it to* HANNAH.

>> If any well-bred youth I knew,
>> Polite and gentle, neat and trim,
>> Then I would hint as much to you,
>> And you could hint as much to him.
(Referring to book.) But here it says, in plainest print,
>> "It's most unladylike to hint"—
>> You *may* not hint,
>> You *must* not hint—
>> It says you mustn't hint, in print!
>> And if I loved him through and through—

>> (True love and not a passing whim),
>> Then I could speak of it to you,
>> And you could speak of it to him.
>> But here I find it doesn't do
>> To speak until you're spoken to.
(Referring to book.) Where can it be? *(Searching book.)*
>> Now let me see— *(Finding reference.)*
>> "Don't speak until you're spoken to"!
>>>> [*Exit* HANNAH.

ROSE. Poor aunt! Little did the good soul think, when she breathed the hallowed name of Robin, that he would do even as well as another. But he resembleth all the youths in this village, in that he is unduly bashful in my presence, and lo, it is hard to bring him to the point. But soft, he is here!
>>> [ROSE *is about to go when* ROBIN *enters and calls her.*

ROB. Mistress Rose!

ROSE *(surprised)*. Master Robin!

ROB. I wished to say that—it is fine.

ROSE. It is passing fine.

ROB. But we do want rain.

ROSE. Ay, sorely! Is that all?

ROB. *(sighing)*. That is all.

ROSE. Good day, Master Robin!

ROB. Good day, Mistress Rose! *(Both going—both stop.)*

ROSE.   I crave pardon, I—

ROB.   I beg pardon, I—

ROSE. You were about to say?

ROB. I would fain consult you.

ROSE. Truly?

ROB. It is about a friend.

ROSE. In truth I have a friend myself.

ROB. Indeed? I mean, of course—

ROSE. And I would fain consult you—

ROB. *(anxiously)*. About him?

ROSE *(prudishly)*. About her.

ROB. *(relieved)*. Let us consult one another.

DUET.—ROBIN *and* ROSE.

ROB. I know a youth who loves a little maid—
>> (Hey, but his face is a sight for to see!)
>> Silent is he, for he's modest and afraid—
>> (Hey, but he's timid as a youth can be!)

ROSE. I know a maid who loves a gallant youth,
>> (Hey, but she sickens as the days go by!)
>> She cannot tell him all the sad, sad truth—
>> (Hey, but I think that little maid will die!)

ROB.   Poor little man!
ROSE.   Poor little maid!
ROB.   Poor little man!
ROSE.   Poor little maid!

BOTH. Now, tell me pray, and tell me true,
>> What in the world should the $\left\{ \begin{array}{l} \text{young man} \\ \text{maiden} \end{array} \right\}$ do?

ROB. He cannot eat and he cannot sleep—
>> (Hey, but his face is a sight for to see!)
>> Daily he goes for to wail—for to weep
>> (Hey, but he's wretched as a youth can be!)

ROSE. She's very thin and she's very pale—
>> (Hey, but she sickens as the days go by!)
>> Daily she goes for to weep—for to wail—
>> (Hey, but I think that little maid will die!)

ROB.   Poor little maid!
ROSE.   Poor little man!
ROB.   Poor little maid!
ROSE.   Poor little man!

BOTH. Now, tell me pray, and tell me true,
>> What in the world should the $\left\{ \begin{array}{l} \text{young man} \\ \text{maiden} \end{array} \right\}$ do?

ROSE. If I were the youth I should offer her my name—
>> (Hey, but her face is a sight for to see!)

ROB. If I were the maid I should feed his honest flame—
>> (Hey, but he's bashful as a youth can be!)

ROSE. If I were the youth I should speak to her to-day—
>> (Hey, but she sickens as the days go by!)

ROB. If I were the maid I should meet the lad half way—
>> (For I really do believe that timid youth will die!)

ROSE.   Poor little man!
ROB.   Poor little maid!
ROSE.   Poor little man!
ROB.   Poor little maid!

BOTH. I thank you, $\left\{ \begin{array}{l} \text{miss,} \\ \text{sir,} \end{array} \right\}$ for your counsel true;
>> I'll tell that $\left\{ \begin{array}{l} \text{youth} \\ \text{maid} \end{array} \right\}$ what $\left\{ \begin{array}{l} \text{he} \\ \text{she} \end{array} \right\}$ ought to do!

[Exit ROSE.

ROB. Poor child! I sometimes think that if she wasn't quite so particular I might venture—but no, no—even then I should be unworthy of her! *[He sits desponding.*

Enter OLD ADAM.

ADAM. My kind master is sad! Dear Sir Ruthven Murgatroyd—

ROB. Hush! As you love me, breathe not that hated name. Twenty years ago, in horror at the prospect of inheriting that hideous title, and with it the ban that compels all who succeed to the baronetcy to commit at least one deadly crime per day, for life, I fled my home, and concealed myself in this innocent village under the name of Robin Oakapple. My younger brother, Despard, believing me to be dead, succeeded to the title and its attendant curse. For twenty years I have been dead and buried. Don't dig me up now.

ADAM. Dear master, it shall be as you wish, for have I not sworn to obey you for ever in all things? Yet, as we are here alone, and as I belong to that particular description of good old man to whom the truth is a refreshing novelty, let me call you by your own right title once more! *(*ROBIN *assents.)* Sir Ruthven Murgatroyd! Baronet! Of Ruddigore! Whew! It's like eight hours at the seaside!

ROB. My poor old friend! Would there were more like you!

ADAM. Would there were indeed! But I bring you good tidings. Your foster-brother, Richard, has returned from sea—his ship the *Tom-Tit* rides yonder at anchor, and he himself is even now in this very village!

ROB. My beloved foster-brother? No, no—it cannot be!

ADAM. It is even so—and see, he comes this way!

Enter CHORUS OF BRIDESMAIDS.

CHORUS.

From the briny sea
Comes young Richard, all victorious!
Valorous is he—
His achievements all are glorious!
Let the welkin ring
With the news we bring
Sing it—shout it—
Tell about it—
Safe and sound returneth he!
All victorious from the sea!

Enter RICHARD. *The* GIRLS *welcome him as he greets old acquaintances.*

BALLAD.—RICHARD.

I shipped, d'ye see, in a Revenue sloop,
And, off Cape Finistere,
A merchantman we see,
A Frenchman, going free,
So we made for the bold Mounseer.
D'ye see?
We made for the bold Mounseer.
But she proved to be a Frigate—and she up with her ports,
And fires with a thirty-two!

It comes uncommon near,
But we answered a cheer,
Which paralyzed the Parly-voo,
D'ye see?
Which paralyzed the Parly-voo!

Then our Captain he up and he says, says he,
"That chap we need not fear—
We can take her, if we like,
She is sartin for to strike,
For she's only a darned Mounseer,
D'ye see?
She's only a darned Mounseer!
But to fight a French fal-lal—it's like hittin' of a gal—
It's a lubberly thing for to do;
For we, with all our faults,
Why, we're sturdy British salts,
While she's only a Parley-voo,
D'ye see?
A miserable Parley-voo!"

So we up with our helm, and we scuds before the breeze,
As we gives a compassionating cheer;
Froggee answers with a shout
As he sees us go about,
Which was grateful of the poor Mounseer,
D'ye see?
Which was grateful of the poor Mounseer!
And I'll wager in their joy they kissed each other's cheek
(Which is what them furriners do),
And they blessed their lucky stars
We were hardy British tars
Who had pity on a poor Parley-voo,
D'ye see?
Who had pity on a poor Parley-voo!

[Exeunt CHORUS, *as* ROBIN *comes forward.*

ROB. Richard!

RICH. Robin!

ROB. My beloved foster-brother, and very dearest friend welcome home again after ten long years at sea! It is such deeds as you have just described that cause our flag to be loved and dreaded throughout the civilized world!

RICH. Why, lord love ye, Rob, that's but a trifle to what we *have* done in the way of sparing life. I believe I may say, without exaggeration, that the marciful little *Tom-Tit* has spared more French frigates than any craft afloat! But 'taint for a British seaman to brag, so I'll just stow my jawin' tackle and belay. *(*ROBIN *sighs.)* But 'vast heavin', messmate, what's brought *you* all a-cockbill?

ROB. Alas, Dick, I love Rose Maybud, and love in vain!

RICH. *You* love in vain? Come, that's too good! Why you're a fine strapping muscular young fellow—tall and strong as a to'-gall'n-m'st—taut as a fore-stay—ay, and a barrow-knight to boot, if all had their rights!

ROB. Hush, Richard—not a word about my true rank, which

none here suspect. Yes, I know well enough that few men are better calculated to win a woman's heart than I. I'm a fine fellow, Dick, and worthy any woman's love—happy the girl who gets me, say I. But I'm timid, Dick; shy, nervous, modest, retiring, diffident, and I cannot tell her, Dick, I cannot tell her! Ah, you've no idea what a poor opinion I have of myself, and how little I deserve it.

RICH. Robin, do you call to mind how, years ago, we swore that, come what might, we would always act upon our hearts' dictates?

ROB. Ay, Dick, and I've always kept that oath. In doubt, difficulty, and danger, I've always asked my heart what I should do, and it has never failed me.

RICH. Right! Let your heart be your compass, with a clear conscience for your binnacle light, and you'll sail ten knots on a bowline, clear of shoals, rocks, and quicksands! Well now, what does my heart say in this here difficult situation? Why, it says, "Dick," it says—(it calls me "Dick" acos its known me from a babby)—"Dick," it says, "*you* ain't shy—*you* ain't modest—speak you up for him as is!" Robin, my lad, just you lay me alongside, and when she's becalmed under my lee, I'll spin her a yarn that shall sarve to fish you two together for life!

ROB. Will you do this thing for me? Can you, do you think? Yes. (*Feeling his pulse.*) There's no false modesty about *you*. Your, what I would call bumptious self-assertiveness (I mean the expression in its complimentary sense), has already made you a bos'n's mate, and it will make an admiral of you in time, if you work it properly, you dear, incompetent old imposter! My dear fellow, I'd give my right arm for one tenth of your modest assurance!

SONG.—ROBIN.

My boy, you may take it from me
That, of all the afflictions accurst
　　With which a man's saddled
　　And hampered and addled,
A diffident nature's the worst.
Though clever as clever can be—
　　A Crichton of early romance—
　　　　You must stir it and stump it,
　　　　And blow your own trumpet,
　　Or, trust me, you haven't a chance,
　　If you wish in the world to advance,
　　Your merits you're bound to enhance,
　　　　You must stir it and stump it,
　　　　And blow your own trumpet,
　　Or, trust me, you haven't a chance!

Now, take, for example, *my* case:
　　I've a bright intellectual brain—
　　　　In all London city
　　　　There's no one so witty—
　　I've thought so again and again.
I've a highly intelligent face—
　　My features cannot be denied—
　　　　But, whatever I try, sir?
　　　　I fail in—and why, sir?
　　I'm modesty personified!
　　If you wish in the world to advance, etc.

As a poet, I'm tender and quaint—
　　　　I've passion and fervour and grace—
　　　　　　From Ovid and Horace
　　　　　　To Swinburne and Morris,
　　　　They all of them take a back place.
Then I sing and I play and I paint:
　　　　Though none are accomplished as I,
　　　　　　To say so were treason:
　　　　　　You ask me the reason?
　　　　I'm diffident, modest, and shy!
　　　　　　If you wish in the world to advance, etc.
　　　　　　　　　　　　　　　　[*Exit* ROBIN.

RICH. (*looking after him*). Ah, it's a thousand pities he's such a poor opinion of himself, for a finer fellow don't walk! Well, I'll do my best for him. "Plead for him as though it was for your own father"—that's what my heart's a remarkin' to me just now. But, here she comes! Steady! Steady it is!

Enter ROSE—*he is much struck by her.*

By the Port Admiral, but she's a tight little craft! Come, come, she's not for you, Dick, and yet—she's fit to marry Lord Nelson! By the Flag of Old England, I can't look at her unmoved.

ROSE. Sir, you are agitated.

RICH. Ay, ay, my lass, well said! I am agitated, true enough!—took flat aback, my girl; but 'tis naught—'twill pass. (*Aside.*) This here heart of mine's a dictatin' to me like anythink. Question is, have I a right to disregard its promptings?

ROSE. Can I do aught to relieve thine anguish, for it seemeth to me that thou art in sore trouble? This apple— (*Offering a damaged apple.*)

RICH. (*looking at it and returning it*). No, my lass, 'taint that. I'm—I'm took flat aback—I never see anything like you in all my born days. Parbuckle me, if you ain't the loveliest gal I've ever set eyes on. There—I can't say fairer than that, can I?

ROSE. No. (*Aside.*) The question is, is it meet that an utter stranger should thus express himself? (*Refers to book.*) Yes,—"Always speak the truth."

RICH. I'd no thoughts of sayin' this here to you on my own account, for, truth to tell, I was chartered by another; but when I see you my heart it up and it says, says it, "This is the very lass for *you*, Dick—speak up to her, Dick," it says—(it calls me Dick acos we was at school together)—"tell her all, Dick," it says, "never sail under false colours—it's mean!" *That's* what my heart tells me to say, and in my rough, common-sailor fashion, I've said it, and I'm a-waiting for your reply. I'm a tremblin', miss. Lookye here. (*Holding out his hand.*) That's narvousness!

ROSE (*aside*). Now, how should a maiden deal with such an one? (*Consults book.*) "Keep no one in unnecessary suspense." (*Aloud.*) Behold, I will not keep you in unnecessary suspense. (*Refers to book.*) "In accepting an offer of marriage, do so with apparent hesitation." (*Aloud.*) I take you, but with a certain show of reluctance. (*Refers to book.*) "Avoid any appearance of eagerness." (*Aloud.*) Though you will bear in mind that I am far from anxious to do so. (*Refers to book.*) "A little show of emotion will not be misplaced!" (*Aloud.*) Pardon this tear! (*Wipes her eye.*)

RICH. Rose, you've made me the happiest blue-jacket in England! I wouldn't change places with the Admiral of the Fleet, no matter who he's a huggin' of at this present moment! But, axin' your pardon, miss (*wiping his lips with his hand*), might I be permitted to salute the flag I'm a-goin' to sail under?

ROSE (*referring to book*). "An engaged young lady should not permit too many familiarities.'' *(Aloud.)* Once! (RICHARD *kisses her.)*

DUET.—RICHARD *and* ROSE.

RICH.
    The battle's roar is over,
        O my love!
    Embrace thy tender lover,
        O my love!
    From tempests' welter,
        From war's alarms,
    O give me shelter
        Within those arms!
    Thy smile alluring,
    All heart-ache curing,
    Gives peace enduring,
        O my love!

ROSE.
    If heart both true and tender,
        O my love!
    A life-love can engender,
        O my love!
    A truce to sighing
        And tears of brine,
    For joy undying
        Shall aye be mine,
    And thou and I, love,
    Shall live and die, love,
    Without a sigh, love—
        My own, my love!

Enter ROBIN, *with* CHORUS OF BRIDESMAIDS.

CHORUS.

If well his suit has sped,
Oh, may they soon be wed!
Oh, tell us, tell us, pray,
What doth the maiden say?
In singing are we justified,
''Hail the Bridegroom—hail the Bride''?

ROB. Well—what news? Have you spoken to her?
RICH. Ay, my lad, I have—so to speak—spoke her.
ROB. And she refuses?
RICH. Why, no, I can't truly say she do.
ROB. Then she accepts! My darling! *(Embraces her.)*

BRIDESMAIDS.

Hail the Bridegroom—hail the Bride!
Let the nuptial knot be tied:
    In fair phrases
    Hymn their praises,
Hail the Bridegroom—hail the Bride!

ROSE *(aside, referring to her book).* Now, what should a maiden do when she is embraced by the wrong gentleman?
RICH. Belay, my lad, belay. You don't understand.
ROSE. Oh, sir, belay, I beseech you!
RICH. You see, it's like this: she accepts—but it's *me!*
ROB. You!   [RICHARD *embraces* ROSE.

BRIDESMAIDS.

Hail the Bridegroom—hail the Bride!
When the nuptial knot is tied

ROB. *(interrupting angrily).* Hold your tongues, will you! Now then, what does this mean?
RICH. My poor lad, my heart grieves for thee; but it's like this: the moment I see her, and just as I was a-goin' to mention your name, my heart it up and it says, says it, ''Dick, you've fell in love with her yourself,'' it says. ''Be honest and sailor-like—don't skulk under false colours—speak up,'' it says, ''take her, you dog, and with her my blessin'!''

BRIDESMAIDS.

''Hail the Bridegroom—hail the Bride!''

ROB. Will you be quiet! Go away! (CHORUS *make faces at him and exeunt.)* Vulgar girls!
RICH. What could I do? I'm bound to obey my heart's dictates.
ROB. Of course—no doubt. It's quite right—I don't mind—that is, not particularly—only it's—it *is* disappointing, you know.
ROSE *(to* ROBIN). Oh, but, sir, I knew not that thou didst seek me in wedlock, or in very truth I should not have hearkened unto this man, for behold, he is but a lowly mariner, and very poor withal, whereas thou art a tiller of the land, and thou hast fat oxen, and many sheep and swine, a considerable dairy farm, and much corn and oil!
RICH. That's true, my lass; but it's done now, ain't it, Rob?
ROSE. Still it maybe that I should not be happy in thy love. I am passing young, and little able to judge. Moreover, as to thy character I know naught!
ROB. Nay, Rose, I'll answer for that. Dick has won thy love fairly. Broken-hearted as I am, I'll stand up for Dick through thick and thin!
DICK *(with emotion).* Thankye, messmate! that's well said. That's spoken honest. Thankye, Rob! *(Grasps his hand.)*
ROSE. Yet methinks I have heard that sailors are but wordly men, and little prone to lead serious and thoughtful lives!
ROB. And what then? Admit that Dick is *not* a steady character, and that when he's excited he uses language that would make your hair curl.—Grant that—he does. It's the truth, and I'm not going to deny it. But look at his *good* qualities. He's as nimble as a pony, and his hornpipe is the talk of the fleet!
RICH. Thankye, Rob! That's well spoken. Thankye Rob!
ROSE. But it maybe that he drinketh strong waters which do bemuse a man, and make him even as the wild beasts of the desert!
ROB. Well, suppose he does, and I don't say he don't, for rum's his bane, and ever has been. He *does* drink—I won't deny it. But what of it. Look at his arms—tattooed to the shoulder! (DICK *rolls up his sleeves.)* No, no—I won't hear a word against Dick!
ROSE. But they say that mariners are but rarely true to those whom they profess to love!
ROB. Granted—granted—and I don't say that Dick isn't as bad as any of 'em. (DICK *chuckles.)* You are, you know you are, you dog! a devil of a fellow—a regular out-and-out Lothario! But what then? You can't have everything, and a better hand at

Eileen Gourlay as Katisha and Murray Melvin as Ko-Ko in a *Bab*-inspired
Mikado at the Theatre Royal, Plymouth and the Cambridge Theatre,
London in 1982. Sets and costumes by Sean Kavanagh.

Set design for Act I of *Princess Ida* by W. Bridges-Adams, first given in a new production at the Princes Theatre, London in December 1920 under Geoffrey Toye. The opera had not been heard in London since its first production in 1884.

Set design for Act II of *Ruddigore* by W. Bridges-Adams in 1927. Compare the idea with that in Gilbert's *Ages Ago* of 1869 (see page 67).

turning-in a dead-eye don't walk a deck! And what an accomplishment *that* is in a family man! No, no—not a word against Dick. I'll stick up for him through thick and thin!

RICH. Thankye, Rob, thankye. You're a true friend. I've acted accordin' to my heart's dictates, and such orders as them no man should disobey.

ENSEMBLE.—RICHARD, ROBIN, ROSE.

In sailing o'er life's ocean wide
Your heart should be your only guide;
With summer sea and favouring wind
Yourself in port you'll surely find.

SOLO.—RICHARD.

My heart says, "To this maiden strike—
　　She's captured you.
She's just the sort of girl you like—
　　You know you do.
If other man her heart should gain,
　　I shall resign."
That's what it says to me quite plain,
　　This heart of mine.

SOLO.—ROBIN.

My heart says, "You've a prosperous lot,
　　With acres wide;
You mean to settle all you've got
　　Upon your bride.
It don't pretend to shape my acts
　　By word or sign;
It merely states these simple facts,
　　This heart of mine!

SOLO.—ROSE.

Ten minutes since my heart said "white"—
　　It now says "black."
It then said "left"—it now says "right"—
　　Hearts often tack.
I must obey its latest strain—
　　You tell me so.　　　　[*To* RICHARD.
But should it change its mind again,
　　I'll let you know.
　　[*Turning from* RICHARD *to* ROBIN *who embraces her.*

ENSEMBLE.

In sailing o'er life's ocean wide
No doubt the heart should be your guide,
But it is awkward when you find
A heart that does not know its mind!
　　[*Exeunt* ROBIN *with* ROSE *and* RICHARD, *weeping.*

Enter MAD MARGARET. *She is wildly dressed in picturesque tatters, and is an obvious caricature of theatrical madness.*

SCENA.—MARGARET.

Cheerily carols the lark
　　Over the cot.

Merrily whistles the clerk
　　Scratching a blot.
　　　But the lark
　　　And the clerk,
　　　I remark,
　　Comfort me not!

Over the ripening peach
　　Buzzes the bee.
Splash on the billowy beach
　　Tumbles the sea.
　　　But the peach
　　　And the beach
　　　They are each
　　Nothing to me!

　　And why?
　　Who am I?
Daft Madge! Crazy Meg!
Mad Margaret! Poor Peg!
He! he! he! he! he! *(Chuckling.)*

　　Mad, I?
　　　Yes, very!
　　But why?
　　　Mystery!
　　　　Don't call!
　　　　　Whisht! whisht!

No crime—
　　'Tis only
That I'm
　　Love—lonely!
　　　That's all!
　　　　Whisht! whisht!

BALLAD.

To a garden full of posies
　　Cometh one to gather flowers,
　　And he wanders through its bowers
Toying with the wanton roses,
　　Who, uprising from their beds,
　　Hold on high their shameless heads,
With their pretty lips a-pouting,
Never doubting—never doubting
　　That for Cytherean posies
　　He would gather aught but roses!

In a nest of weeds and nettles,
　　Lay a violet, half-hidden,
　　Hoping that his glance unbidden
Yet might fall upon her petals,
　　Though she lived alone, apart,
　　Hope lay nestling at her heart,
But, alas, the cruel awakening
Set her little heart abreaking,
　　For he gathered for his posies
　　Only roses—only roses!　　[*Bursts into tears.*

Enter ROSE.

ROSE. A maiden, and in tears? Can I do aught to soften thy sorrow? This apple— *(Offering apple.)*

MAR. *(examines it and rejects it).* No! *(Mysteriously.)* Tell me, are you mad?

ROSE. I? No! That is, I think not.

MAR. That's well! Then you don't love Sir Despard Murgatroyd? All mad girls love him. *I* love him. I'm poor Mad Margaret—Crazy Meg—Poor Peg! He! he! he! he! *(Chuckling.)*

ROSE. Thou lovest the bad Baronet of Ruddigore? Oh, horrible—too horrible?

MAR. You pity me? Then be my mother! The squirrel had a mother; but she drank, and the squirrel fled! Hush! They sing a brave song in our parts—it runs somewhat thus:— *(Sings.)*

"The cat and the dog and the little puppee
Sat down in a—down in a—in a—"

I forget what they sat down in, but so the song goes! Listen—I've come to pinch her!

ROSE. Mercy, whom!

MAR. You mean "who."

ROSE. Nay! it is the accusative after the verb.

MAR. True. *(Whispers melodramatically.)* I have come to pinch Rose Maybud!

ROSE *(aside, alarmed).* Rose Maybud!

MAR. Ay! I love him—he loved me once. But that's all gone. Fisht! He gave me an Italian glance—thus—*(Business.)*—and made me his. He will give *her* an Italian glance, and make *her* his. But it shall not be, for I'll stamp on her—stamp on her—stamp on her! Did you ever kill anybody? No? Why not? Listen—I killed a fly this morning! It buzzed, and I wouldn't have it. So it died—pop! So shall she!

ROSE. But behold, *I* am Rose Maybud, and I would fain not die "pop."

MAR. You are Rose Maybud!

ROSE. Yes, sweet Rose Maybud!

MAR. Strange! They told me she was beautiful! And *he* loves *you!* No, no! If I thought that, I would treat you as the auctioneer and land-agent treated the lady-bird—I would rend you asunder!

ROSE. Nay, be pacified, for behold I am pledged to another, and lo, we are to be wedded this very day!

MAR. Swear me that! Come to a Commissioner and let me have it on affidavit! *I* once made an affidavit—but it died—it died—it died! But see, they come—Sir Despard and his evil crew! Hide, hide—they are all mad—quite mad!

ROSE. What makes you think that?

MAR. Hush! They sing choruses in public. That's mad enough, I think! Go—hide away, or they will seize you. Hush! Quite softly—quite, quite softly!

[Exeunt together, on tiptoe.

Enter CHORUS OF BUCKS AND BLADES, *heralded by* CHORUS OF BRIDESMAIDS.

CHORUS OF BRIDESMAIDS.

Welcome, gentry,
For your entry
Sets our tender hearts a-beating.

Men of station,
Admiration
Prompts this unaffected greeting.
Hearty greeting offer we!

Your exceeding
Easy breeding—
Just the thing our hearts to pillage—
Cheers us, charms us,
Quite disarms us:
Welcome, welcome, to our village;
To our village welcome be

CHORUS OF BUCKS *and* BLADES.

When thoroughly tired
Of being admired
By ladies of gentle degree—degree,
With flattery sated,
High-flown and inflated,
Away from the city we flee—we flee

From charms intramural
To prettiness rural
The sudden transition
Is simply Elysian,
So come, Amaryllis,
Come, Chloe and Phyllis,
Your slaves, for the moment, are we

ALL.   From charms intramural, etc.

CHORUS OF BRIDESMAIDS.

The sons of the tillage
Who dwell in the village
Are people of lowly degree—degree.
Though honest and active
They're most unattractive,
And awkward as awkward can be—can be.
They're clumsy clodhoppers
With axes and choppers,
And shepherds and ploughmen,
And drovers and cowmen,
And hedgers and reapers,
And carters and keepers,
But never a lover for me!

ALL.   They're clumsy, clodhoppers, etc.

ALL.   So welcome, gentry
For $\left\{ \begin{array}{l} your \\ our \end{array} \right\}$ entry
Sets $\left\{ \begin{array}{l} our \\ their \end{array} \right\}$ tender hearts a-beating, etc.

Enter SIR DESPARD MURGATROYD.

SONG AND CHORUS.—SIR DESPARD.

SIR D.   Oh, why am I moody and sad?
CH.   Can't guess!

SIR D. And why am I guiltily mad?
CH. Confess!
SIR D. Because I am thoroughly bad!
CH. Oh yes—
SIR D. You'll see it at once in my face.
Oh, why am I husky and hoarse?
CH. Ah, why?
SIR D. It's the workings of conscience, of course.
CH. Fie, fie!
SIR D. And huskiness stands for remorse,
CH. Oh my!
SIR D. At least it does so in my case!

SIR D. When in crime one is fully employed—
CH. Like you—
SIR D. Your expression gets warped and destroyed:
CH. It do.
SIR D. It's a penalty none can avoid;
CH. How true!
SIR D. I once was a nice-looking youth;
But like stone from a strong catapult—
CH. *(explaining to each other).* A trice—
SIR D. I rushed at my terrible cult—
CH. *(explaining to each other).* That's vice—
SIR D. Observe the unpleasant result!
CH. Not nice.
SIR D. Indeed I am telling the truth!

SIR D. Oh, innocent, happy though poor!
CH. That's we—
SIR D. If I had been virtuous, I'm sure—
CH. Like me—
SIR D. I should be as nice-looking as you're!
CH. May be.
SIR D. You are very nice-looking indeed!
Oh, innocents, listen in time—
CH. We *doe,*
SIR D. Avoid an existence of crime—
CH. Just so—
SIR D. Or you'll be as ugly as I'm—
CH. *(loudly).* No! No!
SIR D. And now, if you please, we'll proceed.

[*All the* GIRLS *express their horror of* SIR DESPARD. *As he approaches them they fly from him, terror-stricken, leaving him alone on the stage.*

SIR D. Poor children, how they loathe me—me whose hands are certainly steeped in infamy, but whose heart is as the heart of a little child! But what *is* a poor baronet to do, when a whole picture-gallery of ancestors step down from their frames and threaten him with an excruciating death, if he hesitate to commit his daily crime? But, ha! ha! I am even with them! *(Mysteriously.)* I get my crime over the first thing in the morning, and then, ha! ha! for the rest of the day I do good—I do good—I do good! *(Melodramatically.)* Two days since, I stole a child and built an orphan asylum. Yesterday I robbed a bank and endowed a bishopric. To-day I carry off Rose Maybud, and atone with a cathedral! This is what it is to be the sport and toy of a Picture Gallery! But I will be bitterly revenged upon them! I will give them all to the Nation, and nobody shall ever look upon their faces again!

Enter RICHARD.

RICH. Ax your honour's pardon, but—
SIR D. Ha! observed! And by a mariner! What would you with me, fellow?
RICH. Your honour, I'm a poor man-o'-war's man, becalmed in the doldrums.
SIR D. I don't know them.
RICH. And I make bold to ax your honour's advice. Does your honour know what it is to have a heart?
SIR D. My honour knows what it is to have a complete apparatus for conducting the circulation of the blood through the veins and arteries of the human body.
RICH. Ay, but has your honour a heart that ups and looks you in the face, and gives you quarter-deck orders that it's life and death to disobey?
SIR D. I have not a heart of that description, but I have a Picture Gallery that presumes to take that liberty.
RICH. Well, your honour, it's like this. Your honour had an elder brother—
SIR D. I had.
RICH. Who should have inherited your title and, with it, its cuss.
SIR D. Ay; but he died. Oh, Ruthven!
RICH. He didn't.
SIR D. He did *not?*
RICH. He didn't. On the contrary, he lives in this here very village, under the name of Robin Oakapple, and he's a-going to marry Rose Maybud this very day.
SIR D. Ruthven alive, and going to marry Rose Maybud. Can this be possible?
RICH. Now the question I was going to ask your honour is— ought I to tell your honour this?
SIR D. I don't know. It's a delicate point. I think you ought. Mind, I'm not sure, but I think so.
RICH. That's what my heart says. It says, "Dick," it says (it calls me Dick acos it's entitled to take that liberty)—"that there young gal would recoil from him if she knowed what he really were. Ought you to stand off and on, and let this young girl take this false step and never fire a shot across her bows to bring her to? No," it says, "you did *not* ought." And I won't ought, accordin'.
SIR D. Then you really feel yourself at liberty to tell me that my elder brother lives—that I may charge him with his cruel deceit, and transfer to his shoulders the hideous thraldom under which I have laboured for so many years! Free—free at last! Free to live a blameless life, and to die beloved and regretted by all who knew me!

DUET.—SIR DESPARD *and* RICHARD.

RICH. You understand?
SIR D. I think I do;
With vigour unshaken
This step shall be taken.
It's neatly planned.
RICH. I think so too;
I'll readily bet it
You'll never regret it!

221

BOTH.	For duty, duty must be done; The rule applies to every one, And painful though that duty be, To shirk the task were fiddle-de-dee!
SIR D.	The bridegroom comes—
RICH.	Likewise the bride— The maidens are very Elated and merry; They are her chums.
SIR D.	To lash their pride Were almost a pity, The pretty committee!
BOTH.	But duty, duty must be done, The rule applies to every one, And painful though that duty be, To shirk the task were fiddle-de-dee!

[*Exeunt* RICHARD *and* SIR DESPARD.

Enter CHORUS OF BRIDESMAIDS *and* BUCKS.

CHORUS OF BRIDESMAIDS.

Hail the bride of seventeen summers;
In fair phrases
Hymn her praises;
Lift your song on high, all comers.
She rejoices
In your voices.
Smiling summer bears upon her,
Shedding every blessing on her:
Maidens, greet her—
Kindly treat her
You may all be brides some day!

CHORUS OF BUCKS.

Hail the bridegroom who advances,
Agitated,
Yet elated.
He's in easy circumstances,
Young and lusty,
True and trusty:
Happiness untold awaits them
When the parson consecrates them;
People near them,
Loudly cheer them—
You'll be bridegrooms some fine day!

Enter ROBIN, *attended by* RICHARD *and* OLD ADAM, *meeting* ROSE,
attended by ZORAH *and* DAME HANNAH. ROSE *and* ROBIN
embrace.

MADRIGAL.

ROSE.	Where the buds are blossoming, Smiling welcome to the spring, Lovers choose a wedding-day— Life is love in merry May!

GIRLS.	Spring is green—Fal lal la! Summer's rose—Fal lal la!
ALL.	It is sad when summer goes, Fal la!
MEN.	Autumn's gold—Fal lal la! Winter's gray—Fal lal la!
ALL.	Winter still is far away— Fal la!

Leaves in autumn fade and fall,
Winter is the end of all.
Spring and summer teem with glee:
Spring and summer, then, for me!
Fal la!

HANNAH.	In the spring-time seed is sown: In the summer grass is mown: In the autumn you may reap: Winter is the time for sleep.
GIRLS.	Spring is hope—Fal lal la! Summer's joy—Fal lal la!
ALL.	Spring and summer never cloy, Fal la!
MEN.	Autumn, toil—Fal lal la! Winter, rest—Fal lal la!
ALL.	Winter, after all, is best— Fal la!
ALL.	Spring and summer pleasure you Autumn, ay, and winter too— Every season has its cheer Life is lovely all the year! Fal la!

GAVOTTE.

After Gavotte, enter SIR DESPARD.

SIR D.	Hold, bride and bridegroom, ere you wed each other, I claim young Robin as my elder brother!
ROB. *(aside)*.	Ah, lost one!
SIR D.	His rightful title I have long enjoyed: I claim him as Sir Ruthven Murgatroyd!
ROSE. *(wildly)*.	Deny the falsehood, Robin, as you should. It is a plot!
ROB.	I would, if conscientiously I could, But I cannot!
ALL.	Ah, base one!

SOLO.—ROBIN.

	As pure and blameless peasant, I cannot, I regret, Deny a truth unpleasant, I am that Baronet!
ALL.	He is that Baronet! But when completely rated Bad baronet am I, That I am what he's stated I'll recklessly deny!
ALL.	He'll recklessly deny!

ROB.	When I'm a bad bart. I will tell taradiddles!
ALL.	He'll tell taradiddles when he's a bad bart.
ROB.	I'll play a bad part on the falsest of fiddles.
ALL.	On very false fiddles he'll play a bad part!
ROB.	But until that takes place I must be conscientious—
ALL.	He'll be conscientious until that takes place.
ROB.	Then adieu with good grace to my morals sententious
ALL.	To mortals sententious adieu with good grace!
ZOR.	Who is the wretch who hath betrayed thee?
	Let him stand forth!
RICH. *(coming forward).* 'Twas I!
ALL.	Die, traitor!
RICH.	Hold, my conscience made me
	Withhold your wrath!

SOLO.—RICHARD.

Within this breast there beats a heart
    Whose voice can't be gainsaid.
It bade me thy true rank impart,
    And I at once obeyed.
I knew 'twould blight thy budding fate—
I knew 'twould cause thee anguish great—
But did I therefore hesitate?
    No! I at once obeyed!

ALL.   Acclaim him who, when his true heart
    Bade him young Robin's rank impart,
        Immediately obeyed!

SOLO.—ROSE *(addressing* ROBIN).

Farewell!
Thou hadst my heart—
    'Twas quickly won!
But now we part—
    Thy face I shun!
Farewell!

Go bend the knee
    At Vice's shrine,
Of life with me
    All hope resign.
    Farewell!
(To SIR DESPARD.) Take me—I am thy bride!
    Hurrah!

BRIDESMAIDS.

Hail the Bridegroom—hail the Bride!
When the nuptial knot is tied;
Every day will bring some joy
That can never, never cloy!

Enter MARGARET, *who listens.*

SIR D.	Excuse me, I'm a virtuous person now—
ROSE.	That's why I wed you!
SIR D.	And I to Margaret must keep my vow!
MAR.	Have I misread you?
	Oh, joy! with newly kindled rapture warmed,
	I kneel before you! *[Kneels.*

SIR D.	I once disliked you; now that I've reformed,
	How I adore you! *[They embrace.*

BRIDESMAIDS.

Hail the Bridegroom—hail the Bride!
When the nuptial knot is tied;
Every day will bring some joy
That can never, never cloy!

ROSE.   Richard, of him I love bereft,
        Through thy design,
    Thou art the only one that's left,
        So I am thine!   *[They embrace.*

BRIDESMAIDS.

Hail the Bridegroom—hail the Bride!
Let the nuptial knot be tied!

DUET.—ROSE *and* RICHARD.

Oh, happy the lily
    When kissed by the bee;
And, sipping tranquilly,
    Quite happy is he;
And happy the filly
    That neighs in her pride;
But happier than any
    A pound to a penny,
A lover is, when he
    Embraces his bride!

DUET.—SIR DESPARD *and* MARGARET.

Oh, happy the flowers
    That blossom in June,
And happy the bowers
    That gain by the boon,
But happier by hours
    The man of descent,
Who, folly regretting,
Is bent on forgetting
His bad baroneting,
    And means to repent!

TRIO.—HANNAH, ADAM, *and* ZORAH.

Oh, happy the blossom
    That blooms on the lea,
Likewise the opossom
    That sits on a tree,
But when you come across 'em,
    They cannot compare
With those who are treading
The dance at a wedding,
While people are spreading
    The best of good fare!

SOLO.—ROBIN.

Oh, wretched the debtor
    Who's signing the deed!
And wretched the letter
    That no one can read!
But very much better
    Their lot it must be
Than that of the person
I'm making this verse on,
Whose head there's a curse on—
    Alluding to me!

Repeat Ensemble with Chorus.

DANCE.

[*At the end of the dance* ROBIN *falls senseless on the stage.*
Picture.

ACT II.

SCENE.—*Picture Gallery in Ruddigore Castle. The walls are covered*
with full-length portraits of the Baronets of Ruddigore from the
time of JAMES I.—*the first being that of* SIR RUPERT, *alluded to*
in the legend; the last, that of the last deceased Baronet, SIR
RODERIC.

Enter ROBIN *and* ADAM, *melodramatically. They are greatly altered in*
appearance, ROBIN *wearing the haggard aspect of a guilty roué;*
ADAM, *that of the wicked steward to such a man.*

DUET.—ROBIN *and* ADAM.

ROB.   I once was as meek as a new-born lamb,
      I'm now Sir Murgatroyd—ha! ha!
        With greater precision,
        (Without the elision)
      Sir Ruthven Murgatroyd—ha! ha!

ADAM.   And I, who was once his *valley-de-sham,*
      As steward I'm now employed—ha! ha!
        The dickens may take him—
        I'll never forsake him!
      As steward I'm now employed—ha! ha!

BOTH.   How dreadful when an innocent heart
      Becomes, perforce, a bad young Bart.,
      And still more hard on old Adam
      His former faithful *valley-de-sham!*

ROB. This is a painful state of things, Old Adam!

ADAM. Painful, indeed! Ah, my poor master, when I swore
that, come what would, I would serve you in all things for ever,
I little thought to what a pass it would bring me! The
confidential adviser to the greatest villain unhung! Now, sir, to
business. What crime do you propose to commit to-day?

ROB. How should I know? As my confidential adviser, it's
your duty to suggest something.

ADAM. Sir, I loathe the life you are leading, but a good old
man's oath is paramount, and I obey. Richard Dauntless is here

with pretty Rose Maybud, to ask your consent to their marriage.
Poison their beer.

ROB. No—not that—I know I'm a bad Bart., but I'm not as
bad a Bart. as all that.

ADAM. Well, there you are, you see! It's no use my making
suggestions if you don't adopt them.

ROB. *(melodramatically).* How would it be, do you think, were
I to lure him here with cunning wile—bind him with good stout
rope to yonder post—and then, by making hideous faces at him,
curdle the heart-blood in his arteries, and freeze the very marrow
in his bones? How say you, Adam, is not the scheme well
planned?

ADAM. It would be simply rude—nothing more. But soft—
they come!

ADAM *and* ROBIN *retire up as* RICHARD *and* ROSE *enter, preceded by*
CHORUS OF BRIDESMAIDS.

DUET.—RICHARD *and* ROSE.

RICH.   Happily coupled are we,
        You see—
    I am a jolly Jack Tar,
        My star,
      And you are the fairest,
      The richest and rarest
    Of innocent lasses, you are,
        By far—
    Of innocent lasses you are!
    Fanned by a favouring gale,
        You'll sail
    Over life's treacherous sea
        With me,
      And as for bad weather,
      We'll brave it together,
    And you shall creep under my lee,
        My wee!
    And you shall creep under my lee!
    For you are such a smart little craft—
    Such a neat little, sweet little craft.
      Such a bright little, tight little,
      Slight little, light little,
    Trim little, prim little craft!

CHORUS.   For she is such, etc.

ROSE.   My hopes will be blighted, I fear,
        My dear;
    In a month you'll be going to sea,
        Quite free,
      And all of my wishes
      You'll throw to the fishes
    As though they were never to be;
        Poor me!
    As though they were never to be,
    And I shall be left all alone
        To moan,
    And weep at your cruel deceit,
        Complete;
    While you'll be asserting

Your freedom by flirting
With every woman you meet,
You cheat—
With every woman you meet!
Though I am such a smart little craft—
Such a neat little, sweet little craft.
Such a bright little, tight little,
Slight little, light little,
Trim little, prim little craft!

CHORUS.   Though she is such, etc.

Enter ROBIN.

ROB. Soho! pretty one—in my power at last, eh? Know ye not that I have those within my call who, at my lightest bidding, would immure ye in an uncomfortable dungeon? *(Calling.)* What ho! within there!

RICH. Hold—we are prepared for this. *(Producing a Union Jack.)* Here is a flag that none dare defy *(all kneel),* and while this glorious rag floats over Rose Maybud's head, the man does not live who would dare to lay unlicensed hand upon her!

ROB. Foiled—and by a Union Jack! But a time will come, and then—

ROSE. Nay, let me plead with him. *(To* ROBIN.) Sir Ruthven, have pity. In my book of etiquette the case of a maiden about to be wedded to one who unexpectedly turns out to be a baronet with a curse on him, is not considered. Time was when you loved me madly. Prove that this was no selfish love by according your consent to my marriage with one who, if he be not you yourself, is the next best thing—your dearest friend!

BALLAD.—ROSE.

In bygone days I had thy love,
Thou hadst my heart.
But Fate, all human vows above,
Our lives did part!
By the old love thou hadst for me,
By the fond heart that beat for thee—
By joys that never now can be,
Grant thou my prayer!

ALL. *(kneeling).*   Grant thou her prayer!

ROB. *(recit.).*   Take her—I yield.
ALL. *(recit.).*   Oh, rapture!
CHORUS.   Away to the parson we go—
               Say we're solicitous very
That he will turn two into one—
               Singing hey, derry down derry!
RICH.   For she *is* such a smart little craft.
ROSE.   Such a neat little, sweet little craft—
RICH.   Such a bright little—
ROSE.   Tight little—
RICH.   Slight little—
ROSE.   Light little—
BOTH.   Trim little, slim little craft!
CHORUS.   Yes she *is* such a smart little craft, etc.

[*Exeunt all but* ROBIN.

ROB. For a week I have fulfilled my accursed doom! I have duly committed a crime a-day! Not a great crime, I trust, but still in the eyes of one as strictly regulated as I used to be, a crime. But will my ghostly ancestors be satisfied with what I have done, or will they regard it as an unworthy subterfuge? *(Addressing Pictures.)* Oh, my forefathers, wallowers in blood, there came at last a day when, sick of crime, you, each and every, vowed to sin no more, and so, in agony, called welcome Death to free you from your cloying guiltiness. Let the sweet psalm of that repentant hour soften your long-dead hearts, and tune your souls to mercy on your poor posterity! *(Kneeling.)*

[*The stage darkens for a moment. It becomes light again, and the Pictures are seen to have become animated.*

CHORUS OF FAMILY PORTRAITS.

Painted emblems of a race,
All accurst in days of yore,
Each from his accustomed place
Steps into the world once more.

[*The Pictures step from their frames and march round the stage.*

Baronet of Ruddigore,
Last of our accursed line,
Down upon the oaken floor—
Down upon those knees of thine.
Coward, poltroon, shaker, squeamer,
Blockhead, sluggard, dullard, dreamer,
Shirker, shuffler, crawler, creeper,
Sniffler, snuffler, wailer, weeper,
Earthworm, maggot, tadpole, weevil!
Set upon thy course of evil
Lest the King of Spectre-Land
Set on thee his grisly hand!

[*The spectre of* SIR RODERIC *descends from his frame.*

SIR ROD.   By the curse upon our race—
CHORUS.   Dead and hearsèd
                         All accursèd!
SIR ROD.   Each inheriting this place—
CHORUS.   Sorrows shake it!
                         Devil take it!
SIR ROD.   Must, perforce, or yea or nay—
CHORUS.   Yea or naying
                         Be obeying!
SIR ROD.   Do a deadly crime each day!
CHORUS.   Fire and Thunder,
                         We knocked under—
               Some atrocious crime committed
               Daily ere the world we quitted!
SIR ROD.   Beware! beware! beware!
ROB.   Gaunt vision, who art thou,
               That thus, with icy glare
                    And stern relentless brow,
                    Appearest, who knows how?
SIR ROD.   I am the spectre of the late
                    Sir Roderic Murgatroyd,
               Who comes to warn thee that thy fate
                    Thou canst not now avoid.
ROB.   Alas, poor ghost!

SIR ROD.   The pity you
                  Express, for nothing goes;
            We spectres are a jollier crew
                  Than you, perhaps, suppose!
CHORUS.   Yes! yes!
            We spectres are a jollier crew
                  Than you, perhaps, suppose!
                              Ha! ha!

SONG.—SIR RODERIC.

When the night wind howls in the chimney cowls, and the bat in
      the moonlight flies,
And inky clouds, like funeral shrouds, sail over the midnight
      skies—
When the footpads quail at the night-bird's wail, and black dogs
      bay the moon,
Then is the spectre's holiday—then is the ghosts' high-noon!
CHORUS.   Ha! ha!
            Then is the ghosts' high-noon!

As the sob of the breeze sweeps over the trees, and the mists lie
      low on the fen,
From grey tomb-stones are gathered the bones that once were
      women and men,
And away they go, with a mop and a mow, to the revel that ends
      too soon,
For cockcrow limits our holiday—the dead of the night's high-
      noon!
CHORUS.   Ha! ha!
            The dead of the night's high-noon!

And then each ghost with his ladye-toast to their churchyard beds
      take flight.
With a kiss, perhaps, on her lantern chaps, and a grisly grim
      "goodnight;"
Till the welcome knell of the midnight bell rings forth its jolliest
      tune,
And ushers our next high holiday—the dead of the night's high-
      noon!
CHORUS.   Ha! ha!
            The dead of the night's high-noon!

ROB. I recognize you now—you are the picture that hangs at the end of the gallery.

SIR ROD. In a bad light. I am.

ROB. Are you considered a good likeness?

SIR ROD. Pretty well. Flattering.

ROB. Because, as a work of art you are poor.

SIR ROD. I am crude in colour, but I have only been painted ten years. In a couple of centuries I shall be an Old Master, and then you will be sorry you spoke lightly of me.

ROB. And may I ask why you have left your frames?

SIR ROD. It is our duty to see that our successors commit their daily crimes in a conscientious and workmanlike fashion. It is our duty to remind you that you are evading the conditions under which you are permitted to exist.

ROB. Really I don't know what you'd have. I've only been a bad baronet a week, and I've committed a crime punctually every day.

SIR ROD. Let us inquire into this. Monday?

ROB. Monday was a Bank Holiday.

SIR ROD. True. Tuesday?

ROB. On Tuesday I made a false income-tax return.

ALL. Ha! ha!

1ST GHOST. That's nothing.

2ND GHOST. Nothing at all.

3RD GHOST. Everybody does that.

4TH GHOST. It's expected of you.

SIR ROD. Wednesday?

ROB. (melodramatically). On Wednesday I forged a will.

SIR ROD. Whose will?

ROB. My own.

SIR ROD. My good sir, you can't forge your own will!

ROB. Can't I, though! I like that! I did! Besides, if a man can't forge his own will, whose will can he forge?

1ST GHOST. There's something in that.

2ND GHOST. Yes; it seems reasonable.

3RD GHOST. At first sight it does.

4TH GHOST. Fallacy somewhere, I fancy!

ROB. A man can do what he likes with his own?

SIR ROD. I suppose he can.

ROB. Well, then, he can forge his own will, stoopid! On Thursday I shot a fox.

1ST GHOST. Hear, hear!

SIR ROD. That's better. (Addressing GHOSTS.) Pass the fox, I think? (They assent.) Yes, pass the fox. Friday?

ROB. On Friday I forged a cheque.

SIR ROD. Whose cheque?

ROB. Old Adam's.

SIR ROD. But old Adam hasn't a banker.

ROB. I didn't say I forged his banker—I said I forged his cheque. On Saturday I disinherited my only son.

SIR ROD. But you haven't got a son.

ROB. No—not yet. I disinherited him in advance, to save time. You see—by this arrangement—he'll be born ready disinherited.

SIR ROD. I see. But I don't think you can do that.

ROB. My good sir, if I can't disinherit my own unborn son, whose unborn son can I disinherit?

SIR ROD. Humph! These arguments sound very well, but I can't help thinking that, if they were reduced to syllogistic form, they wouldn't hold water. Now quite understand us. We are foggy, but we don't permit our fogginess to be presumed upon. Unless you undertake to—well, suppose we say, carry off a lady? (Addressing GHOSTS.) Those who are in favour of his carrying off a lady— (All hold up their hands except a BISHOP.) Those of the contrary opinion? (BISHOP holds up his hands.) Oh, you're never satisfied! Yes, unless you undertake to carry off a lady at once—I don't care what lady—any lady—choose your lady—you perish in inconceivable agonies.

ROB. Carry off a lady? Certainly not, on any account. I've the greatest respect for ladies, and I wouldn't do anything of the kind for worlds! No, no. I'm not that kind of baronet I assure you! If that's all you've got to say, you'd better go back to your frames.

SIR ROD. Very good—then let the agonies commence.

      [GHOSTS make passes. ROBIN begins to writhe in agony.

ROB. Oh! Oh! Don't do that! I can't stand it!

SIR ROD. Painful, isn't it? It gets worse by degrees.

ROB. Oh! Oh! Stop a bit! Stop it, will you? I want to speak.

[SIR RODERIC makes signs to GHOSTS, who resume their attitudes.

SIR ROD. Better?

ROB. Yes—better now! Whew!

SIR ROD. Well, do you consent?

ROB. But it's such an ungentlemanly thing to do!

SIR ROD. As you please. *(To* GHOSTS.*)* Carry on!

ROB. Stop—I can't stand it! I agree! I promise! It shall be done!

SIR ROD. To-day?

ROB. To-day!

SIR ROD. At once?

ROB. At once! I retract! I apologize! I had no idea it was anything like that!

CHORUS.

He yields! He answers to our call!
    We do not ask for more.
A sturdy fellow, after all,
        This latest Ruddigore!
All perish in unheard-of woe
        Who dare our wills defy;
We want your pardon, ere we go,
For having agonized you so—
        So pardon us—
        So pardon us—
        So pardon us—
                Or die!

ROB.   I pardon you!
        I pardon you!

ALL.   He pardons us—
                Hurrah!

[*The* GHOSTS *return to their frames.*

CHORUS. Painted emblems of a race,
            All accurst in days of yore,
        Each to his accustomed place
            Steps unwillingly, once more!

[*By this time the* GHOSTS *have changed to pictures again.*
ROBIN *is overcome by emotion.*

Enter ADAM.

ADAM. My poor master, you are not well—

ROB. Gideon Crawle, it won't do—I've seen 'em—all my ancestors—they're just gone. They say that I must do something desperate at once, or perish in horrible agonies. Go—go to yonder village—carry off a maiden—bring her here at once—any one—I don't care which—

ADAM. But—

ROB. Not a word, but obey! Fly!   [*Exit* ADAM.

RECITATIVE AND SONG.—ROBIN.

Away, Remorse!
            Compunction, hence!
Go, Moral Force!
        Go, Penitence!
To Virtue's plea
        A long farewell—
Propriety,
        I ring your knell!
Come guiltiness of deadliest hue,
Come desperate deeds of derring do!

Henceforth all the crimes that I find in the *Times*
    I've promised to perpetrate daily;
To-morrow I start, with a petrified heart,
    On a regular course of Old Bailey.
There's confidence tricking, bad coin, pocket-picking,
    And several other disgraces—
There's postage-stamp prigging, and then, thimble-rigging,
    The three-card delusion at races!
Oh! a Baronet's rank is exceedingly nice,
But the title's uncommonly dear at the price!

Ye well-to-do squires, who live in the shires,
    Where petty distinctions are vital,
Who found Athenæums and local museums,
    With views to a baronet's title—
Ye butchers and bakers and candlestick makers
    Who sneer at all things that are tradey—
Whose middle-class lives are embarrassed by wives
    Who long to parade as "My Lady,"
Oh! allow me to offer a word of advice,
The title's uncommonly dear at the price!

Ye supple M.P.'s, who go down on your knees,
    Your precious identity sinking,
And vote black or white as your leaders indite
    (Which saves you the trouble of thinking),
For your country's good fame, her repute, or her shame,
    You don't care the snuff of a candle—
But you're paid for your game when you're told that your name
        Will be graced by a baronet's handle—
Oh! allow me to give *you* a word of advice—
The title's uncommonly dear at the price!

[*Exit* ROBIN.

Enter SIR DESPARD *and* MARGARET. *They are both dressed in sober black of formal cut, and present a strong contrast to their appearance in Act I.*

DUET.

DES.   I once was a very abandoned person—

MAR.   Making the most of evil chances.

DES.   Nobody could conceive a worse 'un—

MAR.   Even in all the old romances.

DES.   I blush for my wild extravagances,
                But be so kind
                To bear in mind,

MAR.   We were the victims of circumstances!   [*Dance.*
        That is one of our blameless dances.

MAR.   I was an exceedingly odd young lady—

DES.   Suffering much from spleen and vapours.

MAR.   Clergymen thought my conduct shady—

DES.   She didn't spend much upon linen-drapers.

MAR.   It certainly entertained the gapers.
                My ways were strange
                Beyond all range—

DES.   And paragraphs got into all the papers.   [*Dance.*

DES.   We only cut respectable capers.

DES.   I've given up all my wild proceedings.

MAR. My taste for a wandering life is waning.

DES. Now I'm a dab at penny-readings.

MAR. They are not remarkably entertaining.

DES. A moderate livelihood we're gaining.

MAR.   In fact we rule
          A National School.

DES. The duties are dull, but I'm not complaining, [*Dance.*
This sort of thing takes a deal of training!

DES. We have been married a week.

MAR. One happy, happy week!

DES. Our new life—

MAR. Is delightful indeed!

DES. So calm!

MAR. So unimpassioned! *(Wildly.)* Master, all this I owe to you! See, I am no longer wild and untidy. My hair is combed. My face is washed. My boots fit!

DES. Margaret don't. Pray restrain yourself. Remember, you are now a district visitor.

MAR. A gentle district visitor!

DES. You are orderly, methodical, neat; you have your emotions well under control.

MAR. I have! *(Wildly.)* Master, when I think of all you have done for me, I fall at your feet. I embrace your ankles. I hug your knees! *(Doing so.)*

DES. Hush. This is not well. This is calculated to provoke remark. Be composed, I beg!

MAR. Ah! you are angry with poor little Mad Margaret!

DES. No, not angry; but a district visitor should learn to eschew melodrama. Visit the poor, by all means, and give them tea and barley-water, but don't do it as if you were administering a bowl of deadly nightshade. It upsets them. Then, when you nurse sick people, and find them not as well as could be expected, why go into hysterics?

MAR. Why not?

DES. Because it's too jumpy for a sick-room.

MAR. How strange! Oh, Master! Master!—how shall I express the all-absorbing gratitude that— *(About to throw herself at his feet.)*

DES. Now! *(Warningly.)*

MAR. Yes, I know, dear—it shan't occur again. *(He is seated—she sits on the ground by him.)* Shall I tell you one of poor Mad Margaret's odd thoughts? Well, then, when I am lying awake at night, and the pale moonlight streams through the latticed casement, strange fancies crowd upon my poor mad brain, and I sometimes think that if we could hit upon some word for you to use whenever I am about to relapse—some word that teems with hidden meaning—like "Basingstoke" it might recall me to my saner self. For, after all, I am only Mad Margaret! Daft Meg! Poor Meg! He! he! he!

DES. Poor child, she wanders! But soft—some one comes. Margaret, pray recollect yourself—Basingstoke, I beg! Margaret, if you don't Basingstoke at once, I shall be seriously angry.

MAR. *(recovering herself).* Basingstoke it is!

DES. Then make it so.

Enter ROBIN. *He starts on seeing them.*

ROB. Despard! And his young wife! This visit is unexpected.

MAR. Shall I fly at him? Shall I tear him limb from limb? Shall I rend him asunder? Say but the word, and—

DES. Basingstoke!

MAR. *(suddenly demure).* Basingstoke it is!

DES. *(aside).* Then make it so. *(Aloud.)* My brother—I call you brother still, despite your horrible profligacy—we have come to urge you to abandon the evil courses to which you have committed yourself, and at any cost to become a pure and blameless ratepayer.

ROB. But I've done no wrong yet.

MAR. *(wildly).* No wrong! He has done no wrong! Did you hear that!

DES. Basingstoke.

MAR. *(recovering herself.)* Basingstoke it is.

DES. My brother—I still call you brother, you observe—you forget that you have been, in the eye of the law, a Bad Baronet of Ruddigore for ten years—and you are therefore responsible—in the eye of the law—for all the misdeeds committed by the unhappy gentleman who occupied your place.

ROB. I see! Bless my heart, I never thought of that! Was I very bad?

DES. Awful. Wasn't he? *(To* MARGARET.)

ROB. And I've been going on like this for how long?

DES. Ten years! Think of all the atrocities you have committed —by attorney as it were—during that period. Remember how you trifled with this poor child's affections—how you raised her hopes on high (don't cry, my love—Basingstoke, you know), only to trample them in the dust when they were at the very zenith of their fulness. Oh, fie, sir, fie—she trusted you!

ROB. Did she? What a scoundrel I must have been! There, there—don't cry, my dear *(to* MARGARET, *who is sobbing on* ROBIN's *breast),* it's all right now. Birmingham you know—Birmingham—

MAR. *(sobbing).* It's Ba—Ba—Basingstoke!

ROB. Basingstoke! of course it is—Basingstoke.

MAR. Then make it so!

ROB. There, there—it's all right—he's married you now— that is, *I've* married you. *(Turning to* DESPARD.) I say, which of us has married her?

DES. Oh, *I've* married her.

ROB. *(aside).* Oh, I'm glad of that. *(To* MARGARET.) Yes, *he's* married you now *(passing her over to* DESPARD), and anything more disreputable than my conduct seems to have been I've never even heard of. But my mind is made up—I *will* defy my ancestors. I *will* refuse to obey their behests, thus, by courting death, atone in some degree for the infamy of my career!

MAR. I knew it—I knew it. God bless you. *(Hysterically.)*

DES. Basingstoke!

MAR. Basingstoke it is! *(Recovers herself.)*

PATTER-TRIO.

ROBIN, DESPARD *and* MARGARET.

ROB. My eyes are fully open to my awful situation—
  I shall go at once to Roderic and make him an oration.
  I shall tell him I've recovered my forgotten moral senses,
  And I don't care twopence halfpenny for any consequences.
  Now, I do not want to perish by the sword or by the
      dagger,
  But a martyr may indulge a little pardonable swagger,
  And a word or two of compliment my vanity would
      flatter,
  But I've got to die to-morrow, so it really doesn't matter!

DES.   So it really doesn't matter—

MAR.   So it really doesn't matter—
ALL. So it really doesn't matter, matter, matter, matter, matter!

MAR. If I were not a little mad and generally silly,
    I should give you my advice upon the subject, willy nilly;
    I should show you in a moment how to grapple with the
        question,
    And you'd really be astonished at the force of my
        suggestion.
    On the subject I shall write you a most valuable letter,
    Full of excellent suggestions when I feel a little better,
    But at present I'm afraid I am as mad as any hatter,
    So I'll keep 'em to myself, for my opinion doesn't matter!
DES.   Her opinion doesn't matter—
ROB.   Her opinion doesn't matter—
ALL. Her opinion doesn't matter, matter, matter, matter,
    matter!

DES. If I had been so lucky as to have a steady brother
    Who could talk to me as we are talking now to one
        another—
    Who could give me good advice when he discovered I was
        erring,
    (Which is just the very favour which on you I am
        conferring).
    My story would have made a rather interesting idyll,
    And I might have lived and died a very decent indiwiddle.
    This particularly rapid, unintelligible patter
    Isn't generally heard, and if it is it doesn't matter!
ROB.   If it is it doesn't matter—
MAR.   If it ain't it doesn't matter—
ALL. If it is it doesn't matter, matter, matter, matter, matter!
    [*Exeunt* DESPARD *and* MARGARET.

Enter ADAM.

ADAM (*guiltily*). Master—the deed is done!
ROB. What deed?
ADAM. She is here—alone, unprotected.
ROB. Who?
ADAM. The maiden. I've carried her off—I had a hard task, for
she fought like a tiger-cat!
ROB. Great Heaven, I had forgotten her! I had hoped to have
died unspotted by crime, but I am foiled again—and by a tiger-
cat! Produce her—and leave us!
    [ADAM *introduces* OLD HANNAH, *very much excited, and exit.*
ROB. Dame Hannah! This is—this is not what I expected.
HAN. Well, sir, and what would you with me? Oh, you have
begun bravely—bravely indeed! Unappalled by the calm dignity
of blameless womanhood, your minion has torn me from my
spotless home, and dragged me, blindfold and shrieking, through
hedges, over stiles, and across a very difficult country, and left me
helpless and trembling, at your mercy! Yet not helpless, coward
sir, for, approach one step—nay, but the twentieth part of one
poor inch—and this poniard (*produces a very small dagger*) shall
teach ye what it is to lay unholy hands on old Stephen Trusty's
daughter!
ROB. Madam, I am extremely sorry for this. It is not at all
what I intended—anything more correct—more deeply respectful
than my intentions towards you, it would be impossible for any
one—however particular—to desire.
HAN. Bah, I am not to be tricked by smooth words, hypocrite!

But be warned in time, for there are without, a hundred gallant
hearts whose trusty blades would hack him limb from limb who
dared to lay unholy hands on old Stephen Trusty's daughter!
ROB. And this is what it is to embark upon a career of
unlicensed pleasure!
    [HANNAH, *who has taken a formidable dagger from one of the
        armed figures, throws her small dagger to* ROBIN.

HAN. Harkye, miscreant, you have secured me, and I am your
poor prisoner; but if you think I cannot take care of myself you
are very much mistaken. Now then, it's one to one, and let the
best man win! (*Making for him.*)
ROB. (*in an agony of terror*). Don't! don't look at me like that! I
can't bear it! Roderic! Uncle! Save me!

RODERIC *enters, up trap in centre of stage. He is visible only as far as
        the waist.*

ROD. What is the matter? Have you carried her off?
ROB. I have—she is there—look at her—she terrifies me.
Come quite up and save me!
ROD. (*looking at* HANNAH). Little Nannikin!
HAN. (*amazed.*) Roddy-doddy!
ROD. My own old love! (*Comes completely through trap.*) Why,
how came *you* here?
HAN. This brute—he carried me off! Bodily! But I'll show
him! (*About to rush at* ROBIN.)
ROD. Stop! (*To* ROB.) What do you mean by carrying off this
lady? Are you aware that, once upon a time she was engaged to
be married to me? I'm very angry—very angry indeed.
ROB. Now, I hope this will be a lesson to you in future, not
to—
ROD. Hold your tongue, sir.
ROB. Yes, uncle.
ROD. Have you given him any encouragement?
HAN. (*to* ROB). Have I given you any encouragement? Frankly
now, have I?
ROB. No. Frankly, you have not. Anything more scrupulously
correct than your conduct it would be impossible to desire.
ROD. You go away.
ROB. Yes, uncle.   [*Exit* ROBIN.
ROD. This is a strange meeting after so many years!
HAN. Very. I thought you were dead.
ROD. I am. I died ten years ago.
HAN. And are you pretty comfortable?
ROD. Pretty well—that is—yes, pretty well.
HAN. You don't deserve to be, for I loved you all the while,
dear; and it made me dreadfully unhappy to hear of all your
goings on, you bad, bad boy!

BALLAD.—HANNAH.

There grew a little flower
    'Neath a great oak tree:
When the tempest 'gan to lower
    Little heeded she:
No need had she to cower,
For she dreaded not its power—
She was happy in the bower
    Of her great oak tree!
    Sing hey,
    Lackaday!

Let the tears fall free
For the pretty little flower and the great oak tree!

BOTH.　　　　　　　　Sing hey,
　　　　　　　　　　　Lackaday! etc.

When she found that he was fickle,
　　　　　Was that great oak tree,
She was in a pretty pickle,
　　　　　As she well might be—
But his gallantries were mickle
For Death followed with his sickle,
And her tears began to trickle
　　　　　For her great oak tree!
　　　　　Sing hey,
　　　　　Lackaday! etc.
Said she, "He loved me never,
　　　　　Did that great oak tree,
But I'm neither rich nor clever,
　　　　　And so why should he?

But though fate our fortunes sever
To be constant I'll endeavour,
Ay, for ever and for ever,
　　　　　To my great oak tree!"
　　　　　Sing hey,
　　　　　Lackaday! etc.

[*Falls weeping on* RODERIC'S *bosom.*

Enter ROBIN, *excitedly, followed by all the characters and*
CHORUS OF BRIDESMAIDS.

ROB. Stop a bit—both of you.

ROD. This intrusion is unmannerly.

HAN. I'm surprised at you.

ROB. I can't stop to apologize—an idea has just occurred to me. A Baronet of Ruddigore can only die through refusing to commit his daily crime.

ROD. No doubt.

ROB. Therefore, to refuse to commit a daily crime is tantamount to suicide!

ROD. It would seem so.

ROB. But suicide is, itself, a crime—and so, by your own showing, you ought never to have died at all!

ROD. I see—I understand! Then I'm practically alive!

ROB. Undoubtedly! (SIR RODERIC *embraces* HANNAH.) Rose, when you believed that I was a simple farmer, I believe you loved me?

ROSE. Madly, passionately!

ROB. But when I became a bad baronet, you very properly loved Richard instead?

ROSE. Passionately, madly!

ROB. But if I should turn out *not* to be a bad baronet after all, how would you love me then?

ROSE. Madly, passionately!

ROB. As before?

ROSE. Why, of course!

ROB. My darling! *(They embrace.)*

RICH. Here, I say, belay.

ROSE. Oh, sir, belay, if it's absolutely necessary.

ROB. Belay? Certainly not!

FINALE.

ROB.　　　　Having been a wicked baronet a week,
　　　　　　Once again a modest livelihood I seek,
　　　　　　　　Agricultural employment
　　　　　　　　Is to me a keen enjoyment,
　　　　　　For I'm naturally diffident and meek!

ROSE.　　　When a man has been a naughty baronet,
　　　　　　And expresses his repentance and regret,
　　　　　　　　You should help him if you're able,
　　　　　　　　Like the mousie in the fable.
　　　　　　That's the teaching of my Book of Etiquette.

RICH.　　　If you ask me why I do not pipe my eye,
　　　　　　Like an honest British sailor, I reply,
　　　　　　　　That with Zorah for my missis,
　　　　　　　　There'll be bread and cheese and kisses,
　　　　　　Which is just the sort of ration I enjye!

DES. *and* MAR.　Prompted by a keen desire to evoke,
　　　　　　All the blessed calm of matrimony's yoke,
　　　　　　　　We shall toddle off to-morrow,
　　　　　　　　From this scene of sin and sorrow,
　　　　　　For to settle in the town of Basingstoke!

ALL.　　　　For happy the lily
　　　　　　　　That's kissed by the bee;
　　　　　　And, sipping tranquilly,
　　　　　　　　Quite happy is he;
　　　　　　And happy the filly
　　　　　　　　That neighs in her pride;
　　　　　　But happier than any,
　　　　　　A pound to a penny,
　　　　　　A lover is, when he
　　　　　　　　Embraces his bride!

CURTAIN.

The Yeomen of the Guard

or The Merryman and his Maid

It is necessary to be familiar with the Gilbert and Sullivan idiom before coming to *The Yeomen*, otherwise the melodrama and the banal verses of the pseudo-Tudor speech are difficult to accept; but *in* the idiom, this work ranks with the best and most loved of all the Savoy operas.

After the comparative failure of *Ruddigore*, Sullivan's attitude to Gilbert cooled considerably. He was still disinterested in Gilbert's 'Lozenge Plot' which he termed not human and 'a puppet-show' so there was no new work for Carte to present. Instead, he had to revive old favourites to keep the Savoy going, to avoid bringing in outsiders.

Sullivan was in very poor health, and disillusioned by the successes of others in the operetta field. He was yearning to write grand opera and was hounded by critics, accusing him of wasting his talents. When Gilbert at last proposed the idea of *The Yeomen* to him on Christmas Day 1878, he was much relieved, and took seven numbers to set when he went abroad in the following month. Before the piece was staged, there were rows and disagreements which made the collaborators very uncertain of the commodity they were offering on the first night. But the plot, largely borrowed from other sources, is a compulsive one and Sullivan's evocative and well-ordered score swept the opera along to an enormous success.

Gilbert is said to have been inspired by a poster on Uxbridge Railway Station of a Beefeater advertising The Tower Furnishing Company. However, Beefeaters were a part of the national heritage and appeared almost weekly in the pages of *Punch*; and at the time *The Yeomen* was conceived, the Tower of London had only recently been reopened to the general public after thirty-five years of restoration.

The plot of the piece, which Gilbert has so skilfully manipulated, comes originally from d'Ennery's play *Don César de Bazan* which Vincent Wallace used for his opera *Maritana* of 1845 and which was still in circulation. The critics were quick to see the similarities, and to chide Gilbert mercilessly. No one seems to have pointed out the close affinity that *The Yeomen* also has with Offenbach's operetta *La Périchole* (London 1870). The heroine is a street

singer with a trouping companion Piquillo (compare the verbal likeness to Point), and has to go through a 'blindfold' marriage of convenience, afterwards involving an escape from a prison dungeon. From his own last play for the German Reeds, *Eyes and No Eyes*, Gilbert has lifted the solitary spinner on whom the *Yeomen's* curtain rises. This device was a remarkable departure from the usual Savoy opening chorus.

Although *The Yeomen* was an attempt on Gilbert's part to write a serious work, the usual topsy-turvydom and pantomime characters lurk on the scene. He depicts the Tower as an institution of the State for the extermination of heroes (no mention of traitors); and by compromising two likeable characters who have rescued an innocent man, he condemns them to unsuitable and unsavoury marriages. Thus Sergeant Meryll and his daughter Phoebe fall respectively into the clutches of Dame Carruthers, a Mother Goose figure (the all-knowing

wise woman), and Wilfred Shadbolt, the arch-villain. Gilbert's *Bab* drawings of Shadbolt give him a huge, slightly Caliban-like head, and, furthering this image, he is the most lecherous of all Gilbert's characters. His interlude with Point is reminiscent of the Comics' scene in *The Tempest*.

While writing *The Yeomen*, Gilbert read Shakespeare and Jack Point is said to be based on a Shakespearean fool. All the same, he is a truly Gilbertian character and may have been inspired by Gilbert's personal feelings at the time. Sullivan had recently acted as best man at Carte's wedding, and had been appointed a director of Carte's new Savoy Hotel. Gilbert had been left out. His arrested creative output after *The Mikado* and his fear of being unable to produce an unlimited flow of wit was a sensitive matter, reflected in his characterization of Point. Gilbert's Jester James of 1879 (the joker who ran out

of material and was condemned to shout 'Let well alone!' from its depths) was a forerunner of Point. James and Point (like the Sorcerer) have to yield to popular opinion, and they end up—it is not clear whether they die or not—the odd men out.

SYNOPSIS

The story centres round Colonel Fairfax, imprisoned in the Tower of London and due to be beheaded. He has been falsely accused of sorcery by a treacherous cousin, heir to his wealth, who will inherit if Fairfax dies unmarried. Among Fairfax's brave deeds on the battlefield was the rescue of Sergeant Meryll, now a senior Yeoman Warder at the Tower.

The grand overture, almost Elgarian in its patriotic fervour, is scored to suggest a symphony orchestra, and the scampering violins *in alt* emphasize the effect. The opening theme to the overture, symbolizing the Tower, recurs throughout the opera.

The scene opens on Phoebe, Meryll's daughter, seated at her spinning wheel. Violas perform the onomatopæic effect which recalls Saint-Saëns' *Rouet d'Omphale* (1871). She is approached by the Head

Jailer and Assistant Tormentor, Wilfred Shadbolt, who discusses Fairfax's fate with her. Unknown to Shadbolt, Phoebe has fallen in love with Fairfax and her ardent concern that the Colonel may be reprieved arouses Shadbolt's jealousy, for he considers Phoebe as his property.

A patriotic flourish heralds the Yeomen Warders. Their nostalgic memories are expressed in a chorus, much like that of the exercising prisoners in Beethoven's *Fidelio*. Then Dame Carruthers, Housekeeper of the Tower, comes forward and, as an ancient representative, gives an impartial account 'When our gallant Norman foes ...' (to a plodding march) of the tortures, bleedings and burnings of heroes that it has been the duty of the old building to witness.

Meryll is expecting his son Leonard, a newly-appointed Yeoman, to bring a reprieve for Fairfax, but he arrives without one. Meryll, Leonard and Phoebe therefore plot to rescue Fairfax. It is agreed that he shall impersonate Leonard, with whom no one at the Tower is yet familiar, Leonard shall absent himself and Phoebe will wheedle the dungeon keys from Shadbolt. The trio 'Alas! I waver to and fro ...' is a Verdian pastiche of apprehension.

As Leonard leaves, Fairfax, attended by guards, is seen making his way across Tower Green to his final destination. In reply to the condolences of Sir Richard Cholmondeley, the Lieutenant of the Tower, Fairfax assures him that no one could wish for a better death than the 'business-like' one offered by the Tower. On seeing Phoebe overcome with emotion, Fairfax consoles her and then bids a touching farewell to his old comrade, Meryll. His moving song, 'Is life a boon? ...' captures both the nostalgia and tension of ebbing life. Before Fairfax is led away he explains the necessity for him to marry before he dies, and begs the Lieutenant to find him a bride.

The jester, Jack Point, and his sweetheart Elsie Maynard, a singer, arrive on the Green, pursued by a menacing crowd. The music has definite affinities with a similar scene in Offenbach's *La Périchole* and with the rabble music in *Carmen*. The 'soft and effeminate' Lydian mode underlines Point's failure to please his audience. To pacify their pursuers, Jack and Elsie perform 'The Merryman and his Maid': it is in the style of 'Green Grow the Rushes, O!' with verses progressively lengthening, and concerns the Merryman's fickle sweetheart who sought the affection of a nobleman and was flouted; she returned to her moping lover and all ended happily. This droning ballad of prediction contradicts Point's real, and less fortunate, fate.

After the song, some men in the crowd try to accost Elsie. She draws a dagger and the subsequent furore brings out the Lieutenant. When Elsie explains that she and Point are performing to raise money for her sick mother, the Lieutenant offers her the opportunity of earning 100 crowns in exchange for becoming Fairfax's bride. Point reluctantly agrees to the bargain and Elsie is led away blindfold.

The Lieutenant now questions Point with a view to employing him, and Point gives a demonstration of his talents. The sparely orchestrated woodwind introduction to his song, 'I've wisdom from the East and from the West ...' has a distinctly mediaeval flavour. The jester's trade is outlined with the cynicism of experience:

'When they're offered to the world in merry guise
Unpleasant truths are swallowed with a will ...'

'Were I thy bride'. Sergeant Meryll (Leicester Tunks) returning Shadbolt's keys to Phoebe (Jessie Rose) while Wilfred (Fred Billington) stands bemused by Phoebe's attentions. 1909 production picture photographed at the Tower.

As Point leaves with Sir Richard, Elsie returns, overcome by the realization that she has married a young man, and deeply regretting her imminent widowhood. A moving recitative, weaving Handel with Mozart, precedes her very Victorian song, 'Though tear and long-drawn sigh'.

Shadbolt, who has conveyed the blindfold Elsie to and from the condemned cell, is puzzling over the incident when Meryll approaches. Meryll stands out of Shadbolt's sight while Phoebe, during her wooing song 'Were I thy bride ...' removes the cell keys from his belt, unnoticed, and hands them to her father. By the time she has completed her song, the keys are returned to the unsuspecting Shadbolt, and Phoebe runs from him on her final line, 'I'm not thy bride!'. This scene contains the only moments of sheer dramatic tension in all the operas.

The Yeomen Warders give Fairfax (now in the guise of Leonard) a hero's welcome and enumerate his valiant deeds. Fairfax rightly disclaims their praise and then, to add to his embarrassment, Phoebe demands his brotherly attention. Shadbolt, jealously guarding Phoebe from other suitors, takes the advantage of committing her to her 'brother's' unremitting vigilance. Fairfax willingly accepts guardianship in a martial trio, 'To thy fraternal care ...' which, in the last verse, melts into Fairfax and Phoebe kissing at the end of each line.

To the toll of St Peter's bell the execution party arrives and the block is set up. Ironically, Fairfax is sent with Shadbolt and two Yeomen to fetch the prisoner. During 'The prisoner comes to meet his doom ...', a mournful, Verdian dirge (reminiscent of the Auto de Fé scene in *Don Carlo*), Elsie mourns the fate of her bridegroom.

Suddenly the dirge is interrupted as Fairfax and the Yeomen rush in, proclaiming that the prisoner has escaped. Amid general agitation, Shadbolt is blamed and threatened with death, the conspirators deny all knowledge of the escape and Dame Carruthers suggests enchantment. Elsie is desolate and Point distraught. The chorus, 'All frenzied with despair I rave ...', lamenting the 'cheated grave', is churchy, patriotic and charged with emotion as Elsie faints in Fairfax's arms.

A spacious Tchaikovskian melody reveals Tower Green in moonlight. The community is still in a state of upheaval and Dame Carruthers chides the Yeomen in a tramping song of recrimination, 'Warders are ye? Whom do ye ward? ...'. This has a counter-melody to the opening chorus.

Point and Shadbolt dolefully develop a kind of clownish Shakespearean relationship. Shadbolt expresses his desire to become a jester and Point forthwith embarks on a resumé of the irksome duties. His song, 'Oh! a private buffoon is a light-hearted loon ...' ends with the cynical 'They don't blame you as long as you're funny!'. In return for lessons in jesting, Shadbolt offers to help Point in his

'Hereupon we're both agreed.' Leo Sheffield, Wilfred Shadbolt and Henry Lytton, Jack Point in the roles which they played together from 1916 until 1928.

'Warders are ye? Whom do ye ward?' Dame Carruthers, (Theresa Rassam) leads the female Chorus of accusation against the Yeomen. Savoy Theatre 1907.

Four trade cards designed in 1885 from contemporary cabinet portraits to illustrate the first production of *The Mikado*.

Charles Ricketts was a leading stage designer of the 1920s and 1930s. He designed *The Mikado* for the D'Oyly Carte as well as *The Gondoliers*, and this costume design for the Duke of Plaza Toro shows the simplification and bold economy which was his hallmark, against current trends.

predicament over Elsie's marriage to Fairfax. Point and Shadbolt plan to effect a mock shooting of the prisoner escaping by river, and both will witness that he has been drowned. They joyfully seal their agreement in the 'Cock and Bull' duet.

Fairfax, though free, is haunted by the constraint of his marriage and unknown bride. His ballad, 'Free from his fetters grim ...' is a typical Victorian drawing-room piece and has a melody linked with Elsie's 'Though tear and long-drawn sigh ...'.

Elsie has been convalescing in Meryll's house, tended by Dame Carruthers who is far too attentive to the Sergeant for his liking. Now that her patient has recovered and is about to leave the Tower, Dame Carruthers, seeing a growing relationship between Elsie and 'Leonard', warns him that Elsie has disclosed in her sleep that she is married to Fairfax. The pseudo-Tudor quartet, 'Strange Adventure', reflecting on the extraordinary liaison, includes the minor character of Kate, Dame Carruthers' niece.

Fairfax has now identified his wife and decides to test her fidelity. Still posing as Leonard, he declares his love and, defaming Fairfax, begs Elsie to elope with him. In response to her shocked refusal he begins to excuse himself, but is interrupted by the firing of an arquebus. At once a busy chorus of enquiry ensues. 'Who fired that shot?' the Lieutenant demands, and in reply Wilfred and Point describe Shadbolt's act of bravery. Their contradictory patter-duet, 'Like a ghost his vigil keeping ...', resembles the corroboration trio in *The Mikado*. Shadbolt is redeemed for his act of bravery and carried away shoulder-high.

Elsie, plunged into further emotional indecision, is unable to accept Point's renewed attentions and his denigration of Fairfax; Fairfax is annoyed and, upbraiding Point for his clumsy wooing, gives a demonstration of how it should be done. The trio for Fairfax, Elsie and Phoebe, 'A man who would woo a fair maid ...' is in nursery-rhyme style with an evocative verse for Elsie, now obviously in love, and a more retrospective one for Phoebe. As Fairfax completes his wooing, Point and Phoebe realise, too late, that he is in earnest and has won Elsie. Fairfax and Elsie lead a happy quartet, 'When a wooer goes a-wooing ...' Which Phoebe continues in the minor key and Point turns into a despairing suicide song.

In a jealous fit over Elsie, Phoebe inadvertently discloses Fairfax's identity to Shadbolt. The only way to save herself from a charge of treason is to

marry Wilfred and secure his silence. Similarly, Dame Carruthers discovers that Meryll is guilty of subterfuge. In the comic jig between herself and Meryll, Dame Carruthers crows over her conquest while he reflects, in alternate verses, on his ghastly plight.

A joyous bridal chorus heralds Dame Carruthers, Phoebe and Elsie dressed for her marriage to 'Leonard'. With an exuberant trio they welcome the happy day but their rejoicing is curtailed by a fanfare announcing the Lieutenant. In a *Messiah*-like proclamation, 'Thy husband lives—and he is free ...', he prepares Elsie for Fairfax's arrival.

To a second flourish, Fairfax appears, handsomely dressed. Elsie falls at his feet, begging for mercy and praying aside for Leonard to save her. Sadly she surrenders to Fairfax and, looking up at him for the first time, she is amazed. 'Leonard!' she cries and falls into his arms.

Jack Point is left, brokenly repeating the Merryman song. Elsie takes it up with nostalgic compassion and, as she embraces Fairfax, Point collapses at her feet.

'Sir, I obey! I am thy bride'. Elsie, Ann Dowdall and Fairfax, Thomas Round. City of London Festival 1962, production in the moat of the Tower of London.

THE YEOMEN OF THE GUARD;

OR

THE MERRYMAN AND HIS MAID.

A NEW AND ORIGINAL OPERA,

IN TWO ACTS.

First produced at the Savoy Theatre, 3 October 1888

DRAMATIS PERSONÆ

SIR RICHARD CHOLMONDELEY [*Lieutenant of the Tower*]

bass-baritone

COLONEL FAIRFAX [*under sentence of death*]　　　　　tenor

SERGEANT MERYLL [*of the Yeomen of the Guard*]　　bass-baritone

LEONARD MERYLL [*his Son*]　　　　　　　　　　　tenor

JACK POINT [*a Strolling Jester*]　　　　　　　　baritone

WILFRED SHADBOLT [*Head Jailor and Assistant Tormentor*]

bass-baritone

THE HEADSMAN　　　　　　　　　　　　　　　—

FIRST YEOMAN　　　　　　　　　　　　　　　tenor

SECOND YEOMAN　　　　　　　　　　　　　baritone

FIRST CITIZEN　　　　　　　　　　　　　　　—

SECOND CITIZEN　　　　　　　　　　　　　　—

ELSIE MAYNARD [*a Strolling Singer*]　　　　　　soprano

PHŒBE MERYLL [*Sergeant Meryll's Daughter*]　　soprano

DAME CARRUTHERS [*Housekeeper to the Tower*]　　contralto

KATE [*her Niece*]　　　　　　　　　　　　　soprano

Chorus of Yeomen of the Guard, Gentlemen, Citizens, etc.

SCENE—TOWER GREEN.

DATE—16TH CENTURY.

THE
YEOMEN OF THE GUARD;

OR, THE

MERRYMAN AND HIS MAID.

ACT I.

SCENE.—*Tower Green.* PHŒBE *discovered spinning.*

SONG.—PHŒBE.

When maiden loves, she sits and sighs,
 She wanders to and fro;
Unbidden tear-drops fill her eyes,
And to all questions she replies,
 With a sad heigho!
 'Tis but a little word—"heigho!"
 So soft, 'tis scarcely heard—"heigho!"
  An idle breath—
  Yet life and death
 May hang upon a maid's "heigho!"

When maiden loves, she mopes apart,
 As owl mopes on a tree;
Although she keenly feels the smart,
She cannot tell what ails her heart,
 With its sad "Ah me!"
 'Tis but a foolish sigh—"Ah me!"
 Born but to droop and die—"Ah me!"
  Yet all the sense
  Of eloquence
Lies hidden in a maid's "Ah me!" [*Weeps.*

Enter WILFRED.

WIL. Mistress Meryll!

PHŒ. (*looking up*). Eh! Oh! it's you, is it! You may go away, if you like. Because I don't want you, you know.

WIL. Haven't you anything to say to me?

PHŒ. Oh yes! Are the birds all caged? The wild beasts all littered down! All the locks, chains, bolts, and bars in good order? Is the Little Ease sufficiently uncomfortable? The racks, pincers, and thumbscrews all ready for work? Ugh! you brute!

WIL. These allusions to my professional duties are in doubtful taste. I didn't become a head-jailor because I like head-jailing. I didn't become an assistant-tormentor because I like assistant-tormenting. We can't *all* be sorcerers, you know. (PHŒBE *annoyed.*) Ah! you brought that upon yourself.

PHŒ. Colonel Fairfax is *not* a sorcerer. He's a man of science and an alchemist.

WIL. Well, whatever he is, he won't be one long, for he's to be beheaded to-day for dealings with the devil. His master nearly had him last night, when the fire broke out in the Beauchamp Tower.

PHŒ. Oh, how I wish he had escaped in the confusion! But take care; there's still time for a reply to his petition for mercy.

WIL. Ah! I'm content to chance that. This evening at half-past seven—ah!

PHŒ. You're a cruel monster to speak so unfeelingly of the death of a young and handsome soldier.

WIL. Young and handsome! How do *you* know he's young and handsome?

PHŒ. Because I've seen him every day for weeks past taking his exercise on the Beauchamp Tower. (WILFRED *utters a cry of agony.*) There, I believe you're jealous of *him*, now. Jealous of a man I've never spoken to! Jealous of a poor soul who's to die in an hour!

WIL. I am! I'm jealous of everybody and everything. I'm jealous of the very words I speak to you—because they reach your ears—and I mustn't go near 'em!

PHŒ. How unjust you are! Jealous of the words you speak to me! Why, you know as well as I do, that I don't even like them.

WIL. You used to like 'em.

PHŒ. I used to *pretend* I liked them. It was mere politeness to comparative strangers. [*Exit* PHŒBE, *with spinning wheel.*

WIL. I don't believe you know what jealousy is! I don't believe you know how it eats into a man's heart—and disorders his digestion—and turns his interior into boiling lead. Oh, you are a heartless jade to trifle with the delicate organization of the human interior!

Enter Crowd of MEN *and* WOMEN, *followed by* YEOMEN OF THE GUARD, *led by* SERGEANT MERYLL.

CHORUS (*as* YEOMEN *march on*).

  Tower Warders,
  Under orders,
Gallant pikemen, valiant sworders!
  Brave in bearing,
  Foemen scaring,
In their bygone days of daring!
  Ne'er a stranger
  There to danger—
Each was o'er the world a ranger:
  To the story
  Of our glory
Each a bold contributory!

CHORUS OF YEOMEN.

In the autumn of our life
 Here at rest in ample clover,
 We rejoice in telling over
  Our impetuous May and June.
In the evening of our day,

With the sun of life declining,
We recall without repining,
All the heat of bygone noon.

SOLO —SERGEANT.

This the autumn of our life,
This the evening of our day;
Weary we of battle strife,
Weary we of mortal fray.
But our year is not so spent,
And our days are not so faded,
But that we with one consent,
Were our lovèd land invaded,
Still would face a foreign foe,
As in days of long ago.

PEOPLE.   YEOMEN.

Tower Warders,   In the autumn time of life, etc.
Under orders, etc.

[*Exeunt* CROWD. *Manent* YEOMEN.

Enter DAME CARRUTHERS.

DAME. A good day to you, Sergeant.
SERG. Good day, Dame Carruthers. Busy to-day?
DAME. Busy, ay! The fire in the Beauchamp last night has given me work enough. A dozen poor prisoners—Richard Colfax, Sir Martin Byfleet, Colonel Fairfax, Warren the preacher-poet, and half a score others—all packed into one small cell, not six feet square. Poor Colonel Fairfax, who's to die to-day, is to be removed to No. 14 in the Cold Harbour Tower that he may have his last hour alone with his confessor; and I've to see to that.
SERG. Poor gentleman! He'll die bravely. I fought under him two years since, and he valued his life as it were a feather!
PHŒ. He's the bravest, the handsomest, and the best young gentleman in England! He twice saved my father's life; and it's a cruel thing, a wicked thing, and a barbarous thing that so gallant a hero should lose his head—for it's the handsomest head in England!
DAME. For dealings with the devil. Ay! if all were beheaded who dealt with *him,* there'd be busy doings on Tower Green.
PHŒ. You know very well that Colonel Fairfax is a student of alchemy—nothing more, and nothing less; but this wicked Tower, like a cruel giant in a fairy-tale, must be fed with blood, and that blood must be the best and bravest in England, or it's not good enough for the old Blunderbore. Ugh!
DAME. Silence, you silly girl; you know not what you say. I was born in the old keep, and I've grown grey in it, and, please God, I shall die and be buried in it; and there's not a stone in its walls that is not as dear to me as my own right hand.

SONG.—DAME CARRUTHERS.

When our gallant Norman foes
    Made our merry land their own,
        And the Saxons from the Conqueror were flying,
At his bidding it arose,
    In its panoply of stone,
        A sentinel unliving and undying.

Insensible, I trow,
    As a sentinel should be,
        Though a queen to save her head should come a-suing.
There's a legend on its brow
    That is eloquent to me,
        And it tells of duty done and duty doing.

"The screw may twist and the rack may turn,
    And men may bleed and men may burn,
        On London town and all its hoard
        I keep my solemn watch and ward!"

CHORUS.   The screw may twist, etc.

Within its wall of rock
    The flower of the brave
        Have perished with a constancy unshaken.
From the dungeon to the block,
    From the scaffold to the grave,
        Is a journey many gallant hearts have taken.
And the wicked flames may hiss
    Round the heroes who have fought
        For conscience and for home in all its beauty;
But the grim old fortalice
    Takes little heed of aught
        That comes not in the measure of its duty.

"The screw may twist and the rack may turn,
    And men may bleed and men may burn,
        On London town and all its hoard
        It keeps its silent watch and ward!"

[*Exeunt all but* PHŒBE *and* SERGEANT MERYLL.

PHŒ. Father! No reprieve for the poor gentleman?
MER. No, my lass; but there's one hope yet. Thy brother Leonard, who, as a reward for his valour in saving his standard and cutting his way through fifty foes who would have hanged him, has been appointed a Yeoman of the Guard, will arrive this morning; and as he comes straight from Windsor, where the Court is, it may be—it *may* be—that he will bring the expected reprieve with him.
PHŒ. Oh, that he may!
MER. Amen! For the Colonel twice saved my life, and I'd give the rest of my life to save his! And wilt thou not be glad to welcome thy brave brother, with the fame of whose exploits all England is a-ringing?
PHŒ. Ay, truly, if he brings the reprieve.
MER. And not otherwise?
PHŒ. Well, he's a brave fellow indeed, and I love brave men.
MER. *All* brave men?
PHŒ. Most of them, I verily believe! But I hope Leonard will not be too strict with me—they say he is a very dragon of virtue and circumspection! Now, my dear old father is kindness itself, and—
MER. And leaves thee pretty well to thine own ways, eh? Well, I've no fears for thee; thou hast a feather-brain, but thou'rt a good lass.
PHŒ. Yes, that's all very true, but if Leonard is going to tell me that I may not do this and I may not do that, and I must not talk to this one, or walk with that one, but go through the world with my lips pursed up and my eyes cast down, like a poor nun

who has renounced mankind—why, as I have *not* renounced mankind, and don't mean to renounce mankind, I won't have it—there!

MER. Nay, he'll not check thee more than is good for thee, Phœbe!

Enter LEONARD MERYLL.

LEON. Father!

MER. Leonard! my brave boy! I'm right glad to see thee, and so is Phœbe!

PHŒ. Ay—hast thou brought Colonel Fairfax's reprieve?

LEON. Nay, I have here a despatch for the Lieutenant, but no reprieve for the Colonel!

PHŒ. Poor gentleman! poor gentleman!

LEON. Ay, I would I had brought better news. I'd give my right hand—nay, my body—my life, to save his!

MER. Dost thou speak in earnest, my lad?

LEON. Ay—I'm no braggart. Did he not save thy life? and am I not his foster-brother?

MER. Then hearken to me. Thou hast come to join the Yeomen of the Guard.

LEON. Well!

MER. None has seen thee but ourselves?

LEON. And a sentry, who took but scant notice of me.

MER. Now to prove thy words. Give me the despatch, and get thee hence at once! Here is money, and I'll send thee more. Lie hidden for a space, and let no one know. I'll convey a suit of yeoman's uniform to the Colonel's cell—he shall shave off his beard so that none shall know him, and I'll own him as my son, the brave Leonard Meryll, who saved his flag and cut his way through fifty foes who thirsted for his life. He will be welcomed without question by my brother-yeomen, I'll warrant that. Now, how to get access to his cell? *(To* PHŒBE.) The key is with thy sour-faced admirer, Wilfred Shadbolt.

PHŒ. *(demurely).* I think—I say, I *think*—I can get anything I want from Wilfred. I think—I say, I *think*—you may leave that to me.

MER. Then get thee hence at once, lad—and bless thee for this sacrifice.

PHŒ. And take my blessing too, dear, dear Leonard!

LEON. And thine, eh? Humph! Thy love is new-born, wrap it up, lest it take cold and die.

TRIO.—LEONARD, PHŒBE, MERYLL.

PHŒ.   Alas! I waver to and fro—
          Dark danger hangs upon the deed!

ALL.   Dark danger hangs upon the deed!

LEON.   The scheme is rash and well may fail;
          But ours are not the hearts that quail—
          The hands that shrink—the cheeks that pale
               In hours of need!

ALL.   No, ours are not the hearts that quail,
          The hands that shrink, the cheeks that pale
               In hours of need!

MER.   The air I breathe to him I owe:
          My life is his—I count it naught!
          That life is his—so count it naught!

LEON.   And shall I reckon risks I run
              When services are to be done
              To save the life of such an one?
                   Unworthy thought!

ALL.   And shall we reckon risks we run
              To save the life of such an one?
                   Unworthy thought!

PHŒ.   We may succeed—who can foretell—
              May Heaven help our hope—farewell!

ALL.   We may succeed—who can foretell?
              May Heaven help our hope—farewell!

[LEONARD *embraces* MERYLL *and* PHŒBE, *and then exit.*
      PHŒBE *weeping.*

MER. Nay, lass, be of good cheer, we may save him yet.

PHŒ. Oh, see, father—they bring the poor gentleman from the Beauchamp! Oh, father! his hour is not yet come?

MER. No, no—they lead him to the Cold Harbour Tower to await his end in solitude. But softly—the Lieutenant approaches! He should not see thee weep.

Enter FAIRFAX, *guarded. The* LIEUTENANT *enters,
          meeting him.*

LIEUT. Halt! Colonel Fairfax, my old friend, we meet but sadly.

FAIR. Sir, I greet you with all good-will; and I thank you for the zealous care with which you have guarded me from the pestilent dangers which threaten human life outside. In this happy little community, Death, when he comes, doth so in punctual and business-like fashion; and, like a courtly gentleman, giveth due notice of his advent, that one may not be taken unawares.

LIEUT. Sir, you bare this bravely, as a brave man should.

FAIR. Why, sir, it is no light boon to die swiftly and surely at a given hour and in a given fashion! Truth to tell, I would gadly have my life; but if that may not be, I have the next best thing to it, which is death. Believe me, sir, my lot is not so much amiss!

PHŒ. *(aside to* MERYLL). Oh, father, father, I cannot bear it?

MER. My poor lass!

FAIR. Nay, pretty one, why weepest thou? Come, be comforted. Such a life as mine is not worth weeping for. (*Sees* MERYLL.) Sergeant Meryll, is it not? (*To* LIEUTENANT.) May I greet my old friend? (*Shakes* MERYLL'S *hand.*) Why, man, what's all this? Thou and I have faced the grim old king a dozen times, and never has his majesty come to me in such goodly fashion. Keep a stout heart, good fellow—we are soldiers, and we know how to die, thou and I. Take my word for it, it is easier to die well than to live well—for, in sooth, I have tried both.

BALLAD.—FAIRFAX.

          Is life a boon?
              If so, it must befal
              That Death, whene'er he call,

Must call too soon.
    Though fourscore years he give,
    Yet one would pray to live
Another moon!
    What kind of pliant have I,
    Who perish in July?
    I might have had to die,
Perchance, in June!

Is life a thorn?
    Then count it not a whit!
    Man is well done with it;
Soon as he's born
    He should all means essay
    To put the plague away;
And I, war-worn,
    Poor captured fugitive,
    My life most gladly give—
    I might have had to live
Another morn!

[*At the end* PHŒBE *is led off, weeping, by* MERYLL

FAIR. And now, Sir Richard, I have a boon to beg. I am in this strait for no better reason than because my kinsman, Sir Clarence Poltwhistle, one of the Secretaries of State, has charged me with sorcery, in order that he may succeed to my estate, which devolves to him provided I die unmarried.

LIEUT. As thou wilt most surely do.

FAIR. Nay, as I will most surely *not* do, by your worship's grace! I have a mind to thwart this good cousin of mine.

LIEUT. How?

FAIR. By marrying forthwith, to be sure!

LIEUT. But, Heaven ha' mercy, whom wouldst thou marry?

FAIR. Nay, I am indifferent on that score. Coming Death hath made of me a true and chivalrous knight, who holds all womankind in such esteem that the oldest, and the meanest, and the worst-favoured of them is good enough for him. So, my good Lieutenant, if thou wouldst serve a poor soldier who has but an hour to live, find me the first that comes—my confessor shall marry us, and her dower shall be my dishonoured name and a hundred crowns to boot. No such poor dower for an hour of matrimony!

LIEUT. A strange request. I doubt that I should be warranted in granting it.

FAIR. Tut tut! There never was a marriage fraught with so little of evil to the contracting parties. In an hour she'll be a widow, and I—a bachelor again for aught I know!

LIEUT. Well, I will see what can be done, for I hold thy kinsman in abhorrence for the scurvy trick he has played thee.

FAIR. A thousand thanks, good sir; we meet again on this spot in an hour or so. I shall be a bridegroom then, and your worship will wish me joy. Till then farewell. (*To guard.*) I am ready, good fellows.

[*Exit with guard into Cold Harbour Tower.*

LIEUT. He is a brave fellow, and it is a pity that he should die. Now, how to find him a bride at such short notice? Well, the task should be easy!   [*Exit.*

Enter JACK POINT *and* ELSIE MAYNARD, *pursued by a crowd of* MEN *and* WOMEN. POINT *and* ELSIE *are much terrified;* POINT *however, assuming an appearance of self-possession.*

CHORUS.

Here's a man of jollity,
    Jibe, joke, jollify!
Give us of your quality,
    Come, fool, follify!

If you vapour vapidly,
River runneth rapidly,
    Into it we fling
    Bird who doesn't sing!

Give us an experiment
In the art of merriment;
    Into it we throw
    Cock who doesn't crow!

Banish your timidity,
And with all rapidity
Give us quip and quiddity—
    Willy-nilly, O!

River none can mollify;—
    Into it we throw
Fool who doesn't follify,
    Cock who doesn't crow!

POINT (*alarmed*). My masters, I pray you bear with us, and will satisfy you, for we are merry folk who would make all merry as ourselves. For, look you, there is humour in all things, and the truest philosophy is that which teaches us to find it and to make the most of it.

ELSIE (*struggling with one of the crowd*). Hands off, I say, unmannerly fellow! (*Pushing him away.*)

POINT (*to 1st Citizen*). Ha! Didst thou hear her say, "Hands off?"

1ST CIT. Ay, I heard her say it, and I felt her do it! What then?

POINT. Thou dost not see the humour of that?

1ST CIT. Nay, if I do, hang me!

POINT. Thou dost not? Now observe. She said "Hands off!" Whose hands? Thine. Off what? Off *her.* Why? Because she is a woman. Now had she *not* been a woman, thine hands had not been set upon her at all. So the reason for the laying on of hands is the reason for the taking off of hands, and herein is contradiction contradicted! It is the very marriage of *pro* with *con;* and no such lopsided union either, as times go, for *pro* is not more unlike *con* than man is unlike woman—yet men and women marry every day with none to say "Oh, the pity of it," but I and fools like me! Now wherewithal shall we please you? We can rhyme you couplet, triolet, quatrain, sonnet, rondolet, ballade, what you will. Or we can dance you saraband, gondolet, carole, pimpernel or Jumping Joan.

ELSIE. Let us give them the singing farce of the Merryman and his Maid—therein is song and dance too.

ALL. Ay, the Merryman and his Maid!

DUET.—POINT *and* ELSIE.

POINT.   I have a song to sing, O!

ELSIE.   Sing me your song, O!

POINT.
It is sung to the moon
By a love-lorn loon,
Who fled from the mocking throng, O.
It's the song of a merryman, moping mum,
Whose soul was sad, and whose glance was glum
Who sipped no sup, and who craved no crumb,
As he sighed for the love of a ladye.
Heighdy! heighdy!
Misery me, lackadaydee!
He sipped no sup, and he craved no crumb,
As he sighed for the love of a ladye.

ELSIE.
I have a song to sing, O!

POINT.
Sing me your song, O!

ELSIE.
It is sung with the ring
Of the songs maids sing
Who love with a love life-long, O!
It's the song of a merrymaid, peerly proud
Who loved a lord, and who laughed aloud
At the moan of the merryman, moping mum,
Whose soul was sore, whose glance was glum,
Who sipped no sup, and who craved no crumb,
As he sighed for the love of a ladye!
Heighdy! heighdy!
Misery me, lackadaydee!
He sipped no sup, etc.

POINT.
I have a song to sing, O!

ELSIE.
Sing me your song, O!

POINT.
It is sung to the knell
Of a churchyard bell,
And a doleful dirge, ding dong, O!
It's a song of a popinjay, bravely born,
Who turned up his noble nose with scorn
At the humble merrymaid, peerly proud,
Who loved that lord, and who laughed aloud
At the moan of the merryman, moping mum,
Whose soul was sad, whose glance was glum,
Who sipped no sup, and who craved no crumb,
As he sighed for the love of a ladye!

BOTH.
Heighdy! heighdy!
Misery me, lackadaydee!
He sipped no sup, etc.

ELSIE.
I have a song to sing, O!

POINT.
Sing me your song, O!

ELSIE.
It is sung with a sigh
And a tear in the eye,
For it tells of a righted wrong, O!
It's a song of a merrymaid, once so gay,
Who turned on her heel and tripped away
From the peacock popinjay, bravely born,
Who turned up his noble nose with scorn
At the humble heart that he did not prize:
So she begged on her knees, with downcast eyes,

For the love of the merryman, moping mum,
Whose soul was sad and whose glance was glum,
Who sipped no sup, and who craved no crumb,
As he sighed for the love of a ladye!

BOTH.
Heighdy! heighdy!
Misery me, lackadaydee!
His pains were o'er, and he sighed no more,
For he lived in the love of a ladye!

1ST CIT. Well sung and well danced!

2ND CIT. A kiss for that, pretty maid!

ALL. Ay, a kiss all round.

ELSIE (drawing dagger). Best beware! I am armed!

POINT. Back, sirs—back! This is going too far.

2ND CIT. Thou dost not see the humour of it, eh? Yet there is humour in all things—even in this. (Trying to kiss her.)

ELSIE. Help! help!

Enter LIEUTENANT, *with guard. Crowd falls back.*

LIEUT. What is this bother?

ELSIE. Sir, I sang to these folk, and they would have repaid me with gross courtesy, but for your honour's coming.

LIEUT. (to MOB). Away with ye! Clear the rabble. (Guards push crowd off, and go off with them.) Now, my girl, who are you, and what do you here?

ELSIE. May it please you, sir, we are two strolling players, Jack Point and I, Elsie Maynard, at your worship's service. We go from fair to fair, singing, and dancing, and playing brief interludes; and so we make a poor living.

LIEUT. You two, eh? Are ye man and wife?

POINT. No, sir; for though I'm a fool, there is a limit to my folly. Her mother, old Bridget Maynard, travels with us (for Elsie is a good girl), but the old woman is a-bed with fever, and we have come here to pick up some silver, to buy an electuary for her.

LIEUT. Hark ye, my girl! Your mother is ill?

ELSIE. Sorely ill, sir.

LIEUT. And needs good food, and many things that thou canst not buy?

ELSIE. Alas! sir, it is too true.

LIEUT. Wouldst thou earn a hundred crowns?

ELSIE. An hundred crowns! They might save her life!

LIEUT. Then listen! A worthy, but unhappy gentleman is to be beheaded in an hour on this very spot. For sufficient reasons, he desires to marry before he dies, and he hath asked me to find him a wife. Wilt thou be that wife?

ELSIE. The wife of a man I have never seen!

POINT. Why, sir, look you, I am concerned in this; for though I am not yet wedded to Elsie Maynard, time works wonders, and there's no knowing what may be in store for us. Have we your worship's word for it that this gentleman will die to-day?

LIEUT. Nothing is more certain, I grieve to say.

POINT. And that the maiden will be allowed to depart the very instant the ceremony is at an end.

LIEUT. The very instant. I pledge my honour that it shall be so.

POINT. An hundred crowns?

LIEUT. An hundred crowns!

POINT. For my part, I consent. It is for Elsie to speak.

TRIO.—ELSIE, POINT, LIEUT.

LIEUT. How say you, maiden, will you wed
A man about to lose his head?
For half an hour
You'll be a wife,
And then the dower
Is yours for life
A headless bridegroom why refuse?
If truth the poets tell,
Most bridegrooms, ere they marry, lose
Both head and heart as well!

ELSIE. A strange proposal you reveal,
It almost makes my senses reel.
Alas! I'm very poor indeed,
And such a sum I sorely need.
My mother, sir, is like to die,
This money life may bring,
Bear this in mind, I pray, if I
Consent to do this thing!

POINT. Though as a general rule of life
I don't allow my promised wife,
My lovely bride that is to be,
To marry any one but me,
Yet if the fee is promptly paid,
And he, in well-earned grave,
Within the hour is duly laid,
Objection I will waive!
Yes, objection I will waive!

ALL. Temptation, oh temptation,
Were we, I pray, intended
To shun, whate'er our station,
Your fascinations splendid;
Or fall, whene'er we view you,
Head over heels into you!
Temptation, oh temptation, etc.

[*During this, the* LIEUTENANT *has whispered to* WILFRED *(who has entered).* WILFRED *binds* ELSIE's *eyes with a kerchief, and leads her into the Cold Harbour Tower.*

LIEUT. And so, good fellow, you are a jester?

POINT. Ay, sir, and, like some of my jests, out of place.

LIEUT. I have a vacancy for such an one. Tell me, what are your qualifications for such a post.

POINT. Marry, sir, I have a pretty wit. I can rhyme you extempore; I can convulse you with quip and conundrum; I have the lighter philosophies at my tongue's tip; I can be merry, wise, quaint, grim, and sardonic, one by one, or all at once; I have a pretty turn for anecdote; I know all the jests—ancient and modern—past, present, and to come; I can riddle you from dawn of day to set of sun, and, if that content you not, well on to midnight and the small hours. Oh, sir, a pretty wit, I warrant you—a pretty, pretty wit!

RECIT. AND SONG.—POINT.

I've jest and joke
And quip and crank,
For lowly folk
And men of rank.
I ply my craft
And know no fear,
I aim my shaft
At prince or peer.
At peer or prince—at prince or peer,
I aim my shaft and know no fear!

I've wisdom from the East and from the West,
That's subject to no academic rule;
You may find in it the jeering of a jest,
Or distil it from the folly of a fool.
I can teach you with a quip, if I've a mind;
I can trick you into learning with a laugh;
Oh, winnow all my folly, and you'll find
A grain or two of truth among the chaff!

I can set a braggart quailing with a quip,
The upstart I can wither with a whim;
He may wear a merry laugh upon his lip,
But his laughter has an echo that is grim
When they're offered to the world in merry guise,
Unpleasant truths are swallowed with a will—
For he who'd make his fellow-creatures wise
Should always gild the philosophic pill!

LIEUT. And how came you to leave your last employ?

POINT. Why, sir, it was in this wise. My Lord was the Archbishop of Canterbury, and it was considered that one of my jokes was unsuited to His Grace's family circle. In truth I ventured to ask a poor riddle, sir—Wherein lay the difference between His Grace and poor Jack Point? His Grace was pleased to give it up, sir. And thereupon I told him that whereas His Grace was paid ten thousand pounds a year for being good, poor Jack Point was good—for nothing. 'Twas but a harmless jest, but it offended His Grace, who whipped me and set me in the stocks for a scurril rogue, and so we parted. I had as lief not take post again with the dignified clergy.

LIEUT. But I trust you are very careful not to give offence. I have daughters.

POINT. Sir, my jests are most carefully selected, and anything objectionable is expunged. If your honour pleases, I will try them first on your honour's chaplain.

LIEUT. Can you give me an example? Say that I had sat me down hurriedly on something sharp?

POINT. Sir, I should say that you had sat down on the spur of the moment.

LIEUT. Humph. I don't think much of that. Is that the best you can do?

POINT. It has always been much admired, sir, but we will try again.

LIEUT. Well, then, I am at dinner, and the joint of meat is but half cooked.

POINT. Why then, sir, I should say—that what is *under*done cannot be helped.

LIEUT. I see. I think that manner of thing would be somewhat irritating.

POINT. At first, sir, perhaps; but use is everything, and you would come in time to like it.

LIEUT. We will suppose that I caught you kissing the kitchen wench under my very nose.

POINT. Under *her* very nose, good sir—not under yours! *That* is where *I* would kiss her. Do you take me? Oh, sir, a pretty wit—a pretty, pretty wit!

LIEUT. The maiden comes. Follow me, friend, and we will discuss this matter at length in my library.

POINT. I am your worship's servant. That is to say, I trust I soon shall be. But, before proceeding to a more serious topic, can you tell me, sir, why a cook's brain-pan is like an over wound clock?

LIEUT. A truce to this fooling—follow me.

POINT. Just my luck; my best conundrum wasted!

[*Exeunt.*

Enter ELSIE *from Tower, followed by* WILFRED, *who removes the bandage from her eyes.*

RECITATIVE AND BALLAD.—ELSIE.

'Tis done! I am a bride! Oh, little ring,
   That bearest in thy circlet all the gladness
That lovers hope for, and that poets sing,
   What bringest thou to me but gold and sadness!
A bridegroom all unknown, save in this wise,
To-day he dies! To-day, alas, he dies!

Though tear and long-drawn sigh
   Ill fit a bride,
No sadder wife than I
   The whole world wide!
      Ah me! Ah me!
      Yet maids there be
Who would consent to lose
   The very rose of youth,
      The flower of life,
   To be, in honest truth,
      A wedded wife,
         No matter whose!

Ere half an hour has rung,
   A widow I!
Ah, Heaven, he is too young,
   Too brave to die!
      Ah me! Ah me!
      Yet wives there be
So weary worn, I trow,
   That they would scarce complain,
      So that they could
   In half an hour attain
      To widowhood,
         No matter how!

[*Exit* ELSIE *as* WILFRED *comes down.*

WIL. (*looking after* ELSIE). 'Tis an odd freak, for a dying man and his confessor to be closeted alone with a strange singing girl. I would fain have espied them, but they stopped up the keyhole. *My* keyhole!

Enter PHŒBE *with* MERYLL, *who carries a bundle.* MERYLL *remains in the background, unobserved by* WILFRED.

PHŒ. (*aside*). Wilfred—and alone! Now to get the keys from him. (*Aloud.*) Wilfred—has no reprieve arrived?

WIL. None. Thine adored Fairfax is to die.

PHŒ. Nay, thou knowest that I have naught but pity for the poor condemned gentlemen.

WIL. I know that he who is about to die is more to thee than I, who am alive and well.

PHŒ. Why, that were out of reason, dear Wilfred. Do they not say that a live ass is better than a dead lion! No, I don't mean that!

WIL. They say that, do they?

PHŒ. It's unpardonably rude of them, but I believe they put it in that way. Not that it applies to thee, who art clever beyond all telling!

WIL. Oh yes; as an assistant tormentor.

PHŒ. As a wit, as a humorist, as a most philosophic commentator on the vanity of human resolution.

[PHŒBE *slyly takes bunch of keys from* WILFRED'S *waistband, and hands them to* MERYLL, *who enters the Tower, unnoticed by* WILFRED.

WIL. Truly, I have seen great resolution give way under my persuasive methods. (*Working a small thumbscrew.*) In the nice regulation of a screw—in the hundredth part of a single revolution lieth all the difference between stony reticence and a torrent of impulsive unbosoming that the pen can scarcely follow. Ha! ha! I am a mad wag.

PHŒ. (*with a grimace*). Thou art a most light-hearted and delightful companion, Master Wilfred. Thine anecdotes of the torture-chamber are the prettiest hearing.

WIL. I'm a pleasant fellow an I choose. I believe I am the merriest dog that barks. Ah, we might be passing happy together—

PHŒ. Perhaps. I do not know.

WIL. For thou wouldst make a most tender and loving wife.

PHŒ. Ay, to one whom I really loved. For there is a wealth of love within this little heart, saving up for—I wonder whom? Now, of all the world of men, I wonder whom? To think that he whom I am to wed is now alive and somewhere! Perhaps far away, perhaps close at hand! And I know him not! It seemeth that I am wasting time in not knowing him.

WIL. Now, say that it is I—nay! suppose it for the nonce. Say that we are wed—suppose it only—say that thou art my very bride, and I thy cheery, joyous, bright, frolicsome husband—and that the day's work being done, and the prisoners stored away for the night, thou and I are alone together—with a long, long evening before us!

PHŒ. (*with a grimace*). It is a pretty picture—but I scarcely know. It cometh so unexpectedly—and yet—and yet—*were* I thy bride—

WIL. Ay!—wert thou my bride!

PHŒ. Oh, how I would love thee!

BALLAD.—PHŒBE.

Were I thy bride,
Then the whole world beside
   Were not too wide
      To hold my wealth of love—
Were I thy bride!

Upon thy breast
My loving head would rest,
   As on her nest
      The tender turtle-dove—
Were I thy bride!

This heart of mine
Would be one heart with thine,
    And in that shrine
        Our happiness would dwell—
Were I thy bride!

    And all day long
Our lives should be a song:
    No grief, no wrong
        Should make my heart rebel—
Were I thy bride!

    The silvery flute,
The melancholy lute,
    Were night owl's hoot
        To my love-whispered coo—
Were I thy bride!

    The skylark's trill
Were but discordance shrill
    To the soft thrill
        Of wooing as I'd woo—
Were I thy bride!

MERYLL *re-enters; gives keys to* PHŒBE, *who replaces them at* WILFRED'S *girdle, unnoticed by him.*

    The rose's sigh
Were as a carrion's cry
    To lullaby
        Such as I'd sing to thee,
Were I thy bride!

    A feather's press
Were leaden heaviness
    To my caress.
        But then, of course, you see
I'm not thy bride!

[*Exit* PHŒBE.

WIL. No, thou'rt not—not yet! But, Lord, how she woo'd! I should be no mean judge of wooing, seeing that I have been more hotly woo'd than most men. I have been woo'd by maid, widow, and wife. I have been woo'd boldly, timidly, tearfully, shyly—by direct assault, by suggestion, by implication, by inference, and by innuendo. But this wooing is not of the common order: it is the wooing of one who must needs woo me, if she die for it! [*Exit* WILFRED.

Enter MERYLL, *cautiously, from Tower.*

MER. (*looking after them*). The deed is, so far, safely accomplished. The slyboots, how she wheedled him! What a helpless ninny is a love-sick man! He is but as a lute in a woman's hands—she plays upon him whatever tune she will. But the Colonel comes. I'faith he's just in time, for the Yeomen parade here for his execution in two minutes.

Enter FAIRFAX, *without beard and moustache, and dressed in Yeomen's uniform.*

FAIR. My good and kind friend, thou runnest a grave risk for me!

MER. Tut, sir, no risk. I'll warrant none here will recognize you. You make a brave yeoman, sir! So—this ruff is too high; so—and the sword should hang thus. Here is your halbert, sir, carry it thus. The yeomen come. Now, remember, you are my brave son, Leonard Meryll.

FAIR. If I may not bear mine own name, there is none other I would bear so readily.

MER. Now, sir, put a bold face on it; for they come.

Enter YEOMEN OF THE GUARD.

RECITATIVE.—SERGEANT MERYLL.

Ye Tower Yeomen, nursed in war's alarms,
    Suckled on gunpowder, and weaned on glory,
Behold my son, whose all-subduing arms
    Have formed the theme of many a song and story.
        Forgive his aged father's pride; nor jeer
        His aged father's sympathetic tear!
                [*Pretending to weep.*

CHORUS.

Leonard Meryll!
Leonard Meryll!
Dauntless he in time of peril!
    Man of power,
    Knighthood's flower,
Welcome to the grim old Tower!
To the Tower, welcome thou!

RECITATIVE.—FAIRFAX.

Forbear, my friends, and spare me this ovation,
I have small claim to such consideration:
The tales that of my prowess have been stated
Are all prodigiously exaggerated!

CHORUS.

    'Tis ever thus
Wherever valour true is found,
True modesty will there abound.
    'Tis ever thus;
Wherever valour true is found,
True modesty will there abound.

COUPLETS.

1ST YEOMAN.   Didst thou not, oh, Leonard Meryll!
        Standard lost in last campaign,
    Rescue it at deadly peril—
        Bear it bravely back again?

CHORUS.   Leonard Meryll, at his peril,
        Bore it bravely back again!

2ND YEOMAN. Didst thou not, when prisoner taken,
    And debarred from all escape,
    Face, with gallant heart unshaken,
    Death in most appalling shape?

CHORUS.   Leonard Meryll faced his peril,
    Death in most appalling shape!

FAIR.   Truly I was to be pitied,
    Having but an hour to live,
    I reluctantly submitted,
    I had no alternative!
    Oh! the facts that have been stated
    Of my deeds of derring-do,
    Have been much exaggerated,
    Very much exaggerated,
    Monstrously exaggerated!
    Scarce a word of them is true!

Enter PHŒBE. *She rushes to* FAIRFAX *and embraces him.*

RECITATIVE.

PHŒ. Leonard!
FAIR. *(puzzled).* I beg your pardon?
PHŒ.   Don't you know me?
  I'm little Phœbe!
FAIR. *(still puzzled).* Phœbe? Is this Phœbe?
  My little Phœbe? *(Aside.)* Who the deuce may *she* be?
  It can't be Phœbe, surely?
WIL.   Yes, 'tis Phœbe—
  Thy sister Phœbe!
ALL.   Ay, he speaks the truth;
  'Tis Phœbe!
FAIR. *(pretending to recognize her).* Sister Phœbe!
PHŒ.   Oh, my brother! *(Embrace.)*
FAIR. Why, how you've grown! I did not recognize you!
PHŒ. So many years! Oh, brother! *(Embrace.)*
FAIR.   Oh, my sister!
WIL. Ay, hug him, girl! There are three thou mayst hug—
  Thy father and thy brother and—myself!
FAIR. Thyself, forsooth? And who art thou thyself?
WIL. Good sir, we are betrothed. (FAIRFAX *turns inquiringly to*
  PHŒBE.)
PHŒ.   Or more or less—
  But rather less than more!
WIL.   To thy fond care
  I do commend thy sister. Be to her
  An ever-watchful guardian—eagle-eyed!
  And when she feels (as sometimes she does feel)
  Disposed to indiscriminate caress,
  Be thou at hand to take those favours from her!
ALL.   Yes, yes,
  Be thou at hand to take those favours from her!
PHŒ. *(in* FAIRFAX'S *arms).*   Yes, yes,
  Be thou at hand to take those favours from me!

TRIO.—WILFRED, FAIRFAX, *and* PHOEBE.

WIL.   To thy fraternal care
   Thy sister I commend,
  From every lurking snare

   Thy lovely charge defend:
   And to achieve this end,
  Oh! grant, I pray, this boon—
   She shall not quit thy sight:
  From morn to afternoon—
   From afternoon to night—
  From seven o'clock to two—
   From two to eventide—
  From dim twilight to 'leven at night
   She shall not quit thy side!

ALL. Oh! grant, I pray, this boon, etc.

PHŒ. So amiable I've grown,
   So innocent as well,
  That if I'm left alone
   The consequences fell
   No mortal can foretell.
  So grant, I pray, this boon—
   I shall not quit thy sight:
  From morn to afternoon—
   From afternoon to night—
  From seven o'clock till two—
   From two till day is done—
  From dim twilight to 'leven at night
   All kinds of risk I run!

ALL. So grant, I pray, this boon, etc.

FAIR. With brotherly readiness,
   For my fair sister's sake,
  At once I answer "Yes"—
   That task I undertake—
   My word I never break—
  I freely grant that boon,
   And I'll repeat my plight.

  From morn to afternoon—   [*Kiss.*
   From afternoon to night—   [*Kiss.*
  From seven o'clock to two—   [*Kiss.*
   From two to evening meal—   [*Kiss.*
  From dim twilight to 'leven at night
   That compact I will seal.   [*Kiss.*

ALL. He freely grants that boon, etc.

[*The Bell of St. Peter's begins to toll. The crowd enters; the
block is brought on to the stage, and the* HEADSMAN
takes his place. The YEOMEN OF THE GUARD *form up,*
FAIRFAX *and two others entering the White Tower, to
bring the prisoner to execution. The* LIEUTENANT *enters
and takes his place, and tells off* FAIRFAX *and two others
to bring the prisoner to execution.*

CHORUS.—*(to tolling accompaniment).*

The prisoner comes to meet his doom;
The block, the headsman, and the tomb.
The funeral bell begins to toll—
May Heaven have mercy on his soul!

SOLO.—ELSIE, *with Chorus.*

Oh, Mercy, thou whose smile has shone
 So many a captive on;
Of all immured within these walls,
 The very worthiest falls!

Enter FAIRFAX *and two other* YEOMEN *from Tower in
great excitement.*

My lord! my lord! I know not how to tell
 The news I bear!
I and my comrades sought the prisoner's cell—
 He is not there!
ALL.   He is not there!
They sought the prisoner's cell—he is not there!

TRIO.—FAIRFAX *and* TWO YEOMEN.

As escort for the prisoner
 We sought his cell, in duty bound;
The double gratings open were,
 No prisoner at all we found!
We hunted high, we hunted low,
 We hunted here, we hunted there—
The man we sought, as truth will show,
 Had vanished into empty air!
ALL. Had vanished into empty air!
The man they sought with anxious care
 Had vanished into empty air!
GIRLS. Now, by our troth, the news is fair,
 The man hath vanished into air!
ALL. As escort for the prisoner
  They sought his cell in duty bound, etc.
LIEUT. Astounding news! The prisoner fled.
(To WILFRED). Thy life shall forfeit be instead!
       [WILFRED *is arrested.*
Wilfred. My lord, I did not set him free,
 I hate the man—my rival he!
       [WILFRED *is taken away.*
MERYLL. The prisoner gone—I'm all agape!
 Who could have helped him to escape?
PHŒBE. Indeed I can't imagine who!
 I've no idea at all—have you?
DAME. Of his escape no traces lurk
 Enchantment must have been at work!
ELSIE *(aside to* POINT). What have I done! Oh, woe is me!
 I am his wife, and he is free!
POINT. Oh, woe is *you?* Your anguish sink!
 Oh, woe is *me,* I rather think!
 Oh, woe is *me,* I rather think!
 Yes, woe is *me,* I rather think!
  Whate'er betide
  You are his bride,
  And I am left
  Alone—bereft!
 Yes, woe is *me,* I rather think
 Yes, woe is *me,* I rather think!

ENSEMBLE.

LIEUTENANT.	ELSIE.	POINT.
All frenzied with despair I rave, The grave is cheated of its due.	All frenzied with despair I rave, My anguish rends my heart in two.	All frenzied with despair I rave, My anguish rends my heart in two.
Who is the misbegotten knave Who hath contrived this deed to do?	Unloved, to him my hand I gave; To him, unloved, bound to be true!	Your hand to him you freely gave; It's woe to *me,* not woe to you!
Let search be made throughout the land, Or my vindictive anger dread—	Unloved, unknown, unseen—the brand Of infamy upon his head:	My laugh is dead, my heart unmanned, A jester with a soul of lead!
A thousand marks to him I hand Who brings him here, alive or dead.	A bride that's husbandless, I stand To all mankind for ever dead!	A lover loverless I stand, To womankind for ever dead!

[*The others sing the* LIEUTENANT'S *verse, with altered
pronouns. At the end,* ELSIE *faints in* FAIRFAX'S *arms;
all the* YEOMEN *and populace rush off the stage in
different directions, to hunt for the fugitive, leaving only
the* HEADSMAN *on the stage, and* ELSIE *insensible in*
FAIRFAX'S *arms.*

ACT II.

SCENE.—*Tower Green by Moonlight. Two days have elapsed.*
WOMEN *and* YEOMEN OF THE GUARD *discovered.*

CHORUS OF WOMEN.

Night has spread her pall once more,
 And the prisoner still is free:
Open is his dungeon door,
 Useless now his dungeon key!
He has shaken off his yoke—
 How, no mortal man can tell!
Shame on loutish jailor-folk—
 Shame on sleepy sentinel!
ALL.   He has shaken off his yoke, etc.

SOLO.—DAME CARRUTHERS.

Warders are ye?
 Whom do ye ward?
Bolt, bar, and key,
 Shackle and cord,
Fetter and chain,
 Dungeon of stone,
All are in vain—
 Prisoner's flown!
Spite of ye all, he is free—he is free!
Whom do ye ward? Pretty warders are ye!

CHORUS OF YEOMEN.

Up and down, and in and out,
Here and there, and round about;
Every chamber, every house,
Every chink that holds a mouse,
Every crevice in the keep,
Where a beetle black could creep,
Every outlet, every drain,
Have we searched, but all in vain!

YEOMEN.	WOMEN.
Warders are we:	Warders, are ye?
Whom do we ward?	Whom do ye ward?
Bolt, bar, and key,	Bolt, bar and key;
Shackle and cord,	Shackle and cord,
Fetter and chain,	Fetter and chain,
Dungeon of stone,	Dungeon of stone,
All are in vain.	All are in vain.
Prisoner's flown!	Prisoner's flown!
Spite of us all, he is free!	Spite of ye all, he is free!
he is free!	he is free!
Whom do we ward?	Whom do ye ward?
Warders are we!	Pretty warders are ye!

[*Exeunt all.*

Enter JACK POINT, *in low spirits, reading from a huge volume.*

POINT (*reads*). "The Merrie Jestes of Hugh Ambrose. No. 7863. The Poor Wit and the Rich Councillor. A certayne poor wit, being an-hungered, did meet a well-fed councillor. 'Marry, fool,' quoth the councillor, 'whither away?' 'In truth,' said the poor wag, 'in that I have eaten naught these two dayes, I do wither away, and that right rapidly!' The councillor laughed hugely, and gave him a sausage." Humph! The councillor was easier to please than my new master, the Lieutenant. I would like to take post under that councillor. Ah! 'tis but melancholy mumming when poor heartbroken-jilted Jack Point must needs turn to Hugh Ambrose for original light humour!

Enter WILFRED, *also in low spirits.*

WIL. (*sighing*). Ah, Master Point!
POINT (*changing his manner*). Ha! friend jailor! Jailor that wast—jailor that never shalt be more! Jailor that jailed not, or that jailed, if jail he did, so unjailorly that 'twas but jerry-jailing, or jailing in joke—though no joke to him who, by unjailorlike jailing, did so jeopardize his jailorship. Come, take heart, smile, laugh, wink, twinkle, thou tormentor that tormentest none— thou racker that rackest not—thou pincher out of place—come, take heart, and be merry, as I am!—(*aside, dolefully*)—as I am!
WIL. Ay, it's well for thee to laugh. Thou hast a good post, and hast cause to be merry.
POINT (*bitterly*). Cause? Have we not all cause? Is not the world a big butt of humour, into which all who will may drive a gimlet? See, I am a salaried wit; and is there aught in nature more ridiculous? A poor dull, heart-broken man, who must needs be merry, or he will be whipped; who must rejoice, lest he starve; who must jest you, jibe you, quip you, crank you, wrack you, riddle you, from hour to hour, from day to day, from year to year, lest he dwindle, perish, starve, pine, and die! Why, when there's naught else to laugh at, I laugh at myself till I ache for it!
WIL. Yet I have often thought that a jester's calling would suit me to a hair.
POINT. Thee? Would suit *thee*, thou death's head and crossbones?
WIL. Ay, I have a pretty wit—a light, airy, joysome wit, spiced with anecdotes of prison cells and the torture chamber. Oh, a very delicate wit! I have tried it on many a prisoner, and there have been some who smiled. Now it is not easy to make a prisoner smile. And it should not be difficult to be a good jester, seeing that thou art one.
POINT. Difficult? Nothing easier. Nothing easier. Attend, and I will prove it to thee!

SONG.—POINT.

Oh! a private buffoon is a light-hearted loon,
　　If you listen to popular rumour;
From morning to night he's so joyous and bright,
　　And he bubbles with wit and good humour!
He's so quaint and so terse, both in prose and in verse;
　　Yet though people forgive his transgression,
There are one or two rules that all family fools
　　Must observe, if they love their profession.
　　　　There are one or two rules,
　　　　　　Half a dozen, may be,
　　　　That all family fools,
　　　　　　Of whatever degree,
　　　Must observe, if they love their profession.

If you wish to succeed as a jester, you'll need
　　To consider each person's auricular:
What is all right for B would quite scandalize C
　　(For C is so very particular);
And D may be dull, and E's very thick skull
　　Is as empty of brains as a ladle;
While F is F sharp, and will cry with a carp,
　　That he's known your best joke from his cradle!
　　　　When your humour they flout,
　　　　　　You can't let yourself go;
　　　　And it *does* put you out
　　　　　　When a person says, "Oh,
　　　I have known that old joke from my cradle!"

If your master is surly, from getting up early
　　(And tempers are short in the morning),
An inopportune joke is enough to provoke
　　Him, to give you, at once, a month's warning.
Then if you refrain, he is at you again,
　　For he likes to get value for money.
He'll ask then and there, with an insolent stare,
　　"If you know that your paid to be funny?"
　　　　It adds to the task,
　　　　　　Of a merryman's place,
　　　　When your principal asks,
　　　　　　With a scowl on his face,
　　　If you know that you're paid to be funny?
Comes a Bishop, maybe, or a solemn D.D.—
　　Oh, beware of his anger provoking!
Better not pull his hair—don't stick pins in his chair;

He don't understand practical joking.
If the jests that you crack have an orthodox smack
　　You may get a bland smile from these sages;
But should it, by chance, be imported from France,
　　Half a crown is stopped out of your wages!
　　　　It's a general rule,
　　　　　　Though your zeal it may quench,
　　　　If the family fool
　　　　　　Tell's a joke that's too French,
　　Half a crown is stopped out of his wages!

Though your head it may rack with a bilious attack,
　　And your senses with toothache you're losing,
Don't be mopy and flat—they don't fine you for that,
　　If you're properly quaint and amusing!
Though your wife ran away with a soldier that day,
　　And took with her your trifle of money;
Bless your heart, they don't mind—they're exceedingly
　　kind—
They don't blame you—as long as you're funny!
　　　　It's a comfort to feel
　　　　　　If your partner should flit,
　　　　Though *you* suffer a deal,
　　　　　　They don't mind it a bit—
　　They don't blame you—so long as you're funny.

POINT. And so thou wouldst be a jester, eh? Now, listen! My sweetheart, Elsie Maynard, was secretly wed to this Fairfax half an hour ere he escaped.

WIL. She did well.

POINT. She did nothing of the kind, so hold thy peace and perpend. Now, while he liveth she is dead to me and I to her, and so, my jibes and jokes notwithstanding, I am the saddest and the sorriest dog in England!

WIL. Thou art a very dull dog indeed.

POINT. Now, if thou wilt swear that thou didst shoot this Fairfax while he was trying to swim across the river—it needs but the discharge of an arquebus on a dark night—and that he sank and was seen no more, I'll make thee the very Archbishop of jesters, and that in two days' time! Now, what sayest thou?

WIL. I am to lie?

POINT. Heartily. But thy lie must be a lie of circumstance, which I will support with the testimony of eyes, ears and tongue.

WIL. And thou wilt qualify me as a jester?

POINT. As a jester among jesters. I will teach thee all my original songs, my self-constructed riddles, my own ingenious paradoxes; nay, more, I will reveal to thee the source whence I get them. Now, what sayest thou?

WIL. Why, if it be but a lie thou wantest of me, I hold it cheap enough, and I say yes, it is a bargain!

DUET.—POINT *and* WILFRED.

BOTH.　　Hereupon we're both agreed,
　　　　　　And all that we two
　　　　　　Do agree to
　　　　We'll secure by solemn deed,
　　　　　　To prevent all
　　　　　　Error mental.
　　　　I ⎫
　　　You ⎭ on Elsie ⎰ am ⎱ to call
　　　　　　　　　　⎱ are ⎰

With a story
　　Grim and gory;
How this Fairfax died, and all
　　I ⎫
　　You ⎭ declare to
　　You're ⎫
　　I'm ⎭ to swear to.
　　　　Tell a tale of cock and bull,
　　　　　　Of convincing detail full;
　　　　　　　　Tale tremendous,
　　　　　　　　Heaven defend us!
　　　　What a tale of cock and bull!
In return for ⎰ your ⎱ own part
　　　　　　　　⎱ my ⎰
　　　You are ⎫
　　　I am ⎭ making,
　　Undertaking,
To instruct ⎰ me ⎱ in the art
　　　　　　　⎱ you ⎰
　　　(Art amazing,
　　　　Wonder raising)
Of a jester, jesting free.
　　Proud position—
　　High ambition!
And a lively one ⎰ I'll ⎱ be,
　　　　　　　　　⎱ you'll ⎰
　　　Wag-a-wagging,
　　　Never flagging!
　　　　Tell a tale of cock and bull, etc.
　　　　　　　　　　　　[*Exeunt together.*

Enter FAIRFAX.

FAIR. A day and a half gone, and no news of poor Fairfax! The dolts! They seek him everywhere, save within a dozen yards of his dungeon. So I am free! Free, but for the cursed haste with which I hurried headlong into the bonds of matrimony with—Heaven knows whom! As far as I remember, she should have been young; but even had not her face been concealed by her kerchief, I doubt whether, in my then plight, I should have taken much note of her. Free? Bah! The Tower bonds were but a thread of silk compared with these conjugal fetters which I, fool that I was, placed upon mine own hands. From the one I broke readily enough—how to break the other!

SONG.—FAIRFAX.

Free from his fetters grim—
　　Free to depart;
Free both in life and limb—
　　In all but heart!
Bound to an unknown bride
　　For good and ill;
Ah, is not one so tied
　　A prisoner still?

Free, yet in fetters held
　　Till his last hour,
Gyves that no smith can weld,
　　No rust devour!
Although a monarch's hand

Had set him free,
Of all the captive band
The saddest he!

Enter MERYLL.

FAIR. Well, Sergeant Meryll, and how fares thy pretty charge, Elsie Maynard?

MER. Well enough, sir. She is quite strong again, and leaves us to-night.

FAIR. Thanks to Dame Carruther's kind nursing, eh?

MER. Ay, deuce take the old witch! Ah, 'twas but a sorry trick you played me, sir, to bring the fainting girl to me. It gave the old lady an excuse for taking up her quarters in my house, and for the last two years I've shunned her like the plague. Another day of it and she would have married me! Good Lord, here she is again! I'll·e'en go. *(Going.)*

Enter DAME CARRUTHERS *and* KATE, *her niece.*

DAME. Nay, Sergeant Meryll, don't go. I have something of grave import to say to thee.

MER. *(aside).* It's coming.

FAIR. *(laughing).* I'faith, I think I'm not wanted here. *(Going).*

DAME. Nay, Master Leonard, I've naught to say to thy father that his son may not hear.

FAIR. *(aside).* True. I'm one of the family; I had forgotten!

DAME. 'Tis about this Elsie Maynard. A pretty girl, Master Leonard.

FAIR. Ay, fair as a peach blossom—what then?

DAME. She hath a liking for thee, or I mistake not.

FAIR. With all my heart. She's as dainty a little maid as you'll find in a midsummer day's march.

DAME. Then be warned in time, and give not thy heart to her. Oh, *I* know what it is to give my heart to one who will have none of it!

MER. *(aside).* Ay, *she* knows all about that. *(Aloud.)* And why is my boy to take heed of her? She's a good girl, Dame Carruthers.

DAME. Good enough, for aught I know. But she's no girl. She's a married woman.

MER. A married woman! Tush, old lady—she's promised to Jack Point, the lieutenant's new jester.

DAME. Tush in thy teeth, old man! As my niece Kate sat by her bedside to-day, this Elsie slept, and as she slept she moaned and groaned, and turned this way and that way—and, "How shall I marry one I have never seen?" quoth she—then, "A hundred crowns!" quoth she—then, "Is it certain he will die in an hour?" quoth she—then, "I love him not and yet I am his wife," quoth she! Is it not so, Kate?

KATE. Ay, mother, 'tis eyen so.

FAIR. Art thou sure of all this?

KATE. Ay, sir, for I wrote it all down on my tablets.

DAME. Now, mark my words: it was of this Fairfax she spake, and he is her husband, or I'll swallow my kirtle!

MER. *(aside).* Is this true, sir?

FAIR. True? Why, the girl was raving! Why should she marry a man who had but an hour to live?

DAME. Marry? There be those who would marry but for a minute, rather than die old maids.

MER. *(aside).* Ay, I know one of them!

QUARTETTE.—KATE, FAIRFAX, DAME CARRUTHERS *and* MERYLL.

Strange adventure! Maiden wedded
To a groom she's never seen—
Never, never, never seen!
Groom about to be beheaded,
In an hour on Tower Green!
Tower, Tower, Tower Green!
Groom in dreary dungeon lying,
Groom as good as dead, or dying,
For a pretty maiden sighing—
Pretty maid of seventeen!
Seven—seven—seventeen

Strange adventure that we're trolling,
Modest maid and gallant groom—
Gallant, gallant, gallant groom!—
While the funeral bell is tolling,
Tolling, tolling, Bim-a-boom!
Bim-a, Bim-a, Bim-a-boom!
Modest maiden will not tarry;
Though but sixteen years she carry,
She must marry, she must marry,
Though the altar be a tomb—
Tower—Tower—Tower tomb!

[*Exeunt* DAME CARRUTHERS, MERYLL, *and* KATE.

FAIR. So my mysterious bride is no other than this winsome Elsie! By my hand, 'tis no such ill-plunge in Fortune's lucky bag! I might have fared worse with my eyes open! But she comes. Now to test her principles. 'Tis not every husband who has a chance of wooing his own wife!

Enter ELSIE.

FAIR. Mistress Elsie!

ELSIE. Master Leonard!

FAIR. So thou leavest us to-night?

ELSIE. Yes, Master Leonard. I have been kindly tended, and I almost fear I am loth to go.

FAIR. And this Fairfax. Wast thou glad when he escaped?

ELSIE. Why, truly, Master Leonard, it is a sad thing that a young and gallant gentleman should die in the very fulness of his life.

FAIR. Then when thou didst faint in my arms, it was for joy at his safety?

ELSIE. It may be so. I was highly wrought, Master Leonard, and I am but a girl, and so, when I am highly wrought, I faint.

FAIR. Now, dost thou know, I am consumed with a parlous jealousy?

ELSIE. Thou? And of whom?

FAIR. Why, of this Fairfax, surely!

ELSIE. Of Colonel Fairfax!

FAIR. Ay. Shall I be frank with thee? Elsie—I love thee, ardently, passionately! (ELSIE *alarmed and surprised.*) Elsie, I have loved thee these two days—which is a long time—and I would fain join my life to thine!

ELSIE. Master Leonard! Thou art jesting!

FAIR. Jesting? May I shrivel into raisins if I jest! I love thee with a love that is a fever—with a love that is a frenzy—with a love that eateth up my heart! What sayest thou? Thou wilt not let my heart be eaten up?

ELSIE. *(aside).* Oh, mercy! What am I to say?

FAIR. Dost thou love me, or hast thou been insensible these two days?

ELSIE. I love all brave men.

FAIR. Nay, there is love in excess. I thank Heaven, there are many brave men in England; but if thou lovest them all, I withdraw my thanks.

ELSIE. I love the bravest best. But, sir, I may not listen—I am not free—I—I am a wife!

FAIR. Thou a wife? Whose? His name? His hours are numbered—nay, his grave is dug, and his epitaph set up! Come, his name?

ELSIE. Oh, sir! keep my secret—it is the only barrier that Fate could set up between us. My husband is none other than Colonel Fairfax!

FAIR. The greatest villain unhung! The most ill-begotten, ill-favoured, ill-mannered, ill-natured, ill-omened, ill-tempered dog in Christendom!

ELSIE. It is very like. He is naught to me—for I never saw him. I was blindfolded, and he was to have died within the hour; and he did not die—and I am wedded to him, and my heart is broken!

FAIR. He was to have died, and he did *not* die! The scoundrel! The perjured, traitrous, villain! Thou shouldst have insisted on his dying first, to make sure. 'Tis the only way with these Fairfaxes.

ELSIE. I now wish I had!

FAIR. *(aside).* Bloodthirsty little maiden! *(Aloud.)* A fig for this Fairfax! Be mine—he will never know—he dares not show himself; and if he dare, what art thou to him? Fly with me, Elsie—we will be married to-morrow, and thou shalt be the happiest wife in England!

ELSE. Master Leonard! I am amazed! Is it thus that brave soldiers speak to poor girls? Oh! for shame, for shame! I am wed—not the less because I love not my husband. I am a wife, sir, and I have a duty, and—oh, sir! thy words terrify me—they are not honest—they are wicked words, and unworthy thy great and brave heart! Oh, shame upon thee! shame upon thee!

FAIR. Nay, Elsie, I did but jest. I spake but to try thee.

[Shot heard.

Enter MERYLL, *hastily.*

MER. *(recit.)* Hark! What was that, sir?

FAIR.   Why, an arquebus—
Fired from the wharf, unless I much mistake.

MER. Strange—and at such an hour! What can it mean?

[In the meantime, the CHORUS *have entered.*

CHORUS.

Now what can that have been—
    A shot so late at night,
    Enough to cause affright!
What can the portent mean?

Are foemen in the land?
    Is London to be wrecked?
    What are we to expect?
What danger is at hand?
    Yes, let us understand
    What danger is at hand!

LIEUTENANT *enters, also* POINT *and* WILFRED.

LIEUT. Who fired that shot? At once the truth declare!

WIL. My lord, 'twas I—to rashly judge forbear!

POINT. My lord, 'twas he—to rashly judge forbear!

DUET *and* CHORUS.—WILFRED *and* POINT.

WIL. Like a ghost his vigil keeping—

POINT.   Or a spectre all-appalling—

WIL. I beheld a figure creeping—

POINT.   I should rather call it crawling—

WIL. He was creeping—

POINT.   He was crawling—

WIL. He was creeping, creeping—

POINT.   Crawling!

WIL. Not a moment's hesitation—
    I myself upon him flung,
With a hurried exclamation
    To his draperies I hung;
Then we closed with one another
In a rough-and-tumble smother;
Colonel Fairfax and no other
    Was the man to whom I clung!

ALL. Colonel Fairfax and no other
    Was the man to whom he clung!

WIL. After mighty tug and tussle—

POINT.   It resembled more a struggle—

WIL. He, by dint of stronger muscle—

POINT.   Or by some infernal juggle—

WIL. From my clutches quickly sliding—

POINT.   I should rather call it slipping—

WIL. With the view, no doubt, of hiding—

POINT.   Or escaping to the shipping—

WIL. With a gasp, and with a quiver—

POINT.   I'd describe it as a shiver—

WIL. Down he dived into the river
    And, alas, I cannot swim.

ALL. It's enough to make one shiver,
With a gasp and with a quiver;
Down he dived into the river,
    It was very brave of him!

WIL. Ingenuity is catching;
    With the view my king of pleasing,
Arquebus from sentry snatching—

POINT.   I should rather call it seizing—

WIL.   With an ounce or two of lead
    I despatched him through the head!

ALL.   He despatched him through the head!

WIL. I discharged it without winking,
Little time he lost in thinking,
Like a stone I saw him sinking—

POINT.   I should say a lump of lead.

WIL. Like a stone, my boy, I said—

POINT. Like a heavy lump of lead.

WIL. Anyhow the man is dead.

ALL. Whether stone or lump of lead,
    Arquebus from sentry seizing,
    With the view his king of pleasing.
    Wilfred shot him through the head,
    And he's very, very dead.

And it matters very little whether stone or lump of lead,
It is very, very certain that he's very, very dead!

RECITATIVE.—LIEUTENANT.

The river must be dragged—no time be lost;
The body must be found, at any cost.
To this attend without undue delay;
So set to work with what despatch ye may!   [*Exit.*

ALL.   Yes, yes,
We'll set to work with what despatch we may!

[*Four men raise* WILFRED, *and carry him off on their shoulders.*

CHORUS.

Hail the valiant fellow who
Did this deed of derring-do!
Honours wait on such an one;
By my head, 'twas bravely done

[*Exeunt all but* ELSIE, POINT, FAIRFAX, *and* PHŒBE.

POINT (*to* ELSIE, *who is weeping*). Nay, sweetheart, be comforted. This Fairfax was but a pestilent fellow, and, as he had to die, he might as well die thus as any other way. 'Twas a good death.

ELSIE. Still he was my husband, and had he not been, he was nevertheless a living man, and now he is dead; and so, by your leave, my tears may flow unchidden, Master Point.

FAIR. And thou didst see all this?

POINT. Ay, with both eyes at once—this and that. The testimony of one eye is naught—he may lie. But when it is corroborated by the other, it is good evidence that none may gainsay. Here are both present in court, ready to swear to him!

PHŒ. But art thou sure it was Colonel Fairfax? Saw you his face?

POINT. Ay, and a plaguy ill-favoured face too. A very hang-dog face—a felon face—a face to fright the headsman himself, and make him strike awry. Oh, a plaguy bad face, take my word for 't. (PHŒBE *and* FAIRFAX *laugh*). How they laugh! 'Tis ever thus with simple folk—an accepted wit has but to say, "Pass the mustard," and they roar their ribs out!

FAIR. (*aside*). If ever I come to life again thou shalt pay for this, Master Point!

POINT. Now, Elsie, thou art free to choose again, so behold me: I am young and well-favoured. I have a pretty wit. I can jest you, jibe you, quip you, crank you, wrack you, riddle you—

FAIR. Tush, man, thou knowest not how to woo. 'Tis not to be done with time-worn jests and thread-bare sophistries; with quips, conundrums, rhymes, and paradoxes. 'Tis an art in itself, and must be studied, gravely and conscientiously.

TRIO.—FAIRFAX, ELSIE, *and* PHŒBE.

FAIR.   A man who would woo a fair maid,
Should 'prentice himself to the trade;
    And study all day,
    In a methodical way,
How to flatter, cajole, and persuade.
He should 'prentice himself at fourteen,
And practice from morning to e'en;

And when he's of age,
If he will, I'll engage,
He may capture the heart of a queen!

ALL.   It is purely a matter of skill,
Which all may attain if they will:
    But every Jack,
    He must study the knack
If he wants to make sure of his Jill!

ELSIE.   If he's made the best use of his time,
His twig he'll so carefully lime,
    That every bird
    Will come down at his word,
Whatever its plumage and clime.
He must learn that the thrill of a touch
May mean little, or nothing, or much;
    It's an instrument rare,
    To be handled with care,
And ought to be treated as such.

ALL.   It is purely a matter of skill, etc.

PHŒ.   Then a glance may be timid or free,
It will vary in mighty degree,
    From an impudent stare
    To a look of despair
That no maid without pity can see.
And a glance of despair is no guide—
It may have its ridiculous side;
    It may draw you a tear
    Or a box on the ear;
You can never be sure till you've tried!

ALL.   It is purely a matter of skill, etc.

FAIR. (*aside to* POINT). Now, listen to me—'tis done thus. (*Aloud.*) Mistress Elsie, there is one here who, as thou knowest, loves thee right well!

POINT (*aside*). That he does—right well!

FAIR. He is but a man of poor estate, but he hath a loving, honest heart. He will be a true and trusty husband to thee, and if thou wilt be his wife, thou shalt lie curled up in his heart, like a little squirrel in its nest!

POINT (*aside*). 'Tis a pretty figure. A maggot in a nut lies closer, but a squirrel will do.

FAIR. He knoweth that thou wast a wife—an unloved and unloving wife, and his poor heart was near to breaking. But now that thine unloving husband is dead, and thou art free, he would fain pray that thou wouldst hearken unto him, and give him hope that thou wouldst be his!

PHŒ. (*alarmed*). He presses her hands—and he whispers in her ear! Odds boddikins, what does it mean?

FAIR. Now, sweetheart, tell me—wilt thou be this poor good fellow's wife?

ELSIE. If the good, brave man—*is* he a brave man?

FAIR. So men say.

POINT (*aside*). That's not true, but let it pass this once.

ELSIE. If this brave man will be content with a poor penniless untaught maid—

POINT (*aside*). Widow—but let *that* pass.

ELSIE. I will be his true and loving wife, and that with my heart of hearts!

FAIR. My own dear love! (Embracing her.)

PHŒ. (in great agitation). Why, what's all this? Brother—brother—it is not seemly!

POINT (also alarmed). (Aside.) Oh, I can't let that pass! (Aloud). Hold, enough, master Leonard! An advocate should have his fee, but methinks thou art over-paying thyself!

FAIR. Nay, that is for Elsie to say. I promised thee I would show thee how to woo, and herein is the proof of the virtue of my teaching. Go thou, and apply it elsewhere! (PHŒBE bursts into tears.)

QUARTETTE—ELSIE, FAIRFAX, PHŒBE, and POINT.

ELSIE and FAIR.
When a wooer
Goes a-wooing,
Naught is truer
Than his joy.
Maiden hushing
All his suing—
Boldly blushing—
Bravely coy!

ALL.
Oh, the happy days of doing!
Oh, the sighing and the suing!
When a wooer goes a-wooing,
Oh, the sweets that never cloy.

PHŒ. (weeping)
When a brother
Leaves his sister
For another,
Sister weeps.
Tears that trickle,
Tears that blister—
'Tis but mickle
Sister reaps!

ALL.
Oh, the doing and undoing,
Oh, the sighing and the suing,
When a brother goes a-wooing,
And a sobbing sister weeps!

POINT.
When a jester
Is out-witted,
Feelings fester,
Heart is lead!
Food for fishes
Only fitted,
Jester wishes
He was dead!

ALL.
Oh, the doing and undoing,
Oh, the sighing and the suing,
When a jester goes a-wooing,
And he wishes he was dead!

[Exeunt all but PHŒBE, who remains weeping.

PHŒ. And I helped that man to escape, and I've kept his secret, and pretended that I was his dearly loving sister, and done everything I could think of to make folk believe I was his loving sister, and this is his gratitude! Before I pretend to be sister to anybody again, I'll turn nun, and be sister to everybody—one as much as another!

Enter WILFRED.

WIL. In tears, eh? What a plague art thou grizzling for now?

PHŒ. Why am I grizzling? Thou hast often wept for jealousy—well, 'tis for jealousy I weep now. Ay, yellow, bilious, jaundiced jealousy. So make the most of that, Master Wilfred.

WIL. But I have never given thee cause for jealousy. The Lieutenant's cook-maid and I are but the merest gossips!

PHŒ. Jealous of thee! Bah! I'm jealous of no craven cock-on-a-hill, who crows about what he'd do an he dared! I am jealous of another and a better man than thou—set that down, Master Wilfred. And he is to marry Elsie Maynard, the little pale fool—set that down, Master Wilfred; and my heart is well nigh broken! There, thou hast it all! Make the most of it!

WIL. The man thou lovest is to marry Elsie Maynard? Why, that is no other than thy brother, Leonard Meryll!

PHŒ. (aside). Oh, mercy! what have I said?

WIL. Why, what manner of brother is this, thou lying little jade? Speak! Who is this man whom thou hast called brother, and fondled, and coddled, and kissed—with my connivance too! Oh! Lord, with my connivance! Ha! should it be this Fairfax! (PHŒBE starts.) It is! It is this accursed Fairfax! It's Fairfax! Fairfax, who—

PHŒ. Whom thou hast just shot through the head, and who lies at the bottom of the river!

WIL. A—I—I may have been mistaken. We are but fallible mortals, the best of us. But I'll make sure—I'll make sure. (Going.)

PHŒ. Stay—one word. I think it cannot be Fairfax—mind, I say I think—because thou hast just slain Fairfax. But whether he be Fairfax or no Fairfax, he is to marry Elsie—and—and—as thou hast shot him through the head, and he is dead, be content with that, and I will be thy wife!

WIL. Is that sure?

PHŒ. Ay, sure enough, for there's no help for it! Thou art a very brute—but even brutes must marry, I suppose.

WIL. My beloved! (Embraces her.)

PHŒ. (aside). Ugh!

Enter LEONARD, hastily.

LEON. Phœbe, rejoice, for I bring glad tidings. Colonel Fairfax's reprieve was signed two days since, but it was foully and maliciously kept back by Secretary Poltwhistle, who designed that it should arrive after the Colonel's death. It hath just come to hand, and it is now in the Lieutenant's possession!

PHŒ. Then the Colonel is free? Oh, kiss me, kiss me, my dear! Kiss me, again, and again!

WIL. (dancing with fury). Ods, bobs, death o' my life! Art thou mad? Am I mad? Are we all mad?

PHŒ. Oh, my dear—my dear, I'm well-nigh crazed with joy! (Kissing LEONARD.)

WIL. Come away from him, thou hussy—thou jade—thou kissing, clinging, cockatrice! And as for thee, sir, I'll rip thee like a herring for this! I'll skin thee for it! I'll cleave thee to the chine! I'll— Oh! Phœbe! Phœbe! Phœbe! Who is this man?

PHŒ. Peace, fool. He is my brother!

WIL. Another brother! Are there any more of them? Produce them all at once, and let me know the worst!

PHŒ. This is the real Leonard, dolt; the other was but his substitute. The *real* Leonard, I say—my father's own son.

WIL. How do I know this? Has he ''brother'' writ large on his brow? I mistrust thy brothers! Thou art but a false jade!

[*Exit* LEONARD.

PHŒ. Now, Wilfred, be just. Truly I did deceive thee before—but it was to save a precious life—and to save it, not for me, but for another. They are to be wed this very day. Is not this enough for thee? Come—I am thy Phœbe—thy very own—and we will be wed in a year—or two—or three, at the most. Is not that enough for thee?

Enter MERYLL, *excitedly, followed by* DAME CARRUTHERS
(who listens unobserved).

MER. Phœbe, hast thou heard the brave news?

PHŒ. *(still in* WILFRED's *arms).* Ay, father.

MER. I'm nigh mad with joy! *(Seeing* WILFRED.) Why, what's all this?

PHŒ. Oh, father, he discovered our secret through my folly, and the price of his silence is—

WIL. Phœbe's heart.

PHŒ. Oh dear, no—Phœbe's hand.

WIL. It's the same thing!

PHŒ. *Is* it! [*Exeunt* WILFRED *and* PHŒBE.

MER. *(looking after them).* 'Tis pity, but the Colonel had to be saved at any cost, and as thy folly revealed our secret, thy folly must e'en suffer for it! (DAME CARRUTHERS *comes down.*) Dame Carruthers!

DAME. So this is a plot to shield this arch-fiend, and I have detected it. A word from me, and three heads besides his would roll from their shoulders!

MER. Nay, Colonel Fairfax is reprieved. *(Aside.)* Yet if my complicity in his escape were known! Plague on the old meddler! There's nothing for it! *(Aloud.)* Hush, pretty one! Such bloodthirsty words ill become those cherry lips! *(Aside.)* Ugh!

DAME *(bashfully).* Sergeant Meryll!

MER. Why, look ye, chuck—for many a month I've—I've thought to myself—''There's snug love saving up in that middle-aged bosom for some one, and why not for thee—that's me—so take heart and tell her—that's thee—that thou—that's me—lovest her—thee—and—and—well, I'm a miserable old man, and I've done it—and that's me!'' But not a word about Fairfax! The price of thy silence is—

DAME. Meryll's heart?

MER. No, Meryll's *hand.*

DAME. It's the same thing!

MER. *Is* it!

DUET.—MERYLL *and* DAME CARRUTHERS.

DAME.   Rapture, rapture!
               When love's votary,
          Flushed with capture,
               Seeks the notary,
                    Joy and jollity
                    Then is polity;
                    Reigns frivolity!
          Rapture, rapture!

MER.   Doleful, doleful!
               When humanity,
          With its soul full
               Of satanity,
                    Courting privity,
                    Down declivity
                    Seeks captivity!
          Doleful, doleful!

DAME.   Joyful, joyful!
               When virginity
          Seeks, all coyful,
               Man's affinity;
                    Fate all flowery,
                    Bright and bowery
                    Is her dowery!
          Joyful, joyful!

MER.   Ghastly, ghastly!
               When man, sorrowful,
          Firstly, lastly,
               Of to-morrow full,
                    After tarrying,
                    Yields to harrying—
                    Goes a-marrying.
          Ghastly, ghastly!

FINALE.

Enter YEOMEN, WOMEN, *and* ELSIE *as Bride.*

CHORUS OF WOMEN.

(ELEGIACS.)

Comes the pretty young bride, a-blushing, timidly shrinking—
     Set all thy fears aside—cheerily, pretty young bride!
Brave is the youth to whom thy lot thou art willingly linking!
     Flower of valour is he—loving as loving can be!
               Brightly thy summer is shining,
               Fair is the dawn of the day;
                    Take him, be true to him—
                    Tender his due to him—
                    Honour him, love and obey!

TRIO.—PHŒBE, ELSIE, *and* DAME CARRUTHERS.

'Tis said that joy in full perfection
     Comes only once to womankind—
That, other times, on close inspection,
     Some lurking bitter we shall find.
If this be so, and men say truly,
My day of joy has broken duly.
     With happiness my soul is cloyed—
     This is my joy-day unalloyed!

ALL.   Yes, yes,
     This is her joy-day unalloyed!

Flourish. Enter LIEUTENANT.

LIEUT. Hold, pretty one! I bring to thee
    News—good or ill, it is for thee to say.
    Thy husband lives—and he is free,
    And comes to claim his bride this very day!

ELSIE. No! no! recall those words—it cannot be!
    Leonard, my Leonard, come, oh, come to me!
    Leonard, my own—my loved one—where art thou?
    I knew not how I loved thine heart till now!

ENSEMBLE.

ELSIE and PHŒBE.	CHORUS and OTHERS.	LIEUT. and POINT.
Oh, day of terror! day of tears!	Oh, day of terror! day of tears!	Come, dry these unbecoming tears,
What fearful tidings greet mine ears?	What words are these that greet our ears?	Most joyful tidings greet thine ears.
Oh, Leonard, come thou to my side,	Who is the man who, in his pride,	The man to whom thou art allied
And claim me as thy loving bride.	So boldly claims thee as his bride?	Appears to claim thee as his bride.

Flourish. Enter COLONEL FAIRFAX, *handsomely dressed,
and attended by other* GENTLEMEN.

FAIR. *(sternly.)* All thought of Leonard Meryll set aside.
    Thou art mine own! I claim thee as my bride.
ELSIE. A suppliant at thy feet I fall:
    Thine heart will yield to pity's call!
FAIR. Mine is a heart of massive rock,
    Unmoved by sentimental shock!
ALL.   Thy husband he!
ELSIE. Leonard, my loved one—come to me,
    They bear me hence away!
    But though they take me far from thee,
    My heart is thine for aye!
    My bruisèd heart,
        My broken heart,
    Is thine, my own, for aye!
(To FAIRFAX.*)* Sir, I obey,
    I am thy bride;
    But ere the fatal hour
    I said the say

    That placed me in thy power,
        Would I had died!
    Sir, I obey!
    I am thy bride!
(Looks up and recognizes FAIRFAX.*)* Leonard!
FAIR.   My own!
ELSIE.   Ah! *(Embrace.)*
ELSIE and ⎰ With happiness my soul is cloyed,
FAIR. ⎱ This is my joy-day unalloyed!
ALL.   Yes! yes!
    With happiness their souls are cloyed,
    This is their joy-day unalloyed!
POINT.   Oh thoughtless crew!
    Ye know not what ye do!
    Attend to me, and shed a tear or two—
    For I have a song to sing, O!
ALL.   Sing me your song, O! etc.
POINT.   It is sung to the moon
    By a love-lorn loon,
    Who fled from the mocking throng, O!
It's the song of a merryman moping mum,
Whose soul was sad and whose glance was glum,
Who sipped no sup and who craved no crumb,
    As he sighed for the love of a ladye!
ALL.   Heighdy! Heighdy!
    Misery me, lackadaydee!
He sipped no sup and he craved no crumb,
    As he sighed for the love of a ladye!
ELSIE. I have a song to sing, O!
ALL.   Sing me your song, O!
ELSIE.   It is sung with the ring
    Of the songs maids sing
    Who love with a love life-long, O!
It's the song of a merrymaid, peerly proud,
Who loved a lord, and who laughed aloud
At the moan of the merryman moping mum,
Whose soul was sad and whose glance was glum,
Who sipped no sup and who craved no crumb,
    As he sighed for the love of a layde!
ALL.   Heighdy! Heighdy!
    Misery me, lackadaydee!
He sipped no sup and he craved no crumb,
    As he sighed for the love of a ladye!

[FAIRFAX *embraces* ELSIE *as* POINT *falls insensible at their feet.*

The Gondoliers

or The King of Barataria

The Gondoliers is known as the sunniest of the Savoy operas. Gilbert is at his best, converting his *Bab* plots and interweaving with them an autobiographical kidnap. Sullivan's music is consistently spirited and the first night critics had only praise for the collaborators' Venetian venture. Yet, although the music has great *élan*, it has not the same artistic originality and spontaneous flow of the earlier operas. Sullivan said that its composition was a tremendous effort and a close look at the music reveals his search for evocative prototypes.

Sullivan had been in Venice just before starting work on his score, and in his boisterous gondolier

songs and dances he has caught the 'popular' Italian idiom. The Spanish element and the Italian peasant episodes seem to have been influenced by Bizet's *Carmen* and by Mozart's *Don Giovanni* and *Le Nozze di Figaro*. The two Mozart operas are set in Spain and situations in both works parallel episodes in *The Gondoliers* which are expressed in related music. For the would-be-Royals—a Viennese operetta phenomenon—Sullivan has looked to Johann Strauss. He had previously drawn on French comic opera but *The Gondoliers* is the first opera where he adopts the Viennese style, and this marks a change from his earlier, more subdued, comic writing. Sullivan was a master at manipulating his themes, original or otherwise, and the ear is everlastingly searching for the linked melodies.

Marco, Pacie Ripple and Giuseppe, Richard Green in the Terraine sets for the first repertory season, supervised by Gilbert, at the Savoy Theatre in 1907.

Gilbert has specified the date 1750 for his opera—a time when Venice was in its heyday—the Venice of Tiepolo when the *commedia dell'arte* was at its height. But he has launched out into other fields in order to air his ever-growing satirical views: Republicanism, the disintegration of social rank, religious- and sex-war, all come under attack.

Karl Marx's *Das Kapital* had been published in 1867 and his theories are outrightly condemned by Gilbert in his portrayal of the Baratarian monarchy 'tempered with Republican Equality', the 'monarchs' are happy, with more than enough to do to keep their 'equals' pacified. But their out-of-work 'equals' are surly and indolent despite professed contentment. The Duke of Plaza Toro and Don Alhambra are calculating rogues but, in Gilbert's opinion, it is these men with their insistence on rank and etiquette who make the world tick.

Gilbert was poking fun at religious discrimination when he converted the King of Barataria from Catholicism to Wesleyan Methodism (very topical in 1750). He has created the character of the Grand Inquisitor in order to make the kidnap of the Prince a viable deed. Sullivan has carried the joke in another direction by relating Don Alhambra's song to the tune of 'The Vicar of Bray'—that classical English religious turncoat.

The Duke of Plaza Toro is the most henpecked of all Gilbert's baritone leads and the most unashamedly resilient. His Duchess might be a reflection of Gilbert's mother—the marital disagreements and the tired relationship are so realistically expressed. She is bitingly aggressive and excites less sympathy than any previous contralto.

In *The Gondoliers* there are three heroes and three heroines. At this stage in the annals of the D'Oyly Carte Company the principals had become too self-important, particularly Jessie Bond. To counteract this trend, Gilbert put the *Gondoliers* maxim into practice: 'all shall equal be'. The leading roles are more widely spread, with less emphasis on individuals. This philosophical handling of crises shows Gilbert in a new light. *The Gondoliers* has repeated homilies on taking life calmly: 'Care's a canker that benumbs ...' and

> 'Live to love and love to live—
> You will ripen at your ease,
> Growing on the sunny side—

Gilbert and Sullivan were newly reconciled at this point in their collaboration, but in the quarrel that was to follow *The Gondoliers*, Gilbert did not live up to his mature words of wisdom. Their relationship afterwards became progressively more strained and their two subsequent operas were relatively unsuccessful. The farewell chorus at the end of *The Gondoliers* marks the end of an era.

SYNOPSIS

Architectural chords describe the Piazzetta in Venice. Maidens are binding posies for their two favourite gondoliers, Marco and Giuseppe, who are each coming to choose a bride. 'List and learn, ye dainty roses, ...' is a chorus, perhaps inspired by that of the village girls presenting flowers in Mozart's *Nozze di Figaro*. A solo from Fiametta midway in the graceful waltz expresses the Girls' excitement with flutter-tongue on the flute.

While the Girls are singing, Antonio, Francesco, Giorgio and other gondoliers are watching them unobserved; 'Good morrow, pretty maids, for whom prepare ye?' resembles the auction of servants at Richmond Fair in Flotow's *Martha*. Then, led by Antonio, the Gondoliers give their rendering of a 'Neapolitan' song very like Rossini's 'La Danza'.

Fiametta sees Marco and Giuseppe approaching and all attention turns to them. They greet the Girls formally: 'Buon' giorno, signorine!' and an exchange of Italian greetings follow. The piece has an affinity with the minuet in the finale to Act I of Mozart's *Don Giovanni*, but Sullivan has created a dance rhythm of male display, and the tune links with the previous 'Neapolitan' one.

Marco's and Giuseppe's following duet, 'We're called gondolieri ...' is a song in anticipation of wooing, as 'Expressive glances ...' is in *Princess Ida*. It is another variation on the 'Neapolitan' theme but the country dance from Don Giovanni's party in Act I seems to have had some influence. The verses gradually work up to an abandoned Cachucha.

Marco and Giuseppe now choose their brides in a game of blind-man's-buff. The Girls accuse the men of peeping in arch chatter reminiscent of the maid Adele in Johann Strauss's *Die Fledermaus*. The play begins in true folk-song style: 'My papa he keeps three horses...' are the words given by Kate

Greenaway for the traditional game which has been put into verse by Gilbert.

Giuseppe catches Tessa, and Marco Gianetta. 'Thank you, gallant gondoliers!' the girls' expression of gratitude, has a melody linked with that of 'List and learn, ...', and gradually moves into a reprise of the first song as the couples go to be married.

To fanfares and drums, a gondola arrives at the Piazzetta steps. The down-at-heel Spanish Duke of Plaza Toro disembarks with his Duchess, their daughter Casilda and their attendant Luiz, who carries a drum. Bemoaning the complete lack of ceremonial pomp, the Duke sends Luiz to announce their presence to the Grand Inquisitor. It is then revealed to Casilda that she was married in infancy to the Son of the King of Barataria. But the King became a Wesleyan Methodist so the Grand Inquisitor stole the Prince and brought him to Venice. Now that the King of Barataria has been killed in an insurrection, they have come to find Casilda's husband. Casilda attempts to extricate herself from the match on the grounds of her Father's poverty, but the Duke intends to create a new fashion by turning himself into a limited company. Casilda's scepticism invites a self-appraisal from the Duke:

> 'In enterprise of martial kind,
> When there was any fighting,
> He led his regiment from behind—
> He found it less exciting.'

This is sung over the rhythm of a Spanish Habañera with strumming string accompaniment.

Luiz has meanwhile proclaimed their arrival and the Duke and Duchess go into the Ducal Palace, leaving Luiz with Casilda. She has hitherto been

Don Alhambra del Bolero, the Grand Inquisitor—Kenneth Sandford.

aggressively haughty to him but now, to rapturous chords, they fly to each other's arms. In their simple, *Carmen*-inspired duet, 'Ah, well beloved!' Casilda apologizes for her 'cold disdain'. She tells Luiz of her infant marriage. He is amazed, as the nurse entrusted with the Prince was his mother. Casilda speaks dramatically of their past love and Luiz reflects fondly on days gone by. 'There was a time, ...' is a lament with a tolling chorus, 'Oh, bury, bury—let the grave close o'er ...' This replaced a ballad for Luiz early in the first production, and is a subtly linked melody with their previous duet.

The Duke and Duchess return with Don Alhambra del Bolero, the pompous Grand Inquisitor. He inspects Casilda with approval but she rejects his attentions and when he speaks of some doubt as to the whereabouts of her husband, she sees a ray of hope. 'A doubt? Oh dear, no—no doubt at all!' the Grand Inquisitor assures her, and explains in a ballad with tune re-echoing 'The Vicar of Bray'—'I stole the Prince, and brought him here, ...' He goes on to relate how he left the baby with 'a highly respectable gondolier' so fond of tippling that he was unable to distinguish between the infant

Prince and his own son. Within a year the gondolier died, and both boys grew up and followed his trade. There is no doubt, but to ascertain which gondolier is the Prince, Luiz is to fetch the Nurse, his mother, now married to a Spanish brigand in Cordova.

Casilda remonstrates in a grand operatic recitative and to counter her objection Don Alhambra moralizes

'... Life is one closely complicated tangle:
Death is the only true unraveller!'

'Try we life-long, we can never ...' is a quintet in the style of an anthem, reminiscent of Mozart's prelude to the ordeal by fire and water in *Die Zauberflöte* and reflects 'Care's a canker that benumbers ...'. The conclusion 'Hop and skip to Fancy's fiddle ...' is a reminder of the Fairies' aimless 'tripping hither, tripping thither' from *Iolanthe*.

A drone bass on low strings and bassoons—a bridal march—heralds the arrival of the Gondoliers and Contadine with the newly-wedded couples. They are hailed with 'Bridegroom and Bride!', a variation on Wagner's familiar wedding march. Gilbert's words for Tessa's song of rejoicing, 'When a merry maiden marries, ...' are touchingly evocative and Sullivan's simple melody, interspersed with flowing chorus, creates the atmosphere for 'All the year is merry May!'

The forbidding figure of Don Alhambra enters as the song ends and at the sight of his funereal appearance the crowd disperses. Only the two couples remain. When he discovers that they are married, the Grand Inquisitor—to their amazement—is very concerned. When he condemns their familiarity, Giuseppe expounds on their Republican and socialist beliefs. Don Alhambra then reveals that one of them is a King. 'As you are both Republicans, and hold Kings in detestation, of course you'll abdicate at once!' The Gondoliers, backed by their wives, rapidly change their minds and begin to speculate on the possibilities of an elevated position. Convinced that they are willing to be monarchs, Don Alhambra informs them that he has made arrangements for them to reign jointly in Barataria but that, for the present, 'ladies are not admitted'. The Girls are very upset. Gianetta's song, 'Kind sir, you cannot have the heart ....' with *pizzicato* accompaniment, is emotional, both musically and in sentiment. Gilbert's insistence upon

the differences between male and female love, which he first introduced in *The Yeomen*, is here put more poignantly:'

'Ah me, you men will never understand
That woman's heart is one with
woman's hand!'

In eighteenth-century style recitative, Don Alhambra reassures them that the separation will be temporary and they forthwith renew their joyous speculation in the quartet 'Then one of us will be a Queen, ...'. the rhythm suggests royalty on parade: the spinning of carriage wheels, the prancing of horses and general obeisance. Their fellow gondoliers, observing their mirth, question them and Marco and Giuseppe explain in lordly terms:

'Replying, we sing
As one individual, ...'

Their verse is shared in such a way that each sings half a line, the change of voice splitting the middle word. This entire 'royal' episode has a very definite similarity with Adele's aria of aspiration in Act III of *Die Fledermaus*. In growling chorus, the gondoliers show their disapproval of Marco's and Giuseppe's treachery to the Republican cause. Marco and Giuseppe convince them, in a children's-game-style Tarantella, listing the wide social range of Noble Lords-to-be: 'They all shall equal be'. Marco and Giuseppe, anxious to set forth, regret the parting from their loves, Gianetta and Tessa. Each bids a fond farewell, 'Now, Marco dear, ...' has a linked melody with Tessa's 'When a merry maiden marries'; and 'You'll lay your head ...' with Gianetta's flowing 'Kind sir ...'. Tessa's tearful, sentimental words have a remarkable, Gilbertian originality:

And if so be
You think of me,
Please tell the moon!
I'll read it all
In rays that fall
On the lagoon: ...'

Marco and Giuseppe join in the final chorus 'And O my darling, O my pet, ...'

A xebeque draws up to the quay and the Gondoliers embark to a rousing sea-song interspersed with 'One, two, three, Haul!' and an ecstatic solo for Marco, reminiscent of J.W. Wells's South Sea Island fantasy in *The Sorcerer*. The Girls embrace their lovers and wave farewell as the boat prepares to depart.

The Prelude to Act II begins with a spirited dance linked with 'For the merriest fellows are we ...', but within a few bars a momentary doubt is cast; however it is soon dispelled and the dance is resumed. Three months have passed; Marco and Giuseppe are in Barataria, enthroned in splendour side by side, cleaning the crown and sceptre while their friends, in the guise of ministers and officials,

stand by amusing themselves. In a Tarantella following on from the Prelude, the Gondoliers extol their monarchy, 'tempered with Republican Equality', while Marco and Giuseppe seem perfectly content to be at the mercy of their court on whom they have to wait. Their only complaint is that as one person they are allowed only one ration of food. After much persuasion their Courtiers grudgingly grant an interim order for double rations. Marco and Giuseppe proceed to enumerate their endless duties in a song with chorus—a traditional professional exposé not unlike 'A Policeman's lot is not a happy one!' from *The Pirates of Penzance*. Evocative fanfares and changing, hurrying rhythms give a highly coloured impression of their hectic existence:

'But the privilege and pleasure
That we treasure beyond measure
Is to run on little errands for the Ministers of State.'

The Command Performance of *The Gondoliers* at Windsor Castle on 6 March 1891. *Illustrated London News*, 14 March 1891.

The Plaza Toro Family: Casilda, Valerie Masterson; the Duke, John Reed; the Duchess, Christine Palmer in the last D'Oyly Carte productions of *The Gondoliers*.

Life is delightful, but they miss their wives.

Marco's song, 'Take a pair of sparkling eyes ...' a quasi-serenade with *pizzicato* accompaniment, reflects that a pretty girl and a little cot are all that is necessary for happiness. This is an exceptional tenor number and in looking for Sullivan's inspiration, Mozart's *Don Giovanni* has arias which make interesting comparison.

As this song finishes, the Contadine rush in to the Tarantella (first heard in the Overture). They are full of lively energy despite a rough crossing. An evocative horn solo (a rare event for Sullivan) accompanies Fiametta's sea song, and Vittoria's verse, 'Existence was slow and we wanted variety' is a quotation from *HMS Pinafore*. After a fond reunion, Tessa and Gianetta bombard their husbands with questions:

'Everything is interesting,
Tell us, tell us all about it! ...'

(Their song is reminiscent of the duet in *The Yeomen*, 'Like a ghost his vigil keeping ...'.) At Giuseppe's mention of a celebratory banquet and dance, the music breaks into a boisterous Cachucha in the true Italian popular style.

Amid the dancing and rejoicing, Don Alhambra enters and expresses his horror at the mixing of ranks in the Republican monarchy. In 'There lived a King,

as I've been told ...', he tells how a similar experiment ended disastrously:

'When everyone is somebodee,
Then no one's anybody'.

His song, another going back to 'The Vicar of Bray', is interspersed with bagpipe effects to illustrate the word 'toddy', and snatch of hornpipe at the mention of 'Admirals'.

Don Alhambra then reveals that the Duke of Plaza Toro is on his way, and that one of the Gondoliers is married to Casilda. The old Nurse has arrived and is about to be questioned. The Girls are furious and Marco tries to calm them. The quartet 'In a contemplative fashion ...' begins with studied calm, but emotions rise as the lovers voice their individual reflections, the Girls breaking into unbridled, jealous threats:

'And if I can catch her,
I'll pinch her and scratch her ...'

This scene is similar to one in *The Beggar's Opera*: Macheath's 'How happy could I be with either' followed by 'I'm bubbled, I'm bubbled ...' from the rival women.

A procession of retainers and a grand march herald the Duke of Plaza Toro Limited and his family in magnificent dress. In the absence of a Baratarian Welcome, the Duke and Duchess pay respects to their retinue and sing the praises of their Daughter. Casilda, unwilling to enter into marriage, is lectured by her parents who have, themselves, made the best of a bad job. The Duchess' song, 'On the day when I was wedded ...' follows an interchange of wry remarks. She describes how sweet compliance made no impression on her husband, and to a warhorse rhythm she confesses that the only way to drive him to affection was 'to be wife and husband too'.

Casilda deplores her shady family. But her parents leap to justify their dubious financial dealings. An intoned recitative by the Duke outlines his philanthropic deeds which transpire in the duet 'Small titles and orders ...' to be methods of promoting those less fortunate than himself to his own financial gain. Here one is reminded of the roguish Peachum and Mrs Peachum in *The Beggar's Opera*:

'Through all the employments of Life
Each neighbour abuses his brother ...'

The Gondoliers now arrive to meet the ducal party. They have no idea how to respond to ceremony and are hopelessly gauche. The Duke upbraids them for their failure to provide a Royal Welcome and then proceeds to instruct them in elementary court etiquette. The Gavotte, 'I am a courtier grave and serious ...', for five voices, is a masterpiece of wit, both in words and setting. The melody much resembles the Gavotte from Ambroise Thomas's opera *Mignon*.

When the Duke and Duchess depart, leaving Casilda with the Gondoliers, she confesses that her affections are already elsewhere and they, in turn, tell her that they are married; Tessa and Gianetta arrive at this point. The quintet, 'Here is a case unprecedented ...' is a mathematical fantasy:

'... when excellent husbands are bisected,
and wives divisible into three ...'

This quintet harks back to the Spanish, deriving shamelessly from the Act II quintet in *Carmen*.

Finale of *The Gondoliers*. Set and customes designed by Charles Ricketts in 1929, still used for this late '40s revival.

Carmenesque chords herald the arrival of Don Alhambra with the Duke and Duchess and the entire court. With great pomp, Don Alhambra announces that the Nurse is at hand and he bids everyone prepare to honour the rightful King. ('Long live the King!' from Handel's Coronation Anthem is suggested here.) As the Nurse is brought forward, chattered expectation from those concerned precedes her revelation. In her recitative—almost an incantation—she tells that when Catholic 'traitors' came to fetch the Prince away, she remained faithful to her Methodist King, his father. She gave them her own child and kept the Prince. The rightful King is—Luiz!

To general amazement Luiz, crowned and robed, ascends the throne. Casilda rushes to him. The Chorus expresses wonder and the two married couples are reunited with feelings of relief and disappointment. The ducal party express their pleasure in hymn-like chorus in a linked melody with the Duke of Plaza Toro's autobiographical song.'

Luiz is hailed and all kneel as he crowns Casilda. To a reprise of the Cachucha the company sing:

'So goodbye, cachucha, fandango, bolero—
We'll dance a farewell to that measure—
Old Xeres, adieu—Manzanilla—Montero—
We leave you with feelings of pleasure!'

THE GONDOLIERS;

OR

THE KING OF BARATARIA.

AN ENTIRELY ORIGINAL COMIC OPERA,

IN TWO ACTS.

First performed at the Savoy Theatre, 7 December 1889

DRAMATIS PERSONÆ

THE DUKE OF PLAZA-TORO [*a Grandee of Spain*]	baritone
LUIZ [*his Attendant*]	tenor
DON ALHAMBRA DEL BOLERO [*the Grand Inquisitor*]	baritone
MARCO PALMIERI	tenor
GIUSEPPE PALMIERI	baritone
ANTONIO	baritone
FRANCESCO [*Venetian Gondoliers*]	tenor
GIORGIO	bass
ANNIBALE	—
OTTAVIO	—
THE DUCHESS OF PLAZA-TORO	contralto
CASILDA [*her Daughter*]	soprano
GIANETTA	soprano
TESSA	mezzo-soprano
FIAMETTA [*Contadine*]	soprano
VITTORIA	mezzo-soprano
GIULIA	mezzo-soprano
INEZ [*the King's Foster-mother*]	mezzo-soprano

Chorus of Gondoliers and Contadine, Men-at-Arms, Heralds,
and Pages.

ACT I.

THE PIAZETTA, VENICE.

ACT II.

PAVILION IN THE PALACE OF BARATARIA.

An interval of three months is supposed to elapse between Acts I and II.

DATE—1750.

THE GONDOLIERS;

OR,

THE KING OF BARATARIA.

ACT I.

SCENE.—THE PIAZZETTA, VENICE. *The Ducal Palace on the right.*

FIAMETTA, GIULIA, VITTORIA, *and other* CONTADINE *discovered, each tying a bouquet of roses.*

CHORUS OF CONTADINE.

List and learn, ye dainty roses,
    Roses white and roses red,
Why we bind you into posies
    Ere your morning bloom has fled.
By a law of maiden's making,
Accents of a heart that's aching,
Even though that heart be breaking,
    Should by maiden be unsaid:
Though they love with love exceeding,
They must seem to be unheeding—
Go ye then and do their pleading,
    Roses white and roses red!

FIAMETTA.

Two there are for whom, in duty,
    Every maid in Venice sighs—
Two so peerless in their beauty
    That they shame the summer skies.
We have hearts for them, in plenty,
We, alas, are four-and-twenty!
    They have hearts, but all too few,
    They, alas, are only two!

CHORUS.

Now ye know, ye dainty roses,
Why we bind you into posies
    Ere your morning bloom has fled,
    Roses white and roses red!

[*During this chorus* ANTONIO, FRANCESCO, GIORGIO, *and other* GONDOLIERS *have entered unobserved by the* GIRLS—*at first two, then two more, then four, then half-a-dozen, then the remainder of the* CHORUS.

RECIT.

FRANC.   Good morrow, pretty maids; for whom prepare ye
    These floral tributes extraordinary?

FIA.   For Marco and Giuseppe Palmieri,
    The pink and flower of all the Gondolieri.

GIU.   They're coming here, as we have heard but lately,
    To choose two brides from us who sit sedately.

ANT.   Do all you maidens love them?

ALL.   Passionately!

ANT.   These gondoliers are to be envied greatly!

GIOR.   But what of us, who one and all adore you?
    Have pity on our passion, I implore you!

FIA.   These gentlemen must make their choice before you;

VIT.   In the meantime we tacitly ignore you.

GIU.   When they have chosen two that leaves you plenty—
    Two dozen we, and ye are four-and-twenty.

FIA. *and* VIT. Till then enjoy your *dolce far niente.*

ANT.   With pleasure, nobody *contradicente!*

SONG.—ANTONIO *and* CHORUS.

For the merriest fellows are we, tra la,
That ply on the emerald sea, tra la;
    With loving and laughing,
    And quipping and quaffing,
We're happy as happy can be, tra la—
    As happy as happy can be!
With sorrow we've nothing to do, tra la,
And care is a thing to pooh-pooh, tra la;
    And Jealousy yellow,
    Unfortunate fellow,
We drown in the shimmering blue, tra la—
    We drown in the shimmering blue!

FIA. *(looking off).* See, see, at last they come to make their choice—
    Let us acclaim them with united voice.

[MARCO *and* GIUSEPPE *appear in gondola at back*

ALL THE GIRLS. Hail, gallant gondolieri, ben' venuti!
    Accept our love, our homage, and our duty.

[MARCO *and* GIUSEPPE *jump ashore. The* GIRLS *salute them.*

DUET.—GIUSEPPE *and* MARCO, *with* CHORUS OF GIRLS.

GIU. *and* MAR.   Buon' giorno, signorine!

GIRLS.   Gondolieri carissimi!
    Siamo contadine!

GIU. *and* MAR. *(bowing).* Servitori umilissimi!
    Per chi questi fiori—
    Questi fiori bellissimi?

GIRLS.   Per voi, bei' signori
    O eccellentissimi!

[*The* GIRLS *present their bouquets to* GIUSEPPE *and* MARCO, *who are overwhelmed with them, and carry them with difficulty.*

GIU. *and* MAR. *(their arms full of flowers).* O ciel!
GIRLS. Buon' giorno, cavalieri!
GIU. *and* MAR. *(deprecatingly).* Siamo gondolieri.
(*To* FIA. *and* VIT.) Signorina, io t'amo!
GIRLS *(deprecatingly).* Contadine siamo.
GIU. *and* MAR. Signorine!
GIRLS *(deprecatingly).* Contadine!
(*Curtseying to* GIU. *and* MAR.) Cavalieri.
GIU. *and* MAR. *(deprecatingly).* Gondolieri!
Poveri gondolieri!
CHORUS. Buon' giorno, signorine, etc.

DUET.—MARCO *and* GIUSEPPE.

We're called *gondolieri*,
But that's a vagary,
It's quite honorary
    The trade that we ply.

For gallantry noted
Since we were short-coated,
To ladies devoted,
    My brother and I.

When morning is breaking,
Our couches forsaking,
To greet their awaking
    With carols we come.

At summer day's nooning,
When weary lagooning,
Our mandolins tuning,
    We lazily thrum.

When vespers are ringing,
To hope ever clinging,
With songs of our singing
    A vigil we keep.

When daylight is fading,
Enwrapt in night's shading,
With soft serenading
    We lull them to sleep.

We're called *gondolieri*, etc.

RECIT.—MARCO *and* GIUSEPPE.

And now to choose our brides!
    As all are young and fair,
And amiable besides,
    We really do not care
    A preference to declare.
A bias to disclose
    Would be indelicate—
And therefore we propose
    To let impartial Fate
    Select for us a mate!

ALL. Viva!
A bias to disclose
    Would be indelicate—
But how do they propose
    To let impartial Fate
    Select for them a mate?

MAR. These handkerchiefs upon our eyes be good enough to bind,
GIU. And take good care that both of us are absolutely blind;
BOTH. Then turn us round—and we, with all convenient despatch,
Will undertake to marry any two of you we catch!
ALL. Viva!
They undertake to marry any two of us they catch!

[*The* GIRLS *prepare to bind their eyes as directed.*

TESSA *(to* MARCO). Are you peeping?
    Can you see me?
MAR. Dark I'm keeping,
    Dark and dreamy!
        [*Slyly lifts bandage.*
VIT. *(to* GIUSEPPE). If you're blinded,
    Truly say so.
GIU. All right-minded
    Players play so!
        [*Slyly lifts bandage.*
FIA. *(detecting* MARCO). Conduct shady!
    They are cheating!
    Surely they de-
    Serve a beating!
        [*Replaces bandage.*
VIT. *(detecting* GIUSEPPE). This too much is;
    Maidens mocking—
    Conduct such is
    Truly shocking!
        [*Replaces bandage.*
ALL. You can spy, sir!
Shut your eye, sir!
You may use it by-and-by, sir!
You can see, sir!
Don't tell me, sir!
That will do—now let it be, sir!

ALL THE GIRLS. My papa he keeps three horses,
    Black, and white, and dapple grey, sir;
Turn three times, then take your courses,
    Catch which ever girl you may, sir!

[GIUSEPPE *and* MARCO *turn around, as directed, and try to catch the* GIRLS. *Business of blind-man's buff. Eventually* MARCO *catches* GIANETTA, *and* GIUSEPPE *catches* TESSA. *The two* GIRLS *try to escape, but in vain. The two* MEN *pass their hands over the* GIRLS' *faces to discover their identity.*

GIU. I've at length achieved a capture!
(*Guessing.*) This is Tessa! (*Removes bandage.*) Rapture, rapture!

MAR. *(guessing)* Gianetta fate has granted! *(Removes bandage)*
      Just the very girl I wanted!
GIU. *(politely to* MAR.*)* If you'd rather change—
TESSA.   My goodness!
      This indeed is simple rudeness.
MAR. *(politely to* GIU.*)* I've no preference whatever—
GIA.   Listen to him! Well, I never!

[*Each* MAN *kisses each* GIRL.

GIA. Thank you, gallant *gondolieri:*
          In a set and formal measure
      It is scarcely necessary
          To express our pride and pleasure.
          Each of us to prove a treasure,
      Conjugal and monetary,
          Gladly will devote our leisure,
      Gay and gallant *gondolieri.*
          La, la, la, la, la! etc.

TESSA. Gay and gallant *gondolieri,*
          Take us both and hold us tightly,
      You have luck extraordinary;
          We might both have been unsightly!
          If we judge your conduct rightly,
      'Twas a choice involuntary;
          Still we thank you most politely,
      Gay and gallant *gondolieri!*
          La, la, la, la, la! etc.

ALL THE GIRLS. To these gallant *gondolieri,*
          In a set and formal measure,
      It is scarcely necessary
          To express their pride and pleasure.
          Each of us to prove a treasure,
      Conjugal and monetary,
          Gladly will devote her leisure
      To the other *gondolieri!*
          La, la, la, la, la! etc.

ALL.   Fate in this has put his finger—
          Let us bow to Fate's decree,
      Then no longer let us linger,
          To the altar hurry we!

*They dance off two and two—*GIANETTA *with* MARCO,
      TESSA *with* GIUSEPPE.

Flourish. A gondola arrives at the Piazzetta steps, from which enter the
DUKE *of* PLAZA-TORO, *the* DUCHESS, *their daughter*
CASILDA, *and their attendant* LUIZ, *who carries a drum. All are*
dressed in pompous, but old and faded clothes.

ENTRÉE.

DUKE.   From the sunny Spanish shore,
            His Grace of Plaza-Tor'—
DUCH.   And His Grace's Duchess true—
CAS.   And His Grace's daughter, too—
LUIZ.   And His Grace's private drum
            To Venetia's shores have come:

ALL.   And if ever, ever, ever
                They get back to Spain,
            They will never, never, never
                Cross the sea again!

DUKE.   Neither that Grandee from the Spanish shore,
            The noble Duke of Plaza-Tor'—
DUCH.   Nor his Grace's Duchess, staunch and true—
CAS.   You may add, his Grace's daughter, too—
LUIZ.   And his Grace's own particular drum
            To Venetia's shores any more will come.
ALL.   And if ever, ever, ever
                They get back to Spain,
            They will never, never, never
                Cross the sea again!

DUKE. At last we have arrived at our destination. This is the Ducal Palace, and it is here that the Grand Inquisitor resides. As a Castilian hidalgo of ninety-five quarterings, I regret that I am unable to pay my state visit on a horse. As a Castilian hidalgo of that description, I should have preferred to ride through the streets of Venice; but owing, I presume, to an unusually wet season, the streets are in such a condition that equestrian exercise is impracticable. No matter. Where is our suite?

LUIZ *(coming forward).* Your Grace, I am here.

DUCH. Why do you not do yourself the honour to kneel when you address his Grace?

DUKE. My love, it is so small a matter! *(To* LUIZ.*)* Still, you may as well do it. (LUIZ *kneels.*)

CAS. The young man seems to entertain but an imperfect appreciation of the respect due from a menial to a Castilian hidalgo.

DUKE. My child, you are hard upon our suite.

CAS. Papa, I've no patience with the presumption of persons in his plebeian position. If he does not appreciate that position, let him be whipped until he does.

DUKE. Let us hope the omission was not intended as a slight. I should be much hurt if I thought it was. So would he. *(To* LUIZ.*)* Where are the halberdiers who were to have had the honour of meeting us here, that our visit to the Grand Inquisitor might be made in becoming state?

LUIZ. Your Grace, the halberdiers are mercenary people who stipulated for a trifle on account.

DUKE. How tiresome! Well, let us hope the Grand Inquisitor is a blind gentleman. And the band who were to have had the honour of escorting us? I see no band!

LUIZ. Your Grace, the band are sordid persons who required to be paid in advance.

DUKE. That's so like a band!

DUKE *(annoyed).* Insuperable difficulties meet me at every turn!

DUCH. But surely they know his Grace?

LUIZ. Exactly—they know his Grace.

DUKE. Well, let us hope that the Grand Inquisitor is a deaf gentleman. A cornet-à-piston would be something. You do not happen to possess the accomplishment of tooting like a cornet-à-piston?

LUIZ. Alas, no, your Grace! But I can imitate a farmyard.

DUKE *(doubtfully).* I don't see how that would help us. I don't see how we could bring it in.

CAS. It would not help us in the least. We are not a parcel of graziers come to market, dolt!

DUKE. My love, our suite's feelings! *(To* LUIZ.) Be so good as to ring the bell and inform the Grand Inquisitor that his Grace the Duke of Plaza-Toro, Count Matadoro, Baron Picadoro—

DUCH. And suite—

DUKE. Have arrived at Venice, and seek—

CAS. Desire—

DUCH. Demand!

DUKE. And demand an audience.

LUIZ. Your Grace has but to command. *(Rising.)*

DUKE *(much moved)*. I felt sure of it—I felt sure of it! *(Exit* LUIZ *into Ducal Palace.)* And now, my love—*(aside to* DUCHESS), shall we tell her? I think so. *(Aloud to* CASILDA.) And now, my love, prepare for a magnificent surprise. It is my agreeable duty to reveal to you a secret which should make you the happiest young lady in Venice!

CAS. A secret?

DUCH. A secret which, for State reasons, it has been necessary to preserve for twenty years.

DUKE. When you were a prattling babe of six months old you were married by proxy to no less a personage than the infant son and heir of His Majesty the immeasurably wealthy King of Barataria!

CAS. Married to the infant son of the King of Barataria? It was a most unpardonable liberty!

DUKE. Consider his extreme youth and forgive him. Shortly after the ceremony that misguided monarch abandoned the creed of his forefathers, and became a Wesleyan Methodist of the most bigoted and persecuting type. The Grand Inquisitor, determined that the innovation should not be perpetuated in Barataria, caused your smiling and unconscious husband to be stolen and conveyed to Venice. A fortnight since the Methodist Monarch and all his Wesleyan Court were killed in an insurrection, and we are here to ascertain the whereabouts of your husband, and to hail you, our daughter, as Her Majesty, the reigning Queen of Barataria! *(Kneels.)*

DUCH. Your Majesty! *(Kneels.)*

DUKE. It is at such moments as these that one feels how necessary it is to travel with a full band.

CAS. I, the Queen of Barataria! But I've nothing to wear! We are practically penniless!

DUKE. That point has not escaped me. Although I am unhappily in straightened circumstances at present, my social influence is something enormous; and a Company, to be called the Duke of Plaza-Toro, Limited, is in course of formation to work me. An influential directorate has been secured, and I myself shall join the Board after allotment.

CAS. Am I to understand that the Queen of Barataria may be called upon at any time to witness her honoured sire in process of liquidation?

DUCH. The speculation is not exempt from that drawback. If your father should stop, it will, of course, be necessary to wind him up.

CAS. But it's so undignified—it's so degrading! A Grandee of Spain turned into a public company! Such a thing was never heard of!

DUKE. My child, the Duke of Plaza-Toro does not follow fashions—he leads them. He always leads everybody. When he was in the army he led his regiment. He occasionally led them into action. He invariably led them out of it.

SONG.—DUKE OF PLAZA-TORO.

In enterprise of martial kind,
    When there was any fighting,
He led his regiment from behind—
    He found it less exciting.
But when away his regiment ran,
    His place was at the fore, O—
        That celebrated,
        Cultivated,
        Underrated
          Nobleman,
    The Duke of Plaza-Toro!

ALL.   In the first and foremost flight, ha, ha!
You always found that knight, ha, ha!
        That celebrated,
        Cultivated,
        Underrated
          Nobleman,
    The Duke of Plaza-Toro!

When, to evade Destruction's hand,
    To hide they all proceeded,
No soldier in that gallant band
    Hid half as well as he did.
He lay concealed throughout the war,
    And so preserved his gore, O!
        That unaffected,
        Undetected,
        Well-connected
          Warrior,
    The Duke of Plaza-Toro!

ALL.   In every doughty deed, ha, ha!
He always took the lead, ha, ha!
        That unaffected,
        Undetected,
        Well-connected
          Warrior,
    The Duke of Plaza-Toro!

When told that they would all be shot,
    Unless they left the service,
That hero hesitated not,
    So marvellous his nerve is.
He sent his resignation in,
    The first of all his corps, O!
        That very knowing,
        Over-flowing,
        Easy-going
          Paladin,
    The Duke of Plaza-Toro!

ALL.   To men of grosser clay, ha, ha!
He always showed the way, ha, ha!
        That very knowing,
        Over-flowing,
        Easy-going
          Paladin,
    The Duke of Plaza-Toro!

[*Exeunt* DUKE *and* DUCHESS *into Grand Ducal Palace. As soon as they have disappeared,* LUIZ *and* CASILDA *rush to each other's arms.*

RECITATIVE *and* DUETTINO.—CASILDA *and* LUIZ.

Oh, rapture, when alone together
    Two loving hearts and those that bear them
May join in temporary tether,
    Though Fate apart should rudely tear them,
Necessity, Invention's mother,

Compelled $\begin{Bmatrix} me \\ thee \end{Bmatrix}$ to a course of feigning—

But left alone with one another,

$\left.\begin{matrix} \text{I will} \\ \text{Thou shalt} \end{matrix}\right\}$ atone for $\begin{Bmatrix} my \\ thy \end{Bmatrix}$ disdaining!

CAS.   Ah, well-beloved,
            Mine angry frown
            Is but a gown
            That serves to dress
            My gentleness!

LUIZ.   Ah, well-beloved,
            Thy cold disdain,
            It gives no pain—
            'Tis mercy, played
            In masquerade!

BOTH.   Ah, well-beloved!

CAS. Oh, Luiz, Luiz—what have you said! What have I done! What have I allowed you to do!

LUIZ. Nothing, I trust, that you will ever have reason to repent. *(Offering to embrace her.)*

CAS. *(withdrawing from him).* Nay, Luiz, it may not be. I have embraced you for the last time.

LUIZ *(amazed).* Casilda!

CAS. I have just learnt, to my surprise and indignation, that I was wed in babyhood to the infant son of the King of Barataria!

LUIZ. The son of the King of Barataria? The child who was stolen in infancy by the Inquisition?

CAS. The same. But, of course, you know his story.

LUIZ. Know his story? Why I have often told you that my mother was the nurse to whose charge he was entrusted!

CAS. True. I had forgotten. Well, he has been discovered, and my father has brought me here to claim his hand.

LUIZ. But you will not recognize this marriage? It took place when you were too young to understand its import.

CAS. Nay, Luiz, respect my principles and cease to torture me with vain entreaties. Henceforth my life is another's.

LUIZ. But stay—the present and the future—*they* are another's; but the past—that at least is ours, and none can take it from us. As we may revel in naught else, let us revel in that!

CAS. I don't think I grasp your meaning.

LUIZ. Yet it is logical enough. You say you cease to love me?

CAS. *(demurely).* I say I *may* not love you.

LUIZ. But you do not say you *did* not love me?

CAS. I loved you with a frenzy that words are powerless to express—and that but ten brief minutes since!

LUIZ. Exactly. My own—that is, until ten minutes since, my own—my lately loved, my recently adored—tell me that until, say a quarter of an hour ago, I was all in all to thee!

[*Embracing her.*

CAS. I see your idea. It's ingenious; but don't do that.

[*Releasing herself.*

LUIZ. There can be no harm in revelling in the past.

CAS. None whatever; but an embrace cannot be taken to act retrospectively.

LUIZ. Perhaps not!

CAS. We may recollect an embrace—I recollect many—but we must not repeat them.

LUIZ. Then let us recollect a few! *(A moment's pause, as they recollect, then both heave a deep sigh.)*

LUIZ. Ah, Casilda, you were to me as the sun is to the earth!

CAS. A quarter of an hour ago?

LUIZ. About that.

CAS. And to think that, but for this miserable discovery, you would have been my own for life!

LUIZ. Through life to death—a quarter of an hour ago!

CAS. How greedily my thirsty ears would have drunk the golden melody of those sweet words a quarter—well it's now about twenty minutes since. *(Looking at her watch.)*

LUIZ. About that. In such a matter one cannot be too precise.

CAS. Then, henceforth, our love is but a memory!

LUIZ. It must be so, Casilda!

CAS. Luiz, it must be so!

DUET.—CASILDA *and* LUIZ.

LUIZ.   There was a time—
            A time for ever gone—ah, woe is me!
         It was no crime
            To love but thee alone—ah, woe is me!
         One heart, one life, one soul,
            One aim one goal—
         Each in the other's thrall,
            Each all in all, ah, woe is me!

ENSEMBLE. Oh, bury, bury—let the grave close o'er
         The days that were—that never will be more
         Oh, bury, bury love that all condemn,
         And let the whirlwind mourn its requiem!

CAS.   Dead as the last year's leaves—
            As gathered flowers—ah, woe is me!
         Dead as the garnered sheaves,
            That love of ours—ah, woe is me!
         Born but to fade and die
            When hope was high,
         Dead and as far away
            As yesterday—ah, woe is me!

ENSEMBLE. Oh, bury, bury—let the grave close o'er, etc.

Re-enter from the Ducal Palace the DUKE *and* DUCHESS, *followed by* DON ALHAMBRA BOLERO, *the Grand Inquisitor.*

DUKE. My child, allow me to present to you His Distinction Don Alhambra Bolero, the Grand Inquisitor of Spain. It was His Distinction who so thoughtfully abstracted your infant husband and brought him to Venice.

DON AL. So this is the little lady who is so unexpectedly called upon to assume the functions of Royalty! And a very nice little lady, too!

DUKE. Jimp, isn't she?

DON AL. Distinctly jimp. Allow me. *(Proceeds to inspect her—she turns away scornfully.)* Naughty temper!

DUKE. You must make some allowance. Her Majesty's head is a little turned by her access of dignity.

DON AL. I could have wished that Her Majesty's access of dignity had turned it in this direction. *(Aside.)* Prettily put!

DUCH. Unfortunately, if I am not mistaken, there appears to be some little doubt as to His Majesty's whereabouts.

CAS. A doubt as to his whereabouts? Then I may yet be saved!

DON AL. A doubt? Oh dear, no—no doubt at all! He is here, in Venice, plying the modest but picturesque calling of a gondolier. I can give you his address—I see him every day! In the entire annals of our history there is absolutely no circumstance so entirely free from all manner of doubt of any kind whatever! Listen, and I'll tell you all about it.

SONG.—GRAND INQUISITOR.

I stole the prince, and I brought him here,
    And left him, gaily prattling
With a highly respectable gondolier,
Who promised the Royal babe to rear,
And teach him the trade of a timoneer
    With his own beloved bratling.

    Both of the babes were strong and stout,
        And, considering all things, clever.
    Of that there is no manner of doubt—
    No probable, possible shadow of doubt—
        No possible doubt whatever.

Time sped, and when at the end of a year
    I sought that infant cherished,
That highly respected gondolier
Was lying a corpse on his humble bier—
I dropped a Grand Inquisitor's tear—
    That gondolier had perished.

    A taste for drink, combined with gout,
        Had doubled him up for ever.
    Of *that* there is no manner of doubt—
    No probable, possible shadow of doubt—
        No possible doubt whatever.

But owing, I'm much disposed to fear,
    To his terrible taste for tippling,
That highly respectable gondolier
Could never declare with a mind sincere
Which of the two was his offspring dear,
    And which the Royal stripling!

    Which was which he could never make out,
        Despite his best endeavour.
    Of *that* there is no manner of doubt—
    No probable, possible shadow of doubt—
        No possible doubt whatever.

The children followed his old career—
    (This statement can't be parried)
Of a highly respectable gondolier:
Well, one of the two (who will soon be here)—
But *which* of the two is not quite clear—
    Is the Royal Prince you married!

    Search in and out and round about
        And you'll discover never
    A tale so free from every doubt—
    All probable, possible shadow of doubt—
        All possible doubt whatever!

CAS. Then do you mean to say that I am married to one of two gondoliers, but it is impossible to say which?

DON AL. Without any doubt of any kind whatever. But be reassured: the nurse to whom your husband was entrusted is the mother of the musical young man who is such a past master of that delicately modulated instrument. *(Indicating the drum.)* She can, no doubt, establish the King's identity beyond all question.

LUIZ. Heavens, how did he know that?

DON AL. My young friend, a Grand Inquisitor is always up to date. *(To CAS.)* His mother is at present the wife of a highly respectable and old-established brigand, who carries on an extensive practice in the mountains around Cordova. Accompanied by two of my emissaries, he will set off at once for his mother's address. She will return with them, and if she finds any difficulty in making up her mind, the persuasive influence of the torture-chamber will jog her memory.

RECITATIVE.

CAS.   But, bless my heart, consider my position!
          I am the wife of one, that's very clear;
      But who can tell, except by intuition,
          Which is the Prince, and which the Gondolier?

DON AL. Submit to Fate without unseemly wrangle
          Such complications frequently occur—
      Life is one closely complicated tangle:
          Death is the only true unraveller!

QUINTETTE.

CASILDA, DUCHESS, LUIZ, DUKE, INQUISITOR.

Try we life-long, we can never
    Straighten out life's tangled skein,
Why should we, in vain endeavour,
    Guess and guess and guess again?
    Life's a pudding full of plums,
    Care's a canker that benumbs.
Wherefore waste our elocution
On impossible solution?
Life's a pleasant institution,
    Let us take it as it comes!

Set aside the dull enigma,
    We shall guess it all too soon;
Failure brings no kind of stigma—
    Dance we to another tune!

String the lyre and fill the cup,
Lest on sorrow we should sup.
Hop and skip to Fancy's fiddle,
Hands across and down the middle—
Life's perhaps the only riddle
That we shrink from giving up!

[*Exeunt all except* GRAND INQUISITOR *into Ducal Palace.*

Enter GONDOLIERS *and* CONTADINE, *followed by* MARCO,
GIANETTA, GIUSEPPE, *and* TESSA.

CHORUS.

Bridegroom and bride!
Knot that's insoluble,
Voices all voluble
Hail it with pride.
Bridegroom and bride!
Hail it with merriment;
It's an experiment
Frequently tried.

Bridegroom and bride!
Bridegrooms all joyfully,
Brides, rather coyfully,
Stand at their side.
Bridegroom and bride!
We in sincerity,
Wish you prosperity,
Bridegroom and bride!

SONG.—TESSA.

When a merry maiden marries,
Sorrow goes and pleasure tarries;
    Every sound becomes a song,
    All is right and nothing's wrong!
From to-day and ever after
Let our tears be tears of laughter.
    Every sigh that finds a vent
    Be a sigh of sweet content!
When you marry, merry maiden,
    Then the air with love is laden;
    Every flower is a rose,
    Every goose becomes a swan,
    Every kind of trouble goes
Where the last year's snows have gone!
Sunlight takes the place of shade
When you marry, merry maid!

When a merry maiden marries
Sorrow goes and pleasure tarries;
    Every sound becomes a song—
    All is right, and nothing's wrong.
Gnawing Care and aching Sorrow
Get ye gone until to-morrow;
    Jealousies in grim array,
    Ye are things of yesterday!
When you marry, merry maiden,
Then the air with joy is laden;
    All the corners of the earth

Ring with music sweetly played,
Worry is melodious mirth,
    Grief is joy in masquerade;
    Sullen night is laughing day—
    All the year is merry May!

[*At the end of the song* DON ALHAMBRA *enters at back. The*
    GONDOLIERS *and* CONTADINE *shrink from him, and*
    gradually go off, much alarmed.

GIU. And now our lives are going to begin in real earnest! What's a bachelor? A mere nothing—he's a chrysalis. He can't be said to live—he exists.

MAR. What a delightful institution marriage is! Why have we wasted all this time? Why didn't we marry ten years ago?

TESS. Because you couldn't find anybody nice enough.

GIA. Because you were waiting for *us.*

MAR. I suppose that *was* the reason. We were waiting for you without knowing it. (DON ALHAMBRA *comes forward.*) Hallo!

GIU. If this gentleman is an undertaker, it is a bad omen.

DON AL. Good morning. Festivities of some sort going on.

GIU. *(aside).* He *is* an undertaker! *(Aloud.)* No—a little unimportant family gathering. Nothing in *your* line.

DON AL. Somebody's birthday, I suppose?

GIU. Yes mine!

TESS. And mine!

GIA. And mine!

MAR. And mine!

DON AL. Curious coincidence! And how old may you be.

TESS. It's a rude question—but about ten minutes.

DON AL. Surely you are jesting?

TESS. In other words, we were married about ten minutes since.

DON AL. Married! You don't mean to say you are married?

MAR. Oh yes, we are married.

DON AL. What, both of you?

GIA. All four of us.

DON AL. *(aside).* Bless my heart, how extremely awkward!

GIA. You don't mind, I suppose?

TESS. You were not thinking of either of us for yourself, I presume? Oh, Giuseppe, look at him—he was! He's heart-broken!

DON AL. No, no—I wasn't! I wasn't! *(Aside.)* What will the Duke say?

GIU. Now, my man *(slapping him on the back),* we don't want anything in your line to-day, and if your curiosity's satisfied—

DON AL. You mustn't call me your man. It's a liberty. I don't think you know who I am.

GIU. Not we, indeed! We are jolly gondoliers, the sons of Baptisto Palmieri, who led the last revolution. Republicans, heart and soul, we hold all men to be equal. As we abhor oppression, we abhor kings; as we detest vain-glory, we detest rank; as we despise effeminacy, we despise wealth. We are Venetian gondoliers—your equals in everything except our calling, and in that at once your masters and your servants.

DON AL. Bless my heart, how unfortunate! One of you may be Baptisto's son, for anything I know the contrary; but the other is no less a personage than the only son of the late King of Barataria.

ALL. What!

DON AL. And I trust—I *trust* it was that one who slapped me on the shoulder and called me his man!

GIU. One of us a king!

MAR. Not brothers!

TESS. The King of Barataria!

GIA. Well, who'd have thought it!

MAR. But which is it?

} *Together.*

DON AL. What does it matter? As you are both Republicans, and hold kings in abhorrence, of course you'll abdicate at once. *(Going.)*

TESS. *and* GIA. Oh, don't do that! *(*MARCO *and* GIUSEPPE *stop him.)*

GIU. Well, as to that, of course there are kings and kings. When I say that I detest kings, I mean I detest *bad* kings.

DON AL. I see. It's a delicate distinction.

GIU. Quite so. Now I can conceive a kind of king—an ideal king—the creature of my fancy, you know—who would be absolutely unobjectionable. A king, for instance, who would abolish taxes and make everything cheap, except gondolas.

MAR. And give a great many free entertainments to the gondoliers.

GIU. And let off fireworks on the Grand Canal, and engage all the gondolas for the occasion.

MAR. And scramble money on the Rialto among the gondoliers.

GIU. Such a king would be a blessing to his people, and if I were a king, that is the sort of king I would be.

DON AL. Come, I'm glad to find your objections are not insuperable.

MAR. *and* GIU. Oh, they're not insuperable.

TESS. *and* GIA. No, they're not insuperable.

GIU. Besides, we are open to conviction. Our views may have been hastily formed on insufficient grounds. They may be crude, ill-digested, erroneous. I've a very poor opinion of the politician who is not open to conviction.

TESS. *(to* GIA.*)*. Oh, he's a fine fellow!

GIA. Yes, that's the sort of politician for *my* money!

DON AL. Then we'll consider it settled. Now, as the country is in a state of insurrection, it is absolutely necessary that you should assume the reins of Government at once; and, until it is ascertained which of you is to be king, I have arranged that you will reign jointly, so that no question can arise hereafter as to the validity of any of your acts.

MAR. As one individual?

DON AL. As one individual.

GIU. *(linking himself with* MARCO*)*. Like this?

DON AL. Something like that.

MAR. And we may take our friends with us, and give them places about the Court?

DON AL. Undoubtedly.

MAR. I'm convinced!

GIU. So am I!

TESS. Then the sooner we're off the better.

GIA. We'll just run home and pack up a few things. *(Going.)*

DON AL. Stop, stop—that won't do at all—we can't have any ladies. *(Aside.)* What will Her Majesty say!

ALL. What!

DON AL. Not at present. Afterwards, perhaps. We'll see.

GIU. Why, you don't mean to say you are going to separate us from our wives!

DON AL. *(aside)*. This is very awkward! *(Aloud.)* Only for a time—a few months. After all, what is a few months?

TESS. But we've only been married half an hour! *(Weeps.)*

SONG.—GIANETTA.

Kind sir, you cannot have the heart
Our lives to part
From those to whom an hour ago
We were united!
Before our flowing hopes you stem,
Ah, look at them,
And pause before you deal this blow,
All uninvited!
You men can never understand,
That heart and hand
Cannot be separated when
We go a-yearning-;
You see, you've only women's eyes
To idolize,
And only women's hearts, poor men,
To set *you* burning!
Ah me, you men will never understand
That woman's heart is one with woman's hand!

Some kind of charm you seem to find
In womankind—
Some source of unexplained delight
(Unless you're jesting),
But what attracts you, I confess,
I cannot guess,
To me a woman's face is quite
Uninteresting!
If from my sister I were torn,
It could be borne—
I should, no doubt, be horrified.
But I could bear it;—
But Marco's quite another thing—
He is my King,
He has my heart, and none beside
Shall ever share it!
Ah me, you men will never understand
That woman's heart is one with woman's hand!

FINALE.

RECITATIVE.—GRAND INQUISITOR.

Do not give way to this uncalled-for grief,
Your separation will be very brief.
To ascertain which is the King
And which the other,
To Barataria's Court I'll bring
His foster-mother;
Her former nurseling to declare
She'll be delighted.
That settled, let each happy pair
Be reunited.

MAR., GIU., TESS., GIA. Viva! His argument is strong!
Viva! We'll not be parted long!
Viva! It will be settled soon!
Viva! Then comes our honeymoon!

[*Exit* DON ALHAMBRA.

QUARTETTE.—TESSA, GIANETTA, MARCO, GIUSEPPE.

GIA.　Then one of us will be a Queen,
　　　　And sit on a golden throne,
　　　　　　With a crown instead
　　　　　　Of a hat on her head,
　　　　And diamonds all her own!
　　　　With a beautiful robe of gold and green,
　　　　I've always understood;
　　　　　　I wonder whether
　　　　　　She'd wear a feather?
　　　　I rather think she should!

ALL.　Oh! 'tis a glorious thing, I ween,
　　　　To be a regular Royal Queen!
　　　　No half-and-half affair, I mean,
　　　　But a right-down regular Royal Queen!

MAR.　She'll drive about in a carriage and pair,
　　　　With the King on her left-hand side,
　　　　　　And a milkwhite horse,
　　　　　　As a matter of course,
　　　　Whenever she wants to ride!
　　　　With beautiful silver shoes to wear
　　　　Upon her dainty feet;
　　　　　　With endless stocks
　　　　　　Of beautiful frocks,
　　　　And as much as she wants to eat!

ALL.　Oh! 'tis a glorious thing, I ween, etc.

TESS.　Whenever she condescends to walk,
　　　　Be sure she'll shine at that,
　　　　　　With her haughty stare,
　　　　　　And her nose in the air,
　　　　Like a well-born aristocrat!
　　　　At elegant high society talk
　　　　She'll bear away the bell,
　　　　　　With her "How de do?"
　　　　　　And her "How are you?"
　　　　And her "Hope I see you well!"

ALL.　Oh! 'tis a glorious thing, I ween, etc.

GIU.　And noble lords will scrape and bow,
　　　　And double them into two,
　　　　　　And open their eyes
　　　　　　In blank surprise
　　　　At whatever she likes to do.
　　　　And everybody will roundly vow
　　　　She's fair as flowers in May,
　　　　　　And say, "How clever!"
　　　　　　At whatsoever
　　　　She condescends to say!

　　　　Oh! 'tis a glorious thing, I ween,
　　　　To be a regular Royal Queen!
　　　　No half-and-half affair, I mean,
　　　　But a right-down regular Queen!

Enter CHORUS OF GONDOLIERS *and* CONTADINE.

CHORUS.

Now, pray, what is the cause of this remarkable hilarity?
　　This sudden ebullition of unmitigated jollity?
Has anybody blessed you with a sample of his charity?
　　Or have you been adopted by a gentleman of quality?

MAR. *and* GIU.　Replying, we sing
　　　　　　As one individual,
　　　　　　As I find I'm a king
　　　　　　　　To my kingdom I bid you all.
　　　　　　I'm aware you object
　　　　　　　　To pavilions and palaces,
　　　　　　But you'll find I respect
　　　　　　　　Your Republican fallacies.

CHORUS.　　As they know we object
　　　　　　　　To pavilions and palaces.
　　　　　　How can they respect
　　　　　　　　Our Republican fallacies?

MARCO *and* GIUSEPPE.

For every one who feels inclined,
Some post we undertake to find
Congenial with his peace of mind—
　　And all shall equal be.

The Chancellor in his peruke—
The Earl, the Marquis, and the Dook,
The Groom, the Butler, and the Cook—
　　They all shall equal be.

The Aristocrat who banks with Coutts,
The Aristocrat who hunts and shoots,
The Aristocrat who cleans our boots—
　　They all shall equal be!

The Noble Lord who rules the State—
The Noble Lord who cleans the plate—
The Noble Lord who scrubs the grate—
　　They all shall equal be!

The Lord High Bishop orthodox—
The Lord High Coachman on the box—
The Lord High Vagabond in the stocks—
　　They all shall equal be!
　　　　Sing high, sing low,
　　　　Wherever they go,
　　　　　　They all shall equal be!

CHORUS.　　　Sing high, sing low,
　　　　　　Wherever they go,
　　　　　　　　They all shall equal be!

The Earl, the Marquis, and the Dook,
The Groom, the Butler, and the Cook,
The Aristocrat who banks with Coutts,
The Aristocrat who cleans the boots,
The Noble Lord who rules the State,

The Noble Lord who scrubs the grate,
The Lord High Bishop orthodox,
The Lord High Vagabond in the stocks—
    Sing high, sing low,
    Wherever they go,
        They all shall equal be!

Then, hail! O King,
    Whichever you may be,
To you we sing,
    But do not bend the knee.
It may be thou—
    Likewise it may be thee—
So, hail! O King,
    Whichever you may be!

MARCO *and* GIUSEPPE *(together)*.

Then let's away—our island crown awaits me—
Conflicting feelings rend my soul apart!
The thought of Royal dignity elates me,
But leaving thee behind me breaks my heart!

[*Addressing* TESSA *and* GIANETTA.

TESSA *and* GIANETTA *(together)*.

Farewell, my love; on board you must be getting;
But while upon the sea you gaily roam,
Remember that a heart for thee is fretting—
The tender little heart you've left at home!

GIA. Now, Marco dear,
 My wishes hear:
  While you're away
 It's understood
 You will be good,
  And not too gay,
 To every trace
 Of maiden grace
  You will be blind,
 And will not glance
 By any chance
  On womankind!
 If you are wise,
 You'll shut your eyes
  'Till we arrive,
 And not address
 A lady less
  Than forty-five.
 You'll please to frown
 On every gown
  That you may see:
 And, oh, my pet
 You won't forget
  You've married me!

Oh, my darling, oh, my pet,
Whatever else you may forget,
In yonder isle beyond the sea,
Oh, don't forget you've married me!

TESS. You'll lay your head
 Upon your bed
  At set of sun.
 You will not sing
 Of anything
  To any one.
 You'll sit and mope
 All day, I hope,
  And shed a tear
 Upon the life
 Your little wife
  Is passing here.
 And if so be
 You think of me,
  Please tell the moon:
 I'll read it all
 In rays that fall
  On the lagoon;
 You'll be so kind
 As tell the wind
  How you may be,
 And send me words
 By little birds
  To comfort me!

And, oh, my darling, oh, my pet,
Whatever else you may forget,
In yonder isle beyond the sea,
Oh, don't forget you've married me!

CHORUS *(during which a "Xebeque" is hauled alongside the quay)*.

Then away we go to an island fair
 That lies in a Southern sea:
We know not where, and we don't much care,
 Wherever that isle may be.

THE MEN *(hauling on boat)*. One, two, three,
   Haul!
  One, two, three,
   Haul!
  One, two, three,
   Haul!
  With a will!

ALL. Then away we go, etc.

SOLO.—MARCO.

Away we go
 To a balmy isle,
Where the roses blow
 All the winter while.

ALL. Then pull, yeo ho! and again yeo ho! *(Hoisting sail.)*
 And again yeo ho! with a will!
 When the breezes are a-blowing,
 Then our ship will be a-going,
 When they don't we shall all stand still!

And away we go to the island fair,
That lies in a Southern sea,
We } now not where, and { we } don't much care,
They } { they }
Wherever that isle may be!

[*The* MEN *embark on the* "Xebeque". MARCO *and*
GIUSEPPE *embracing* GIANETTA *and* TESSA. *The*
GIRLS *wave a farewell to the* MEN *as the curtain falls.*

ACT II.

SCENE.—*Pavilion in the Court of Barataria.* MARCO *and* GIUSEPPE,
*magnificently dressed, are seated on two thrones, occupied in
cleaning the crown and the sceptre. The* GONDOLIERS *are
discovered dressed, some as courtiers, officers of rank, etc., and
others as private soldiers and servants of various degrees. All are
enjoying themselves without reference to social distinctions—
some playing cards, others throwing dice, some reading, others
playing cup and ball, "morra," etc.*

CHORUS.

Of happiness the very pith
In Barataria you may see,
A monarchy that's tempered with
Republican Equality.
This form of government we find
The beau ideal of its kind—
A despotism strict, combined
With absolute equality!

MARCO *and* GIUSEPPE.

Two kings, of undue pride bereft,
Who act in perfect unity,
Whom you can order right and left
With absolute impunity.
Who put their subjects at their ease
By doing all they can to please!
And thus, to earn their bread-and-cheese,
Seize every opportunity.

MAR. Gentlemen, we are much obliged to you for your
expressions of satisfaction and good-feeling. We are delighted, at
any time, to fall in with sentiments so charmingly expressed.

GIU. At the same time there is just one little grievance that we
should like to ventilate.

ALL (*angrily*). What!

GIU. Don't be alarmed—it's not serious. It is arranged that,
until it is decided which of us two is the actual King, we are to
act as one person.

GIORGIO. Exactly.

GIU. Now, although we act as *one* person, we are, in point of
fact, *two* persons.

ANNIBALE. Ah, I don't think we can go into that. It is a legal
fiction, and legal fictions are solemn things. Situated as we are,
we can't recognize two independent responsibilities.

GIU. No; but you can recognize two independent appetites.
It's all very well to say we act as one person, but when you

supply us with only one ration between us, I should describe it as
a legal fiction carried a little too far.

ANNI. It's rather a nice point. I don't like to express an opinion
off-hand. Suppose we reserve it for argument before the full
Court?

MAR. Yes, but what are we to do in the mean time?

ANNI. I think we may take an interim order for double rations
on their Majesties entering into the usual undertaking to
indemnify in the event of an adverse decision?

GIORGIO. That, I think, will meet the case. But you must
work hard—stick to it—nothing like work.

GIU. Oh, certainly. We quite understand that a man who
holds the magnificent position of King should do something to
justify it. We are called "Your Majesty," we are allowed to buy
ourselves magnificent clothes, our subjects frequently nod to us
in the streets, the sentries always return our salutes, and we enjoy
the inestimable privilege of heading the subscriptions to all the
principal charities. In return for these advantages the least we can
do is to make ourselves useful about the Palace.

SONG.—GIUSEPPE.

Rising early in the morning,
We proceed to light our fire,
Then our Majesty adorning
In its workaday attire,
We embark without delay
On the duties of the day.

First, we polish off some batches
Of political despatches,
And foreign politicians circumvent;
Then, if business isn't heavy,
We may hold a Royal *levée,*
Or ratify some acts of parliament.
Then we probably review the household troops—
With the usual "Shalloo humps!" and "Shalloo hoops!"
Or receive with ceremonial and state
An interesting Eastern potentate.
After that we generally
Go and dress our private *valet*—
(It's a rather nervous duty—he's a touchy little man)—
Write some letters literary
For our private secretary—
He is shaky in his spelling, so we help him if we can.
Then, in view of cravings inner,
We go down and order dinner;
Then we polish the Regalia and the Coronation Plate—
Spend an hour in titivating
All our Gentlemen-in-Waiting;
Or we run on little errands for the Ministers of State.
Oh, philosophers may sing
Of the troubles of a king;
Yet the duties are delightful, and the privileges great;
But the privilege and pleasure
That we treasure beyond measure
Is to run on little errands for the Ministers of State.
After luncheon (making merry
On a bun and glass of sherry),
If we've nothing particular to do,
We may make a Proclamation,
Or receive a Deputation—

Then we possibly create a Peer or two.
Then we help a fellow-creature on his path
With the Garter or the Thistle or the Bath.
Or we dress and toddle off in semi-State
To a festival, a function, or a *fête.*
    Then we go and stand as sentry
    At the Palace (private entry),
Marching hither, marching thither, up and down and to
    and fro,
    While the warrior on duty
    Goes in search of beer and beauty
(And it generally happens that he hasn't far to go).
    He relieves us, if he's able,
    Just in time to lay the table,
Then we dine and serve the coffee, and at half-past twelve
    or one,
    With a pleasure that's emphatic,
    We retire to our attic
With the gratifying feeling that our duty has been done!
    Oh, philosophers may sing
    Of the troubles of a King,
But of pleasures there are many and of troubles there are
    none;
    And the culminating pleasure
    That we treasure beyond measure
Is the gratifying feeling that our duty has been done!

[*Exeunt all but* MARCO *and* GIUSEPPE.

GIU. Yes it really is a very pleasant existence. They're all so extraordinarily kind and considerate. You don't find them wanting to do this, or wanting to do that, or saying, "It's my turn now". No, they let us have all the fun to ourselves, and never seem to grudge it.

MAR. It makes one feel quite selfish. It almost seems like taking advantage of their good nature.

GIU. How nice they were about the double rations.

MAR. Most considerate. Ah! there's only one thing wanting to make us thoroughly comfortable—the dear little wives we left behind us three months ago.

GIU. It *is* dull without female society. We can do without everything else, but we can't do without that.

MAR. And if we have that in perfection, we have everything. There is only one recipe for perfect happiness.

SONG.—MARCO.

Take a pair of sparkling eyes,
    Hidden, ever and anon,
        In a merciful eclipse—
Do not heed their mild surprise—
    Having passed the Rubicon.
        Take a pair of rosy lips;
Take a figure trimly planned—
    Such as admiration whets
        (Be particular in this);
Take a tender little hand,
    Fringed with dainty fingerettes,
        Press it—in parenthesis;—
Take all these, you lucky man—
Take and keep them, if you can!

Take a pretty little cot—
    Quite a miniature affair—
        Hung about with trellised vine,
Furnish it upon the spot
    With the treasures rich and rare
        I've endeavoured to define.
Live to love and love to live—
    You will ripen at your ease,
        Growing on the sunny side—
Fate has nothing more to give.
    You're a dainty man to please
        If you are not satisfied.
Take my counsel, happy man;
Act upon it, if you can!

Enter CHORUS OF CONTADINE, *running in, led by* FIAMETTA *and* VITTORIA. *They are met by all the* EX-GONDOLIERS, *who welcome them heartily.*

CHORUS OF CONTADINE.

Here we are, at the risk of our lives,
From ever so far, and we've brought your wives—
And to that end we've crossed the main,
And we don't intend to return again!

FIA.   Though obedience is strong,
                Curiosity's stronger—
            We waited for long,
                Till we couldn't wait longer.

VIT.   It's imprudent, we know,
                But without your society
            Existence was slow,
                And we long for variety—

ALL.   So here we are, at the risk of our lives,
        From ever so far, and we've brought your wives—
        And to that end we've crossed the main,
        And we don't intend to return again!

Enter TESSA *and* GIANETTA. *They rush to the arms of* GIUSEPPE *and* MARCO.

GIU. Tessa!
TESS.   Giuseppe!
GIA.   Marco!
MAR.   Gianetta!   [*Embrace.*

TESSA *and* GIANETTA. (*Alternate lines.*)

After sailing to this island—
        Tossing in a manner frightful,
We are all once more on dry land—
        And we find the change delightful.
As at home we've been remaining—
        We've not seen you both for ages,
Tell me, are you fond of reigning?
        How's the food, and what's the wages?
Does your new employment please ye?—
        How does Royalizing strike you?
Is it difficult or easy?

Do you think your subjects like you?
    I am anxious to elicit,
        Is it plain and easy steering?
Take it altogether, is it—
        Better fun than gondoliering?

CHORUS. We shall all go on requesting,
        Till you tell us, never doubt it,
    Everything is interesting,
        Tell us, tell us all about it!

Is the populace exacting?
        Do they keep you at a distance?
All unaided are you acting,
        Or do they provide assistance?
When you're busy, have you got to
        Get up early in the morning?
If you do what you ought not to,
        Do they give the usual warning?
With a horse do they equip you?
        Lots of trumpeting and drumming?
Do the Royal tradesmen tip you?
        Ain't the livery becoming?
Does your human being inner
        Feed on everything that nice is?
Do they give you wine for dinner?
        Peaches, sugar-plums, and ices?

CHORUS. We shall all go on requesting,
        Till you tell us, never doubt it;
    Everything is interesting,
        Tell us, tell us all about it!

MAR. This is indeed a most delightful surprise!

TESS. Yes, we thought you'd like it. You see, it was like this: After you left we felt very dull and mopey, and the days crawled by, and you never wrote; so at last I said to Gianetta, "I can't stand this any longer; those two poor Monarchs haven't got any one to mend their stockings, or sew on their buttons, or patch their clothes—at least, I hope they haven't—let us all pack up a change and go and see how they're getting on." And she said, "Done," and they all said, "Done;" and we asked old Giacopo to lend us his boat, and *he* said, "Done;" and we've crossed the sea, and, thank goodness, *that's* done; and here we are, and—and—*I've* done!

GIA. And now—which of you is King?

TESS. And which of us is Queen?

GIU. That we shan't know until Nurse turns up. But never mind that—the question is, how shall we celebrate the commencement of our honeymoon? Gentlemen, will you allow us to offer you a magnificent banquet?

ALL. We will!

GIU. Thanks very much; and what do you say to a dance?

TESS. A banquet *and* a dance! Oh, it's too much happiness!

CHORUS.

We will dance a cachucha, fandango, bolero,
Old Xeres we'll drink—Manzanilla, Montero—
For wine, when it runs in abundance, enhances
The reckless delight of that wildest of dances!

To the pretty pitter-pitter-patter,
And the clitter-clitter-clitter-clatter—
    Clitter-clitter-clatter,
    Pitter-pitter-patter
We will dance a cachucha, fandango, bolero;
Old Xeres we'll drink—Manzanilla, Montero—
For wine, when it runs in abundance, enhances
The reckless delight of that wildest of dances!

CACHUCHA.

The dance is interrupted by the unexpected appearance of DON ALHAMBRA, *who looks on with astonishment.* MARCO *and* GIUSEPPE *appear embarrassed. The others run off.*

DON AL. Good evening. Fancy ball?

GIU. No, not exactly. A little friendly dance. That's all.

DON AL. But I saw a groom dancing, and a footman!

GIU. Yes. That's the Lord High Footman.

DON AL. And, dear me, a common little drummer-boy!

MAR. Oh no! That's the Lord High Drummer Boy.

DON AL. But surely, surely the servants' hall is the place for these gentry?

GIU. Oh dear, no! *We* have appropriated the servants' hall. It's the Royal Apartment, and we permit no intruders.

MAR. We really must have some place that we can call our own.

DON AL. (*puzzled*). I'm afraid I'm not quite equal to the intellectual pressure of the conversation.

GIU. You see, the Monarchy has been re-modelled, on Republican principles. All departments rank equally, and everybody is at the head of his department.

DON AL. I see.

MAR. I'm afraid you're annoyed.

DON AL. No. I won't say that. It's not quite what I expected.

GIU. I'm awfully sorry.

MAR. So am I.

GIU. By-the-by, can I offer you anything after your voyage? A plate of macaroni and a rusk?

DON AL. (*preoccupied*). No, no—nothing—nothing.

GIU. Obliged to be careful?

DON AL. Yes—gout. You see, in every Court there are distinctions that must be observed.

GIU. (*puzzled*). There are, are there?

DON AL. Why, of course. For instance, you wouldn't have a Lord High Chancellor play leapfrog with his own cook.

GIU. Why not?

DON AL. Because a High Lord Chancellor is a personage of great dignity, who should never under any circumstances, place himself in the position of being told to tuck in his tuppenny, except by noblemen of his own rank.

GIU. Oh, I take you.

DON AL. For instance, a Lord High Archbishop might tell a Lord High Chancellor to tuck in his tuppenny, but certainly not a cook.

GIU. Not even a Lord High Cook?

DON AL. My good friend, that is a rank that is not recognised at the Lord Chamberlain's office. No, no, it won't do. I'll give you an instance in which the experiment was tried.

SONG.—DON ALHAMBRA.

There lived a King, as I've been told,
In the wonder-working days of old,
When hearts were twice as good as gold,
  And twenty times as mellow.
Good-temper triumphed in his face,
And in his heart he found a place
For all the erring human race
  And every wretched fellow.
When he had Rhenish wine to drink
It made him very sad to think
That some, at junket or at jink,
  Must be content with toddy.
He wished all men as rich as he
(And he was rich as rich could be),
So to the top of every tree
  Promoted everybody.

MAR. *and* GIU. Now, that's the kind of King for me—
  He wished all men as rich as he,
  So to the top of every tree
    Promoted everybody!

Lord Chancellors were cheap as sprats,
And Bishops in their shovel hats
Were plentiful as tabby cats—
  In point of fact, too many.
Ambassadors cropped up like hay,
Prime Ministers and such as they
Grew like asparagus in May,
  And Dukes were three a penny.
On every side Field Marshals gleamed,
Small beer were Lords Lieutenant deemed,
With Admirals the ocean teemed
  All round his wide dominions.
And Party Leaders you might meet
In twos and threes in every street,
Maintaining, with no little heat,
  Their various opinions.

MAR. *and* GIU. Now that's a sight you couldn't beat—
  Two Party Leaders in each street,
  Maintaining, with no little heat,
    Their various opinions!

That King, although no one denies,
His heart was of abnormal size,
Yet he'd have acted otherwise,
  If he had been acuter.
The end is easily foretold,
When every blessed thing you hold
Is made of silver, or of gold,
  You long for simple pewter.
When you have nothing else to wear
But cloth of gold and satins rare,
For cloth of gold you cease to care—
  Up goes the price of shoddy.
In short, whoever you may be,
To this conclusion you'll agree,
When every one is somebodee,
  Then no one's anybody!

MAR. *and* GIU. Now that's as plain as plain can be,
  To this conclusion we agree—
  When every one is somebodee,
    Then no one's anybody!

TESSA *and* GIANETTA *enter unobserved. The two* GIRLS, *impelled by curiosity, remain listening at the back of the stage.*

DON AL. And now I have some important news to communicate. His Grace the Duke of Plaza-Toro, Her Grace the Duchess, and their beautiful daughter Casilda—I say their beautiful daughter Casilda—have arrived at Barataria, and may be here at any moment.

MAR. The Duke and Duchess are nothing to us.

DON AL. But the daughter—the beautiful daughter! Aha! Oh, you're a lucky fellow, one of you!

GIU. I think you're a very incomprehensible old gentleman.

DON AL. Not a bit—I'll explain. Many years ago when you (whichever you are) were a baby, you (whichever you are) were married to a little girl who has grown up to be the most beautiful young lady in Spain. That beautiful young lady will be here to claim you (whichever you are) in half an hour, and I congratulate that one (whichever it is) with all my heart.

MAR. Married when a baby!

TESS. *and* GIA. *(aside).* Oh!

GIU. But we were married three months ago!

DON AL. One of you—only one. The other (whichever it is) is an unintentional bigamist.

MAR. *and* GIU. *(bewildered).* Oh, dear me!

TESS. *and* GIA. *(coming forward).* Well, upon my word!

DON AL. Eh? Who are these young people?

TESS. Who are we? Why, their wives, of course. We've just arrived.

DON AL. Their wives! Oh dear, this is very unfortunate. Oh, dear, this complicates matters! Dear, dear, what will the Duke say?

GIA. And do you mean to say that one of these Monarchs was already married?

TESS. And that neither of us will be a Queen?

DON AL. That is the idea I intended to convey. (TESSA *and* GIANETTA *begin to cry.*)

GIU. *(to* TESSA). Tessa, my dear, dear child—

TESS. Get away! perhaps it's you!

MAR. *(to* GIANETTA). My poor, poor little woman?

GIA. Don't. Who knows whose husband you are!

TESS. And pray, why didn't you tell us all about it before they left Venice?

DON AL. Because if I had, no earthly temptation would have induced these gentlemen to leave two such extremely fascinating and utterly irresistible little ladies! *(Aside.)* Neatly put!

TESS. There's something in that.

DON AL. I may mention that you will not be kept long in suspense, as the old lady who nursed the Royal child is at present in the Torture Chamber, waiting for me to interview her.

GIU. Poor old girl. Hadn't you better go and put her out of her suspense?

DON AL. Oh no—there's no hurry—she's all right. She has all the illustrated papers. However, I'll go and interrogate her, and, in the mean time, may I suggest the absolute propriety of your regarding yourselves as single young ladies.

[*Exit* DON ALHAMBRA.

TESS. Well, here's a pleasant state of things!

MAR. Delightful. One of us is married to two young ladies, and nobody knows which; and the other is married to one young lady whom nobody can identify!

GIA. And one of us is married to one of you, and the other is married to nobody.

TESS. But which of you is married to which of us, and what's to become of the other? *(About to cry.)*

GIU. It's quite simple. Two husbands have managed to acquire three wives. Three wives—two husbands. *(Reckoning up.)* That's two-thirds of a husband to each wife.

TESS. Oh, Mount Vesuvius, here we are in arithmetic! My good sir, one can't marry a vulgar fraction!

GIU. You've no right to call me a vulgar fraction.

MAR. We are getting rather mixed. The situation is entangled. Let's try and comb it out.

QUARTETTE.—MARCO, GIUSEPPE, TESSA, GIANETTA.

In a contemplative fashion,
    And a tranquil frame of mind,
Free from every kind of passion,
    Some solution let us find.
Let us grasp the situation,
    Solve the complicated plot—
Quiet, calm deliberation
    Disentangles every knot.

TESS. I, no doubt, Giuseppe wedded— THE OTHERS. In
    That's, of course, a slice of luck. [a contemplative
He is rather dunder-headed, [fashion, etc.
    Still distinctly, he's a duck.

GIA. I, a victim too of Cupid, *The Others.* Let
    Marco married—that is clear. [us grasp the
He's particularly stupid, [situation, etc.
    Still distinctly, he's a dear.

MAR. To Gianetta I was mated; THE OTHERS. In
    I can prove it in a trice: [a contemplative
Though her charms are overrated, [fashion, etc.
    Still I own she's rather nice.

GIU. I to Tessa, willy-nilly, THE OTHERS. Let
    All at once a victim fell. [us grasp the
She is what is called a silly, [situation, etc.
    Still she answers pretty well.

MAR. Now when we were pretty babies
    Some one married us, that is clear—
GIA. And if I can catch her
    I'll pinch her and scratch her,
    And send her away with a flea in her ear.

GIU. He, whom that young lady married,
    To receive her can't refuse.
TESS. If I overtake her
    I'll warrant I'll make her
    To shake in her aristocratical shoes!

GIA. *(to TESS.).* If she married your Giuseppe
    You and he will have to part—
TESS. *(to GIA.).* If I have to do it
    I'll warrant she'll rue it—
    I'll teach her to marry the man of my heart!

TESS. *(to GIA.).* If she married Messer Marco
    You're a spinster, that is plain—
GIA. *(to TESS.).* No matter—no matter,
    If I can get at her
    I doubt if her mother will know her again!

ALL. Quiet, calm deliberation
    Disentangles every knot!

[Exeunt, pondering.

MARCH. *Enter procession of* RETAINERS, *heralding approach of* DUKE, DUCHESS, *and* CASILDA. *All three are now dressed with the utmost magnificence.*

CHORUS.

With ducal pomp and ducal pride
    (Announce these comers,
    O ye kettle-drummers!)
Comes Barataria's high-born bride.
    (Ye sounding cymbals clang!)
She comes to claim the Royal hand—
    (Proclaim their Graces,
    O ye double basses!)
Of the King who rules this goodly land.
    (Ye brazen brasses bang!)

DUKE. This polite attention touches
    Heart of Duke and heart of Duchess,
DUCH. Who resign their pet
    With profound regret.
DUKE. She of beauty was a model
    When a tiny tiddle-toddle,
DUCH. And at twenty-one
    She's excelled by none!
ALL. With ducal pomp and ducal pride, etc.

DUKE *(to the attendants).* Be good enough to inform His Majesty that His Grace the Duke of Plaza-Toro, Limited, has arrived, and begs—

CAS. Desires.

DUCH. Demands.

DUKE. And demands an audience. *(Exeunt, attendants.)* And, now, my child, prepare to receive the husband to whom you were united under such interesting and romantic circumstances.

CAS. But which is it? There are two of them!

DUKE. It is true that at present His Majesty is a double gentleman; but as soon as the circumstances of his marriage are ascertained, he will, *ipso facto,* boil down to a single gentleman—thus presenting a unique example of an individual who becomes a single man and a married man by the same operation.

DUCH. *(severely).* I have known instances in which the characteristics of both conditions existed concurrently in the same individual.

DUKE. Ah, he couldn't have been a Plaza-Toro.

CAS. Well, whatever happens, I shall of course be a dutiful wife, but I can never love my husband.

DUKE. I don't know. It's extraordinary what unprepossessing people one can love if one gives one's mind to it.

DUCH. I loved your father.

DUKE. My love—that remark is a little hard, I think? Rather cruel, perhaps? Somewhat uncalled for, I venture to believe?

DUCH. It was very difficult, my dear; but I said to myself, "That man is a Duke, and I *will* love him." Several of my relations bet me I couldn't, but I did—desperately!

SONG.—DUCHESS.

On the day when I was wedded
    To your admirable sire,
I acknowledge that I dreaded
    An explosion of his ire.
I was overcome with panic—
For his temper was volcanic,
    And I didn't dare revolt,
    For I feared a thunderbolt!
I was always very wary,
    For his fury was ecstatic—
His refined vocabulary
    Most unpleasantly emphatic.
        To the thunder
            Of this Tartar
        I knocked under
            Like a martyr:
        When intently
            He was fuming,
        I was gently
            Unassuming—
        When reviling
            Me completely,
        I was smiling
            Very sweetly:
Giving him the very best, and getting back the very worst—
That is how I tried to tame your great progenitor—at first!

But I found that a reliance
    On my threatening appearance,
And a resolute defiance
    Of marital interference,
And a gentle intimation
Of my firm determination
    To see what I could do
    To be wife and husband too,
Was all that was required
    For to make his temper supple,
And you couldn't have desired
    A more reciprocating couple.
        Ever willing
            To be wooing,
        We were billing—
            We were cooing;
        When I merely
            From him parted

We were nearly
    Broken-hearted—
When in sequel
    Reunited,
We were equal
    Ly delighted.
So with double-shotted guns and colours nailed unto the mast,
I tamed your insignificant progenitor—at last!

CAS. My only hope is that when my husband sees what a shady family he has married into he will repudiate the contract altogether.

DUKE. Shady? A nobleman shady, who is blazing in the lustre of unaccustomed pocket-money? A nobleman shady, who can look back upon ninety-five quarterings? It is not every nobleman who is ninety-five quarters in arrear—I mean, who can look back upon ninety-five of them! And this, just as I have been floated at a premium! Oh, fie!

DUCH. Your Majesty is surely unaware that directly your Majesty's father came before the public he was applied for over and over again.

DUKE. My dear, her Majesty's father was in the habit of being applied for over and over again—and very urgently applied for, too—long before he was registered under the Limited Liability Act.

RECITATIVE.—DUKE.

To help unhappy commoners, and add to their enjoyment,
Affords a man of noble rank congenial employment;
Of our attempts we offer you examples illustrative:
The work is light, and, I may add, it's most remunerative!

DUET.—DUKE *and* DUCHESS.

DUKE.	Small titles and orders
	For Mayors and Recorders
	I get—and they're highly delighted—
DUCH.	They're highly delighted!
DUKE.	M.P.'s baroneted,
	Sham Colonel's gazetted,
	And second-rate Aldermen knighted—
DUCH.	Yes, Aldermen knighted.
DUKE.	Foundation-stone laying
	I find very paying:
	It adds a large sum to my makings—
DUCH.	Large sum to his makings.
DUKE.	At charity dinners
	The best of speech-spinners,
	I get ten per cent. on the takings—
DUCH.	One-tenth of the takings.
DUCH.	I present any lady
	Whose conduct is shady
	Or smacking of doubtful propriety—
DUKE.	Doubtful propriety,
DUCH.	When Virtue would quash her,
	I take and whitewash her,
	And launch her in first-rate society—
DUKE.	First-rate society!

DUCH. I recommend acres
Of clumsy dressmakers—
Their fit and their finishing touches—

DUKE. Their finishing touches.

DUCH. A sum in addition
They pay for permission
To say that they make for the Duchess—

DUKE. They make for the Duchess!

DUKE. Those pressing prevailers,
The ready-made tailors,
Quote me as their great double-barrel—

DUCH. Their great double-barrel.

DUKE. I allow them to do so,
Though Robinson Crusoe
Would jib at their wearing-apparel!

DUCH. Such wearing-apparel!

DUKE. I sit, by selection,
Upon the direction
Of several Companies' bubble—

DUCH. All Companies' bubble!

DUKE. As soon as they're floated
I'm freely bank-noted—
I'm pretty well paid for my trouble!

DUCH. He's paid for his trouble!

DUCH. At middle-class party
I play at *écarté*—
And I'm by no means a beginner—

DUKE *(significantly)*. She's not a beginner.

DUCH. To one of my station
The remuneration—
Five guineas a-night and my dinner—

DUKE. And wine with her dinner.

DUCH. I write letters blatant
On medicines patent—
And use any other you mustn't—

DUKE. Believe me, you mustn't—

DUCH. And vow my complexion
Derives its perfection
From somebody's soap—which it doesn't—

DUKE *(significantly)*. It certainly doesn't!

DUKE. We're ready as witness
To any one's fitness
To fill any place or preferment—

DUCH. A place or preferment.

DUCH. We're often in waiting
At junket or *fêting,*
And sometimes attend an interment—

DUKE. We like an interment.

BOTH. In short, if you'd kindle
The spark of a swindle,
Lure simpletons into your clutches—
Yes; into your clutches.
Or hoodwink a debtor,
You cannot do better

DUCH. Than trot out a Duke or a Duchess—

DUKE. A Duke or a Duchess!

Enter MARCO *and* GIUSEPPE.

DUKE. Ah! their Majesties. *(Bows with great ceremony.)*

MAR. The Duke of Plaza-Toro, I believe?

DUKE. The same. *(*MARCO *and* GIUSEPPE *offer to shake hands with him. The* DUKE *bows ceremoniously. They endeavour to imitate him.)* Allow me to present—

GIU. The young lady one of us married?

[MARCO *and* GIUSEPPE *offer to shake hands with her.* CASILDA *curtsies formally. They endeavour to imitate her.*

CAS. Gentlemen, I am the most obedient servant of one of you. *(Aside.)* Oh, Luiz!

DUKE. I am now about to address myself to the gentleman whom my daughter married; the other may allow his attention to wander if he likes, for what I am about to say does not concern him. Sir, you will find in this young lady a combination of excellences which you would search for in vain in any young lady who had not the good fortune to be my daughter. There is some little doubt as to which of you is the gentleman I am addressing, and which is the gentleman who is allowing his attention to wander; but when that doubt is solved, I shall say (still addressing the attentive gentleman), "Take her, and may she make you happier than her mother has made me."

DUCH. Sir!

DUKE. If possible. And now there is a little matter to which I think I am entitled to take exception. I come here in State with Her Grace the Duchess and Her Majesty, my daughter, and what do I find? Do I find, for instance, a guard of honour to receive me? No. The town illuminated? No. Refreshment provided? No. A Royal salute fired? No. Triumphal arches erected? No. The bells set ringing? Yes—one—the Visitors', and I rang it myself. It is not enough.

GIU. Upon my honour, I'm very sorry; but, you see, I was brought up in a gondola, and my ideas of politeness are confined to taking off my hat to my passengers when they tip me.

DUCH. That's all very well, but it is not enough.

GIU. I'll take off anything else in reason.

DUKE. But a Royal Salute to my daughter—it costs so little.

CAS. Papa, I don't want a salute.

GIU. My dear sir, as soon as we know which of us is entitled to take that liberty she shall have as many salutes as she likes.

MAR. As for guards of honour and triumphal arches, you don't know our people—they wouldn't stand it.

GIU. They are very off-hand with us—very off-hand indeed.

DUKE. Oh, but you mustn't allow that—you must keep them in proper discipline, you must impress your Court with your importance. You want deportment—carriage—manner—dignity. There must be a good deal of this sort of thing—*(business)*—and a little of this sort of thing—*(business)*—and possibly just a *soupçon* of this sort of thing!—*(business)*—and so on. Oh, it's very useful, and most effective. Just attend to me. You are a king—I am a subject. Very good—

QUINTETTE.—DUKE, DUCHESS, CASILDA, MARCO, GIUSEPPE

DUKE. I am a courtier grave and serious
Who is about to kiss your hand:
Try to combine a pose imperious
With a demeanour nobly bland.

MAR. *and* GIU. Let us combine a pose imperious
With a demeanour nobly bland.

[MARCO *and* GIUSEPPE *endeavour to carry out his instructions*

DUKE. That's, if anything, *too* unbending—
Too aggressively stiff and grand!
[*They suddenly modify their attitudes.*
Now to the other extreme you're tending—
Don't be so deucedly condescending!

DUCH. *and* } Now to the other extreme you're tending—
CAS. } Don't be so dreadfully condescending!

MAR. *and* } Oh, hard to please some noblemen seem!
GIU. } At first, if anything, *too* unbending!
Off we go to the other extreme—
Too confoundedly condescending;

DUKE Now a gavotte perform sedately—
Offer your hand with conscious pride;
Take an attitude not too stately,
Still sufficiently dignified.

MAR. *and* } Now for an attitude not too stately,
GIU. } Still sufficiently dignified.
[*They endeavour to carry out his instructions.*

DUKE (*beating time.*)
Oncely, twicely—oncely, twicely—
Bow impressively ere you glide.
[*They do so.*
Capital both—you've caught it nicely!
That is the sort of thing precisely!

DUCH. *and* } Capital both—they've caught it nicely!
CAS. } That is the sort of thing precisely!

MAR. *and* } Oh, sweet to earn a nobleman's praise!
GIU. } Capital both—we've caught it nicely!
Supposing he's right in what he says,
This is the sort of thing precisely!

[GAVOTTE. *At the end exeunt* DUKE *and* DUCHESS, *leaving* CASILDA
with MARCO *and* GIUSEPPE.

GIU. (*to* MARCO.) The old birds have gone away and left the young chickens together. That's called tact.

MAR. It's very awkward. We really ought to tell her how we are situated. It's not fair to the girl.

GIU. Undoubtedly, but I don't know how to begin. (*To* CASILDA.) A—Madam—

CAS. Gentlemen, I am bound to listen to you; but it is right to tell you that, not knowing I was married in infancy, I am over head and ears in love with somebody else.

GIU. Our case exactly! *We* are over head and ears in love with somebody else! (*Enter* TESSA *and* GIANETTA.) In point of fact, with our wives!

CAS. Your wives! Then you are married?

TESS. It's not our fault, you know. We knew nothing about it. We are sisters in misfortune.

CAS. My good girls, I don't blame you. Only before we go any further we must really arrive at some satisfactory arrangement, or we shall get hopelessly complicated.

QUINTETTE.—MARCO, GIUSEPPE, TESSA, GIANETTA, CASILDA

ALL Here is a fix unprecedented!
Here are a King and Queen ill-starred!
Ever since marriage was first invented
Never was known a case so hard!

MAR. *and* } I may be said to have been bisected,
GIU. } By a profound catastrophe!

GIA., TESS., } Through a calamity unexpected
AND CASS. } I am divisible into three!

ALL. Oh, moralists all,
How can you call
Marriage a state of unitee,
When excellent husbands are bisected,
And wives divisible into three?

Enter DON ALHAMBRA, *followed by* DUKE, DUCHESS, *and all the*
CHORUS.

FINALE.

RECITATIVE.—DON ALHAMBRA.

Now let the loyal lieges gather round—
The Prince's foster-mother has been found!
She will declare, to silver clarion's sound,
The rightful King—let him forthwith be
crowned!

CHORUS. She will declare, etc.

[DON ALHAMBRA *brings forward* INEZ, *the Prince's foster-mother.*

TESS. Speak, woman, speak—
DUKE. We're all attention—
GIA. The news we seek—
CAS. This moment mention,
DUCH. To us they bring—
DON. AL. His foster-mother.
MAR. Is he the King?
GIU. Or this my brother?
ALL. Speak, woman, speak, etc.

RECITATIVE.—INEZ.

The Royal Prince was by the King entrusted
To my fond care, ere I grew old and crusted;
When traitors came to steal his son reputed,
My own small boy I deftly substituted!
The villains fell into the trap completely—
I hid the Prince away—still sleeping sweetly;
I called him "son" with pardonable slyness—
His name, Luiz! Behold his Royal Highness!

[*Sensation.* LUIZ *ascends the throne, crowned and robed as King*

CAS. (*rushing to his arms.*) Luiz!
LUIZ. Casilda! (*Embrace*).

ALL Is this indeed the King,
Oh, wondrous revelation!
Oh, unexpected thing!
Unlooked-for situation!
[*They kneel.*

MARCO, GIANETTA, GIUSEPPE, TESSA.

This statement we receive
  With sentiments conflicting;
Our thoughts rejoice and grieve,
  Each other contradicting;
To those who we adore
  We can be reunited—
On one point rather sore,
  But, on the whole, delighted!

CASILDA, LUIZ, DUKE, AND DUCHESS.

LUIZ. When others claimed thy dainty hand,
     I waited—waited—waited—waited,
DUKE. As prudence (so I understand)
     Dictated—tated—tated—tated.

CAS. By virtue of our early vow
     Recorded—corded—corded—corded,
DUCH. Your pure and patient love is now
     Rewarded—warded—warded—warded.

ALL. Then hail, O King of a Golden Land,
And the high-born bride who claims his hand.
The past is dead, you gain your own,
A royal crown and a golden throne!

MAR. *and* GIU. Once more *gondolieri,*
     Both skilful and wary.
     Free from this quandary
      Contented are we.
     From Royalty flying,
     Our gondolas plying
     And merrily crying,
      Our *"premê," "stali!"*

ALL So, good-bye cachucha, fandango, bolero—
     We'll dance a farewell to that measure—
Old Xeres, adieu—Manzanilla—Montero—
     We leave you with feelings of pleasure!

CURTAIN.

Utopia, Limited

or The Flowers of Progress

George Bernard Shaw wrote: 'I enjoyed the score of *Utopia* more than that of the previous Savoy operas'. Gilbert's good-natured mockery of the artificiality of Victorian society, and his socialist 'Flowers of Progress', the colonial officials sent to reform Utopia in the name of virtuous England, was a rather Shavian concept.

Gilbert's Utopia is a tribal South Pacific island in the nature of Gauguin's Tahiti, happy and prosperous in its primitivity. It is ruled by a so-called despot, King Paramount. But he is in thrall to two Wise Men who watch his every move. They have been very subtly conceived—clowns and rogues—yet living up to their name in that they have devised a working method of government. The King is a paragon of virtue (the Wise Men take care of that) and yet he is forced by them to defame his own character in farce and satire as a kind of release mechanism to provide the populace with an outlet from strict rule. His mentors tell Paramount: 'It is not every monarch who enjoys the privilege of undoing by night all the despotic absurdities he's committed during the day—'.

Utopians are simple people, all too ready to take the word of colonials at face value. Conversely, the Flowers of Progress take matters into their own hands using personal initiative in reform whether or not sanctioned by England. The ingenious Christy Minstrel Cabinet Council carries this licence to the extreme. The Flowers of Progress clean up so thoroughly that Utopia becomes 'swamped with dull prosperity', and revolution is imminent —Government by party is the suggested solution—a similar, but far more complicated, method than that of the Wise Men. Despite Lord Dramaleigh's and Mr Goldbury's maxim that 'Art is wrong and Nature's right', Princess Zara, by importing the Flowers of Progress, has merely introduced Art at the expense of Nature.

When Gilbert first read his proposed plot for *Utopia, Limited* to Sullivan and George Grove at Roquebrune in January 1893, the composer was delighted with it and thought it was the best Gilbert had devised. Unfortunately it did not develop on the lines that Sullivan had expected as Gilbert's infatuation for the young American girl, Nancy McIntosh, upset the balance of the plot entirely. The part of Princess Zara was given to her (though she was neither a professional singer nor actress) and the libretto was written so as to provide her with a star part. For this reason the plots and sub-plots are inconclusive and the interest of the piece lies in the satire.

However, this dry political mockery was no inspiration for Sullivan. His music is witty, more skilled than that of the earlier operas, far more fluent and untidy than *The Gondoliers,* but generally lacking

Nancy McIntosh (1874-1954), later Gilbert's adopted daughter, as Princess Zara, her stage début.

in the heart that is such an integral part of his previous work. For the uninspiring Flowers of Progress and the grotesque tenor song, Sullivan cleverly borrows from his earlier operas. Goldbury, the Company Promoter, is the one interesting character, and to him Sullivan has given a dare-devil, carefree type of music which pervades episodes in the opera connected with the Utopia Company Limited that Goldbury has created.

The languorous Utopians express themselves in waltz music. The influence of Brahms's *Liebeslieder Walzer* can be traced, but Sullivan's compositions are, by comparison, vastly simplified despite interesting orchestration. There are many linked melodies interchanging between these waltz numbers. King Paramount has a strange mixture of styles—British patriotism mixed with Utopianism—giving a subtle impression of broken English. Sullivan is at his best in the music for the Wise Men. It is barbaric, tigerish and extremely original and witty.

In Lady Sophy, Sullivan refused to depict yet another love-starved, middle-aged predator, and Gilbert fell over himself to make his stock character palatable as well as sympathetic. They have succeeded here in creating a touching role from the prototype, but contemporary critics felt that the softening process was a failure. Certainly the pantomime-dame aspect of the contralto part was obliterated in Lady Sophy.

In *The Gondoliers* we saw a philosophic Gilbert: in *Utopia* he appears middle-aged, engrossed in business interests and the course of life in general. Paramount is one of his most complex characters, laughing at life, laughing at himself and yet afraid of being laughed at:

> 'Time's teetotum,
> If you spin it,
> Gives its quotum
> Once a minute ...'

> 'Joke beginning.
> Never ceases,
> Till your inning
> Time releases,
> On your way
> You blindly stray,
> And day by day
> The joke increases!'

SYNOPSIS

Fanfares and languid patriotic music breaking into birdsong serves as a prelude to introduce the Utopian Kingdom. Reclining Girls are discovered in a palm grove in the royal gardens overlooking the sea. They are enjoying themselves in 'lotus-eating fashion' and their opening chorus 'In lazy languor—motionless ...' resembles—but is more voluptuous than—the lilting song of the love-sick maidens in *Patience*. Sullivan has created an echo, evoking shimmering heat and a limpid sound with low strings and soprano solo for

> 'The rippling play
> Of waterway; ...'

Punch's view of the new concoction. October 1893.

The Utopian Vice-Chamberlain Calynx arrives with news that King Paramount's eldest daughter, Princess Zara, is to return after spending five years in England and taking a degree at Girton. The Girls receive the idea of the reforms she may bring with mixed feelings, but their speculations are interrupted by the dramatic entrance of Tarara, the Public Exploder, uttering a string of 'strong expressions' in Utopian. Everyone is shocked, as King Paramount has ordered that all communication must be made in English. The Exploder (producing a party cracker as an aid with which to accustom himself to his duties) goes on to explain that he has been newly appointed to blow up the King should His Majesty in any way abuse his autocratic powers. The King is watched day and night by two Wise Men whose duty it is to report any transgression to the Exploder. A scurrilous 'society' paper (*The Palace Peeper*) has been brought to the Exploder's notice—a scandal sheet relating to the King's abominable immoralities. The Exploder is furious with the Wise Men for condoning the King's behaviour.

A brash march, with unison chorus, heralds the arrival of the Wise Men, Scaphio and Phantis. There is a similarity, both in words and tune, between this march and the gospel hymn 'O, this is my land'. This episode also echoes Don Alhambra's two songs in *The Gondoliers*. The roguish duet for the Wise Men, 'In every mental lore ...', has shared sentences and skipping rhythm which is carried on into the repeat of 'So make way for the wise men ...'.

Phantis (aged fifty-five) now confesses to Scaphio (aged sixty-six) that he is in love. Scaphio has not yet found his ideal, '—a semi-transparent Being, filled with an inorganic pink jelly—', but Phantis has fallen for Princess Zara. In the duet, 'Let all your doubts take wing', resembling 'The truth is found' in *Princess Ida*, each performs a fantastic dance of which the other must divine the meaning.

A trumpet call on a repeated note followed by a flute passage heralds the arrival of the King's procession preceded by dancing girls. They usher him in with their lush chorus, 'Quaff the nectar—cull the roses—'. The musical introduction to the King's song is an uncertain blend of some of his numbers to come combined with Schubertian snatches. This song, 'A King of autocratic power we—' is quasi-patriotic in flavour, with a short quotation from *Rule Britannia* when Paramount speaks of modelling Utopia on Great Britain. His

Daughters of King Paramount, Nekaya and Kalyba—Emmie Owen and Florence Perry in their exotic Utopian costumes. Savoy Theatre, 7 October 1893.

two younger daughters have been 'finished' by an English Lady (his tone reveals his obvious affection for her) and Paramount intends that they shall be exhibited in public daily, as examples of 'maidenly perfection'.

Nekaya and Kalyba, twins of about fifteen, then appear. They are dressed in sober English costume and in a demure balletic episode, with solo violin obbligato, they pose before the populace. 'How fair! How modest! how discreet!' is a hymn-like Schubertian chorus of adulation. The Schubertian vein continues in their duet, 'Although of native maids the cream, ...'. The bouncing string accompaniment colours the gauche teenager impression Sullivan has created. Their governess, Lady Sophy, complete with lecturer's wand, is led on by the King. She puts the Princesses through their haughty paces as she simulates 'A course of maiden courtship, from the start to the triumphant matrimonial finish'. Her song, 'Bold-faced ranger' has a pulsating waltz rhythm as though it came from Brahms's *Liebeslieder Walzer*.

At the end of the lengthy demonstration, all the women move on for a repeat lecture in the market-place. The King, alone with Scaphio and Phantis (after being made to remove his crown) discusses his latest scurrilous writings, particularly his Comic Opera in which he has devised an outrageous impersonation of himself as an English Tenor. Paramount feels that, in his own interests, he has gone too far, but the Wise Men assure him to the contrary. The King muses on the quaint world:

'First you're born—and I'll be bound you
Find a dozen strangers round you.'

is an Irish jogging tune, a wry reflection on the progress of life, interspersed with a series of 'Ho! ho! ho! ho! ho! ho! ho!'

Scaphio and Phantis leave the King still pondering on the detrimental effect of his writings and the consequences of their falling into the hands of Princess Zara or Lady Sophy. He is interrupted by the Governess and intends to make overtures to her, but she gently forestalls him, telling him, 'I am not for you!' Confessing that she had formerly thought of lowering her respectability in order to accept Paramount's hand, she now produces *The Palace Peeper*, given her by the Public Exploder. The King tries to convince her of the untruth of the scandalous writings. Sophy questions no more statements but is puzzled that the King has not punished the offending journalist. Paramount excuses himself with reference to the Mikado—'I have the ground plan and sectional elevations of several punishments in my desk at this moment,' but as yet the ideal has

not been found. Their love duet, 'Subjected to your heavenly gaze ...' is once more reminiscent of the Brahms *Walzer*. Sophy gently pursues her objective of making Paramount punish the 'contemptible worm' but he is adamant—

'To treat this pest
As you suggest
Would pain my Majesty greatly.'

She finally exits on a dance of repudiation. This song re-echoes Phyllis's 'For riches and rank I do not long—' in *Iolanthe*.

The Utopian Court enters to British fanfares and a quick march which herald the arrival of Princess Zara, escorted by Captain Fitzbattleaxe and four Life Guards. She is welcomed by the Utopian Girls. The Princess then introduces herself in a Utopian solo, and then her entourage, who give a spirited military account of themselves and their sea journey. All join in their reminiscence of those left behind, 'Knightsbridge nursemaids—serving fairies—' and then Zara's trumpet call 'Tantantarara-rara-rara!' is blasted out. Against a reprise of the final chorus, Zara and Fitzbattleaxe sing a love duet.

As the Troopers stand at ease they are surrounded by gazing Utopian Girls of whom they take no notice. Lady Sophy is shocked, and at once removes Nekaya and Kalyba, but Fitzbattleaxe assures the King that the Guards are used to being stared at on sentry duty. The King, after reassuring himself that the practice is English, allows the Girls to continue. Zara thanks her gallant escort and he replies, taking up her song, that 'pleasure merely masquerades as Regimental Duty!' Then, to a reprise of the rousing march and love duet, they disperse, Zara going with her father.

As they leave, the two Wise Men see Zara. Scaphio instantly falls in love with her. Despite the dissuasion of Phantis, Scaphio remains in a state of high excitement. Zara, returning with Fitzbattleaxe, is at once accosted by the Wise Men and Scaphio declares love on behalf of both of them. Fitzbattleaxe acts quickly and proposes that, before they duel, they should give the lady to an officer of the Household Cavalry to hold in trust for the victor, as is done in England under the Rival Admirers' Clauses Consolidation Act.

In the rather prosaic manner of Pish-Tush in *The Mikado*, Fitzbattleaxe opens the quartet which clinches the agreement: 'It's understood, I think, all round ...' that he 'will hold the lady safe and sound'.

> 'If I should die and he should live,
> To you, without reserve, I give
> Her heart ...'

Both Wise Men address a similar speech to Fitzbattleaxe. Once more Zara and her lover express their feelings aside, against the repetition of the agreement in double-time by Scaphio and Phantis.

Zara and Fitzbattleaxe celebrate their triumph in a duet beginning with a reminiscence of that of the dragoon guards' entrance in *Patience*, and this becomes gentler for their love song, which is closely related to Nanki-Poo's kissing song in *The Mikado* (with a hint, too of *Am Donaus Strande* from the *Liebeslieder Walzer*). The words of the first verse are comic, but in the second verse Gilbert produces this philosophy of experience:

> 'There's no such case
> As perfect rest;
> Some pretty blight
> Asserts its sway—
> Some crumpled roseleaf light
> Is always in the way!'

Paramount finds Zara alone and she confronts him with a copy of *The Palace Peeper* which she has been given by Lady Sophy. After denouncing the paper, Zara guesses: 'If you were a free agent, you would never permit these outrages.' Paramount then tells her of the evil influence of the Wise Men and Zara advises him to put himself in the hands of the six select Representatives of prosperous England that she has imported.

Paramount is ready to try anything to rid himself of the Wise Men, and orders his Court to be summoned at once.

A blowzy, hurrying fanfare brings in the Assembly. The King addresses them, mentioning the Representatives from England to the patriotic strains of *Rule, Britannia*. The Court is joyful, with the exception of Scaphio and Phantis rumbling 'What does this mean?'

Now Zara addresses her 'Barbarian' Utopians with a trumpet-like proclamation and introduces the six English Flowers of Progress. First she presents Fitzbattleaxe. 'When Britain sounds the trump of war' has an elaborate patriotic introduction and is a reminder—in quick march time—of 'When Britain

really ruled the waves' in *Iolanthe*. The Utopians are impressed and hail him with their 'Ulahlica!' which follows each of her introductions. Sir Bailey Barre, QC, MP is next: 'Of all the arts and faculties the terse embodiment ...'. Zara's busy description (in the same rhythm as the Notary's song in *The Sorcerer*) is followed by Sir Bailey's own self-appraisal.

Lord Dramaleigh (a British Lord Chamberlain) and the County Councillor are introduced together. Strains of Phyllis's music from *Iolanthe* and the *Liebeslieder Walzer* accompany Lord Dramaleigh's attributes of moral cleanliness, both at Court and on the stage. Similarly, the County Councillor sings:

> 'I dwelling-houses sanitate,
> And purify the Halls!'

Mr Goldbury, the Company Promoter, has a busy song, echoing the rhythm of the speculating Duke of Plaza Toro.

Lastly, Captain Sir Edward Corcoran RN introduces himself after a lugubrious rendering of the sailor's hornpipe. Gradually his *Pinafore*-like song moves into the real thing with 'What, never?' and its usual follow-up by the whole Assembly.

A hymn of adulation from the Utopians precedes a short quartet, 'Ye wanderers from a mighty State, ...' from Zara, Lady Sophy, Fitzbattleaxe and the King. The somewhat incongruous waltz tune is again reminiscent of the previously quoted Brahms collection. The Flowers of Progress each deliver a characteristic sentence of advice, ending with Goldbury who proposes to float Utopia 'as a Company Limited'. The King and populace are puzzled. 'What does he mean? What does he mean?' growl Scaphio and Phantis. Goldbury explains in his jaunty, music-hall style song 'some seven men form an Association ... (It's shady, but it's sanctified by custom)' and

> 'Make the money-spinner spin,
> For you only stand to win ...'

typify the discourse ending:

> 'But the Liquidators say,
> "Never mind—you needn't pay,"
> So you start another Company to-morrow!'

The King feels it is dishonest, 'But if it's good enough for virtuous England ...'. Despite the warnings of the Wise Men, Paramount becomes very excited at the prospect of Utopia becoming a registered Company, and the proposal is unanimously hailed with 'Ulahlica!'

In a short solo the King rejoices:

'We'll go down to posterity
Of Sovereigns all the pink!'

Aside, in the manner of 'It really doesn't matter' from *Ruddigore,* Tarara the Public Exploder sings 'He'll go *up* to Posterity ...' while the Wise Men contradict him. The joke explained, they repeat his phrase while the Chorus joins with the King, and Zara and Fitzbattleaxe have another loving aside. In a trotting final chorus the act ends with an 'All hail!'

Ominous strains of *Ruddigore* are heard as Zara and Fitzbattleaxe are discovered at night in the Palace Throne Room. Uncertain snatches of Tolloller's song from *Iolanthe* follow. Fitzbattleaxe is attempting to serenade Zara but 'the fervour of his love' is affecting his voice. His attempted high C is a squawk. His neurotic song 'A tenor all singers above' is a mixture of Richard Dauntless's, the Defendant's and Tolloller's music interspersed with an ill-judged high note and cadenza.

'Why Arthur, what does it matter?' Fitzbattleaxe's lack of voice pales into insignificance when Zara thinks of the improvements made by the Flowers of Progress. As regards the services, they have been remodelled and reforms have been introduced which, even in England, were never dreamt of. In Mr Goldbury's department he has arranged things so that every Utopian is his own Limited Company. English dress has been introduced and the first Drawing-Room is about to take place.

Zara is just leaving to try on her Court Dress when Fitzbattleaxe declares his love for her. Zara reproves him:

'Words of love too loudly spoken
Ring their own untimely knell; ...'

Their duet starts in the same mood as Ralph's 'The Nightingale' from *Pinafore,* but continues with the lilting 'Sweet and Low', another waltz, with reference to the Tennyson-Barnby contemporary ballad. Fitzbattleaxe remains in the Throne Room as Paramount, dressed as a Field Marshal, makes his entrance. He is self-conscious and wonders, confidentially, whether he is not being made fun of.

The other Flowers of Progress now converge for an English Cabinet Council. Paramount, unfamiliar with the procedure, asks the Lord Chamberlain for instruction. Dramaleigh arranges the chairs in a line, as for a Christy Minstrel show, with the King presiding in the centre. When he asks for assurance that all 'is in accordance with the practice at the Court of St James's' Dramaleigh replies that 'it is in accordance with the practice at the Court of St James's Hall' (music hall). Then to the American plantation song, 'Johnny get a gun', in nigger-minstrel style, they embark on an appraisal of their remodelling. They have created England with improvements (an extremely revolutionary version of the real English social and political status quo). There is an exceedingly clever instrumental impersonation of this elementary jazz band (two violins, ukelele, banjo, tambourine and bones) by means of clarinets and bowed strings in a low register. King Paramount quickly adjusts to the medium, and executes a 'breakdown'—or wild dance, singing in falsetto voice.

A *marche dansante,* with a Polonaise snap, is played for the splendid entrance of the entire Royal Household. (This has a theme relating both to the Tower motif in *Yeomen* and to 'The threatened cloud ...' from *The Mikado*). The Princesses' trains are carried by Pages of Honour, and Lord Dramaleigh arranges the King on the throne with the Princesses on either side.

A complicated ceremonial of presentation takes place (in this instance closely related to reality). The background gavotte has more than a similarity with the opening Dance of the Hours from Ponchielli's *La Gioconda.* In a patriotic recitative based on *God Save the Queen*, Paramount vows 'We'll gloriously succeed or nobly fail!' His subjects respond in a hymn-like, unaccompanied chorus, in the mood of 'Hail, Poetry!' from *The Pirates*, to the words 'Eagle high in cloudland soaring' evocative of the native island. The orchestra takes up the melody as the Court disperses.

Scaphio and Phantis, dressed as judges, now come forward melodramatically. Their introductory music suggests preying animals and their words, 'With fury deep we burn—We do—' have seething string accompaniment. They mean to banish the Flowers of Progress and get the King into their power once more.

The King, witnessing their fury, demands to know their complaints. All their devious schemes have been ruined by the Flowers of Progress. Paramount merely refers them to the Secretary of Utopia Limited who will lay their written list of complaints before the Board. The Wise Men threaten him but the King is firm. In a trio the King demonstrates, to a reprise of the Wise Men's 'guessing' dance, that his mood means 'complete indifference'. The Wise Men's reply typifies 'remorselessness' while the King counteracts with 'unruffled cheerfulness'.

Together with the ineffectual Tarara, Scaphio and Phantis devise a plot to overthrow the King. Their trio 'With wily brain upon the spot' is one of Sullivan's most skilful and witty songs. It begins with a verse harking back to the conspiratorial element in *The Pirates* and then, over a pouncing dance *continuo* they make suggestions. Only the initial part of the sentence is heard, and the secret plan is tantalizingly whispered. However, it is clear that Scaphio's suggestions are not acceptable. The first verse ends:

> SCA. You're a drivelling barndoor owl!
> PHAN. You're a vapid and vain old muff!

After a short interlude they continue and this time Scaphio's proposals meet with absolute approval. However, the 'capital plan' is never revealed.

Dramaleigh and Goldbury now discuss the Drawing-Room with approval. Goldbury congratulates him on the innovation of tea and biscuits in particular. Then they turn to the subject of the timid young Princesses who forthwith appear without Lady Sophy. The two men soon disillusion the girls about the behaviour of English girls. Goldbury's song, 'A wonderful joy our eyes to bless ...' is in praise of the bright and beautiful English girl. Again

'At last a capital plot we've got'. Tarara the Public Exploder with Scaphio and Phantis. (L to r) W. H. Denny, Walter Passmore, John le Hay.

in waltz time, it is large and unornamented, but strangely ingratiating, just as is Gilbert's description.

In the following waltz quartet, the Girls rejoice in their newly-found licence while Dramaleigh and Goldbury instruct them (ironically) that Art is wrong and Nature's right. To a variation on 'Oh happy the blossom ...' from *Ruddigore* in a linked melody with Goldbury's Company Song, the Girls vow to undo their primness:

> 'And when I wish
> To hum a tune
> It needn't be a hymn one?'

'No! No!' the men sing in hymn-like chorus.

Lady Sophy, alone, bemoans the restrictive vows she has imposed upon herself in a sad recitative. Her song, 'When but a maid of fifteen year ...' is in the same nostalgic vein as Dr Daly's shy young curate from *The Sorcerer*. She tells of her ambition to marry 'a spotless King' but though she has searched in many lands, her paragon still remains undiscovered.

> 'Even Paramount's angelic grace—
> Ah me!
> Is but a mask on Nature's face!'

'Ah, Lady Sophy—then you love me!' the King cries, having overheard her, but in dramatic, heart-beating recitative (*The Palace Peeper* in hand) she denounces him. In equally emotional recitative, Paramount enlightens Lady Sophy, who cries

> 'And *that* is why you did not boil
> The author on the spot!'

Their duet of love and reconciliation, 'Oh, the rapture unrestrained ...' is a trotting variation on the Christy Minstrels episode. During their subsequent dance, Dramaleigh and Goldbury enter unobserved with the young Princesses. Zara and Fitzbattleaxe follow and are amazed to see the King kiss Lady Sophy. All restraint is thrown to the winds as the company breaks into a wild Tarantella, a disguised variation on the previous number.

At this point, Scaphio, Phantis and Tarara lead the populace in revolt. A chromatic shout from the Chorus, 'Down with the Flowers of Progress!', introduces Scaphio, their spokesman. He denounces the reforms which have brought Utopia to a stand-still—no wars, no illness, no litigation.

The King and Zara are perplexed, but Sir Bailey Barre whispers a solution to Zara. 'Of course! ... Why, I had forgotten ... Government by Party!' One party will undo all that the other has done and there will be a reversion to all the former ills.

'Ulahlica! Ulahlica!' shout the populace while Scaphio and Phantis, thwarted, are led off in custody. The King proclaims the adoption of Government by Party and pronounces Utopia not only a monarchy Limited, but a Limited Monarchy. Following a snatch of *Rule, Britannia* Zara leads the stirring, martial finale which is a skilfully blended variation on both Goldbury's songs. She describes Great Britain in glowing terms and then a slight doubt creeps in:

> 'Let us hope, for her sake,
> That she makes no mistake—
> That she's all she professes to be!'

Paramount takes up the song and holds Great Britain up as an example, but the opera ends on the note of doubt.

UTOPIA, LIMITED;

OR,

THE FLOWERS OF PROGRESS.

AN ORIGINAL COMIC OPERA,

IN TWO ACTS.

First performed at the Savoy Theatre, 7 October 1893

DRAMATIS PERSONÆ

KING PARAMOUNT THE FIRST [*King of Utopia*]	baritone
SCAPHIO ⎱	baritone
⎰ [*Judges of the Utopian Supreme Court*]	
PHANTIS ⎰	bass
TARARA [*the Public Exploder*]	baritone
CALYNX [*the Utopian Vice-Chamberlain*]	baritone

IMPORTED FLOWERS OF PROGRESS.

LORD DRAMALEIGH [*a British Lord Chamberlain*]	baritone
CAPTAIN FITZBATTLEAXE [*First Life Guards*]	tenor
CAPTAIN SIR EDWARD CORCORAN, K.C.B. [*of the Royal Navy*]	baritone
MR. GOLDBURY [*a Company Promoter—afterwards Comptroller of the Utopian Household*]	tenor
SIR BAILEY BARRE, Q.C., M.P.	tenor
MR. BLUSHINGTON [*of the County Council*]	baritone
THE PRINCESS ZARA [*Eldest Daughter of King Paramount*]	soprano
THE PRINCESS NEKAYA ⎱	soprano
⎰ [*her Younger Sisters*]	
THE PRINCESS KALYBA ⎰	mezzo-soprano
THE LADY SOPHY [*their English Gouvernante*]	contralto
SALATA ⎱	soprano
MELENE ⎰ [*Utopian Maidens*]	soprano
PHYLLA ⎰	soprano

ACT I.

A UTOPIAN PALM GROVE.

ACT II.

THRONE ROOM IN KING PARAMOUNT'S PALACE.

UTOPIA, LIMITED;

OR,

THE FLOWERS OF PROGRESS.

SCENE.—*A Utopian Palm Grove in the gardens of* KING PARA-MOUNT'S *Palace, showing a picturesque and luxuriant Tropical landscape, with the sea in the distance.* SALATA, MELENE, PHYLLA, *and other* MAIDENS *discovered, lying lazily about the stage and thoroughly enjoying themselves in lotus-eating fashion.*

OPENING CHORUS.

In lazy langour—motionless,
We lie and dream of nothingness;
　　For visions come
　　From Poppydom
　　　　Direct at our command:
Or, delicate alternative,
In open idleness we live,
　　With lyre and lute
　　And silver flute,
　　　　The life of Lazyland!

SOLO.—PHYLLA.

The song of birds
　　In ivied towers;
　　　　The rippling play
　　　　Of waterway;
The lowing herds;
　　The breath of flowers;
　　　　The languid loves
　　　　Of turtle doves—
These simple joys are all at hand
Upon thy shores, O Lazyland!

CHORUS.

In lazy languor, etc.

Enter CALYNX.

CAL. Good news! Great news! His Majesty's eldest daughter, Princess Zara, who left our shores five years since to go to England—the greatest, the most powerful, the wisest country in the world—has taken a high degree at Girton, and is on her way home again, having achieved a complete mastery over all the elements that have tended to raise that glorious country to her present pre-eminent position among civilized nations!

SAL. Then in a few months Utopia may hope to be completely Anglicized?

CAL. Absolutely and without a doubt.

MEL. *(lazily)*. We are very well as we are. Life without a care—every want supplied by a kind and fatherly monarch, who, despot though he be, has no other thought than to make his people happy—what have we to gain by the great change that is in store for us?

SAL. What have we to gain? English institutions, English tastes, and oh, English fashions!

CAL. England has made herself what she is because, in that favoured land, every one has to think for himself. Here we have no need to think, because our monarch anticipates all our wants, and our political opinions are formed for us by the journals to which we subscribe. Oh, think how much more brilliant this dialogue would have been, if we had been accustomed to exercise our reflective powers! They say that in England the conversation of the very meanest is a coruscation of impromptu epigram!

Enter TARARA *in a great rage.*

TAR. Lalabalele talala! Callabale lalabalica falahle!

CAL. *(horrified)*. Stop—stop, I beg!

[*All the ladies close their ears.*

TAR. Callamalala galalate! Caritalla lalabalee kallalale poo!

LADIES. Oh, stop him! stop him!

CAL. My Lord, I'm surprised at you. Are you not aware that His Majesty, in his despotic acquiescence with the emphatic wish of his people, has ordered that the Utopian language shall be banished from his court, and that all communications shall henceforward be made in the English tongue.

TAR. Yes, I'm perfectly aware of it, although— *(Suddenly presenting an explosive "cracker".)* Stop—allow me.

CAL. *(pulls it)*. Now, what's that for?

TAR. Why, I've recently been appointed Public Exploder to His Majesty, and as I'm constitutionally nervous, I must accustom myself by degrees to the startling nature of my duties. Thank you. I was about to say that although, as Public Exploder, I am next in succession to the throne, I nevertheless do my best to fall in with the royal decree. But when I am over-mastered by an indignant sense of overwhelming wrong, as I am now, I slip into my native tongue without knowing it. I am told that in the language of that great and pure nation, strong expressions do not exist, consequently when I want to let off steam I have no alternative but to say, "Lalabalele molola lililah kallalale poo!"

CAL. But what is your grievance?

TAR. This—by our Constitution we are governed by a Despot who, although in theory, absolute—is, in practice, nothing of the kind—being watched day and night by two Wise Men whose duty it is, on his very first lapse from political or social propriety, to denounce him to me, the Public Exploder, and it then becomes my duty to blow up His Majesty with dynamite—allow me. *(Presenting a cracker, which* CALYNX *pulls.)* Thank you—and, as some compensation to my wounded feelings, I reign in his stead.

CAL. Yes. After many unhappy experiments in the direction of an ideal Republic, it was found that what may be described as a Despotism tempered by Dynamite provides, on the whole, the most satisfactory description of ruler—an autocrat who dares not abuse his autocratic power.

TAR. That's the theory—but in practice, how does it act? Now, do you ever happen to see the *Palace Peeper?*

[*Producing a "Society" Paper.*

CAL. Never even heard of the journal.

TAR. I'm not surprised, because His Majesty's agents always buy up the whole edition; but I have an aunt in the publishing department, and she has supplied me with a copy. Well, it actually teems with circumstantially convincing details of the King's abominable immoralities! If this high-class journal may be believed, His Majesty is one of the most Heliogabalian profligates that ever disgraced an autocratic throne! And *do* these Wise Men denounce him to me? Not a bit of it! They wink at his immoralities! Under the circumstances I really think I am justified in exclaiming, "Lalabalele molola lililah kalabalele poo!" *(All horrified.)* I don't care—the occasion demands it.

[*Exit* TARARA

MARCH. *Enter* GUARD, *escorting* SCAPHIO *and* PHANTIS.

CHORUS.

Oh, make way for the Wise Men!
  They are prizemen—
  Double-first in the world's university!
For though lovely this island,
  (Which is *my* land,)
  She has no one to match them in *her* city.
They're the pride of Utopia—
  Cornucopia
  Is each in his mental fertility.
Oh, they never make blunder,
  And no wonder,
  For they're triumphs of infallibility.

DUET.—SCAPHIO *and* PHANTIS.

In every mental lore,
  (The statement smacks of vanity,)
We claim to rank before
  The wisest of humanity.
As gifts of head and heart
  We wasted on "utility,"
We're "cast" to play a part
  Of great responsibility.

Our duty is to spy
  Upon our King's illicities,
And keep a watchful eye
  On all his eccentricities.
If ever a trick he tries
  That savours of rascality,
At our decree he dies
  Without the least formality.

We fear no rude rebuff,
  Or newspaper publicity;
Our word is quite enough,
  The rest is electricity.
A pound of dynamite
  Explodes in his auriculars,
It's not a pleasant sight—
  We'll spare you the particulars.

It's force all men confess,
  The King needs no admonishing—
We may say its success
  Is something quite astonishing.
Our despot it imbues

With virtues quite delectable;
He minds his P's and Q's,—
  And keeps himself respectable.

Of a tyrant polite
He's a paragon quite.
He's as modest and mild
In his ways as a child;
And no one ever met
With an autocrat, yet,
So delightfully bland
To the least in the land!

So make way for the wise men, etc.

[*Exeunt all but* SCAPHIO *and* PHANTIS. PHANTIS *is pensive.*

SCA. Phantis, you are not in your customary exuberant spirits. What is wrong?

PHAN. Scaphio, I think you once told me that you have never loved?

SCA. Never! I have often marvelled at the fairy influence which weaves its rosy web about the faculties of the greatest and wisest of our race; but I thank Heaven I have never been subjected to its singular fascination. For, oh Phantis! there is that within me that tells me that when my time *does* come, the convulsion will be tremendous! When *I* love, it will be with the accumulated fervour of sixty-six years! But I have an ideal—a semi-transparent Being—filled with an inorganic pink jelly—and I have never yet seen the woman who approaches within measurable distance of it. All are opaque—opaque—opaque!

PHAN. Keep that ideal firmly before you, and love not until you find her. Though but fifty-five, I am an old campaigner in the battle-fields of Love; and, believe me, it is better to be as you are, heart-free and happy, than as I am—eternally racked with doubting agonies! Scaphio, the Princess Zara returns from England to-day!

SCA. My poor boy, I see it all!

PHAN. Oh! Scaphio, she is so beautiful. Ah! you smile, for you have never seen her. She sailed for England three months before you took office.

SCA. Now, tell me, is your affection requited?

PHAN. I do not know—I am not sure. Sometimes I think it is, and then come these torturing doubts! I feel sure that she does not regard me with absolute indifference, for she could never look at me without having to go to bed with a sick headache.

SCA. That is surely something. Come, take heart, boy! you are young and beautiful. What more could maiden want?

PHAN. Ah! Scaphio, remember she returns from a land where every youth is as a young Greek god, and where such poor beauty as I can boast is seen at every turn.

SCA. Be of good cheer! Marry her, boy, if so your fancy wills, and be sure that love will come.

PHAN. *(overjoyed).* Then you will assist me in this?

SCA. Why, surely! Silly one, what have you to fear? We have but to say the word, and her father must consent. Is he not our very slave? Come, take heart. I cannot bear to see you sad.

PHAN. Now I may hope, indeed! Scaphio, you have placed me on the very pinnacle of human joy!

DUET.—SCAPHIO *and* PHANTIS.

SCA. Let all your doubts take wing—
   Our influence is great.
  If Paramount our King
   Presume to hesitate,
    Put on the screw,
     And caution him
    That he will rue
     Disaster grim
    That must ensue
     To life and limb,
    Should he pooh-pooh
     This harmless whim.

BOTH. This harmless whim—this harmless whim.
  It is, as { I / you } say, a harmless whim.

PHAN. *(dancing).* Observe this dance
    Which I employ
    When I, by chance,
     Go mad with joy.
    What sentiment
     Does this express?

[PHANTIS *continues his dance while* SCAPHIO *vainly endeavours to discover its meaning.*

    Supreme content
     And happiness

BOTH. And happiness—and happiness—
  Of course it does—and happiness

PHAN. Your friendly aid conferred
   I need no longer pine.
  I've but to speak the word.
   And lo! the maid is mine!
    I do not choose
     To be denied.
    Or wish to lose
     A lovely bride—
    If to refuse
     The King decide,
    The Royal shoes
     Then woe betide!

BOTH. Then woe betide—then woe betide
  The Royal shoes then woe betide.

SCA. *(dancing).* This step to use
    I condescend
    Whene'er I chose
     To serve a friend.
    What it implies
     Now try to guess;

[SCAPHIO *continues his dance while* PHANTIS *is vainly endeavouring to discover its meaning.*

    It typifies
     Unselfishness!

BOTH. *(dancing).* Unselfishness! Unselfishness!
   Of course it does—unselfishness!
    This step to use
    We condescend! etc.

[*Exeunt* SCAPHIO *and* PHANTIS.

MARCH. *Enter* KING PARAMOUNT, *attended by* GUARDS *and* NOBLES, *and preceded by* GIRLS *dancing before him.*

CHORUS.

Quaff the nectar—cull the roses—
 Gather fruit and flowers in plenty!
For our King no longer poses—
 Sing the songs of *far niente!*
Wake the lute that sets us lilting,
 Dance a welcome to each comer;
Day by day our year is wilting—
 Sing the sunny songs of summer
     La, la, la, la!

SONG.—KING.

A King of autocratic power we—
 A despot whose tyrannic will is law—
Whose rule is paramount o'er land and sea,
 A Presence of unutterable awe!
But though the awe that I inspire
Must shrivel with imperial fire
 All foes whom it may chance to touch,
To judge by what I see and hear,
It does not seem to interfere
 With popular enjoyment, much.

CHORUS. No, no—it does not interfere
     With our enjoyment much.

RECITATIVE.—KING.

My subjects all, it is your wish emphatic
That all Utopia shall henceforth be modelled
Upon that glorious country called Great Britain—
To which some add—but others do not—Ireland.

ALL. It is!

KING. That being so, as you insist upon it,
  We have arranged that our two younger daughters
  Who have been "finished" by an English Lady—
(Tenderly.) A grave, and good, and gracious English Lady—
  Shall daily be exhibited in public,
  That all may learn what, from the English stand-point,
  Is looked upon as maidenly perfection!
  Come hither, daughters!

Enter NEKAYA *and* KALYBA. *They are twins, about fifteen years old; they are very modest and demure in their appearance, dress, and manner. They stand with their hands folded and their eyes cast down.*

CHORUS.

How fair! how modest! how discreet
 How bashfully demure!

See how they blush, as they've been taught,
At this publicity unsought!
How English and how pure!

DUET.—NEKAYA *and* KALYBA.

BOTH. Although of native maids the cream,
We're brought up on the English scheme—
The best of all
For great and small
Who modesty adore.

NEK. For English girls are good as gold,
Extremely modest (so we're told),
Demurely coy—divinely cold—

KAL.   And we are that—and more.

To please papa, who argues thus—
All girls should mould themselves on us
Because we are,
By furlongs far
The best of all the bunch,
We show ourselves to loud applause
From ten to four without a pause—

NEK. Which is an awkward time because
It cuts into our lunch.

BOTH.   Oh, maids of high and low degree,
Whose social code is rather free,
Please look at us and you will see
What good young ladies ought to be!

NEK. And as we stand, like clockwork toys,
A lecturer whom papa employs
Proceeds to praise
Our modest ways
And guileless character—

KAL. Our well-known blush—our downcast eyes—
Our famous look of mild surprise

NEK. (Which competition still defies)—

KAL.   Our celebrated "Sir!!!"

Then all the crowd take down our looks
In pocket memorandum books.
To diagnose
Our modest pose
The Kodaks do their best:

NEK. If evidence you would possess
Of what is maiden bashfulness,
You only need a button press—

KAL.   And *we* do all the rest

Enter LADY SOPHY—*an English lady of mature years and extreme
gravity of demeanour and dress. She carries a lecturer's wand
in her hand. She is led on by the* KING, *who expresses great
regard and admiration for her.*

RECITATIVE.—LADY SOPHY.

This morning we propose to illustrate
A course of maiden courtship, from the start
To the triumphant matrimonial finish.

[*Through the following song the two* PRINCESSES *illustrate in
gesture the description given by* LADY SOPHY.

SONG.—LADY SOPHY.

Bold-faced ranger
(Perfect stranger)
Meets two well-behaved young ladies.
He's attractive,
Young and active—
Each a little bit afraid is.
Youth advances,
At his glances
To their danger they awaken;
They repel him
As they tell him
He is very much mistaken.
Though they speak to him politely,
Please observe they're sneering slightly,
Just to show he's acting vainly.
This is Virtue saying plainly,
"Go away, young bachelor,
We are not what you take us for!"
When addressed impertinently,
English ladies answer gently,
"Go away, young bachelor,
We are not what you take us for!"
As he gazes,
Hat he raises,
Enters into conversation.
Makes excuses—
This produces
Interesting agitation.
He, with daring,
Undespairing,
Gives his card—his rank discloses—
Little heeding
This proceeding,
They turn up their little noses.
Pray observe this lesson vital—
When a man of rank and title
His position first discloses,

Always cock your little noses.
When at home, let all the class
Try this in the looking-glass.
English girls of well-bred notions,
Shun all unrehearsed emotions,
English girls of highest class
Practise them before the glass.

His intentions
Then he mentions
Something definite to go on—
Makes recitals
Of his titles,
Hints at sentiments, and so on.
Smiling sweetly,
They, discreetly,
Ask for further evidences:
Thus invited,
He, delighted,

Gives the usual references.
This is business. Each is fluttered
When the offer's fairly uttered.
"Which of them has his affection?"
He declines to make selection.
        Do they quarrel for his dross?
        Not a bit of it—they toss!
Please observe this cogent moral—
English ladies never quarrel.
        When a doubt they come across,
        English ladies always toss.

RECITATIVE.—LADY SOPHY.

The lecture's ended. In ten minutes' space
'Twill be repeated in the market-place!

[*Exit* LADY SOPHY, *followed by* NEKAYA *and* KALYBA

CHORUS.

Quaff the nectar—cull the roses—
    Bashful girls will soon be plenty!
Maid who thus at fifteen poses
    Ought to be divine at twenty!

[*Exit* CHORUS. *Manet* KING.

KING. I requested Scaphio and Phantis to be so good as to favour me with an audience this morning.

Enter SCAPHIO *and* PHANTIS.

Oh, here they are!

SCA. Your Majesty wished to speak with us, I believe. You—you needn't keep your crown on, on our account, you know.

KING. I beg your pardon. (*Removes it.*) I always forget that! Odd, the notion of a King not being allowed to wear one of his own crowns in the presence of two of his own subjects.

PHAN. Yes—bizarre, is it not?

KING. Most quaint. But then it's a quaint world.

PHAN. Teems with quiet fun. I often think what a lucky thing it is that you are blessed with such a keen sense of humour!

KING. Do you know, I find it invaluable. Do what I will, I *cannot* help looking at the humorous side of things—for, properly considered, everything has its humorous side—even the *Palace Peeper*. (*Producing it.*) See here—"Another Royal Scandal," by Junius Junior. "How long is this to last?" by Senex Senior. "Ribald Royalty," by Mercury Major. "Where is the Public Exploder?" by Mephistopheles Minor. When I reflect that all these outrageous attacks on my morality are written by me, at your command—well, it's one of the funniest things that have come within the scope of my experience.

SCA. Besides, apart from that, they have a quiet humour of their own which is simply irresistible.

KING. (*gratified*). Not bad, I think. Biting, trenchant sarcasm—the rapier, not the bludgeon—that's my line. But then it's so easy—I'm such a good subject—a bad King but a good Subject—ha! ha!—a capital heading for next week's leading article! (*Makes a note.*) And then the stinging little paragraphs about our Royal goings-on with our Royal Second Housemaid—delicately sub-acid, are they not?

SCA. My dear King, in that kind of thing no one can hold a candle to you.

PHAN. But the crowning joke is the Comic Opera you've written for us—"King Tuppence; or, A Good Deal Less than Half a Sovereign"—in which the celebrated English tenor, Mr. Wilkinson, burlesques your personal appearance and gives grotesque imitations of your Royal pecularities. It's immense!

KING. Ye—es. That's what I wanted to speak to you about. Now, I've not the least doubt but that even *that* has its humorous side, too—if one could only see it. As a rule, I'm pretty quick at detecting latent humour—but I confess I do *not* quite see where it comes in, in this particular instance. It's so horribly personal!

SCA. Personal? Yes, of course it's personal—but consider the antithetical humour of the situation.

KING. Yes. I—I don't think I've quite grasped that.

SCA. No? You surprise me. Why, consider. During the day thousands tremble at your frown, during the night (from 8 to 11) thousands roar at it. During the day your most arbitrary pronouncements are received by your subjects with abject submission—during the night, they shout with joy at your most terrible decrees. It's not every monarch that enjoys the privilege of undoing by night all the despotic absurdities he's committed during the day.

KING. Of course! Now I see it! Thank you very much. I was sure it had its humorous side, and it was very dull of me not to have seen it before. But, as I said just now, it's a quaint world.

PHAN. Teems with quiet fun.

KING. Yes. Properly considered, what a farce life is, to be sure!

SONG.—KING.

First you're born—and I'll be bound you
Find a dozen strangers round you.
"Hallo," cries the new-born baby,
"Where's my parents? which may they be?"
    Awkward silence—no reply—
    Puzzled baby wonders why!
Father rises, bows politely—
Mother smiles, (but not too brightly)—
Doctor mumbles like a dumb thing—
Nurse is busy mixing something—
    Every symptom tends to show
    You're decidedly *de trop*—

ALL.   Ho! ho! ho! ho! ho! ho! ho! ho!
                    Time's teetotum,
                        If you spin it,
                    Gives it's quotum
                        Once a minute.
                    I'll go bail
                    You hit the nail,
                    And if you fail
                        The deuce is in it!

You grow up, and you discover
What it is to be a lover.
Some young lady is selected—
Poor, perhaps, but well-connected
    Whom you hail (for Love is blind)

As the Queen of fairy kind.
Though she's plain—perhaps unsightly,
Makes her face up—laces tightly,
In her form your fancy traces
All the gifts of all the graces.
    Rivals none the maiden woo,
    So you take her and she takes you!

ALL.　　　　　Ho! ho! ho! ho! ho! ho! ho!
        Joke beginning,
            Never ceases,
        Till your inning
            Time releases,
        On your way
        You blindly stray,
        And day by day
            The joke increases!

Ten years later—Time progresses—
Sours your temper—thins your tresses
Fancy, then, her chin relaxes;
Rates are facts and so are taxes.
    Fairy Queen's no longer young—
    Fairy Queen has got a tongue.
Twins have probably intruded—
Quite unbidden—just as you did—
They're a source of care and trouble—
Just as you were—only double.
    Comes at last the final stroke—
    Time has had his little joke!

ALL.　　　　　Ho! ho! ho! ho! ho! ho! ho! ho!
        Daily driven
            (Wife as drover)
        Ill you've thriven—
            Ne'er in clover:
        Lastly, when
        Three-score and ten
        (And not till then),
            The joke is over!
        Ho! ho! ho! ho! ho! ho! ho! ho!
        Then—and then
            The joke is over!

[*Exeunt* SCAPHIO *and* PHANTIS. *Manet* KING.

KING. *(putting on his crown again).* It's all very well. I always like to look on the humorous side of things; but I do *not* think I ought to be required to write libels on my own moral character. Naturally, I see the joke of it—anybody would—but Zara's coming home to-day; she's no longer a child, and I confess I should *not* like her to see my Opera—though it's uncommonly well written; and I should be sorry if the *Palace Peeper* got into her hands—though it's certainly smart—very smart indeed. It is almost a pity that I have to buy up the whole edition, because it's really too good to be lost. And Lady Sophy—that blameless type of perfect womanhood! Great heavens, what would *she* say if the Second Housemaid business happened to meet *her* pure blue eye!

Enter LADY SOPHY.

LADY S. My monarch is soliloquizing. I will withdraw. *(Going.)*

KING. No—pray don't go. Now I'll give you fifty chances, and you won't guess whom I was thinking of.

LADY S. Alas, sir, I know too well. Ah! King, it's an old, old story, and I'm well nigh weary of it! Be warned in time—from my heart I pity you, but I am not for you! *(Going.)*

KING. But hear what I have to say.

LADY S. It is useless. Listen. In the course of a long and adventurous career in the principal European Courts, it has been revealed to me that I unconsciously exercise a weird and supernatural fascination over all Crowned Heads. So irresistible is this singular property, that there is not a European Monarch who has not implored me, with tears in his eyes, to quit his kingdom, and take my fatal charms elsewhere. As time was getting on it occurred to me that by descending several pegs in the scale of Respectability I might qualify your Majesty for my hand. Actuated by this humane motive and happening to possess Respectability enough for Six, I consented to confer Respectability enough for Four upon your two younger daughters—but although I have, alas, only Respectability enough for Two left, there is still, as I gather from the public press of this country *(producing the* Palace Peeper*)*, a considerable balance in my favour.

KING *(aside).* Da—! *(Aloud.)* May I ask how you came by this?

LADY S. It was handed to me by the officer who holds the position of Public Exploder to your Imperial Majesty.

KING. And surely, Lady Sophy, surely you are not so unjust as to place any faith in the irresponsible gabble of the Society press!

LADY S. *(referring to paper).* I read on the authority of Senox Senior that your Majesty was seen dancing with your Second Housemaid on the Oriental Platform of the Tivoli Gardens. That is untrue?

KING. Absolutely. Our Second Housemaid has only one leg.

LADY S. *(suspiciously).* How do you know that?

KING. Common report, I give you my honour.

LADY S. It may be so. I further read—and the statement is vouched for by no less an authority than Mephistopheles Minor—that your Majesty indulges in a bath of hot rum-punch every morning. I trust I do not lay myself open to the charge of displaying an indelicate curiosity as to the mysteries of the royal dressing-room when I ask if there is any foundation for this statement?

KING. None whatever. When our medical adviser exhibits rum-punch it is as a draught, not as a fomentation. As to our bath, our valet plays the garden hose upon us every morning.

LADY S. *(shocked).* Oh, pray—pray spare me these unseemly details. Well you are a Despot—have you taken steps to slay this scribbler?

KING. Well, no—I have *not* gone so far as that. After all, it's the poor devils living, you know.

LADY S. It is the poor devil's living that surprises me. If this man lies, there is no recognized punishment that is sufficiently terrible for him.

KING. That's precisely it. I—I am waiting until a punishment is discovered that will exactly meet the enormity of the case. I am in constant communication with the Mikado of Japan, who is a leading authority on such points; and moreover, I have the ground plans and sectional elevations of several capital punishments in my desk at this moment. Oh, Lady Sophy, as you are powerful, be merciful!

DUET.—KING *and* LADY SOPHY.

KING. Subjected to your heavenly gaze
                (Poetical phrase)
        My brain is turned completely.
            Observe me now,
            No Monarch, I vow,
                Was ever so far afflicted?
LADY S. I'm pleased with that poetical phrase,
                "A heavenly gaze,"
        But though you put it neatly,
            Say what you will,
            These paragraphs still
                Remain uncontradicted.
        Come, crush me this contemptible worm
                (A forcible term),
        If he's assailed you wrongly.
            The rage display,
            Which, as you say,
                Has moved your Majesty lately.
KING. Though I admit that forcible term,
                "Contemptible worm,"
        Appeals to me most strongly,
            To treat this pest
            As you suggest
                Would pain my Majesty greatly.
LADY S. This writer lies!
KING. Yes, bother his eyes!
LADY S. He lives, you say?
KING. In a sort of way.
LADY S. Then have him shot.
KING. Decidedly not.
LADY S. Or crush him flat.
KING. I cannot do that.
BOTH. O royal Rex,
        My ⎱
        Her ⎰ blameless sex.

        Abhors such conduct shady.

        You ⎱
        I ⎰ plead in vain,

        You ⎱
        I ⎰ never will gain

        Respectable English lady!

[*Dance of repudiation by* LADY SOPHY. *Exit, followed by* KING.

March. Enter all the COURT, *heralding the arrival of the* PRINCESS
ZARA, *who enters, escorted by* CAPTAIN FITZBATTLEAXE *and
four* TROOPERS, *all in the full uniform of the First Life Guards.*

CHORUS.

        Oh, maiden, rich
            In Girton lore,
        That wisdom which
            We prized before,
        We do confess
        Is nothingness,
        And rather less,
            Perhaps, than more.
        On each of us
            Thy learning shed.

On calculus
    May we be fed.
And teach us, please,
To speak with ease
All languages,
    Alive and dead!

SOLO.—PRINCESS *and* CHORUS.

ZARA. Five years have flown since I took wing—
                Time flies, and his footstep ne'er retards—
        I'm the eldest daughter of your king.
TROOPERS. And we are her escort—First Life Guards!
            On the royal yacht,
                When the waves were white,
            In a helmet hot
                And a tunic tight,
            And our great big boots,
                We defied the storm:
            For we're not recruits.
                And his uniform
        A well-drilled trooper ne'er discards—
        And we are her escort—First Life Guards!

ZARA. These gentlemen I present to you,
                The pride and boast of their barrack-yards;
        They've taken, oh, such care of me!
TROOPERS. For we are her escort—First Life Guards!
            When the tempest rose,
                And the ship went *so*—
            Do you suppose
                We were ill? No, no!
            Though a qualmish lot
                In a tunic tight,
            And a helmet hot,
                And a breastplate bright
        (Which a well-drilled trooper ne'er discards),
        We stood as her escort—First Life Guards!

FULL CHORUS.

        Knightsbridge nursemaids—serving fairies—
        Stars of proud Belgravian airies;
        At stern duty's call you leave them,
        Though you know how that must grieve them!
ZARA. Tantantarara-rara-rara!
CAPT. FITZ. Trumpet-call of Princess Zara!
CHORUS. That's trump-call, and they're all trump cards—
        They are her escort—First Life Guards!

ENSEMBLE.

CHORUS.	PRINCESS ZARA *and* FITZBATTLEAXE *(aside).*
LADIES. Knightsbridge nursemaids, etc.	Oh! the hours are gold, And the joys untold,
MEN. When soldier seeks, etc.	When my eyes behold My beloved Princess; And the years will seem But a brief day-dream,

In the joy extreme
Of our happiness.

FULL CHORUS. Knightsbridge nursemaids—serving fairies, etc.

Enter KING, PRINCESSES NEKAYA *and* KALYBA, *and* LADY SOPHY.
As the KING *enters the escort present arms.*

KING. Zara! my beloved daughter! Why, how well you look, and how lovely you have grown! *(Embraces her.)*

ZARA. My dear father! *(Embracing him.)* And my two beautiful little sisters! *(Embracing them.)*

NEK. Not beautiful.

KAL. Nice looking.

ZARA. But first let me present to you the English warrior who commands my escort, and who has taken, oh! such care of me during the voyage—Captain Fitzbattleaxe!

TROOPERS.   The First Life Guards.
When the tempest rose,
And the ship went *so*—

[CAPT. FITZBATTLEAXE *motions them to be silent. The* TROOPERS *place themselves in the four corners of the stage, standing at ease, immovably, as if on sentry. Each is surrounded by an admiring group of young* LADIES, *of whom they take no notice.*

KING *(to* CAPT. FITZ.). Sir, you come from a country where every virtue flourishes. We trust that you will not criticize too severely such shortcomings as you may detect in our semi-barbarous society.

FITZ. *(looking at* ZARA). Sir, I have eyes for nothing but the blameless and the beautiful.

KING. We thank you—he is really very polite! (LADY SOPHY, *who has been greatly scandalized by the attentions paid to the* LIFEGUARDSMEN *by the young* LADIES, *marches the* PRINCESSES NEKAYA *and* KALYBA *towards an exit.)* Lady Sophy, do not leave us.

LADY S. Sir, your children are young, and, so far, innocent. If they are to remain so, it is necessary that they be at once removed from the contamination of their present disgraceful surroundings. *(She marches them off.)*

KING *(whose attention has thus been called to the proceedings of the young* LADIES—*aside).* Dear, dear! They really shouldn't. *(Aloud.)* Captain Fitzbattleaxe.

FITZ. Sir.

KING. Your troopers appear to be receiving a troublesome amount of attention from those young ladies. I know how strict you English soldiers are, and I should be extremely distressed if anything occurred to shock their puritanical British sensitiveness.

FITZ. Oh, I don't think there's any chance of that.

KING. You think not? They won't be offended?

FITZ. Oh no! They are quite hardened to it. They get a good deal of that sort of thing, standing sentry at the Horse Guards.

KING. It's English, is it?

FITZ. It's particularly English.

KING. Then, of course, it's all right. Pray proceed, ladies, it's particularly English. Come, my daughter, for we have much to say to each other.

ZARA. Farewell, Captain Fitzbattleaxe! I cannot thank you too emphatically for the devoted care with which you have watched over me during our long and eventful voyage.

DUET.—ZARA *and* CAPTAIN FITZBATTLEAXE.

ZARA.   Ah! gallant soldier, brave and true
In tented field and tourney,
I grieve to have occasioned you
So very long a journey.
A British soldier gives up all—
His home and island beauty—
When summoned by the trumpet-call
Of Regimental duty!

ALL.   Tantantarara-rara-rara!
Trumpet-call of Princess Zara!

ENSEMBLE.

MEN.	FITZBATTLEAXE *and* ZARA *(aside).*
A British warrior gives up all, etc.	Oh, my joy, my pride, My delight to hide,
LADIES.	Let us sing, aside, What in truth we feel.
Knightsbridge nursemaids, etc.	Let us whisper low Of our love's glad glow, Lest the truth we show We would fain conceal.

FITZ.   Such escort duty, as his due,
To young Lifeguardsman falling
Completely reconciles him to
His uneventful calling.
When soldier seeks Utopian glades
In charge of Youth and Beauty,
Then pleasure merely masquerades
As Regimental Duty!

ALL.   Tantantarara-rara-rara!
Trumpet-call of Princess Zara!

ENSEMBLE.

CHORUS.	FITZBATTLEAXE *and* ZARA *(aside).*
MEN.	
A British warrior, etc.	Oh, the hours are gold, And the joys untold, When my eyes behold
WOMEN.	My beloved Princess; And the year will seem
Knightsbridge nursemaids, etc.	But a brief day-dream, In the joy extreme, Of our happiness!

[*Exeunt* KING *and* PRINCESS *in one direction,* LIFEGUARDSMEN *and* CROWD *in opposite direction.*

Enter, at back, SCAPHIO *and* PHANTIS, *who watch the* PRINCESS *as she goes off.* SCAPHIO *is seated, shaking violently, and obviously under the influence of some strong emotion.*

PHAN. There—tell me, Scaphio, is she not beautiful? Can you wonder that I love her so passionately?

SCA. No. She is extraordinarily—miraculously lovely! Good heavens, what a singularly beautiful girl!

PHAN. I knew you would say so!

Sca. What exquisite charm of manner! What surprising delicacy of gesture! Why, she's a goddess! a very goddess!

Phan. *(rather taken aback).* Yes—she's—she's an attractive girl.

Sca. Attractive? Why, you must be blind! She's entrancing—enthralling!—intoxicating! *(Aside.)* God bless my heart, what's the matter with me?

Phan. *(alarmed).* Yes. You—you promised to help me to get her father's consent, you know.

Sca. Promised! Yes, but the convulsion has come, my good boy! It is she—my ideal! Why, what's this? *(Staggering.)* Phantis! Stop me—I'm going mad—mad with the love of her!

Phan. Scaphio, compose yourself, I beg. The girl is perfectly opaque! Besides, remember—each of us is helpless without the other. You can't succeed without my consent, you know.

Sca. And you dare to threaten? Oh, ungrateful! When you came to me, palsied with love for this girl, and implored my assistance, did I not unhesitatingly promise it? And this is the return you make? Out of my sight, ingrate! *(Aside.)* Dear! dear! what is the matter with me?

Enter Capt. Fitzbattleaxe *and* Zara.

Zara. Dear me. I'm afraid we are interrupting a *tête-à-tête*.

Sca. *(breathlessly).* No, no. You come very appropriately. To be brief, we—we love you—this man and I—madly—passionately!

Zara. Sir!

Sca. And we don't know how we are to settle which of us is to marry you.

Fitz. Zara, this is very awkward.

Sca. *(very much overcome).* I—I am paralyzed by the singular radiance of your extraordinary loveliness. I know I am incoherent. I never was like this before—it shall not occur again. I—shall be fluent presently.

Zara *(aside).* Oh, dear Captain Fitzbattleaxe, what *is* to be done?

Fitz. *(aside).* Leave it to me—I'll manage it. *(Aloud.)* It's a common situation. Why not settle it in the English fashion?

Both. The English fashion? What is that?

Fitz. It's very simple. In England, when two gentlemen are in love with the same lady, and until it is settled which gentleman is to blow out the brains of the other, it is provided, by the Rival Admirers' Clauses Consolidation Act, that the lady shall be entrusted to an officer of Household Cavalry as stakeholder, who is bound to hand her over to the survivor (on the Tontine principle) in a good condition of substantial and decorative repair.

Sca. Reasonable wear and tear and damages by fire excepted?

Fitz. Exactly.

Phan. Well, that seems very reasonable. *(To* Scaphio.) What do you say—Shall we entrust her to this officer of Household Cavalry? It will give us time.

Sca. *(trembling violently).* I—I am not at present in a condition to think it out coolly—but if he *is* an officer of Household Cavalry, and if the Princess consents—

Zara. Alas, dear sirs, I have no alternative—under the Rival Admirers' Clauses Consolidation Act!

Fitz. Good—then that's settled.

Quartette.

Fitzbattleaxe, Zara, Scaphio, *and* Phantis.

Fitz.
It's understood, I think, all round
That, by the English custom bound,
I hold the lady safe and sound
    In trust for either rival,
Until you clearly testify
By sword or pistol, by-and-by,
Which gentleman prefers to die,
    And which prefers survival.

Ensemble.

Sca. *and* Phan.	Zara *and* Fitz. *(aside).*
It's clearly understood, all round,	We stand, I think, on safish ground;
That, by your English custom bound,	Our senses weak it will astound
He holds the lady safe and sound	If either gentleman is found
In trust for either rival,	Prepared to meet his rival,
Until we clearly testify	Their machinations we defy;
By sword and pistol, by-and-by,	We won't be parted, you and I—
Which gentleman prefers to die,	Of bloodshed each is rather shy—
And which prefers survival.	They both prefer survival!

Phan. *(aside to* Fitz.).	If I should die and he should live,
	To you, without reserve, I give
	Her heart so young and sensitive,
	And all her predilections.
Sca. *(aside to* Fitz.).	If he should live and I should die,
	I see no kind of reason why
	You should not, if you wish it, try
	To gain her young affections.

Ensemble.

Sca. *and* Phan. *(angrily to each other).*	Fitz. *and* Zara *(aside).*
If I should die and you should live,	As both of us are positive
To this young officer I give	That both of them intend to live,
Her heart so soft and sensitive,	There's nothing in the case to give,
And all her predilections.	Us cause for grave reflections.
If you should live and I should die,	As both will live and neither die
I see no kind of reason why	I see no kind of reason why
He should not, if he chooses try,	I should not, if I wish it, try
To win her young affections.	To gain your young affections!

[*Exeunt* Scaphio *and* Phantis *together.*

DUET.—ZARA and FITZBATTLEAXE.

ENSEMBLE.

Oh, admirable art!
  Oh, neatly-planned intention!
  Oh, happy intervention—
    Oh, well-constructed plot!
When sages try to part
  Two loving hearts in fusion,
  Their wisdom's a delusion,
    And learning serves them not!

FITZ.
    Until quite plain
      Is their intent,
    These sages twain
      I represent.
    Now please infer
      That, nothing loth,
    You're henceforth, as it were,
      Engaged to marry both—
  Then take it that I represent the two—
  On that hypothesis, what would you do?

ZARA (aside). What would I do? what would I do?
ZARA.
    In such a case,
      Upon your breast,
    My blushing face
      I think I'd rest— (Doing so.)
    Then perhaps I might
      Demurely say
    "I find this breastplate bright
      Is sorely in the way!"
  That is, supposing it were true
  That I'm engaged to both—and both were you!

ENSEMBLE.

  Our mortal rao
    Is never blest—
  There's no such case
    As perfect rest:
  Some petty blight
    Asserts its sway!
  Some crumpled roseleaf light
    Is always in the way!

[*Exit* FITZBATTLEAXE. *Manet* ZARA.

ZARA (*looking off, in the direction in which* SCAPHIO *and* PHANTIS *have gone*). Poor, trusting, simple-minded, and affectionate old gentlemen! I'm really sorry for them! How strange it is that when the flower of a man's youth has faded, he seems to lose all charm in a woman's eyes; and how true are the words of my expurgated Juvenal—

      "*Festinat decurrere velox*
Flosculus, angustæ, miseræque brevissima vitæ
Portio!"

Enter KING.

KING. My daughter! At last we are alone together.
ZARA. Yes, and I'm glad we are, for I want to speak to you very seriously. Do you know this paper?

KING (*aside*). Da—! (*Aloud.*) Oh yes—I've—I've seen it. Where in the world did you get this from?
ZARA. It was given to me by Lady Sophy—my sisters' governess.
KING (*aside*). Lady Sophy's an angel, but I do sometimes wish she'd mind her own business! (*Aloud.*) It's—ha! ha!—it's rather humorous.
ZARA. I see nothing humorous in it. I only see that you, the despotic King of this country, are made the subject of the most scandalous insinuations. Why do you permit these things?
KING. Well, they appeal to my sense of humour. It's the only really comic paper in Utopia, and I wouldn't be without it for the world.
ZARA. If it had any literary merit I could understand it.
KING. Oh, it *has* literary merit. Oh, distinctly, it has literary merit.
ZARA. My dear father, it's mere ungrammatical twaddle.
KING. Oh, it's not ungrammatical. I can't allow that. Unpleasantly personal, perhaps, but written with an epigrammatical point that is very rare nowadays—very rare indeed.
ZARA (*looking at cartoon*). Why do they represent you with such a big nose?
KING. (*looking at cartoon*). Eh? Yes, it *is* a big one! Why, the fact is that, in the cartoons of a comic paper, the size of your nose always varies inversely as the square of your popularity. It's the rule.
ZARA. Then you must be at a tremendous discount, just now! I see a notice of a new piece called "King Tuppence," in which an English tenor has the audacity to personate you on a public stage. I can only say that I am surprised that any English tenor should lend himself to such degrading personalities.
KING. Oh, he's not really English. As it happens he's a Utopian, but he calls himself English.
ZARA. Calls himself English?
KING. Yes. Bless you, they wouldn't listen to any tenor who didn't call himself English.
ZARA. And you permit this insolent buffoon to caricature you in a pointless burlesque! My dear father—if you were a free agent, you would never permit these outrages.
KING (*almost in tears*). Zara—I—I admit I am not altogether a free agent. I—I am controlled. I try to make the best of it, but sometimes I find it very difficult—very difficult indeed. Nominally a Despot, I am, between ourselves, the helpless tool of two unscrupulous Wise Men, who insist on my falling in with all their wishes and threaten to denounce me for immediate explosion if I remonstrate! (*Breaks down completely.*)
ZARA. My poor father! Now listen to me. With a view to remodelling the political and social institutions of Utopia, I have brought with me six representatives of the principal causes that have tended to make England the powerful, happy, and blameless country which the consensus of European civilization has declared it to be. Place yourself unreservedly in the hands of these gentlemen, and they will reorganize your country on a footing that will enable you to defy your persecutors. They are all now washing their hands after their journey. Shall I introduce them?
KING. My dear Zara, how can I thank you? I will consent to anything that will release me from the abominable tyranny of these two men. (*Calling.*) What ho! Without there!

Enter CALYNX.

Summon my court without an instant's delay!

[*Exit* CALYNX.

FINALE.

Enter EVERY ONE, *except the* FLOWERS OF PROGRESS.

CHORUS.

Although your Royal summons to appear
From courtesy was singularly free,
Obedient to that summons we are here—
What would your Majesty?

RECITATIVE.—KING.

My worthy people, my beloved daughter
Most thoughtfully has brought with her from England
The types of all the causes that have made
That great and glorious country what it is.

CHORUS.   Oh, joy unbounded!

SCA., TAR., *and* PHAN. (*aside*). Why, what *does* this mean?

RECITATIVE.—ZARA.

Attend to me, Utopian populace,
Ye South Pacific Island viviparians;
All in the abstract, types of courtly grace,
Yet, when compared with Britain's glorious race,
But little better than half-clothed barbarians!

CHORUS.

That's true—we South Pacific viviparians,
Contrasted when
With Englishmen,
Are little better than half-clothed barbarians!

Enter all the FLOWERS OF PROGRESS, *led by* FITZBATTLEAXE.

SONG.—ZARA. (*Presenting* CAPTAIN FITZBATTLEAXE.)

When Britain sounds the trump of war
(And Europe trembles),
The army of that conqueror
In serried ranks assembles;
'Tis then this warrior's eyes and sabre gleam
For our protection—
He represents a military scheme
In all its proud perfection!

FITZ.   Yes—yes—
I represent a military scheme
In all its proud perfection!

CHORUS.   Ulahlica! Ulahlica! Ulahlica!

SOLO.—ZARA. (*Presenting* SIR BAILEY BARRE, Q.C., M.P.)

A complicated gentleman allow me to present,
Of all the arts and faculties the terse embodiment,
He's a great Arithmetician who can demonstrate with ease
That two and two are three, or five, or anything you
please;
An eminent Logician who can make it clear to you
That black is white—when looked at from the proper
point of view;
A marvellous Philologist who'll undertake to show
That "yes" is but another and a neater form of "no."
SIR BAILEY.   Yes—yes—yes—
Oh "yes" is but another and a neater form of "no."
All preconceived ideas on any subject I can scout,
And demonstrate beyond all possibility of doubt,
That whether you're an honest man or whether you're a
thief
Depends on whose solicitor has given me my brief.

CHORUS.   Yes—yes—yes
That whether you're an honest man, etc.
Ulahlica! Ulahlica! Ulahlica!

SOLO.—ZARA. (*Presenting* LORD DRAMALEIGH *and*
COUNTY COUNCILLOR.)

What these may be, Utopians all
Perhaps you'll hardly guess—
They're types of England's physical
And moral cleanliness.
This is a Lord High Chamberlain
Of purity the gauge—
He'll cleanse our Court from moral stain
And purify our Stage.

LORD DRAM.   Yes—yes—yes—
Court reputations I revise,
And presentations scrutinize,
New plays I read with jealous eyes,
And purify the Stage.

CHORUS.   Yes—yes—yes—
New plays, etc.

ZARA.   This County Councillor acclaim,
Great Britain's latest toy—
On anything you like to name
His talents he'll employ—
All streets and squares he'll purify
Within your city walls,
And keep meanwhile a modest eye
On wicked music halls.

C.C.   Yes—yes—yes—
In towns I make improvements great,
Which go to swell the County Rate—
I dwelling-houses sanitate,
And purify the Halls!

CHORUS.   Yes—yes—yes—
He'll dwelling-houses, etc.
Ulahlica! Ulahlica! Ulahlica!

SOLO.—ZARA. *(Presenting* MR. GOLDBURY.)

A Company Promoter this, with special education,
Which teaches what Contango means and also
    Backwardation—
To speculators he supplies a grand financial leaven,
Time was when *two* were company—but now it must be
    seven.

MR. GOLD.   Yes—yes—yes—
    Stupendous loans to foreign thrones
      I've largely advocated;
    In ginger-pops and peppermint-drops
      I've freely speculated;
    Then mines of gold, of wealth untold,
      Successfully I've floated,
    And sudden falls in apple-stalls
      Occasionally quoted:
    And soon or late I always call
      For Stock Exchange quotation—
    No scheme's too great and none too small
      For Companification!

CHORUS.   Then soon or late, etc.
Ulahlica! Ulahlica! Ulahlica!

ZARA. *(Presenting* CAPTAIN SIR EDWARD CORCORAN, R.N.)

And lastly I present
    Great Britain's proudest boast,
Who from the blows
Of foreign foes
    Protects her sea-girt coast—
And if you ask him in respectful tone,
He'll show you how you may protect your own!

SOLO.—CAPTAIN CORCORAN.

I'm Captain Corcoran, K.C.B.,
I'll teach you how we rule the sea,
    And terrify the simple Gaul.
And how the Saxon and the Celt
Their Europe-shaking blows have dealt
With Maxim gun and Nordenfelt
    (Or will, when the occasion calls),
If sailor-like you'd play your cards
Unbend your sails, and lower your yards,
    Unstep your masts—you'll never want 'em more.
Though we're no longer hearts of oak,
Yet we can steer and we can stoke,
    And, thanks to coal, and thanks to coke,
      We never run a ship ashore!
ALL.   What never?
CAPT.   No, never!
ALL.   What, *never?*
CAPT.   Hardly ever!
ALL.   Hardly ever run a ship ashore!

Then give three cheers, and three cheers more,
For the tar who never runs his ship ashore;
Then give three cheers, and three cheers more,
For he never runs his ship ashore!

CHORUS.

All hail, ye types of England's power—
    Ye heaven-enlightened band!
We bless the day, and bless the hour
    That brought you to our land.

QUARTETTE.

Ye wanderers from a mighty State
Oh, teach us how to legislate—
Your lightest word will carry weight
    In our attentive ears.
Oh, teach the natives of this land
(Who are not quick to understand)
How to work off their social and
    Political arrears!

CAPT. FITZ.   Increase your army!
LORD DRAM.   Purify your Court!
CAPT. COR.   Get up your steam and cut your canvas short!
SIR B. BAR.   To speak on both sides teach your sluggish
    brains!
MR. B., C.C.   Widen your thoroughfares, and flush your
    drains!
MR. GOLD.   Utopia's much too big for one small head—
    I'll float it as a Company Limited!

KING.   A Company Limited? What may that be?
    The term, I rather think, is new to me.

CHORUS.   A Company Limited? etc.

SCA., PHAN., *and* TARARA *(aside).*
    What does he mean? What does he mean?
      Give us a kind of clue!
    What does he mean? What does he mean?
      What is he going to do?

SONG.—MR. GOLDBURY.

Some seven men form an Association
    (If possible, all Peers and Baronets),
They start off with a public declaration
    To what extent they mean to pay their debts.
That's called their Capital: if they are wary
    They will not quote it at a sum immense.
The figure's immaterial—it may vary
    From eighteen million down to eighteenpence.
    I should put it rather low;
    The good sense of doing so
Will be evident at once to any debtor,
    When it's left to you to say
    What amount you mean to pay,
Why, the lower you can put it at, the better.
CHORUS.   When it's left to you to say, etc.

They then proceed to trade with all who'll trust 'em,
    Quite irrespective of their capital
      (It's shady, but it's sanctified by custom);
      Bank, Railway, Loan, or Panama Canal.
You can't embark on trading too tremendous—
    It's strictly fair, and based on common sense—
If you succeed, your profits are stupendous—
    And if you fail, pop goes your eighteenpence.
      Make the money-spinner spin!
      For you only stand to win,
    And you'll never with dishonesty be twitted.
      For nobody can know,
      To a million or so,
    To what extent your capital's committed!

CHORUS.   No, nobody can know, etc.

If you come to grief, and creditors are craving,
    (For nothing that is planned by mortal head
Is certain in this Vale of Sorrow—saving
    That one's Liability is Limited),—
Do you suppose that signifies perdition?
    If so you're but a monetary dunce—
You merely file a Winding-up Petition,
    And start another Company at once!
      Though a Rothschild you may be
      In your own capacity,
    As a Company you've come to utter sorrow—
      But the Liquidators say,
      "Never mind—you needn't pay,"
    So you start another company to-morrow!

CHORUS.   But the Liquidators say, etc.

RECITATIVE.

KING.   Well, at first sight it strikes us as dishonest,
      But if it's good enough for virtuous England—
      The first commercial country in the world—
      It's good enough for us.

SCA. PHAN., and TARARA. You'd best take care—
(aside to KING). Please recollect *we* have not been consulted.
KING (not   And do I understand you that Great Britain
heeding them). Upon this Joint Stock principle is governed?

MR. GOLD.   We haven't come to that, exactly—but
      We're tending rapidly in that direction.
      The date's not distant.

KING (enthusiastically). We will be before you!

      We'll go down to Posterity renowned
      As the First Sovereign in Christendom
      Who registered his Crown and Country under
      The Joint Stock Company's Act of Sixty-Two.

ALL.   Ulahlica! Ulahlica! Ulahlica!

SOLO.—KING.

Henceforward, of a verity,
    With Fame ourselves we link—

    We'll go down to Posterity
      Of sovereigns all the pink!

SCA., PHAN., and TAR. (aside to KING). If you've the
      mad temerity
      Our wishes thus to blink,
    You'll go down to Posterity
      Much earlier than you think!

TARARA (correcting them). He'll go *up* to Posterity,
      If *I* inflict the blow!

SCA. and PHAN. (angrily). He'll go *down* to Posterity.
      We think we ought to know!

TARARA (explaining). He'll go *up* to Posterity,
      Blown up with dynamite!

SCA. and PHAN. (apologetically). He'll go *up* to Posterity;
      Of course he will, you're right!

ENSEMBLE.

KING, LADY SOPHY, NEK., KAL., CAL., and CHORUS.	SCA., PHAN., and TARARA (aside)	FITZBATTLEAXE and ZARA (aside)
Henceforward of a verity With fame ourselves we link, And go down to Posterity Of sovereigns all the pink!	If he has the temerity Our wishes thus to blink, He'll go up to Posterity Much earlier than they think!	Who love with all sincerity, Their lives may safely link; And as for our Posterity— We don't care what they think!

CHORUS.

Let's seal this mercantile pact—
    The step we ne'er shall rue—
It gives whatever we lacked—
    The statement's strictly true.
All hail, astonishing Fact!
    All hail, Invention new—
The Joint Stock Company's Act—
    The Act of Sixty-Two!

CURTAIN.

ACT II.

SCENE.—*Throne Room in the Palace. Night.* FITZBATTLEAXE
discovered, singing to ZARA.

RECITATIVE.—FITZ.

Oh, Zara, my beloved one, bear with me!
Ah, do not laugh at my attempted C!
Repent not, mocking maid, thy girlhood's choice—
The fervour of my love affects my voice!

SONG.—FITZ.

A tenor, all singers above,
    (This doesn't admit of a question)
        Should keep himself quiet,
        Attend to his diet
And carefully nurse his digestion:
But when he is madly in love
    It's certain to tell on his singing—
        You can't do chromatics
        With proper emphatics
    When anguish your bosom is wringing!
When distracted with worries in plenty,
And his pulse is a hundred and twenty,
And his fluttering bosom the slave of mistrust is,
A tenor can't do himself justice.
        Now observe—*(sings a high note)*,
You see, I can't do myself justice!

I could sing, if my fervour were mock,
    It's easy enough if you're acting—
        But when one's emotion
        Is born of devotion
    You mustn't be over-exacting.
One ought to be firm as a rock
    To venture a shake in *vibrato*,
        When fervour's expected
        Keep cool and collected
    Or never attempt *agitato*.
But, of course, when his tongue is of leather,
And his lips appear pasted together,
And his sensitive palate as dry as a crust is,
A tenor can't do himself justice.
        Now observe—*(sings a cadence)*,
It's no use—I can't do myself justice!

ZARA. Why, Arthur, what *does* it matter? When the higher qualities of the heart are all that can be desired, the higher notes of the voice are matters of comparative insignificance. Who thinks slightingly of the cocoanut because it is husky? Besides *(demurely)* you are not singing for an engagement. *(Putting her hand in his.)* You have that already!

FITZ. How good and wise you are! How unerringly your practised brain winnows the wheat from the chaff—the material from the merely incidental!

ZARA. My Girton training, Arthur. At Girton all is wheat, and idle chaff is never heard within its walls! But tell me, is not all working marvellously well? Have not our Flowers of Progress more than justified their name?

FITZ. We have indeed done our best. Captain Corcoran and I have, in concert, thoroughly remodelled the sister-services—and upon so sound a basis that the South Pacific trembles at the name of Utopia!

ZARA. How clever of you!

FITZ. Clever? Not a bit. It's as easy as possible when the Admiralty and Horse Guards are not there to interfere. And so with the others. Freed from the trammels imposed upon them by idle Acts of Parliament, all have given their natural talents full play and introduced reforms which, even in England, were never dreamt of!

ZARA. But perhaps the most beneficent change of all has been effected by Mr. Goldbury who, discarding the exploded theory that some strange magic lies hidden in the number Seven, has applied the Limited Liability principle to individuals, and every man, woman, and child is now a Company Limited with liability restricted to the amount of his declared Capital! There is not a christened baby in Utopia who has not already issued his little Prospectus!

FITZ. Marvellous is the power of a Civilization which can transmute, by a word, a Limited Income into an Income *(Limited)*.

ZARA. Reform has not stopped here—it has been applied even to the costume of our people. Discarding their own barbaric dress, the natives of our land have unanimously adopted the tasteful fashions of England in all their rich entirety. Scaphio and Phantis have undertaken a contract to supply the whole of Utopia with clothing designed upon the most approved English models—and the first Drawing-Room under the new state of things is to be held here this evening.

FITZ. But Drawing-Rooms are always held in the afternoon.

ZARA. Ah, we've improved upon that. We all look so much better by candle-light! And when I tell you, dearest, that my court train has just arrived, you will understand that I am longing to go and try it on.

FITZ. Then we must part?

ZARA. Necessarily, for a time.

FITZ. Just as I wanted to tell you, with all the passionate enthusiasm of my nature, how deeply, how devotedly I love you!

ZARA. Hush! Are these the accents of a heart that really feels? True love does not indulge in declamation—its voice is sweet, and soft, and low. The west wind whispers when he woos the poplars!

DUET.—ZARA *and* FITZBATTLEAXE.

Zara.   Words of love too loudly spoken
                Ring their own untimely knell;
        Noisy vows are rudely broken,
                Soft the song of Philomel.

        Whisper sweetly, whisper slowly,
                Hour by hour and day by day;
        Sweet and low as accents holy
                Are the notes of lover's lay!

BOTH.   Sweet and low, etc.

FITZ.   Let the conqueror, flushed with glory,
                Bid his noisy clarions bray;
        Lovers tell their artless story
                In a whispered virelay.
        False is he whose vows alluring,
                Make the listening echoes ring;
        Sweet and low when all-enduring,
                Are the songs that lovers sing!

BOTH.   Sweet and low, etc.   [*Exit* ZARA.

Enter KING, *dressed as Field Marshal.*

KING. To a Monarch who has been accustomed to the uncontrolled use of his limbs, the costume of a British Field Marshal is, perhaps, at first, a little cramping. Are you sure that this is all right? It's not a practical joke, is it? No one has a keener sense of humour than I have, but the First Statutory Cabinet Council of Utopia *(Limited)* must be conducted with dignity and impressiveness. Now, where are the other five who signed the Articles of Association?

FITZ. Sir, they are here.

Enter LORD DRAMLEIGH, CAPTAIN CORCORAN, SIR BAILEY BARRE, MR. BLUSHINGTON, *and* MR. GOLDBURY *from different entrances.*

KING. Oh! *(Addressing them.)* Gentlemen, our daughter holds her first Drawing-Room in half an hour, and we shall have time to make our half-yearly report in the interval. I am necessarily unfamiliar with the forms of an English Cabinet Council—perhaps the Lord Chamberlain will kindly put us in the way of doing the thing properly, and with due regard to the solemnity of the occasion.

LORD DRAM. Certainly—nothing simpler. Kindly bring your chairs forward—his Majesty will, of course, preside.

[*They range their chairs across stage like Christy Minstrels.* KING *sits centre,* LORD DRAMLEIGH *on his left,* MR. GOLDBURY *on his right,* CAPTAIN CORCORAN *left of* LORD DRAMLEIGH, CAPTAIN FITZBATTLEAXE *right of* MR. GOLDBURY, MR. BLUSHINGTON *extreme right,* SIR BAILEY BARRE *extreme left.*

KING. Like this?

LORD DRAM. Like this.

KING. We take your word for it that this is all right. You are not making fun of us? This is in accordance with the practice at the Court of St. James's?

LORD DRAM. Well, it is in accordance with the practice at the Court of St. James's Hall.

KING. Oh! it seems odd, but never mind.

SONG.—KING.

Society has quite forsaken all her wicked courses,
  Which empties our police courts, and abolishes
    divorces.
CHORUS.   Divorce is nearly obsolete in England.
KING. No tolerance we show to undeserving rank and
    splendour;
  For the higher his position is the greater the
    offender.
CHORUS.   That's a maxim that is prevalent in
    England.
KING. No peeress at our Drawing-Room before the
    Presence passes
  Who wouldn't be accepted by the lower-middle
    classes,
  Each shady dame, whatever be her rank, is bowed
    out neatly.
CHORUS. In short, this happy country has been Anglicized
    completely!
        It really is surprising
        What a thorough Anglicizing
  We have brought about—Utopia's quite another
    land;
        In her enterprising movements,
        She is England—with improvements,
  Which we dutifully offer to our mother-land!

KING. Our city we have beautified—we've done it willy-
    nilly—
  And all that isn't Belgrave Square is Strand and
    Piccadilly.
CHORUS.   We haven't any slummeries in England!
KING. We have solved the labour question with
    discrimination polished,
  So poverty is obsolete and hunger is abolished—
CHORUS.   We are going to abolish it in England.
KING. The Chamberlain our native stage has purged,
    beyond a question,
  Of "risky" situation and indelicate suggestion;
  No piece is tolerated if it's costumed indiscreetly—
CHORUS. In short, this happy country has been Anglicized
    completely!
        It really is surprising, etc.
KING. Our Peerage we've remodelled on an intellectual
    basis,
  Which certainly is rough on our hereditary races—
CHORUS.   We are going to remodel it in England.
KING. The Brewers and the Cotton Lords no longer seek
    admission,
  And Literary Merit meets with proper recognition—
CHORUS.   As Literary Merit does in England!
KING. Who knows but we may count among our
    intellectual chickens
  Like you, an Earl of Thackeray and p'r'aps a Duke of
    Dickens—
  Lord Fildes and Viscount Millais (when they come)
    we'll welcome sweetly—
CHORUS. In short, this happy country has been Anglicized
    completely!
        It really is surprising, etc.

[*At the end all rise and replace their chairs.*

KING. Now then, for our First Drawing-room. Where are the Princesses? What an extraordinary thing it is that since European looking-glasses have been supplied to the Royal bedrooms my daughters are invariably late!

LORD DRAM. Sir, their Royal Highnesses await your pleasure in the Ante-Room.

KING. Oh. Then request them to do us the favour to enter at once.

MARCH. *Enter all the* Royal Household, *including (besides the* Lord Chamberlain) *the* Vice-Chamberlain, *the* Master of the Horse, *the* Master of the Buckhounds, *the* Lord High Treasurer, *the* Lord Steward, *the* Comptroller of the Household, *the* Lord-in-Waiting, *the* Groom-in-Waiting, *the* Field Officer in Brigade Waiting, *the* Gold and Silver Stick, *and the* Gentlemen Ushers. *Then enter the three* Princesses *(their trains carried by* Pages of Honour), LADY SOPHY, *and the* Ladies-in-waiting.

KING. My daughters, we are about to attempt a very solemn ceremonial, so no giggling, if you please. Now, my Lord Chamberlain, we are ready.

LORD DRAM. Then, ladies and gentlemen, places if you please, His Majesty will take his place in front of the throne, and will be so obliging as to embrace all the *débutantes.*(LADY SOPHY, *much shocked.)*

KING. What—must I really?

LORD DRAM. Absolutely indispensable.

KING. More jam for the *Palace Peeper!*

[*The* KING *takes his place in front of the throne, the* PRINCESS ZARA *on his left. The two younger* Princesses *on the left of* ZARA.

KING. Now, is every one in his place?

LORD DRAM. Every one is in his place.

KING. Then let the revels commence.

Enter the Ladies *attending the Drawing-room. They give their cards to the* Groom-in-Waiting, *who passes them to the* Lord-in-Waiting, *who passes them to the* Vice-Chamberlain, *who passes them to the* Lord Chamberlain, *who reads the names to the* KING *as each lady approaches. The* Ladies *curtsy in succession to the* KING, *and the three* Princesses, *and pass out. When all the presentations have been accomplished, the* KING, Princesses, *and* LADY SOPHY *come forward, and all the* Ladies *re-enter.*

RECITATIVE—KING

This ceremonial our wish displays
To copy all Great Britain's courtly ways,
Though lofty aims catastrophe entail,
We'll gloriously succeed or nobly fail!

UNACCOMPANIED CHORUS

Eagle high in cloudland soaring—
    Sparrow twittering on a reed—
Tiger in the jungle roaring—
    Frightened fawn in grassy mead—
Let the eagle, not the sparrow,
Be the object of your arrow—
    Fix the tiger with your eye—
    Pass the fawn in pity by.
    Glory then will crown the day—
    Glory, Glory, anyway!   [*Then exeunt all.*

Enter SCAPHIO *and* PHANTIS, *now dressed as judges in red and ermine robes and undress wigs. They come down stage melodramatically— working together.*

DUET.—SCAPHIO AND PHANTIS

SCA.   With fury deep we burn—

PHAN.   We do—
           We fume with smothered rage.
      These Englishmen who rule supreme
      Their undertaking they redeem
      By stifling every harmless scheme
          In which we both engage—

SCA.   They do—
      In which we both engage.

BOTH (*with great energy*). For this mustn't be, and this won't do,
      If you'll back me, then I'll back you,
      Let's both agree, and we'll pull things through,
      For this mustn't be, and this won't do.
          No, this won't do,
          No, this won't do,
          No, this mustn't be,
          And this won't do.

Enter the KING.

KING. Gentlemen, gentlemen—really! This unseemly display of energy within the Royal Precincts is altogether unpardonable. Pray what do you complain of?

SCA. (*furiously*). What do we complain of? Why, though the innovations introduced by the Flowers of Progress all our harmless schemes for making a provision for our old age are ruined. Our Matrimonial Agency is at a standstill, our Cheap Sherry business is in bankruptcy, our Army Clothing contracts are paralyzed, and even our Society paper, the *Palace Peeper*, is practically defunct!

KING. Defunct? Is that so? Dear, dear, I am truly sorry.

SCA. Are you aware that Sir Bailey Barre has introduced a law of libel by which all editors of scurrilous newspapers are publicly flogged—as in England? And six of our editors have resigned in succession! Now, the editor of a scurrilous paper can stand a good deal—he takes a private thrashing as a matter of course—it's considered in his salary—but no gentleman likes to be publicly flogged.

KING. Naturally. I shouldn't like it myself.

PHAN. Then our burlesque Theatre is absolutely ruined!

KING. Dear me, Well, theatrical property is not what it was.

PHAN. Are you aware that the Lord Chamberlain, who has his own views as to the best means of elevating the national drama, has declined to license any play that is not in blank verse and three hundred years old—as in England?

SCA. And as if that wasn't enough, the County Councillor has ordered a four-foot wall to be built up right across the proscenium, in case of fire—as in England.

PHAN. It's so hard on the company—who are liable to be roasted alive—and this has to be met by enormously increased salaries—as in England.

SCA. You probably know that we've contracted to supply the entire nation with a complete English outfit. But perhaps you do *not* know that, when we send in our bills, our customers plead liability limited to a declared capital of eighteenpence, and apply to be dealt with under the Winding-up Act—as in England?

KING. Really, gentlemen, this is very irregular. If you will be so good as to formulate a detailed list of your grievances in writing, addressed to the Secretary of Utopia (*Limited*), they will be laid before the Board, in due course, at their next monthly meeting.

SCA. Are we to understand that we are defied?

KING. That is the idea I intended to convey.

PHAN. Defied! We are defied!

SCA. (*furiously*). Take care—you know our powers. Trifle with us, and you die!

TRIO—SCAPHIO, PHANTIS, *and* KING

SCA.   If you think that when banded in unity,
      We may both be defied with impunity,
          You are sadly misled of a verity!

PHAN.   If you value repose and tranquillity,
      You'll revert to a state of docility,
          Or prepare to regret your temerity!

KING   If my speech is unduly refractory
      You will find it a course satisfactory
          At an early Board meeting to show it up.
      Though if proper excuse you can trump any,

Percy Anderson's costume design for King Paramount in Act I of the original *Utopia, Limited* production, October 1893. Rutland Barrington played the role and changed out of this somewhat barbaric clothing into a British Field Marshal's uniform for Act II.

The Christy Minstrels scene from the 1975 *Utopia* (l to r)
Colin Wright as Sir Bailey Barre, Meston Reid as Captain
Fitzbattleaxe, Michael Rayner as Goldbury, Kenneth Sandford
(standing) as King Paramount, James Conroy-Ward as Lord
Dramaleigh, John Broad as Captain Corcoran and David
Porter as Blushington.

Utopia, Limited was not heard again in London until 1975
when, in Peter Rice's sets and costumes, it was transported
from its former South Sea Island to a benign Gulf State.
Kenneth Sandford is King Paramount, John Reed is Scaphio
and John Ayldon, Phantis in their Act I trio.

310

Poster for *The Mikado* in Tokyo (*c.*1950). In 1907 all performances of the opera in Britain had been banned by the Lord Chamberlain because of a visit by the Japanese Prince Fushimi. A special correspondent of a Japanese newspaper, travelling in advance of the Prince, found only 'bright music, much fun and no insults' exactly what subsequent Tokyo audiences experienced.

You may *wind* up a Limited Company,
　　You cannot conveniently *blow* it up!
　　　　[SCAPHIO *and* PHANTIS *thoroughly baffled.*

KING (*dancing quietly*).　　Whene'er I chance to baffle you
　　　　I, also, dance a step or two—
　　　　Of this now guess the hidden sense:

　　[SCAPHIO *and* PHANTIS *consider the question as*
　　KING *continues dancing quietly—then give it up.*

　　　　It means—complete indifference

ALL THREE (*dancing quietly*).　　Indifference—indifference—
　　Of course it does—indifference!
　　You ⎫
　　　　⎬ might have guessed its hidden sense.
　　We ⎭
　　It means complete indifference!

　　　　　[SCAPHIO *and* PHANTIS *dancing furiously.*

KING (*dancing quietly*).　　As we've a dance for every mood
　　　　With *pas de trois* we will conclude.
　　　　What this may mean you all may
　　　　　　　guess—

SCA. *and* PHAN.　⎫　It typifies remorselessness!
KING　　　　　　⎬
　　　　　　　　⎭　It means unruffled cheerfulness!

　　[KING *dances off placidly as* SCAPHIO *and* PHANTIS *dance
　　furiously.*

PHAN. (*breathless*). He's right—we are helpless! He's no longer
a human being—he's a Corporation, and so long as he confines
himself to his Articles of Association we can't touch him! What
are we to do?

SCA. Do? Raise a Revolution, repeal the Act of Sixty-Two,
reconvert him into an individual, and insist on his immediate
explosion! (TARARA *enters.*) Tarara, come here; you're the very
man we want.

TAR. Certainly, allow me. (*Offers a cracker to each, they snatch
them away impatiently.*) That's rude.

SCA. We have no time for idle forms. You wish to succeed to
the throne?

TAR. Naturally.

SCA. Then you won't unless you join us. The King has defied
us, and, as matters stand, we are helpless. So are you. We must
devise some plot at once to bring the people about his ears.

TAR. A plot?

PHAN. Yes, a plot of superhuman subtlety. Have you such a
thing about you?

TAR. (*feeling*). No, I think not. No. There's one on my
dressing-table.

SCA. We can't wait—we must concoct one at once, and put it
into execution without delay. There is not a moment to spare!

　　　　TRIO.—SCAPHIO, PHANTIS, *and* TARARA.

　　　　　　ENSEMBLE.

With wily brain upon the spot
　　A private plot we'll plan,
　　The most ingenious private plot

Since private plots began.
That's understood. So far we've got
And, striking while the iron's hot,
　　We'll now determine like a shot
　　The details of this private plot.

SCA.　　I think we ought—　　　　　　　[*Whispers.*
PHAN. *and* TAR.　　Such bosh I never heard!
PHAN.　　Ah, happy thought!—　　　　　　[*Whispers.*
SCA. *and* TAR.　　How utterly dashed absurd!
TAR.　　*I'll* tell you how—　　　　　　　[*Whispers.*
SCA. *and* PHAN.　　Why, what put that in your head?
SCA.　　I've got it now—　　　　　　　　[*Whispers.*
　　　　Oh! take him away to bed!
PHAN.　　　　Oh, put him to bed!
TAR.　　　　Oh, put him to bed!
SCA.　　　　What! put *me* to bed?
PHAN. *and* TAR.　　Yes, put him to bed!
SCA.　　But, bless em, don't you see—
PHAN.　　　　Do listen to me, I pray—
TAR.　　It certainly seems to me—
SCA.　　　　Bah—this is the only way!
PHAN.　　It's rubbish absurd you growl!
TAR.　　　　You talk ridiculous stuff!
SCA.　　You're a drivelling barndoor owl!
PHAN.　　　　You're a vapid and vain old muff!

　　　　　　[*All coming down to audience*
So far we haven't quite solved the
　　plot—
They're not a very ingenious lot—
　　　　But don't be unhappy,
　　　　It's still on the *tapis*
We'll presently hit on a capital plot.

SCA.　　Suppose we all—　　　　　　　[*Whispers.*
PHAN.　　　　Now *there* I think you're right.
　　　　Then we might all—　　　　　　[*Whispers.*
TAR.　　　　That's true—we certainly might.
　　　　I'll tell you what—　　　　　　[*Whispers.*
SCA.　　　　We will if we possibly can.
　　　　Then on the spot—　　　　　　[*Whispers.*
PHAN. *and* TAR.　　Bravo! a capital plan!
SCA.　　　　That's exceedingly neat and new!
PHAN.　　　　Exceedingly new and neat!
TAR.　　I fancy that that will do.
SCA.　　　　Its certainly very complete!
PHAN.　　Well done, you sly old sap!
TAR.　　　　Bravo, you cunning old mole!
SCA.　　You very ingenious chap!
PHAN.　　　　You intellectual soul!

　　[*All, coming down, and addressing audience.*

At last a capital plan we've got;
Never mind why and never mind what:
　　　　It's safe in my noddle—
　　　　Now off we will toddle,
And slyly develop this capital plot!

313

[*Business. Exeunt* Scaphio *and* Phantis *in one direction, and* Tarara *in the other.*

Enter Lord Dramaleigh *and* Mr. Goldbury.

Lord Dram. Well, what do you think of our first South Pacific Drawing-Room? Allowing for a slight difficulty with the trains, and a little want of familiarity with the use of the rouge-pot, it was, on the whole, a meritorious affair?

Gold. My dear Dramaleigh, it rebounds infinitely to your credit.

Lord Dram. One or two judicious innovations, I think?

Gold. Admirable. The cup of tea and the plate of mixed biscuits were a cheap and effective inspiration.

Lord Dram. Yes—my idea, entirely. Never been done before.

Gold. Pretty little maids, the king's youngest daughters, but timid.

Lord Dram. That'll wear off. Young.

Gold. *That'll* wear off. Ha! here they come, by George. And without the Dragon! What can they have done with her?

Enter Nekaya *and* Kalyba, *timidly.*

Nek. Oh, if you please Lady Sophy has sent us in here, because Zara and Captain Fitzbattleaxe are going on, in the garden, in a manner which no well conducted young ladies ought to witness.

Lord Dram. Indeed, we are very much obliged to her Ladyship.

Kal. Are you? I wonder why.

Nek. Don't tell us if it's rude.

Lord Dram. Rude? Not at all. We are obliged to Lady Sophy because she has afforded us the pleasure of seeing you.

Nek. I don't think you ought to talk to us like that.

Kal. It's calculated to turn our heads.

Nek. Attractive girls cannot be too particular.

Kal. Oh, pray, pray do not take advantage of our unprotected innocence.

Gold. Pray be reassured—you are in no danger whatever.

Lord Dram. But may I ask—is this extreme delicacy—this shrinking sensitiveness—a general characteristic of Utopian young ladies?

Nek. Oh no; we are crack specimens.

Kal. We are the pick of the basket. *Would* you mind not coming quite so near? Thank you.

Nek. And please don't look at us like that; it unsettles us.

Kal. And we don't like it. At least, we *do* like it; but it's wrong.

Nek. *We* have enjoyed the inestimable privilege of being educated by a most refined and easily-shocked English lady, on the very strictest English principles.

Gold. But, my dear young ladies—

Kal. Oh, don't. You mustn't. It's too affectionate.

Nek. It really does unsettle us.

Gold. Are you really under the impression that English girls are so ridiculously demure? Why, an English girl of the highest type is the best, the most beautiful, the bravest, and the brightest creature that Heaven has conferred upon this world of ours. She is frank, open-hearted, and fearless, and never shows in so favourable a light as when she gives her own blameless impulses full play!

Nek. *and* Kal. Oh, you shocking story!

Gold. Not at all. I'm speaking the strict truth. I'll tell you all about her.

Song.—Mr. Goldbury.

A wonderful joy our eyes to bless,
In her magnificent comeliness,
Is an English girl of eleven stone two,
And five foot ten in her dancing shoe!
She follows the hounds, and on she pounds—
　　The "field" tails off and the muffs diminish—
Over the hedges and brooks she bounds
　　Straight as a crow, from find to finish.
At cricket, her kin will lose or win—
　　She and her maids, on grass and clover,
Eleven maids out—eleven maids in—
　　And perhaps an occasional "maiden over!"
Go search the world and search the sea,
Then come you home and sing with me
There's no such gold and no such pearl
As a bright and beautiful English girl!

With a ten mile spin she stretchers her limbs,
She golfs, she punts, she rows, she swims—
She plays, she sings, she dances, too,
From ten or eleven till all is blue!
　　At ball or drum, till small hours come,
　　　(Chaperon's fan conceals her yawning)
　　She'll waltz away like a teetotum,
　　　And never go home till daylight's dawning.
Lawn-tennis may share her favours fair—
　　Her eyes a-dance and her cheeks a-glowing—
Down comes her hair, but what does she care?
　　It's all her own and it's worth the showing!
　　　Go search the world, etc.

Her soul is sweet as the ocean air,
For prudery knows no haven there;
To find mock-modesty, please apply
To the conscious blush and the downcast eye.
　　Rich in the things contentment brings,
　　　In every pure enjoyment wealthy,
　　Blithe as a beautiful bird she sings,
　　　For body and mind are hale and healthy.
Her eyes they thrill with right goodwill—
　　Her heart is light as a floating feather—
As pure and bright as the mountain rill
　　That leaps and laughs in the Highland heather!
　　　Go search the world, etc.

Quartette

Nek.	Then I may sing and play?
Lord. Dram.	You may!
Kal.	And I may laugh and shout?
Gold.	No doubt!
Nek.	These maxims you endorse?
Lord. Dram	Of course!
Kal.	You won't exclaim "Oh fie!"
Gold.	Not I!

GOLD. Whatever you are—be that:
  Whatever you say—be true:
   Straightforwardly act—
   Be honest—in fact,
  Be nobody else but *you.*

LORD DRAM. Give every answer pat—
  Your character true unfurl;
   And when it is ripe,
   You'll then be a type
  Of a capital English girl!

ALL   Oh, sweet surprise—oh, dear delight,
  To find it undisputed quite,
  All musty, fusty rules despite,
  That Art is wrong and Nature right!

NEK.   When happy I,
   With laughter glad
    I'll wake the echoes fairly,
  And only sigh
   When I am sad—
    And that will be but rarely!

KAL.   I'll row and fish,
   And gallop, soon—
    No longer be a prim one—
  And when I wish
   To hum a tune,
    It needn't be a hymn one?

GOLD. *and* LORD DRAM. No, no!
  It needn't be a hymn one!

ALL   Oh, sweet surprise and dear delight
[*dancing*] To find it undisputed quite—
  All musty, fusty rules despite—
  That Art is wrong and Nature right!

[*Dance, and off.*

Enter LADY SOPHY.

RECITATIVE.—LADY SOPHY.
Oh, would some demon power the gift impart
To quell my over-conscientious heart—
Unspeak the oaths that never had been spoken,
And break the vows that never shall be broken!

SONG.—LADY SOPHY.

When but a maid of fifteen year,
 Unsought—unplighted—
Short petticoated—and, I fear,
 Still shorter-sighted—
I made a vow, one early spring,
That only to some spotless king
Who proof of blameless life could bring
 I'd be united.

For I had read, not long before,
Of blameless kings in fairy lore,
And thought the race still flourished here—
 Well, well—
I was a maid of fifteen year!

The KING *enters and overhears this verse.*

Each morning I pursued my game
 (An early riser);
For spotless monarchs I became
 An advertiser:
But all in vain I searched each land,
So, kingless, to my native strand
Returned, a little older, and
 A good deal wiser!
I learnt that spotless King and Prince
Have disappeared some ages since—
Even Paramount's angelic grace,
 Ah, me!
Is but a mask on Nature's face!

[KING *comes forward*

RECITATIVE.

KING. Ah, Lady Sophy—then you love me!
  For so you sing—
LADY S. No, by the stars that shine above me
[*indignant and surprised*]. Degraded King!
[*Producing* PALACE PEEPER.]
  For while these rumours, through the city bruited
  Remain uncontradicted, unrefuted,
  The object thou of my aversion rooted,
   Repulsive thing!
KING. Be just—the time is now at hand
   When truth may published be,
  These paragraphs were written and
   Contributed by me!
LADY S. By you? no, no!
KING.   Yes, yes, I swear, by me!
  I, caught in Scaphio's ruthless toil,
   Contributed the lot!
LADY S. And *that* is why you did not boil
   The author on the spot!
KING. And *that* is why *I* did not boil
   The author on the spot!
LADY S. I *couldn't* think why you did not boil.
KING. But *I* know why I did not boil
   The author on the spot!

DUET.—LADY SOPHY AND KING.

LADY S. Oh, the rapture unrestrained
   Of a candid retractation;
  For my sovereign has deigned
   A convincing explanation—
  And the clouds that gathered o'er,
   All have vanished in the distance
  And of Kings of fairy lore
   One, at least, is in existence!

KING.
    Oh, the skies are blue above,
      And the earth is red and rosal,
    Now the lady of my love
      Has accepted my proposal!
    For that *asinorum pons*
      I have crossed without assistance,
    And of prudish paragons
      One, at least, is in existence!

[KING *and* LADY SOPHY *dance gracefully. While this is going on* LORD DRAMALEIGH *enters unobserved with* NEKAYA *and* MR. GOLDBURY *with* KALYBA. *Then enter* ZARA *and* CAPT. FITZBATTLEAXE. *The two Girls direct* ZARA'S *attention to the* KING *and* LADY SOPHY, *who are still dancing affectionately together. At this point the* KING *kisses* LADY SOPHY, *which causes the* PRINCESSES *to make an exclamation. The* KING *and* LADY SOPHY *are at first much confused at being detected, but eventually throw off all reserve, and the four couples break into a wild Tarantella, and at the end exeunt severally.*

Enter all the male CHORUS, *in great excitment, from various entrances, led by* SCAPHIO, PHANTIS, *and* TARARA, *and followed by the female* CHORUS.

CHORUS.

    Upon our sea-girt land
    At our enforced command
    Reform has laid her hand
      Like some remorseless ogress—
    And make us darkly rue
    The deeds she dared to do—
    And all is owing to
      Those hated Flowers of Progress!

ALL.
      So down with them!
      So down with them!
    Reform's a hated ogress.
      So down with them!
      So down with them!
    Down with the Flowers of Progress!

Flourish. Enter KING, *his three* DAUGHTERS, LADY SOPHY, *and the* FLOWERS OF PROGRESS.

KING.
What means this most unmannerly irruption?
Is this your gratitude for boons conferred?

SCA.
Boons? Bah! A fico for such boons, say we!
These boons have brought Utopia to a standstill!
Our pride and boast—the Army and the Navy—
Have both been re-constructed and re-modelled
Upon so irresistible a basis
That all the neighbouring nations have disarmed—
And War's impossible! Your County Councillor
Has passed such drastic Sanitary laws
That all the doctors dwindle, starve, and die!
The laws, remodelled by Sir Bailey Barre,
Have quite extinguished crime and litigation:
The lawyers starve, and all the jails are let
As model lodgings for the working-classes!
In short—
Utopia, swamped by dull Prosperity,
Demands that these detested Flowers of Progress

Be sent about their business, and affairs
Restored to their original complexion!

KING. (*to* ZARA). My daughter, this is a very unpleasant state of things. What is to be done?

ZARA. I don't know—I don't understand it. We must have omitted something,

KING. Omitted something? Yes, that's all very well, but—
          [SIR BAILEY BARRE *whispers to* ZARA.

ZARA (*suddenly*). Of course, Now I remember! Why, I had forgotten the most essential element of all!

KING. And that is—

ZARA. Government by Party! Introduce that great and glorious element at once the bulwark and foundation of England's greatness—and all will be well! No political measures will endure, because one Party will assuredly undo all that the other party has done; and while grouse is to be shot, and foxes worried to death, the legislative action of the country will be at a standstill. Then there will be sickness in plenty, endless lawsuits, crowded jails, interminable confusion in the Army and Navy, and, in short, general and unexampled prosperity!

ALL. Ulahlica! Ulahlica!

PHAN. (*aside.*) Baffled!

SCA. But an hour *will* come!

KING. Your hour has come already—away with them, and let them wait my will! (SCAPHIO *and* PHANTIS *are led off in custody.*) From this moment Government by Party is adopted, with all its attendant blessings; and henceforward Utopia will no longer be a Monarchy (Limited), but, what is a great deal better, a Limited Monarchy!

FINALE.

ZARA.
    There's a little group of isles beyond the wave—
      So tiny, you might almost wonder where it is—
    That nation is the bravest of the brave,
      And cowards are the rarest of all rarities.
    The proudest nations kneel at her command;
      She terrifies all foreign-born rapscallions;
    And holds the peace of Europe in her hand
      With half a score invincible battalions!
      Such, at least, is the tale
      Which is borne on the gale,
        From the island which dwells in the sea.
      Let us hope, for her sake,
      That she makes no mistake—
        That she's all she professes to be!

KING.
    Oh, may we copy all her maxims wise,
      And imitate her virtues and her charities;
    And may we, by degrees, acclimatize
      Her Parliamentary peculiarities!
    By doing so, we shall, in course of time,
      Regenerate completely our entire land—
    Great Britain is that monarchy sublime,
      To which some add (but others do not) Ireland
        Such, at least, is the tale, etc.

CURTAIN

The Grand Duke

or The Statutory Duel

There were twenty-five years between *Thespis* and *The Grand Duke*, and yet these first and last collaborations have two identical elements in the plot: a company of actors and a Greek scene.

Although all Gilbert and Sullivan's operas (except for *Thespis*) have a close resemblance throughout, there are surprising progressions to be found in each. Both librettist and composer were always up to date with the times, and because the brash and vulgar atmosphere of the 1890s was all-pervading, they naturally caught it in *The Grand Duke*. The 'proper' Gilbert even resorts to risqué lines, and Sullivan broadens his style to the full-blown. His score for *The Grand Duke* is a development—a bridge—between the old pattern and something which he was never to develop with another librettist. It is this style, much influenced by continental operetta and its increasing blowziness, which Ivor Novello was to take up and again refine in his musical plays, Ruritanian in setting, but decidedly British in a Sullivanesque style.

Gilbert and Sullivan, near the end of their joint working lives, were together again under a flag of truce; yet while social decorum prevailed between them, there was a tense atmosphere beneath the surface.

Gilbert's sources for *The Grand Duke* were a short story and an American newspaper article. The story was 'The Duke's Dilemma' published in *Blackwood's Magazine* for September 1853. It was about an impoverished nobleman whose rich fiancée was likely to jilt him unless he put on a show of affluence when they met. He engages a company of actors to replace the courtiers who have left him, and the ruse is entirely successful. This story was made into a play, staged in London in 1889 under the title of *The Prima Donna*, although it was originally to have been called *The Grand Duke*. It is more likely that Gilbert's use of this title was inclining towards Offenbach's *Grande Duchesse (de Gérolstein)* who is mentioned in the opera. The eccentric newspaper article, written at about the time when the electric chair was instituted in the United States, discussed

the results, legal and otherwise, were a 'dead' person to be resuscitated and brought back to life. This idea may be indirectly compared with the old 'Lozenge Plot'.

A fresh agreement between Carte, Gilbert and Sullivan after their latest disagreement, allowed Carte to mount revivals of the operas at the Savoy again; but it disallowed Nancy McIntosh from appearing in the new opera. By way of pacification, Gilbert was at liberty to find another ingénue whom he would build up into a star.

In early 1896, Gilbert found his new leading lady at Drury Lane Theatre, singing Briefchristel in Zeller's operetta *Der Vogelhändler*. Mme Ilka von Palmay (in married life the Countess Kinsky) was a true middle-European comédienne. She had a

Ilka von Palmay, Gilbert's new 'discovery', as Julia Jellicoe, the 'English' leading lady.

delicious sense of humour and she could sing. The idea of casting such a performer, so arch and coy, as a typical English actress of the 1890s was a truly Gilbertian stroke. Curiously enough, she had been the subject of an injunction by Carte when the Royal Court Theatre, Berlin billed her to appear there as Nanki-Poo in *Der Mikado* three years before.

Gilbert's minor infatuation for von Palmay led to a complete *bouleversement* of the *Grand Duke* libretto. The work that Sullivan had seen and approved and declared himself willing to set now suffered a great change. The role of Julia Jellicoe was built up, new numbers were written for her, and the balance of the whole piece was so disturbed that the Grand Duke himself has hardly anything to do in the second act. The intrigues and politics between actors and actresses (as in *Thespis*) take up far too much of the first act dialogue, which is not in Gilbert's best vein anyway. Who would have imagined that theatrical 'bitchery', or puns on Greece and grease (however hidden in the two acts) would replace his old wit?

Unfortunately Gilbert allowed more than this to mar his libretto. He manages to invest some of it with spiteful and cynical tilts at Queen Victoria (her German accent and her minor continental princeling relatives); at Sullivan (the inviolability of dramatic contracts and disparaging asides about Ireland); and at those people who never stop talking about money (Carte?) because the characters in *The Grand Duke* scarcely ever let the matter drop.

It is a disappointing libretto in its final form, especially as two rather good numbers in Act II—a Brindisi for the Baroness, and the Roulette Song for the Prince of Monte Carlo—together with a final, angry song for Rudolph have all been cut (though they are to be heard on the Decca recording). The libretto would stand more effectively were sensible cuts to be made in the Act I dialogue. Even Gilbert was dissatisfied with it, for after the first night he declared that he never wanted to see 'the ugly, misshapen little brat again!'; while Sullivan, recovering from it all in Monte Carlo, wrote 'Another week's rehearsal with WSG and I should have gone raving mad. I had already ordered some straw for my hair.'

The Grand Duke had only 123 performances at the Savoy in 1896 and was never given again professionally in London until a single concert performance at the same theatre on 5 April 1975.

Music cover of 'The Grand Duke Quadrille'.

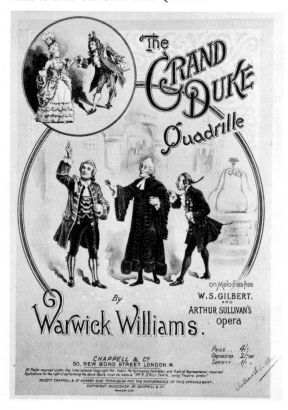

SYNOPSIS

The pot-pourri Overture is promising. It begins with the Grand Duke's March containing a very German quotation from Beethoven's incidental music to 'The Ruins of Athens' and sets the scene for the decadent plot.

Act I opens on a jolly party in the marketplace in Speisesaal, capital of the Grand Duchy of Pfennig-Halbpfennig in 1750. A company of actors seated at small tables are celebrating the forthcoming marriage of their chief comedian Ludwig, to the soubrette Lisa. 'Won't it be a pretty wedding?' is a chattering chorus of carousal. The waltz duet for Ludwig and Lisa which follows adds to the middle-European operetta idea.

The theatrical company represents the residents of the Grand Duchy who are plotting to overthrow the Grand Duke Rudolph *on the morrow*. Notary Tannhäuser, their solicitor in the conspiracy, is surprised to find that the wedding has not yet taken place. This, he is told, is because the Grand Duke has suddenly called a convocation of clergy 'to settle the details of his approaching marriage with the enormously wealthy Baroness von Krakenfeldt'. Because no parson will be available until six, and the company are due to perform *Troilus and Cressida* at seven, they are all anticipating the wedding in this manner.

Ludwig checks a casual remark about the conspiracy from one of the actresses by singing a song 'You must eat a sausage roll', which is the secret sign between friends. Ernest Dummkopf, manager of the theatrical company and Grand Duke elect (among the conspirators) joins the company and, like Thespis in that opera, voices the opinion that anyone who can rule a theatrical company can equally well govern 'All Europe—with Ireland thrown in!' Ernest is in love with his leading actress, Julia Jellicoe, the only English girl in his company. She informs him that if he is to become Grand Duke, she must—in accordance with her contract—play every leading part in his productions, and so must become Grand Duchess. In her ballad, 'How would I play this part ...?' she confesses that in spite of disliking Ernest, she would throw herself into the role so thoroughly that (even to the extent of having children) she would be a complete success in the eyes of the world. Ernest is absolutely willing to accept her on these terms, due to the 'delicate touches' she has outlined.

Ludwig returns, followed by an agitated Chorus, for he has given away the secret of the plot to the Grand Duke's private detective whom he saw eating *three* sausage rolls and concluded, wrongly, that he was of the fraternity. The choral interjections in canon are the best part of this number. Notary Tannhäuser calms them down with a description of the Statutory Duel. Duellists each take a card from a pack and the higher one wins. He who takes the lowest is socially 'dead' ('a legal ghoest') for twenty-four hours, and must disappear from everyone's sight. The winner is obliged to discharge the loser's debts, 'pay all his bets, and take his obligations'. But this *Code of the Duello*, instituted a century ago, will lapse *on the morrow*.

In the quintet 'Strange the views some people hold!' with its refrain 'Ding! Dong!', Julia, Lisa, Ludwig, Ernest and the Notary have a closely harmonized ensemble—late *Gondoliers* in spirit, but lacking in 'lift'. Ernest and Ludwig then duel with the cards because of Ludwig's misdemeanour, and

Ernest loses with a King against Ludwig's Ace. Consequently Ludwig the comedian now becomes manager of the company. A jolly number in a gambling spirit, 'Sing Hearts, Clubs, Diamonds, Spades and all!' celebrates the fact.

The Grand Duke's March—first heard at the opening of the Overture—announces the impending arrival of the Monarch. Seven Chamberlains enter first and discuss him in disparaging terms. The mean, miserable and melancholy Grand Duke Rudolph enters, dressed in old, patched clothes blazing 'with a profusion of orders and decorations'. He looks 'very weak and ill, from low living'. Grand Duke Rudolph reveals to his Chamberlains his intention to marry the (equally mean) Baroness von Krakenfeldt *on the morrow*. One by one, in order of seniority, the seven Chamberlains pass up his snuff-box, then his handkerchief, which is protocol. He then outlines his stingy arrangements for the wedding celebrations.

The Baroness arrives and notes her fiancé's seedy appearance. He explains to her that he was betrothed

'Observe. My handkerchief!' Grand Duke Rudolph, Walter Passmore, in his opening number. Savoy Theatre, 7 March 1896.

Rosina Brandram as the Baroness von Krakenfeldt with the detective's letter concealed in her newspaper.

in infancy to the Princess of Monte Carlo, but it doesn't matter because 'it's practically off'. The betrothal is void once the Princess has come of age, and she will do so *on the morrow*. Because her father is so in debt, he dare not leave his palace, and so their arrival in Pfennig-Halbpfennig can be discounted. The Baroness accepts this proposition and they both dwell on the delights of a frugal partnership: 'As o'er our penny rolls we sing ...'

Rudolph reads his detective's report when the Baroness has left, and learns about the dethronement plot, due *on the morrow*. His nightmare song— 'When you find you're a broken-down critter ...' has a variety of onomatopœic instrumental accompaniments, to accord with the words representing a serious physical and mental condition, that are unusual for Sullivan and make the number worthy of an encore. Instead of trying to avert the revolution, Rudolph sinks down beside the well in the marketplace 'exhausted and weeping'.

Here Ludwig discovers him when he comes to confess his part in the conspiracy and hope for

pardon—having taken on at least one of Ernest's responsibilities. But seeing how dejected Rudolph is, and calling him a cry-baby, he offers the solution of a Statutory Duel to get him out of his unenviable situation. The Grand Duke finally agrees but insists that there must be 'a devil of a quarrel' first.

He calls in all the people, who are nervous because of their implication in the plot, to witness a feeble quarrel between the Grand Duke and Ludwig: 'Big bombs, small bombs ...' well set as duet with full chorus. Again the Notary explains how the Statutory Duel works. The two contestants have previously palmed their cards so that Ludwig's Ace beats the Grand Duke Rudolph's King. Three female members of the company bid mocking farewells to Rudolph, while the rest pretend to weep. Even Lisa is ironical in her charming 'Though malcontents abuse you ...'. Rudolph leaves them, enraged at their behaviour, and warns them of dire punishment on his return in twenty-four hours. 'We hail you, sir!' is a miniature, mock national anthem of greeting to the new Grand Duke Ludwig.

But Ludwig has no intention of yielding his new title. As well as announcing that 'our rule shall be merry', he abolishes the twenty-four hour clause in the Statutory Duel Act, and extends the Act by another hundred years. He consequently commits both Rudolph and Ernest to eternal 'death' but they, being incommunicado, do not know it. Ludwig tells the crowd: 'Till I perish your Monarch am I!' 'The Court appointments will be given out ...' he continues, 'according to professional position.'

Julia immediately comes forward (with Lisa 'clinging to her') and in her charming aria 'Our duty, if we're wise ...' proposes that, in consequence of her contract as leading actress, she must become Grand Duchess. Ludwig is not at all pleased and reminds her that it is a part she must play for life, but she is coldly adamant. Lisa is appalled. In the duet, Julia-Lisa, 'Oh, listen to me, dear ...' the tender-hearted little soubrette is firmly put down by the calculating and 'bitchy' Julia by stagey words and insincere sentiment. The Notary declares that Julia is in the right for, 'though marriage contracts ... are very solemn, dramatic contracts ... are even more so!'

Lisa's heart-broken song, 'The die is cast ...' touches Ludwig, but Julia drags him away. Promise of fun at last in Pfennig-Halbpfennig is interrupted by Julia with demands for 'dress original and novel'.

Ludwig says that they shall all wear Greek dress for the celebrations (their 'Troilus and Cressida shall be played out') and the act ends with a reprise of the cheerful number 'Sing hey, the jolly jinks of Pfennig-Halbpfennig!'

Act II takes place in the Grand Ducal Hall and begins with the wedding of Ludwig and Julia. All the members of the theatrical company in their Greek costumes are playing on appropriate instruments or singing 'As before you we defile …'. It is a dirge in C that never quite becomes A minor, and is somehow reminiscent of 'Twenty lovesick maidens' from *Patience*.

Ludwig answers their thanks (and reminds them that he did not choose his new Grand Duchess) with a quasi-patter song, full of Greek epithets and having a linked melody with the 'Sausage Roll'. Lisa can no longer contain her misery at losing Ludwig, and in a passionate number, 'Take care of him—', she instructs Julia upon how to treat him. It is not an easy song to sing and is probably the most tenderly expressed, in music and in words, of any in this opera.

Julia and Ludwig privately discuss their respective attitudes to one another. Ludwig's uncertain 'Now Julia, come, Consider it …' is answered at length by this young virago in a complicated *scena* which gives ample opportunity for the 'first-rate part' she is always after. She goes through the agonies of an assumed jealousy, the pursuit and strangling of her rival, remorse and finally madness. Sullivan scarcely matches the Lady Macbeth-like requirements by accompanying the scene with merely melodramatic ideas; nor has it any of the charm inherent in the only other mad scene in the operas: Mad Margaret's in *Ruddigore*.

This frantic atmosphere suddenly changes into the choral number 'Your Highness, there's a party at the door—' when the crowd bursts in to announce the arrival of the Baroness von Krakenfeldt. She is incensed because her bridegroom Rudolph is not waiting to meet her. Ludwig has no idea who she is, and treats her in an aloof manner through their sprightly jig (reminiscent of 'The truth is found' in *Princess Ida*).

When the Baroness hears that Rudolph 'Isn't at home just now' and that he expired yesterday on account of a Statutory Duel, she understands entirely and—after an exceedingly bitter altercation with Julia—demands Ludwig's hand, for of all Rudolph's

Rutland Barrington as Ludwig, wearing Inigo Jones-style Troilus costume.

responsibilities which Ludwig must now accept, she is 'the most overwhelming of them all!'

Krakenfeldt begins a *postillon galop* (Auber not entirely forgotten) 'Now away to the wedding we go …' in which everyone (excepting Julia) joins as Ludwig allows himself to be dragged by the Baroness into yet another marriage.

Julia, for the first time, finds herself cut out, and the sugary sentiment of her Viennese operetta-like recitative and aria 'So ends my dream … Broken every promise plighted …' shows her, in this German folk-tune, to be irrepressively determined. She decides to forget the past and to look forward to tomorrow.

The 'dead' Ernest enters and Julia affects not being able to see him. When he realizes that she is not married to Ludwig and understands all that Ludwig has done, he proposes to her again. In the duet 'If the light of love's lingering ember' she rejects him, and Ernest threatens to haunt her for ever.

A march brings back the Chorus to enquire who is now approaching (rather in the style of *The Mikado*), and a Herald announces, in an attractive number, the arrival in Pfennig-Halbpfennig, of 'The Prince of Monte Carlo and his be-autiful daughter!' Their entrance music is again a linked melody with the 'Sausage Roll', and the Prince's aria shows a paucity of musical invention. He tells how he has engaged six supernumeraries from the Theatre Monaco ('at a salary immense, quite regardless of expense') who must not speak, because they are illiterate, and must wear gloves because their nails are not presentable. Since they are, in any case, wealthy members of 'the brewing interest', they have all been raised to the Peerage.

Ludwig's 'Greek' followers, who have all been in hiding, spring out—to general amazement—and everyone joins in their 'reckless dance' until they fall, exhausted. The Prince explains to Ludwig the reason for his arrival and introduces his daughter who embraces her supposed fiancé. Ludwig explains that he already has three Grand Duchesses, and when he realizes that the Monte Carlos are looking for Rudolph, he explains that Rudolph died, quite suddenly, of 'a pack of cardiac affection'. In any case,

the Grand Duke had been engaged to the Baroness for three weeks, and Ludwig is obliged to take her over with the rest of the obligations. When the Princess reminds him that she had been engaged to Rudolph for twenty years, her father insists that she has the right to Ludwig. She takes him too to get married and they all sing 'Away to the wedding we'll go ...' a reprise of the Baroness's earlier song.

Suddenly Rudolph, Ernest and the Notary enter, and everyone kneels in astonishment. They declare in unison that 'The Law forbids the banns!' Rudolph, speechless with rage, leaves it to the Notary to disclose the awful truth that the Act has been misinterpreted because 'the Ace shall count invariably as lowest!'

Ernest tells Julia that he is about to come to life again, and she submits to him. The Princess of Monte Carlo and Rudolph pair off, after all; Ludwig claims Lisa and on the stroke of three, the Act expires. They depart for the joint marriage to a reprise of the opening number with the words 'Happy couples, lightly treading ... such a pretty, pretty wedding!'

THE GRAND DUKE;

OR

THE STATUTORY DUEL.

First produced at the Savoy Theatre, 7 March 1896

DRAMATIS PERSONÆ

RUDOLPH [*Grand Duke of Pfennig Halbpfennig*]	baritone
ERNEST DUMMKOPF [*a Theatrical Manager*]	tenor
LUDWIG [*his Leading Comedian*]	baritone
DR. TANNHAUSER [*a Notary*]	tenor
THE PRINCE OF MONTE CARLO	bass
BEN HASHBAZ [*a Costumier*]	baritone
HERALD	baritone
THE PRINCESS OF MONTE CARLO [*betrothed to* RUDOLPH]	soprano
THE BARONESS VON KRAKENFELDT [*betrothed to* RUDOLPH]	contralto
JULIA JELLICOE [*an English Comédienne*]	soprano
LISA [*a Soubrette*]	soprano
OLGA)	soprano
GRETCHEN)	soprano
BERTHA) [*Members of Ernest Dummkopf's Company*]	mezzo-soprano
ELSA)	soprano
MARTHA)	soprano

Chamberlains, Nobles, Actors, Actresses, etc.

ACT I.

SCENE, PUBLIC SQUARE OF SPEISESAAL

ACT II.

SCENE, HALL IN THE GRAND DUCAL PALACE

DATE 1750

THE GRAND DUKE;

OR

THE STATUTORY DUEL.

ACT I.

SCENE—*Market Place of Speisesaal, in the Grand Duchy of Pfennig Halbpfennig. A well, with decorated iron-work, up* L.C. GRETCHEN, BERTHA, OLGA, MARTHA, *and other members of* ERNEST DUMMKOPF'S *theatrical company are discovered, seated at several small tables, enjoying a repast in honour of the nuptials of* LUDWIG, *his leading comedian, and* LISA, *his soubrette.*

CHORUS.

Won't it be a pretty wedding?
    Doesn't Lisa look delightful?
Smiles and tears in plenty shedding—
    Which in brides of course is rightful.
    One might say, if one were spiteful,
Contradiction little dreading,
    Her bouquet is simply frightful—
Still, it is a pretty wedding!
Oh, it is a pretty wedding!
    Such a pretty, pretty wedding!

ELSA.   If her dress *is* badly fitting,
    Theirs the fault who made her *trousseau.*

BERTHA. If her gloves *are* always splitting,
    Cheap kid gloves, we know, will do so.

OLGA.   If her wreath *is* all lop-sided,
    That's a thing one's always dreading.

GRETCHEN.If her hair *is* all untidied,
    Still, it is a pretty wedding!

CHORUS. Oh, it is a pretty wedding!
    Such a pretty, pretty wedding!

CHORUS.

Here they come, the couple plighted—
    On life's journey gaily start them.
Soon to be for aye united,
    Till divorce or death do part them.

LUDWIG *and* LISA *come forward.*

DUET—LUDWIG *and* LISA

LUDWIG. Pretty Lisa, fair and tasty,
    Tell me now, and tell me truly,
    Haven't you been rather hasty?
    Haven't you been rash unduly?
    Am I quite the dashing *sposo*

That your fancy could depict you?
Perhaps you think I'm only so-so?
        [*She expresses admiration.*]
    Well, I will not contradict you!

CHORUS.   No, he will not contradict you!

LISA.   Who am I to raise objection?
    I'm a child, untaught and homely—
    When you tell me you're perfection,
        Tender, truthful, true, and comely—
    That in quarrel no one's bolder,
        Though dissensions always grieve you—
    Why, my love, you're so much older
        That, of course, I must believe you!

CHORUS.   Yes, of course, she must believe you!

CHORUS.

If he ever acts unkindly,
Shut your eyes and love him blindly—
Should he call you names uncomely,
Shut your mouth and love him dumbly—
Should he rate you, rightly—leftly—
Shut your ears and love him deafly.
    Ha! ha! ha! ha! ha! ha! ha!
    Thus and thus and thus alone,
    Ludwig's wife may hold her own!
        [LUDWIG *and* LISA *sit at table*]

Enter NOTARY TANNHAUSER.

NOTARY. Hallo! Surely I'm not late? *(All chatter unintelligibly in reply.)* But, dear me, you're all at breakfast! Has the wedding taken place? *(All chatter unintelligibly in reply.)* My good girls, one at a time, I beg. Let me understand the situation. As solicitor to the conspiracy to dethrone the Grand Duke—a conspiracy in which the members of this company are deeply involved—I am invited to the marriage of two of its members. I present myself in due course, and I find, not only that the ceremony has taken place—which is not of the least consequence—but the wedding breakfast is half eaten—which is a consideration of the most serious importance.

        [LUDWIG *and* LISA *come down*]

LUDWIG. But the ceremony has *not* taken place. We can't get a parson!

NOTARY. Can't get a parson! Why, how's that? They're three a penny!

LUDWIG. Oh, it's the old story—the Grand Duke!

ALL. Ugh!

LUDWIG. It seems that the little imp has selected this, our wedding day, for a convocation of all the clergy in the town to settle the details of his approaching marriage with the enormously wealthy Baroness von Krakenfeldt, and there won't be a parson to be had for love or money until six o'clock this evening!

LISA. And as we produce our magnificent classical revival of *Troilus and Cressida* to-night at seven, we have no alternative but to eat our wedding-breakfast before we've earned it. So sit down, and make the best of it.

GRETCHEN. Oh, I should like to pull his Grand Ducal ears for him, that I should! He's the meanest, the cruellest, the most spiteful little ape in Christendom!

OLGA. Well, we shall soon be freed from his tyranny. Tomorrow the Despot is to be dethroned!

LUDWIG. Hush, rash girl! You know not what you say.

OLGA. Don't be absurd! We're all in it—we're all tiled, here.

LUDWIG. That has nothing to do with it. Know ye not that in alluding to our conspiracy without having first given and received the secret sign, you are violating a fundamental principle of our Association?

SONG.—LUDWIG.

By the mystic regulation
Of our dark Association,
Ere you open conversation
  With another kindred soul,
  You must eat a sausage-roll!

[*Producing one*

ALL.   You must eat a sausage-roll!

LUDWIG.   If, in turn, he eats another,
That's a sign that he's a brother—
Each may fully trust the other.
  It is quaint and it is droll,
  But it's bilious on the whole.

ALL.   Very bilious on the whole.

LUDWIG.   It's a greasy kind of pasty,
Which, perhaps, a judgment hasty
Might consider rather tasty:
  Once (to speak without disguise)
  It found favour in our eyes.

ALL.   It found favour in our eyes.

LUDWIG.   But when you've been six months feeding
(As we have) on this exceeding
Bilious food, it's no ill-breeding
  If at these repulsive pies
  Our offended gorges rise!

ALL.   Our offended gorges rise!

MARTHA. Oh, bother the secret sign! I've eaten it until I'm quite uncomfortable! I've given it six times already to-day—and (*whimpering*) I can't eat any breakfast!

BERTHA. And it's so unwholesome. Why, we should all be as yellow as frogs if it wasn't for the make-up!

LUDWIG. All this rank treason to the cause. I suffer as much as any of you. I loathe the repulsive thing—I can't contemplate it without a shudder—but I'm a conscientious conspirator, and if

you won't give the sign I will. (*Eats sausage roll with an effort.*)

LISA. Poor martyr! He's always at it, and it's a wonder where he puts it!

NOTARY. Well, now, about *Troilus and Cressida.* What do *you* play!

LUDWIG (*struggling with his feelings*). If you'll be so obliging as to wait until I've got rid of this feeling of warm oil at the bottom of my throat, I'll tell you all about it. (LISA *gives him some brandy.*) Thank you, my love; it's gone. Well, the piece will be produced upon a scale of unexampled magnificence. It is confidently predicted that my appearance as King Agamemnon, in a Louis Quatorze wig, will mark an epoch in the theatrical annals of Pfennig Halbfennig. I endeavoured to persuade Ernest Dummkopf, our manager, to lend us the classical dresses for our marriage. Think of the effect of a real Athenian wedding procession cavorting through the streets of Speisesaal! Torches burning—cymbals banging—flutes tootling—citharæ twanging—and a throng of fifty lovely Spartan virgins capering before us, all down the High Street, singing "Eloia! Eloia! Opoponax, Eloia!" It would have been tremendous!

NOTARY. And he declined?

LUDWIG. He did, on the prosaic ground that it might rain, and the ancient Greeks didn't carry umbrellas! If, as is confidently expected, Ernest Dommkopf is elected to succeed the dethroned one, mark my words, he will make a mess of it.

OLGA. He's sure to be elected. His entire company has promised to plump for him on the understanding that all the places about the Court are filled by members of his troupe, according to professional precedence.

[*He strolls up and off with* LISA, *as* ERNEST *enters in great excitement.*]

BERTHA (*looking off*). Here comes Ernest Dummkopf. Now we shall know all about it!

ALL. Well—what's the news? How is the election going?

ERNEST. Oh, it's a certainty—a practical certainty! Two of the candidates have been arrested for debt, and the third is a baby in arms—so, if you keep your promises, and vote solid, I'm cocksure of election!

OLGA. Trust to us. But you remember the conditions?

ERNEST. Yes—all of you shall be provided for, for life. Every man shall be ennobled—every lady shall have unlimited credit at the Court Milliner's, and all salaries shall be paid weekly in advance!

GRETCHEN. Oh, it's quite clear he knows how to rule a Grand Duchy!

ERNEST. Rule a Grand Duchy? Why, my good girl, for ten years past I've ruled a theatrical company! A man who can do that can rule anything!

SONG.—ERNEST.

Were I king in very truth,
And had a son—a guileless youth—
  In probable succession;
To teach him patience, teach him tact,
How promptly in a fix to act,
He should adopt, in point of fact,
  A manager's profession.
To that condition he should stoop
(Despite a too fond mother),

325

With eight or ten "stars" in his troupe,
    All jealous of each other!
Oh, the man who can rule a theatrical crew,
Each member a genius (and some of them two),
And manage to humour them, little and great,
    Can govern this tuppenny State!

ALL.   Oh, the man, etc.

    Both A and B rehearsal slight—
    They say they'll be "all right at night"
        They've both to go to school yet);
    C in each act *must* change her dress,
    D *will* attempt to "square the press";
    E won't play Romeo unless
        His grandmother plays Juliet;
    F claims all hoydens as her rights
        (She's played them thirty seasons);
    And G must show herself in tights
        For two convincing reasons—
        Two very well-shaped reasons!
Oh, the man who can drive a theatrical team.
With wheelers and leaders in order supreme,
Can govern and rule, with a wave of his fin,
    All Europe—with Ireland thrown in!

ALL.   Oh, the man, etc.   *[Exeunt all but* ERNEST]

ERNEST. Elected by my fellow conspirators to be Grand Duke of Pfennig Halbpfennig as soon as the contemptible little occupant of the historical throne is deposed—here is promotion indeed! Why, instead of playing Troilus of Troy for a month, I shall play Grand Duke of Pfennig Halbpfennig for a lifetime! Yet am I happy? No—far from happy! The lovely English *comédienne* —the beautiful Julia, whose dramatic ability is so overwhelming that our audiences forgive even her strong English accent—that rare and radiant being treats my respectful advances with disdain unutterable! And yet, who knows? She is haughty and ambitious, and it may be that the splendid change in my fortunes may work a corresponding change in her feelings towards me!

Enter JULIA JELLICOE.

JULIA. Herr Dummkopf, a word with you, if you please.
ERNEST. Beautiful English maiden—
JULIA. No compliments, I beg. I desire to speak with you on a purely professional matter, so we will, if you please, dispense with allusions to my personal appearance, which can only tend to widen the breach which already exists between us.
ERNEST *(aside)*. My only hope shattered! The haughty Londoner still despises me! *(Aloud)*. It shall be as you will.
JULIA. I understand that the conspiracy in which we are all concerned is to develop to-morrow, and that the company is likely to elect you to the throne of the understanding that the posts about the court are to be filled by members of your theatrical troupe, according to their professional importance.
ERNEST. That is so.
JULIA. Then all I can say is that it places me in an extremely awkward position.

ERNEST *(very depressed)*. I don't see how it concerns you.
JULIA. Why, bless my heart, don't you see that, as your leading lady, I am bound under a serious penalty to play the leading part in all your productions?
ERNEST. Well?
JULIA. Why, of course, the leading part in this production will be the Grand Duchess!
ERNEST. My wife?
JULIA. That is another way of expressing the same idea.
ERNEST *(aside—delighted)*. I scarcely dared even to hope for this!
JULIA. Of course, as your leading lady, you'll be mean enough to hold me to the terms of my agreement. Oh, that's so like a man! Well, I suppose there's no help for it—I shall have to do it!
ERNEST *(aside)*. She's mine! *(Aloud.)* But—do you really think you would care to play that part? *(Taking her hand.)*
JULIA *(withdrawing it)*. Care to play it? Certainly not—but what am I to do? Business is business, and I am bound by the terms of my agreement.
ERNEST. It's for a long run, mind—a run that may last many, many years—no understudy—and once embarked upon there's no throwing it up.
JULIA. Oh, we're used to these long runs in England: they are the curse of the stage—but, you see, I've no option.
ERNEST. You think the part of Grand Duchess will be good enough for you?
JULIA. Oh, I think so. It's very good part in Gerolstein, and oughtn't to be a bad one in Pfennig Halbpfennig. Why, what did you suppose I was going to play?
ERNEST *(keeping up a show of reluctance)*. But, considering your strong personal dislike to me and your persistent rejection of my repeated offers, won't you find it difficult to throw yourself into the part with all the impassioned enthusiasm that the character seems to demand? Remember, it's a strongly emotional part, involving long and repeated scences of rapture, tenderness, adoration, devotion—all in luxuriant excess, and all of the most demonstrative description.
JULIA. My good sir, throughout my career I have made it a rule never to allow private feeling to interefere with my professional duties. You may be quite sure that (however distasteful the part may be) if I undertake it, I shall consider myself professionally bound to throw myself into it with all the ardour at my command.
ERNEST *(aside—with effusion)*. I'm the happiest fellow alive! *(Aloud.)* Now—would you have any objection—to—to give me some idea—if it's only a mere sketch—as to how you would play it? It would be really interesting—to me—to known your conception of—of—the part of my wife.
JULIA. How would I play it? Now, let me see—let me see. *(Considering.)* Ah, I have it!

BALLAD—JULIA

    How would I play this part—
        The Grand Duke's Bride?
    All rancour in my heart
        I'd duly hide—
        I'd drive it from my recollection
        And 'whelm you with a mock affection,
        Well calculated to defy detection—
    That's how I'd play this part—
        The Grand Duke's Bride.

With many a winsome smile
    I'd witch and woo;
With gay and girlish guile
    I'd frenzy you—
I'd madden you with my caressing,
Like turtle, her first love confessing—
That it was "mock", no mortal would
    be guessing,
With so much winsome wile.
    I'd witch and woo!

Did any other maid
    With you succeed,
I'd pinch the forward jade—
    I would indeed!
With jealous frenzy agitated
(Which would, of course, be simulated),
I'd make her wish she'd never been
    created—
Did any other maid
    With you succeed!

And should there come to me,
    Some summers hence,
In all the childish glee
    Of innocence,
Fair babes, aglow with beauty vernal,
My heart would bound with joy diurnal!
This sweet display of sympathy maternal,
Well, that would also be
    A mere pretence!

My histrionic art,
    Though you deride,
That's how I'd play that part—
    The Grand Duke's Bride!

ENSEMBLE.

ERNEST.

Oh joy! when two glowing
    young hearts,
From the rise of the curtain,
Thus throw themselves
    into their parts,
Success is most certain!
If the *rôle* you're
    prepared to endow
With such delicate touches,
    By the heaven above us,
    I vow
You shall be my
    Grand Duchess!

JULIA.

My boy, when two glowing
    young hearts,
    From the rise of the curtain,
Thus throw themselves
    into their parts,
Success is most certain!
The *rôle* I'm prepared
    to endow
With most delicate touches,
    By the heaven above us,
    I vow
I will be your Grand
    Duchess!   *(Dance)*

Enter all the Chorus with LUDWIG, NOTARY, *and* LISA—
all greatly agitated.

EXCITED CHORUS

My goodness me! what shall be do! Why, what
    a dreadful situation!

(To LUDWIG.*)* It's all your fault, you booby
    you—you lump of indiscrimination!
I'm sure I don't know where to go—it's put
    me into such a tetter—
But this at all events I know—the sooner we are
    off, the better!

ERNEST. What means this *agitato?* What d'ye seek?
    As your Grand Duke elect I bid you speak!

SONG.—LUDWIG.

Ten minutes since, I met a chap
    Who bowed an easy salutation—
Thinks I, "This gentleman, mayhap,
    Belongs to our Association."
    But, on the whole,
      Uncertain yet,
    A sausage-roll
      I took and eat—
That chap replied (I don't embellish)
By eating *three* with obvious relish.

CHORUS *(angrily).* Why, gracious powers,
      No chum of ours
    Could eat three sausage-rolls with relish!

LUDWIG.   Quite reassured, I let him know
    Our plot—each incident explaining;
That stranger chuckled much, as though
    He thought me highly entertaining.
    I told him all,
      Both bad and good;
    I bade him call—
      He said he would:
I added much—the more I muckled,
The more that chuckling chummy chuckled!

ALL *(angrily).*   A bat could see
      He couldn't be
    A chum of ours if he chuckled!

LUDWIG.   Well, as I bowed to his applause,
    Down dropped he with hysteric bellow—
And *that* seemed right enough, because
    I *am* a devilish funny fellow.
    Then suddenly,
      As still he squealed,
    It flashed on me
      That I'd revealed
Our plot, with all details effective,
To Grand Duke Rudolph's own detective!

ALL.   What folly fell,
      To go and tell
    Our plot to any one's detective!

CHORUS *(attacking* LUDWIG*).* You booby dense—
      You oaf immense,
      With no pretence
      To common sense!
      A stupid muff

Who's made of stuff
Not worth a puff
Of candle-snuff!
Pack up at once and off we go, unless we're
anxious to exhibit
Our fairy forms all in a row, strung up upon the
Castle gibbet!
[*Exeunt Chorus. Manet* LUDWIG, LISA, ERNEST, JULIA *and*
NOTARY.

JULIA. Well, a nice mess you've got us into! There's an end of our precious plot! All up—pop—fizzle—bang—done for!

LUDWIG. Yes, but—ha! ha!—fancy my choosing the Grand Duke's private detective, of all men, to make a confidant of! When you come to think of it, it's really devilish funny!

ERNEST *(angrily)*. When you come to think of it, it's extremely injudicious to admit into a conspiracy every pudding-headed baboon who presents himself!

LUDWIG. Yes—I should never do that. If I were chairman of this gang, I should hesitate to enroll *any* baboon who couldn't produce satisfactory credentials from his Zoological Gardens.

LISA. Ludwig is far from being a baboon. Poor boy, he could not help giving us away—it's his trusting nature—he was deceived.

JULIA *(furiously)*. His trusting nature! (*To* LUDWIG.) Oh, I should like to talk to you in my own language for five minutes—only five minutes! I know some good, strong, energetic English remarks that would shrivel your trusting nature into raisins—only you wouldn't understand them!

LUDWIG. Here we perceive one of the disadvantages of a neglected education!

ERNEST *(to* JULIA). And I suppose you'll never be my Grand Duchess, now!

JULIA. Grand Duchess? My good friend, if you don't produce the piece how can I play the part?

ERNEST. True. (*To* LUDWIG). You see what you've done.

LUDWIG. But, my dear sir, you don't seem to understand that the man ate three sausage-rolls. Keep that fact steadily before you. Three large sausage-rolls.

JULIA. Bah!—Lots of people eat sausage-rolls who are not conspirators.

LUDWIG. Then they shouldn't. It's bad form. It's not the game. When one of the Human Family proposes to eat a sausage-roll, it is his duty to ask himself, "Am I a conspirator?" And if, on examination, he finds that he is *not* a conspirator, he is bound in honour to select some other form of refreshment.

LISA. Of course he is. One should always play the game. (*To* NOTARY, *who has been smiling placidly through this.*) What are you grinning at, you greedy old man?

NOTARY. Nothing—don't mind me. It is always amusing to the legal mind to see a parcel of laymen bothering themselves about a matter which to a trained lawyer presents no difficulty whatever.

ALL. No difficulty!

NOTARY. None whatever! The way out of it is quite simple.

ALL. Simple?

NOTARY. Certainly! Now attend. In the first place, you two men fight a Statutory Duel.

ERNEST. A Statutory Duel?

JULIA. A Stat-tat-tatutory Duel! Ach! what a crack-jaw language this German is!

LUDWIG. Never heard of such a thing.

NOTARY. It is true that the practice has fallen into abeyance through disuse. But all the laws of Pfennig Halbfennig (which are framed upon those of Solon, the Athenian law-giver) run for a hundred years, when (again like the laws of Solon) they die a natural death, unless, in the meantime, they have been revived for another century. The act that institutes the Statutory Duel was passed a hundred years ago, and as it has never been revived, it expires to-morrow. So you're just in time.

JULIA. But what is the use of talking to us about Statutory Duels when we none of us know what a Statutory Duel is?

NOTARY. Don't you? Then I'll explain.

SONG.—NOTARY.

About a century since,
    The code of the duello
        To sudden death
        For want of breath
    Sent many a strapping fellow.
The then presiding Prince
    (Who useless bloodshed hated),
        He passed an Act,
        Short and compact,
    Which may be briefly state:
Unlike the complicated laws
A Parliamentary draughtsman draws,
    It may be briefly stated.

ALL. We know that complicated laws,
    Such as a legal draughtsman draws,
        Cannot be briefly stated.

NOTARY. By this ingenious law,
    If any two shall quarrel,
        They may not fight
        With falchions bright
    (Which seemed to him immoral);
But each a card shall draw,
    And he who draws the lowest
        Shall (so 'twas said)
        Be thenceforth dead—
    In fact, a legal "ghoest"
    (With exigence of rhyme compels,
Orthography foregoes her spells,
    And "ghost" is written "ghoest.")

ALL *(aside)*. With what an emphasis he dwells
    Upon "orthography" and "spells"!
        That kind of fun's the lowest.

NOTARY. When off the loser's popped
    (By little legal fiction),
        And friend and foe
        Have wept their woe
    In counterfeit affliction,
The winner must adopt
    The loser's poor relations—
        Discharge his debts,
        Pay all his bets,
    And take his obligations.
In short, to briefly sum the case,

The winner takes the loser's place,
With all its obligations.

ALL. How neatly lawyers state a case!
The winner takes the loser's place,
With all its obligations!

LUDWIG. I see. The man who draws the lowest card—

NOTARY. Dies, *ipso facto,* a social death. He loses all his civil rights—his identity disappears—the Revising Barrister expunges his name from the list of voters, and the winner takes his place, whatever it may be, discharges all his functions and adopts all his responsibilities.

ERNEST. This is all very well, as far as it goes, but it only protects one of us. What's to become of the survivor?

LUDWIG. Yes, that's an interesting point, because *I* might be the survivor.

NOTARY. The survivor goes at once to the Grand Duke, and, in a burst of remorse, denounces the dead man as the moving spirit of the plot. He is accepted as King's evidence, and, as a matter of course, receives a free pardon. To-morrow, when the law expires, the dead man will, *ipso facto,* come to life again—the Revising Barrister will restore his name to the list of voters, and he will resume all his obligations as though nothing unusual had happened.

JULIA. When he will be at once arrested, tried, and executed on the evidence of the informer! Candidly, my friend, I don't think much of your plot!

NOTARY. Dear, dear, dear, the ignorance of the laity! My good young lady, it is a beautiful maxim of our glorious Constitition that a man can only die once. Death expunges crime, and when he comes to life again, it will be with a clean slate.

ERNEST. It's really very ingenious.

LUDWIG. (*to* NOTARY). My dear sir, we owe you our lives!

LISA. (*aside to* LUDWIG). May I kiss him?

LUDWIG. Certainly not: you're a big girl now. (*To* ERNEST). Well, miscreant, are you prepared to meet me on the field of honour?

ERNEST. At once. By Jove, what couple of fire-eaters we are!

LISA. Ludwig doesn't know what fear is.

LUDWIG. Oh, I don't mind this sort of duel!

ERNEST. It's not like a duel with swords. I hate a duel with swords. It's not the blade I mind—it's the blood.

LUDWIG. And I hate a duel with pistols. It's not the ball I mind—it's the bang.

NOTARY. Altogether it is a great improvement on the old method of giving satisfaction.

QUINTETTE.

LUDWIG, LISA, NOTARY, ERNEST, JULIA.

Strange the views some people hold!
Two young fellows quarrel—
Then they fight, for both are bold—
Rage of both is uncontrolled—
Both are stretched out, stark and cold!
Prithee where's the moral?
Ding dong! Ding dong!
There's an end to further action,
And this barbarous transaction
Is described as "satisfaction"!

Ha! ha! ha! ha! satisfaction!
Ding dong! Ding dong!
Each is laid in churchyard mould—
Strange the views some people hold!
Better than the method old,
Which was coarse and cruel,
Is the plan that we've extolled.
Sing thy virtues manifold
(Better than refinéd gold),
Statutory Duel!
Sing song! Sing song!
Sword or pistol neither uses—
Playing card he lightly chooses,
And the loser simply loses!
Ha! ha! ha! ha! simply loses.
Sing song! Sing song!
Some prefer the churchyard mould!
Strange the views some people hold!

NOTARY (*offering a card to* ERNEST). Now take
a card and gaily sing
How little you care for Fortune's rubs—

ERNEST (*drawing a card*). Hurrah, hurrah!—
I've drawn a King!

ALL. He's drawn a King!
He's drawn a King!
Sing Hearts and Diamonds, Spades and
Clubs!

ALL (*dancing*). He's drawn a King!
How strange a thing!
An excellent card—his chance it aids—
Sing Hearts and Diamonds, Spades and Clubs—
Sing Diamonds, Hearts and Clubs and Spades!

NOTARY (*to* LUDWIG). Now take a card with heart of grace—
(Whatever our fate, let's play our parts).

LUDWIG (*drawing card*). Hurrah, hurrah!—I've drawn an Ace!

ALL. He's drawn an Ace!
He's drawn an Ace!
Sing Clubs and Diamonds, Spades and Hearts!

ALL
(*dancing*). He's drawn an Ace!
Observe his face—
Such very good fortune falls to few—
Sing Clubs and Diamonds, Spades and Hearts—
Sing Clubs, Spades, Hearts and Diamonds too!

NOTARY. That both these maids may keep their troth,
And never misfortune them befall,
I'll hold 'em as trustee for both—

ALL He'll hold 'em both!
He'll hold 'em both!
Sing Hearts, Clubs, Diamonds, Spades and all!

ALL By joint decree
(*dancing*). As $\left\{ \begin{array}{l} \text{our} \\ \text{your} \end{array} \right\}$ trustee

This Notary $\left\{ \begin{array}{l} \text{we} \\ \text{you} \end{array} \right\}$ will now install—

In custody let him keep $\left\{ \begin{array}{l} \text{their} \\ \text{our} \end{array} \right\}$ hearts,

Sing Hearts, Clubs, Diamonds, Spades and all!
[Dance and exeunt LUDWIG, ERNEST, *and* NOTARY *with
the two Girls.]*

March. Enter the seven Chamberlains of the
GRAND DUKE RUDOLPH.

CHORUS OF CHAMBERLAINS.

The good Grand Duke of Pfennig Halbpfennig,
Though, in his own opinion, very very big,
In point of fact he's nothing but a miserable prig,
Is the good Grand Duke of Pfennig Halbpfennig!
Though quite contemptible, as every one agrees,
We must dissemble if we want our bread and cheese,
So hail him in a chorus, with enthusiasm big,
The good Grand Duke of Pfennig Halbpfennig!

Enter the GRAND DUKE RUDOLPH. *He is meanly and
miserably dressed in old and patched clothes, but blazes
with a profusion of orders and decorations. He is very
weak and ill, from low living.*

SONG—RUDOLPH.

A pattern to professors of monarchial autonomy,
I don't indulge in levity or compromising *bon-homie*,
But dignified formality, consistent with economy,
    Above all other virtues I particularly prize.
I never join in merriment—I don't see joke or jape any—
I never tolerate familiarity in shape any—
This, joined with an extravagant respect for tuppence
ha'penny,
    A keynote to my character sufficiently supplies.

(Speaking.) Observe. *(To Chamberlains.)* My snuff-box!
*(The snuff-box is passed with much ceremony from the Junior
Chamberlain, through all the others, until it is presented
by the Senior Chamberlain to* RUDOLPH, *who uses it.)*
That incident a keynote to my character supplies.
ALL That incident, etc.
RUDOLPH. I weigh out tea and sugar with precision
mathematical—

Instead of beer, a penny each—my orders are emphatical—
(Extravagance unpardonable, any more than that I call),
    But, on the other hand, my Ducal dignity to keep—
All Courtly ceremonial—to put it comprehensively—
I rigidly insist upon (but not, I hope, offensively)
Whenever ceremonial can be practised inexpensively—
    And, when you come to think of it, it's really very
cheap!
(Speaking.) Observe. *(To Chamberlains.)* My handkerchief!
*(Handkerchief is handed by Junior Chamberlain to the next in
order, and so on until it reaches* RUDOLPH, *who is much
inconvenienced by the delay.)*
It's sometimes inconvenient, but it's always very cheap!
ALL. It's stately and impressive, etc.
RUDOLPH. My Lord Chamberlain, as you are aware, my
marriage with the wealthy Baroness von Krakenfeldt will take
place to-morrow, and you will be good enough to see that the

rejoicings are on a scale of unusual liberality. Pass that on.
*(Chamberlain whispers to Vice-Chamberlain, who whispers to the next,
and so on.)* The sports will begin with a Wedding Breakfast Bee.
The leading pastry-cooks of the town will be invited to compete,
and the winner will not only enjoy the satisfaction of seeing his
breakfast devoured by the Grand Ducal pair, but he will also be
entitled to have the Arms of Pfennig Halbpfennig tattoo'd
between his shoulder-blades. The Vice-Chamberlain will see to
this. All the public fountains of Speisesaal will run with
Gingerbierheim and Currantweinmilch at the public expense.
The Assistant Vice-Chamberlain will see to this. At night,
everybody will illuminate; and as I have no desire to tax the
public funds unduly, this will be done at the inhabitants' private
expense. The Deputy Assistant Vice-Chamberlain will see to
this. All my Grand Ducal subjects will wear new clothes, and the
Sub-Deputy Assistant Vice-Chamberlain will collect the usual
commission on all sales. Wedding presents (which, on this
occasion, should be on a scale of extraordinary magnificence) will
be received at the Palace at any hour of the twenty-four, and the
Temporary Sub-Deputy Assistant Vice-Chamberlain will sit up
all night for this purpose. The entire population will be
commanded to enjoy themselves, and with this view the Acting-
Temporary Sub-Deputy Assistant Vice-Chamberlain will sing
comic songs in the Market Place from noon to nightfall. Finally,
we have composed a Wedding Anthem, with which the entire
population are required to provide themselves. It can be obtained
from our Grand Ducal publishers at the usual discount price, and
all the Chamberlains will be expected to push the sale.
(Chamberlains bow and exeunt.) I don't feel at all comfortable. I
hope I'm not doing a foolish thing in getting married. After all,
it's a poor heart that never rejoices, and this wedding of mine is
the first little treat I've allowed myself since my christening.
Besides, Caroline's income is very considerable, and as her ideas
of economy are quite on a par with mine, it ought to turn out
well. Bless her tough old heart, she's a mean little darling! Oh,
here she is, punctual to her appointment!

Enter BARONESS VON KRAKENFELDT.

BARONESS. Rudolph! Why, what's the matter?
RUDOLPH. Why, I'm not quite myself, my pet. I'm a little
worried and upset. I want a tonic. It's the low diet, I think. I am
afraid, after all, I shall have to take the bull by the horns and have
an egg with my breakfast.
BARONESS. I shouldn't do anything rash, dear. Begin with a
jujube. *(Gives him one.)*
RUDOLPH. *(about to eat it, but changes his mind.)* I'll keep it for
supper. *(He sits by her and tries to put his arm round her waist.)*
BARONESS. Rudolph, don't! What in the world are you
thinking of?
RUDOLPH. I was thinking of embracing you, my sugarplum.
Just as a little cheap treat.
BARONESS. What, here? In public? Really you appear to have
no sense of delicacy.
RUDOLPH. No sense of delicacy, Bon-bon!
BARONESS. No. I can't make you out. When you courted me,
all your courting was done publicly in the Market Place. When
you proposed to me, you proposed in the Market Place. And now
that we're engaged you seem to desire that our first *tête-à-tête* shall
occur in the Market Place! Surely you've a room in your
Palace—with blinds—that would do?

RUDOLPH. But, my own, I can't help myself. I'm bound by my own decree.

BARONESS. Your own decree?

RUDOLPH. Yes. You see, all the houses that give on the Market Place belong to me, but the drains (which date back to the reign of Charlemagne) want attending to, and the houses wouldn't let—so, with a view of increasing the value of the property, I decreed that all love-episodes between affectionate couples should take place, in public, on this spot, every Monday, Wednesday, and Friday, when the band doesn't play.

BARONESS. Bless me, what a happy idea! So moral too! And have you found it answer?

RUDOLPH. Answer? The rents have gone up fifty per cent., and the sale of opera glasses (which is a Grand Ducal monopoly) has received an extraordinary stimulus! So, under the circumstances, *would* you allow me to put my arm round your waist? As a source of income. Just once!

BARONESS. But it's so very embarrassing. Think of the opera glasses!

RUDOLPH. My good girl, that's just what I *am* thinking of. Hang it all, we must give them *something* for their money! What's that?

BARONESS. *(unfolding paper, which contains a large letter, which she hands to him).* It's a letter which your detective asked me to hand to you. I wrapped it up in yesterday's paper to keep it clean.

RUDOLPH. Oh, it's only his report! That'll keep. But, I say, you've never been and bought a newspaper?

BARONESS. My dear Rudolph, do you think I'm mad? It came wrapped round my breakfast.

RUDOLPH *(relieved).* I thought you were not the sort of girl to go and buy a newspaper! Well, as we've got it, we may as well read it. What does it say?

BARONESS. Why—dear me—here's your biography! "Our Detested Despot!"

RUDOLPH. Yes—I fancy that refers to me.

BARONESS. And it says—Oh it can't be!

RUDOLPH. What can't be?

BARONESS. Why, it says that although you're going to marry me to-morrow, you were betrothed in infancy to the Princess of Monte Carlo!

RUDOLPH. Oh yes—that's quite right. Didn't I mention it?

BARONESS. Mention it! You never said a word about it!

RUDOLPH. Well, it doesn't matter, because, you see, it's practically off.

BARONESS. Practically off?

RUDOLPH. Yes. By the terms of the contract the betrothal is void unless the Princess marries before she is of age. Now, her father, the Prince, is stony-broke, and hasn't left his house for years for fear of arrest. Over and over again he has implored me to come to him to be married—but in vain. Over and over again he has implored me to advance him the money to enable the Princess to come to me—but in vain. I am very young, but not as young as that; and as the Princess comes of age at two to-morrow, why at two to-morrow I'm a free man, so I appointed that hour for our wedding, as I shall like to have as much marriage as I can get for my money.

BARONESS. I see. Of course, if the married state is a happy state, it's a pity to waste any of it.

RUDOLPH. Why, every hour we delayed I should lose a lot of you and you'd lose a lot of me!

BARONESS. My thoughtful darling! Oh, Rudolph, we ought to be very happy!

RUDOLPH. If I'm not, it'll be my first bad investment. Still there *is* such a thing as a slump even in Matrimonials.

BARONESS. I often picture us in the long, cold, dark December evenings, sitting close to each other and singing impassioned duets to keep us warm, and thinking of all the lovely things we could afford to buy if we chose, and, at the same time, planning out our lives in a spirit of the most rigid and exacting economy!

RUDOLPH. It's a most beautiful and touching picture of connubial bliss in its highest and most rarefied development!

DUET—BARONESS *and* RUDOLPH.

BARONESS.　　As o'er our penny roll we sing,
　　　　　　　　It is not reprehensive
　　　　　　To think what joys our wealth would bring
　　　　　　Were we disposed to do the thing
　　　　　　　　Upon a scale extensive.
　　　　　　There's rich mock-turtle—thick and clear—

RUDOLPH *(confidentially).* Perhaps we'll have it once a year!

BARONESS *(delighted.)* You *are* an open-handed dear!

RUDOLPH.　　Though, mind you, it's expensive.

BARONESS.　　No doubt it *is* expensive.

BOTH　　　　Oh, he who has an income clear
　　　　　　Of fifty thousand pounds a year
　　　　　　Can purchase all his fancy loves—

BARONESS.　　Conspicuous hats—

RUDOLPH.　　　　Two-shilling gloves—

BARONESS *(doubtfully).* Two-shilling gloves?

RUDOLPH *(positively).* Two-shilling gloves—

BOTH　　　　Cheap shoes and ties of gaudy hue,
　　　　　　And Waterbury watches, too—
　　　　　　And think that he could buy the lot
　　　　　　Were he a donkey—

RUDOLPH.　　Which he's *not!*

BARONESS.　　Oh no, he's *not!*

RUDOLPH.　　Oh no, he's *not!*

BOTH.　　　　That kind of donkey he's *not!*
　　　　　　(Dancing). Then let us be modestly merry,
　　　　　　And rejoice with a derry down derry.
　　　　　　　　For to laugh and to sing
　　　　　　　　Is a rational thing—
　　　　　　It's a joy economical, very!　　[*Exit* BARONESS.]

RUDOLPH. Oh, now for my detective's report. *(Opens letter.)* What's this! Another conspiracy! A conspiracy to depose *me!* And my private detective was so convulsed with laughter at the notion of a conspirator selecting him for a confidant that he was physically unable to arrest the malefactor! Why, it'll come off! This comes of engaging a detective with a keen sense of the ridiculous! For the future I'll employ none but Scotchmen. And the plot is to explode to-morrow! My wedding day! Oh, Caroline, Caroline! *(Weeps)*. This is perfectly frightful! What's to be done? I don't know! I ought to keep cool and think, but you *can't* think when your veins are full of hot soda water, and your brain's fizzing like a firework, and all your faculties are jumbled in a perfect whirlpool of tumblication! and I'm going to be ill! I know I am! I've been living too low, and I'm going to be very ill indeed!

SONG—RUDOLPH.

When you find you're a broken-down critter,
Who is all of a trimmle and twitter,
With your palate unpleasantly bitter,
    As if you'd just eaten a pill—
When your legs are as thin as dividers,
And you're plagued with unruly insiders,
And your spine is all creepy with spiders,
    And you're highly gamboge in the gill—
When you've got a beehive in your head,
    And a sewing machine in each ear,
And you feel that you've eaten your bed,
    And you've got a bad headache *down here*—
        When such facts are about,
        And these symptoms you find
            In your body or crown—
        Well, you'd better look out,
        You may make up your mind
            You have better lie down!

When your lips are all smeary—like tallow,
And your tongue is decidedly yellow,
With a pint of warm oil in your swallow,
    And a pound of tin-tacks in your chest—
When you're down in the mouth with the
        vapours,
And all over your new Morris papers
Black-beetles are cutting their capers,
    And crawly things never at rest—
When you doubt if your head is your own,
    And you jump when an open door slams—
Then you've got to a state which is known
    To the medical world as "jim-jams."
        If such symptoms you find
        In your body or head,
            They're not easy to quell—
        You may make up your mind
        You are better in bed,
            For you're not at all well!
            [*Sinks exhausted and weeping at foot of well.*]

Enter—LUDWIG.

LUDWIG. Now for my confession and full pardon. They told me the Grand Duke was dancing duets in the Market Place, but I don't see him. *(Sees* RUDOLPH). Hallo! Who's this? *(Aside.)* Why, it *is* the Grand Duke!

RUDOLPH *(sobbing)*. Who are you, sir, who presume to address me in person? If you've anything to communicate, you must fling yourself at the feet of my Acting Temporary Sub-Deputy Assistant Vice-Chamberlain, who will fling himself at the feet of his immediate superior, and so on, with successive foot-flingings through the various grades—your communication will, in course of time, come to my august knowledge.

LUDWIG. But when I inform your Highness that in me you see the most unhappy, the most unfortunate, the most completely miserable man in your whole dominion—

RUDOLPH *(still sobbing)*. *You* the most miserable man in my whole dominion? How can you have the face to stand there and say such a thing? Why, look at me! Look at me! *(Bursts into tears.)*

LUDWIG. Well, I wouldn't be a cry-baby.

RUDOLPH. A cry-baby? If you had just been told that you were going to be deposed to-morrow, and perhaps blown up with dynamite for all I know, wouldn't *you* be a cry-baby? I do declare, if I could only hit upon some cheap and painless method of putting an end to an existence which has become insupportable, I would unhesitatingly adopt it!

LUDWIG. You would? *(Aside.)* I see a magnificent way out of this! By Jupiter, I'll try it! *(Aloud).* Are you, by any chance, in earnest?

RUDOLPH. In earnest? Why, look at me!

LUDWIG. If you are really in earnest—if you really desire to escape scot free from this impending—this unspeakably horrible catastrophe—without trouble, danger, pain, or expense—why not resort to a Statutory Duel?

RUDOLPH. A Statutory Duel?

LUDWIG. Yes. The Act is still in force, but it will expire to-morrow afternoon. You fight—you lose—you are dead for a day. To-morrow, when the Act expires, you will come to life again and resume your Grand Duchy as though nothing had happened. In the meantime, the explosion will have taken place and the survivor will have had to bear the brunt of it.

RUDOLPH. Yes, that's all very well, but who'll be fool enough to *be* the survivor?

LUDWIG. *(kneeling)*. Actuated by an overwhelming sense of attachment to your Grand Ducal person, I unhesitatingly offer myself as the victim of your subjects' fury.

RUDOLPH. You do? Well, really that's very handsome. I daresay being blown up is not nearly as unpleasant as one would think.

LUDWIG. Oh, yes it is. It mixes one up, awfully!

RUDOLPH. But suppose I were to lose?

LUDWIG. Oh, that's easily arranged. *(Producing cards.)* I'll put an Ace up my sleeve—you'll put a King up yours. When the drawing takes place, I shall seem to draw the higher card and you the lower. And there you are!

RUDOLPH. Oh, but that's cheating.

LUDWIG. So it is. I never thought of that *(going)*.

RUDOLPH *(hastily)*. Not that I mind. But I say—you won't take an unfair advantage of your day of office? You won't go tipping people, or squandering my little savings in fireworks, or any nonsense of that sort?

LUDWIG. I am hurt—really hurt—by the suggestion.

RUDOLPH. You—you wouldn't like to put down a deposit, perhaps?

LUDWIG. No. I don't think I should like to put down a deposit.

RUDOLPH. Or give a guarantee?

LUDWIG. A guarantee would be equally open to objection.

RUDOLPH. It would be more regular. Very well, I suppose you must have your own way.

LUDWIG. Good. I say—we must have a devil of a quarrel!

RUDOLPH. Oh, a devil of a quarrel!

LUDWIG. Just to give colour to the thing. Shall I give you a sound thrashing before all the people? Say the word—it's no trouble.

RUDOLPH. No, I think not, though it would be very convincing and it's extremely good and thoughtful of you to suggest it. Still, a devil of a quarrel!

LUDWIG. Oh, a devil of a quarrel!

RUDOLPH. No half-measures. Big words—strong language—rude remarks. Oh, a devil of a quarrel!

LUDWIG. Now the question is, how shall we summon the people?

RUDOLPH. Oh, there's no difficulty about that. Bless your heart, they've been staring at us through those windows for the last half hour!

FINALE.

RUDOLPH. Come hither, all you people—
    When you hear the fearful news,
    All the pretty women weep'll,
      Men will shiver in their shoes.

LUDWIG. And they'll all cry "Lord, defend us!"
    When they learn the fact tremendous
    That to give this man his gruel
      In a Statutory Duel—

BOTH. This plebeian man of shoddy—
    This contemptible nobody—
      Your Grand Duke does not refuse!

During this, Chorus of men and women have entered, all trembling with apprehension under the impression that they are to be arrested for their complicity in the conspiracy.

CHORUS.

With faltering feet,
    And our muscles in a quiver,
Our fate we meet
    With our feelings all unstrung!
If our plot complete
    He has managed to diskiver,
There is no retreat—
    We shall certainly be hung!

RUDOLPH (*aside to* LUDWIG). Now *you* begin and pitch it strong—walk into me abusively—

LUDWIG (*aside to* RUDOLPH). I've several epithets that I've reserved for you exclusively.

A choice selection I have here when you are ready *to* begin.

RUDOLPH. Now *you* begin—

LUDWIG.   No, *you* begin—

RUDOLPH.   No, *you* begin—

LUDWIG.   No, *you* begin!

CHORUS (*trembling*). Has it happed as we expected?
    Is our little plot detected?

DUET—RUDOLPH *and* LUDWIG.

RUDOLPH (*furiously*). Big bombs, small bombs,
    great guns and little ones!
    Put him in a pillory!
    Rack him with artillery!

LUDWIG (*furiously*). Long swords, short swords,
    tough swords and brittle ones!
    Fright him into fits!
    Blow him into bits!

RUDOLPH. You muff, sir!
    You lout, sir!

LUDWIG. Enough, sir!
    Get out, sir!   [*Pushes him.*]

RUDOLPH. A hit, sir?
    Take that, sir!   [*Slaps him.*]

LUDWIG. (*slapping* RUDOLPH) It's tit, sir,
    For tat, sir!

CHORUS (*appalled.*) When two doughty heroes thunder,
    All the world is lost in wonder;
      When such men their temper lose,
      Awful are the words they use!

LUDWIG. Tall snobs, small snobs, rich snobs and needy ones!

RUDOLPH (*jostling him*). Whom are you alluding to?

LUDWIG (*jostling him*). Where are you intruding to?

RUDOLPH. Fat snobs, thin snobs, swell snobs and seedy ones!

LUDWIG. I rather think you err.
    To whom do you refer?

RUDOLPH. To you, sir!

LUDWIG. To me, sir?

RUDOLPH. I do, sir!

LUDWIG. We'll see, sir!

RUDOLPH. I jeer, sir!
    (*Makes a face at* LUDWIG.). Grimace, sir!

LUDWIG. Look here, sir—
    (*Makes a face at* RUDOLPH.) A face, sir!

CHORUS (*appalled.*) When two heroes, once pacific,
    Quarrel, the effect's terrific!
      What a horrible grimace!
      What a paralysing face!

ALL. Big bombs, small bombs, etc.

LUDWIG and RUDOLPH (*recit.*). He has insulted me, and,
    in a breath,
    This day we fight a duel to the death!

NOTARY (*checking them*). You mean, of course,
    by duel (*verbum sat.*),
    A Statutory Duel.

ALL. Why, what's that?

NOTARY. According to established legal uses,
    A card apiece each bold disputant chooses—
    Dead as a doornail is the dog who loses—
    The winner steps into the dead man's shoeses!

ALL. The winner steps into the dead man's shoeses!

RUDOLPH and LUDWIG. Agreed! Agreed!

RUDOLPH. Come, come—the pack!

NOTARY (*producing one*). Behold it here!

RUDOLPH. I'm on the rack!

LUDWIG.   I quake with fear!
               [NOTARY *offers card to* LUDWIG.]

LUDWIG. First draw to you!

RUDOLPH.   If that's the case,
    Behold the King! [*Drawing card from his sleeve,*]

LUDWIG. *(same business.).* Behold the Ace!
CHORUS. Hurrah, hurrah! Our Ludwig's won,
        And wicked Rudolph's course is run—
        So Ludwig will as Grand Duke reign
        Till Rudolph comes to life again—
RUDOLPH. Which will occur to-morrow!
        I come to life to-morrow!
GRETCHEN *(with mocking curtsey).*
        My Lord Grand Duke, farewell!
          A plesant journey, very,
        To your convenient cell
          In yonder cemetery!
  LISA. *(curtseying).* Though malcontents abuse you,
        We're much distressed to lose you!
        You were, when you were living,
        So liberal, so forgiving!
BERTHA. So merciful, so gentle!
        So highly ornamental!
OLGA.   And now that you've departed,
        You leave us broken-hearted!
ALL *(pretending to weep).* Yes, truly, truly, truly, truly—
        Truly broken-hearted!
        Ha! ha! ha! ha! ha! ha! [*Mocking him.*]
RUDOLPH *(furious).* Rapscallions, in penitential fires,
        You'll rue the ribaldry that from you falls!
        To-morrow afternoon the law expires,
        And then—look out for squalls!
          [*Exit* RUDOLPH, *amid general ridicule.*]

CHORUS. Give thanks, give thanks to wayward fate—
          By mystic fortune's sway,
        Our Ludwig guides the helm of State
          For one delightful day!

(To LUDWIG*).* We hail you, sir!
          We greet you, sir!
          Regale you, sir!
          We treat you, sir!
            Our ruler be
            By fate's decree
          For one delightful day!

NOTARY. You've done it neatly! Pity that your powers
        Are limited to four-and-twenty hours!
LUDWIG. No matter, though the time will quickly run,
        In hours twenty-four much may be done!

SONG—LUDWIG.

Oh, a monarch who boasts intellectual graces
  Can go, if he likes, a good deal in a day—
He can put all his friends in conspicuous places,
  With plenty to eat and with nothing to pay!
You'll tell, no doubt, with unpleasant grimaces,
  To-morrow, deprived of your ribbons and laces,
  You'll get your dismissal—with very long faces—
    But wait! on that topic I've something to say!
(Dancing) I've something to say—I've something to say—I've
        something to say!
Oh, our rule shall be merry—I'm not an ascetic—
  And while the sun shines we will get up our hay

By a pushing young Monarch, of turn energetic,
  A very great deal may be done in a day!

CHORUS. Oh, his rule will be merry, etc.

[*During this,* LUDWIG *whispers to* NOTARY, *who writes.*]

For instance, this measure (his ancestor drew it),
        (Alluding to NOTARY.)
  This law against duels—to-morrow will die—
The Duke will revive, and you'll certainly rue it—
  He'll give you "what for" and he'll let you
        know why!
But in twenty-four hours there's time to renew it—
  With a century's life I've the right to imbue it—
  It's easy to do—and, by Jingo, I'll do it!

[*Signing paper, which* NOTARY *presents.*]

It's done! Till I perish your Monarch am I!
  Your Monarch am I—your Monarch am I—your
        Monarch am I!
  Though I do not pretend to be very prophetic,
    I fancy I know what you're going to say—
  By a pushing young Monarch, of turn energetic,
    A very great deal may be done in a day!

ALL *(astonished).* Oh, it's simply uncanny, his power prophetic—
  It's perfectly right—we *were* going to say.
      By a pushing, etc.

Enter JULIA, *at back.*

LUDWIG *(recit.)* This very afternoon—at two (about)—
        The Court appointments will be given out.
        To each and all (for that was the condition)
        According to professional position!
ALL.   Hurrah!
JULIA *(coming forward).* According to professional position?
LUDWIG. According to professional position!
ALL.   Then, horror!
JULIA. Why, what's the matter? What's the matter?
          What's the matter?

SONG—JULIA *(*LISA *clinging to her).*

Ah, pity me, my comrades true,
Who love, as well I know you do,
    This gentle child,
      To me so fondly dear!

ALL.   Why, what's the matter?

JULIA.   Our sister-love so true and deep
        From many an eye unused to weep
          Hath oft beguiled
            The coy, reluctant tear!

ALL.   Why, what's the matter?

JULIA. Each sympathetic heart 'twill bruise
When you have learnt the frightful news
(Oh, will it not?)
That I must now impart!

ALL. Why, what's the matter?

JULIA. Her love for him is all in all!
Ah, cursed fate! that it should fall
Unto *my* lot
To break my darling's heart!

ALL. Oh, *that's* the matter!

LUDWIG. What means our Julia by those fateful
looks?
Please do not keep us all on tenter-
hooks—
Now, what's the matter?

JULIA. Our duty, if we're wise,
We never shun.
This Spartan rule applies
To every one.
In theatres, as in life,
Each has her line—
This part—the Grand Duke's wife
(Oh agony!) is mine!
A maxim new I do not start—
The canons of dramatic art
Decree that this repulsive part
(The Grand Duke's wife)
Is mine!

LISA (*appalled, to* LUDWIG). Can that be so?

LUDWIG. I do not know—
But time will show
If that be so.

CHORUS. Can that be so? etc.

LISA (*recit.*) Be merciful!

DUET—LISA *and* JULIA.

LISA. Oh, listen to me, dear—
I love him only, darling!
Remember, oh, my pet,
On him my heart is set!
This kindness do me, dear—
Nor leave me lonely, darling!
Be merciful, my pet,
Our love, do not forget!

JULIA. Now don't be foolish, dear—
You couldn't play it, darling!
It's "leading business," pet,
And you're but a soubrette.
So don't be mulish, dear—
Although I say it, darling,
It's not your line, my pet—

I play that part, you bet!
I play that part—
I play that part, you bet!
[LISA *overwhelmed with grief.*]

NOTARY. The lady's right. Though Julia's engagement
Was the stage meant—
It certainly frees Ludwig from his
Connubial promises.
Though marriage contracts—or whate'er you call
'em—
Are very solemn,
Dramatic contracts (which you all adore so)
Are even more so!

ALL. That's very true!
Though marriage contracts, etc.

SONG—LISA.

The die is cast,
My hope has perished!
Farewell, O Past,
Too bright to last,
Yet fondly cherished!
My light has fled,
My hope is dead,
Its doom is spoken—
My day is night,
My wrong is right
In all men's sight—
My heart is broken! [*Exit, weeping.*]

LUDWIG. (*recit.*). Poor child, where will she go?
What will she do?
JULIA. *That* isn't in your part, you know.
LUDWIG. (*sighing*). Quite true!
(*With an effort.*). Depressing topics we'll not touch upon—
Let us begin as we are going on!
For this will be a jolly Court, for little and for big!
ALL. Sing hey, the jinks of Pfennig Halbpfennig!
LUDWIG. From morn to night our lives shall be as merry as a
grig!
ALL. Sing hey, the jolly jinks of Pfennig Halbpfennig!
LUDWIG. All state and ceremony we'll eternally abolish—
We don't mean to insist upon unnecessary polish—
And, on the whole, I rather think you'll find our
rule tollolish!
ALL. Sing hey, the jolly jinks of Pfennig Halbpfennig!
JULIA. But stay—your new-made Court
Without a courtly coat is—
We shall require
Some Court attire,
And at a moment's notice.
In clothes of common sort
Your courtiers must not grovel—
Your new *noblesse*
Must have a dress
Original and novel!

LUDWIG. Old Athens we'll exhume!
The necessary dresses,
　　Correct and true
　　And all brand-new
The company possesses:
Henceforth our Court costume
Shall live in song and story,
　　For we'll upraise
　　The dead old days
Of Athens in her glory!

ALL. 　Yes, let's upraise
　　The dead old days
Of Athens in her glory!

ALL. 　Agreed! Agreed!
For this will be a jolly Court for little and for big!
　etc.
[*They carry* LUDWIG *round stage and deposit him on the ironwork of well.* JULIA *stands by him, and the rest group round them.*]

ACT DROP

Act II

SCENE.—*Entrance Hall of the Grand Ducal Palace, the next morning. Enter a procession of the members of the theatrical company (now dressed in the costumes of* TROILUS AND CRESSIDA*), carrying garlands, playing on pipes, citharæ, and cymbals, and heralding the return of* LUDWIG *and* JULIA *from the marriage ceremony, which has just taken place.*

CHORUS.

As before you we defile,
　Eloia! Eloia!
Pray you, gentles, do not smile
If we shout, in classic style,
　Eloia!
Ludwig and his Julia true
Wedded are each other to—
So we sing, till all is blue,
　Eloia! Eloia!
　Opoponax! Eloia!

Wreaths of bay and ivy twine,
　Eloia! Eloia!
Full the bowl with Lesbian wine,
And to revelry incline—
　Eloia!
For as gaily we pass on
Probably we shall, anon,
Sing a Deirgeticon—
　Eloia! Eloia!
　Opoponax! Eloia!

RECITATIVE—LUDWIG.

Your loyalty our Ducal heartstrings touches:
Allow me to present your new Grand Duchess.
Should she offend, you'll graciously excuse her—
And kindly recollect *I* didn't choose her!

SONG—LUDWIG.

At the outset I may mention it's my sovereign intention
　To revive the classic memories of Athens at its best,
For the company possesses all the necessary dresses
　And a course of quiet cramming will supply us with the rest.
We've a choice hyporchematic (this is, ballet-operatic)
　Who respond to the *choreutæ* of that cultivated age,
And our clever chorus-master, all but captious criticaster,
　Would accept as the *choregus* of the early Attic stage.
This return to classic ages is considered in their wages,
　Which are always calculated by the day or by the week—
And I'll pay 'em (if they'll back me) all in *oboloi* and *drachmæ*,
　Which they'll get (if they prefer it) at the Kalends that are Greek!
　　　　　　[*Confidentially to audience*]
　　　At this juncture I may mention
　　　That this erudition sham
　　　Is but classical pretension,
　　　The result of steady "cram":
　　　Periphrastic methods spurning,
　　　To this audience discerning
　　　I admit this show of learning
　　　　Is the fruit of steady "cram"!

CHORUS. Periphrastic methods, etc.
　In the period Socratic every dining-room was Attic
　　(Which suggests an architecture of a topsy-turvy kind),
　There they'd satisfy their thirst on a *recherché* cold ἄριστον,
　　Which is what they called their lunch—and so may you, if you're inclined.
As they gradually got on, they'd τρέπεσθαι πρὸς τὸν πότον
　(Which is Attic for a steady and a conscientious drink).
But they mixed their wine with water—which I'm sure they didn't oughter—
　And we modern Saxons know a trick worth two of that, I think!
Then came rather risky dances (under certain circumstances)
　Which would shock that worthy gentleman, the Licenser of Plays,
Corybantian man*ia*c kick—Dionysiac or Bacchic—
　And the Dithryambic revels of those undecorous days.
　　　　　　[*Confidentially to audience.*]

And perhaps I'd better mention,
  Lest alarming you I am,
That it isn't our intention
  To perform a Dithyramb—
It displays a lot of stocking,
Which is always very shocking,
And of course I'm only mocking
  At the prevalence of "cram."

CHORUS.   It displays a lot, etc.

Yes, on reconsideration, there are customs of that nation
  Which are not in strict accordance with the habits of
    our day,
And when I come to codify, their rules I mean to modify,
Or Mrs. Grundy, p'r'aps, may have a word or two to
    say.
  For they hadn't macintoshes or umbrellas or goloshes—
  And a shower with their dresses must have played the
    very deuce,
  And it must have been unpleasing when they caught a
    fit of sneezing,
  For, it seems, of pocket-handkerchiefs they didn't know
    the use.
They wore little underclothing—scarcely anything—or no
    thing—
And their dress of Coan silk was quite transparent in
    design—
Well, in fact, in summer weather, something like the
    "altogether."
And it's *there*, I rather fancy, I shall have to draw the
    line!

[*Confidentially to audience.*]

      And again I wish to mention
        That this erudition sham
      Is but classical pretension,
        The result of steady "cram."
      Yet my classic love aggressive
      (If you'll pardon the possessive)
      Is exceedingly impressive
        When you're passing an exam.

CHORUS.   Yet his classic love, etc.
[*Exeunt* CHORUS. *Manent* LUDWIG, JULIA, *and* LISA.]
LUDWIG. *(recit.).* Yes, Ludwig and his Julia are mated!
  For when an obscure comedian, whom the law backs,
  To sovereign rank is promptly elevated,
  He takes it with its incidental drawbacks!
  So Julia and I are duly mated!
    [LISA, *through this, has expressed intense distress at having to*
    surrender LUDWIG.]

SONG—LISA.

Take care of him—he's much too good to live!
  With him you must be very gentle:
Poor fellow, he's so highly sensitive,
  And O, so sentimental!
Be sure you never let him sit up late
  In chilly open air conversing—
Poor darling, he's extremely delicate,
  And wants a deal of nursing!

LUDWIG. I want a deal of nursing!
LISA.   And O, remember this—
            When he is cross with pain,
         A flower and a kiss—
         A simple flower— a tender kiss
            Will bring round again!

His moods you must assiduously watch:
  When he succumbs to sorrow tragic,
Some hardbake or a bit of butter-scotch
  Will work on him like magic.
To contradict a character so rich
  In trusting love were simple blindness—
He's one of those exalted natures which
  Will only yield to kindness!

LUDWIG. I only yield to kindness!
LISA.   And O, the bygone bliss!
            And O, the present pain!
         That flower and that kiss—
         That simple flower—that tender kiss
            I ne'er shall give again!

[*Exit, weeping.*]

JULIA. And now that everybody has gone, and we're happily
and comfortably married, I want to have a few words with my
new-born husband.

LUDWIG *(aside).* Yes, I expect you'll often have a few words
with your new-born husband! *(Aloud).* Well, what is it?

JULIA. Why, I've been thinking that as you and I have to play
our parts for life, it is most essential that we should come to a
definite understanding as to how they shall be rendered. Now,
I've been considering how I can make the most of the Grand
Duchess.

LUDWIG. Have you? Well, if you'll take my advice, you'll
make a very fine part of it.

JULIA. Why, that's quite *my* idea.

LUDWIG. I shouldn't make it one of your hoity-toity vixenish
viragos.

JULIA. You think not?

LUDWIG. Oh, I'm quite clear about that. I should make her a
tender, gentle, submissive, affectionate (but not too affectionate)
child-wife—timidly anxious to coil herself into her husband's
heart, but kept in check by an awestruck reverence for his exalted
intellectual qualities and his majestic personal appearance.

JULIA. Oh, that is your idea of a good part?

LUDWIG. Yes—a wife who regards her husband's slightest
wish as an inflexible law, and who ventures but rarely into his
august presence, unless (which would happen seldom) he should
summon her to appear before him. A crushed, despairing voilet,
whose blighted existence would culminate (all too soon) in a
lonely and pathetic death-scene! A fine part, my dear.

JULIA. Yes. There's a good deal to be said for your view of it.
Now there are some actresses whom it would fit like a glove.

LUDWIG *(aside.).* I wish I'd married one of 'em!

JULIA. But, you see I *must* consider my temperament. For
instance, my temperament would demand some strong scenes of
justifiable jealousy.

LUDWIG. Oh, there's no difficulty about that. You shall have
them.

JULIA. With a lovely but detested rival—

LUDWIG. Oh, *I'll* provide the rival.

JULIA. Whom I should stab—stab—stab!

LUDWIG. Oh, I wouldn't stab her. It's been done to death. I should treat her with a silent and contemptuous disdain, and delicately withdraw from a position which, to one of your sensitive nature, would be absolutely untenable. Dear me, I can see you delicately withdrawing, up centre and off!

JULIA. *Can* you?

LUDWIG. Yes. It's a fine situation—and in your hands, full of quiet pathos!

DUET.—LUDWIG *and* JULIA.

LUDWIG.   Now Julia, come,
   Consider it from
    This dainty point of view—
 A timid tender
 Feminine gender,
   Prompt to coyly coo—
 Yet silence seeking
 Seldom speaking
   Till she's spoken to—
 A comfy, cosy,
 Rosy-posy
   Innocent *ingenoo!*
    The part you're suited to—
    (To give the deuce her due)
   A sweet (O, jiminy!)
   Miminy-piminy
    Innocent ingen*oo!*

ENSEMBLE.

LUDWIG.	JULIA.
The part you're suited to—	I'm much obliged to you,
(To give the deuce her due)	I don't think that would do—
A sweet (O, jiminy!)	To play (O, jiminy!)
Miminy-piminy,	Miminy-piminy,
Innocent ingen*oo!*	Innocent ingen*oo!*

JULIA.   You forgot my special magic
   (In a high dramatic sense)
 Lies in situations tragic—
  Undeniably intense.
 As I've justified promotion
  In the histrionic art,
 I'll submit to you my notion
  Of a first-rate part.

LUDWIG.   Well, let us see your notion
  Of a first-rate part.

JULIA *(dramatically)*.
  I have a rival! Frenzy-thrilled,
   I find you both together!
  My heart stands still—with horror chilled—
   Hard as the millstone nether!
  Then softly, slyly, snaily, snaky—
  Crawly, creepy, quaily, quaky—
   I track her on her homeward way,
   As panther tracks her fated prey!

(Furiously.) I fly at her soft white throat—
  The lily-white laughing leman!
 On her agonized gaze I gloat
  With the glee of a dancing demon!
 My rival she—I have no doubt of her—
 So I hold on—till the breath is out of her!
   —till the breath is out of her!

And then—Remorse! Remorse!
O cold unpleasant corse,
 Avaunt! Avaunt!
That lifeless form
 I gaze upon—
That face, still warm
 But weirdly wan—
Those eyes of glass
 I contemplate—
And then, alas,
 Too late—too late!
I find she is—your Aunt!

(Shuddering.) Remorse! Remorse!
 Then, mad—mad—mad!
  With fancies wild—chimerical—
 Now sorrowful—silent—sad—
 Now, hullabaloo hysterical!
  Ha! ha! ha! ha!
 But whether I'm sad or whether I'm glad,
  Mad! mad! mad! mad!

This calls for the resources of a high-class art,
And satisfies my notion of a first-rate part!

    [*Exit* JULIA.]

Enter all the CHORUS, *hurriedly, and in great excitement*

CHORUS.

 Your Highness, there's a party at the door—
  Your Highness, at the door there is a party—
   She says that we expect her,
   But we do not recollect her,
 For we never saw her countenance before!

 With rage and indignation she is rife,
  Because our welcome wasn't very hearty—
   She's as sulky as a super,
   And she's swearing like a trooper,
 O, you never heard such language in your life!

Enter BARONESS VON KRAKENFELDT, *in a fury.*

BARONESS. With fury indescribable I burn!
  With rage I'm nearly ready to explode!
 There'll be grief and tribulation when I learn
  To whom this slight unbearable is owed!
 For whatever may be due I'll pay it double—
 There'll be terror indescribable and trouble!
  With a hurly-burly and a hubble-bubble
 I'll pay you for this pretty episode!

ALL. Oh, whatever may be due she'll pay it double!
It's very good of her to take the trouble—
But we don't know what she means by "hubble-bubble"—
No doubt it's an expression *à la mode*.

BARONESS. *(to* LUDWIG*).* Do you know who I am?

LUDWIG *(examining her).* I don't;
Your countenance I can't fix, my dear.

BARONESS. This proves I'm not a sham.
[*Showing pocket-handkerchief.*]

LUDWIG. *(examining it).* It won't:
It only says "Krakenfeldt, Six," my dear.

BARONESS. Express your grief profound!

LUDWIG. I sha'n't!
This tone I never allow, my love.

BARONESS. Rudolph at once produce!

LUDWIG. I can't;
He isn't at home just now, my love.

BARONESS *(astonished).* He isn't at home just now!

ALL. He isn't at home just now,
(Dancing derisively.). He has an appointment particular, very—
You'll find him, I think, in the town cemetery;
And that's how we come to be making so merry,
For he isn't at home just now!

BARONESS. But bless my heart and soul alive, it's impudence personified!
I've come here to be matrimonially matrimonified!

LUDWIG. For any disappointment I am sorry unaffectedly.
But yesterday that nobleman expired quite unexpectedly—

ALL *(sobbing).* Tol the riddle lol!
Tol the riddle lol!
Tol the riddle, lol the riddle, lol lol lay!
(Then laughing wildly.) Tol the riddle, lol the riddle, lol lol lay!

BARONESS. But this is most unexpected. He was well enough at a quarter to twelve yesterday.

LUDWIG. Yes. He died at half-past eleven.

BARONESS. Bless me, how very sudden!

LUDWIG. It *was* sudden.

BARONESS. But what in the world am I to do? I was to have been married to him to-day!

ALL. *(singing and dancing).* For any disappointment we are sorry unaffectedly.
But yesterday that nobleman expired quite unexpectedly—
Tol the riddle lol!

BARONESS. Is this Court Mourning or a Fancy Ball?

LUDWIG. Well, it's a delicate combination of both effects. It is intended to express inconsolable grief for the decease of the late Duke and ebullient joy at the accession of his successor. *I* am his successor. Permit me to present you to my Grand Duchess. *(Indicating* JULIA*).*

BARONESS. Your Grand Duchess? Oh, your Highness! *(Curtseying profoundly.)*

JULIA. *(sneering at her.).* Old frump!

BARONESS. Humph! A recent creation, probably?

LUDWIG. We were married only half-an-hour ago.

BARONESS. Exactly. I thought she seemed new to the position.

JULIA. Ma'am, I don't know who you are, but I flatter myself I can do justice to *any* part on the very shortest notice.

BARONESS. My dear, under the circumstances you are doing admirably—and you'll improve with practice. It's so difficult to be a lady when one isn't born to it.

JULIA. *(in a rage, to* LUDWIG*).* Am I to stand this? Am I not to be allowed to pull her to pieces?

LUDWIG *(aside to* JULIA*).* No, no—it isn't Greek. Be a violet, I beg.

BARONESS. And now tell me all about this distressing circumstance. How did the Grand Duke die?

LUDWIG. He perished nobly—in a Statutory Duel.

BARONESS. In a Statutory Duel? But that's only a civil death!—and the Act expires to-night, and then he will come to life again!

LUDWIG. Well, no. Anxious to inaugurate my reign by conferring some inestimable boon on my people, I signalized this occasion by reviving the law for another hundred years.

BARONESS. For another hundred years! Am I to understand that you, having taken upon yourself all Rudolph's responsibilities, will occupy the Grand Ducal throne for the ensuing century?

LUDWIG. If I should live so long.

BARONESS. Set the merry joy-bells ringing! Let festive epithalamia resound through these ancient halls! Cut the satisfying sandwich—broach the exhilarating Marsala—and let us rejoice to-day, if we never rejoice again!

LUDWIG. But I don't think I quite understand. We have already rejoiced a good deal.

BARONESS. Happy man, you little reck of the extent of the good things you are in for. When you killed Rudolph you adopted all his overwhelming responsibilities. Know then that I, Caroline von Krakenfeldt, am the most overwhelming of them all!

LUDWIG. But stop, stop—I've just been married to somebody else!

JULIA. Yes, ma'am, to somebody else, ma'am! Do you understand, ma'am? To somebody else!

BARONESS. Do keep this young woman quiet; she fidgets me!

JULIA. Fidgets you!

LUDWIG *(aside to* Julia*).* Be a violet—a crushed despairing violet!

JULIA. Do you suppose I intend to give up a magnificent part without a struggle?

LUDWIG. My good girl, she has the law on her side. Let us both bear this calamity with resignation. If you must struggle, go away and struggle in the seclusion of your chamber.

CHORUS.

Now away to the wedding we go,
So summon the charioteers—
No kind of reluctance they show
To embark on their married careers.
Though Julia's emotion may flow
For the rest of her maidenly years,
To the wedding we eagerly go,
So summon the charioteers!

Now away, etc.
[*All dance off to the wedding except* JULIA]

RECITATIVE—JULIA.

So ends my dream—so fades my vision fair!
Of hope no gleam—distraction and despair!
My cherished dreams, the Ducal throne to share,
That aim supreme has vanished into air!

SONG—JULIA.

Broken every promise plighted—
    All is darksome—all is dreary.
Every new-born hope is blighted!
    Sad and sorry—weak and weary!
Death the Friend or Death the Foe,
Shall I call upon thee? No!
I will go on living, though
    Sad and sorry—weak and weary!

No, no! Let the bygone go by!
    No good ever came of repining:
If to-day there are clouds o'er the sky,
    To-morrow the sun may be shining !
        To-morrow, be kind,
        To-morrow, to me!
        With loyalty blind
        I curtsey to thee!
To-day is a day of illusion and sorrow,
So *viva* To-morrow, To-morrow, To-morrow!
    God save you, To-morrow!
    Your servant, To-morrow!
God save you, To-morrow, To-morrow,
    To-morrow!   [*Exit* JULIA]

Enter ERNEST.

ERNEST. It's of no use—I can't wait any longer. At any risk I
must gratify my urgent desire to know what is going on.
(*Looking off*). Why, what's that? Surely I see a wedding
procession winding down the hill, dressed in my *Troilus and
Cressida* costumes! That's Ludwig's doing! I see how it is—he
found the time hang heavy on his hands, and is amusing himself
by getting married to Lisa. No—it can't be to Lisa, for here she
is!

ENTER LISA.

LISA (*not seeing him*). I really cannot stand seeing my Ludwig
married twice in one day to somebody else!
    ERNEST. Lisa!
            [LISA *sees him, and stands as if transfixed with horror.*]
    ERNEST. Come here—don't be a little fool—I want you.
                    [LISA *suddenly turns and bolts off.*]
    ERNEST. Why, what's the matter with the little donkey? One
would think she saw a ghost! But if he's not marrying Lisa,
whom *is* he marrying? (*Suddenly.*) Julia! (*Much overcome.*) I see it
all! The scoundrel! He had to adopt all my responsibilities, and
he's shabbily taken advantage of the situation to marry the girl
I'm engaged to! But no, it can't be Julia, for here *she* is!

Enter JULIA.

JULIA (*not seeing him*). I've made up my mind. I won't stand it!
I'll send in my notice at once!
    ERNEST. Julia! Oh, what a relief!
                    [JULIA *gazes at him as if transfixed.*]
    ERNEST. Then you've not married Ludwig? You are still true
to me?
            [JULIA *turns and bolts in grotesque horror.* ERNEST *follows and
                stops her.*]
    ERNEST. Don't run away! Listen to me. Are you all crazy?
    JULIA (*in affected terror*). What would you with me, spectre?
Oh, ain't his eyes sepulchral! And ain't his voice hollow! What
you are doing out of your tomb at this time of day—apparition?
    ERNEST. I do wish I could make you girls understand that I'm
only technically dead, and that physically I'm as much alive as
ever I was in my life!
    JULIA. Oh, but it's an awful thing to be haunted by a technical
bogie!
    ERNEST. You won't be haunted much longer. The law must be
on its last legs, and in a few hours I shall come to life
again—resume all my social and civil functions, and claim my
darling as my blushing bride!
    JULIA. Oh—then you haven't heard?
    ERNEST. My love, I've heard nothing. How could I? There are
no daily papers where I come from.
    JULIA. Why, Ludwig challenged Rudolph and won, and now
he's Grand Duke, and he's revived the law for another century!
    ERNEST. What! But you're not serious—you're only joking!
    JULIA. My good sir, I'm a light-hearted girl, but I don't chaff
bogies.
    ERNEST. Well, that's the meanest dodge I ever heard of!
    JULIA. Shabby trick, *I* call it.
    ERNEST. But you don't mean to say that you're going to cry
off!
    JULIA. I really can't afford to wait until your time is up. You
know, I've always set my face against long engagements.
    ERNEST. Then defy the law and marry me now. We will fly to
your native country, and I'll play broken-English in London as
you play broken-German here!
    JULIA. No. These legal technicalities cannot be defied. Situated
as you are, you have no power to make me your wife. At best
you could only make me your widow.
    ERNEST. Then be my widow—my little, dainty, winning,
winsome widow!
    JULIA. Now what would be the good of that? Why, you
goose. I should marry again within a month!

DUET—ERNEST *and* JULIA.

ERNEST.   If the light of love's lingering ember
                Has faded in gloom,
            You cannot neglect, O remember,
                A voice from the tomb!
            That stern supernatural diction
            Should act as a solemn restriction,
            Although by a mere legal fiction
                A voice from the tomb!

JULIA (*in affected terror*). I own that that utterance chills me—
                It withers my bloom!
            With awful emotion it thrills me—

That voice from the tomb!
Oh, spectre, won't anything lay thee?
Though pained to deny or gainsay thee,
In this case I cannot obey thee,
    Thou voice from the tomb!

(*Dancing*). So, spectre appalling,
    I bid you good-day—
Perhaps you'll be calling
    When passing this way.
Your bogeydom scorning,
And all your love-lorning,
I bid you good-morning,
    I bid you good-day.

ERNEST (*furious*). My offer recalling,
    Your words I obey—
Your fate is appalling,
    And full of dismay.
To pay for this scorning
I give you fair warning
I'll haunt you each morning,
    Each night, and each day!

[*Repeat Ensemble, and exeunt in opposite directions.*]

Re-enter the Wedding Procession of LUDWIG *and* BARONESS, *dancing.*

CHORUS.

Now bridegroom and bride let us toast
    In a magnum of merry champagne—
Let us make of this moment the most,
    We may not be so lucky again.
So drink to our sovereign host
    And his highly intelligent reign—
His health and his bride's let us toast
    In a magnum of merry champagne!

[*March heard.*]

LUDWIG (*recit.*). Why, who is this approaching,
    Upon our joy encroaching?
    Some rascal come a-poaching
    Who's heard that wine we're broaching?

ALL.   Who may this be?
            Who may this be?
        Who is he? Who is he? Who is he?

Enter HERALD.

HERALD. The Prince of Monte Carlo,
    From Mediterranean water,
    Has come here to bestow
        On you his beautiful daughter.
    They've paid off all they owe,
        As every statesman oughter—
    That Prince of Monte Carlo, etc.
        And his be-eautiful daughter!

CHORUS.   The Prince of Monte Carlo, etc.

HERALD. The Prince of Monte Carlo
    Who is so very particklar,
    Has heard that you're also
        For ceremony a stickler—
    Therefore he lets you know
        By word of mouth auric'lar—
    (That Prince of Monte Carlo
        Who is so very particklar)—

CHORUS.   The Prince of Monte Carlo, etc.

HERALD. That Prince of Monte Carlo,
    From Mediterranean water,
    Has come here to bestow
        On you his be-eautiful daughter!

LUDWIG (*recit.*). His Highness we know not—
        nor the locality
    In which is situate his Principality;
    But, as he guesses by some odd fatality,
    This *is* the shop for cut and dried formality!
        Let him appear—
        He'll find that we're
    Remarkable for cut and dried formality.
[*Reprise of March. Exit* HERALD. LUDWIG *beckons his Court.*]

LUDWIG. I have a plan—I'll tell you all the plot of it—
    He wants formality—he shall have a lot of it!
            [*Whispers to them, through symphony.*]
    Conceal yourselves, and when I give the cue,
    Spring out on him—you all know what to do!
[*All conceal themselves behind the draperies that enclose the stage.*]

Pompous March. Enter the PRINCE *and* PRINCESS *of* MONTE CARLO, *attended by six theatrical-looking nobles and the Court Costumier.*

DUET—PRINCE *and* PRINCESS.

PRINCE. We're rigged out in magnificent array
        (Our own clothes are much gloomier)
    In costumes which we've hired by the day
        From a very well-known costumier.

COSTUMIER (*bowing*). I am the well-known costumier.

PRINCESS. With a brilliant staff a Prince should make a show
        (It's a rule that never varies),
    So we've engaged from the Theatre Monaco
        Six supernumeraries.

NOBLES. We're the supernumeraries.

ALL.   At a salary immense,
            Quite regardless of expense,
        Six supernumeraries!

PRINCE. They do not speak, for they break our grammar's
        laws,
        And their language is lamentable—
    And they never take off their gloves, because
        Their nails are not presentable.

NOBLES. Our nails are not presentable!

PRINCESS. To account for their shortcomings manifest,
　　　　We explain, in a whisper bated,
　　　　They are wealthy members of the brewing interest,
　　　　To the Peerage elevated.

NOBLES. To the Peerage elevated.

ALL.　　$\left\{\begin{array}{l}\text{They're}\\\text{We're}\end{array}\right\}$ very, very rich
　　　　And accordingly, as sich,
　　　　To the Peerage elevated.

PRINCE. Well, my dear, here we are at last—just in time to compel Duke Rudolph to fulfil the terms of his marriage contract. Another hour and we should have been too late.

PRINCESS. Yes, papa, and if you hadn't fortunately discovered a means of making an income by honest industry, we should never have got here at all.

PRINCE. Very true. Confined for the last two years within the precincts of my palace by an obdurate bootmaker who held a warrant for my arrest, I devoted my enforced leisure to a study of the doctrine of chances—mainly with the view of ascertaining whether there was the remotest chance of my ever going out for a walk again—and this led to the discovery of a singularly fascinating little round game which I have called Roulette, and by which, in one sitting, I won no less than five thousand francs! My first act was to pay my bootmaker—my second, to engage a good useful working set of second-hand nobles—and my third, to hurry you off to Pfennig Halbpfennig as fast as a *train de luxe* could carry us!

PRINCESS. Yes, and a pretty job-lot of second-hand nobles you've scraped together!

PRINCE *(doubtfully).* Pretty, you think? Humph! I don't know. I should say tol-lol, my love—only tol-lol. They are not wholly satisfactory. There is a certain air of unreality about them—they are not convincing.

COSTUMIER. But, my goot friend, vhat can you expect for eighteenpence a day!

PRINCE. Now take this Peer, for instance. What the deuce do you call *him?*

CUSTOMIER. Him? Oh, he's a swell—he's the Duke of Riviera.

PRINCE. Oh, he's a Duke, is he? Well, that's no reason why he should look so confoundedly haughty. *(To* NOBLE.*)* Be affable, sir! (NOBLE *takes attitude of affability.)* That's better. Now *(passing to another)* here's a nobleman's coat all in holes!

CUSTOMIER *(to* NOBLE*).* Vhat a careless chap you are! Vhy don't you take care of the clo's? These cost money, these do! D'ye think I stole 'em?

PRINCE. It's not the poor devil's fault—it's yours. I don't wish you to end our House of Peers, but you might at least mend them. *(Passing to another.)* Now, who's this with his moustache coming off?

CUSTOMIER. Why, you're Viscount Mentone, ain't you?

NOBLE. Blest if I know. *(Turning up sword belt.)* It's wrote here—yes, Viscount Mentone.

COSTUMIER. Then vhy don't you say so? 'Old yourself up—you ain't carryin' sandwich boards now. *(Adjusts his moustache and hat—and handkerchief falls out.)*

PRINCE. And we may be permitted to hint to the Noble Viscount, in the most delicate manner imaginable, that it is not the practice among the higher nobility to carry their handkerchiefs in their hats.

NOBLE. I ain't got no pockets.

PRINCE. Then tuck it in here. *(Sticks it in his breast.)* Now, once for all, you Peers—when His Highness arrives, don't stand like sticks, but appear to take an intelligent and sympathetic interest in what is going on. You needn't say anything, but let your gestures be in accordance with the spirit of the conversation. Now take the word from me. Affability! *(Attitude.)* Submission! *(Attitude.)* Surprise! *(Attitude.)* Shame! *(Attitude.)* Grief! *(Attitude.)* Joy! *(Attitude.)* That's better! You can do it if you like!

PRINCESS. But, papa, where in the world is the Court? There is positively no one here to receive us!

PRINCE. Well, my love, you must remember that we have taken Duke Rudolph somewhat by surprise. These small German potentates are famous for their scrupulous adherence to ceremonial observances, and it may be that the etiquette of this Court demands that we should be received with a certain elaboration of processional pomp—which Rudolph may, at this moment, be preparing.

PRINCESS. I can't help feeling that he wants to get out of it. First of all you implored him to come to Monte Carlo and marry me there, and he refused on account of the expense. Then you implored him to advance us the money to enable us to go to him—and again he refused, on account of the expense. He's a miserly little wretch—that's what he is.

PRINCE. Well, I should'nt go so far as to say that. I should rather describe him as an enthusiastic collector of coins—of the realm—and we must not be too hard upon a numismatist if he feels a certain disinclination to part with some of his really very valuable specimens. It's a pretty hobby: I've often thought I should like to collect some coins myself.

PRINCESS. Papa, I'm sure there's some one behind that curtain. I saw it move!

PRINCE. Then no doubt they are coming. Now mind, you Peers—haughty affability combined with a sense of what is due to your exalted ranks, or I'll fine you half a franc each—upon my soul I will!

Gong. The curtains fly back and the Court are discovered. They give a wild yell and rush on to the stage dancing wildly, with PRINCE, PRINCESS, *and* NOBLES, *who are taken by surprise at first, but eventually join in a reckless dance. At the end all fall down exhausted.*

LUDWIG. There, what do you think of that? That's our official ceremonial for the reception of visitors of the very highest distinction.

PRINCE *(puzzled).* It's very quaint—very curious indeed. Prettily footed, too. Prettily footed.

LUDWIG. Would you like to see how we say "good-bye" to visitors of distinction? That ceremony is also performed with the foot.

PRINCE. Really, this tone—ah, but perhaps you have not completely grasped the situation?

LUDWIG. Not altogether.

PRINCE. Ah, then I'll give you a lead over. *(Significantly.)* I am the father of the Princess of Monte Carlo. Doesn't that convey any idea to the Grand Ducal mind?

LUDWIG *(stolidly).* Nothing definite.

PRINCE (aside). H'm—very odd! Never mind—try again! (Aloud.) This is the daughter of the Prince of Monte Carlo. Do you take?

LUDWIG (still puzzled). No—not yet. Go on—don't give it up—I daresay it will come presently.

PRINCE. Very odd—never mind—try again. (With sly significance.) Twenty years ago! Little doddle doddle! Two little doddle doddles! Happy father—hers and yours. Proud mother—yours and hers! Hah! Now you take? I see you do! I see you do!

LUDWIG. Nothing is more annoying than to feel that you're not equal to the intellectual pressure of the conversation. I wish he'd say something intelligible.

PRINCE. You didn't expect me?

LUDWIG (jumping at it). No, no. I grasp that—thank you very much. (Shaking hands with him.) No, I did not expect you!

PRINCE. I thought not. But ha! ha! at last I have escaped from my enforced restraint. (General movement of alarm.) (To crowd, who are stealing off.) No, no—you misunderstand me. I mean I've paid my debts!

ALL. Oh! (They return).

PRINCESS (affectionately). But, my darling, I'm afraid that even now you don't quite realise who I am! (Embracing him).

BARONESS. Why, you forward little hussy, how dare you? (Takes her away from LUDWIG.)

LUDWIG. You mustn't do that, my dear—never in the presence of the Grand Duchess, I beg!

PRINCESS (weeping). Oh, papa, he's got a Grand Duchess!

LUDWIG. A Grand Duchess! My good girl, I've got three Grand Duchesses!

PRINCESS. Well, I'm sure! Papa, let's go away—this is not a respectable Court.

PRINCE. All these Grand Dukes have their little fancies, my love. This Potentate appears to be collecting wives. It's a pretty hobby—I should like to collect a few myself. This (admiring BARONESS) is a charming specimen—an antique, I should say—of the early Merovingian period, if I'm not mistaken; and here's another—a Scotch lady, I think (alluding to JULIA), and (alluding to LISA) a little one thrown in. Two half-quarterns and a makeweight! (To LUDWIG.) Have you such a thing as a catalogue of the Museum?

PRINCESS. But I cannot permit Rudolph to keep a museum—

LUDWIG. Rudolph? Get along with you, I'm not Rudolph! Rudolph died yesterday!

PRINCE and PRINCESS. What!

LUDWIG. Quite suddenly—of—of—a cardiac affection.

PRINCE and PRINCESS. Of a cardiac affection?

LUDWIG. Yes, a pack-of-cardiac affection. He fought a Statutory Duel with me and lost, and I took over all his engagements—including this imperfectly preserved old lady, to whom he has been engaged for the last three weeks.

PRINCESS. Three weeks! But I've been engaged to him for the last twenty years!

BARONESS, LISA, and JULIA. Twenty years!

PRINCE (aside). It's all right, my love—they can't get over that. (Aloud.) He's yours—take him, and hold him as tight as you can!

PRINCESS. My own! (Embracing LUDWIG.)

LUDWIG. Here's another!—the fourth in four-and-twenty hours! Would anybody else like to marry me? You, ma'am—or you—anybody! I'm getting used to it!

⎧ Baroness. But let me tell you, ma'am—
⎨ Julia. Why, you impudent little hussy—
⎩ Lisa. Oh, here's another—here's another! (Weeping.)

PRINCESS. Poor ladies, I'm very sorry for you all; but, you see, I've a prior claim. Come, away we go—there's not a moment to be lost!

CHORUS (as they dance towards exit).

Away to the wedding we'll go
To summon the charioteers,
Though her rival's emotion may flow
In the form of impetuous tears—
[At this moment RUDOLPH, ERNEST, and
NOTARY appear. All kneel in
astonishment.]

RECITATIVE.
RUDOLPH, ERNEST, and NOTARY.

Forbear! This may not be!
Frustrated are your plans!
With paramount decree
The Law forbids the banns!

ALL. The Law forbids the banns!

LUDWIG. Not a bit of it! I've revived the law for another century.

RUDOLPH. You didn't revive it! You couldn't revive it! You—you are an impostor, sir—a tup-penny rogue sir! You—you never were, and in all human probability never will be—Grand Duke of Pfennig Anything!

ALL. What!!!

RUDOLPH. Never—never, never! (Aside). Oh, my internal economy!

LUDWIG. That's absurd, you know. I fought the Grand Duke. He drew a King, and I drew an Ace. He perished in inconceivable agonies on the spot. Now, as that's settled, we'll go on with the wedding.

RUDOLPH. It—it isn't settled. You—you can't. I—I—[to NOTARY]. Oh, tell him—tell him! I can't!

NOTARY. Well, the fact is, there's been a little mistake here. On reference to the Act that regulates Statutory Duels, I find it is expressly laid down that Ace shall count invariably as lowest!

ALL. As lowest!

RUDOLPH [breathlessly]. As lowest—lowest—lowest? So you're the ghoest—ghoest—ghoest! [Aside.] Oh, what is the matter with me inside here!

ERNEST. Well, Julia, as it seems that the Law hasn't been revived—and as, consequently, I shall come to life in about three minutes—[consulting his watch]

JULIA. My objection falls to the ground. (Resignedly.) Very well!

PRINCESS. And am I to understand that I was on the point of marrying a dead man without knowing it? [To RUDOLPH, who revives.] Oh, my love, what a narrow escape I've had!

RUDOLPH. Oh—you are the Princess of Monte Carlo, and you've turned up just in time! Well, you're an attractive little girl, you known, but you're as poor as a rat! [They retire up together].

LISA. That's all very well, but what is to become of me? [To LUDWIG]. If you're a dead man—[Clock strikes three.]

LUDWIG. But I'm not. Time's up—the Act has expired—I've come to life—the parson is still in attendance, and we'll all be married directly.

ALL. Hurrah!

FINALE

Happy couples, lightly treading,
Castle chapel will be quite full!
Each shall have a pretty wedding,

As, of course, is only rightful,
Though the bride be fair or
frightful.
Contradiction little dreading,
This will be a day delightful—
Each shall have a pretty wedding!
Such a pretty, pretty wedding!
Such a pretty wedding!

[*All dance off to get married as the curtain falls.*)

Notes on the recordings and films of the Savoy Operas

Sir Arthur Sullivan was the most recorded of any British composer in the days of 78 rpm discs, and so it is not surprising that the operas have received considerable treatment from 1906/7 and onwards. The individual songs and concerted numbers (that began with H. Scott Russell singing 'Take a Pair of Sparkling Eyes in 1898) are legion. The enterprising Pearl Records have issued a handsome set of the best individual numbers relative to creators, but only the 'sets'— complete and otherwise—can be discussed here.

The first G&S operas to appear on records were on G&T single-sided discs. *Pinafore, Mikado* and *Yeomen* were quite substantially recorded by a group of contract singers, including Peter Dawson, who were billed as 'The Sullivan Operatic Party' and who sang all the main roles in each opera between the four or five of them. Coincidentally the English Odeon Company produced double-sided records of *Pinafore* (in late 1907) followed by *The Mikado* (mysteriously lacking 'The Sun whose Rays') and *Yeomen*. This *Mikado* has been well transferred and reissued on LP by Pearl; in it, Walter Passmore sings Ko-Ko and becomes the first member of the D'Oyly Carte Company (though no longer with it in 1908) to feature in a more or less complete opera.

From 1918 the D'Oyly Carte office exercised almost a monopoly of recordings of the operas. Their acoustic *Mikado* appeared in 1918, followed by *Gondoliers, Yeomen, Pirates, Patience* and *Iolanthe* at yearly intervals, but principal roles were not sung by members of the Company. Instead they were given to such established recording artists as George Baker, Peter Dawson, Robert Radford, Frederick Ranalow, Bessie Jones and others.

Fourteen more 'complete' recordings followed (always HMV), with duplications but still with a few non-D'Oyly Carte singers, until 1936, covering the usual eleven though only an abridged *Sorcerer*. This is on a Pearl transfer.

In 1949 The Decca Record Company obtained the D'Oyly Carte franchise, used only Company singers, and issued musically complete versions of the standard eleven up to 1955. Eventually all of them were on mono LP. From 1958, re-recordings in stereo, with new D'Oyly Carte voices, appeared in mono and stereo.

HMV re-entered the lists in 1957 with *The Gondoliers* sung by British opera singers like Elsie Morison, Monica Sinclair, Richard Lewis and Owen Brannigan supported by a larger orchestra than usual and conducted by Sir Malcolm Sargent. It was followed during the next five years with the next six, predictable operas done equally well. All these performances have great authority, verve and musicianship.

Utopia, Limited and *The Grand Duke* received premier recordings in 1964 and 1974 respectively by the enterprising Pearl Records from semi-professional, 'live' performances; while *Thespis* was taken from another performance in 1971 by Rare Recorded Editions. The concocted score does no more than prolong speculation.

With the advent of video, Brent-Walker commissioned the production of eleven operas, cast from British and American stars. An indication of the new film look from *HMS Pinafore* may be found on page 76 where it can be discerned that there is a tendency to wide screen performance on the small screen. However, if this is regarded as the beginning, and compared with the distance travelled in the recording field, Brent-Walker are pioneers in the video line.

So far as cinema films are concerned, the first serious attempt was in 1938, with *The Mikado* in colour from Pinewood studios and full D'Oyly Carte approval. Martyn Green was the Ko-Ko, Sidney Granville Pooh-Bah and Kenny Baker was imported for Nanki-Poo. Despite the affectionate hand of Geoffrey Toye as producer, it did not transfer altogether successfully to the cinema.

The 1982 *Pirates of Penzance* film (as distinct from the uneven Brent-Walker video *Pirates*) did not attract good reviews in the USA, nor in the UK. But even if these first essays, in what must be considered a new G&S medium, are merely exploratory, our age of *the picture* will demand repeated versions, probably more competitive with one another than the gramophone recordings of the last eighty years.

Select bibliography

ADAIR-FITZGERALD, S. J., *The Story of Gilbert and Sullivan* London, 1924

ASLIN, ELIZABETH, *The Aesthetic Movement* London, 1981

ALLEN, REGINALD, *The First Night Gilbert and Sullivan* New York/London, 1958

BAILY, LESLIE, *The Gilbert and Sullivan Book* London, 1967
Gilbert and Sullivan and their World London, 1973

BOND, J. & MacGEORGE, E., *The Life and Reminiscences of Jessie Bond* London, 1930

BRADLEY, IAN, *An Annotated Gilbert and Sullivan* London, 1982

BRAHMS, CARYL, *Gilbert and Sullivan: Lost Chords and Discords* London, 1975

CELLIER, F. & BRIDGEMAN, C., *Gilbert, Sullivan and D'Oyly Carte* London, 1914

CRANE, WALTER, *An Artist's Reminiscences* London, 1907

DARLINGTON, W. A., *The World of Gilbert and Sullivan* London, 1951

DUNHILL, T. F., *Sullivan's Comic Operas* London, 1928

GILBERT, W. S., *The Bab Ballads* London, 1869;
The Bab Ballads London, 1898; *The Bab Ballads and Songs of a Savoyard* London, 1924; *The Savoy Operas* London, 1926; *The Bab Ballads* (ed. Ellis) New York/London, 1970; *Plays of Gilbert and Sullivan* New York/London, 1976

GROSSMITH, GEORGE, *A Society Clown* London, 1888

GROVE, GEORGE (ED.), *Dictionary of Music and Musicians* Oxford, 1899
The New Grove (ed. SADIE, S.) London, 1982

HAREWOOD, EARL OF (ED.), *Kobbé's Complete Opera Book* London, 1976

HILLIER, JACK, *Japanese Masters of the Colour Print* London, 1954

HOLME, BRYAN, *The Kate Greenaway Book* London, 1976

HUGHES, GERVASE, *The Music of Arthur Sullivan* London, 1959

JONES, J. B. (ED.), *W S Gilbert: A Centenary of Scholarship* New York, 1970

PEARSON, HESKETH, *Gilbert, His Life and Strife* London, 1957

Punch, 1870-1908 *passim*

REES, TERENCE, *Thespis: A Gilbert and Sullivan Enigma* London, 1964

ROLLINS, C. & WITTS, R. J., *The D'Oyly Carte Opera Company, A Record of Performances* London, 1962

SHAW, G. B., *Shaw's Music Vols I-III* London, 1981

STEDMAN, JANET, *Gilbert Before Sullivan* London, 1969

SULLIVAN, J. & FLOWER, N., *Sir Arthur Sullivan* London, 1927

TENNYSON, ALFRED LORD, *Collected Works* London, 1892

WILLIAMSON, AUDREY, *Gilbert and Sullivan Opera* London, (1953) 1982

WOLFSON, JOHN, *Final Curtain* London, 1975

YOUNG, PERCY M., *Sir Arthur Sullivan* London, 1971

Acknowledgements

PICTURE CREDITS

The author and publishers are grateful to the
following for supplying illustrations:

COLOUR

Sven Arnstein 217; British Theatre Museum 218,
236, 309, 312; Decca International 310, 311;
Dyson Perrins Museum 49 (top); Peter Joslin 67
(top), 68, 152, 235; Martha Swope 133; Victoria
& Albert Museum 50, 67 (below); Reg Wilson
134, 151.

BLACK AND WHITE

Author's collection 21; John Blomfield 22; Brent-
Walker 76; BBC Hulton Picture Library 14
(right), 115, 136, 207, 233; British Library 14
(left), 15 (below), 53 (below), 56, 77, 208;
Guildhall Library 184; Peter Joslin 17, 18, 19
(left), 20, 23, 25, 42, 54, 138, 165 (left), 187, 237,
318; Mander & Mitchenson 19 (right), 92 (below),
93, 210 (right); Mansell Collection 261; Pierpont
Morgan Library 13, 24 (below), 39 (below); Peter
Pratt 162; John Reed 262; Terence Rees 72
(right), 160; Martha Swope 92 (above); Theatre
Museum 22, 40, 55, 73 (below), 75, 91, 94, 111,
112, 114, 132, 137, 139, 140, 164, 165 (right),
185, 186, 209, 210 (left), 234, 257, 263, 284, 286,
290, 317, 319, 320, 321; Victoria & Albert
Museum 24 (above); Reg Wilson 250.

The publishers have made every reasonable
endeavour to trace the owners of copyright
material used in *The Complete Gilbert and Sullivan
Opera Guide*.

Index